D1169055

Nova Scotia,
New Brunswick &
Prince Edward Island

Karla Zimmerman
Celeste Brash

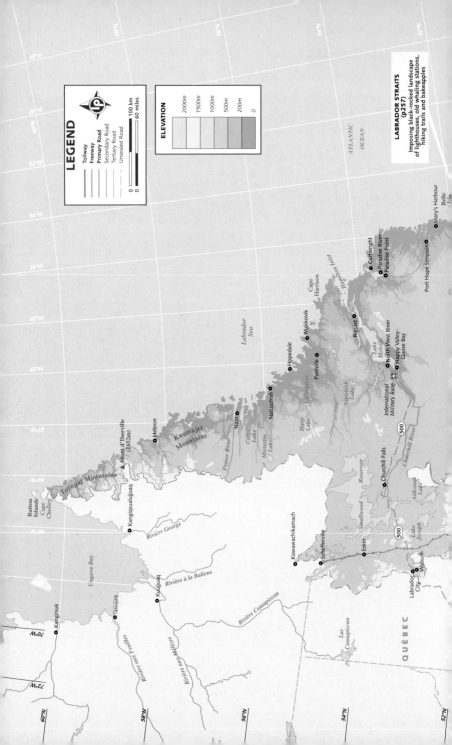

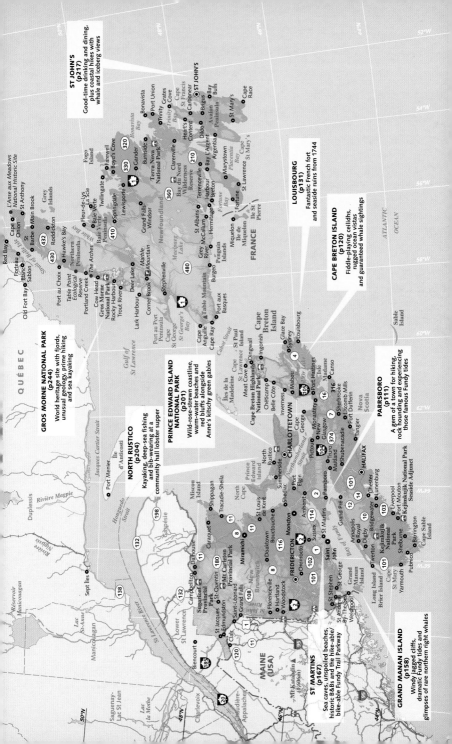

ST JOHN'S (p217)
Good-time drinking and dining, plus coastal hikes with whale and iceberg views

GROS MORNE NATIONAL PARK (p244)
World heritage site with fjords, unusual geology, prime hiking and sea kayaking

NORTH RUSTICO (p204)
Kayaking, deep-sea fishing and bib-wearing at a community hall lobster supper

PRINCE EDWARD ISLAND NATIONAL PARK (p201)
Wild-rose-strewn coastline, red-water beaches and red bluffs alongside Anne's kitschy green gables

LOUISBOURG (p131)
Fantastic French fort and seaside ruins from 1744

CAPE BRETON ISLAND (p120)
Fiddle-playing ceilidhs, rugged ocean vistas and guaranteed whale sightings

PARRSBORO (p111)
A gem of a town for hiking, rock hounding and experiencing those famous Fundy tides

ST MARTINS (p167)
Sea caves, unspoiled beaches, historic B&Bs and the hike-able/bike-able Fundy Trail Parkway

GRAND MANAN ISLAND (p158)
Windy, rugged cliffs, dramatic Fundy tides and glimpses of rare northern right whales

Destination Nova Scotia, New Brunswick & Prince Edward Island

'Water everywhere,' you think, as you scan around from the cliff top to which this path has brought you. The surf crashes, the tides pull, the wind slaps you with a briny smell. It's forever about the sea here.

Then you see it. No, not the bank of fog rolling in over the hill. You see that too, and curse it, but what you see out on the water is this: a fine spray emanating from what appears to be a log. Then it happens! The log morphs into two giant tail flukes arching up, cascading water from their scalloped edges. The whale is gone quick as a wink, and the surface returns to its regular roil.

'One more time,' you will the giant, and she concurs, a little to the left this time. Your game of hide-and-seek continues, and even when the fog arrives and you can't see the whale, you can still hear her spouting.

It's a freeze-frame moment, one of many to experience in the Atlantic provinces. Such flashes might occur when you crack into a buttery lobster in peaceful, red-headed Prince Edward Island, or fly-fish the mythical rivers of French-tinged New Brunswick. Or in Nova Scotia, when you dance to fiddle music at a Cape Breton pub, or feed your inner foodie at a Halifax restaurant. These three provinces are known as the Maritimes. Ratchet it up a notch with rocky, offbeat Newfoundland and Labrador, and it becomes Atlantic Canada. And its tops for hiking, kayaking, whale watching or anything having to do with the sea.

It doesn't matter what you call it or where you anchor: the music rocks, seafood steams up plates, and whales spout throughout the region. So just jump in – Atlantic Canada is sure to float your boat.

BRENT WINEBRENN

Nova Scotia

Stunning cycling trails (p50) traverse the region

NOVA SCOTIA TOURISM, CULTURE AND HERITAGE

Jig it up at Cape Breton's Celtic Colours Fest (p120)

ALISON WRIGHT

Wildflowers (p46) abound in Atlantic Canada

CHERYL FORBES

ABBOT MOFFAT

Joe's Scarecrow Theatre (p123) offers a funky roadside stop along the coastal highway leading to Chéticamp

ALISON WRIG

Nova Scotians are renowned for their friendly nature

Visit the port of Lunenburg (p83) for a taste of the sea

ABBOT MOF

CHERYL FORBES

Hike or drive the famous Cabot Trail (p124), where moose wander and bald eagles swoop

Long-dormant cannons stand guard over the fascinating Louisbourg National Historic Site (p131)

BRENT WINEBRENNER

New Brunswick

JOHN NEUBAUER

Visit the attractive Acadian town of Caraquet (p179)

CHERYL FORBE

The Hopewell Rocks (p170) are a sight to behold

Disappear down the longest covered bridge in the world in Hartland (p148)

CHERYL FORBE

JOHN NEUBAUER

Go back in time at the Acadien Historic Village (p180), a re-creation of the lives of Acadian settlers

JOHN NEUBAUER

The lighthouse at Grand Anse (p181) is painted in the traditional colors of the Acadian flag

LEE FOSTE

Fishing is still a big part of the region's economy and livelihood

TOURISM AND PARKS NEW BRUNSWIC

TOURISM AND PARKS NEWS BRUNSWIC

The peaks of Mt Carleton Provincial Park (p148) offer sightings of moose, bear, deer and even the 'extinct' Eastern cougar

Prince Edward Island

EMILY RIDDELL

Malpeque (p208) presents typical Maritime scenery such as these lobster boats near store sheds

This lighthouse looks out over warm waters and pristine sand of Cavendish Beach (p201)

ALISON WRIGHT

EMILY RIDDE

No visit to the island would be complete without a tour of the house (p206) that inspired *Anne of Green Gables*

Cavendish (p206) is surrounded by charming riverside villages

EMILY RIDDELL

The island's lush countryside (p184) complements its famed red hues

JIM WA

One way to cross into 'Anne's land' is over the Confederation Bridge (p200), the longest bridge in Canada

Capture the essence of Atlantic Canada with a visit to tiny Rustico (p203)

Newfoundland & Labrador

'Iceberg Alley' (p250) drifts through Newfoundland's waters from late spring to early summer

L'Anse aux Meadows (p248) is the site of the first European settlement in Canada

A dream to geologists, the awe-inspiring Tablelands (p244) are a highlight of Gros Morne National Park

ABBOT MOFFAT

EMILY RIDDELL

Costumed soldiers perform a tattoo (p220) in St John's

The bright, bold architecture of St John's (p217) is just one of its many attractions

Trinity (p233) brings visitors from far and wide who delight in its storybook-like charm

EMILY RIDDELL

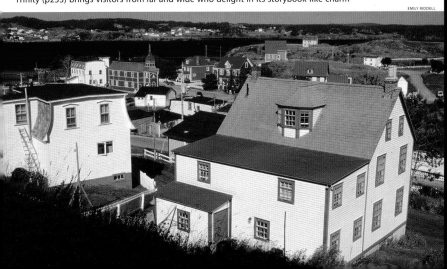

STEPHEN SAKS

The remains of Fort Amherst (p221) cling to a cliff
that's ideal for whale- and iceberg-spotting

ABBOT MO

Culinary delights (p225) such as
moose soup, are Newfie favorites

Signal Hill (p220) offers expansive views of Newfoundland's capital, St John's

EMILY RIDDE

Contents

Regional Map Contents

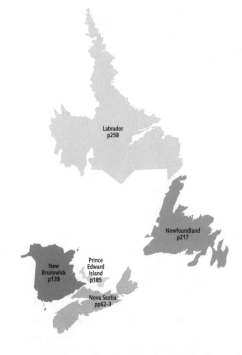

Labrador
p258

Newfoundland
p217

Prince
Edward
Island
p185

New
Brunswick
p139

Nova Scotia
pp62-3

The Authors

KARLA ZIMMERMAN   Coordinating Author, Newfoundland & Labrador

Karla became an honorary Newfoundlander after indulging in a drop o' Screech, and is thrilled to be a citizen of the big-hearted, good-humored province. To further her assimilation, Karla munched cod tongues and caribou in Labrador, hit the high seas whale-watching in St Anthony, drove by moose in Burgeo and inhaled an embarrassing number of éclairs in St-Pierre.

When she's not north of the border, Karla lives in Chicago with husband Eric (another honorary Newfoundlander) and writes travel features for newspapers, books, magazines and radio. She has authored or coauthored several of Lonely Planet's US and Canadian titles.

My Favorite Trip

It's gotta be Newfoundland's Northern Peninsula and the Labrador Straits. The region gets bigger, bolder and more savage with each kilometer northward. I start in Gros Morne National Park (p244) and think that's pretty outlandish with the bald, golden tablelands and blistering wind (makes for a helluva thigh-grinding bike ride). Then I take the Viking Trail north to L'Anse aux Meadows. I love the simplicity of the Viking site (p248) – pretty much the same desolate expanse of bog and shore that Leif Eriksson must have encountered 1000 years ago. I jump a quick ferry over to the Labrador Straits (p257), and the landscape becomes positively primeval. Black basalt cliffs and rocks dwarf the lone road. Clouds tear across mammoth skies. People are few and far between, so the hikes I take by whale bones and warship fragments make me feel like a true voyager.

Labrador Straits L'Anse aux Meadows National Park Gros Morne National Park

CELESTE BRASH   Nova Scotia, New Brunswick & Prince Edward Island

'So this is where people from Tahiti go on vacation?' This question was asked of Celeste several times during her voyage through the Maritimes. Lighthouses and lupine are a far cry from palm trees and hibiscus but that's just what she was hoping for. Celeste fell in love with the crisp air, became certain that Atlantic lobster is the best food on earth and came unabashedly out of the closet as an Anne fan. Satiated, she returned to her island home, husband and two children to eat mangoes instead of blueberries. She is still dreaming of lobsters.

My Favorite Trip

With crisp air, green hills fringed by the icy Atlantic and a lively mix of Scottish, Mi'kmaw and Acadian cultures, Cape Breton Island (p120) won me over in an instant. From the blustery fort of Louisbourg (p131) and the damp, underground mines of Glace Bay (p131) to the Alexander Graham Bell Historic Site in Baddeck (p132), this is history, hands-on. Of course nothing rivals watching eagles soar over pods of minke whales at Meat Cove (p127), pulling over to the side of the road to get close-up to moose in Cape Breton Highlands National Park (p124) and looking a humpback whale in the eye from a zodiac in Pleasant Bay (p126). I learned to love fiddle music at the Red Shoe Pub in Mabou (p120) then continued on to ceilidhs in Baddeck (p132). One of my favorite experiences was meeting the Mi'kmaw community in Wagmatcook (p133) and learning about the cultures' colorful past at their village museum.

CONTRIBUTING AUTHOR

David Lukas wrote the Environment chapter (p43). David works as a professional naturalist, leading nature tours, conducting biological surveys and writing about natural history. His articles have appeared in *Audubon,* the *Los Angeles Times, Orion, Sunset* and elsewhere. David has contributed chapters to more than 10 Lonely Planet titles including *Yosemite National Park, Grand Canyon National Park, Dominican Republic* and *Costa Rica.*

Getting Started

Atlantic Canada's tourism infrastructure caters mostly to midrange travelers rather than backpackers and jetsetters, though both of these groups will certainly find options. An important thing to keep in mind is travel time: distances can be deceivingly long and travel times slow due to single-lane highways and even a lack of highways (when you must board a ferry). Don't try to pack too much into your itinerary and do consider limiting your explorations to one or two regions in depth. Public transportation is limited, so you'll likely need to rent a car for at least a portion of your trip. Room and transportation reservations are a good idea in the peak times of July and August.

WHEN TO GO

You can visit Atlantic Canada at any time of year, but most people arrive in summer when temperatures are pleasant and they can take advantage of the region's abundant outdoor activities and festivals. July and August are the busiest months due to the warm weather and US and Canadian summer holidays.

See Climate Charts (p266) for more information.

In general, tourist facilities are open May through October, though in colder climes the season can get compressed to July and August only. Peak summer season technically runs from mid-June to Labor Day (which is in early September), and you may find that facilities can be quite crowded at this time.

The shoulder season – from mid-May to mid-June and in September – offers a good compromise between the summer throngs and the winter cold; during these times you'll enjoy mostly good weather and have the place to yourself.

The long, dark and snowy winter, from November through April, is strictly for the brave. A small but dedicated group of cold-weather operators offer skiing, snowmobiling and other outdoor activities, but beyond that tourists won't find a whole lot to do.

COSTS & MONEY

Accommodation is likely to be your biggest expense, although as fuel prices rise, transportation ranks up there too. Because the tourist season is so compressed – just eight to 10 weeks over summer in most cases – businesses ratchet up prices then for lodging, rental cars and attractions. If you find the prices asked in July and August too steep, try to visit between mid-May and mid-June, when many prices are a third lower, or defer your trip until September.

DON'T LEAVE HOME WITHOUT...

- Checking the border-crossing (p276) and visa requirements (p274), as these may change
- Valid travel insurance (p269)
- Your driver's license and vehicle registration papers, plus adequate liability insurance (p282)
- Bug spray (p287)
- Your sea legs and motion sickness medication (useful for whale-watch cruises)
- Transportation and sleeping reservations, especially in July and August

In most parts of Atlantic Canada, single travelers who rent a car, stay in decent B&Bs and eat at least one meal out will spend about $165 per day. The total cost is only a little bit more for a couple traveling together. For those on a tight budget, costs can be brought down by staying in hostels or camping, self-catering from local markets, taking public transportation when available and limiting entertainment options. This will reduce your daily costs to about $70.

To break down the expenses you'll incur: comfortable midrange accommodations start at around $80 to $90 for a double room, usually including breakfast. A full restaurant midrange meal with wine or beer costs between $15 and $20 plus tax and a tip. The bill is lower if you stick to cafés and casual restaurants and skip alcoholic drinks. Rental cars cost from $35 to $55 a day for a compact-size vehicle, not including gas. Attraction admissions range from $3 to $10.

Discounts are widely available to children, students and seniors throughout the region. Most attractions also offer a family admission price, which can save dough for two adults and their brood.

Taxes of 14% and up are added to nearly all goods and services, but you can get at least a portion of them back through the Visitor Rebate Program (p271).

TRAVEL LITERATURE

Get stoked for your journey to Atlantic Canada by reading the tales of those who've gone before you.

Love-him-or-hate-him Canadian author Farley Mowat spins a good yarn in *The Boat Who Wouldn't Float* (1984), about sailing his woebegone schooner *Happy Adventure* around Newfoundland. The boat's perpetual leak only enhances exploits involving rum-running, heavy drinking and hanging out with various coastal characters. He also penned *A Whale for the Killing* (1991), a somber man-versus-nature narrative that pits the townsfolk in the Newfoundland outport of Burgeo against an 80-ton fin whale trapped in a nearby lagoon. Let's just say the whale's outcome is not a happy one.

Walter Stewart first zipped across the Trans-Canada Hwy in 1964. Thirty-five years later he did it again, and this time he wrote a book about what he saw. In *My Cross-Country Checkup* (2000), Stewart moves beyond clichés and explores the Evangeline legend in Nova Scotia and the real Lucy Maud Montgomery of Green Gables, as well as controversies such as the Sydney tar ponds and Irving oil empire.

In *Welcome Home: Travels in Small Town Canada* (1992), Stuart McLean shares his impressions of Sackville, New Brunswick; Pleasantville, Nova Scotia (where we meet a mechanic who makes sculptures out of sledgehammered engine parts); and Ferryland, Newfoundland, among other Canadian outposts. Though written more than a decade ago, a lot of these places and their residents haven't changed much.

The Sea's Voice, An Anthology of Atlantic Canadian Nature Writing (2005), edited by Harry Thurston, brings together 24 essays by regional writers focusing on nature, be they pieces on personal healing in the natural world or sorrow caused by environmental destruction.

It's true, shipwrecks and whale collisions may not inspire you so much as make you wary, but *Ocean of Storms, Sea of Disaster: North Atlantic Shipwrecks of the Strange and Curious* (2005) by Robert C Parsons is intriguing reading. Who can resist 70 stories of piracy, mutiny, rum-running and iceberg wrecks? If you can't find it in a store or via an online retailer, check with publisher Pottersfield Press (www.pottersfieldpress.com).

HOW MUCH?

Fish-and-chips $7

Whale-watch cruise $45-60

B&B double room $90

Pack of cigarettes $6-7

Newspaper $1

See Quick Reference (inside front cover) for additional prices.

TOP FIVES AND 10'S

Top 10 Bashes

For a list of more swinging parties, see p269. For food fests, see p55.

Pictou Landing First Nation Powwow (p117; June) Drumming and craft demonstrations in Pictou.

Festival Western (p150; July) Cowgirl beauty contests, poker games and country music in St Quentin.

New Brunswick Highland Games Festival (p144; July) Whiskey, haggis and kilts in Fredericton.

Privateer Days (p87; July) Avast, it's pirate re-enactments in Liverpool.

Royal St John's Regatta (p224; July) Rowing event that empties St John's streets.

Stan Rogers Folk Festival (p135; July) A whopping musical hootenanny – and Nova Scotia's largest festival – in Canso.

Evolve (p71; August) Renewable energy demonstrations along with music at this green fest in Antigonish.

Festival Acadien (p180; August) Acadians from around the world celebrate their culture in Caraquet.

PEI International Shellfish Festival (p190; September) Oyster shucking and chowder eating in Charlottetown.

Celtic Colours (p120; October) Foot-stompin' music and flame-colored foliage in Cape Breton.

Top 10 Historical Sights

See the History chapter (p31) for more information on the region's past.

Acadian Historic Village (p179) Witness Acadian culture and the hard life post-expulsion.

Alexander Graham Bell National Historic Site (p133) Examine the inventor's telegraphs, telephones, kites and seaplanes.

Citadel National Historic Site (p65) Hike the hill to Canada's most-visited historic site, a star-shaped beauty.

Fort Anne National Historic Site p100) Tour the French fort by day, its lantern-lit graveyard by night.

King's Landing Historical Settlement (p147) Live the early 1800s life in horse-drawn carts and candlelit pubs.

L'Anse aux Meadows National Historic Site (p248) Walk in the 1000-year-old footsteps of Viking Leif Eriksson.

Louisbourg National Historic Site (p131) Munch on French soldiers' rations and bribe the guards at this 1744 fort.

Province House National Historic Site (p187) See the 'birthplace of Canada,' where 23 guys created a country.

Red Bay National Historic Site (p259) Learn how Basque whalers hunted mighty prey from tiny dinghies.

Signal Hill National Historic Site (p220) Take in views, cannon fire and ham radio above the harbor.

Top Five Regional Reads

These are tales of Acadian separation, Beothuk times and quirky village life, among others. For more reads and more details on these titles, see p39.

Anne of Green Gables (1908) by Lucy Maud Montgomery

Evangeline (1847) by Henry Wadsworth Longfellow.

No Great Mischief (1999) by Alistair MacLeod.

Rare Birds (1997) by Edward Riche.

River Thieves (2001) by Michael Crummey.

Top Five Regional Reels

Whether they make you laugh or cry, these films give a sense of the region, its culture and its history. For additional flicks and further details on those listed below, see p39.

Margaret's Museum (1995) directed by Mort Ransen.

Random Passage mini-series (2002) directed by John N Smith.

The Shipping News (2001) directed by Lasse Hallström.

Titanic (1997) directed by James Cameron.

Trailer Park Boys TV series (2001–2003) directed by Mike Clattenburg.

INTERNET RESOURCES

Environment Canada (www.weatheroffice.ec.gc.ca) Is it raining in Halifax? Snowing in Corner Brook? Check here for the forecast.

Government of Canada (www.gc.ca) The mother of all Canada websites, with information both national (immigration rules, national anthem lyrics) and regional (ice conditions off Labrador, provincial tourism offices) in scope.

Lonely Planet (www.lonelyplanet.com) Fire up Atlantic Canada travel news and summaries.

Podcast Alley (www.podcastalley.com) Type in an Atlantic city or province, and hear podcasts covering niches from the electronic music scene in Halifax to hockey in St John's.

Sierra Club of Canada Atlantic Chapter (www.sierraclub.ca/atlantic) The Sierra Club's site provides background on local environmental concerns such as the Sydney tar ponds.

Itineraries
CLASSIC ROUTES

Drive into the land the Acadians cherished and see lighthouses, wineries, giant pumpkins and more stars than you can possibly imagine. What? You want yoga and lobster fishing too? Done, on this 530km loop that rolls through Nova Scotia's South Shore and Annapolis Valley.

LUSH NOVA SCOTIA — Four Days / South Shore & Annapolis Valley

Soak up **Halifax** (p61) then travel to nearby **Peggy's Cove** (p78). Jostle for position to snap the most photographed lighthouse in the world, or have a more subdued experience picnicking in equally pretty **Prospect** (p78). Unfurl the yoga mat in ecominded **Mahone Bay** (p81) before moving on to **Lunenburg** (p83), a world heritage site known for its colorful boxy buildings, *Bluenose* schooner and lobstering tours. The **Kejimkujik Seaside Adjunct** (p89) provides miles of unspoiled white beaches (and maybe seals), while its big brother **Kejimkujik National Park** (p88) lies inland and is a prime place to float a canoe and drift through the woods. Move on to **Annapolis Royal** (p100) and explore its fort by day and graveyard by night; don't forget to look up at the zillions of fat stars smudging the sky. The next day go river tubing and wolf down a meal in **Wolfville** (p105), before stopping at the winery in **Grand Pré** (p106). Visit **Windsor** (p107) to see Howard Dill's scale-busting pumpkins before returning to Halifax.

HEART OF THE MARITIMES   One Week / Nova Scotia, New Brunswick & PEI

Eat and drink your way through **Halifax** (p61), then make a break northwest toward **Amherst** (p114) perhaps detouring to **Maitland** (p108) for a tidal-bore rafting excursion. Your real goal is to reach Prince Edward Island, but to do so you'll first have to cross into New Brunswick. Crustacean lovers won't mind since **Shediac** (p175) is just up the road. It's the home of the world's biggest lobster sculpture and – no surprise – the cooked version of the creature gets served in eateries all over town. It's even used as a pizza topping.

Barrel over the 12.9km **Confederation Bridge** (p200) that links New Brunswick to Prince Edward Island and begin the pilgrimage to Anne's Land. Anne, of course, is the fictional redheaded orphan of *Green Gables* fame, and **Cavendish** (p206) is the wildly developed town that pays homage to her. It's now a cavalcade of kitsch, complete with a wax museum and glow-in-the-dark minigolf.

Spurting lobster all over your shirt at a lobster supper initiates you into the local lifestyle; **North Rustico** (p204) is a good place to get juicy. Go from red shellfish to red sandstone bluffs at **Prince Edward Island National Park** (p201); there's bird-watching, beach walking and swimming, too. Stop in PEI's compact, colonial capital **Charlottetown** (p186) before taking the ferry from **Wood Islands** (p195) back to **Pictou** (p116) in Nova Scotia. You can stroll Pictou's boardwalk and if you're lucky, the town might be hosting its **First Nations Powwow** (p117). It takes about two hours to return to Halifax from here.

> You'll get a bit of everything on this 650km loop that starts and ends in Halifax: the bundle of Maritime provinces (**Nova Scotia, New Brunswick and Prince Edward Island**), a looooong bridge, a ferry ride, high kitsch, beachy solitude and a whole lotta lobster.

CABOT & VIKING TRAILS

**Two to Three Weeks /
Halifax to L'Anse aux Meadows**

Wild, windswept
and whale-riddled,
this 1400km route
calls for some
serious time
behind the wheel.
Thankfully, the
sea-and-cliff vistas
you'll spot from the
car make up for the
stiff knee joints. Do
try and keep your
eyes at least
partially on
the road.

Spend a couple days in **Halifax** (p61) enjoying the cosmopolitan life, then hit the road to Cape Breton Island. In between, raft the tidal bore's waves in **Maitland** (p108) and climb the 13 sand dunes at **Pomquet** (p119). As you approach Baddeck (about halfway up Cape Breton Island) hook up with the **Cabot Trail** (p124), a well-marked 300km loop through the region. Aah, now you're getting your money's worth. First up as you swing around to the northwest is **Chéticamp** (p123), a deeply Acadian town. Next you can watch whales or chant with monks at the Tibetan monastery in **Pleasant Bay** (p126). Look for moose and nesting bald eagles in **Cape Breton Highlands National Park** (p124). It's always nice to stretch your legs with a hike at **Meat Cove** (p127). And don't forget to get your art fix at the studios along the **St Ann's Loop** (p128) before arriving in industrial North Sydney for the ferry to Newfoundland.

It's a six-hour sail over the sometimes-rough swell of the Cabot Strait to **Port aux Basques** (p253). Alight and drive north to **Gros Morne National Park** (p244), rich with mountain hikes, sea-kayak tours, fjords and weird rock formations. Take the Viking Trail from here to its awe-inspiring endpoint: **L'Anse aux Meadows National Historic Site** (p248), North America's first settlement. Leif Eriksson and his Viking pals homesteaded the place 1000 years ago, and it probably looked much the same then as it does now. After coming all this way, you too will feel like an Atlantic explorer.

TAILORED TRIPS

FEEDING FRENZY

Loosen the belt: you've got several hundred kilometers of eating ahead.

It's no surprise, given the watery environs, that seafood rules the tables in Atlantic Canada. Foodies around the globe salivate over giant **scallops** (p98) from Digby. Nothing beats a cold beer to chase down Malpeque's **oysters** (p208), famous for their moist, briny taste. Seaside cafés steam up batches of fresh **mussels** (p209) on Prince Edward Island, especially the western side in towns such as Summerside. And don't dare leave the island without strapping on a bib and making a squirty mess at a traditional **lobster** (p205) supper in New Glasgow.

Newfoundland and Labrador have unusual foods on their provincial plate, including **caribou meat** (p249), surprisingly tender and rich-tasting, available in Northern Peninsula towns such as L'Anse aux Meadows; and **bakeapples** (p259), an apricot-meets-raspberry fruit that shows up in jams and syrups for which Labrador's Forteau is famous.

New Brunswick's Miramichi River Valley is renowned for **fiddleheads** (p179), a distinctive green that's only edible in springtime.

You're probably getting thirsty thinking about all this food. Vineyards carpet several hectares of the Annapolis Valley; **Grand Pré's winery** (p106) is highly regarded. The air is sweeter in Mabou thanks to the aroma of single-malt whiskey from the **Glenora Distillery** (p120) wafting forth.

And for dessert? Glad you asked: sweet and smooth **Ganong's Chocolate** (p152) is in St Stephen.

GET CULTURED

Impress your friends by returning from vacation more knowledgeable.

Cape Breton Island combines cultures. See **Acadian traditions** (p123) in action, such as the art of hooked rug–making, at Chéticamp. Get your **Gaelic fix** (p128) near Englishtown, where the Gaelic College of Celtic Arts & Crafts offers classes in playing bagpipes or dancing like a true Scot. The 1744 fortress and ruins at Louisbourg provide your full dose of **French-versus-English regional history** (p131).

Set foot on PEI and discover how a fictional orphan became a worldwide **phenomenon** (p206); *Anne*-mania peaks in Cavendish. Lennox Island's Aboriginal Ecotourism Complex is an ideal place to explore **Mi'kmaw culture** (p213). Charlottetown's **Province House** (p187) is one of the country's most important historic sites.

In New Brunswick, visit King's Landing Historical Settlement to see the life of the **British Loyalists** (p147). Compare it to the not-so-plush **French Acadian** (p180) lifestyle at Acadian Historic Village. Finally, see where it all began 1000 years ago when **Viking Leif Eriksson** (p248) built a sod house at L'Anse aux Meadows.

Snapshot

Sit down at any dinner table in Atlantic Canada, and you'll hear the same thing:

'My ___ [fill in the blank: sister, cousin, neighbor] just left for Alberta to work in the oil fields.'

Outward migration, or 'outmigration,' is the single biggest issue facing Nova Scotia, New Brunswick and especially Newfoundland and Labrador. As the provinces' traditional industries – fishing, logging and mining – fall deeper into decline, and as Alberta's oil fields gush high-paying industrial jobs, people are leaving in droves to make their living where it makes economic sense.

Who can blame them? Newfoundland's unemployment rate hovers near 16%, the highest in Canada. Prince Edward Island is second-highest at 10%. The problem is nothing new: Atlantic economies have been taking a beating for the past 15 years as their resource base – codfish, timber and coal – was depleted and little effort was made to diversify early on. Newfoundland is the most extreme case of what happens as a result. Its population has spiraled downward for 14 years in a row (a statistic that happens to correlate to the 1992 codfish moratorium), and in 2006 the province had more deaths than births for the first time.

While people of all ages migrate, it's mostly younger folks who are bidding adieu to the region. As one local said, 'we're Canada's greatest exporters of youth.' Local governments worry about the future as the population that remains gets older and no younger generation comes in to take over and foot the bill for the oldsters.

Right now it's a conservative government that's figuring out how to deal with the situation. Each province is led by a center-right party, in line with Canada's current federal administration. In general, Atlantic Canada skews conservative, perhaps due to its ruralness. For instance, Nova Scotians recently went to the polls to vote on whether stores should be allowed to open on Sundays. The result? The province decided to keep them shuttered in accordance with the 'Lord's day' and to encourage family time.

It's true that many people kick and scream about the waning economy and population decline, and they expect the government to bail them out. But this is also a region that embraces an independent and entrepreneurial spirit. Plenty of creative folks see it all as an opportunity: they refurbish fishing boats into whale-watch boats, or turn mines into attractions that teach about ecology. The region's abundant natural resources are still there for the taking, they just come in new forms. Codfishing may be on its way out, but offshore oil drilling has arrived to take its place. What remains to be seen is how these resources are developed from now on: hopefully the region has learned from past mistakes (see p46) and will move forward responsibly and sustainably. It's this struggle that will loom largest over Atlantic Canada in coming years.

FAST FACTS

Population: 2.34 million

Unemployment rate: 10.4%

Median family income: $49,725

Hours per week of TV watched: 22.3

Average life expectancy: 66.5 years

Number of homicides (2005): 38

Nova Scotians who smoke: 23.4%

New Brunswickers for whom French is their mother tongue: 33%

Number of annual moose–vehicle collisions in Newfoundland: 700

Potato production per capita on PEI: 8000kg

History

For the region's top historical sights see the boxed text, p24.

THE FIRST FISHERMEN

Atlantic Canada's first inhabitants, the Paleoindians, walked into Labrador 9000 years ago. The harsh, frozen land didn't make life easy or lengthy for these folks. Next came the Maritime Archaic Indians, hunters and gatherers who survived on the sea's bountiful fish-and-seal dinners. They ranged throughout Atlantic Canada, Maine and into parts of Labrador between 7500 and 3500 years ago and are known for their ceremonial burials and other religious and magical practices, evidenced at sites such as Newfoundland's Port au Choix. They mysteriously disappeared around 1000 BC.

The next to tend the land were the Mi'kmaw and Maliseet peoples in the Maritimes and the Beothuk people in Newfoundland – all members of the Algonquin-speaking eastern woodlands tribes. The Mi'kmaq and Maliseet practiced agriculture and lived in fairly permanent settlements. The Beothuk were seminomadic and paddled the area in their birch-bark canoes. It was the Beothuk and their ceremonially ochre-coated faces who were dubbed 'red men' by the arriving Europeans, a name soon applied to all of North America's indigenous groups.

None of these people fared well once Europeans arrived and introduced diseases, land conflict and war to the mix. While the Mi'kmaq and Maliseet still occupy parts of Atlantic Canada, the Beothuk died out in 1829.

AGE OF DISCOVERY

Viking celebrity Leif Eriksson was the first European to reach Atlantic Canada's shores. Actually, he and his tribe of adventurous seafarers from Iceland and Greenland were the first Europeans in all of North America. Around AD 1000 they poked around the eastern shores of Canada, establishing winter settlements and way stations for repairing ships and restocking supplies, such as at L'Anse aux Meadows (p248) in Newfoundland. The local tribes did not exactly roll out the welcome mat for these intruders, who eventually tired of the hostilities and withdrew. There would be no more visits from the outside for another 300 to 400 years.

Call it a cartographic detective story: *The Viking Deception* (2005), a Public Broadcasting Service (PBS) documentary, examines the fabled scrap of parchment that shows North America's eastern seaboard. Is it a true Viking map, or a fake?

The action heated up again in the late 15th century. In 1492, backed by the Spanish crown, Christopher Columbus went searching for a western sea route to Asia and instead stumbled upon some small islands in the Bahamas. Other European monarchs, excited by his 'discovery,' quickly sponsored expeditions of their own. In 1497 Giovanni Caboto, better known as John Cabot, sailed under a British flag as far west as Newfoundland and Cape Breton. Although there's no evidence of where he first made landfall, the village of Bonavista (p234) in eastern Newfoundland usually gets the nod.

Cabot didn't find a passage to China but he did find cod, then a much-coveted commodity in Europe. In short order, hundreds of boats were shuttling between Europe and the fertile new fishing grounds. Basque whalers from northern Spain soon followed. Several were based at Red Bay (p259) in Labrador, which became the world's biggest whaling port during the 16th century.

TIMELINE	**1000 BC**	**AD 1000**
	After hanging around for a few thousand years, Maritime Archaic Indians inexplicably disappear	Viking Leif Eriksson and crew wash up at L'Anse aux Meadows and smelt iron

About this time, French explorer Jacques Cartier also was sniffing around Labrador. He was looking for gold and precious metals, but found only 'stones and horrible rugged rocks,' as he wrote in his journal in 1534. So he moved on to Québec – but not before bestowing Canada with its name. Scholars say it comes from *kanata,* a Huron-Iroquois word for 'village' or 'settlement,' which was written in Cartier's journal and later transformed by mapmakers to 'Canada.'

SETTLING IN

So we've got fish, furs and nice juicy chunks of land – is it any wonder Europe starts salivating?

In the margin: *In 2006, seven navigators of Basque heritage completed a 3500km voyage from Québec City to Red Bay, Labrador using an 8.4m chalupa, an exact replica of the 16th-century craft their whaling forefathers used.*

St John's lays claim to being the oldest town in North America, first settled in 1528. It belonged to no nation; rather it served fishing fleets from all over Europe. By 1583 the British claimed it, and St John's had the distinction of being the first colony of the Empire. The Brits also threw down stakes in Trinity (mid-1500s, though this was an unofficial group of merchants living together versus a chartered colony), Cupids (1610) and the Colony of Avalon (1621), all in Newfoundland.

The French weren't just sitting on their butts during this time. In 1604 explorer Samuel de Champlain and his party spent the winter on St Croix Island, a tiny islet in the river on the present international border with Maine. The next year Champlain and his fur-trader patron Sieur de Monts moved their small settlement to Port Royal in the Annapolis Valley, which would soon become an English–French flash point.

The French revved up their colonization in 1632 by bringing in a load of immigrants to LaHave on Nova Scotia's south shore. More settlers arrived in 1635, and soon the French had spread throughout the Annapolis Valley and the shores of the Bay of Fundy – a rich farming region they called Acadia.

FRENCH & ENGLISH: SMACKDOWN

By this time, the French were galling the English, and the English were infuriating the French. Both had claims to the land – hadn't Cabot sailed here first for England? or was it Cartier for France? – but each wanted regional dominance. They skirmished back and forth in hostilities that mirrored those in Europe, where wars raged throughout the first half of the 18th century.

Things came to a head in 1713 with the Treaty of Utrecht, which ended Queen Anne's War (1701–13) overseas. Under its provisions the majority of Nova Scotia and Newfoundland went to the British, and Cape Breton Island, Prince Edward Island and what is today New Brunswick went to the French. That Acadia was now British was a particularly bitter spoonful for the French; the Brits had even overtaken Port Royal and renamed it Annapolis Royal (p100), after Queen Anne.

The French reorganized and decided to give regional dominance another shot. In 1719 they began construction of a fortress at Louisbourg (p131) on Cape Breton Island to protect their interests. Bit by bit the fortified town grew.

The British took note and in 1745 sent out a colonial army from Massachusetts to capture Louisbourg. It fell after a 46-day siege. A treaty a few years later returned it to France.

1528	1755
Fishing village of St John's bobs up as North America's first European settlement	English round up and deport thousands of French Acadians from Bay of Fundy region

And so it went, with control of the region ping-ponging, until 1754 when the French and Indian Wars (sometimes called the Seven Years' War) began and ramped up the fighting to a new level.

MEMO TO ACADIANS: GET OUT

Charles Lawrence, the security-conscious British governor of Nova Scotia, had had enough. A war was going on, and when the French Acadian citizens in his territory refused to swear allegiance to Britain, his suspicions mounted to a fever pitch. In 1755, he ordered the Acadians to be rounded up and deported.

In a tragic chapter of history known as the Great Expulsion, the British burned villages and forced some 14,000 men, women and children onto ships. (The exact number varies, but scholars agree somewhere between 10,000 and 18,000 people were displaced.) Grand Pré (p106) was the heart of the area from which the Acadians were removed. Many headed for Louisiana and New Orleans; others went to various Maritime points, Martinique in the Caribbean, Santo Domingo in the Dominican Republic, or back to Europe.

The government gave their lands in the Annapolis Valley to 12,000 New England colonists called 'planters.' After peace was restored, some Acadians chose to return from exile but they were forced to settle on the less favorable 'French Shore' between Yarmouth and Digby.

Ultimately the English won the French and Indian Wars, and the French colonial era in the region ended. At the Treaty of Paris in 1763, France handed Canada over to Britain – except for two small islands off the coast of Newfoundland named St-Pierre and Miquelon (p244), which remain staunchly French to this day.

A PERFECT UNION IN PEI

All through the first half of the 19th century, shipbuilding made New Brunswick and Nova Scotia wealthy, and Nova Scotia soon boasted the world's fourth-largest merchant marine. The Cunard Line was founded at Halifax in 1840, and immigration from Scotland and Ireland flourished (as a look at the lengthy Mac and Mc sections of today's phone book confirms).

In 1864, Charlottetown, Prince Edward Island (PEI), served as the birthing room for modern Canada. At the town's Province House (p187), a group of representatives from Nova Scotia, New Brunswick, PEI, Ontario and Québec got together and hammered out the framework for a new nation. It took two more meetings – one in Québec City, the other in London – before Parliament passed the British North America Act in 1867. And so began the modern, self-governing state of Canada, originally known as the Dominion of Canada. The day the act became official, July 1, is celebrated as Canada's national holiday; it was called Dominion Day until it was renamed Canada Day in 1982.

Newfoundland, ever true to its independent spirit, did not join the confederation until 1949.

WORLD WARS

During both world wars Atlantic Canada played a key role as a staging area for the convoys that supplied Britain. The wars also boosted local economies and helped transition the region from an agricultural to an industrial base.

For those searching for their Cajun roots, the Acadian Genealogy Homepage (www.acadian.org) has compiled census reports harking back to 1671, plus maps and histories of local Acadian communities.

The Nova Scotia government maintains a website (http://titanic.gov.ns.ca) of all things *Titanic*, including a list of passengers buried in local graveyards and artifacts housed in the local museums.

1763	1864
Treaty of Paris boots France out of Canada after France loses the Seven Years' War	Fathers of the Confederation meet in Charlottetown and create a new country called Canada

Halifax was the only city in North America to suffer damage during WWI. In December, 1917 the *Mont Blanc*, a French munitions ship carrying TNT and highly flammable benzol, collided with the *Imo* in Halifax Harbour. The 'Halifax Explosion' ripped through the city, leveling most of Halifax' north end, injuring 9000 and killing 1900 people. It was the world's biggest man-made explosion prior to A-bombs being dropped on Japan in 1945.

Newfoundland had the dubious honor of being the only place in North America directly attacked by German forces during WWII. Just offshore from Bell Island (p228) near St John's, German U-boats fired on four allied ore carriers in 1942. All of them sank, with a loss of 69 lives. The Germans fired a torpedo at yet another carrier, but the projectile missed and instead struck inland at Bell Island's loading pier – thus making it the sole spot on the continent to take a straight-on German hit. That same year the Germans also torpedoed a Newfoundland ferry sailing in the Cabot Strait near Port aux Basques; 137 people died.

For a big-picture look at the rise and fall of the mighty cod, and its historical impact, read Cod: A Biography of the Fish that Changed the World *(1997) by Mark Kurlansky.*

MODERN TIMES

It wasn't until 1960 that Canada's Aboriginal people – including the Mi'kmaq, Maliseet and Innu – were finally granted Canadian citizenship. Even into the late 1960s Aboriginal children were being removed from their families and sent away to residential schools to 'civilize' them; many were abused. Land-rights claims and settlements regarding the schools are still winding their way through Canadian courts, while the damage such policies inflicted continues to haunt the Aboriginal communities.

Meanwhile, in Newfoundland in the 1950s the provincial government also was enforcing a resettlement program upon its citizens. People living in small, isolated fishing communities (aka outports) were being strongly 'encouraged' to pack it up and move inland where the government could deliver schools, health care and other services more economically. One method for 'encouraging' villagers was to cut ferry services to their communities, thus making them inaccessible since there were no roads. Many people were squeezed out of their ancestral homes in this way.

A Way of Life that Does not Exist: Canada & the Extinguishment of the Innu *(2003), by Colin Samson, studies what has happened to Labrador's northern indigenous people since the government tried to assimilate them in the 1950s and 1960s.*

FIRST PLACE PRIZE

Atlantic Canada was the site for a number of historic 'firsts' in 20th century:

- In St John's, Newfoundland Guglielmo Marconi received the world's first wireless transatlantic message from atop Signal Hill (1901).

- Robert E Peary gave his first news conference at Battle Harbour, Labrador after becoming the first man to reach the North Pole (1909).

- The wireless operators at the lighthouse at Cape Race, Newfoundland were the first to receive *Titanic*'s 'have struck iceberg' distress call (1912).

- Aviatrix Amelia Earhart took off from Harbour Grace, Newfoundland and became the first woman to cross the Atlantic Ocean solo (1932).

- Scientists from around the world held their first conference on disarmament issues in Pugwash, Nova Scotia, which led to 1963's Partial Test Ban Treaty (1957).

1912	**1942**
Titanic sinks off southern coast of Newfoundland	Bell Island, Newfoundland, torpedoed by German forces

AVAST! PIRATES ON THE HORIZON

Pirates began to ply and plunder Atlantic Canada's waters soon after Europeans arrived to colonize the area.

Peter Easton was one of the region's most famous pirates. He started out as an English naval officer in 1602. But when King James downsized the Royal Navy the next year, stranding Easton and his men in Newfoundland without any money, they – perhaps understandably – got pissed off and decided to use the resources at hand (ie boats and a bad attitude) to become pirates. By 1610 Easton was living large in Harbour Grace (p232), commanding a fleet of 40 ships and a crew of 5000 men. The money piled in for several more years, until he eventually retired to France, married a noblewoman and became the Marquis of Savoy.

Black Bart, aka Bartholomew Roberts, was another boatsman who made quite a splash in the local plundering business. He became a pirate after being captured by another, and he took to the lifestyle. Sort of. He liked the booty and the clothing it enabled (crimson waistcoat, scarlet plumed hat, gold necklaces), but he disliked booze and gambling. He also encouraged prayer among his employees. No one mutinied though, because his pirating prowess was legendary. For example, in 1720 he sailed into Newfoundland's Trepassey Bay aboard a 10-gun sloop with a crew of 60 men, and they were able to capture 21 merchant ships manned by 1200 sailors. He died in battle off the coast of Africa a few years later.

Halifax, always a well-sailored port, put a unique spin on its pirate history when the local government began sponsoring the plunder. The pirates were called 'privateers,' and during the War of 1812 the government sanctioned them to go out and get the goods and then provided them with waterfront warehouses to store it all. You can see where the action took place at the Privateer's Warehouse (p68). The South Shore town of Liverpool commemorates the era by hosting a rollicking Privateer Days festival (p87).

The latter 20th century was particularly harsh to two of the region's biggest industries: coal mining and fishing. Cape Breton's coal mines started to tank in the 1960s as their high-sulphur, high-pollution product fell out of favor in the marketplace; the mines shuttered for good in the 1990s. In 1992, the codfishing moratorium (see the boxed text, p236) was put in place, and many fisherfolk and fish-plant workers – a huge percentage of the population, especially in Newfoundland – lost their livelihoods. The offshore oil and tourism industries have been trying to pick up the slack, but many people are leaving the region to find work elsewhere in Canada.

1963	1992
Trans-Canada Hwy completed, spanning 7821km from St John's to Victoria, BC	Cod moratorium imposed, and thousands of fisherfolk lose their livelihood

The Culture

REGIONAL IDENTITY

A down-home vibe as thick as the fog blankets Atlantic Canada. It's the kind of place where two perfect strangers can sit next to each other on a bus, start talking, and within 15 minutes:

'You live next door to William? Why, his daughter is married to my brother's son!'

'It's a small world, luv.'

It's the kind of place where neighbors walk into each other's unlocked homes, borrow a cup of sugar, and leave a note saying, 'I'll pay you back later.'

It's the kind of place where the provincial ferry sails off its route to help a fisherman who has run into trouble at sea.

The hospitality and sense of community here are every bit as legendary as the stories you've heard, and memories of it will linger beyond the whale watches and lobster dinners. Locals extend their kindness to people from 'away' in many fashions: Need a ride? Hop in. Going to St John's? My cousin lives there; I've called and she'll pick you up at the airport. Don't have a place to sleep? Let me call Bonnie, she usually has a room.

The flip side of the small-town ambience is the stereotype that Atlantic Canadians, particularly Newfoundlanders, are all bumpkins. Yet the rural communities here are no different from those anywhere else in Canada.

If you've been hankering to know who invented the first snowplow for trains (Fredericton's John Hamilton) or the linguistic derivation of 'shoeshoe' (Mi'kmaw word), then read Calling the Maritimes Home: Origins, Attitudes, Quirks and Curiosities *(2004) by Julie V Watson.*

LIFESTYLE

Folks live a simple lifestyle, more functional than flashy. Despite an average income below the rest of Canada, most people own a home. In fact, they often own more than one: the 'cottage' is ubiquitous, a small, simple dwelling (maybe even a campervan) located outside of town where the family goes to relax for the weekend.

Family is important here. The divorce rate is well below Canada's average of 38%; indeed, Newfoundland and Labrador's rate is the nation's lowest at 22%. Multiple generations often work together in family businesses, and families often live near each other, though this is changing due to out-migration (see p30).

Atlantic Canadians spend a good deal of time outdoors – fishing, hunting, skiing, perhaps building their own home or cottage. However, it doesn't necessarily translate into fit and healthy, as the rising diabetes rate (among Canada's highest) attests.

Downhome (www .downhomelife.com) is a monthly lifestyle magazine for Atlantic Canadians. Residents offer up folksy tidbits like favorite places to fly a kite, best berry recipes and the latest on that albino moose roaming the 'hood.

ECONOMY

Let's just say when your financial planner up and leaves town to go drive a truck in Alberta, it's a sign of a weak economy.

Such is the recent case of a New Brunswick couple in their 50s: the husband was a financial planner in Fredericton, the wife a nurse. They said 'enough of this low-pay crap,' bolted to Fort McMurray, and are now making heaps more money than they ever did at home. It's a common scenario.

Atlantic Canada's economy is based on natural resources including fish, timber, minerals, natural gas and oil, a foundation that hasn't served it well in recent years. After the government imposed the cod moratorium in 1992, the fishing industry took a beating. Many people do still fish – it's herring now, followed by hake and haddock, as well as shellfish, with lobster being the most valuable, followed by shrimp, crab and scallops. But these species

---

FLYING THE ACADIAN FLAG

The French knew prime real estate when they saw it, and that's why they put down stakes around the Minas Basin in the 1630s. They called the region Arcadia, a Greek and Roman term for 'pastoral paradise.' It soon got shortened to Acadia, and by the 18th century, the Acadians felt more connection with the land they worked than with the distant Loire Valley they'd said *au revoir* to years earlier.

To the English, however, they would always be French, with whom rivalry and suspicion were constant. The hatred boiled over in 1755. The English had 'won' Nova Scotia by that time, but the Acadians refused to take an oath of allegiance to the English king, considering it an affront to their Catholic faith. This act of rebellion prompted the English to round up some 14,000 Acadians and deport them (p33).

In later years many of the displaced people returned. In Nova Scotia, Acadians resettled the Chéticamp area (p123) on Cape Breton Island and the French Shore (p95) north of Yarmouth. New Brunswick has a large French population stretching up the east coast past the Acadian Peninsula at Caraquet (p179) and around Edmundston and Moncton. On PEI, French speakers live from Miscouche to Mont-Carmel in the Région Évangéline (p212).

In all of these areas you'll see vibrant communities that speak French and have their own festivals, foods (p54) and red-white-and-blue, yellow-starred flag.

---

have not enabled the industry to recapture its former glory (though Nova Scotia's fishery remains the most lucrative in Canada).

Then there is the forest industry and its trail of pulp and paper mills throughout New Brunswick, Nova Scotia and Newfoundland. In New Brunswick alone, more than 24,000 jobs depend on forestry, and pulp and paper exports are worth a billion dollars a year. But that industry too has bled jobs, for reasons such as a general decline in construction.

For the future, the word on everyone's lips is – no, Benjamin, not plastics. It's oil, and hopefully it will rejuvenate the economy so that folks like the aforementioned financial planner will return to the region. Companies have begun drilling offshore from Cape Breton and St John's, in particular, and money is starting to trickle in. In Labrador, the hydroelectric plant at Churchill Falls and the nickel plant at Voisey's Bay are also being sized up as boons to the economy.

For more information on employment rates and the economy, see p30.

> Nova Scotia is the world's largest exporter of lobsters, Christmas trees, gypsum and wild blueberries.

POPULATION

About 53% of residents live in a city or town – rendering Atlantic Canada much more rural than Canada as a whole, where 80% of people live in an urban setting. And while Prince Edward Island (PEI) wins the prize as Canada's most densely populated province, it's still on the light side in world terms. It has 23.8 people per sq km, a figure that places it near USA proportions (29.4 per sq km) but a far cry from UK (244.1) or Netherlands (390.3) proportions. The other Atlantic provinces are even more lightly populated, culminating in Newfoundland and Labrador's lonely figure of 1.4 people per sq km.

Almost 16.5% of the region's population is under age 15, 13.8% is over age 65, and the rest are in between – a basic age distribution that parallels Canada's.

MULTICULTURALISM

Most immigrants came ashore in the 17th to 19th centuries from England, Ireland, Scotland and France, and their descendants can be found in

---

BUDDING BUDDHISTS

Halifax is home to one of the largest communities of Buddhist converts on the continent. In the late 1970s, Chögyam Trungpa, spiritual leader of the Tibetan-influenced Shambhala Buddhists, chose the city to be the sect's world headquarters. He admired Halifax' sense of tradition and lack of materialism. Today, about 600 Buddhists live inconspicuously in the city, and more live at Gampo Abbey (p126) on Cape Breton Island. The group emphasizes meditation, which can be studied at any of its 150 Shambhala centers worldwide; check www.shambhala.org for further enlightening information.

---

distinct pockets. Cape Breton Island and PEI have deep Scottish roots, while Newfoundland maintains its English and Irish ancestry. In New Brunswick, people of French descent comprise 37% of the population, a number that trickles down to 12% on PEI and 9% in Nova Scotia. For the French communities' geographic distribution see the boxed text, p37.

The great waves of European immigrants coming to Canada post-1900 blew right over the Atlantic region and instead headed west by train to colonize the prairies. Even today, there aren't many foreign-born people in Atlantic Canada. The statistics range from a low of 1.6% of Newfoundland and Labrador's population, to a high of 4.6% in Nova Scotia. Compare that with Canada as a whole, where 18.4% of the population is foreign-born – a number that keeps rising, whereas foreign-born numbers have declined recently in the Atlantic provinces. Immigration is not the issue here. Rather, the story has become one of emigration; see p30 for details.

Blacks, located mostly in Nova Scotia, are the region's largest visible minority (see the boxed text, p91). See the boxed text on p40 for details on the Aboriginal population.

The website www.off darock.com contains all you ever wanted to know about Newfoundlanders – their jokes, music, slang and recipes. You can even download a 'screeched in' certificate.

MEDIA

The hand of Transcontinental Media reaches far and wide. The company publishes nine daily newspapers (including the *Charlottetown Guardian* and *St John's Telegram*) and 26 community newspapers throughout Atlantic Canada, mostly in Nova Scotia and Newfoundland, with a combined circulation of more than 300,000.

The region's small but high-quality book-publishing industry actively promotes works by and about locals. Fredericton's **Goose Lane Editions** (www .gooselane.com), St John's-based **Creative Book Publishing** (www.nfbooks.com) and Halifax-based **Nimbus Publishing** (www.nimbus.ns.ca) crank out fiction books as well as nonfiction art, history and cookbooks.

RELIGION

Thanks to forefathers from the British Isles and France, Protestantism and Catholicism linger as the region's main religions. The Protestants have a slight edge overall, but the Catholics rule in New Brunswick and on PEI. Regardless, formal religion plays an ever-diminishing role in local life.

A small but powerful group of Buddhists lives in Nova Scotia; see the boxed text, above for details.

Which province is the most generous? Smartest? Richest? Find out at Statistics Canada (www.statcan.ca), where they've crunched census data on multiple topics.

SPORTS

Just because there are no professional teams in the region doesn't mean that people aren't rabid about certain sports – hockey, to be specific. Ah yes, Canada's de facto national game is skated with enthusiasm in the Atlantic provinces. You can literally be in the middle of nowhere, a tiny town with just a few hundred people, and what is the lone community building you'll see? An ice-hockey rink.

Allegedly the game was invented in Windsor, Nova Scotia (p107), so it's no wonder hockey remains ingrained in the local culture. In lieu of the pros, check out teams such as the St John's Fog Devils, Halifax Mooseheads and PEI Rockets, all part of the Québec Major Junior Hockey League. The season runs from mid-September to mid-March.

Newfoundlander Brad Gushue and his team won the gold medal for curling at the 2006 Olympic Games. Provincial schools and business closed early to watch the final match.

ARTS

The more isolated and woeful the landscape, the more it inspires local artists. Or so it seems, with Cape Breton Island and Newfoundland producing the most writers and musicians.

Literature

Nova Scotian Thomas Chandler Haliburton (1796–1865) endures as one of the region's top writers. What? You've never heard of him? How about phrases such as 'the early bird gets the worm' and 'you can't get blood out of stone'? Haliburton coined these sayings in his humorous 1836 novel *The Clockmaker*.

It's hard to argue against Lucy Maud Montgomery (1877–1942) being the region's most famous writer, given the mania that takes place in her name in Cavendish (p206). Though her children's book *Anne of Green Gables* (1908) initially was rejected by five publishers, the story of the lively orphan on a farm at Avonlea has since become a worldwide classic, and the book's sites have become literary shrines.

Alistair MacLeod (b 1936) conveys the Gaelic melancholy and loneliness of Cape Breton Island through his short stories and novels such as *No Great Mischief* (1999), which traces a family from Scotland to Cape Breton over several generations.

The face of Acadian literature is New Brunswickan Antonine Maillet (b 1929). She wrote *La Sagouine* (1971), 16 monologues by a disheveled Acadian fisherman's wife (also adapted into a play), and *Pélagie* (1982), about Acadians returning from exile in Louisiana. Maillet is a skillful folklorist, and her writings are immensely popular in French Canada and France. Though not Acadian himself, Henry Wadsworth Longfellow wrote the most enduring work about the culture: his poem *Evangeline* (1847) reveals the Acadian deportation through the eyes of two lovers separated by the events.

Newfoundland has a clutch of local novelists. Edward Riche penned *Rare Birds* (1997), in which a Newfoundlander tries to save his restaurant by hatching (pun!) a plot using phony rare bird sightings to draw tourists. Bernice Morgan's *Random Passage* (1992) follows a courageous woman's journey from servitude in England to the harsh outport life. Michael Crummey's *River Thieves* (2001) delves into the tension between settlers and the Beothuk Aboriginals in the early 1800s. And E Annie Proulx won the Pulitzer Prize for *The Shipping News* (1994), about a man's redemption upon returning to his ancestral home in Newfoundland. A lot of locals dislike Proulx' book because they think it perpetuates negative cultural stereotypes, such as incest.

Cinema & Television

Nova Scotia and Newfoundland are the two main players in the region's small filmmaking scene.

Parts of *Titanic* (1997; directed by James Cameron) were shot in Nova Scotia. Leonardo DiCaprio's character supposedly was based on J Dawson, age 23, one of *Titanic*'s engine room workers. His grave is in Halifax's Fairview Cemetery, where he was buried after the legendary ship sank in 1912. *Margaret's Museum* (1995; directed by Mort Ransen), starring Helena Bonham Carter, was filmed on windswept Cape Breton Island and depicts the bleak life of the local Glace Bay coal miners.

The popular TV comedy *Trailer Park Boys* focuses on Ricky and Julian, two ex-cons living in Sunnyvale Trailer Park near Halifax. They're constantly trying to make money, but misguided schemes like a homemade porno titled *From Russia With the Lovebone* land them in trouble. The Boys have been airing since 2001, and they also have a self-titled movie out.

Several books by Newfoundland authors (see Literature, p39) have been made into films that give tantalizing glimpses of the province's scenery. The limited-release *Rare Birds* (2002; directed by Sturla Gunnarsson) stars William Hurt. *The Shipping News* (2001; directed by Lasse Hallström) got the full Hollywood treatment with an all-star cast led by Kevin Spacey and Dame Judi Dench. *Random Passage* (2002; directed by John N Smith) is a sprawling miniseries with a mostly Irish cast.

For further information on what's filming in the region, check the provincial film websites: New Brunswick (www.nbfilm.com), Newfoundland (www.nlfdc.ca), Nova Scotia (www.film.ns.ca) and Prince Edward Island (www.techpei.com).

Music

Music is the region's artistic strong suit, with tunes emanating from an epicenter on Cape Breton Island. Fiddles, accordions, vocal harmonies, vivid storytelling and other Celtic traits form the music's backbone – no

---

THE MI'KMAQ, MALISEETS & INNU: A FIRST NATIONS PRIMER

Some 23,500 Mi'kmaq and Maliseets live in the three Maritime provinces. Roughly 10,000 members of both bands live in New Brunswick, the Maliseets in the upper Saint John River valley in the west and the Mi'kmaq to the east. Some 1000 Mi'kmaqs are on PEI. About 12,500 Mi'kmaqs live in Nova Scotia in 14 communities, mostly around Bras d'Or Lake on Cape Breton and near Truro. Together Aboriginal peoples account for just over 1% of the Maritimes' total population. Included in these figures are 2000 Métis, the name used to denote those of mixed Aboriginal and European blood.

In Newfoundland and Labrador (mostly the latter), the cold weather–dwelling Inuit and Innu join the Métis and Mi'kmaw. About 8400 Aboriginal peoples live in Labrador today, comprising 30% of the total population.

Many residents of the Maritimes' 36 reserves as well as those in Labrador live in poverty. Rates of infant mortality, life expectancy, literacy and incarceration are disproportionately high compared with other Canadians. This situation is largely a result of Canadian governmental policy. When great numbers of Aboriginal people died from European diseases during the 18th century, the survivors were relocated on small reserves in remote, unfavorable areas. Their hereditary hunting and fishing rights were largely abolished, and their traditional beliefs – in which there was no sharp division between the sacred and the secular – were attacked by Christian missionaries.

During the past two decades a revitalization movement has emerged to encourage a return to traditional ways. A revival of local song and dance, language programs, and healing and ritual ceremonies now accompanies the legal battles being waged across the region for fishing and timber rights and political autonomy.

For further information, visit the websites for the Mi'kmaq Resource Center (http://mrc.uccb .ns.ca) at Cape Breton University; the Innu Nation (www.innu.ca); and www.native-languages .org/maliseet.htm for Maliseet links.

surprise since much of it originated in 18th-century Scotland. Performances called 'ceilidhs' (*kay*-lees), 'shindigs' or 'kitchen parties' occur regularly in summer throughout the region and feature fancy fiddling and step dancing. Popular Cape Breton musicians include fiddlers Ashley MacIsaac, Buddy MacMaster and Natalie MacMaster, and multi-instrumentalist JP Cormier.

Newfoundland's music is similar to Cape Breton's, though the latter is more lyrical and tender-sounding whereas Newfoundland music gets played with an edge. Singer-songwriter Ron Hynes embodies the local style and can be found strumming his guitar in St John's pubs. The Navigators play driving Celtic tunes reminiscent of the Pogues, while the Novaks evoke Tom Petty with the whoop-ass amped up.

The band that translates this music to a larger stage most successfully is Newfoundland's Great Big Sea. They tour throughout the USA and Canada, filling mighty venues with their Celtified rave-ups and kitchen-party enthusiasm. They are a definite must-see live.

Acadian/Cajun music often parallels Celtic music, especially in regard to traditional fiddling and step dancing. Notable groups include Blou, creators of Acadico, a new category of world music that mixes traditional and contemporary sounds. Jacobus et Maleco is the first Acadian rap group, and internationally renowned Grand Dérangement sings movingly of Acadian reality through its traditional tunes.

And let's not overlook rock. The new front man for supergroup INXS is JD Fortune from Salt Springs, Nova Scotia. He won TV's inaugural *Rock Star* series to land the gig.

> In the 1950s, folklorist MacEdward Leach traveled around Cape Breton and Newfoundland to record the region's traditional songs. Hear them at www.mun.ca/folklore/leach/songs/index.html.

Architecture

Traditional wood-framed fishing cottages dominate the architecture in Atlantic Canada, and you'll see them everywhere, frequently coated with colorful paint. The well-preserved fishing buildings of Lunenburg helped earn the town its Unesco world heritage designation; see p83 for architectural details.

The English left a legacy of Victorian homes. Often these houses are much finer than the surrounding residences and that's because this is where the local fish merchant or paper-mill supervisor lived, lording over his employees. Many of the homes are now B&Bs.

Painting

The region's most celebrated artist is the realist painter Alex Colville (b 1920), who lives in Wolfville, Nova Scotia. His works have a peculiar, geometric foundation prompting many critics to dub his style 'magic realist.'

Fellow realist painter Mary Pratt (b 1935) was born and raised in New Brunswick. She moved to Newfoundland in 1963, where she has been painting ever since and where she was a driving force behind the establishment of The Rooms (p221).

Folk artist Maud Lewis (1903–70) of Digby, Nova Scotia, overcame polio to produce delightful paintings of outdoor scenes. These now hang in the Art Gallery of Nova Scotia (p65). The Acadian regions are also full of folk artists; watch for signs along the highways, especially near the Chéticamp area.

Aboriginal artists such as Alan Syliboy (b 1952), of the Millbrook First Nation at Truro, Nova Scotia, have drawn inspiration from ancient petroglyphs found in Kejimkujik National Park and elsewhere. Syliboy's website (www.redcrane.ca) provides an excellent introduction to contemporary Mi'kmaw art.

Theater & Dance

The region's theatrical offerings can be divided into two categories: serious academic or avant-garde productions, generally staged for local audiences during the winter season; and summer-only theaters (sometimes called 'dinner theaters') that deal with folkloric or historic themes and depend almost entirely on the patronage of visitors.

The *Anne of Green Gables* musical (p193) presented each summer in Charlottetown is easily the most celebrated tourist production. The French equivalent is *Évangéline* (p96) at Church Point, Nova Scotia.

Other summer theaters of note include the Ship's Company Theatre (p112) in Parrsboro, Nova Scotia, which stages new Canadian and Maritime works in an old ferryboat. In New Brunswick there is the French-language Le Pays de la Sagouine at Bouctouche, dedicated to Acadian writer Antonine Maillet (see Literature, p39). In Newfoundland, Trinity's Rising Tide Theatre (p234) has garnered accolades. Check any of these in July and August.

Environment David Lukas

From unexplored wilderness to dramatic coastlines and phenomenal wildlife, the provinces of Atlantic Canada are a nature-lover's dream. It's a place where you are as likely to see thousands of seabirds resting on a passing iceberg as a moose crossing the road, and, if you're lucky, you may spot feeding blue whales or a wandering polar bear. This rich and varied landscape is easily explored courtesy of the region's many parks, ranging from the alluring sandy beaches of Prince Edward Island National Park to the soaring fjords of Gros Morne National Park in Newfoundland.

At the Fundy Geological Museum (http://museum .gov.ns.ca/fgm/index .html; p112), 'time travel' with interactive exhibits and visit a lab where dinosaur bones are being cleaned and assembled.

THE LAND

The spectacular landscapes of Atlantic Canada are both their charm and their challenge. Due to the rugged land and crumpled coastlines the traditions of isolated villages and homesteads have been preserved to a greater extent than perhaps anywhere else in North America, but the difficulty of coaxing crops from the rocky soil or transporting goods to market keeps much of the region economically depressed.

For geologists, however, this region hides great wealth, not just in the shape of rich ore deposits but in the record of earth history preserved by the rocks. This is where two significant geologic provinces converge: Labrador forms the eastern rim of the vast Canadian Shield, the greatest exposure of ancient rocks on the earth's surface; while the other Atlantic provinces perch at the northern tip of the Appalachian Mountains, the single most important topographic feature of eastern North America.

You could plan your entire trip around visiting the stunning geologic features presented in the splendidly illustrated *The Last Billion Years: A Geological History of the Maritime Provinces of Canada,* published by the Atlantic Geoscience Society.

Sitting at this great convergence, Atlantic Canada offers a visually dramatic snapshot of more than one billion years of earth history, ranging from the red sandstone cliffs of Northumberland Strait to the famed granite headlands at Peggy's Cove, Nova Scotia. And perhaps even more fascinating for the

---

TRAVELING RESPONSIBLY: DOS & DON'TS

The impact you have on other people's as well as your own experience while traveling are functions of being responsible and having respect for another region's environment. Common sense and awareness are your best guides.

- *Don't* litter. *Do* patronize hotels that have recycling programs. *Do* carry out all of your trash from trails and parks.

- *Do* stay on trails: they lessen the erosion caused by human transit. *Don't* disturb animals or damage plants. *Do* observe wildlife from a distance with binoculars.

- *Don't* feed the animals! Doing so interferes with the animals' natural diets. They can be susceptible to bacteria transferred by humans, or pesticides contained within fruit, which may cause illness or death. Not only do the animals become more vulnerable to hunting and trapping, but they may stop seeking out their own natural food sources and become dependent on this human source.

- *Do* follow the instructions of trained naturalist guides. *Don't* request that guides disturb animals or plants so you can have a better look.

- *Do* learn about wildlife and local conservation, environmental and cultural issues before your trip and during your visit. *Do* ask questions and listen to what locals have to say. *Do* support tourism companies and environmental groups that promote conservation initiatives and long-term management plans.

visitor are the many signs of the massive Pleistocene ice sheet that smothered the region with ice a mile deep as recently as 20,000 years ago: the thrilling fjords of the north, the rounded mounds of Nova Scotia (known locally as drumlins), the tens of thousands of small shallow lakes.

In its simplest form, the geologic story is that Atlantic Canada formed from the fragments and pieces left over after North America and Africa collided and crushed an ocean between them 400 million years ago. In the process of swinging into each other with tremendous force, the two continents compressed and folded seafloor sediments into a giant mountain chain that has eroded over millions of years into the rolling hills we now call the Appalachian Mountains. Mixed into this mélange are the many different pieces of smaller land masses trapped between the colliding continents.

When North America and Africa went their separate ways 180 million years ago, they each left part of their coastline behind. This may be best observed in Newfoundland, for its western third is a remnant of the ancestral North American coastline, its middle third is a slice of ancient seafloor, and its eastern third once belonged to northern Africa.

The Nova Scotia Museum of Natural History (http://museum.gov .ns.ca/mnh/index.htm) is a fabulous resource, both online and in person, for learning about local plants and critters.

Kids may be especially intrigued by the region's fossils, many of which are on display in various parks and museums, including fossil footprints, dinosaur bones, and fossilized creatures that look like they're from outer space. In New Brunswick, see remains of the first life to walk on land in North America (a giant centipede, in case you're wondering) and evidence of the most primitive terrestrial plants.

But geology never stops at the simple story, and for the traveler who's enthusiastic about the subject this region never runs out of surprises. Even if you don't study rocks or get excited by fossils, you cannot ignore the stunning outcroppings and rock types visible at nearly every stage of your journey. There are, for example, sea stacks, drowned coastlines, glacial grooves, and erratics everywhere – what more could you ask for?

WILDLIFE

Whether you come for a glimpse of polar bear, caribou, whales or moose, Atlantic Canada will not disappoint the wildlife enthusiast. In fact this is a marvelous wildlife destination no matter what season you visit. Many people travel to the region to see the incredible numbers of seabirds and whales that can be spotted from coastal bluffs or on whale-watch trips, but some of the most unusual wildlife is seen in the far north where few travelers journey.

The white hairs on a polar bear are hollow and trap sunlight to help keep the animal warm in frigid temperatures.

The plants and animals of Atlantic Canada are even more amazing when you realize that the entire region was completely buried in ice only 20,000 years ago and was not accessible for life until about 10,000 years ago. Where all these critters came from and how they got here so quickly is anybody's guess!

Animals

If you needed one single reason to visit Atlantic Canada, it might be to have world-class encounters with some of the whales that gather in great numbers in these food-rich waters. Somewhere in the neighborhood of 22 species of whale and porpoise can be seen on the numerous whale-watch tours (p49) offered from countless coastal harbors. Humpback whales are a perennial favorite because of their spectacular leaps and dives, but people are just as eager to catch a glimpse of the highly endangered North Atlantic right whale or the largest leviathan of all, the blue whale.

Closer to shore or hauled out on the ice, it is common to see a variety of seals, including in winter the snowy white young of the harp seal. Sadly these drew worldwide horror in the 1970s when it was revealed that they

---

THE GRAND BANKS

Banks are a funny name for a shallow area, but in the case of the Grand Banks off Newfoundland's southeast coast it's no laughing matter. Until recently this was considered the greatest site in the world for ocean fish and the animals that came to feed on them. Even today, with the fish nearly hunted out, millions of seabirds and uncounted whales come to feed in the rich waters. This area is incredibly productive because the continental shelf off the coast of Newfoundland sticks out like a thumb to intercept the south-flowing waters of the frigid Labrador Current right at the point where they mingle with the warm north-flowing waters of the Gulf Stream. The mix of warmth and nutrient-rich Arctic waters creates an explosion of plankton that feeds everything from the smallest fish to the biggest whale. And because the shallow waters allow sunlight to penetrate to the ocean floor, the food chain is active at all depths.

---

were being clubbed to death for their furs. Harbor and gray seals are easily observed, though in winter they seek out the edges of the pack ice. (Both species are nonmigratory, though they make some local movements in response to breeding season and development of ice floes.)

Land animals are also a powerful draw. Fox, bear, and otter are widespread throughout the region. On Newfoundland there are more than 100,000 moose and there are many more on Cape Breton Island, so you'd have to work hard *not* to see one. As you travel north the animals become even more exotic. From Newfoundland north you will find polar bear, arctic fox, wolf, lynx, and musk oxen. Labrador has the largest herd of caribou in the world, as well as wolves that follow the long lines of migrating caribou.

Seabirds are the primary wildlife attraction in Atlantic Canada, and rightly so. There are few places in North America where it is easier to see outstanding numbers of seabirds such as razorbill, Atlantic puffin, common murre, and northern gannet. Huge nesting colonies on rocky islands and promontories may contain more than a million birds, but these merely hint at the numbers that once nested here before market hunters slaughtered uncounted millions of birds.

Mudflats and shorelines, especially along the Bay of Fundy, are world famous for the tremendous quantities of shorebirds they attract during the May and August migration. Upwards of two million birds stop here annually. On nearby beaches, the diminutive and endangered piping plover tries to hold its own against the trespass of invading sunbathers and beach walkers – please respect signs that warn you of this bird's home.

More than any other animal, fish have placed Atlantic Canada on the map, in particular the northern cod (see the boxed text, above). With the collapse of the great cod fishery, other species such as halibut, mackerel, haddock, and herring have grown in economic importance. In the region's many lakes and rivers, fishermen seek out trout, bass, salmon, and river herring (with the quaint name alewives).

Although it is easy to focus on the region's showiest animals, we cannot ignore the one that is smallest but not least in Atlantic Canada. It has been said that the diminutive black fly has single-handedly maintained the wild splendor of Labrador. This may sound like an exaggeration until you step foot onto the shore in midsummer and are virtually blanketed in biting insects against which you are defenseless. Getting into eyes, nose, mouth, and ears these insects have literally driven people mad with their painful itching bites. Second only to the black fly, though it's a close call, are mosquitoes so prolific that it has been estimated they would drain half your blood in two hours if you let them. If it's any consolation, you can tell yourself that

It seems like every bend in the road is rich with birds when you use the detailed maps and descriptions in *Birding Sites of Nova Scotia,* by Blake Maybank.

every animal from ant to moose is tormented equally by these creatures, so they're not picking on you.

Plants

Although the Atlantic Canada provinces present some tree diversity in their southern reaches with a mix of birch, maple, and ash, vast areas of forest are completely dominated by spruce as you head north. And at some point even those homogenous forests give way to soggy tundra that stretches to the Arctic. Surprisingly the area can be rich with abundant wildflowers during the short growing season.

The yellow dandelion-like flowers of the coltsfoot may be the first ones to come out each spring, but far more attention is given to the region's delightful midsummer orchid displays, including showy lady's slipper, which may carpet entire boggy areas. Blue lupines seem to bloom everywhere, and many other varieties and colors can be found.

The most common shrubs, especially in Newfoundland and Labrador, are those in the heath family, including blueberries, cranberries, and other delicious berries that grow in profusion in August. Tolerant of the acidic soils, these shrubs are prolific beyond comprehension, which isn't such a bad thing since their berries are highly sought after by both humans and animals.

Perhaps the most curious plant is the odd lichen called caribou moss. Growing in such a dense spongy carpet that other plants cannot get a toehold, this pale greenish moss may be the most dominant plant in the northern forests. It is an important food source for caribou, hence its name, and is often mixed with seal meat to vary the diets of sled dogs.

NATIONAL & PROVINCIAL PARKS

Atlantic Canada has taken its park systems seriously and that many important sites are protected within both national and provincial parks. Nova Scotia alone has more than 120 parks, but even Newfoundland and Labrador, which are so sparsely settled as to be parks in their own right, have a total of 34 parks.

Not all parks are set up for camping, but they are all worthy of a visit. In a few parks it is possible to plan extended hiking and camping trips, but all of them offer splendid opportunities for activities ranging from picnicking to beachcombing to kayaking and cycling. Those that are open in the winter are favored by cross-country skiers and snowshoers.

Even though it's not a designated park, Bras d'Or Lake (p133) on Cape Breton Island has 967km of shoreline with unspoiled coves and islands, and fantastic numbers of bald eagles.

ENVIRONMENTAL ISSUES

Early Europeans explorers were dumbfounded by the apparently inexhaustible numbers of animals they encountered in Atlantic Canada. It was a scene of such incredible abundance that they thought it would never end, so they bent their will toward exploiting and profiting from the natural wealth in every way possible. The result is only too predictable and sad: animals lost forever include the mythical great auk, the Labrador duck and the sea mink. Today Atlantic Canada is facing the horrifying prospect that the greatest fishery in the world, the uncounted millions of cod that sustained their provincial livelihood for 400 years, may have come to an end when cod were listed as endangered in 2003. In the end, not only has the environment suffered great damage, but so have the villages and traditions that needed the fish for their survival.

Unfortunately resource exploitation continues unabated on several other fronts. Some $3 billion a year is generated from logging, with half of the production coming from New Brunswick. Vast ore deposits are being explored and developed all the time, with huge areas stripped of their forest and soil

ATLANTIC CANADA'S TOP NATURAL AREAS

Park	Features	Activities	Best time to visit	Page
Nova Scotia				
Cape Chignecto Provincial Park	largest and newest park in province, rugged wilderness; old growth forest deer, moose, eagles	hiking and back-country camping	Jun-Oct	(p113)
Kejimkujik National Park	pristine wilderness network of glacial lakes; otter, loon, bald eagles	canoeing, camping, hiking	late Sep-early Oct	(p88)
Cape Breton Highlands National Park	dramatic oceanside cliffs, world-famous scenic drive; whales, bald eagles, seabirds, bear, moose, wild orchids	hiking, camping, sightseeing, whale-watching	May-Oct	(p124)
New Brunswick				
Fundy National Park	sandstone cliffs, extensive beach, dramatic tides; bear, moose, beaver, peregrine falcons	mountain biking, bird-watching,hiking	year-round	(p168)
Kouchibouguac National Park	lagoons, white-sand beaches; moose, deer, bear	strolling, clam digging, kayaking, bird-watching cycling, skiing,	year-round	(p176)
Prince Edward Island				
Prince Edward Island National Park	red sandstone bluffs, dunes, beaches; red fox, piping plover, sandpiper	bird-watching, beach walking, swimming, picnicking	May-Sep	(p201)
Newfoundland				
Cape St Mary's Ecological Reserve	rugged ocean cliffs, one of the most accessible seabird colonies in North America; nesting gannets, whales	bird-watching	Mar-Aug	(p233)
Terra Nova National Park	craggy cliffs and many sheltered inlets, lakes, bogs; moose, beaver, bald eagles, whales	kayaking, fishing, camping	mid-May-mid-Oct	(p239)
Witless Bay Ecological Reserve	offshore islands; over a million breeding seabirds, feeding whales, icebergs	bird-watching, whale-watching	Jun-Aug	(p229)
World Heritage–Listed Sites				
Gros Morne National Park, Newfoundland	stunning mix of barren plateaus and deep fjords considered one of Canada's premier treasures; world-famous geology, wild orchids	camping, hiking, sightseeing	mid-May–mid-Oct	(p244)
L'Anse aux Meadows National Historic Site, Newfoundland	first European settlement in North America; historical interpretation, reconstructed huts, buildings, and port	Viking boat building course	Jun-early Oct	(p248)
Old Town Lunenburg, Nova Scotia	original colonial settlement; Victorian architecture, historic inns, wooden boats	sightseeing	year-round	(p83)

cover to access coal, iron, nickel and other mineral resources. Recently there has been a spate of oil and natural gas development, especially on the ocean floor, with untold consequences for marine life. What is particularly troubling is how much exploitation occurs in seldom-visited parts of Labrador, where there is little public scrutiny or attention.

Outdoors

Atlantic Canada has only recently begun to harness its cliffy, wet, marine-mammaled terrain for outdoor adventures. Visitors can now get out in the sun (or rain or fog, as the case may be) to hike, kayak, whale-watch, or even surf. The season is short for most activities (May to October in a good year), but you'll find plenty of tour operators eager to set you up for action. It's also easy to arrange independent adventures with your own or rented equipment.

HIKING

Trails – from gentle jaunts around an interpretive path to breath-sapping slogs up a mountain – crisscross the area's national and provincial parks. Even the most confirmed couch-dweller will be able to find somewhere suitable to trek. And hiking – aside from being low-cost – is the most enjoyable way to absorb the region.

The hiking season runs from May to October, with optimal conditions from July onward, when the trails have dried out. Maps are available at park information centers, although for extended hikes you may need topographic maps (see p270).

So strap on your hiking boots and hit the pathways. In Nova Scotia, highlights include Taylor Head Provincial Park (p136), which occupies a slender sprig of land on the eastern shore and has trails traversing forest and beach. Cape Breton Highlands National Park (p125) offers exquisite hiking over stark, dramatic coastline; the Skyline Trail is the most popular path, but it's hard to go wrong with any of them. The trails over Cape Mabou Highlands' (p122) hills and dunes reward hardy souls (and legs).

New Brunswick is no slouch in the hiking department either. Grand Manan Island (p159) shines as the provincial jewel for hikes, as it does with so many outdoor activities. Cliffs, marshes and lighthouses are all on the paths. There's more rugged coast to be explored at Fundy National Park (p169) and on the Fundy Trail Parkway (p168), though you'll have more company than on lonesome Grand Manan.

Newfoundland's trails are remnants of old walking paths that used to connect local communities and provided escape routes inland from pirates. They make for fantastic hiking since most clutch the shoreline and often provide whale views. The East Coast Trail (p222) on the Avalon Peninsula, Discovery Trail (p233) on the Bonavista Peninsula and trails throughout Gros Morne National Park (p245) are renowned for their vistas.

On Prince Edward Island (PEI), you can hike along many parts of the Confederation Trail (p199) or in the national park (p201).

Finally, don't forget that Canada is also home to one of the most ambitious paths ever conceived, the **Trans Canada Trail** (www.tctrail.ca), an 18,078km-long ribbon from Cape Spear (p229) in Newfoundland all the way to Victoria, British Columbia. It's still a work in progress, but trails in the provinces sometimes coincide with it.

KAYAKING & CANOEING

Atlantic Canada is chock-full of possibilities to get out on the water, be it a lazy canoe trip or a battle with roiling white water. Sea kayaking has exploded here, with myriad places to paddle; see the boxed text, opposite, for details. A unique activity in the region is tidal-bore rafting, where you harness the blasting force of the famous Fundy tides; see p108 for how to get outfitted.

SEA KAYAKING

If there's any one activity that is Atlantic Canada's specialty, it's sea kayaking. It's everywhere; it's absolutely the best way to see the remarkable coastlines, and oftentimes you'll be kayaking alongside whales.

Most companies cater to beginners, so no need to feel unworthy if you've never kayaked before. Conversely, advanced paddlers can rent crafts and head out on their own. It can be very rough out there due to volatile weather, high winds and strong currents, so know your limits. The Canadian government publishes an excellent resource titled *Sea Kayaking Safety Guide*, available via download from **Transport Canada** (www.tc.gc.ca/BoatingSafety/pubs/kayak/menu.htm). It details each province's weather and kayaking terrain, and also provides trip-planning tips.

Nova Scotia's top kayaking spots are along the Eastern Shore, including Tangier (p137) where waters are warmish, and along the South Shore, including well-serviced Mahone Bay (p81) and Kejimkujik Seaside Adjunct (p89. Cape Breton (p120) is scenically stunning though the winds can be brutal.

In New Brunswick the Fundy Isles (p155) from St Andrews to Grand Manan are prime kayak terrain, rich in marine and birdlife, though beware of the tides. Paddling along the eastern Fundy shore (p167) rewards with sea caves and seabirds.

Newfoundland and Labrador offers the region's most remote paddling. Way the hell up in Cartwright (p260) an outfitter offers tours to the Wonderstrands, the giant beach that captivated the Vikings 1000 years ago. Many south-coast outports (p255) provide tours where it will just be you and the great big sea. More accessible jaunts – and your best shot at hanging out with whales – can be had at Witless Bay (p229), Terra Nova (p239) and Gros Morne (p246) national parks.

National and provincial parks are excellent places to start if you've never dipped an oar. Maps and equipment rentals are usually available from the park information centers, where the staff can also give route recommendations.

Canoeing

Canoeing doesn't have the cachet of sea kayaking in the region, but there are still some lovely opportunities. The sport is best suited to inland lakes and rivers, so it's no shocker that Kejimkujik National Park (p88) ranks high on the list, given its setting in Nova Scotia's lake-washed interior. It's a good place to paddle into the backcountry and camp. In New Brunswick, canoeing in untouched, moose- and bear-trodden Mt Carleton Provincial Park (p149) is sweet; those wishing to remain closer to city life can push off from Fredericton (p143) and paddle the Saint John River. Canoeing in Newfoundland centers on Terra Nova National Park (p239).

The **Canadian Recreational Canoeing Association** (☎ 613-269-2910, 888-252-6292; www.paddlingcanada.com) publishes *Kanawa* paddling magazine and has an extensive online bookstore. For regional information, check **Canoe Kayak Nova Scotia** (☎ 902-425-5454; www.ckns.ca) and **Canoe/Kayak New Brunswick** (www.canoekayaknb.org).

WHALE-WATCHING

The region's most precious gift to visitors is whale-watching. The thrill of spotting a whale's spout followed by its giant tail flukes arching and descending is unbeatable.

More than 22 species of whale and porpoise lurk offshore throughout Atlantic Canada, drawn to the rich fishy feeding waters like Homer Simpson to doughnuts. The standout species include the leaping and diving humpback whale, the highly endangered North Atlantic right whale and the largest leviathan of all, the mighty blue whale.

Kayakers, fisherfolk and anyone else sailing out to sea can check www.buoy weather.com for marine conditions all around Atlantic Canada.

To learn more about the right, humpback and other whales that swim the Bay of Fundy – as well as hear their songs – go to http://new-brunswick.net /new-brunswick/whales /avi.html.

TOP FIVE PLACES TO WHALE-WATCH

- Twillingate Island (p241), Newfoundland
- Grand Manan Island (p159), New Brunswick
- Witless Bay Ecological Reserve (p229), Newfoundland
- Long Island (p97), Nova Scotia
- Pleasant Bay (p126), Nova Scotia

Whale-watch boat operators are ubiquitous and will bring you close to the creatures. Popular tour areas include Cape Breton's Cabot Trail coastline, with more than 20 operators in the region, especially around Pleasant Bay; the most common sightings are humpback, minke and pilot whales. In New Brunswick, excellent whale-watching concentrates along the Eastern Fundy Shore and around the Fundy Isles; right whales and blue whales are viewable. Newfoundland pretty much has whales swimming all around its shores, with humpback and minke commonly seen; tour operators cluster near Witless Bay Ecological Reserve and Twillingate.

Some whale-watches provide the opportunity to do more than just take a tour. Operators such as Ocean Contact (p234) in Trinity, Newfoundland, and Ocean Explorations (p97) on Long Island, Nova Scotia, are run by biologists conducting whale research, so by touring with them you become a helper in their scientific endeavors.

Most tours last about two hours and cost around $45 to $60 per adult. Sighting success rate often is posted, but if not ask (and ask if there's any sort of money-back guarantee if you do not see whales). Remember, you're heading out on open sea for many of these tours, so be prepared for a wavy ride. If you're at all prone to seasickness, medicate beforehand. It's also cold out there, so take a jacket or sweater. The season varies by location but usually is in July and August.

And while whale-watch tours are great, never underestimate what you can see from shore, especially from places such as Cape Breton's Cabot Trail and throughout Newfoundland's Avalon Peninsula.

A good resource is the *Pocketguide to Whale Watching on Canada's East Coast* (2003; Formac Publishing), by Jeffrey C Domm. Its illustrations of local sea creatures will help you identify what you see rising from the water.

Whoa! The male humpback whale has a penis that's 2m long.

CYCLING & MOUNTAIN BIKING

Cycling is where PEI shines. Several years ago, the province converted a defunct 357km railway bed into a cycling route called the Confederation Trail (p200), and it landed PEI on the map as an international cycling destination. The trail runs along the length of the island, with feeder paths down to most towns. Good services and facilities line it, many provided in reconditioned train stations. This easy service availability, combined with compact distances and flat terrain, make cycling here doable even for those with limited experience. The seaside stretch from St Peters to Mt Stewart (p199) is particularly inspiring.

New Brunswick is working hard to do something similar, and you'll find finished but as yet unconnected sections of the New Brunswick Trail (www .nbtrail.com) around the province. Rewarding rides include the Fundy Trail Parkway (p168) along coastal wilderness, and paths through the backcountry in Kouchibouguac National Park (p176).

In Nova Scotia the area around Lunenburg (p83) is a cyclist's dream with few hills, sweet ocean views and little vehicle traffic. Cape Breton Highlands National Park (p125) certainly has the scenery going for it, but it's tough riding due to the hilliness and traffic – not a good place for beginners.

Rugged terrain, high winds, poor road conditions and long stretches of road between towns make Newfoundland a difficult cycling destination. If you want to give it a try, Gros Morne National Park (p246) and CA Pippy Park (p222) in St John's are options.

Atlantic Canada Cycling (☎ 902-423-2453; www.atlanticcanadacycling.com) is a great resource with user-generated information on routes and road ratings. The **Canadian Cycling Association** (☎ 613-248-1353; www.canadian-cycling.com) is another good resource.

For more ideas and for bike-rental information, see the 'Activities' sections for individual destinations throughout this book. For cycling regulations and costs, see p280.

Trails Nova Scotia (www
.trails.gov.ns.ca) provides
maps and route descrip-
tions for snowmobile
trails, canoe and sea-
kayak waterways, and
cycling and walking paths
in the province.

FISHING

Fly-fishing in this region is downright mythical. Avid anglers get all slack-jawed and weak-kneed when names such as 'Miramichi' and 'Margaree' are invoked. No, these aren't beautiful women, but rather places to cast a line for Atlantic salmon and trout (speckled and brown, among the many).

On the tranquil Miramichi River (p178) in New Brunswick, everyone from Prince Charles to Dick Cheney to Marilyn Monroe has reeled one in. Cape Breton Island's Margaree Valley (p123) inspires similar reverence and catches. The Humber River (p250) in Newfoundland and Pinware River (p259) in Labrador Straits are known for salmon fishing. If the latter isn't remote enough, Labrador offers several fly-in lodges that host the likes of George Bush Sr. (Why is it that Republicans seem to be the most keen fishermen?)

These places all have experienced ups and downs with overfishing, poaching and unknown causes (perhaps climate change) affecting stocks, but they seem to be at sustainable levels presently.

Unleash your inner sailor
(or fisherperson or rock
climber) by learning to tie
a half hitch, bowline and
others with *Knots and
Splices* (2006) by Cyrus
Day and Colin Jarman.
Also helpful for budding
escape artists.

Staff at any tourist office will have the most current information about fishing regulations and outfitters. Each province also produces its own 'angler's guide' booklet that includes licensing rules. License prices vary by province and by species fished; a seven-day license costs anywhere from $30 to $90. Check with each province's environmental or natural resources department for further information:

Newfoundland & Labrador (☎ 709-637-2409; www.env.gov.nl.ca)
New Brunswick (☎ 506-453-2440; www.gnb.ca)
Nova Scotia (☎ 902-426-5433; www.gov.ns.ca/nsaf)
Prince Edward Island (☎ 902-368-6080; www.gov.pe.ca)

And finally, lobster fishing provides a unique experience, one that kids will love. Haul up crustacean-filled pots in Lunenburg (p84) in Nova Scotia.

WHERE TO OM AWAY FROM HOME

Yoga isn't exactly prevalent in Atlantic Canada, but with a little effort you can find studios and other practitioners with whom to salute the sun. Nova Scotia is the premier land of lotus positions, and serene, organic-minded Mahone Bay (p81) sits at the top of the heap. Several B&Bs here offer free yoga each morning; one even has its own yoga studio on-site. The seaside Whitman Wharf House B&B (p135) in Canso operates on a similar premise, and has a yoga room and mats guests can use.

For yoga courses, the Tatamagouche Centre in the northern part of the province offers workshops (p116). Those looking for a unique slant on the concept can hook up with Freewheeling Adventures (p274), a bicycle-tour company based near Mahone Bay that incorporates yoga into some of its cycling trips. The owners also offer a class teaching bike skills interwoven with gentle yoga exercises to help with balance, skill and confidence while pedaling.

BIRD-WATCHING

No need to be a binocular-toting ornithologist to get into the scene here. Birds swarm the region, and whether you're a birder or not, you'll find it tough to resist the charm of a funny-looking puffin or common murre.

Seabirds are the top draw. Many whale-watch tours also take visitors to seabird colonies; since whales and birds share a taste for the same fish, they often lurk in the same areas. So you'll be able to feast your eyes upon razorbills, kittiwakes, arctic terns, and yes, puffins and murres. The colonies can be up to one million strong, their shrieks deafening and their smell, well, not so fresh. Still, it's an amazing sight to behold. The preeminent places to get feathered are New Brunswick's Grand Manan Island (p159) and Newfoundland's Witless Bay (p229) and Cape St Mary's (p233).

Also impressive to watch are the Arctic-nesting shorebirds that migrate south through the Bay of Fundy. Each year millions of tiny sandpipers refuel in the rich mudflats exposed by the world's highest tides. The prime time is mid-August, and the prime places are around Windsor and Grand Pré in Nova Scotia's Annapolis Valley.

Eagles soar through Atlantic Canada, too. Visitors to Cape Breton often are rewarded with sightings in St Ann's Loop (p128) and Whycocomagh (p134) around Bras d'Or Lake. In the Annapolis Valley, Canning's (p104) chicken farms draw hundreds of hungry eagles between November and March.

The *Sibley Field Guide to Birds of Eastern North America* (2003) by David Sibley makes an excellent, illustrated and portable companion for birdwatchers. Further bird details and resources can be found in the Environment chapter (p44).

Hook up with the Nova Scotia Bird Society (http://nsbs.chebucto .org) for free local field trips as well as the lowdown on birding books and rare bird alerts. These enthusiasts know their stuff.

SURFING

Surfing seems an unusual sport for Atlantic Canada – too damn cold, right? Think again. People do surf here and not only is it cold, it's bloody freezing, since the best waves break in winter.

The place to partake of the madness is Lawrencetown Beach (p137) on Nova Scotia's eastern shore. L-town, as it's called, faces due south and picks up stormy weather from hundreds of kilometers away; this results in exceptional wrapping waves, especially plentiful in the colder months. So bundle up in your 7mm wetsuit, try not to freeze your ass off in the 0° C water, and join the line-up. People do surf at warmer times of the year, too. Board rentals cost about $25 per day, lessons about $75.

Kejimkujik Seaside Adjunct (p89) provides additional waves and dude, the prices are similar.

Perhaps even more radical than surfing is kite-surfing, in which you cruise in, over and out of waves using some funky equipment. Shippagan (p181) in northeastern New Brunswick is a good place to try it.

Check www.wavewatch.com for wave forecasts for the region.

SKIING & SNOWBOARDING

Atlantic Canada's best skiing and snowboarding take place at Newfoundland's **Marble Mountain** (☎ 709-637-7616; www.skimarble.com; Hwy 1; day pass $45; ✆ 10am-4:30pm Tue-Thu, 9am-9:30pm Fri, to 4:30pm Sat-Mon mid-Dec–early Apr) outside Corner Brook (p250). It may not have the height of Whistler or other top resorts, but it's lower cost with far fewer queues, so you get more time on the slopes.

Marble has 35 trails, four lifts, a 488m vertical drop and annual snowfall of 4.8m. There are snowboarding and tubing parks, as well as night skiing on Friday. The region caters to cross-country skiers at **Blow-Me-Down Cross Country Ski Park** (☎ 709-639-2754; www.blowmedown.ca; ✆ sunrise-9pm early Dec-Apr), about 10 minutes from the mountain.

ADVENTURES IN SNOW-KITING

This will impress the friends at the next beer-up: tell them you went snow-kiting in Newfoundland. Of course, it will entail actually going to Newfoundland – in winter – but you'll be going to Corner Brook, near the renowned ski resort of Marble Mountain, so you won't feel too out of place.

Snow-kiting is sort of a windsurfing-meets-snowboarding endeavor, and the patient folks at **My Newfoundland Adventures** (☎ 866-469-6353; www.mynewfoundland.ca) teach how to do it, no experience required. Just bring some very, very warm clothes for the 3½-hour lesson ($99) and off you'll zip across the tundra. (OK, it's not really tundra, but it's cold enough to be!)

Uber cross-country skiers will want to head far north to where the Canadian national team trains in Labrador West. The Wapusakatto Mountains (p262) let loose with good, cold, dry snow from late October to late April, a much longer season than elsewhere in the region – or anywhere in Canada.

For further information contact the **Canadian Ski Council** (☎ 905-212-9040; www.canadianskicouncil.org).

ROCK CLIMBING

Bouldering has muscled onto the outdoor scene in Nova Scotia, with the active community based in Halifax. Have a look at *Halifax Bouldering* (Hignell Printing; $30), by Ghislain Losier, for recommended climbs at Crystal Crescent Beach, Prospect and elsewhere in the area. Another resource is the website for **Climb Nova Scotia** (www.climbnovascotia.ca).

SCUBA DIVING

Visitors won't find many opportunities for scuba diving in the region. The places you see scattered around are mostly clubs for locals. One exception is diving off St Paul Island in Cape Breton. Several shipwrecks lie on the ocean floor here, and the St Paul Island Trading Company (p128) organizes dives on them.

Food & Drink

Inventive chefs and their sophisticated dishes do crop up in surprisingly remote outposts, but for the most part Atlantic Canada's food and drink is plain and simple. Most often it's fish or shellfish, fried or boiled, with a veggie thrown in for good measure. Odd local specialties liven up many menus; don't be shy to give them a try.

For a culinary road trip, see p29.

STAPLES & SPECIALTIES

The sea defines Atlantic Canada, so it's no surprise seafood defines the local cuisine.

Cod gets battered and fried and brought to your table as fish-and-chips; it's the one dish you can trust to be on every menu. Atlantic salmon, cousin of the better-known Pacific salmon, usually arrives broiled and sauced, perhaps with dill or hollandaise. 'Nova' is lightly smoked salmon (akin to lox), for which Nova Scotia is deservedly famous.

Nova Scotia, New Brunswick and Prince Edward Island (PEI) boil more lobster than you can shake a stick of butter at. Crikey, even McDonald's is in on the action, serving a McLobster sandwich at its regional outlets. One of the best places to get down and dirty with the crustacean is at a community-hall lobster supper (p205). Throw yourself into the mussels, potato salad and hearty seafood chowder while you're waiting, but don't eat too much; you'll need to leave room for the bulging fruit pie that'll come your way afterward.

Nova Scotia visitors should also save their appetites for Digby scallops. Those touring in PEI will notice the preponderance of potatoes for which the island is famous.

French Acadians have cooked up several specialties over the centuries. In Acadian towns you might see menu items such as *rappie* pie (also known as *la rapure*), a potato and salted-pork dish. *Tourtière* is a meat pie. *Poutine râpée* is a mixture of grated raw and mashed potatoes wrapped around fresh pork.

Newfoundland and Labrador may be boggy, rocky and cruddy for growing most things, but berries flourish here. Thus blueberries, partridgeberries (similar to cranberries) and bakeapples (p260) get shoveled into muffins, pies and jams. For more on the province's cuisine, see p225.

DRINKS

Everyone loves Alexander Keith's crisp beer from the eponymous, good-time brewery (p65) in Halifax. Moosehead (p163) is the region's best-known suds, brewed in Saint John. In Newfoundland, Quidi Vidi microbrews (p221) flow through the provincial taps; try Eric the Red.

New Brunswick and Nova Scotia join Québec and Ontario as Canada's main maple-syrup producers. It's tapped in February or March, and takes a hefty 40L of sap to make 1L of syrup.

Lobster once was viewed as poor man's food and used as fertilizer for farmers' fields.

TRAVEL YOUR TASTEBUDS

Head-scratching foods you may encounter in Nova Scotia and Prince Edward Island include Solomon Gundy (a pickled-herring and chopped-meat combo) and Lunenburg pudding (pork and spices cooked in the intestines of a pig). Dulce is an edible seaweed; New Brunswick's Grand Manan Island (p158) is famous for it. Fiddleheads are a fern's first shoots that are served like vegetables in the region. Figgy duff and jig's dinner are just a few of Newfoundland's colorfully named dishes; see p225 for more.

DO-IT-YOURSELF SEAFOOD CHOWDER

You've sipped and slurped chowder throughout the region and now you want to do it yourself. The ingredients below await your cooking pot.

Ingredients

500mL lobster meat
500g fish fillets
125mL chopped onions
50mL butter or margarine
25mL all-purpose flour
1L peeled and diced potatoes
500g mussels or clams, steamed and shucked.

250mL water
500g scallops
1L cream
750g milk
5mL salt
pinch of white cayenne pepper

Method

If frozen, thaw lobster reserving the lobster liquor. Remove any bits of shell or cartilage and cut into bite-size pieces. De-bone fish fillets and cut into 2.5cm pieces. Set aside.

In a heavy saucepan, sauté onions in butter until tender. Stir in flour and cook for one minute. Add potatoes and enough water to cover, bring to a boil and cook until tender. Add fish and scallops, and simmer for five minutes, stirring once or twice. Add cream, milk, lobster, lobster juice, mussels and seasonings. Heat gently and serve.

Makes 12 servings.

Recipe from *Taste of Nova Scotia* © 2006 www.tasteofnovascotia.ns.ca

Boutique wineries are uncorking bottles in Nova Scotia, mostly in the Annapolis Valley. Domaine de Grand Pré (p107), Blomidon Estate Winery (p104) and Jost Vineyards (p115) are popular, and all offer tours.

The Glenora Distillery (p120) on Cape Breton Island produces a very sip-worthy single-malt whiskey. Newfoundland is famous for its Screech (p227), a brand of rum that's actually made in Jamaica. Give it a shot.

You can get quality coffee, including espresso and cappuccino, in cities. Barring that, the ubiquitous Tim Hortons doughnut shops brew a respectable cup.

CELEBRATIONS

Food and drink are a big part of celebrating in Atlantic Canada, where summer's seafood festivals, autumn's Thanksgiving Day, winter's Christmas get-togethers and spring's Easter holidays traditionally feature generous family feasts with plenty of meat dishes, salad bowls, giant desserts, and beer and wine. A hearty, family-focused Sunday dinner is also a common event.

Several towns showcase their special cuisines with annual festivals:

Lobster Carnival (p117) Pictou, Nova Scotia; early July.
Tyne Valley Oyster Festival (p212) Tyne Valley, PEI; early August.
Digby Scallop Days (p99) Digby, Nova Scotia; mid-August.
PEI International Shellfish Festival (p190) Charlottetown, PEI; late September.

WHERE TO EAT & DRINK

Even the smallest town usually has a midpriced restaurant. In places where this is not the case, your lodging host will likely serve food; for instance, many B&Bs serve meals beyond breakfast for a price and if you prearrange it. Atlantic Canada doesn't feature many fine-dining establishments, but a few do turn up in unexpected, out-of-the-way places; see the boxed text, p59, for further information on these. A pub is often the cheapest place to get a good cooked meal.

Longing for the perfect cup of chowder or ways to scratch the bakeapple pie itch? Visit the culinary tourism websites for Nova Scotia (www.taste ofnovascotia.ns.ca) and Newfoundland (www .tastenl.com) for recipes and restaurants.

For those who've been wondering how to roast a porcupine, *Taste of Acadie*, published by Goose Lane Editions, reveals the answer along with 150 traditional Acadian recipes.

FARMERS' MARKETS FORAGES

Saturday mornings are usually prime time to graze.

- Halifax Farmers' Brewery Market (p76) is the region's top farmers' market, with jewelry, clothes and crafts, too.
- Moncton Market (p173) is another good one, with a huge selection of local eats.
- Pick up fresh foods or take a seat at the on-site restaurant at Boyce Farmers' Market (p145).
- Old City Market (p166) is busy, busy, busy with fresh fruits, prepared meals, even lobster.
- Charlottetown Farmers' Market (p192) has a good sampling of island foods.
- Bidgood's (p229) is Newfoundland's prime place to get seal flippers or moose heart.

While there are many variations, most restaurants open for lunch (usually between 11.30am and 2:30pm) and dinner from 5:30pm (some fancy establishments only open for dinner). Midrange and family restaurants often stay open all day. Closing times vary and often depend on how busy the restaurant is that day.

Budget eateries include takeouts, cafés, markets and basic restaurants where you can fill up for less than $10 including taxes. At midrange establishments you get full menus, beer and wine lists and a bill that shouldn't exceed $20 per person for an appetizer, main course and one drink, not including tax and tip. Top-end places are typically gourmet affairs with fussy service, creative and freshly prepared food. At these establishments, main courses alone can cost $25 or more.

See p271 for information on taxes, and the boxed text, p58, for information on tipping.

Eight Nova Scotia wineries strut their surprisingly good stuff at www.winesns.com. The website includes information on tours, tastings and grape stomps.

Quick Eats

In addition to farmers' markets (see the boxed text, above) in cities, roadside stands offer enticing seasonal produce in rural areas. Do yourself a favor and pick up a container of strawberries (best in June) or blueberries (August).

You might come across the occasional roadside van selling fish-and-chips. Barring that, well, there's always Tim Hortons or a McLobster: fast food is everywhere.

VEGETARIANS & VEGANS

Vegetarians will be well catered for in the region's principal cities such as Halifax, Fredericton and St John's, but as you move away from urban areas your options become extremely limited. Not surprisingly, vegans can expect an even rougher ride. Strict adherents should stick to any vegetarian-only eateries they come across, since 'vegetarian' items in mainstream restaurants may well have been prepared with meat stock or lard. Chinese eateries occasionally pop up in remote areas and may be another option.

EATING WITH KIDS

The majority of restaurants in Atlantic Canada are ready, willing and able to deal with families, offering crayons, booster seats and child-adept servers. Special kids menus usually rely heavily on breaded chicken and fries and brightly colored minipizzas. As an alternative, ask for a half-order of something more nutritious from the adult menu.

See p266 for further details on prices and resources for children.

HABITS & CUSTOMS

Atlantic Canadians follow the North American tradition of eating morning breakfast, midday lunch and early-evening dinner. Expect the generally high standards of North American restaurant and bar service to apply here. Table service is common at most pubs, although you can still order at the bar as well. Don't forget to give a tip to your table server, and consider dropping some change in the bar-server's pot if you stick around for a few beers.

All of the Atlantic provinces have adopted widespread smoking bans. Nova Scotia's law is the toughest in the nation, prohibiting smoking at outdoor eating and drinking establishments in addition to all indoor public areas.

COOKING COURSES

While the cuisine-tourism boom that has blazed its way through provinces such as British Columbia and Ontario hasn't come to Atlantic Canada just yet, you can still get intimate with pots and pans at a number of places. Hunt for mushrooms, including the namesake chanterelle, and then learn to cook them at Chanterelle Country Inn's (p129) Field, Farm and Foraging workshops. Or learn about the Annapolis Valley's reds and whites with sommelier-led **Wine Valley Tours** (☎ 902-404-9463; www.valleywinetours.ca).

In *Newfoundland Home-style & Traditional Recipes*, by Hillcrest Publishing, all of the province's time-honored dishes are given their due. Go ahead, see if you can stomach the seal-flipper pie. There's blueberry wine and figgy duff, too.

LOCAL VOICE

Dennis Johnston
Chef-Owner of Fid, Halifax, Nova Scotia

After 20 years spent cooking in Montréal and Europe, Dennis Johnston returned to his home province and opened Fid (p74) with wife Monica Bauche in 2000. Their mission: focus on local foods and seasonality, and make people mindful of where the food on their plate comes from. Yep, Johnston is a slow-food proponent. Each Saturday he shops at the Halifax Farmers' Market to pick out Fid's ingredients for the week, so his Franco-Asian-tinged menu changes every seven days based on what area farmers have plucked from the ground. Below he explains the local food scene:

What are some season-by-season examples of regional foods? In winter we have leeks and root vegetables (mostly stuff that's been holding in the cellar, like beets), kale, beef and pork belly.

Spring brings the first flushing of baby spinach and the first root vegetables like white beets and golden beets. We have goat cheese. Quail and squab appear, as do foods from the sea: cod, haddock, halibut, mussels, whelks, oysters, and snow crab.

In summer we get a full variety of tomatoes, herbs and greens. We have chicken and big-eye tuna. Chanterelle mushrooms. We ease out of strawberries and into other berries like raspberries and gooseberries.

In fall we have fresh swordfish and more root vegetables: cabbages, kales, parsley roots and potatoes.

What are the origins of regional foods? A lot is grown in the Annapolis Valley [in Nova Scotia], which is home to many people who fled the Vietnam War. They were doing organic farming when no one had even heard of it, and they've been organic since the 1970s.

Many farmers have French Acadian roots. For instance, the Halifax Farmers' Market originated with Acadians who farmed on the outskirts of the city, and who would come in to sell their produce to the English living in the city. Dutch, Swiss and German farmers also came to the region.

Any local foods that you missed while living abroad? Fried clams-and-chips from **John's Lunch** (☎ 902-469-3074; www.johnslunch.com; 352 Pleasant St, Dartmouth, NS; ☺ 10am-9pm Mon-Sat, 11am-9pm Sun).

EAT YOUR WORDS

A few French phrases might come in handy, especially in New Brunswick's Acadian regions or on the islands of St-Pierre and Miquelon (off the coast of Newfoundland).

Useful Phrases

I'd like to reserve a table.
Je voudrais réserver une table.   zher voo·dray ray·zair·vay ewn ta·bler

A table for (two), please.
Une table pour (deux), s'il vous plaît.   ewn ta·bler poor (der) seel voo play

Do you have a specialty?
Avez-vous une spécialité?   a·vay·voo zewn spay·sya·lee·tay

I'm a vegetarian.
Je suis végétarien/végétarienne. (m/f)   zher swee vay·zhay·ta·ryun/vay·zhay·ta·ryen

Do you have a kids' menu?
Avez-vous un menu pour enfants?   a·vay·voo zun mer·new poor on·fon

Where are the restrooms?
Où sont les toilettes?   oo son lay twa·let

Food Glossary

BASICS

fromage	fro·mazh	cheese
lait	lay	milk
pain	pun	bread

MEATS

jambon	zhom·bon	ham
porc	por	pork
poulet	poo·lay	chicken
poutine râpée	poo·teen ra·pay	Acadian dish of grated potatoes wrapped around pork
Solomon Gundy		marinated-herring and chopped-meat combo
tourtière	toor·tyair	meat pie

FRUIT & VEGETABLES

fiddlehead		edible fern
fraise	frez	strawberry
partridgeberry		red, cranberrylike fruit

DOS & DON'TS

Do...

- Tip around 15% (pretax) in restaurants and bars with good table service.
- Make reservations for popular restaurants, especially top-end establishments.
- Take a bottle of wine if you're invited to a dinner party at someone's home.

Don't...

- Tip the full 15% unless the service has been good.
- Tip if a gratuity has been automatically added to your bill – a growing and annoying practice.

TOP FIVE FOODIE RESTAURANTS

All of these places use local and/or organic ingredients.

- Chanterelle Country Inn (p129), St Ann's Loop, Nova Scotia
- Fid (p74), Halifax, Nova Scotia
- Inn at Bay Fortune (p197), Bay Fortune, Prince Edward Island
- Norseman Restaurant (p249), L'Anse aux Meadows, Newfoundland
- Rossmount Inn (p155), St Andrews by-the-Sea, New Brunswick

patates frites	pa·tat freet	French fries
poutine	poo·teen	fries served under gravy and cheese curds

DRINKS

bière	bee·yair	beer
café	ka·fay	coffee
eau	o	water
jus	zhew	juice
pint		a large glass of beer (rarely a pint in volume)
sleeve		a medium-sized glass of beer
vin	vun	wine

Nova Scotia

At first glance, Nova Scotia appears sweet as a storybook: lupin-studded fields meet gentle rolling hills; in summer there's golf, in winter ice-skating; living history museums are ubiquitous. Words like 'cute' and 'quaint' roll off the tongue at every bend in the road. The gingerbread-like houses, picture-perfect lighthouses and lightly lapping waves on sandy shores make you want to wrap it all up and give it to a cuddly kid as a Christmas gift.

Then, the antithesis creeps up on you: the Canada of fishermen braving icy seas, laboring coal miners, moose, horseflies, hockey – it's all here despite the sugar coating. It gets terrifically cold during the winter and you have to be of sturdy stock to live the life of a fisherman, miner or mill worker. Add to this that industry is down; the coal mines and mills have all but shut, the fishing is low. Despite their hardships, these robust Maritime people remain some of the warmest and down-to-earth folk you'll ever meet.

Nova Scotia has scarcely scratched the surface of its potential as a destination for kayaking, biking and hiking. While the season is short for these activities you'll find plenty of tour operators eager to get you on the trip of your dreams. When you're tired of roughing it, head to chic, cosmopolitan Halifax for some world-class dining and a rocking music scene.

HIGHLIGHTS

- People-watch along the waterfront, stroll aimlessly through the chic downtown and take in a world-class meal in **Halifax** (opposite)

- Hop a seaworthy vessel (and pop a seasickness pill) on **Briar Island** (p98) to look for the world's largest and rarest whales

- Hike the steep hill at **Meat Cove** (p127) to watch whales pass below while bald eagles soar above or get your adrenalin fix by smashing through the tidal bore waves at **Maitland** (p108)

- Spend a day visiting artists' studios along **St Ann's Loop** (p128)

- Wander through the lantern-lit graveyard of **Annapolis Royal** (p100) and learn the town's history through tales of the deceased

- Sit back with a beer and a hearty slice of Acadian meat pie while listening to live Celtic music at the Red Shoe Pub in **Mabou** (p120)

- Explore the white sand beaches and rocky outcrops of **Kejimkujic Seaside Adjunct** (p89)

- Sample French soldiers' rations c 1744 at **Louisbourg National Historic Site** (p131)

- Voyage under the ocean floor of **Glace Bay** (p131) to the damp coal-mines while listening to the yarns of a retired miner

▪ AREA: 55,491 SQ KM	▪ POPULATION: 937,000	▪ CAPITAL: HALIFAX

HALIFAX

Halifax (population 360,000) is a hotbed for everything that is young, hip and culturally diverse in the Maritimes. The hilly agglomeration of heritage buildings, arty shops and cosmopolitan eateries slope down to the second-largest harbor in the world and its majestic views. Several universities keep the population young and the bars and nightclubs full. It's estimated that 36 different ethnic groups make up this lively population; you can get fish-and-chips, curry or sushi all within the same few blocks. Sea breezes keep the air clean, parks and trees grace the central areas. This is the kind of town that people flock to, not so much for the opportunities, but for the quality of life it has to offer.

HISTORY

Pirates, Indians, warring colonialists, exploding ships and sinking ships makes Halifax history read like an adventure story. The Mi'kmaq called present-day Halifax Che-book-took, meaning 'great long harbor,' and the British eagerly took advantage of its potential as a port. From 1749, when Edward Cornwallis founded Halifax along what is today Barrington St, the settlement expanded and flourished. The complete destruction of the French fortress at Louisbourg in 1760 increased British dominance and sealed Halifax as Nova Scotia's most important city.

In the early 1800s the growing port town became home to St Mary's University, followed shortly after by Dalhousie University. Despite being a seat of higher education, Halifax was still a rough-and-ready sailor's nest that, during the War of 1812, became a center for privateer black market trade. As piracy lost its government endorsement, Halifax sailed smoothly into a mercantile era, the city streets (particularly Market and Brunswick Sts) became home to countless taverns and brothels.

On April 14, 1912 three Halifax ships were sent in response to a distress call; the *Titanic*, hailed as unsinkable, had hit an iceberg. More than 1500 people were killed in the tragedy and many were buried at Fairview Cemetery.

During WWI and WWII, hundreds of ships massed in the extensive Bedford Basin before traveling in convoys across the North Atlantic. In 1917 the *Mont Blanc*, a French munitions ship carrying TNT and highly flammable benzol, collided with another ship. The 'Halifax Explosion,' the world's biggest manmade explosion prior to A-bombs being dropped on Japan in 1945, ripped through the city. More than 1900 people were killed and 9000 injured. Almost the entire northern end of Halifax was leveled and many buildings and homes that were not destroyed by the explosion burned to the ground when winter stockpiles of coal in the cellars caught fire.

Halifax faced its most natural disaster in September 2003 when the 185km per hour winds of Hurricane Juan ripped out thousands of trees, severely damaged buildings and scarred Halifax forever. Despite the violence of the storm only eight people were killed.

ORIENTATION

The downtown area, three universities and older residential neighborhoods are contained on a compact peninsula that juts out from the mainland area of Halifax West. Almost all sights of interest to visitors are concentrated in this area, making walking the best way to get around.

Two bridges span the harbor, connecting Halifax to Dartmouth and leading to highways north (for the airport) and east. The MacDonald Bridge at the eastern end of North St is closest to downtown. The airport is 40km northwest of town on Hwy 102.

INFORMATION
Bookstores

Book Room (☎ 902-423-8271; 1546 Barrington St; ⏲ 9am-7:30pm Mon-Fri, 9am-5pm Sat Jul-Sep, to 5:30pm Mon & Tue Oct-Jun) Founded in 1839, Canada's oldest bookshop specializes in Nova Scotian and Canadian books.

Bookmark (☎ 902-423-0419; 5686 Spring Garden Rd; ⏲ 9am-10pm Mon-Fri, 9am-6pm Sat, 11am-6pm Sun) Good selection of maps and travel guides.

Mountain Equipment Co-op (☎ 902-421-2667; 1550 Granville St; ⏲ 10am-9pm Mon-Fri, 9am-6pm Sat Jul & Aug, 10am-7pm Mon-Wed, 10am-9pm Thu & Fri, 9am-6pm Sat Sep-Jun) Topographical maps and guides to hiking, kayaking and biking in Nova Scotia.

Internet Access

Many B&Bs, hotels and hostels have wi-fi and computer terminals for guests' use.

Blowers St Paper Chase (☎ 902-423-0750; 5228 Blowers St; per hr $8; ⏲ 8am-8pm Mon-Sat, 9am-8pm Sun) This cool café charges by the minute or the hour; wireless is free.

NOVA SCOTIA

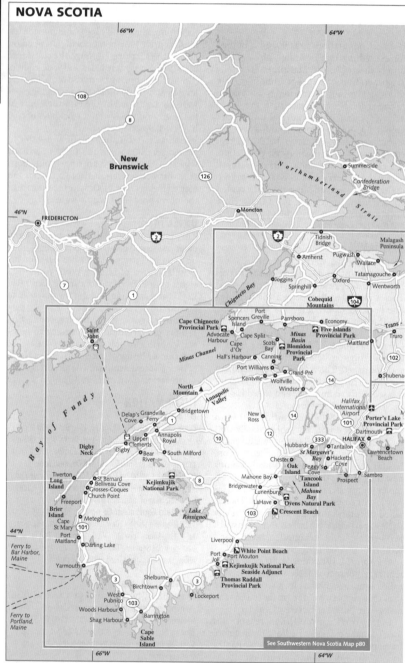

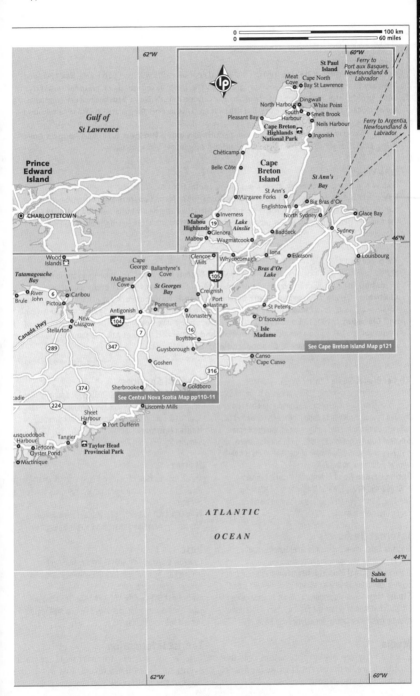

NOVA SCOTIA

NOVA SCOTIA IN...

Two Days

Get lost in downtown **Halifax** (p61). If it's Saturday, foot traffic will lead you to **Halifax Farmers' Brewery Market** (p76) where you can grab a coffee, fresh baked goods or seasonal fruit. From here, stroll to the waterfront boardwalk to **Alexander Keith's Nova Scotia Brewery** (opposite) for a rollicking brewery tour. If the **Bluenose II** (p71) is in port take a cruise under sail around the harbor.

The next day, get out of town heading south to explore **Prospect** (p78) and **Peggy's Cove** (p78). Don't forget to eat as much fresh seafood as you can along the way!

One Week

Follow the two-day itinerary, then keep going south. Plan to windowshop downtown **Mahone Bay** (p81) before heading to historic **Lunenburg** (p83) for a **Lobstermen Tour** (p84) to learn hands-on about Nova Scotia's most divine shellfish. Hike the **Kejimkujic Seaside Adjunct** (p89) for the day before driving to **Annapolis Royal** (p100) to tour historic gardens and the Fort Anne graveyard by night.

Two Weeks

Follow the two-day itinerary, then drive to **Cape Breton Island** (p120). Take in some live music in **Mabou** (p120), swim in warm(ish) ocean waters off **Inverness** (p122) and visit museums in **Chéticamp** (p123). Then explore **Cape Breton Highlands National Park** (p124), leaving time for whale-watching from **Pleasant Bay** (p126). Continue around the island via **St Ann's Loop** (p128) and **Glace Bay** (p131) to **Louisbourg** (p131). Return to Halifax stopping at the stunning dunes of **Pomquet** (p119), to ride the tidal bore at **Maitland** (p108) and to meet Atlantic Canada's wildlife up-close at the animal park in **Shubenacadie** (p108).

Khyber Digital Media Centre(☎ 902-446-4053; http://khyberarts.ns.ca/kdmc; 1588 Barrington St; per hr $5; ☽ noon-8pm Tue-Fri, to 6pm Sat) Friendly staff here on the 2nd floor of the Khyber Centre for the Arts (opposite) can help you upload video and audio; you can also check email.
Second Cup (☎ 902-429-0883; 5425 Spring Garden Rd; ☽ 7am-midnight) A half-hour of Internet access is free with any purchase at this café.
Spring Garden Road Memorial Public Library (☎ 902-490-5723; 2285 Gottingen St; ☽ 10am-9pm Tue-Thu, 10am-5pm Fri & Sat) Free Internet on a first-come, first-served basis.

Internet Resources

Halifax Info (www.halifaxinfo.com) Details about festivals, sights and tours.
Halifax Regional Municipality (www.halifax.ca) Info on everything from bus schedules to recreation programs.
Studio Map (www.studiorally.ca) An up-to-date guide to art and craft studios across the province, plus a shortlist of spot-on recommendations for eateries and B&Bs.

Media

The *Coast*, a free weekly publication available around town, is the essential guide for music, theater, film and events.

Medical Services

Family Focus (☎ 902-420-2038; 5991 Spring Garden Rd; consultation $60; ☽ 8:30am-9pm Mon-Fri, 11am-5pm Sat & Sun) Walk-in or same-day appointments.
Halifax Infirmary (☎ 902-473-3383/7605; 1796 Summer St; ☽ 24hr) For emergencies.

Money

Bank branches clustered around Barrington and Duke Sts change traveler's checks for a $3 fee.
Travelex (☎ 902-873-3612; Halifax International Airport; ☽ 6am-9pm) Charges $5.50 per transaction.

Post

Lawton's Drugs (☎ 902-429-0088; 5675 Spring Garden Rd; ☽ 8am-9pm Mon-Fri, 8am-6pm Sat, noon-5pm Sun) Post office inside.
Main Post Office (☎ 902-494-4670; 1680 Bedford Row; ☽ 7:30am-5:15pm Mon-Fri) Pick up mail sent to General Delivery, Halifax, NS B3J 2L3 here.

Tourist Information

Check out posters for performances and events on the bulletin boards just inside the door of the Halifax Public Library.

NOVA SCOTIA

Tourism Nova Scotia (☎ 902-425-5781, 800-565-0000; www.novascotia.com) Operates visitor information centers in Halifax and in strategic locations across the province, plus a free booking service for accommodations, which is useful when rooms are scarce in midsummer. It publishes the free *Doers & Dreamers Guide*, which lists places to stay, attractions and tour operators.

Visitor Information Centres (VICs) Barrington St (☎ 902-490-5963; cnr Duke & Barrington Sts; ☑ 8:30am-8pm Jul & Aug, 8:30am-7pm May, Jun & Sep, 8:30am-4:30pm Mon-Fri rest of year); Halifax International Airport (☎ 902-873-1223; ☑ 9am-9pm); Sackville St (☎ 902-490-5963; cnr Argyle & Sackville Sts; ☑ 8:30am-8pm Jul & Aug, 8:30am-7pm May, Jun & Sep, 8:30am-4:30pm Mon-Fri rest of year); Waterfront (☎ 902-424-4248; 1655 Lower Water St; ☑ 8:30am-8pm Jun-Sep, 8:30am-4:30pm Wed-Sun Oct-May)

SIGHTS
Historic Downtown
CITADEL HILL NATIONAL HISTORIC SITE
Canada's most visited national historic site, the huge **Citadel** (☎ 902-426-5080; off Sackville St; adult/child/senior/family $9/4.50/7.75/22.50, 30% discount May & mid-Sep–early Nov; ☑ 9am-6pm Jul & Aug, 9am-5pm rest of year) is an eight-pointed star-shaped fort on top of Halifax' big central hill. Construction began in 1749 with the founding of Halifax; this version of the Citadel is the fourth, built from 1818 to 1861. Guided tours explain the fort's intriguingly peaceful shape and surprisingly peaceful history – give yourself three hours. The grounds inside the fort are open year-round, with free admission when the exhibits are closed.

KHYBER CENTRE FOR THE ARTS
This historic building was saved from demolition by community activists and converted into a nonprofit artist-run **center** (☎ 902-422-9668; www.khyberarts.ns.ca; 1588 Barrington St; admission free; ☑ noon-5pm Tue-Sat) with several galleries devoted primarily to emerging artists. There's also a digital media center (p61) and an entertainment venue (see Khyber Club, p75). It's a great place to browse and carouse with the interesting side of Halifax.

ALEXANDER KEITH'S NOVA SCOTIA BREWERY
Come hither ye lovers of ale! If you drink beer or not, a tour of this **brewery** (☎ 902-455-1474; www.keiths.ca; The Brewery Market, 1496 Lower Water St; adult/child/senior/family $15/6/12/36; ☑ 11am-8pm Mon-Thu, 11am-9pm Fri & Sat, noon-4pm Sun late May-Oct, 5-8pm Fri, noon-8pm Sat, noon-4pm Sun rest of year) brings you right back to 19th-century Halifax via costumed thespians, quality brew and some dark corridors. Learn the history, check out the beer-making techniques then finish your hour-long visit with a party in the basement pub complete with beer on tap, singing, pub games and some ale-inspired yarns. Note that you'll need your ID and the kids are served lemonade.

OTHER SIGHTS
At the corner of Barrington and Bishop, **Government House** has been the residence of the provincial lieutenant governor since 1807, when it was built for Governor John Wentworth. It's currently not open to the public. Across the street, the **Old Burying Ground** (cnr Spring Garden Rd & Barrington St) is the final resting place of some 12,000 people buried between 1749 and 1843. A display points out graves of historical significance.

The **Province House** (☎ 902-424-4661; 1726 Hollis St; guided tours free; ☑ 9am-5pm Mon-Fri, 10am-4pm Sat & Sun Jul & Aug, 9am-4pm Mon-Fri Sep-Jun) is one of the finest examples of 19th-century Georgian architecture in all of North America and was the first legislature in a British colony to win local self-government. After Charles Dickens visited the

---

NOVA SCOTIA BLUENOSES

If you visit Nova Scotia during winter months you might think that the origin of the nickname 'bluenose' for these Easterners is obvious – you yourself might end up with an icy-blue nose, fingers, toes, ears... The history of the term is, in fact, more complicated, unclear and probably dates back to the late 18th century. One explanation is that the name came from the Irish Bluenose potato that was widely planted and exported by early settlers; another is that it comes from blue smudges often seen on fishermen's noses from their blue mittens. Whatever the reason, the moniker has stuck and today Nova Scotians proudly bear their endearing nickname and use it to name everything from publications to businesses to boats. The most famous *Bluenose* is the famous fishing schooner now used for harbor tours around Lunenburg and Halifax (see p71).

HALIFAX

0 ————— 800 m
0 ————— 0.5 miles

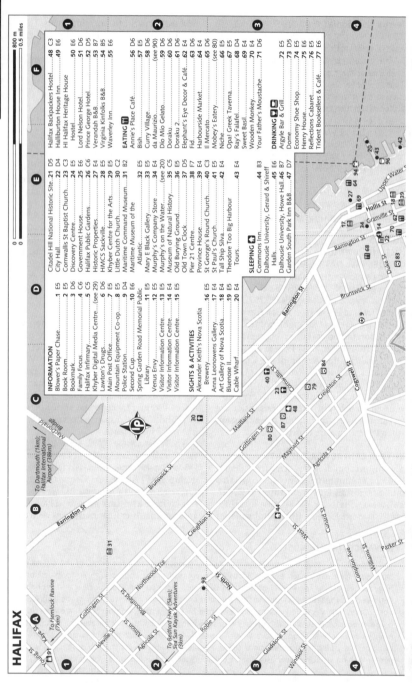

To Dartmouth (1km);
Halifax International
Airport (38km)

To Bedford Hwy (5km);
Sea Sun Kayak Adventures
(3km)

To Hemlock Ravine
(7km)

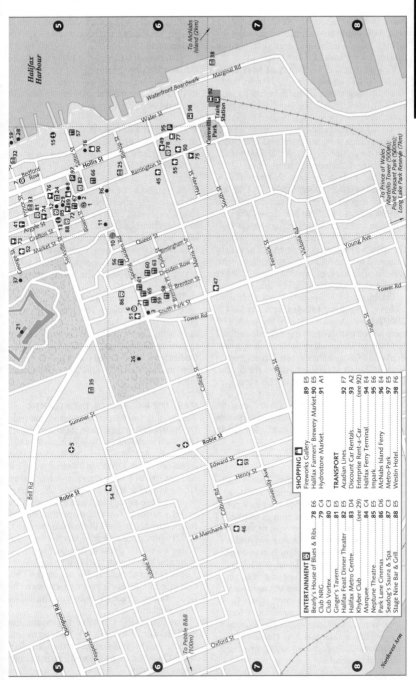

Nova Scotia legislature in 1842, he wrote 'it was like looking at Westminster through the wrong end of a telescope.' A guided tour will take up 15 minutes of your time.

The provincial **Art Gallery of Nova Scotia** (☎ 902-424-7542; www.agns.gov.ns.ca; 1723 Hollis St; adult/child 6-17yr/student/family $12/3/5/25, by donation 5-9pm Thu; ☺ 10am-5pm Fri-Wed, 10am-9pm Thu), the largest art gallery in Nova Scotia, is housed in the impressive Dominion Building (c 1868). The 35 galleries range from historical and traditional folk art to contemporary art. Daily tours at 2:30pm are included with admission.

Off the pedestrian area on Granville St, the **Anna Leonowens Gallery** (☎ 902-494-8184; 1891 Granville St; admission free; ☺ 11am-5pm Tue-Fri, noon-4pm Sat, show openings 5:30-7:30pm Mon) shows work by students and faculty of the Nova Scotia College of Art & Design, which occupies much of the Historic Properties (see right). The gallery is named for the founder of the college, who was immortalized in *The King and I* for her relationship with the King of Siam.

Established in 1749 with the founding of Halifax, Anglican **St Paul's Church** (☎ 902-429-2240; 1749 Argyle St; admission free; ☺ 9am-4pm Mon-Fri) once served parishioners from Newfoundland to Ontario. Designed by James Gibbs, a student of Sir Christopher Wren, it resembles St Peter's Church in London. Across the square, Halifax' **City Hall** (cnr Duke & Argyle Sts) is a true gem of Victorian architecture.

Mary E Black Gallery (☎ 902-424-4062; www.craft-design.gov.ns.ca/mebgal.html; 1683 Barrington St; admission free; ☺ 10am-9pm Mon-Thu, 10am-4pm Fri, 9am-5pm Sat

---

HURRICANE JUAN

Many Haligonians didn't really believe the weather forecast on September 28, 2003. Despite hurricane warnings, townsfolk put their garbage out on the curb as usual or walked down to the waterfront to see the big waves. But Hurricane Juan hit Halifax with a vengeance, toppling hundreds of the stately, mature trees that line Halifax streets. Enormous root systems lifted up sidewalks. Thousands spent the next week without power, some without water. The hurricane traced a path across Nova Scotia, exiting near Tatamagouche en route to Prince Edward Island. In Point Pleasant Park, Hurricane Juan destroyed 57,000 trees, or 70% of the total.

& Sun), in the Nova Scotia Centre for Craft & Design, has changing exhibits by Nova Scotian craftspeople.

At the top of George St, at Citadel Hill, the **Old Town Clock** has been keeping time for 200 years. The inner workings arrived in Halifax in 1803 after being ordered by Prince Edward, the Duke of Kent.

Waterfront Boardwalk
HISTORIC PROPERTIES

The Historic Properties is a group of restored buildings at 1869 Upper Water St built between 1800 and 1905. Originally designed as huge warehouses for easy storage of goods, cargo, and privateers' booty, they now house shops, cafés and pubs and are connected by the waterfront boardwalks. The three blocks were nearly lost to urban development but luckily were made into a national historic site in 1963. Artisans, merchants and buskers do business around the buildings in the summer.

The 1814 **Privateer's Warehouse** is the area's oldest stone building. The privateers were government-sanctioned and -sponsored pirates who stored their booty here. Among the other vintage buildings are the wooden **Old Red Store** – once used for shipping operations and as a sail loft – and **Simon's Warehouse**, built in 1854.

MARITIME MUSEUM OF THE ATLANTIC

Part of this impressive waterfront **museum** (☎ 902-424-7490; http://museum.gov.ns.ca/mma; 1675 Lower Water St; adult/child 6-17yr/senior/family $8/4/7/21, half-price Nov-Apr; ☺ 9:30am-5:30pm Wed-Mon, to 8pm Tue Jun-Sep, 9:30am-5:30pm Mon & Wed-Sat, to 8pm Tue, 1-5:30pm Sun May & Oct, 9:30am-5pm Wed-Sat, to 8pm Tue, 1-5pm Sun Nov-Apr) was once a chandlery, where all the equipment needed to outfit a vessel was sold. You can smell the charred ropes, cured to protect them from saltwater, and try pumping a hand-operated foghorn. There's a wildly popular display on the *Titanic* and another on the Halifax Explosion. The 3-D film about the *Titanic* costs $3.50. Outside at the dock you can explore the CSS *Acadia*, a retired hydrographic vessel from England.

You'll find the last WWII corvette, the **HMCS Sackville** (adult/child $3/2; ☺ 10am-5pm Jun-Sep), docked nearby and staffed by the Canadian Navy. Count on spending a little over an hour at this museum.

PIER 21 CENTRE

Pier 21 was to Canada what Ellis Island was to the USA. Between 1928 and 1971 more than a million immigrants came through these halls to begin their lives as Canadians. Their stories and the historical context that led them to abandon their homelands are presented in this **museum** (☎ 902-425-7770; www.pier21.ca; 1055 Marginal Rd; adult/child/student/family $7.75/4.30/5.50/18; ☼ 9:30am-5:30pm May-Nov, 10am-5pm Tue-Fri, noon-5pm Sat Dec-Mar; 10am-5pm Apr). Researchers fanned out across Canada to get first-hand testimonials from immigrants who passed through Pier 21. These videos are shown in screening rooms off a railcar; don't miss it – and bring your hanky.

North End

The North End has been a distinct neighborhood for almost as long as Halifax has existed. The town center was still within palisades in the early 1750s when the 'North Suburbs' became popular because of its larger building lots.

The Admiral of the British navy for all of North America was based in Halifax until 1819 and threw grand parties at Admiralty House, now the **Maritime Command Museum** (☎ 902-427-0550 ext 6725; 2725 Gottingen St; admission free; ☼ 9:30am-3:30pm Mon-Fri). Apart from the beautiful Georgian architecture, the museum is worth a visit for its eclectic collections: cigarette lighters, silverware and ships' bells, to name a few. One notable bell is a cracked specimen from the victorious *Shannon,* which took the USS *Chesapeake* in a famous skirmish of the War of 1812.

St George's Round Church (☎ 902-423-1059; http://collections.ic.gc.ca/churchandcommunity; 2222 Brunswick St), built in 1800 according to the design specifications of the Duke of Kent, included separate seating areas for naval and civilian congregants. A rare circular Palladian church with a main rotunda 18m in diameter, it was damaged by fire in 1994. Tours are by arrangement. Tours of the 1756 **Little Dutch Church** (2405 Brunswick St), the second-oldest building in Halifax, can also be arranged through St George's. The **Cornwallis St Baptist Church** (5457 Cornwallis St) has been serving African Nova Scotians since the 1830s. Walk by on Sunday morning and hear the gospel music overflow its walls.

Halifax Public Gardens

At the corner of Spring Garden Rd and South Park St, these are considered the finest Victorian city gardens in North America. Oldies bands perform off-key concerts in the gazebo on Sunday afternoons in summer, tai chi practitioners go through their paces, and anyone who brings checkers can play on outside tables. The 7 hectares make a great detour when walking across the city on foot – you feel as if you've left metropolis for a quirky, bustling countryside. The gardens are open daily from dawn till dusk.

Point Pleasant Park

Some 39km of nature trails, picnic spots and the **Prince of Wales Martello Tower** – a round 18th-century defensive structure – are all positioned within this 75-hectare sanctuary that juts out into the Atlantic Ocean. Trails around the perimeter of the park offer views of McNabs Island, the open ocean and the North West Arm. Bus 9 along Barrington St will take you to Point Pleasant, and there's ample free parking off Point Pleasant Dr. For many people Point Pleasant Park is a strong symbol of Halifax – an example of how city inhabitants keep close to nature and close to the sea.

McNabs Island

Fine sand and cobbled-stone shorelines, salt marshes, abandoned military fortifications and forests of maple, beech and red spruce paint the scenery of this 400-hectare island in Halifax Harbour. In all there are 30km of roads and trails to explore close to the city yet far away from its clatter and clamor. Staff of the **McNabs Island Ferry** (☎ 902-465-4563; http://mcnabsisland.com; Government Wharf; round-trip ticket adult/senior & child $10/8; ☼ 24hr) will provide you with a map and an orientation to the island. For camping reservations contact the **Department of Natural Resources** (☎ 902-861-2560; www.parks.gov.ns.ca/mcnabs.htm); due to increased fire risks from rotting trees ploughed down by Hurricane Juan (see opposite) be aware that campfires are currently prohibited on the island. The ferry runs from Fisherman's Cove in Eastern Passage, a short drive through Dartmouth. When the ferry staff are not too busy, they'll pick you up in Halifax for the same fare. The ferry's captain Mike Tilly (aka Redbeard) will also lead nature tours and charters from $49 per hour for groups. Another option to get to McNabs is the **harbor taxi** (☎ 902-830-3181; round-trip fare for up to 8 people $60), based at Cable Wharf.

NOVA SCOTIA

ACTIVITIES
Cycling

Cycling is a great way to see sights on the outskirts of Halifax – you can take bikes on the ferries to Dartmouth or cycle over the MacDonald Bridge. **Velo Bicycle Club** (www .velohalifax.ca) organizes several rides each week; it's a way to meet locals and go on some fun rides but you'll have to join the club which costs $45. See the website for ride schedules and the club application form.

Pedal & Sea Adventures (☎ 902-857-9319, 877-772-5699; www.pedalandseaadventures.com; per day/week incl tax $30/130) will deliver the bike right to you, complete with helmet, lock and repair kit. It also leads good-value tours; one-/two-day trips including taxes and meals will cost you $95/225.

Hiking

There are both short and long hikes surprisingly close to downtown Halifax. **Hemlock Ravine** is an 80-hectare wooded wilderness that was once home to Nova Scotia's 1780s lieutenant governor, John Wentworth. It is located within a heavily populated area, but the five trails, suitable for all levels, really feel removed from the city. To get there take the Bedford Hwy from central Halifax then turn left at Kent Ave – there is parking and a map of the trail at the end of this road. **Long Lake Park Reserve Trail** is an easy trail that makes its way to a dreamy lake setting; the trail can get a little muddy around the lake but will lead you to a small waterfall. There is parking for the trailhead right before the road leading to Exhibition Park along St Mararet's Bay Rd. See www.novatrails.com for more detailed trail descriptions and directions to trailheads. There's also hiking in Point Pleasant Park (p69) and on McNabs Island (p69).

Kayaking

Ideally you'll do this further away from polluted Halifax Harbour. But if you can't wait to get on the ocean, try **Sea Sun Kayak Adventures** (☎ 902-471-2732; www.paddlenovascotia.com; St Mary's Boat Club, 1741 Fairfield Rd, off Jubilee Rd), which offers enjoyable day-long tours ($80) of sights along the sheltered North West Arm. It also has a second location in Terrence Bay, a short drive from Halifax, that rents kayaks (half-/full day $40/58) and offers a range of other trips. Its 'Kayak Bus' will pick up

paddlers at their place of lodging within the Halifax area.

WALKING TOUR

At a leisurely pace, you could take a day for this walk although the distance is only 1.8km. Begin with a stop at **Khyber Centre for the Arts** (**1**; p65) to browse exhibits, fuel up on espresso and check email before strolling up Barrington St to **Mary E Black Gallery** (**2**; p65). Once you've finished perusing the crafts, swing right onto Prince St then take your second left onto Hollis St. On your left you come across **Province House** (**3**; p65). Ogle the architecture and imagine Charles Dickens visiting here in 1842. Cross the street to the **Art Gallery of Nova Scotia** (**4**; p65) to browse this contemporary and historical collection. From here, turn left on George St then right onto Barrington once more. A block later you are at **City Hall** (**5**; p65), another gem of Victorian architecture; take it in for a minute before hanging a right onto Duke St then your first left onto Granville St. A few steps along will bring you to **Anna Leonowens Gallery** (**6**; p65). Make a U-turn to backtrack, then a left onto Duke St and a left onto Upper Water St – walk about 75m from here to the **Historic Properties** (**7**; p68) to take in views of the harbor and browse the shops. You are on your own from here to enjoy the waterfront boardwalk, visit the **Maritime Museum of the Atlantic** (**8**; p68) see the **Bluenose II** (**9**; opposite) if it's in town, and stop in for a brewery tour at **Alexander Keith's Nova Scotia Brewery** (**10**; p65).

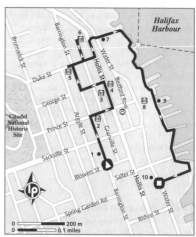

HALIFAX FOR CHILDREN

Discovery Centre (☎ 902-492-4422; www.discovery centre.ns.ca; 1593 Barrington St; adult/child $7.50/5; 😊 10am-5pm Mon-Sat, 1-5pm Sun) Science is fun! Hands-on exhibits, live shows and movies are all part of the road to discovery for all ages. The gift shop is hard to get through with out dropping a chunk of change.

Museum of Natural History (☎ 902-424-7353; http://museum.gov.ns.ca/mnh/index.htm; 1747 Summer St; adult/family mid-Jun–mid-Oct $5/15, late Oct-early Jun $3/9, admission free 5-8pm Wed year-round; 😊 9:30am-5pm Mon-Sat, to 8pm Wed, 1-5pm Sun, to 5:30pm Thu-Tue Jun–mid-Oct) Daily summer programs introduce children to Gus the toad and demonstrate the cooking of bugs. Exhibits on history and the natural world will keep parents engaged, too. It's just a couple of blocks north of Spring Garden Rd or west of Citadel Hill.

Theodore Too Big Harbour Tours (☎ 902-492-8847; www.theodoretoo.com; 1751 Lower Water St; adult/child under 1yr/under 6yr/under 15yr $20/free/9/15; 😊 mid-Jun–Oct) Yes, you can chug around on this cartoon character boat of children's book and TV fame. One-hour tours leave every hour-and-a-half (from 9:30am till 8pm) and are designed especially with children in mind – it's particularly good for under-sixes.

TOURS

For whale-watching and deep-sea fishing, check out the tours in Dartmouth (p77).

Murphy's on the Water (☎ 902-420-1015; murphys onthewater.com; 1751 Lower Water St, Cable Wharf) runs a range of tours on Halifax Harbour, from two-hour tours to dinner cruises to the popular Harbour Hopper Tours (55-minute tours adult/child under seven/child eight to 15 years/family $23/8/14/66), which tours on the *Lark 5*, a seaworthy tour bus. **Murphy's Company Store** (☎ 902-422-8972; 1903 Barrington St), off the Granville St pedestrian area, also sells tickets.

There are several other options on both sea and land:

Bluenose II (☎ 902-634-1963, 800-763-1963; www .bluenose2.ns.ca; Lower Water St, near Maritime Museum; adult/child 3-12yr $20/10) This replica of the famous two-masted racing schooner, the *Bluenose* (see p65), seen on the back of Canada's 10¢ coin, runs harbor tours when it's in town.

HFX Adventures (☎ 902-209-5255; www.hfxad ventures.ca; 2-/3-/4hr tours $70/90/100) Need a little adrenalin after all those harbor cruises? Hop in a hummer for some off-roading through remote terrain.

Tall Ship Silva (☎ 902-429-9463; www.tallshipsilva.com; Queen's Wharf at Prince St; tours adult/child $20/14; 😊 noon, 2pm & 4pm May-Oct) Lend a hand or sit back and relax while taking a 1½-hour cruise on Halifax' square-masted tall ship.

Tattle Tours (☎ 902-494-0525; www.tattletours.ca; per person $10; 😊 walking tours by demand – ask at any VIC, ghost tours Wed-Sun 7:30pm) Lively two-hour tours departing from the Old Clock Tower are filled with local gossip, pirate tales and ghost stories.

FESTIVALS & EVENTS

Check out volunteering opportunities through festival websites.

Halifax Celtic Feis (www.halifaxcelticfeis.com) A rich celebration of Celtic music, dance, literature and the arts held in early June.

Royal Nova Scotia International Tattoo (www.ns tattoo.ca; tickets $19-53) One of Nova Scotia's largest festivals has nothing to do with skin tattoos but everything to do with parading Scottish bagpipers; early July.

Atlantic Jazz Festival (www.jazzeast.com; tickets $15-30) A full week of free outdoor jazz concerts each afternoon and evening; performances range from world music to classic jazz trios. Takes place mid-July.

Halifax International Busker Festival (www.busk ers.ca) Comics, mimics, daredevils and musicians from all

---

TOP FIVE NOVA SCOTIAN SHINDIGS

■ Cruise the coast for parties, ceilidhs (*kay*-lees) and live music at Mabou and on Hwy 19 (p120).

■ All genres of grassroots music from Canada and around the word fill a secluded peninsula at the Stan Rogers Folk Festival (p135).

■ Canada's largest 'green' festival is Evolve Festival (p118) and it brings more than 200 artists – from funk and hip-hop to bluegrass and experimental – to the stage. Renewable and alternative energy sources are used and demonstrated.

■ Mi'kmaw, Acadian, African Nova Scotian, and the British Isles are just some of the 'roots' represented at the rocking Canadian Deep Roots Festival (p105).

■ Celebrate Celtic culture through foot-stomping music – all to the tune of flame-colored foliage at Celtic Colours (p120).

over the world perform along the Halifax waterfront from early to mid-August.

Atlantic Fringe Festival (www.atlanticfringe.com) Offbeat and experimental theater from both emerging and established artists; held mid-September.

Atlantic Film Festival (www.atlanticfilm.com; tickets $9.50-15) A week-and-a-half of great flicks from the Atlantic region and around the world held in September.

Grou Tyme Acadian Festival (www.groutyme.com; tickets from $7) Meaning 'Huge Celebration' you'll find entertainment from every pocket of Acadian culture during the third week of September.

SLEEPING

Budget

HI Halifax Heritage House Hostel (☎ 902-422-3863; www.hihostels.ca; 1253 Barrington St; member/nonmember dm $20/25, r $50/57; check-in 2pm-midnight) Nova Scotia's largest hostel has a prime downtown location in a historic house. There's a friendly staff and a spacious common kitchen but because of the sheer size of this place and all the ins and outs, you should exercise the usual precautions and keep an eye on your valuables. The 65 beds fill up in the summer; reserve ahead.

Halifax Backpackers Hostel (☎ 902-431-3170, 888-431-3170; www.halifaxbackpackers.com; 2193 Gottingen St; dm/d/f $20/50/65; P) Young, funky and caffeinated, this 36-bed North End hostel is bright, well run and has a common kitchen. If the punk band is practicing across the street, don't expect to get much sleep before midnight (or bring earplugs) but at least you can get high quality coffee the next morning at the friendly downstairs café. The café also has cheap breakfasts and draws in all sorts of interesting local characters. City buses stop right out the front, but walking alone at night is ill-advised in this rough-edged neighborhood.

Dalhousie University (☎ 902-494-8840; www.dal.ca/confserv; s/d $40/65; mid May-mid Aug; P) Re-live your college days, or experience dorm life for the first time at one of Halifax' universities. Without wall-hangings or your friends down the hall, it feels more like a hospital than a great moment of youth, but it's central, clean and the best deal in town if you don't want to share a room with four other people. Howe Hall (6230 Coburg St) is adjacent to all the university amenities such as the cafeteria and library, but Gerard and Shireff Halls (5303 Morris St) are closer to downtown. Check the website for student and senior rates.

Midrange

Commons Inn (☎ 902-484-3466; www.commonsinn.ca; 5780-8 West St; s/d/ste $80/100/150; P) The Commons Inn is rather common and motel-like, but it's friendly, reasonable priced and in a good area not too far from downtown. Some rooms have a funny smell to 'em.

Verandah B&B (☎ 902-494-9500; www.theverandahbb.com; 1394 Edward St; d/ste $95/125) The brightest front terrace near downtown Halifax welcomes you to the Verandah. The rooms and interior are no bleaker, with plenty of cheerful, country comforters and well-managed color schemes. Two rooms have shared bath and there's one entirely self-contained suite. Owner/manager Joan is an opinionated Newfoundlander who will tell you what's on her mind.

Virginia Kinfolks B&B (☎ 902-423-6687; www.members.aol.com/vakinfolkz; 1722 Robie St; r $100-175;) Southern hospitality has found its way to Halifax in the form of a simple B&B in a central location right across from the hospital. The decor is nothing too fancy but there are fireplaces and Jacuzzi tubs in every room. This long-standing favorite books up fast during high season.

Garden Southpark Inn B&B (☎ 902-492-8577, 877-414-8577; www.gardeninn.ns.ca; 1263 South Park St; d/tw $110/120; P) The 23 rooms of this 1875 Victorian feel slightly more hotel-like than a B&B but the friendly service makes you feel right at home. One side of the house borders a beautiful, historic graveyard; rooms on this side offer better views if it's not too creepy for you. Downtown is only a five-minute stroll away; parking costs $6.

our pick **Waverley Inn B&B** (☎ 902-423-9346, 800-565-9346; www.waverleyinn.com; 1266 Barrington St; d $125-280; P) Period antique decor moves into a higher realm at this quirky gem. A Halifax Inn since 1876, the Waverley has housed notables such as Oscar Wilde, PT Barnum and Anna Leonowens (AKA 'Anna' from *The King and I*). Today, it's still a circus for the senses and poetry to the eyes. Although the less expensive rooms are less extraordinary than higher-end ones, each is unique, culminating with the penthouse 'Chinese Wedding Suite', which is furnished in eclectic Victorian and Chinese art and antiques. All this fun is in a central downtown location perfect for exploring the city's other historical whims.

Halliburton House Inn B&B (☎ 902-420-0658; www.halliburton.ns.ca; 5184 Morris St; r $145-350; P) This class-act was once home to the first chief justice of Nova Scotia. Today it's one of the finest B&Bs in town noted for excellent service and its rooms, which are discreetly decorated with antiques. Some of the smallest – and least expensive – rooms have balconies overlooking the garden patio. Rooms at the front of the building have more light.

Top End

Pebble B&B (☎ 902-423-3369, 1-888-303-5056; www.the pebble.ca; 1839 Armview Tce; d $150-225) Bathroom aficionados will find heaven at this luxurious B&B. The tub and shower are in a giant room that leads to a terrace overlooking a leafy garden. The bedrooms are equally generous with plush, high beds and a modern-meets-antique decor. Irish owner Elizabeth O'Carroll grew up with a pub-owning family and brings lively, joyous energy from the Emerald Isle to her home in a posh, waterside residential area.

Lord Nelson Hotel (☎ 902-423-5130, 800-565-2020; www.lordnelsonhotel.com; 1515 South Park St; d $155-215, ste $250; P ⬛ ♿) This elegant 1920s hotel is across from Halifax Public Gardens and is considered the most luxurious in Halifax. Use the in-house fitness center, or there are free passes to the YMCA next door. Parking is $15.

Prince George Hotel (☎ 902-425-1986, 800-565-1567; www.princegeorgehotel.com; 1725 Market St; d $180-250, ste $450; P ⬛ 🐾) A suave and debonair gem, central Prince George has all the details covered. Garden patios are a great place to take a drink, a meal or even work as an alternative to indoor meeting areas. Parking is $15.

EATING

The only downfall of dining in Halifax is that it can be downright difficult deciding which great place to go. From cheap eats to candle-lit dining on the harbor, this town has it all.

Budget

Annie's Place Café (☎ 902-420-0098; 1513 Birmingham St; breakfast & light meals $3-4; ⏱ 7am-5pm Mon-Fri, 8am-4pm Sat) A slice of small town in the heart of Halifax, Annie welcomes you in and cooks up a hearty breakfast. She also makes smoothies, homemade Chai and espresso drinks.

Ray's Falafel (☎ 902-492-0233; Scotia Square Mall, cnr Barrington & Duke Sts; meals $4-5; ⏱ 8am-6pm Mon-Wed, 8am-9pm Thu & Fri, 9am-6pm Sat) Ray's has been voted the best falafel in Halifax for 10 years running by readers of the *Coast*.

Dío Mío Gelato (☎ 902-492-3467; 5670 Spring Garden Rd; meals $5-8; ⏱ 8am-10pm Mon-Fri, noon-10pm Sat & Sun)

Italian-style ice cream and fruit ices are concocted from all-natural ingredients, and nearby Halifax Public Gardens is the perfect place to enjoy them. For lunch, choose from three different veggie burgers or the healthy and flavorful salads and sandwiches.

Elephant's Eye Decor & Café (☎ 902-420-1225; 1727 Barrington St; meals $5-11; ⏱ 9am-4pm Mon-Fri, 9am-3pm Sat) This understated little place offers a soup, crepe or vegetarian main of the day, and a seafood dish of the day. Browse the eccentric collection of antique knick-knacks while you eat.

Harbourside Market (Historic Properties, 1869 Upper Water St; meals $9-12; ⏱ 7am-9pm Mon-Thu, 7am-10pm Fri, 7:30am-10pm Sat, 7:30am-9pm Sun) If you've got kids with you, this is a great place for lunch. There's something for everyone from pizzas to seafood and you can enjoy your meal on a deck overlooking the harbor. A brewpub offers a selection of lagers and ales.

Midrange

Your Father's Moustache (☎ 902-423-6766; 5686 Spring Garden Rd; mains $8-15; ⏱ 11am-midnight) This is one of Halifax' most popular outdoor decks. Enjoy pub-style seafood steaks and pastas often accompanied by live music. Don't miss brunch on Saturdays for the blues matinee.

Curry Village (☎ 902-429-5010; 5677 Brenton Pl; mains $8-16; ⏱ 11:30am-2pm & 5-10pm Tue-Sat, 5-10pm Sun) Tucked away in a corner a block or two from Spring Garden Rd, this is Halifax' favorite stop for a biryanis, tandooris and curries.

ourpick Sweet Basil (☎ 902-425-2133; 1866 Upper Water St; mains lunch $8-18, dinner $18-20; ⏱ 11:30am-10pm) Halifax' finest cuisine need not cost a fortune; lunch at this chic, country-style bistro will appease your inner gourmet, guilt-free. Try the creative lunch crepe special ($9) that changes daily, or the walnut-crusted chicken breast ($19) at dinner. And whatever you do, save room for dessert; a separate kitchen is dedicated to fantastical creations that make Haligonians' mouths water. Vegetarian and gluten-free options are available.

Opa! Greek Taverna (☎ 902-492-7999; 1565 Argyle St; mains $9-16; ⏱ lunch & dinner) Souvlaki, stuffed tomatoes, soups and a smorgasbord of Greek specialties add a splash of sunshine to grey city streets. If the giant fake olive tree in the center doesn't bring you to European shores, the Mediterranean blues and yellows will.

Il Mercato (☎ 902-422-2866; 5650 Spring Garden Rd; mains $10-20; ⏱ 11am-11pm) This long-standing Italian favorite doesn't take reservations;

come early or late on weekends, or wait a short while. Talk and laugh loudly while filling your belly with homestyle pasta.

Doraku (sushi combo plates $13-26; 5:30-9:30pm Tue-Sat) Dresden Row (☎ 902-425-8888; 1579 Dresden Row); Spring Garden Rd (☎ 902-423-8787; 5640 Spring Garden Rd) One of Halifax' better sushi restaurants remains affordable and now has two downtown locations. The Dresden Row location is more upscale than the one on Spring Garden Rd.

Niche (☎ 902-423-6632; 1505 Barrington St; mains $14-18; lunch & dinner) This open-feeling restaurant has live jazz most nights during the summer and serves everything from grilled meats to pizzas to seafood jambalaya. The fake trees and wrought-iron detail make the inside feel like outside; there is dining next to real foliage on the patio when the weather is warm.

Wooden Monkey (☎ 902-444-3844; 1685 Argyle St; mains $15-20; 11am-10pm) 'A restaurant with a conscience,' the monkey was modeled with wood salvaged from Hurricane Juan and is decorated with recycled furniture. The result feels like an artistic living room; stained-glass pieces, beaded curtains and local art make you want to cosy up with a grilled breast of free-range chicken. The restaurant adamantly supports local organics and is a fab place to get gluten-free and vegan meals as well as humane meat dishes.

Top End

Fid (☎ 902-422-9162; www.fidcuisine.ca; 1569 Dresden Row; mains lunch $14-16, dinner $22-27; lunch Wed-Fri, dinner Tue-Sun) Slow food proponent Dennis Johnston (p57) buys all his ingredients from the local farmers' market, then sautées in Franco-Asian flavors to concoct dishes such as monkfish with shell peas, maple/asparagus-glazed pork belly with sweet potato and a beautiful pad thai. It's a great place to sample regional foods; the menu changes weekly and carries vegetarian options.

da Maurizio (☎ 902-423-0859; Brewery Market Bldg, 1496 Lower Water St; mains $28-30; 5-10pm Mon-Sat) This is Northern Italian class, pure and simple. Many locals cite da Maurizio as their favorite Halifax restaurant. The ambience is as fine as the cuisine; exposed brick and clean lines bring out all the flavors of this heritage brewery building. Reservations are strongly recommended.

Bish (☎ 902-425-7993; 1475 Lower Water St; mains $29-33; 5-10pm Mon-Sat) If grilled lobster tail with truffle butter doesn't up the ante of Maritime cuisine, not much will. There's no better place to celebrate or get very, very romantic than waterside Bishop's Harbour. Put it on plastic and enjoy yourself.

DRINKING

Halifax rivals St John's, Newfoundland, for the most drinking holes per capita. The biggest concentration of attractive bars is on Argyle St, where temporary streetside patios expand the sidewalk each summer. Pubs and bars close at 12:30am, a few hours earlier on Sunday.

Economy Shoe Shop (☎ 902-423-8845; 1663 Argyle St) This has been the 'it' place to drink and people-watch in Halifax for a decade now. On weekend nights actors and journalists figure heavily in the crush. It's a pleasant place for afternoon drinks but note that this is one of the more expensive establishments in town. The kitchen dishes out tapas ($6 to $10) until last call at 1:45am.

Henry House (☎ 902-423-5660; 1222 Barrington St) The most atmospheric pub in town is close to inns and hostels in the southern end of downtown. The basement is inviting and dark.

Argyle Bar & Grill (☎ 902-492-8844; 1575 Argyle St) The Argyle comes into its own each too-short summer, when the rooftop patio attracts a crowd for daiquiris.

Dome (☎ 902-422-5453; 1740 Argyle St) Dubbed the 'Liquordome,' with four venues under one roof. 'The Attic' has live music; the others are nightclubs open until 3am. It's a bit of a meat market and a favorite for heavy drinkers.

Reflections Cabaret (☎ 902-422-2957; www.reflectionscabaret.com; 5184 Sackville St) If you're looking for a wild night out look no further. A mainly gay disco that attracts a mixed crowd, nightly entertainment ranges from wrestling to drag shows to sensory stage shows. It opens at 4pm, but the action really starts after 10pm and it stays open until 3am.

Trident Booksellers & Café (☎ 902-423-7100; 1256 Hollis St; 8am-5pm Mon-Fri, 8:30am-5pm Sat, 11am-5pm Sun) This sedate café is the place to linger with your journal or novel.

ENTERTAINMENT

Check out the *Coast* (p64) to see what's on.

Live Music

Halifax' music scene began in the mid-1990s when Nirvana's label signed local band Sloan. Halifax was declared the 'new Seattle' and everyone wore flannel. Since then, the town's live music scene has diversified, with folk, hip-hop, alternative country and rock gigs every weekend. Many restaurants listed in 'Eating' also have live music – see p73 for details.

Khyber Club (☎ 902-446-4053; http://khyberarts.ns.ca/kdmc; 1588 Barrington St; membership $10, weekend cover $6; ☺ 5pm-1am Tue-Fri, 8pm-1am Sat) On the 1st floor of the Khyber Centre for the Arts (p65), this is a happening venue with spoken word on Tuesday, hip-hop on Wednesday and pop, rock or folk musicians on weekends.

Stage Nine Bar & Grill (☎ 902-444-7800; www.stagenine.ca; 1567 Grafton St; cover free-$25; ☺ 4pm-2am Tue-Sun) This venue has three stories of fun including two smoking rooms, live local music daily and a summer rooftop patio. There's also a full kitchen so you can grab a meal before shaking your booty.

Marquee (☎ 902-429-3020; www.themarqueeclub.ca; 2037 Gottingen St; cover $6-25) This is the choice venue for touring bands and big-name locals; shows start around 10:30pm. Up-and-coming musicians play downstairs in Hell's Kitchen. Admission to the Marquee gets you into Hell's Kitchen, but not vice versa. Check the website for information on upcoming events.

Ginger's Tavern (☎ 902-425-5020; 1662 Barrington St; cover $5; ☺ 11am-2am) This mellow venue showcases folk and alternative country acts. It was popular in the '70s and '80s and is now experiencing a sort of rebirth.

Bearly's House of Blues & Ribs (☎ 902-423-2526; 1269 Barrington St; cover $3; ☺ 11:30am-9pm Mon, 11:30am-10pm Tue-Sat & noon-10pm Sun) The best blues musicians found in Atlantic Canada play here at incredibly low cover charges. Wednes-day karaoke nights draw a crowd and some fine singers.

Theater
The two professional theaters in Halifax – Neptune Theatre and Eastern Front Theatre – take a break in summer, when their last shows typically playing in May. However, Shakespeare by the Sea provides diversion through the summer.

Halifax Feast Dinner Theatre (☎ 902-420-1840; www.feastdinnertheatre.com; 1505 Barrington St; dinner & show adult/child $45/23; ☺ 7pm nightly) Get whisked away to another era while enjoying a three-course meal at this acclaimed dinner theater.

Neptune Theatre (☎ 902-429-7070; www.neptunetheatre.com; 1593 Argyle St) This downtown theater presents musicals and well-known plays on its main stage ($37), and edgier stuff in the studio ($20).

Shakespeare by the Sea (☎ 902-422-0295; www.shakespearebythesea.ca; Point Pleasant Park; suggested donation $10; ☺ Jun-Sep) Fine performances of the Bard's works at the Cambridge Battery, an old fortification in the middle of the park. Check the website for a map and details.

Film
Park Lane Cinemas (☎ 902-423-4598; Park Lane Mall, Spring Garden Rd & Dresden Row) Hollywood flicks and occasional screenings of independent films.

Sports
Halifax Metro Centre (☎ 902-451-1221; 5284 Duke St; tickets $13.50) Halifax Mooseheads junior hockey team play here.

GAY & LESBIAN HALIFAX

Halifax has a thumping and thriving gay and lesbian scene with most of the nightlife action being concentrated around Gottingen St. **Club NRG** (☎ 902-422-4368; 2099B Gottingen St; ☺ 4pm-2am) is popular for dancing on Friday night. **Club Vortex** (☎ 902-420-1323; 2215 Gottingen St; ☺ 11:30am-2am) hosts occasional Womyn's nights and promises high-energy dancing on weekends. In the club is **Mobey's Eatery** (mains $8-15; ☺ lunch & dinner Wed-Sun), which is packed on Sunday for brunch. Lesbian travelers can stop by **Venus Envy** (☎ 902-422-0004; 1598 Barrington St; ☺ 10am-6pm Mon-Wed & Sat, 10am-7pm Thu & Fri, noon-5pm Sun) to network, browse books and check out fun toys. Squeaky clean **Seadog's Sauna & Spa** (☎ 444-3647; 2199 Gottingen St; www.seadogs.ca; ☺ 4pm-1am Mon-Thu, open from 4pm Fri through 1am Mon) is the largest private men's club east of Québec City and has all the spa fixings as well as private rooms, high-speed Internet and more. About once a month the spa gets turned over to the womyn of Venus Envy and becomes **Shedogs** (www.venusenvy.ca). **Halifax Pride Week** (www.halifaxpride.com) takes place every year around the second week of June. Enjoy film screenings, comedy, art exhibits, drag shows and more; the week culminates on Pride Day with a big, flamboyant parade through the downtown area.

SHOPPING

Halifax Farmers' Brewery Market (☎ 902-492-4043; 1496 Lower Water St; ◷ 7am-1pm Sat May-Dec, 8am-1pm Sat Jan-May) North America's oldest farmers' market, in the 1820s Keith's Brewery Building, is the ultimate Maritime shopping experience. Head here to people-watch and buy organic produce, jewelry, clothes and crafts. Come early or late to avoid the crowds.

Fireworks Gallery (☎ 902-420-1735; 1569 Barrington St; ◷ 10am-5:30pm Mon-Thu & Sat, 10am-8pm Fri) Beautiful jewelry by resident goldsmiths is for sale; other pieces by artisans from across the Maritimes are on display. Prices vary widely.

Hydrostone Market (5515-47 Young St; ◷ 10am-6pm Tue-Fri, 10am-5pm Sat, noon-5pm Sun) This was reconstructed following the Halifax Explosion. The quaint row of shops, cafés and restaurants includes the Bogside Gallery (☎ 902-453-3063; open from 10am to 6pm Monday, Tuesday and Friday, 10am to 8pm Wednesday and Thursday, 10am to 5pm Saturday and noon to 5pm Sunday), featuring fine crafts.

GETTING THERE & AWAY
Air

Air Canada and Westjet have multiple flights daily between Halifax and major Canadian cities such as Toronto ($300, 2½ hours), Montréal ($300, 1½ hours) and Ottawa ($300, 1¾ hours). Air Canada also flies between Halifax and other Maritime destinations (Saint John $200, 45 minutes, four times daily; Moncton $350, 40 minutes, four times daily), to St John's ($380, one hour, five time daily) and to Boston ($250, 2¼ hours, twice daily). In summer, there's a daily direct flight to London ($700, six hours). All prices vary widely depending on sales and how far in advance the ticket is purchased. See p278 for information.

Bus

The **Acadian Lines** (☎ 902-454-9321; www.acadianbus .com; 1161 Hollis St) terminal is at the VIA Rail station next to the Westin Hotel. Its buses travel to Truro and Amherst and connect to Montréal and New York. It also goes to Digby ($40, four hours), with stops throughout the Annapolis Valley, and to Sydney ($62, 6½ hours) stopping in Antigonish ($35, 3½ hours).

Trius Lines has a daily route from Halifax to Yarmouth (4½ hours; approximately $50) that serves towns along the South Shore. Call Acadian (above) for information on prices and departure points.

Shuttle

Private shuttle buses compete with the major bus companies. They usually pick you up and drop you off and, with fewer stops, they also travel faster. The slight trade-off is a more cramped ride – per passenger price is determined by the number of people taking the shuttle. **Cloud Nine Shuttle** (☎ 902-742-3992, 888-805-3335; www.thecloudnineshuttle.com) goes to Yarmouth ($50, 3½ hours), stopping along the South Shore each afternoon, returning to the Halifax area each morning. Airport pickup or drop-off is an extra $5. **Amero's Shuttle** (☎ 888-283-2222; www.ameroshuttle.com; Halifax to Yarmouth $45-60) travels to Yarmouth through the Annapolis Valley; book several days ahead. **Try Town Transit** (☎ 877-521-0855, 902-521-0855) goes to Mahone Bay ($22, 50 minutes) and Lunenburg ($23, one hour).

Scotia Shuttle (☎ 902-435-9686, 800-898-5883; www.atyp.com/scotiashuttle) travels to Sydney on Cape Breton Island ($50, five hours, once daily). **MacLeod's Shuttle** (☎ 902-539-2700, 800-471-7775) does this route also. **Inverness Shuttle Service** (☎ 902-945-2000, 888-826-2477) travels between Halifax and Inverness, Cape Breton Island (adult/student $40/35) every day but Saturday.

PEI Express Shuttle (☎ 902-462-8177, 877-877-1771; www.peishuttle.com) and **Go-Van** (☎ 866-463-9660) both charge $50 per person to Charlottetown, PEI, with early morning pickups; Go-Van charges $15 per bicycle. **Advanced Shuttle** (☎ 877-886-3322, 902-886-3322) leaves Halifax in the afternoon for Charlottetown; it charges $10 per bicycle.

Train

One of the few examples of monumental Canadian train station architecture left in the Maritimes is found at 1161 Hollis St. Options with **VIA Rail** (www.viarail.ca) include overnight service to Montréal (one-week advance purchase adult/child two to 11 years $133/66, 21 hours, daily except Tuesday).

GETTING AROUND
To/From the Airport

Halifax International Airport is 40km northeast of town on Hwy 102 toward Truro. **Airbus** (☎ 902-873-2091; one-way/return $16/21) runs between 5am and 11pm and picks up at major hotels. **Share-A-Cab** (☎ 902-429-5555, 800-565-8669; one-way $24) must be booked a day ahead. A taxi to or from the airport costs $53.

Car & Motorcycle

Pedestrians almost always have the right-of-way in Halifax. Watch out for cars stopping suddenly!

Outside the downtown core, you can usually find free on-street parking for up to two hours. Otherwise, try private **Impark** (1245 Hollis St; per hr/12hr $1/6) or the municipally owned **Metro-Park** (☎ 902-830-1711; 1557 Granville St; per hr/12hr $2/14). Halifax' parking meters are enforced from 8am to 6pm Monday to Friday.

It costs considerably more to rent a car at the airport than in town. All the major national chains (see p282) are represented there and also have offices in Halifax. **Enterprise Rent-a-Car** (☎ 902-492-8400; www.enterprise.com; 1161 Hollis St) has an office in the train station and at several other locations near downtown. It has some of the lowest rates. **Discount Car Rentals** (☎ 902-453-5153; www.discountcar.com; 2710 Agricola St) also has good deals, depending on availability. It's 1.25km north of the northwest corner of Citadel Hill.

Public Transportation

Metro Transit (☎ 902-490-6600; one-way $1.75, 20 tickets $30) runs the city bus system and the ferries to Dartmouth. Transfers are free when traveling in one direction within a short time frame. Maps and schedules are available at the ferry terminals and at the information booth in Scotia Sq Mall.

Bus 7 cuts through downtown and North End Halifax via Robie St and Gottingen St, passing both hostels. Bus 1 travels Spring Garden Rd, Barrington St, and the south part of Gottingen St before crossing the bridge to Dartmouth. 'Fred' is a free city bus that loops around downtown every 30 minutes in the summer.

Taking the ferry to Dartmouth from the Halifax waterfront is a nice way of getting on the water, even if it's just for 12 minutes. Woodside, where another ferry goes in peak periods, is a good place to start a bike ride to Eastern Passage or Lawrencetown.

AROUND HALIFAX
Dartmouth

Much more residential than Halifax, Dartmouth (population 94,779) has 23 lakes, which have earned it the nickname 'City of Lakes.' Founded in 1750, one year after Halifax, the sister cities are linked via two bridges, the Angus L McDonald and the A Murray MacKay. The best way to get to Dartmouth, however, is by the Maritime's best budget harbor cruise, the ferry, which is the oldest saltwater ferry system in North America, dating back to 1752.

Alderney Gate houses the ferry terminal, the Dartmouth public library and Eastern Front Theatre (below). The term 'Dartmouth' often means a much broader area that encompasses everything to Eastern Passage.

The city swells during the **Nova Scotia Multicultural Festival** (www.mans.ns.ca) in late June. This weekend festival on the waterfront celebrates diversity with great performances and even better food.

SIGHTS & ACTIVITIES

Dartmouth Heritage Museum (☎ 902-464-2300; www.dartmouthheritagemuseum.ns.ca; 26 Newcastle St; admission $2; ☉ 10am-5pm Tue-Sun mid-Jun–Aug, 1:30-5pm Wed-Sat Sep–mid-Jun) displays an eclectic collection in historic **Evergreen House**, the former home of folklorist Helen Creighton (who traversed the province in the early 20th century recording stories and songs). Tickets include admission on the same day to the 1786 **Quaker House** (59 Ochterloney St; ☉ 10am-5pm Tue-Sun Jun-Aug), the oldest house in the Halifax area, which was built by Quaker whalers from Nantucket who were fleeing the American Revolution. Guides in costume lead visitors around the house, and there's a children's dress-up box.

Dartmouth Sportsplex (☎ 902-460-2600; www.dartmouthsportsplex.com; 110 Wyse Rd; ☉ 5:30am-10:30pm Mon-Fri, 6am-9pm Sat, 9am-10:30pm Sun, extended hr Sep-Jun) has a warm-water pool, and Pirate's Cove (for children at least 1.22m tall) within the same complex has three waterslides. More grown-up entertainment can be found at **Eastern Front Theatre** (☎ 902-463-7529; www.easternfront.ns.ca; Alderney Gate, Dartmouth; tickets $20-25) which debuts several works by Atlantic playwrights each year.

TOURS

Dartmouth is the best location in this area to head out on a sea adventure.

Seadawgs Historical Walking Tour (☎ 902-465-2357; www.seadawgs.ca; Fisherman's Cove, Eastern Passage; adult/child/family $10/5/25; ☉ 1:30pm & 3:30pm May-Oct) Cavort with a properly clad pirate, your guide through the times of pirates and privateers via the seaside of Eastern passage.

Some Sites 2 Sea Eco Tours & Charters (☎ 902-489-7401; wwwsomesites2sea.com; Alderny Landing,

Dartmouth; whale-watching adult/child $25/15; half-day fishing adult/child $45/35) Located beside the ferry terminal, this safe, well-equipped vessel takes folks out whale-watching, deep-sea fishing and catch-and-release shark fishing.

SLEEPING & EATING

Shubie Campground (☎ 902-435-8328, 800-440-8450; www.shubiecampground.com; Jaybee Dr, off Waverley Rd) This privately run, municipality-owned Dartmouth campground is the only one accessible from Halifax on public transportation. A grassy field with little shade, facilities include showers and a laundromat.

Caroline's B&B (☎ 902-469-4665; 134 Victoria Rd; s/d $40/50; ☺ Apr-Dec) This Dartmouth B&B is an economical alternative to staying in Halifax and it's close to both bus routes and the ferry. Three rooms share two bathrooms.

Wharf Wraps (☎ 902-465-3476; 104 Fisherman's Cove, Eastern Passage; mains $6-12; ☺ lunch & dinner) Known far and wide as serving some of the best fish-and-chips, you'd better be hungry before diving into these huge portions.

Eastern Shore Beaches

When downtown dwellers venture over the bridge to Dartmouth on a hot summer's day, it's most likely en route to a beach. There are beautiful, long, white-sand beaches all along the Eastern Shore, and several are a reasonable drive from Halifax. The water never gets very warm, but brave souls venture in for a swim or a surf, particularly if the fog stays offshore.

The closest – and busiest – of the Eastern Shore beaches, **Rainbow Haven**, is 1km long. It has washrooms, showers, a canteen and a boardwalk with wheelchair access to the beach. Lifeguards supervise a sizable swimming area. To get there, take Portland St from downtown Dartmouth through Cole Harbour, where it becomes Cole Harbour Rd/Hwy 207, and turn right on Bissett Rd. Turn left at the end of Bissett Rd and then right at the beach entrance.

Porters Lake Provincial Park (☎ 902-827-2250; http://parks.gov.ns.ca; 1160 Crowell Rd; campsites $18) is a campground on a peninsula and small island in Porters Lake, with 158 nicely separated, shady campsites. It's best to reserve for Friday or Saturday nights from mid-July to mid-August.

With more than 3km of white sand, **Martinique** is the longest beach in Nova Scotia. Even if you find the water too cold for a swim, this is a beautiful place to walk, watch birds or throw a Frisbee. Follow the signs for Hwy 7 from Dartmouth, drive about 40km, and then turn right onto East Petpeswick Rd in Musquodoboit Harbour.

Sambro

Just 18km south of Halifax, **Crystal Crescent Beach** is on the outskirts of the fishing village of Sambro. There are actually three beaches here in distinct coves; the third one out – toward the southwest – is clothing-optional and gay-friendly. An 8.5km **hiking trail** begins just inland of Crystal Crescent Beach and heads through barrens, bogs and boulders to Pennant Point. To get here, take Herring Cove Rd from the roundabout in Halifax all the way to Sambro, then follow the signs.

Prospect

As pretty as Peggy's Cove, Prospect (population 200) doesn't attract a fraction of the tourist traffic. This quiet little seaside village is a perfect escape and has the feel of being completely surrounded by water. An undeveloped **trail** starts at the end of Indian Point Rd and leads 3km along the coast past plenty of perfect picnic spots. There's not a lot of room to park at the trailhead, so you may need to leave your vehicle on the roadside into the village.

Prospect B&B (☎ 902-543-2233; www.nsinns.com; 1758 Prospect Bay Rd; r $95-165) in a gorgeous old nunnery, has recently gotten a face-lift. The warm owners use organics for everything from soaps to the ingredients of their tasty breakfasts. Your host is an accomplished musician who likes to play music with her guests; with all the scenery and revelry you'll never want to leave.

Peggy's Cove

The Cove (population 60) is one of the most visited sites in Atlantic Canada and there's a reason for it: it is exceptionally picturesque in a province famed for its beauty. Peggy wears her visitors well. Tour buses and hordes of people don't take anything away from that perfect image of a white-and-red lighthouse perched on rolling hills of granite. There is only one B&B in town and three little restaurants. Dating from 1811 and with just 60 residents, the little fishing village shines with simplicity.

It's best to visit before 11am in the summer as tour buses tend to arrive in the middle of the day. There's a free parking area with washrooms and a **tourist information office** (☎ 902-823-2253; 109 Peggy's Cove Rd; ☺ 9am-7pm Jul &

Aug, 9am-5pm mid-May–Jun, Sep & Oct) as you enter the village. Free half-hour and one-hour walking tours are led from the tourist office five days a week. The tour days are variable through the week but they are guaranteed on weekends. Across the street from the tourist office, and included in the walking tour, **deGarthe Gallery** (☎ 902-823-2256; admission $2; ⏰ 9am-5pm mid-May–Oct) has paintings by local artist William deGarthe (1907–83), who sculpted the magnificent 30m-high **Fishermen's Monument** out of a rock face in front of the gallery.

The famous **lighthouse** is now a small post office with its own lighthouse-shaped stamp cancellation mark. A poignant **memorial** to those who perished aboard the 1998 Swissair Flight 111 just offshore is off Hwy 333, about 1.8km north of the turnoff to Peggy's Cove.

New to the cove is the **Peggy Show** (☎ 902-823-2099; www.thepeggyshow.net; Old Red Schoolhouse, 126 Peggy's Point Rd; requested donation $10; ⏰ 2pm & 4pm Wed-Sun end Jun-Sep) the 'unauthorized autobiography of Peggy from the cove.' The creative comedy has been a big hit and is a must-see if you enjoy watching men dressed as women.

SLEEPING
Wayside Camping Park (☎ 902-823-2271; wayside@hfx .eastlink.ca; 10295 Hwy 333, Glen Margaret; tent/RV sites $20/30) This large park, 10km north of Peggy's Cove and 36km from Halifax, has lots of shady sites up on the hill. It's crowded in midsummer.

Oceanstone Inn & Cottages (☎ 902-823-2160, 866-823-2160; www.oceanstone.ns.ca; 8650 Peggy's Cove Rd, Indian Harbour; r $85-175, cottages $185-365; 🖵 ♿) A short drive from Peggy's Cove, Oceanstone feels miles away from everything. Take a walk through the pines, past English gardens and sunny lawns, to the sea. Whimsical, Maritime-style cottages are a stone's throw from the beach. Guests can use paddleboats to venture to small islands and outcroppings, some with lighthouses. Don't miss the restaurant (see Eating, right), which offers some of the finest dining in the area. The inn and cottages are open year-round, with great off-season specials and discounts.

Peggy's Cove Bed & Breakfast (☎ 902-543-2233, 800-725-8732; www.nsinns.com; 19 Church Rd; r $95-165) The only place to stay in the cove itself, this B&B has an enviable position on a slope overlooking the fishing docks and the lighthouse. Once an old fisherman's home, it was once lived in by the artist William deGarthe. You'll definitely need advance reservations here.

EATING
Beale's Bailwick (☎ 902-823-2009; 124 Peggy's Point Rd; espresso $2.50; ⏰ 9am-5pm) Stop in for an organic espresso and leave with a fridge magnet or a wind chime; this gift shop has a sunny terrace at the back which is a perfect place to rest the feet and fuel up on caffeine.

Murray's Wharfside Lobster Pound (☎ 902-823-3249; 13 Rocky Rd; chowder $6.50, lobster $22; ⏰ 11am-8pm) Shake off the tourist crowd at this funky fisherman's shack hidden along a little dirt road. Dine on superb seafood on plastic tables right on the cove.

Rhubarb (☎ 902-823-2160; 8650 Peggy's Cove Rd; mains $20-30; ⏰ dinner Jul-Sep, Sat & Sun only May, Jun & Oct) Owned by Oceanstone Inn & Cottages, this fine dining option serves scrumptious seafood dinners and appetizers (reservations recommended). The very refined and glamorous dining area verges on stuffy – you'll want to dress correctly when taking an evening meal.

ST MARGARET'S BAY
The scenery from Peggy's Cove continues south, down the coast of St Margaret's Bay. Rolling granite slowly gives way to rocky beaches; little evergreen islands dot the twisting and curving shoreline so that you almost feel you are beside a lake. It's no wonder this tranquil area is popular with cruising yachts. From east to west, this area includes the towns of Hacketts Cove, Tantallon and Hubbards.

No rip currents and the sheltered bay mean perfect (although cold) swimming conditions – you couldn't hope to find a nicer beach than **Queensland Beach** near Hubbards at the base of St Margaret's Bay. On sunny days this small stretch of sand becomes one of the most popular family spots in the province.

Flying Dutchman B&B (☎ 902-823-1728, 866-859-5044; doreenlangille@eastlink.ca; 9758 Peggy's Cove Rd, Hacketts Cove; r $75-145; 🖵) has an oceanfront lawn with swimming and boating as well as some swings for the kids. This Cape Cod–style home is spacious and has all the amenities. Dutch and German are also spoken.

SOUTH SHORE

Much of what might be considered stereotypical Nova Scotia – lighthouses, rugged Atlantic coastline and charming fishing villages – is found along this stretch. Highway 3 – labeled the 'Lighthouse Route' by tourism officials –

can be slow, particularly on weekends, as a result of day-trippers from Halifax, Yarmouth or the Maine ferry. If you're not pressed for time and want to enjoy some spectacular scenery, take Hwy 3 all the way. Travel times can be halved by taking Hwy 103 directly to the closest exit for your destination, but as one local put it, 'the only sights you'll see is roadkill.'

CHESTER

Overlooking Mahone Bay, the old village of Chester (established 1759) has had a colorful history as the haunt of pirates and Prohibition-era bathtub-gin smugglers. Over the past several decades, it's become a northern Martha's Vineyard: a choice spot for well-to-do Americans and Haligonians to have a summer home.

There's a large **regatta** in the attractive harbor in mid-August. Browse the town's few streets for an uncommonly high concentration of shops and galleries, pottery studios and candle-making workshops.

Information

Tourist office (☎ 902-275-4616; Hwy 3; ⏰ 9am-7pm Jul & Aug, 10am-6pm Jun & Sep, 10am-5pm May & Oct) in the old train depot near the Chester turnoff.

Sights & Activities

A fine example of Georgian architecture from 1806, the **Lordly House Museum** (☎ 902-275-3842; 133 Central St; admission free; ⏰ 10am-5pm Tue-Sat, 1-5pm Sun mid-May–mid-Oct) has three period rooms illustrating 19th-century upper-class life and

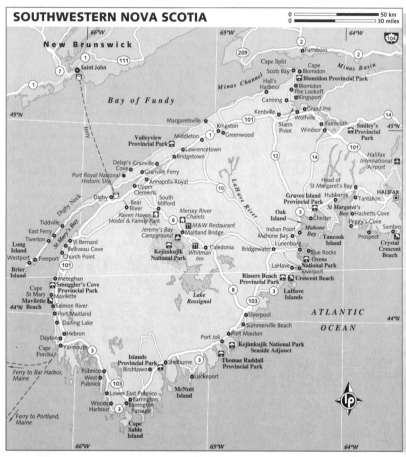

SOUTHWESTERN NOVA SCOTIA

Chester history. The museum is also an artists' studio.

Tancook Island (population 190) is a 45-minute ferry ride from Government Wharf in Chester (return $5, four runs Monday to Friday, two on weekends; exact schedule at http://freepages.history.rootsweb.com /~tancook/ferry.htm). Walking trails crisscross the island. Settled by Germans and French Huguenots in the early 19th century, the island is famous for its sauerkraut. The last ferry from Chester each day overnights in Tancook Island.

Sleeping & Eating

Graves Island Provincial Park (☎ 902-275-4425; http://parks.gov.ns.ca; 3km northeast of Chester off Hwy 3; campsites $18) An island in Mahone Bay connected by a causeway to the mainland has 64 wooded and open campsites. RVs usually park in the middle of the area, but some shady, isolated tent sites are tucked away on the flanks of the central plateau. Graves Island is very popular in midsummer; it will be full Friday and Saturday nights.

Mecklenburgh Inn B&B (☎ 902-275-4638; www .mecklenburghinn.ca; 78 Queen St; s/d with shared bathroom $85/95, with private bathroom $125/135; ☯ May-Dec) This casual four-room inn, built in 1890, has a breezy 2nd-floor veranda; some rooms have private adjacent balconies, most have private bathrooms.

Julien's Pastry Shop Bakery (☎ 902-275-2324; 43 Queen St near Pleasant St; sandwiches $4-5; ☯ 8am-5pm Tue-Sun) Julien's freshly baked French pastries are addictive.

Kiwi Café (☎ 902-275-1492; 19 Pleasant St; light lunches $6-9; ☯ 7:30am-4pm) A New Zealand chef prepares fabulous sandwiches and delicious breakfasts here. You can't miss the kiwi-green awning.

Rope Loft (☎ 902-275-3430; 36 Water St; mains around $15; ☯ food served 11:30am-9pm Sun-Thu, till 10pm Fri & Sat, pub open daily till 11pm) You couldn't find a better setting than this bayside pub. Hearty pub food is served indoors or out on the open deck when there's sunshine.

Entertainment

Chester Playhouse (☎ 902-275-3933; www.chesterplay house.ns.ca; 22 Pleasant St; tickets $24; ☯ Mar-Dec) This older theater space has great acoustics for live performances. Plays or dinner theater are presented most nights, except Monday, in July and August, with occasional concerts during spring and fall. During the summer festival months of July and August there are matinees at 2pm and evening performances at 8pm.

MAHONE BAY

Tranquil Mahone Bay (population 991), on a bay with more than 100 islands, gets more than its fair share of tourists but keeps smiling through them all. About 100km from Halifax, it's a great base for exploring this section of the South Shore. This is one of the most environmentally aware hubs in the region and you'll find plenty of eco-minded lodgings and yummy organic cooking – not to mention yoga everywhere! Thanks to having some of the best weather on the coast, this is a fab place for a stroll, a kayak or a bike ride.

Information

Biscuit Eater Booktrader & Cafe (☎ 902-624-2665; 16 Orchard St; free wi-fi, terminals per hr $5; ☯ 9am-5pm Mon-Sat, 11am-5pm Sun, closed Tue) The best place to check email with a fair-trade coffee and a light organic meal.

Mahone Bay (www.mahonebay.com) Links to restaurants and accommodations.

VIC (☎ 902-624-6151; 165 Edgewater St; ☯ 9am-7pm Jul & Aug, 9am-6pm Jun & Sep, 10am-5pm Oct, 10am-5pm Sat & Sun only May) Has walking-tour brochures.

Sights & Activities

Facing the waterfront in a row along Edgewater St are three historic **churches** belonging to the Anglican, Lutheran and United denominations.

Settlers' Museum & Cultural Centre (☎ 902-624-6263; 578 Main St; admission free; ☯ 10am-5pm Tue-Sat, 1-5pm Sun Jun–mid-Oct) shows exhibits on the settlement of this area by 'Foreign Protestants' in 1754 and local architecture. Pick up a walking-tour map for a self-guided walk through Mahone Bay's architectural history.

Amos Pewter (☎ 800-565-3369; www.amospewter .com; 589 Main St; admission free; ☯ 9am-6:30pm Mon-Sat, 10am-5:30pm Sun Jul & Aug, 9am-5:30pm Mon-Sat, noon-5:30pm Sun May, Jun, Sep & Oct) is both a museum demonstrating the art of pewter-making and a store where wares are sold.

East Coast Outfitters (☎ 877-852-2567; www.east coastoutfitters.net; 617 Main St; half-/full-day kayak rental $45/65, half-/full-day bike rental $20/35) Rents kayaks and bikes plus leads kayak tours and lessons.

A PIRATE'S TREASURE

Nova Scotia's Oak Island, near Mahone Bay, is home to a so-called 'money pit' that has cost over $2 million in excavation costs and six lives. There is still not a shred of information about what the pit is or what might be buried there.

The mystery began 1795 when three inhabitants of the island came across a depression in the ground. Knowing that pirates had once frequented the area, they decided to dig and see what they could find. Just over half a meter down they hit a layer of neatly placed flagstone; another 2.5m turned up one oak platform, then another. After digging to 9m, the men temporarily gave up but returned eight years later with the Onslow Company, a professional crew.

The Onslow excavation made it down 27.5m; when the crew returned the next morning, the shaft had flooded and they were forced to halt the digging. A year later, the company returned to dig 33.5m down in a parallel shaft, which also flooded. While the dig was on, it was noticed that the floodwaters were salty and rose and fell with the tides. This formed the idea that the pit was booby trapped with flood channels. This was confirmed in 1850 with the discovery that the beach at Smith Cove, 150m away from the pit, was artificial. The original clay had been removed and round beach stones, dead eel grass, coconut fibre then sand, had been laid in its place. At the bottom of all this were five box drains that would have merged at some point near the pit. This ingenious design prevented the flood shafts from clogging.

Over the next couple hundred years, as people have come to seek their fortune at the 'money pit,' the only things that have been found are a few links of a gold chain, some parchment, a cement vault and an inscribed stone. What the pit has produced is a bounty of rumor and mystery. Speculation as to what might be or have been in the hole range from the Holy Grail to the original manuscripts of Shakespeare to millions of British pounds to Viking treasure. Today the mystery is no closer to being solved although treasure seekers are still risking their fate and their money in hopes of uncovering the truth, and maybe an early retirement.

Courses

Mahone Bay is a haven for artists and is a popular spot for those seeking inspiration. **Mahone Arts** (☎ 902-624-9215; www.mahonearts.com; workshops from $425) organize a three-day or one-week art workshop by the sea with local artists. Check the website for scheduling; there is also an art trek to mysterious Oak Island (see above).

Festivals & Events

On the weekend prior to the first Monday in August, the **Mahone Bay Classic Boat Festival** (☎ 902-624-0348; www.woodenboatfestival.org) celebrates the town's heritage with workshops in boatbuilding, daily races of small craft, parades and fireworks.

Sleeping

Kip & Kaboodle Backpackers Hostel (☎ 902-531-5494, 866-549-4522; www.kiwikaboodle.com; Hwy 3; dm incl breakfast $25) This great, helpful and friendly hostel, 3km from the attractions of Mahone Bay's Main St and 7km from Lunenburg, has nine beds, an outdoor pool, and a superior location. Owners offer town pickup.

Hammock Inn the Woods B&B (☎ 902-624-0891; www.hammockinnthewoods.com; 198 Woodstock Rd; d $85)

Any stress you might have will vanish at this wonderfully calm B&B up a quiet road from Main St. There are two beckoning hammocks nestled in a wooded garden, the house is bright and soothing and rooms are a restful blend of modern plush and country comfort. The healthy breakfasts are cooked using organic produce and there's free yoga every morning.

Fisherman's Daughter B&B (☎ 902-624-0483; www.fishermans-daughter.com; 97 Edgewater St; d/ste $85/125) Original woodwork, Gothic-revival windows and an ideal location overlooking the bay makes the Fisherman's Daughter one of the best-looking girls in the village. Rooms are spacious and all have en suite baths. The British reception is a bit cooler than the standard over-the-top friendliness of the Maritimes.

Three Thistles B&B (☎ 902-624-0517; www.three-thistles.com; 389 West Main St; s/d $85/110) One of the most environmentally friendly B&Bs in this half of Nova Scotia, owner Phyllis Wiseman uses environmentally conscious cleaning agents as well as cooking with organic foods. Rooms are sparkling and clean, and there's a back garden that stretches to a wooded area. A newly constructed yoga studio downstairs inspires morning stretches or meditation.

Mahone Bay B&B (☎ 902-624-6388, 866-239-6252; www.bbcanada.com/4078.html; 558 Main St; r $85-125) Enjoy a view of the three churches from this friendly, ornate 1860s shipbuilder's home. Right in the center of town, all comforts are included, from cable TV to bathrobes. This place fills up fast during the summer.

Eating

Cheesecake Gallery (☎ 902-624-0579; 533 Main St; mains $7-21; ☽ 11am-8pm, closed Thu) A truly stunning gallery of works from Nova Scotian artists doubles as one of the best places in town for creative sandwiches, seafood, vegetarian mains and a tempting display of cheesecakes.

Mug & Anchor (☎ 902-624-6378; 643 Main St; mains $8-16; ☽ 11am-12:30am) There's a great view of Mahone Bay from the waterfront deck of this upmarket pub. The fish isn't deep-fried and there are some decent vegetarian options, plus there's a nice microbrew on tap.

Innlet Café (☎ 902-624-6363; 249 Edgewater St; mains $9-17; ☽ 11:30am-9pm) Great on a sunny day. Get a tan while you eat on the front deck overlooking the bay. Dig in to the house specialty, Mahone Mussle Bay Stew ($9), or simpler fare such as burgers and pasta.

Shopping

Main St, which skirts the harbor, is scattered with shops selling antiques, quilts, chocolates and pottery.

Shuttles & Seawinds (☎ 902-624-6177; 446 Main St; ☽ 9am-5pm Tue-Sat, 11am-5pm Sun) This long-standing institution offers Nova Scotia–made quilts and unique gifts.

Redden's Fine Whale Sculptures (☎ 902-624-1232; 788 Main St; ☽ 10am-5pm Mon-Sat) Visit the studio of Susan Redden, who produces sumptuous whale and dolphin replicas out of fine mahogany. The warm wood mixed with fine detail pay a just homage to the endangered creatures.

Moorings Gallery (☎ 902-624-6208; 575 Main St; ☽ 10:30am-5pm Mon-Sat, 1-5pm Sun Jun-Aug, 11am-5pm Thu-Sat, 1-5pm Sun May & Oct-Dec) This gallery features pottery, jewelry and fine art by Maritime artists and craftspeople.

LUNENBURG

Red, blue and yellow historic fishing buildings grace the ship-filled seaport in Lunenburg (population 2781), the region's only Unesco world heritage site. The *Bluenose* sailing schooner was built here in 1921 and

Lunenburg was the first British settlement outside Halifax. Look for the distinctive 'Lunenburg Bump,' a five-sided dormer window on the 2nd floor that overhangs the 1st floor of many houses. You'll find that most of the well-preserved practical fishing architecture is rather boxy compared with the Victorian homes in town and throughout Nova Scotia, but that's what makes this town stand out against the rest.

Lunenburg was settled largely by Germans, Swiss and Protestant French who were first recruited by the British as a workforce for Halifax; most became fishermen. Nova Scotia has been hard hit by dwindling fish stocks and severely curtailed limits imposed by the federal government, but Lunenburg's burgeoning tourism trade has helped shore up the local economy.

Be warned: even on a rainy Monday you're guaranteed to find considerable throngs of tourists in Lunenburg. The top-notch festivals draw even more visitors.

Information

Explore Lunenburg (www.explorelunenburg.ca) Local history and tourism information.
Lunenburg Public Library (☎ 902-634-8008; 19 Pelham St; ☽ 10am-6pm Tue, Wed & Fri, 10am-8pm Thu, 10am-5pm Sat) Free Internet access.
Lunenburg VIC (☎ 902-634-8100, 888-615-8305; 11 Blockhouse Hill Rd; ☽ 9am-6pm May-Oct, to 8pm Jul & Aug) Tourist brochures and help with accommodations.

Sights & Activities

The fishing schooner *Theresa E Connor* and the dragger *Cape Sable* are just two of the exhibits at the **Fisheries Museum of the Atlantic** (☎ 902-634-4794; http://fisheries.museum.gov.ns.ca; 68 Bluenose Dr; adult/child under 18yr/family $9/3/22; ☽ 9:30am-5:30pm early May-late Oct). The knowledgeable staff includes a number of retired fishers who can give firsthand explanations of the fishing industry. An awesome aquarium on the 1st floor lets you get eye-to-eye with flounder, halibut and other sea creatures. Films screen regularly in the 3rd-floor theater.

Considered the finest example of Georgian architecture in the province, the 1793 **Knaut-Rhuland House** (☎ 902-634-3498; 125 Pelham St; admission $3; ☽ 11am-5pm Tue-Sat, 1-5pm Sun early Jun-Sep) has costumed guides who point out its features.

Lunenburg Academy (97 Kaulbach St) is the huge black-and-white turreted hilltop structure visible on your way in from Halifax. Built entirely of wood in 1895 as a prestigious high school, it is now a public school. In July and August, it's home to the **Lunenburg Seaside Craft School** (☎ 902-634-3242; www.lunenburgcraftschool.com; 5-day course $490). Preregistration is required for courses in basket weaving, paper art and a host of other crafts, but you can call to check for openings.

The **Captain Angus J Walters House** (☎ 902-634-2020; 37 Tannery Rd; admission $2; 1-7pm Mon-Fri, 1-5pm Sat) was donated to the town by the descendants of Captain Walters, who skippered the famous *Bluenose*. It's dedicated to preserving the history of the man and the schooner.

Bicycles can be rented and repaired at the **Bike Barn** (☎ 902-634-3426; www.bikelunenburg.com; 579 Blue Rocks Rd; hybrid/tandem bikes per day $20/40), almost 2km east of town toward the small fishing community of Blue Rocks. On a small peninsula with no commercial development, this area is a cyclist's dream with few hills, great ocean views, and little vehicle traffic. Owner Merrill Heubach will gladly help you plan your trip.

Tours

Tours depart from the wharf adjacent to the Fisheries Museum on Bluenose Dr.

Bluenose II (☎ 902-634-1963, 800-763-1963; www .bluenose2.ns.ca; 2hr cruise adult/child 3-12yr $20/10) This classic replica of the *Bluenose* racing schooner is sometimes in Halifax and sometimes in Lunenburg. Clambering about the schooner when it's in port is free.

Lunenburg Whale Watching (☎ 902-527-7175; adult/child under 14yr $42/30; Jun–mid-Oct) Offers three-hour trips that promise sightings of birds and seals as well as whales.

Lobstermen Tours (☎ 902-634-3434; www.lobster mentours.com; 45min tours adult/child $12/6) The two-hour tour includes hauling lobster pots and examining their contents in a touch tank. The minitour cruises around Lunenburg Harbour.

Festivals & Events

Lunenburg Heritage Bandstand Summer Concerts (www.lunenburgheritagesociety.ca) Free Sunday afternoon concerts from Big Band to Jazz over July and August.

Boxwood Festival (www.boxwood.org; festival pass $50) Flautists and pipers from around the world put on stellar public concerts in the last week of July.

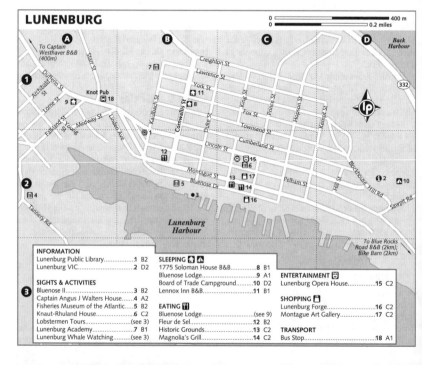

LOCAL VOICES

Judy Strong

Retired office manager for the Victorian Order of Nurses, age 67, Lunenburg

If your best friend was coming to visit, where would you go for the weekend? The Kejimkujik Seaside Adjunct. It hasn't been tampered with. There are unspoiled rock formations, miles of beach and you can sit and have lunch with the seals. **What do you think is the most controversial issue facing your area today and why?** It's the same issue that's faced this province since I was 17 years old: if you have a secondary education, you are out of the Maritimes. The Maritimes have become known in Canada as the 'greatest exporters of youth.' There's just not much industry to keep people here. There's not even really a fishing industry in Lunenburg anymore, just seasonal tourism work.

Lunenburg Folk Harbour Festival (☎ 902-634-3180; www.folkharbour.com) Singer-songwriters from Canada and beyond, plus traditional music and gospel, come here in early August.

Nova Scotia Folk Art Festival (www.nsfolkartfestival .com) The first Sunday in August sees the sale and display of works from more than 40 folk artists.

Sleeping

Make reservations as far ahead as possible, especially if you want to visit during a summer festival.

Board of Trade Campground (☎ 902-634-8100/3656; lbt@aliantzinc.ca; 11 Blockhouse Hill Rd; tent/RV sites $18/$27; 🖳) Atop the hill locally called the 'blockhouse' this RV-dominated campsite next to the VIC has great views over the water. Grassy tent sites are closely packed together and lack shade.

Captain Westhaver B&B (☎ 902-634-4937; www3 .ns.sympatico.ca/westhaver.haus; 102 Dufferin St; s/d $55/65; 🖳) One of the best bargains in Nova Scotia, Steve and Sue Olliver skimp neither on luxury of accommodation nor on service. If you don't mind sharing the bathroom, this place is worth every penny.

Blue Rocks Road B&B (☎ 902-634-8033; www.bike lunenburg.com; 579 Blue Rocks Rd; r with shared/private bathroom $80/95; 🖳) Bike all day then sleep it off at this B&B-cum–bike rental shop (see Bike Barn, opposite) on the outskirts of town. Rooms are brightly painted, rustically charming and undeniably cosy. The owner cooks up a hearty breakfast and makes you feel right at home.

Lennox Inn (☎ 902-634-4043, 888-379-7605; www .lennoxinn.com; 69 Fox St; r $85/140) This place feels authentically old, with electric candles lighting the halls and massive plank wood floors. The Inn is the oldest in Canada and you get to eat breakfast in what was once the tavern.

1775 Solomon House (☎ 902-634-3477; www.bb canada.com/5511.html; 69 Townsend St; r $95-120; 🖳) This well tended, classic Lunenburg box-style home has real seaside flavor. The breakfasts here are known to be the best in town and the welcome is un-equalled.

Bluenose Lodge (☎ 902-634-8851, 800-565-8851; www.bluenoselodge.ca; 10 Falkland St; r $80-190; 🖳) A landmark building impossible to miss, the Bluenose is an elegant place to sleep and dine (see below). While the big blue building is anything but subtle, the interior decor is gently Victorian.

Eating

Try some offbeat Lunenburg specialties like Solomon Gundy (pickled herring with onions) or Lunenburg pudding (pork and spices cooked in the intestines of a pig).

Historic Grounds (☎ 902-634-9995; 100 Montague St; breakfast $5-12; 🕒 7:30am-4pm Mon-Fri, 8am-4pm Sat & Sun) Get an espresso fix along with baked goods or stop in for one of the best breakfasts in town. The outdoor patio overlooks the water and fills up quickly on summer weekends. Weekdays this is a great place to kick back and hang out with the locals.

Magnolia's Grill (☎ 902-634-3287; 128 Montague St; mains $7-15; 🕒 lunch & dinner) This diner-style favorite of local and traveling foodies is often busy. Try one of the many soups of the day, from creole-peanut (very rich) to potato-leek, or the gently spicy Tunisian vegetable stew. Seafood (including Solomon Gundy) and an extensive wine list are available.

Bluenose Lodge (☎ 902-634-8851; 10 Falkland St; mains lunch $8-14, dinner $17-36; 🕒 11am-9pm Mon-Sat, 10am-9pm Sun) Treat yourself to a creative gourmet sandwich at lunch or splurge on the chef's sampler ($36) at dinner. The elegant dining room makes you feel like a movie star.

Fleur de Sel (☎ 902-640-2121; 53 Montague St; mains lunch $8-12, dinner $22-29; 🕒 11am-2pm & 5-10pm)

Owned by a young and dynamic couple – he's the chef and she's the hostess – this is by far the most elegant eating option in the region. French-inspired seafood, meat and vegetarian dishes use organic produce and are served in the classic, bright dining area. If dinner is a bit steep for you, definitely stop here for lunch.

Entertainment

Lunenburg Opera House (☎ 902-634-4010; 290 Lincoln St; www.lunenburgoperahouse.com; tickets $5-20) This rickety old 400-seat theater is rumored to have a resident ghost. Built as an Oddfellows Hall in 1907, it's now a favorite venue for rock and folk musicians. Check the posters in the window or the website for what's coming up.

Shopping

Lunenburg Forge (☎ 902-634-7125; 146 Bluenose Dr; ☺ 10am-6pm) This is the summertime studio of metalworkers Laurie Fisher Huck and Christopher Huck (their winter studio is located in Mexico). Laurie created the whimsical sea creatures that hang from Lunenburg's street poles.

Montague Art Gallery (☎ 902-634-8955; 139 Montague St; ☺ 10am-7pm) Daniel Richards' marine- and fisheries-inspired art is a favorite in Nova Scotia. This is his primary studio.

Getting There & Away

Trius Lines buses serve Lunenburg on their once-daily Halifax-to-Yarmouth route; best source of information on Trius' prices and departure locations is **Acadian Lines** (☎ 902-454-9321, 800-567-5151). For alternative shuttles, see p76.

BRIDGEWATER

Bridgewater (population 7315), an industrial town with a big Michelin tire plant, is the largest center on the South Shore. **Wile Carding Mill** (☎ 902-543-8233; museum.gov.ns.ca/wcm; 242 Victoria Rd; adult/child $2/1; ☺ 9:30am-5:30pm Mon-Sat, 1-5:30pm Sun Jun-Sep) is an authentic water mill dating from 1860. Carding is the straightening and untangling of wool fibers in preparation for spinning. This mill did in an hour what would otherwise take a woman a whole week.

LAHAVE

Sleepy LaHave is a tiny village on the south bank of the LaHave River, famous for its great bakery. Besides fresh bread, the area has good kayaking, and several kayak tour companies lead trips through this area.

Once you've gotten your sandwich and coffee from the bakery, head up to **Fort Point Museum** (☎ 902-688-2696; Fort Point Rd; admission free; ☺ 10am-5pm Jun-Aug), 1km west of the village. It was here, in 1632, that returning French settlers, who would become known as Acadians, landed after the Treaty of St Germain-en-Laye when England ceded Acadia to France. The museum in the former lighthouse keeper's house at the site tells the story of this early settlement and its leader, Isaac de Razilly.

Sleeping options in LaHave do not abound but you could try **LaHave Marine Hostel** (☎ 902-688-2908; 3421 Hwy 331; dm $12-15; ☺ Jun-Sep). When it's open (and nothing is set in stone), it's ideal for cyclists, backpackers or any like-minded soul looking for a low-budget place. There's a well-equipped kitchen where you can prepare meals, a sitting room and a library. The riverside dock behind the hostel is a great place to linger. There is no email address or website so you'll need to call to make sure someone will be there to receive you.

The tasty baked goods from **La Have Bakery** (☎ 902-688-2908; 3421 Hwy 331; sandwiches $4-6; ☺ 8:30am-6:30pm) can be found throughout

---

DETOUR: OVENS NATURAL PARK

Just south of Lunenburg is **Ovens Natural Park** (☎ 902-766-4621; www.ovenspark.com; admission adult/child & senior $6/3), so-named for its massive, seaside caves. Although the 77 hectares of dramatic, rocky coastline and boat-accessible sea caves are a draw, the most fun reason to visit the park is to try your hand at panning for gold. The gold rush of 1861 has long since gone but many regulars still pan here and have enough success to keep coming back.

Besides looking for gold, there are **boat tours** (adult/child $23/20; ☺ 8:30am-5:30pm on the hr Jun-Sep) run by the park and a self-guided cave trail **walking tour** (free). Great **campsites** (incl park entry $23) and **RV hook-up sites** ($31-40) are available as well as a few **cabins** (d $50-85, q $125-180). At night the Chapin family (the park's owners) are known to strike up some music and get everyone involved. There's a general store and a family-style restaurant also in park boundaries.

Nova Scotia and you can stop in at the bakery for a hearty sandwich on big, thick slabs of bread straight from the oven. There's also pizza, soups, fresh loaves, cookies and hot and cold drinks.

Most people visiting the village will experience the **LaHave Ferry** which connects Hwys 332 and 331, saving motorists a 40km drive up and down the river to use the bridges at Bridgewater. The five-minute cable ferry trip goes every half-hour and costs $5 per car. Pedestrians can ride back and forth as often as they like for free.

LAHAVE ISLANDS

Just southwest of LaHave are the LaHave Islands, a handful of small, pleasant-to-look-at islands connected to the mainland by a 2km causeway along Crescent Beach and to each other by one-lane iron bridges. You're allowed to drive a car along the sands of Crescent Beach!

On Bell Island just past Government Wharf is the **Marine Museum** (☎ 902-688-2973; www.fortpoint museum.com; 100 Bells Island; admission free; ☺ 10am-5pm Jun-Aug). The museum is housed in St John's Anglican Church and services are occasionally still held among the marine artifacts.

Rissers Beach Provincial Park (☎ 902-688-2034; http://parks.gov.ns.ca/parks/rissers.htm; 5463 Hwy 331; campsites $18; ☺ mid-May–early Oct) is a kilometer west of the causeway to the islands and 10km from LaHave. Rissers Beach is a very busy campground (in July and August) and an excellent long, sandy beach. There's also a saltwater marsh with a boardwalk trail and a good interpretive display with information on the natural environment. The 92-site campground has two sections, one along the beach and another inland. Rissers Beach is close enough to Halifax/Dartmouth to get rather crowded on midsummer weekends. Thomas Raddall Provincial Park near Port Joli to the southwest gets a lot less traffic, and the campsites are larger and more private.

LIVERPOOL

Liverpool (population 11,694) was once ruled by British privateers who protected British trade routes from incursions by the USA during the War of 1812, and did the odd bit of plundering for their own coffers. Today, the locals are mild, upstanding folk that make this otherwise mediocre town an inviting place. There is plenty to do in the village itself and

it's well situated for exploring several gorgeous white-sand beaches, Kejimkujik National Park (68km north, see p88) and its Seaside Adjunct (15km southwest, see p89).

Information

Tourist office (☎ 902-354-5421; 28 Henry Hensey Dr; ☺ 9am-7pm Jul & Aug, 10am-5pm Jun & early–mid-Sep) Near the river bridge, it has a walking-tour pamphlet and brochures of scenic drives.

Sights & Activities

Sherman Hines is behind a number of new cultural attractions in Liverpool. One of Atlantic Canada's most prolific photographers, and a wealthy Liverpudlian, his most ambitious venture is the **Rossignol Cultural Centre** (☎ 902-354-3067; www.rossignolculturalcentre.com; 205 Church St; adult/child/student $4/2/3; ☺ 10am-5:30pm Mon-Sat). It contains minimuseums of wildlife and folk art, outhouses and a couple of galleries. Admission includes entry to **Sherman Hines Museum of Photography & Galleries** (☎ 902-354-2667; www.shermanhinesphotographymuseum.com; 219 Main St; ☺ 10am-5:30pm Mon-Sat), where six galleries in the old town hall run the gamut of media.

Perkins House Museum (☎ 902-354-4058; http://museum.gov.ns.ca/peh; 105 Main St; adult/child $2/1; ☺ 9:30am-5:30pm Mon-Sat, 1-5:30pm Sun Jun–mid-Oct) displays articles and furniture from colonial times. Built in 1766, it's the oldest house belonging to the Nova Scotia Museum. Next door, the **Queen's County Museum** (☎ 902-354-4058; www.queensmuseum.netfirms.com; 109 Main St; admission $1; ☺ 9:30am-5:30pm Mon-Sat, 1-5:30pm Sun Jun–mid-Oct, 9am-5pm Mon-Sat rest of year) has First Nations artifacts and more materials relating to town history, as well as writings by early citizens.

At **Fort Point**, a cairn marks the site where Frenchman Samuel de Champlain landed in 1604. You can blow the hand-pumped foghorn in the **lighthouse** (☎ 902-354-5260; 21 Fort Lane, at the end of Main St; admission free; ☺ 10am-6pm mid-May–mid-Oct).

Hank Snow Country Music Centre (☎ 902-354-4675; www.hanksnow.com; 148 Bristol Ave; admission $3; ☺ 9am-5pm Mon-Sat, noon-5pm Sun late May-early Oct) sheds light on Nova Scotia's status as a northern Nashville. In the old train station, it captures the history of Snow, Wilf Carter and other crooners and yodelers.

Festivals

Step back to 1780 for **Privateer Days** (www .privateerdays.com; early July), which re-creates the privateer era through re-enactments, sporting events, music and a downtown festival; this is one of the better festivals in Nova Scotia. In mid-May, catch the **Liverpool International Theatre Festival** (www.astortheatre.ns.ca) with five days of performances that celebrate theater from around the world.

Sleeping & Eating

Geranium House (☎ 902-354-4484; 87 Milton Rd; r $50) This board-and-battens-style B&B on a large wooded property next to the Mersey River welcomes cyclists and families. The three rooms share a bathroom.

Lane's Privateer Inn B&B (☎ 902-354-3456, 800-794-3332; www.lanesprivateerinn.com; 27 Bristol Ave; s/d $80/95) Originally the home of a swashbuckling privateer, this inn has been in the same family for three generations. It now has a bookshop and gourmet food store. Its cosy pub and dining room (open 7am to 10pm) offer seafood with surprising sauces and some Mexican dishes (mains $9 to $25). Try a pear and blue-cheese salad.

Woodpile Carving Cafe (☎ 902-354-4494; 181 Main St; light meal $3-6; ☉ 8am-4pm Mon-Sat) This atmospheric café has the owner's wood-carving workshop right in its center. A local's favorite, grab a specialty coffee, soups, sandwiches and salads.

Golden Pond (☎ 902-354-5186; 73 Henry Hensey Dr; mains around $9; ☉ 11am-11pm Mon-Fri) Great Chinese food but also some local flavors such as fish-and-chips.

Entertainment

Astor Theatre (☎ 902-354-5250; www.astortheatre.ns .ca; 59 Gorham St) The Astor is the oldest continuously operating performance venue in the province. Built in 1902 as the Liverpool Opera House, it presents films, plays and live music.

KEJIMKUJIK NATIONAL PARK

This is one of the only places in Nova Scotia where you feel far from the sea. Driving through the little communities and wooded areas, this region feels distinctly off-the-beaten-track even though, if you're still in your car, it's not. In the park you'll find some of Nova Scotia's most pristine wilderness and best backcountry adventure opportunities. Less than 20% of Kejimkujik's 381 sq km is accessible by car; the rest is reached either on foot or by paddle. Bird-watchers can hope to see plenty

of water fowl, barred owls, scarlet tanagers and pileated woodpeckers among other species, while wildlife ranges from porcupines to black bear. Canoeing is an ideal way to explore this area of glacial lakes; the park is well set up for extended, overnight paddles. On a less joyful note, biting insects are rampant; watch out for mosquitoes the size of hummingbirds and eel-like leeches in the lakes.

The only close town of any size is Caledonia (population 1500), which has an information office, a grocery store, gas station, pharmacy, post office, bank (with ATM) and a B&B (see below). It's about 18km southeast of the park and everything is easily spotted roadside.

Information

There is a visitors center in Caledonia and a bigger one inside the park.

Visitor Center Caledonia (☎ 902-682-2470; Hwy 8; ☉ 9am-5pm Mon-Sat) This local-flavored info center is very helpful.

Visitor center (☎ 902-682-2772, 800-414-6765; www.parkscanada.gc.ca/keji; Hwy 8; adult/child/family $4.50/2.25/11.25; ☉ 8:30am-9pm mid-Jun–early Sep, to 4pm rest of year, closed weekends Nov-Mar) Get an entry permit and reserve backcountry sites here.

Activities

The main **hiking** loop is a 60km trek that begins at the east end of George Lake and ends at the Big Dam Lake trailhead. September to early October is prime hiking time; the bugs in the spring would drive you mad. A shorter loop, ideal for an overnight trek, is the 26km Channel Lake Trail that begins and ends at Big Dam Lake. More than a dozen lakes are connected by a system of portages, allowing canoe trips of up to seven days. A topographical map ($10; available at the park visitors center) may be required for ambitious multi-day trips. Rent canoes and other equipment in the park at **Jake's Landing** (☎ 902-682-5253; www .friendsofkeji.ns.ca/jakes; ☉ 8am-9pm Jun-Sep, off-season by appointment). One-hour hire of a kayak, bike or rowboat is $6, double kayak or canoe is $8; 24-hour hire is $30/33 and one-week hire is $125 for single or double.

Sleeping & Eating

Forty-five backcountry campsites ($8 per person plus a $5 booking fee) are scattered among the lakes of Kejimkujik. You must book them in advance by calling or stopping at the park's visitors center, but it's worth it. There's a 14-

day maximum; you can't stay more than two nights at any site.

Raven Haven Hostel & Family Park (☎ 902-532-7320; www.annapoliscounty.ns.ca/rec/ravhav/hostel.htm; 2239 Virginia Rd, off Hwy 8, South Milford; dm member/nonmember $16/18, tent/RV sites $16/19; ☯ mid-Jun–early Sep) This community-run HI hostel and small family campground is 25km south of Annapolis Royal and 27km north of the national park. The clean four-bed hostel is in a cabin near the white-sand beach; it's only a five-second jog between your bed and the cool waters of the lake. There are 15 campsites, including some private wooded ones, but the camping in the park is better. Canoes and paddleboats can be rented.

Jeremy's Bay Campground (☎ 902-682-2772, 800-414-6765; campsites summer/winter $21/15) Its 360 campsites within the park include a handful of walk-in sites near the shoreline. Thirty percent of the sites are assigned on a first-come, first-served basis. These will be taken by midafternoon Friday on any midsummer weekend. There is only one shower area for all the camp area so be prepared to wait for a stall or stay dirty. It costs $10 to reserve a site.

Aunt Nettie's B&B (☎ 902-682-3030; auntnetties bb@hotmail.com; 9865 Hwy 8, Caledonia; s/d $65/85; ▢) As cute as the country town it's in, Caledonia's sole B&B feels like your grandparents house. Abbie the feisty little dog keeps everyone entertained. The B&B is scent- and smoke-free.

Whitman Inn (☎ 902-682-2226, 800-830-3855; www .whitmaninn.com; 12389 Hwy 8; r $70-120; ☯ Feb-Oct, dinner by reservation; ▣) About 4km south of the park near Caledonia, this gracious older inn has a wide veranda and great facilities, like a sauna and games room. Breakfast and picnic lunches ($7) are available for guests. Anyone is welcome for dinner (mains $13 to $20) from 6pm to 8pm July and August; call for hours the rest of the year.

Mersey River Chalets (☎ 902-682-2447, 877-667-2583; www.merseyriverchalets.ns.ca; 2537 River Rd; tepee $70, d $110, cabins $150-175; ▢ ⴲ) With a winding, rapid river, the scent of pine and artistically constructed river walkway, this is the perfect place to live comfortably in a dreamily rustic wilderness. Free canoes and kayaks are available for guests. One of the owners is in a wheelchair so the entire place has been made wheelchair accessible, from the boardwalk to the on-site restaurant. Comfy cabins have woodsy pine floors, wood-burning stoves and very private porches complete with barbecue; rooms in the lodge have private decks with lake views and cosy tepees have fully equipped kitchens.

M&W Restaurant & Variety Store (☎ 902-682-2189; Hwy 8; mains $4-10; ☯ 8am-9pm mid-May–mid-Oct) Only 500m from the park entrance this convenient and friendly place serves 'hungry camper' breakfasts ($6) as well as lunch and dinner. It's also a general store stocked with camping supplies (including firewood) and a Laundromat.

SEASIDE ADJUNCT (KEJIMKUJIK NATIONAL PARK)

Welcome to some of the most divinely undeveloped coastline of Eastern Nova Scotia. The 'Keji Adjunct' protects the oceanfront beach areas between Port Joli and Port Mouton (ma-*toon*) Bay; the landscapes of rolling low brush, wildflowers, white sandy coves and granite outcrops are angelically serene. The only access from Hwy 103 is along a 6.5km gravel road. From road's end, two mostly flat trails lead to the coast. **Harbour Rocks Trail** (5.2km return) follows an old cart road through mixed forest to a beach where seals are often seen. A loop trail around **Port Joli Head** is 8.7km return. Take a picnic and feel the troubles of the world melt away.

The Port Joli Basin contains **Point Joli Migratory Bird Sanctuary** with waterfowl and shorebirds in great numbers (*Nova Scotia Birding on the Lighthouse Route* is an excellent resource available at VICs). It's only easily accessible by kayak. The **Rossignol Surf Shop** (☎ 902-683-2550; www.surfnovascotia.com; 600 St Catherine's River Rd, Port Joli; half-/full-day kayak rentals $30/45, tours $55/95, surf clinics $75) rents kayaks, offers guided tours and surf instruction.

Summerville Beach and **White Point** are beach and surf areas a short detour off exit 20 from Port Mouton, near the park.

Thomas Raddall Provincial Park (☎ 902-683-2664; www.parks.gov.ns.ca; campsites $18), across Port Joli Harbour from Keji Adjunct, has large, private campsites with eight walk-in ones. The forested campground extends out onto awesome beaches. If you don't have camping gear, **Port Mouton International Hostel** (☎ 902-947-3140; www .wqccda.com/PMhostel; 8100 Hwy 3;dm $20; ▢), only five minutes from 'Keji Adjunct,' is a great budget place to stop for the night. It's in a closed-down 1960s-built school so you might feel like you've reverted back to kindergarten;

NOVA SCOTIA

its converted-garage decor gives it a high-school vibe as well. The common area and full kitchen inspire group meals.

More upscale in the resort area of Summerville Beach, **Quarterdeck Beachside Villas & Grill** (☎ 902-683-2998, 800-565-1119; www.quarterdeck.ns.ca; Hwy 3; cottages $129-339; 🖳) has plush condo-style apartments that look out over a beach worthy of a Californian soap opera. You can also just stop in for a meal at the seaside grill. Serving all-day brunch, burgers and the like, this restaurant is perched over crashing waves.

LOCKEPORT

An unpretentious fishing village set behind beautiful Crescent Beach, Lockeport (population 701) is worth a detour from Hwy 103. The **Crescent Beach Centre** (☎ 902-656-3123; 157 Locke St; 🕙 9am-7pm Jul & Aug, 9am-4pm Jun & Sep, 10am-4pm Tue-Sat rest of year) has tourist information and a memorial quilt for 17 local fishermen lost at sea in 1964. Follow the boardwalk to get to the beach. It's a nesting site for the endangered piping plover, so dogs should always be on a leash and people should be careful where they walk.

Little School Museum (☎ 902-656-2850; 29 Locke St; admission by donation; 🕙 10am-5pm Jul & Aug), just up from the beach, captures early local history. One room is restored as an 1890s village schoolroom, another has a collection of old fishing implements.

Five houses overlooking the harbor on South St are protected as a heritage streetscape. Built between 1836 and 1876 by descendants of town father Jonathan Locke, they show the distinct style of Colonial, Georgian and Victorian times. A plaque at the far end of South St examines the history of the homes and the families who once lived there.

Hire surfboards and bodyboards at the Crescent Beach Centre (per hour/half-day/day $10/20/40, with wetsuit $20/30/50). Lockeport's back harbor, accessible via a long boardwalk, is a good site for **birding**.

The best place to stay in the area is **Ocean Mist Cottages** (☎ 902-656-3200; www.oceanmistcottages .com; Crescent Beach; cottages $160; 🖳). These self-contained pine units have two bedrooms and can comfortably sleep a family of four. The location, right on a half moon of white sand with views of the lighthouse, couldn't be better.

SHELBURNE

One of the most attractive towns on the South Shore (imagine a mini-Lunenburg without the throngs of tourists), Shelburne's (population 2132) center runs along the waterfront and has 17 homes older than 1800. These early buildings once housed Loyalists who retreated here from the American Revolution. Life in the USA was not easy for those loyal to the British crown, and thousands left for Canada; many of those who came here were from New York aristocracy. This shipbuilding town is known as the birthplace of yachts.

Shelburne's early history is celebrated with **Founders' Days** during the last weekend of July. A more modern festival, the **Waterfront Jazz & Blues Festival** (☎ 902-875-2202; www.waterfrontjazz.org) rocks the town for three days in mid-July.

Information

Tourist office (☎ 902-875-4547; 31 Dock St; 🕙 8am-8pm Jul & Aug, 11am-5pm mid-May–Jun & Sep) Has copies of a self-guided historic district walking tour.

Sights & Activities

Four museums in the historic district relate Shelburne's history as a Loyalist community and a shipbuilding center. Admission to all four museums costs $8, a single admission is $3.

Built in 1784, **Ross-Thomson House** (☎ 902-875-3141; www.rossthomson.museum.gov.ns.ca; 9 Charlotte Lane; admission free; 🕙 9:30am-5:30pm Mon-Sat, 9:30am-noon Sun Jun–mid-Oct) and the store adjacent to it belonged to well-to-do Loyalist merchants who arrived from Cape Cod. Furniture, paintings and original goods from the store are on display. The house is surrounded by authentic period gardens.

Another Loyalist house (c 1787) is now the **Shelburne County Museum** (☎ 902-875-3219; cnr Maiden Lane & Dock St; 🕙 9:30am-5:30pm Jun–mid-Oct, 10am-noon & 2-5pm Mon-Fri rest of year) with a collection of Loyalist furnishings, displays on the history of the local fishery and a small collection of Mi'kmaw artifacts, including typical porcupine-quill decorative work.

The **Muir-Cox Shipyard** (☎ 902-875-1114; www .historicshelburne.com/muircox.htm; 18 Dock St; 🕙 9:30am-5:30pm Jun-Sep) has been in almost continuous operation since 1820, turning out barques, yachts and fishing boats. It's still active year-round, but the interpretive center is seasonal. Likewise, Shelburne dories (small open boats once used for fishing from a mother schooner) are still made to order at the **Dory Shop Museum** (☎ 902-875-3219; http://museum.gov.ns.ca/dory; 11 Dock St; 🕙 9:30am-5:30pm Jun-Sep) for use as lifeboats.

There's a **trail** for hiking or biking the 6km to Birchtown across from Spencer's Garden Centre at the far south end of Main St.

Sleeping

Islands Provincial Park (☎ 902-875-4304; www.parks .gov.ns.ca; off Hwy 3; campsites $18) Across the harbor from Shelburne are 65 campsites in mature forest and a beach for swimming.

Water Street Lighthouse B&B (☎ 902-875-2331; www.shelburnelighthouse.com; 263 Water St; r $65; ✆ May-Oct) Not luxurious, but comfy and friendly, this is a great B&B to shack up your bike for the night. A lighthouse theme runs throughout the house and the breakfasts will satisfy even the hungriest traveler.

Millstones B&B (☎ 902-875-4525, 866-240-9110; www.millstonesbedandbreakfast.com; 2 Falls Lane; r $90-140; ▢) This butter-yellow stunner sits gracefully by the river 1km from town center. Rooms are decorated in a modern, country style and each has a different flower theme.

Shady Pines Farm Country Inn (☎ 902-875-3495; www.countryvacations.info; 12 Roger Lane; r $95) It's not far off the main road yet you'll feel like you're lost in the woods at this place. Pine is definitely king here, but rooms are tastefully decorated and comfortable. A river runs right past the property and a few llamas liven up the farm.

Cooper's Inn B&B (☎ 902-875-4656, 800-688-2011; www.thecoopersinn.com; 36 Dock St; r $100-150; ▢) Across from a rare working cooperage that still makes barrels for the fishing industry,

this was once home to generations of coopers. Part of the building dates back to 1784 and was actually brought here from Boston. Now it's a comfortable, unique inn with six rooms. The smallest room opens directly into the heritage garden.

Eating & Drinking

Shelburne Pastry & Tea House (☎ 902-875-1164; 151 Water St; mains $7-14; ✆ 8am-8pm Mon-Fri, 8am-2pm Sat) Enjoy breakfast, lunch and dinner of seafood specialties including fresh poached haddock with lemon dill wine sauce ($13) and an array of lobster sandwiches (from $8). The garden terrace lets you sit back and enjoy.

Charlotte Lane (☎ 902-875-3314; 13 Charlotte Lane; mains $15-30; ✆ lunch & dinner Tue-Sat) People drive from Halifax and Yarmouth to eat here, and then rave about it; evening reservations are highly recommended. Try salmon glazed with miso and mustard ($16) or chicken baked with camembert ($15). The chef is constantly revising an extensive annotated wine list.

Beandock (☎ 902-875-1302; 10 John St; ✆ 8am-5pm Mon-Sat) The funky, hip patio is one of the best places in town to enjoy the view with a good coffee. It's right on the water at the corner of Dock St.

Sea Dog Saloon (☎ 902-875-2862; 1 Dock St; ✆ 11am-midnight Mon-Sat, noon-8pm Sun) Coffee's not what you had in mind? Shuffle over to this harborview patio for a pint. There's also an extensive pub menu.

AFRICAN NOVA SCOTIANS

While Nova Scotia was a haven for freed and escaped African slaves compared with the southern US, it was far from a paradise for this displaced population. After the American Revolution, about 3500 Black Loyalists were rewarded by the British with land for settlements near Shelburne, Halifax, Digby and Guysborough. Nine years later, in 1792, after barely surviving harsh winters and unequal treatment, 1200 of them boarded 15 ships bound for Sierra Leone, in West Africa, where they founded Freetown. An additional 2000 from the USA settled in the Maritimes after the War of 1812, and still others came from the Caribbean in the 1890s to work in the Cape Breton Island coal mines.

The future was no brighter. Underfunded, segregated schools existed until the 1950s. In 1970 the City of Halifax forcibly removed residents of Africville from their homes on the shore of the Bedford Basin in order to build the MacKay Bridge; the community and its church were bulldozed and the people moved to cramped public housing projects in North End Halifax. Today, African Nova Scotians are under-represented in high-school graduation ceremonies and over-represented in courtrooms and prisons.

The United Baptist Church has been a pillar of this community almost since the beginning, something poet George Elliott Clarke writes about in *Whylah Falls*, an award-winning collection of linked poems set in an imagined settlement of Black Loyalist descendants. A self-guided tour of African heritage in Nova Scotia is available online (www.gov.ns.ca/nsarm/virtual/africanns/).

NOVA SCOTIA

BIRCHTOWN

Just as Shelburne was once the largest Loyalist settlement in British North America, so Birchtown was once the largest settlement of freed African slaves in North America. Named for British General Samuel Birch who signed the freedom papers of many Black Loyalists at the end of the American Revolution, it was home to close to 1500 freed Blacks in 1784 (see the boxed text, p91).

The **Black Loyalist Heritage Society Historical Site & Museum** (☎ 902-875-1381, 888-354-0722; www .blackloyalist.com; 104 Birchtown Rd; ⊙ 11am-6pm Tue-Fri, noon-6pm Sat, noon-5pm Sun) includes a museum, an old burial ground and a walking trail that leads to a 'pit house', which archaeologists think was once a temporary shelter. There are also pleasant picnic areas and a **trail** for hiking or cycling the 6km to Shelburne (see p90).

BARRINGTON & BARRINGTON PASSAGE

Barrington was settled in 1760 by 50 families from Cape Cod. Several **museums** (☎ 902-637-2185; per museum adult/child $2/1; ⊙ 9:30am-5:30pm Mon-Sat, 1-5:30pm Sun Jun-Sep) are run by the local historical society. Other than the museums, there's not much reason to visit this industrial backwash of a town.

The **Information Center** (☎ 902-637-2625; 2517 Hwy 3; ⊙ 9am-5pm Mon-Sat) is very helpful and can help you with ideas for Shelburne as well. For years, church services of all faiths and community meetings happened in the New England–style meeting house, now the **Old Meeting House Museum** (http://museum.gov.ns.ca/omh; 2408 Hwy 3). Many town founders are buried in the graveyard next door. Interpreters at the **Barrington Woolen Mill Museum** (http://museum.gov .ns.ca/bwm; 2368 Hwy 3) demonstrate handspinning, dyeing and weaving in what was a thriving community enterprise in the late 19th century. The **Seal Island Light Museum** (2422 Hwy 3) is a replica of a lighthouse, including the original light.

The **Old Schoolhouse Restaurant & Motel** (☎ 902-637-3770; oldschol@klis.com; Hwy 3; mains $5-16; ⊙ dining 7am-9pm, lounge 9pm-2am; 🖳) was built in 1889 and was a working schoolhouse till 1969. The historic building was bought by the North-East Kingdom Community Church – known locally as 'the cult,' who turned it into a popular health food restaurant. The religious group left, and now the once-stylish establishment sells burgers and fries, has a blaring TV and a linoleum add-on – the lovely rooms are now replaced with generic motel-style rooms ($85 to $90). The old school janitor apparently still haunts the grounds. Maybe he's looking for tofu.

BARRINGTON TO PUBNICO

At Barrington, you can choose to take the fast, not-very-scenic Hwy 103 to Yarmouth, or to meander along about 100km of interesting coastline via Hwy 3. If you stop and have a chat with locals – and local wharves are fine spots to stretch your legs – you'll notice two distinct accents in this small corner of Nova Scotia. In **Cape Sable Island** (see boxed text, opposite) and **Woods Harbour** people speak with a Boston drawl, testament to the close relationship between this part of Nova Scotia and that US city. Then, starting in **Lower East Pubnico**, English is spoken with an Acadian French accent.

WEST PUBNICO

Not to be confused with Middle West Pubnico, Lower West Pubnico, East Pubnico (and its derivatives) or Pubnico proper, West Pubnico is an old Acadian community. You'll notice that a large percentage of the town's population bear the name d'Entremont, which was the name of the man who founded the village in 1653; for more on Acadians, see p37. **Le Village Historique Acadien** (☎ 902-762-2530; Old Church Rd; adult/child under 6yr/child 7-18yr $4/free/2; ⊙ 9am-5pm mid-Jun–Sep) recreates an Acadian village, with a blacksmith shop, a timber-frame house and a fish store. There are only a handful of houses but the enthusiasm of the staff and the wistful hillside setting make this a worthwhile stop. Opposite the firehall, the **Musée Acadien & Archives** (☎ 902-762-3380; www .museeacadien.ca; 898 Hwy 335; admission $3; ⊙ 9am-5pm Mon-Sat, 12:30-4:30pm Sun) displays household items, original maps and a collection of more than 300 cameras. You'll see the tops of *Star Wars*–like windmills turning in the distance at the **Pubnico Point Windfarm**. This farm of 30 megawatts supplies the needs of approximately 13,000 homes. Drive toward the point to stand under a 118m-high windmill to listen to the wisping, turning blade.

YARMOUTH

It's been said that Yarmouth (population 7561) is too big to be cute and too small to be interesting. While 'practical' might be a better adjective for the city, it does boast some interesting sights worth at least a day's exploration. Yarmouth is the largest town in western Nova Scotia and the destination for ferries from Portland and Bar Harbor, Maine (see p279). If you're around mid-July, expect bigger crowds for the **Yarmouth Seafest** (www .playarmouthevents.com), which includes a fish feast, rum-running races, parades and fireworks as well as a gigantic sidewalk sale.

Information

About Yarmouth (www.aboutyarmouth.com) Has a calendar of events and accommodations and dining options.
VIC (☎ 902-742-5033; 228 Main St; ☉ 7:30am-9pm Jul & Aug, 7.30am-4:30pm May, Jun, Sep & Oct) Also has a money exchange counter.
Yarmouth Public Library (☎ 902-742-2486; 405 Main St; ☉ 10am-8pm Mon-Thu, 10am-5pm Fri, 10am-4pm Sat, 1-4pm Sun) Free Internet access.

Sights & Activities

First settled by New Englanders from Massachusetts in 1761, Yarmouth reached its peak of growth and prosperity in the 1870s. The Collins Heritage Conservation District protects many fine Victorian homes built around that time. Check out the VIC for a self-guided walking tour.

Walk off the streets of no-nonsense Yarmouth into a cosmopolitan place of art and culture at the **Art Gallery of Nova Scotia** (☎ 902-749-2248; www .agns.gov.ns.ca/yarmouth_agns; 341 Main St; entry adult/ child/student/senior $5/1/2/4; ☉ noon-8pm). The new three-story building has well-selected works from mostly Maritime artists in large rooms, perfect for taking it all in. While there you can also check the Internet for free.

Yarmouth County Museum (☎ 902-742-5539; http://yarmouthcountymuseum.ednet.ns.ca; 22 Collins St; adult/student/family $3/2/6; ☉ 9am-5pm Mon-Sat, 2-5pm Sun Jun–mid-Oct, 2-5pm Tue-Sat mid-Oct–May), in

a former church, contains five period rooms related to the sea. A combined admission ticket (adult/child/student/family $5/1/2/10) includes **Pelton-Fuller House** (☉ 9am-5pm Mon-Sat Jun-Oct) next door. It's a Victorian home typical of the heritage district, filled with period artwork, glassware and furniture.

Firefighters' Museum (☎ 902-742-5525; http:// museum.gov.ns.ca/fm; 431 Main St; adult/family $3/6; ☉ 9am-9pm Mon-Sat, 10am-5pm Sun Jul & Aug, 9am-5pm Mon-Sat Jun & Sep, closed Sat other months) has fire engines from 1819 to 1935 and an exhibit where kids can pretend to fight a fire.

W Laurence Sweeney Museum (☎ 902-742-3457; 112 Water St; adult/family $3/7.50; ☉ 10am-6pm Mon-Sat late May–mid-Oct) shows the business of fishing, from catching to processing and selling.

Yarmouth Light (☎ 902-742-1433; Hwy 304; admission free; ☉ 9am-9pm Jul & Aug, 10am-3pm May, Jun, Sep & Oct) is at the end of Cape Forchu, a left on Hwy 304 from Main St. The lighthouse affords spectacular views.

Sleeping

Yarmouth Backpacker's Accommodation (☎ 902-749-0941; www.yarmouthbackpackers.com; 6 Trinity Pl; dm/s/d $20/25/50; ☐) This affable little hostel is in a sparkling 1865 Italianate mansion. It's just a short walk to town center and you won't find more helpful folks than the Australian-Canadian couple who own the place. The dorm room only has four beds plus there are two double rooms and a single. It's best to reserve in advance. Everyone from students to families to elderly couples mingle together in the relaxed atmosphere.

Lakelawn Motel (☎ 902-742-3588, 1-877-664-0664; www.lakelawnmotel.com; 641 Main St; s/d $59/89) For a motel, this place is as cute as they come. Rooms are clean and basic, you can buy homemade quilts in the lobby and breakfast is available in the country-style dining area for as little as $3.50.

DETOUR: CAPE SABLE ISLAND

If you are in this neck of the southwest, take a detour to **Cape Sable Island** (not to be confused with 'Sable Island' – see p136), a puddle-flat appendage that is Nova Scotia's most southerly point. Many of the island's windy, white-sand beaches are designated as 'important bird areas.' The Hawk, the most southern point, has thousands of Atlantic Brant flocking the coast during spring months. Sweeping Daniel's Head Beach is a protected nesting habitat for the endangered piping plover during the months from April to August. The best beach for picnicking is clean, bright-white Stoney Island beach.

The whole island from its wooded areas to its marshes, tends to get banked in fog which might explain why its lighthouse is 31.1m tall, the tallest in Nova Scotia.

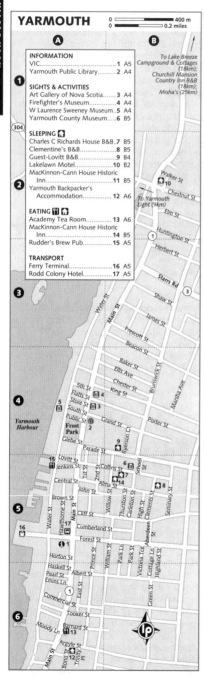

Clementines B&B (☎ 902-742-0079; clementinesb-b@klis.com; 21 Clements St; d $95;) Run by Ron and Evelyn Gray for over 20 years, Clementines hasn't faded a bit. Rooms with shared bath are unpretentiously decorated with country antiques and Evelyn's breakfasts are famous throughout Yarmouth. The B&B is in one of the town's more quiet, residential neighborhoods but is only a few minutes' walk to Main St.

MacKinnon-Cann House Historic Inn (☎ 902-742-0042; www.mackinnoncanninn.com; 27 Willow St; r $100-195;) This B&B was brought to life by the same team as the Charles C Richards House and they've had even more fun here. Each of the six rooms represents a decade from the 1900s to the '60s. The '60s room is different from anything else you're likely to find in Nova Scotia, with leopard-print wallpaper, an orange flower floor lamp and beaded curtains. Each room depicts the century at its most stylish while managing to stay calming and comfortable. Two rooms can be joined to create a family suite. The innkeepers have also opened a small restaurant (see below).

Guest-Lovitt B&B (☎ 902-742-0372, 866-742-0372; www.guestlovitt.ca; 12 Parade St; r $100-200;) This beautiful Italianate-style heritage property has been rightfully decorated with lovely heirloom furnishings. Central and comfortable with great breakfasts, you can't go wrong here. Don't miss the view from the widow's walk.

Charles C Richards House B&B (☎ 902-742-0042; www.charlesrichardshouse.ns.ca; 17 Collins St; r/ste $125/210) The owners of this Queen Anne Victorian mansion won a provincial award for returning a neglected rooming house to its former glory. Stained-glass windows abound, as do plants in the conservatory. It's gay friendly as well as being just generally friendly.

Eating

Yarmouth would be greatly improved by a good restaurant or two. If you are into fast food, you'll be in to-go heaven.

Academy Tea Room (☎ 902-749-0193; 113 Main St; sandwiches $7-8; 10am-4pm Tue-Sat) This is a nice alternative for a pot of tea ($2.50) or lunch. The menu of sandwiches includes interesting vegetarian creations and good deli meats.

MacKinnon-Cann House Historic Inn (☎ 902-742-0042; 27 Willow St; mains $8-11; 5:30-10:30pm) For elegant dining without a ritzy price tag, try the dining room at this classy B&B. Simple, gourmet light meals include seafood gumbo ($8), rappie pie ($8) a nightly pasta special and vegetarian options. There's a decent wine list and excellent service.

Rudders Brew Pub (☎ 902-742-7311; 96 Water St; pub menu $9-12, dinner mains $16-29) Three-hundred seat, waterfront Rudders gets packed during summer. It brews up a mean ale on site, and has a wide-ranging menu. Drinks are poured until the wee hours on busy summer nights and there is often live music.

Getting There & Away

Anyway you shake it, getting to Halifax from Yarmouth will take you around four-and-a-half hours and cost approximately $50. The **Trius Lines** (☎ call Acadian Lines at 902-454-9321 or 800-567-5151; ☷ 6:20am Mon-Sat, 11:20am Sun & holidays) bus leaves from the Rodd Colony Hotel and travels along the southwestern shore. Private shuttles **Cloud Nine Shuttle** (☎ 902-742-3992, 888-805-3335; www.thecloudnineshuttle.com) and **Amero's Shuttle** (☎ 888-283-2222; www.ameroshuttle.com) all make the trip daily. Yarmouth is also a jumping-off point to Maine via ferry (see p279).

DARLING LAKE & PORT MAITLAND

Only 14.5km from Yarmouth, it's worth coming out this way for the country atmosphere and some interesting dining options.

Lake Breeze Campground & Cottages (☎ 902-649-2332; www.lakebreezecampground.com; 2000 Hwy 1, Darling Lake; sites unserviced $17, serviced $20-25, cabins $60-100; ☷ mid-May–mid-Oct), a wee campground on a delicately wooded area bordering Darling Lake, is the closest camping option to Yarmouth. The best tent sites are to the back, although if the camping is full you won't have much privacy. The cottages range from a double unit with no kitchen to a two-bedroom cottage with full kitchen. Canoe and rowboat rentals are $5/10 an hour/day and you can swim and fish in the lake.

Right out of a classic mystery novel, **Churchill Mansion Country Inn B&B** (☎ 902-649-2818, www .churchillmansion.com; off Hwy 1 in Darling Lake; r $54-140; ☷ May-Nov) has several ghosts that mingle in the dark drapes and heavy antiques of this rambling old mansion. The inn is a favorite for psychics and is mentioned in a number of ghost story books – it's even been on TV. Apparently 'orbs' of light appear in photos taken within the inn. Don't worry, the spirits are friendly, as is the talkative owner. Even if you don't choose to sleep here, you can

stop in for the nightly all-you-can-eat seafood buffet for $14 or a delicious breakfast from $5 – ghost stories are free. It's best to call in advance for a meal.

It's worth driving the 15 minutes from Yarmouth to eat at **Misha's** (Hwy 1, Port Maitland; daily specials $8; ☷ 7am-8pm Mon-Sat, 11am-8pm Sun, closed Wed), a four-table roadside café. Country breakfasts from $4 are served all day or you can get delicious sandwiches or the daily special (usually a seafood option or a pizza and pita plate). This is a local haunt so chances are you'll be up on all the region's gossip by meal's end. The Mexican coffee blended with chocolate and cinnamon is another good reason to come here.

ANNAPOLIS VALLEY & FRENCH SHORE

The red, white, blue and yellow Acadian flag is omnipresent along the coast north of Yarmouth as this is the heart of Acadian Nova Scotia. With views of the Bay of Fundy, historic farmhouses, and overflowing farmers' markets, there are things to do and see in the region, but it's best to linger in any one of these small towns for a few days to get a real taste of Acadian spirit – don't forget to sample a local live-music performance. From Digby, things turn decidedly British (although the Acadian roots are here). Moving into the Annapolis Valley, you'll find much of Nova Scotia's fresh produce: wineries that have taken advantage of the sandy soil and hills and plains of shady apple orchards that bloom in spring. Dykes protecting the rich agricultural land are evidence of hard work by early Acadians.

The French shore, on the mainland directly across St Mary's Bay from Digby Neck, is the heart of Acadian Nova Scotia. This is where Acadians settled when, after trekking back to Nova Scotia following the deportation, they found their homesteads in the Annapolis Valley already occupied. Now linked by Hwy 1 – pretty much the only road in town – these are small fishing communities.

The highway passes through all the major towns in the valley, but to really get into the countryside, try making your own tracks along the smaller roads that run parallel to Hwy 1 where picture-perfect farms and orchards come into view. In the summer months you can find live Acadian music nightly along the coast from Cape St Mary to St Bernard.

CAPE ST MARY

A long, wide arc of fine sand, just 900m off Hwy 1, **Mavilette Beach** is great for collecting seashells, and the marsh behind it is good for bird-watching. The crumbling **Cape View Motel** (☎ 902-645-2258; http://nsonline.com/capeview; off Hwy 1; r $65-85, cottages $85-120), just above the beach, offers motel rooms and self-contained cottages with great views. One of this region's most secluded options is **À La Maison D'Amité B&B** (☎ 902-645-2601; www.houseoffriendship.ca; 169 Baseline Rd; r from $125; 🖵), which is perched dramatically on a cliff within 6 private hectares. The huge, brand new American-style home, with cathedral ceilings and sky-high windows has views on all sides. Ask about rappelling down the sea cliffs or taking the walking trail to the lighthouse; from the forest to the beach, you could wander the outdoors around this place for days.

Across from the motel, **Cape View Restaurant** (☎ 902-645-2519; lunch $5-8, dinner $12-20; 🕙 lunch & dinner) serves seafood and Acadian dishes. The view of the beach and of Cape St Mary is spectacular. Come on a Wednesday night during the summer to enjoy live Acadian music.

METEGHAN

The largest community on the French shore, Meteghan is home to AF Thétiault and Sons, one of Canada's largest private shipbuilding companies. **Smuggler's Cove Provincial Park**, at the southern edge of town, is named for its popularity with 19th-century pirates. A hundred wooden stairs take you down to a rocky beach and a good cave for hiding treasure. There are picnic sites with barbecue pits at the top of the stairs, with a view across St Mary's Bay to Brier Island.

L'Auberge au Havre du Capitaine (☎ 902-769-2001; capitaine@auracom.com; 9118 Hwy 1; r $75-100) has one wheelchair-accessible room. From the cosy seating area to the handmade quilts, this stylish inn says *bienvenue* (welcome) in true Acadian style. Try scrambled eggs with lobster ($12) for breakfast at the on-site **restaurant** (breakfast $5-7, mains lunch $7-8, dinner $12-15; 🕙 7am-9pm Jul & Aug, 7-9am & 5-7:30pm rest of year). There's live Acadian entertainment on Friday evening.

CHURCH POINT (POINTE D'ÉGLISE)

Église Ste Marie (☎ 902-769-2808; Hwy 1; admission incl guide $2; 🕙 9am-5pm mid-May–mid-Oct) towers over the town, also commonly known as Pointe de l'Église. Built between 1903 and 1905, the church is said to be the tallest and biggest wooden church in North America. An informative guide will show you around. Adjacent is the **Université Ste-Anne**, the only French university in the province and a center for Acadian culture, with 300 students.

The oldest of the annual Acadian cultural festivals, **Festival Acadien de Clare** is held during the second week of July. In July and August the musical *Evangeline*, based on Longfellow's romantic poem about the Acadian deportation, is presented in the **Théâtre Marc-Lescarbot** (☎ 902-769-2114; adult/child & student/senior $25/15/20) at the Université Ste-Anne. Performances are given in English on Saturday, in French with headset translation Tuesday and Friday, and outdoors in French only on Wednesday.

GROSSES-COQUES

With a name that sounds romantic in French but like something out of the mouths of Beavis and Butthead in English, this tidy Acadian town takes its appellation from the unusually large clams found along the shore. If you've got a bucket, you can try your luck at clam-digging at the rocky beach.

Most people come to town for **Chez Christophe Guesthouse & Restaurant** (☎ 902-837-5817; www.chezchristophe.ca; 2655 Hwy 1; breakfast from $8, mains dinner $12-36; 🕙 6am-9pm, closed Mon). Master Chef Paul Comeau has turned the house that his grandfather built in 1837 into a guesthouse (rooms $60 to $85) and respected restaurant; this is probably the most renowned Acadian restaurant in Nova Scotia. Rooms here are simple but well priced if you want to indulge in a little too much wine with your meal. Live Acadian music is performed from 6pm to 8pm Thursday nights through June and nearly every night of the week in July and August.

BELLIVEAU COVE

Belliveau Beach, near the southern end of this community, is reached by turning right onto Major's Point. The beach is made up of masses of sea-polished stones broken only by small clumps of incredibly hardy fir trees. Just behind the beach, a cemetery and monument recall the struggles of the early Acadian settlers of the French shore.

Piau's trail, named for Pierre (Piau) Belliveau, who led Acadians here during the deportation (p33), starts here and winds 5km along the beach before ending up in the backyard of **Chez Jean Dairy Twirl** (☎ 902-837-5750; 3139 Hwy 1; meals $7-12; ⌚ 11am-10pm Sun-Thu, to midnight Fri & Sat). This casual eatery with a great view serves ice-cream as well as seafood.

If you happen to be passing through on a Saturday morning, check out the Acadian **farmers' market** (Belliveau Cove Wharf; ⌚ 9am-2pm Sat May-Oct) to browse meats, produce, prepared foods, herbs, plants, arts and crafts and more. For a basic bite to eat, **Roadside Grill** (☎ 902-837-5047; 3334 Hwy 1; meals $7-13; ⌚ 8am-9pm Jul & Aug, 9am-7pm Sep-Jun) is a pleasantly old-fashioned local restaurant serving Acadian favorites. Try the steamed clams or the rappie pie. It also rents three small cabins (singles/doubles $45/60) with cable TV and microwaves. There's live Acadian music Tuesday nights from 5:30pm to 7:30pm June through August.

ST BERNARD

St Bernard's overwhelming attraction is **St Bernard Church** (☎ 902-837-5637; Hwy 1; ⌚ tours Jun-Sep), a huge granite structure built by locals who added one row of blocks each year between 1910 and 1942. It has incredible acoustics, which are showcased each summer through the **Musique St-Bernard** (http://wvcn.ns.ca/~msb; adult/under 18yr $15/5) concert series.

DIGBY NECK

It looks more like a finger than a neck, but whatever you want to call it, this appendage points out to form St Mary's Bay; its northern side skirts the wild and marine-mammal-filled Bay of Fundy. Long and Brier Islands make up the middle and end joints of the digit and are connected by ferry with the rest of the peninsula.

Plankton stirred up by the strong Bay of Fundy tides attracts heaps of finback, minke and humpback whales but this is also the best place in the world to see the endangered North Atlantic right whale. Blue whales, the world's largest animal are also sighted on occasion and you're almost certain to see plenty of seals.

Bring plenty of warm clothing (regardless of how hot a day it seems), sunblock and binoculars. A motion-sickness pill taken before leaving the dock may not be a bad idea either.

GETTING THERE & AWAY

Two ferries connect Long and Brier Islands to the rest of Digby Neck. The Petit Passage ferry leaves East Ferry (on Digby Neck) on the half-hour and Tiverton on the hour; ferries are timed so that if you drive directly from Tiverton to Freeport (18km) there is no wait for the Grand Passage ferry to Westport. Both ferries operate hourly 24 hours a day year-round. Passage is $4 for a car and all its passengers (you pay only in the westerly direction). Pedestrians ride free.

Long Island

Most people head straight to Briar Island, but Long Island has better deals on whale-watching as well as a livelier community. At the northeastern edge of Long Island, **Tiverton** is an active fishing village. The tourist information desk is found at the **Island Museum** (☎ 902-839-2853; 3083 Hwy 217; admission free; ⌚ 9:30am-7:30pm Jul & Aug, 9:30am-4:30pm late May-Jun & Sep–mid-Oct), 2km west of the Tiverton ferry, and has exhibits on local history.

One of the best whale-watch tours in the province is found just near the Tiverton ferry dock: **Ocean Explorations Zodiac Whale Tours** (☎ 902-839-2417, 877-654-2341; www.oceanexplorations.ca; Tiverton; half-day tour adult/child $55/40, discount given for groups of 3 or more; ⌚ depends on weather & demand Jun-Oct), led by biologist Tom Goodwin, has the adventurous approach of getting you low to whale-level in a Zodiac. Shimmy into a coastguard-approved orange flotation suit and hold on tight! Goodwin has been leading whale-watch tours since 1980 and donates part of his proceeds to wildlife conservation and environmental education organizations.

A 4km round-trip trail to the **Balancing Rock** starts 2km southwest of the museum. The trail features rope railings, boardwalks and an extensive series of steps down a rock bluff to the bay. Be careful with children; it's very slippery. At the end there is a viewing platform where you can see a 7m-high stone column perched precariously just above the pounding surf of St Mary's Bay.

Near the center of Long Island, **Central Grove Provincial Park** has a 2km hiking trail to the Bay of Fundy. Welcoming and fun camping (there's also a cabin and a trailer to rent if you don't have gear) can be found at **Whale Cove Campground** (☎ 902-834-2025; www.whalecovecampground.com; Hwy 217; serviced/unserviced sites $23/15, cabin or trailer $45-55; ▢ ♿) in Tiddville, about

5km before Freeport. Owners Vaughn and Gloria are real characters and will keep you informed and entertained (he plays bluegrass).

At the southwestern end of Long Island, **Freeport** is central for exploring both Brier Island and Long Island. **Summer Solstice B&B** (☎ 902-839-2170; www.summersolstice.ca; 325 Over Cove Rd; s/d $75/95, discounts for families taking more than 1 room) is an absolutely gorgeous, gay-friendly, century-old house. Four sparkling, modern rooms have views over the Bay of Fundy. Start your day with a ray of sunshine in the bright breakfast room and cuddle up at night in the warm fluffy beds.

Lavena's Catch Café (☎ 902-839-2517; 15 Hwy 217; mains $5-15; ❤ lunch & dinner) is a cute-as-can-be café directly above the wharf at Freeport; it's the perfect spot to enjoy a sunset and you might even see a whale from the balcony. There are lots of seafood and a few vegetarian options on the menu. Inside the restaurant is the office for **Freeport Whale & Seabird Tours** (☎ 902-839-2923; www.valleyweb.com/freeportwhaleand seabird/main.html; half-day tours adult/child/senior $32/17/19; ❤ 3 tours daily Jun-Sep), which offers the most competitively priced whale tour in the region. Boats leave right in front of the café and sightings are guaranteed.

Briar Island

Westport, Briar Island's only town, was the home of Joshua Slocum, the first man to sail solo around the world. This quaint little fishing village is a great base to explore the numerous excellent, if not rugged, hiking trails around the island. The island is grassy, nearly always windy and is marked by columnar basalt rocks all along the coast. Agates can be found on the beaches and seals bask on the rocks.

Brier Island Backpackers Hostel (☎ 902-839-2273; www.brierislandhostel.com; 223 Water St; dm adult/child 6-12yr $15/7.50; 🖳) is a tiny, spotless place about 1.5km to the left as you come off the ferry. The common room and kitchen area has big windows with views over the water. Because of the centrality of the living space, you'll be mingling with other backpackers. There's a general store, gas station and basic **café** (mains $5-8; ❤ 8am-9pm Mon-Sat, 10am-8pm Sun) next door that are owned by the same people.

Bay of Fundy Inn (☎ 902-839-2346; www.novasco tiawhalewatching.ca/guesthouse.php; d $75), directly opposite the ferry landing at Westport,

then just up the hill, is a hard-to-miss yellow, old-fashioned fisherman's home. It's central and comfy. The same owners run **Mariner Cruises** (☎ 902-839-2346, 800-239-2189; www .novascotiawhalewatching.ca; adult/child/senior $46/25/39; ❤ Jun-Oct), which have trips, complete with homemade muffins, that can last anywhere from 2½ to five hours depending on where the whales are.

On top of cliffs 1km east of Westport is **Brier Island Lodge** (☎ 902-839-2300, 800-662-8355; www .brierisland.com; s $70, d $60-120; 🖳 ⑤), a 40-room hotel reminiscent of a 1950s summer family camp. Nearly all the rooms have a view and the place is kept in tip-top shape. Its **restaurant** (mains $14-31; ❤ breakfast, dinner & boxed lunches) is the best dining option on the island with views on two sides, perfect service and fabulously fresh seafood.

DIGBY

Digby (population 2111) has been a tourist mecca for more than a century. Other than a mild climate and the somewhat picturesque waterfront, there's not much going on here unless you are catching the ferry to New Brunswick. The people here, perhaps from having too many tourists flock to their streets, can be less friendly than the rest of Nova Scotia.

Digby is nestled in a protected inlet off the Bay of Fundy. Settled by United Empire Loyalists in 1783, it's home to the largest fleet of scallop boats in the world; if you are going to do anything in Digby it should be to treat yourself to the most amazing scallops you will ever taste. The daily ferry (p166) to Saint John, New Brunswick, squeezes through the small channel known affectionately as the Digby Gut.

Information

Digby (www.klis.com/digby) Has a virtual tour of Digby as well as links to useful information.

VIC (☎ 902-245-2201; Shore Rd; ❤ 8:30am-8:30pm mid-Jun–mid-Sep, 9am-5pm May–mid-Jun & mid-Sep–Oct) A large provincial tourist office, 2km from the ferry wharf, with hundreds of brochures.

Western Counties Regional Library (☎ 902-245-2163; 84 Warwick St; ❤ 12:30-5pm & 6-8pm Tue-Thu, 10am-5pm Fri, 10am-2pm Sat) Free Internet access.

Sights & Activities

Stroll the boardwalk and watch the scallop draggers come and go. The **Lady Vanessa** (☎ 902-245-4950; 34 Water St; admission $2; ❤ 9am-7pm

Jul & Aug, 9am-5pm May, Jun, Sep & Oct), a 30m wooden dragger, is now permanently mounted on the sidewalk for visitors to tour. There are exhibits and a video on the scallop fishery inside.

A mid-19th century Georgian home is now the **Admiral Digby Museum** (☎ 902-245-6322; 95 Montague Row; admission by donation; ☿ 9am-5pm Tue-Sat, 1-5pm Sun mid-Jun–Aug, 9am-5pm Tue-Fri Sep–mid-Oct, 9am-5pm Wed & Fri mid-Oct–mid-May), which contains exhibits of the town's marine history and early settlement.

Sleeping & Eating

If you're in town mid-August, you don't know how lucky you are! Don't miss the chance to taste how many succulent ways the region's scallops can be prepared at **Digby Scallop Days** (www.townofdigby.ns.ca) – be sure to reserve lodging well in advance.

Digby Campground (☎ 902-245-1985; www.angelfire.com/biz2/digbycamping; Hwy 303; serviced/unserviced sites $25/18; ☐) There are some nice wooded sites and you can walk to town from this roadside campground.

Bayside Inn (☎ 888-754-0555, 902-245-2247; www.baysideinn.ca; 115 Montague Row; r incl breakfast $58-98; ℗ ☐) In continuous operation since the late 1800s, this is Digby's oldest inn. It's a large inn, less intimate than the B&Bs, but it's friendly and clean. Floral patterns dominate the rooms.

Thistle Down Country Inn (☎ 902-245-4490, 800-565-8081; www.thistledown.ns.ca/theinn; 98 Montague Row; r $85-120; ☿ May-Nov) Opulent brocades and heavy fabrics dominate this rich Victorian B&B. It's right on the water, has a grassy lawn for lounging and an elegant dining area. There's an annex of six motel-style rooms at the back, which are much more plain.

Boardwalk Café & Suites (☎ 902-245-5497; www.boardwalkcafé.netfirms.com; 40 Water St; mains $8-15; ☿ 11am-8pm Mon-Sat, 11am-5pm Sun) One of Digby's best eating venues happens to also be the finest place to stay in town (suites $110). The little waterfront café serves light mains such as chowder, rappie pie and lasagne as well as espresso and tempting baked goods. Upstairs, the two suites, one modern and the other antique style, have sea views, private terraces, sitting areas, full kitchens and bath. This is a phenomenal value for the price. There's also a shared laundry area for guests.

Royal Fundy Seafood Market (☎ 902-245-5411; 144 Prince William; mains $6-10; ☿ 9am-9pm Mon-Sat, 11am-7pm Sun) Get your seafood from the source at this little fishmonger-cum-café. You can buy mussels, scallops and other seafood by the pound or let the chatty staff cook it up for you – catch up on the local gossip while you enjoy your meal.

Getting There & Away

Bay Ferries (☎ 506-649-7777, 888-249-7245; www.bayferries.com; 1-way walk-on adult/child/senior $35/25/20 children under 5yr free, car $80; ☿ 2-3 trips daily) offers year-round service between and Digby and Saint John, New Brunswick (see p167 for details).

Acadian Lines buses from Halifax ($40, four hours, daily) stop at the **Irving gas station** (☎ 902-245-2048; 77 Montague Row).

BEAR RIVER

With the hyperbolic nickname of 'the Switzerland of Nova Scotia,' Bear River (population 89) has enough out-of-sync character that it deserves its own designation, thank you very much. The village attracts off-beat artists and other quirky folk. Unlike many Nova Scotian towns Mi'kmaq and Scottish blend together in the community creating a palpable air of spirituality, calm and the great outdoors. The fog doesn't reach this far inland so the town stays blissfully warmer than the coast, which is only minutes away. Some buildings near the river are on stilts while other historic homes nestle on the steep hills of the valley. The locals relish the fact that cell phones don't work here.

Information

VIC (☎ 902-467-3200; 109 Wharf Rd; ☿ 9am-4pm mid-Jun–mid-Oct, to 6pm Jul & Aug) In a windmill beside the river, where there is also parking and several picnic tables.

Sights & Activities
DOWNTOWN BEAR RIVER

Up the hill from the VIC, the **Oakdene Centre** (1913 Clementsvale Rd) is a former elementary school now reborn as artists' studios. Wander the studios and check the bulletin board for details of performances, classes and other community happenings.

The founder of the **Riverview Ethnographic Museum** (☎ 902-467-4321; 18 Chute Rd; admission $2; ☿ 10am-5pm Tue-Sat) is a retired costume designer who collected traditional clothing from around the world, now on display.

Bear River Heritage Museum (☎ 902-467-0902; 1890 Clementsvale Rd; admission free; ☿ 10am-4pm Mon-Sat, 1-4pm Sun Jul–mid-Sep) has five rooms of exhibits on local history, including Mi'kmaw artifacts.

BEAR RIVER FIRST NATION

The Bear River First Nation is a five-minute drive from the heart of town: turn left after crossing the bridge from the VIC, then take a left where the road forks. In a beautiful new building, with a wigwam-shaped foyer, its **Heritage & Cultural Centre** (☎ 902-467-0301; 194 Reservation Rd; admission $2.50; ☻ 10am-6pm mid-May–mid-Oct) offers demonstrations of traditional crafts and hands-on workshops. A 1km **trail** starts behind the center and highlights plants with traditional medicinal uses.

Sleeping & Eating

Inn Out of the Fog (☎ 902-467-0268; www.innoutofthe fog.com; 1 Wharf Rd; r $75-85) Sparkling tapestries and old kimonos grace the brightly painted walls of this whimsically artistic inn. The gardens surrounding the historic marine warehouse are just as vibrant as the rooms with explosions of flowers, chirping birds and a fat, friendly cat. The downstairs craft and clothing shop, Oddacity Designs (open 10am to 5pm Monday to Saturday), will make you want to buy everything you need to recreate a room like this at home, or at least dress like it.

Changing Tides Diner (☎ 902-467-3008; 1882 Main St; mains $7-14; ☻ 7:30am-8pm Jul & Aug, to 5pm rest of year) The only place to eat in town, this café is a great place to chat with locals, grab a sandwich ($3 to $8) and enjoy the view of Bear River. The kids' menu starts at $3.50.

Shopping

Flight of Fancy (☎ 902-467-4171; Main St, at the bridge; ☻ 9am-7pm Mon-Sat, 11am-7pm Sun Jul & Aug, 9am-5pm Mon-Sat, 11am-5pm Sun rest of year) This is an exquisitely curated craft store and gallery with work by more than 200 artists and craftspeople. If you want to buy one unique treasure to take

---

GREEN SEWAGE

Just past the windmill, check out the greenhouse that houses Bear River's award-winning **sewage treatment facility**. Beautiful, lush aquatic plants do the dirty work and thrive in the process. Ask at the VIC – if you're lucky you might be able to catch someone at the facility to get a tour. Unfortunately this revolutionary treatment system has received little outside support and rocky finances have stagnated the project.

---

away from Nova Scotia, this is a good place to find it.

Bear Town Baskets (☎ 902-467-3060; 44 Maple Ave, Bear River First Nation; ☻ 10am-10pm) Baskets sold here are made by a retired chief of the Bear River First Nation. Follow the signs to the studio in his front yard where he makes traditional ash baskets.

ANNAPOLIS ROYAL

From the tidy, traditional town center to the historical fort and enchanting graveyard, this bite-sized town will charm you senseless. A community passionate for preserving its history, the efforts of village restoration have made this one of the most delightful places to visit in the region. In fact, Annapolis Royal (population 800) is one of the only well-trodden towns of its size in Nova Scotia *sans* Tim Hortons (a ubiquitous fast-food franchise). The site was Canada's first permanent European settlement, Port Royal, founded by French explorer Samuel de Champlain in 1605. As the British and French battled (see p32), the settlement often changed hands. In 1710 the British had a decisive victory and changed the town's name to Annapolis Royal in honor of Queen Anne.

Orientation & Information

Most sights are on or near long, curving St George St. A waterfront boardwalk behind King's Theatre on St George St provides views of the village and Granville Ferry across the Annapolis River.

Annapolis Royal (www.annapolisroyal.com) Links to history, festivals and everything else.

VIC (☎ 902-532-5769; 236 Prince Albert Rd; ☻ 10am-6pm mid-May–mid-Oct) At the Tidal Power Project site by the Annapolis River Causeway; pick up a historic walking tour pamphlet.

Sights & Activities

Fort Anne National Historic Site (☎ 902-532-2397; www.parkscanada.gc.ca/fortanne; Upper St George St; adult/child 6-16yr/family $4/2/10; ☻ 9am-6pm), in the town center, preserves the memory of the early Acadian settlement plus the remains of the 1635 French fort. Entry to the extensive grounds is free, but you'll also want to visit the museum where artifacts are contained in various period rooms. An extraordinary four-panel tapestry, crafted in needlepoint by more than 100 volunteers (including Queen Elizabeth II), depicts 400 years of history.

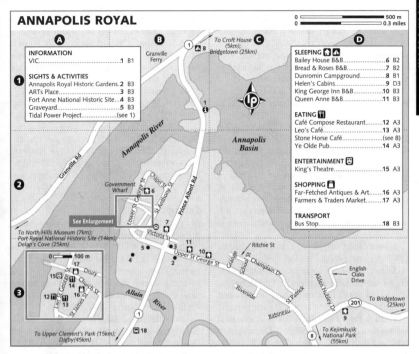

ANNAPOLIS ROYAL

INFORMATION	
VIC.....................................**1** B1	

SIGHTS & ACTIVITIES	
Annapolis Royal Historic Gardens..**2** B3	
ARTs Place...............................**3** B3	
Fort Anne National Historic Site....**4** B3	
Graveyard.................................**5** B3	
Tidal Power Project.................(see 1)	

SLEEPING	
Bailey House B&B.....................**6** B2
Bread & Roses B&B..................**7** B2
Dunromin Campground..............**8** B1
Helen's Cabins.........................**9** D3
King George Inn B&B...............**10** B3
Queen Anne B&B....................**11** B3

EATING	
Café Compose Restaurant.........**12** A3
Leo's Café..............................**13** A3
Stone Horse Café.................(see 8)
Ye Olde Pub..........................**14** A3

ENTERTAINMENT	
King's Theatre........................**15** A3

SHOPPING	
Far-Fetched Antiques & Art.......**16** A3
Farmers & Traders Market.........**17** A3

TRANSPORT	
Bus Stop................................**18** B3

Annapolis Royal Historic Gardens (☎ 902-532-7018; www.historicgardens.com; 441 Upper St George St; adult/student/family $6/5/15; ☼ 9am-5pm May-Oct, 8am-dusk Jul & Aug) is the perfect place to spend a sunny day. The winding trails lead through 6.5 hectares of lush gardens, including a rose collection of more than 2000 plants and the Innovative and Acadian Gardens, where you can explore the gardening methods of the early settlers to techniques of the future. Munch on blueberries, ogle the veggies and look for frogs. The Secret Garden Café offers lunches (from $5) and tasty German-style baked goods.

Tidal Power Project (☎ 902-532-5454; admission free; ☼ 10am-6pm mid-May–mid-Oct), a hydroelectric prototype at the Annapolis River Causeway, has been harnessing power from the Bay of Fundy tides since 1984 (see p104). The guides are passionate about the project and can answer even the most complicated questions; the interpretive center includes models, exhibits and a video.

ARTsPLACE (☎ 902-532-7069; 396 Upper St George St; admission free; ☼ 10am-5pm Tue-Fri, 1-4pm Sat & Sun) is a tiny artist-run center that hosts exhibits and workshops. Stop in for a chat.

Tours

Be escorted by an undertaker-garbed guide for a tour of the Fort Anne **graveyard** (adult/child $7/1; Fort Anne; ☼ 9:30pm Tue, Thu & Sun Jun-Sep). Everyone carries a lantern to wind through the headstones and discover this town's history through stories of those who've passed away. This tour has become so popular that it's not uncommon for groups of 50 to form in summer; proceeds go to the Annapolis Royal Historical Society.

Starting from the lighthouse on St George St, **daytime tours** (adult/child $7/1; ☼ 2pm Mon-Fri), run by the same group, focus on the Acadian heritage of Annapolis Royal or the architecture of the historic district.

Festivals & Events

West of Jazz East (☎ 902-532-2741; www.tallships.ca /jazz; 1-day tickets/festival passes $15/40) Three days of jazz over the third weekend in July.

Arts Festival (☎ 902-532-7069; www.arcac.ca) Readings, exhibits and workshops in late September.

Sleeping

Annapolis Royal offers one of the finest B&B selections in Nova Scotia.

Dunromin Campground (☎ 902-532-2808; www.dunromincampsite.com; Hwy 1, Granville Ferry; serviced/unserviced sites $22/23, cabins/tepees/caravan $65/50/50; ☐) This off-beat campground has some secluded riverside sites as well as nifty options like a tepee (an elevated sheet of plywood covered with a tent; sleeps six) and a gypsy caravan. You can rent canoes here for $10 per hour and there is also a good on-site restaurant (see right).

Croft House B&B (☎ 902-532-0584; www.bbcanada.com/crofthouse; 51 Riverview Lane; s/d $55/70; ☺ May-Nov) This sturdy old farmhouse down a dirt road 3km out of Annapolis Royal has two good-sized rooms. Peace is the word on 16 hectares of land used for planting, among other things, organic berries used in guests' breakfasts. The owners compost and recycle everything, and even supply handmade soaps in the bathrooms.

Helen's Cabins (☎ 902-532-5207; 106 Hwy 201; s/d $60/70) A perfect choice for families, these two-bedroom, two-bath cottages with kitchenette are a steal. You can get pizza and donair at the connected Tom's Pizzeria (pizza from $6; open 11am to 10pm), which is popular with locals.

Bread & Roses B&B (☎ 902-532-5727; www.breadandroses.ns.ca; 82 Victoria St; r $75-140) This massive building differs from the other B&Bs in the area, not only for its sheer size and spaciousness, but because it is built of brick. Besides feeling solid and stable, there is an open atmosphere to the building, from the hallways and elegant sitting area to the vast bedrooms. The decor is antique while remaining light and uplifting.

our pick **Bailey House B&B** (☎ 902-532-1285, 877-532-1285; www.baileyhouse.ca; 150 Lower St George St; r $90-110, f $130; ☐) The only B&B on the waterfront, Bailey House is also the oldest inn in the area. The friendly owners have managed to keep the vintage charm (anyone over six feet might hit their head on the doorways!) while adding all the necessary modern comforts and conveniences. A little driftwood archway and sitting area are right on the water and there's a flowery back garden to putter around in. The dining room takes you back to the 18th century and has been the site of an historic culinary re-creation: the original owner's moose nose soup. The B&B is gay friendly.

Queen Anne B&B (☎ 902-532-7850, 877-536-0403; www.queenanneinn.ns.ca; 494 St George St; r $90-170, ste $180-240; ☐ ☺) Arguably the most elegant property in Annapolis Royal, this B&B is the perfect balance of period decor and subtle

grace. It's so beautiful, with the Tiffany lamp replicas, manicured grounds and sweeping staircases, that it might seem stuffy were it not for the over-the-top friendly owners who make you feel like you could (almost) kick your feet up on the antique coffee table.

King George Inn B&B (☎ 902-532-5286, 888-799-5464; www.kinggeorgeinn.20m.com; 548 Upper St George St; r $99-190, ste $150-225; ☐) A wooden statue of King George welcomes you to the door of this Victorian B&B of character. Antique mirrors, lamps, stuffed animals and more decorate the rooms without being overwhelmingly knick-knacky. The environment is scent- and smoke-free.

Eating

Many of the B&Bs, such as the Queen Anne, are open for elegant lunches and dinners.

Stone Horse Café (☎ 902-532-2808; Hwy 1, Granville Ferry; mains $5-10; ☺ 7am-9pm Mon-Sat) At the Dunromin Campground (see p101), this nook of a café serves yummy homemade soups, sandwiches, breakfasts and healthy fare. Dine on the sunny, flower-filled patio.

Leo's Café (☎ 902-532-7424; 222 St George St; mains $6-9; ☺ 9am-8pm Mon-Sat, noon-4pm Sun Jul-Sep, 9am-4pm Mon-Sat off-season) Nestled in the brightest gardens in town, be prepared to wait for a delicious sandwich. Specials combine sandwiches with salad or soup.

Ye Olde Pub (☎ 902-532-2244; 9-11 Church St; mains $8-15; ☺ 11am-11pm Mon-Sat, noon-8pm Sun) It calls itself the smallest pub in Nova Scotia, but that was when it was only licensed to serve alcohol to a few seats at the bar. Today it's a cosy café-bar serving standard pub fare. On sunny days the outdoor terrace is hopping. Try the marinated scallop appetizer ($7).

Café Compose Restaurant (☎ 902-532-1251; 235 Lower St George St; mains $18-23; ☺ 11:30am-8pm Wed-Mon) Watch the sunset across the river at this bustling place. Nearly all the food is prepared with organic, local ingredients and European flair. Every plate that comes out of the kitchen is a medley of colors played out to the sounds of classical music.

Entertainment

King's Theatre (☎ 902-532-7704; www.kingstheatre.ca; 209 Lower St George St; movie ticket $6, live shows $14-22) This waterfront theater presents musicals, dramas and concerts most evenings in July and August, and occasionally during the rest of the year. Hollywood films are screened on most weekends, and independent films most Tuesdays, year-round.

Shopping

Farmers & Traders Market (cnr St George & Church Sts; ☺ Sat am & Wed pm) Annapolis Royal's thriving community of artists and artisans offer their wares alongside local farmers at this popular market. There's live entertainment most Saturday mornings.

Far-Fetched Antiques & Art (☎ 902-532-0179; 27 Church St; ☺ 10am-6pm Mon-Fri, 9am- 6pm Sat, noon-6pm Sun Jun-Sep, 10am-5pm Mon-Fri, 9am-5pm Sat, noon-5pm Sun Oct) This labyrinth of fun stuff features treasures gathered from Southeast Asia.

Getting There & Away

Acadian Lines stops at the Port Royal Wandlyn Inn **bus stop** (☎ 902-532-2323; 3924 Hwy 1) from Halifax ($34, 3½ hours, daily) en route to Digby ($6, 30 minutes).

AROUND ANNAPOLIS ROYAL

North Hills Museum (☎ 902-532-2168; http://museum .gov.ns.ca/nhm; 5065 Granville Rd, Granville Ferry; adult/child $3/2; ☺ 9:30am-5:30pm Mon-Sat, 1-5:30pm Sun Jun–mid-Oct), overlooking the Annapolis Basin, has a superb collection of Georgian antiques displayed in a farmhouse dating from 1764.

If you're traveling with kids, don't miss **Upper Clements Park & Wildlife Park** (☎ 902-532-7557, 888-248-4567; www.upperclementspark.com; Upper Clements; admission basic/premium $17/21; ☺ 11am-7pm May-Sep). Atlantic Canada's largest amusement park manages to stay surprisingly pleasant, not cheesy. A basic pass gets you into the main and wildlife parks and on all the smaller rides, but you'll need the premium pass to ride the waterslides and roller coasters. The bears are fed at 3pm – they eat at a picnic bench, which makes them look like giant teddy bears.

Some 14km northwest of Annapolis Royal, **Port Royal National Historic Site** (☎ 902-532-2898; www.pc.gc.ca/lhn-nhs/ns/portroyal/index_e.asp; 53 Historic Lane; adult/child $4/2; ☺ 9am-6pm mid-May–mid-Oct) is the actual location of the first permanent European settlement north of Florida. It's a replica, reconstructed in the original manner of de Champlain's 1605 fur-trading habitation. Costumed workers help tell the story of this early settlement with panoramic views of the valley and basin in the backdrop.

Over the North Mountain from Annapolis Royal, **Delap's Cove Wilderness Twrail** takes you to the Fundy shore. It consists of two loop trails connected by an old inland road that used to serve a Black Loyalist community, now just old foundations and apple trees in the woods. With both loops, the trail is 9km return.

Fundy Trail Campground & Cottages (☎ 902-532-7711, 877-519-2267; www.fundytrail.com; 62 Delap's Cove; serviced/unserviced sites $22/30; 🖳) caters mostly to RVs but it has 24 unserviced sites. Of these, sites 70 to 77 are hidden in the woods next to a creek that runs down to the fishing wharf at Delap's Cove, just minutes from the trailhead for the hike. Bring coins for the showers.

KENTVILLE

Kentville is the county seat for the area, with a number of government offices along with stately old homes and some good pubs. During the colorful spring bloom of the valley, the **Annapolis Valley Apple Blossom Festival** (www .appleblossom.com) in early June brings folks together with concerts, a parade, barbecues and art shows.

Information

Tourist office (☎ 902-678-7170; 125 Park St; ☺ 9:30am-7pm Jul & Aug, 9:30am-5:30pm mid-May–Jun & Sep-early Oct) West of the town center.

Sights & Activities

Local artifacts, history and an art gallery can be seen at the **Old King's Courthouse Museum** (☎ 902-678-6237; 37 Cornwallis Ave; admission free; ☺ 9:30am-4:30pm Mon-Sat). At the eastern end of town, the **Agriculture Research Station** (☎ 902-678-1093; off Hwy 1; admission free; ☺ 8:30am-4:30pm Jun-Aug) includes a museum on the area's farming history and the apple industry in particular. Guided museum tours are offered during summer. The 4km-return **Ravine Trail** begins from the gravel parking lot immediately east of the entrance to the research station. No bicycles are allowed on this pleasant walking trail through the old-growth hemlock woods.

Sleeping & Eating

Wickwire House B&B (☎ 902-679-1188, 877-679-1188; www.the-wickwire.ca; 183 Main St; d $85-100) This grand mansion overlooks a river valley and has ample oak and maple gardens perfect for playing croquet. The rooms are as noble as the surroundings with color-coordinated period decor and plenty of hardwoods. There's a piano downstairs and the owners love it when guests strike up a tune.

TIDAL POWER

With all that water flowing in and out every day, it seems only logical that someone would try to harness it to convert it into usable energy. Annapolis Tidal began in 1984 as a pilot project and today it employs the largest straight-flow turbine in the world to generate more than 30 million kilowatt-hours of electricity per year, enough for 4500 homes. It is one of only two tidal plants of this kind in the world.

Technology has taken some major steps since 1984 and it is now known that the ebb-generating system (which involves a dam across an estuary) at Annapolis Royal has negative environmental implications, which include changes to the natural processes of sedimentation. The new direction of tidal power is with Instream tidal systems that look like underwater windmills anchored to the sea floor. Water's greater density means fewer and smaller turbines are needed to produce the same amount of electricity as wind turbines. Studies conclude that these 'windmills' don't disturb local critters or sedimentation although they are considerably less efficient than the ebb method. As it becomes more apparent that the world needs more alternative power sources, Nova Scotia is the most likely candidate to house the first major tidal power plant in North America. Plans to use Instream turbines are already forming with prospective sites being around the Minas Basin (see p113).

Paddy's Pub & Rosie's (☎ 902-678-3199; 30 Aberdeen St; mains $7-12; ☯ brunch, lunch & dinner) Paddy's and Rosie's share the same building and menu, but Rosie's is a family-friendly restaurant. Paddy's brews its own gems such as Annapolis Valley Ale. Try the Irish stew ($7.50) made with Paddy's Porter.

Getting There & Away

Acadian Lines (☎ 902-678-2000; 66 Cornwallis St) has an office in the old train station; buses run to Halifax ($18, two hours, twice daily). **Kings Transit** (☎ 888-546-4442; 66 Cornwallis St; flat fare $2.50; ☯ 6am-7pm Mon-Fri, 8am-3pm Sat) is an excellent regional bus service that runs between Cornwallis and Wolfville with free transfers between buses at Kentville and Greenwood. It could take five hours to do a one-hour trip by car, but the price is right.

NORTH OF HIGHWAY 1

The North Mountain, which ends at dramatic Cape Blomidon, defines one edge of the Annapolis Valley. On the other side of the mountain are fishing communities on the Bay of Fundy. The valley floor between Hwy 1 and the North Mountain is crisscrossed with small highways lined with farms and orchards. It's a great place to throw out your road map and explore. To start the adventure, turn north on Hwy 358 just west of Wolfville (at exit 11 of Hwy 101). The historic town of Canning is en route to Scots Bay, where Hwy 358 ends and a dramatic hiking trail leads to views of the Minas Basin and the Bay of Fundy.

Port Williams

This village is so close to Wolfville, you might not even realize you've changed towns. Turn off Hwy 1 and you're there. Before you blink, stop at **Tin Pan** (☎ 902-691-0020; 978 Main St; mains $3-7; ☯ breakfast, lunch & dinner Mon-Sat), for an honest, if not completely unique Maritime dining experience. Owner Dee Cook (and yes, she is dee cook) has created an atmosphere that is the opposite of intimate. The three rickety tables are packed close together and everyone ends up chatting together, with Dee piping in on occasion from the kitchen. Her breakfasts and basic fare are famous in Wolfville. Saturday mornings there's a group of bikers loudly breakfasting.

Prescott House Museum (☎ 902-542-3984; http://prescott.museum.gov.ns.ca; 1633 Starr's Point Rd; adult/student $3/2; ☯ 9:30am-5:30pm Mon-Sat, 1-5:30pm Sun Jun–mid-Oct), c 1814, is the finest example of Georgian architecture in Nova Scotia, and former home of the horticulturalist who introduced many of the apple varieties grown in the Annapolis Valley. To get to here, turn right on Starr's Point Rd at the flashing light in Port Williams, 2km north of Hwy 1, and follow it for 3.25km.

Canning

From November to March, hundreds of **bald eagles** gather in the Canning area, attracted by local chicken farms – a photographers' and nature-lovers' dream. Just west of Canning on Hwy 221 **Blomidon Estate Winery** (☎ 902-582-7565; 10318 Hwy 221; ☯ 11am & 3pm, Jun-Sep) offers free tours and tastings. Further along Hwy 358, stop at the **Lookoff**. About 200m above the Annapolis Valley, this is the best view of its rows of fruit trees and picturesque farmhouses.

Fireside Café (☎ 902-582-7270, 888-809-1555; 9819 Main St, Canning; mains $6-10; ☽ 7am-6pm Mon-Sat, 10am-6pm Sun, to 8pm Wed-Fri Jul & Aug) exhibits work by local artists. It has surprising selections (such as carrot cashew curry) and great prices. Call ahead to order a picnic lunch or wait around while one is made up.

Scots Bay

The hike to the end of **Cape Split** starts in Scots Bay. This is probably the most popular hiking trail in Nova Scotia. It's about 15km return, taking 4½ hours with little elevation change if you follow the easier inland route. To do that, follow the trail along the fence as you leave the parking area, and then choose the trail on your right when you come to a fork. (The trail on the left leads to a coastal route, which is poorly marked and subject to erosion. Give yourself extra time – and consider carrying a compass – if you want to explore that route.) The hike ends in a grassy meadow on cliffs high above the Bay of Fundy. Here you can see the tides creating waves called tidal rips.

Take time before or after the hike to look for agates along the beach at Scots Bay.

Blomidon Provincial Park (☎ 902-582-7319; http://parks.gov.ns.ca; off Hwy 358; campsites $18) is on the opposite side of Cape Blomidon from Scots Bay. There are a number of routes to get here from Hwy 358, all well signed. One begins 15km south of Scots Bay, and involves driving 10km along the Minas Basin. The campground is set atop high cliffs that overlook the basin. There's a beach and picnic area at the hill's base and a 14km system of hiking trails within the park.

Hall's Harbour

Further southeast on the Bay of Fundy (take any route west from Hwy 358 until you hit Hwy 359, then take it over the North Mountain), **Hall's Harbour** is a great spot to spend an afternoon hiking along the beach and in the surrounding hills. It's also the best place in Nova Scotia to eat lobster.

Pick your own lobster at **Hall's Harbour Lobster Pound** (☎ 902-679-5299; ☽ noon-8pm Jul & Aug, noon-7pm May, Jun, Sep & Oct). The price is determined by the market – a whole one will rarely cost below $25. Seafood baskets with scallops or clams cost $12.

WOLFVILLE

Thanks to the students and faculty of Acadia University, who represent some 3500 of Wolfville's 7000 residents, the town's one main street is one of this coast's best places to stop for a meal. With easy access to the Acadian dykes, enjoyable hikes and fine architecture, Wolfville is a great place to spend a day or two. If you're in town early fall, rock out to modern roots music at the annual **Canadian Deep Roots Festival** (www.deeprootsmusic.ca; mid-September).

Information

Odd Book (☎ 902-542-9491; 112 Front St) Secondhand books of all genres.

Tourist office (☎ 902-542-7000; 11 Willow Ave; ☽ 9am-9pm Jul-Sep, 9am-5pm early May-Jun & Oct) A very helpful office at the east end of Main St.

Wolfville (www.wolfville.info) Information on Wolfville, Acadia University and exploring Nova Scotia.

Wolfville Memorial Library (☎ 902-542-5760; 21 Elm Ave; ☽ 11am-5pm & 6:30-8:30pm Tue-Thu, 11am-5pm Fri & Sat, 1-5pm Sun) Free Internet access.

Sights

Waterfront Park (cnr Gaspereau Ave & Front St) offers a stunning view of the tidal mudflats, Minas Basin and the red cliffs of Cape Blomidon. Displays explain the tides, dykes, flora, fauna and history of the area. This is an easy spot to start a walk or bike ride on top of the dykes.

Randall House Museum (☎ 902-542-9775; 171 Main St; admission by donation; ☽ 10am-5pm Mon-Sat, 2-5pm Sun mid-Jun–mid-Sep) relates the history of the New England planters and colonists who replaced the expelled Acadians. Tea ($3) is served on antique china at 2:30pm.

Activities

Locals fought to save the home of hundreds of chimney swifts, birds that migrate annually to Wolfville from Peru. As a result, the chimney of a now-demolished dairy has become the focal point of the **Robie Tufts Nature Centre** (Front St), opposite the public library. Drop by in the late evening in spring or summer to see the birds swooshing down for a night's rest.

When the water is high enough, **tubing** down the Gaspereau River is a unique experience. Locals such as **Kevin Schofield & Joy Power** (☎ 902-542-3002; 3498 Black River Rd, Gaspereau; rentals per day $3; ☽ Jun–mid-Jul or longer) rent inner tubes for this purpose.

Rent bikes at **Valley Stove & Cycle** (☎ 902-542-7280; 234 Main St; rentals half-/full day $25/30).

NOVA SCOTIA

Sleeping

Garden House B&B (☎ 902-542-1703; www.gardenhouse
.ca; 220 Main St; s/d $65/75) This antique house re-
tains its old-time feel in the most comfortable
way. Creaky floors, a rustic breakfast table
decorated with wildflowers and the fact that
everyone is encouraged to take off their shoes,
creates a lived-in vibe you instantly feel a part
of. The fun and friendly owners make it that
much better.

Gingerbread House Inn (☎ 902-542-1458; www
.gingerbreadhouse.ca; 8 Robie Tufts Dr; d $80-130, ste $130-
190) The exterior of this unique B&B looks like
it was created by a master pastry chef; it's like a
big pink birthday cake with lacy white edging
and texture everywhere. Enter the modern
and relaxing lounge to find a bright gallery
of the colorful works of Lunenburg-based
painter Daniel Richards (p86). If you haven't
been floored yet, move on to the rooms, several of which have a hot tub in them, creating
an atmosphere of your own candle-lit spa.

Blomidon Inn (☎ 902-542-2291, 800-565-2291; www
.theblomidon.net; d $99-140, ste $160-270) Lofty Victorian architecture meets Old World extrava-
gance at this very uppercrust-feeling inn. On
2.5 hectares of perfectly maintained gardens
the rooms are just as well groomed and the
dining area might inspire you to shine your
shoes. This place might feel a bit stuffy were
it not for the smiling, easy-going staff.

Victoria's Historic Inn (☎ 902-542-5744, 800-556-
5744; www.victoriashistoricinn.com; r $145-245) This ele-
gant inn has 16 rooms with modern amenities
and timeless charm. Rooms on the 3rd floor
are decorated with more modern furnishings
while the rest of the inn is Victorian without
feeling too heavy.

Eating & Drinking

A farmers' market is held on Saturday mornings in the spring and summer on Front St
by the library.

Coffee Merchant & Library Pub (☎ 902-542-4315;
472 Main St; ☼ 11:30am-midnight Mon-Sat) Downstairs
the café serves up good fair-trade coffee and
baked goods, while you can get a pint and a
square meal at the cosy upstairs pub. During
daytime hours the well-lit pub is a popular
place to read a book over a meal; at night
studying goes to the wayside.

Ivy Deck (☎ 902-542-1868; 8 Elm Ave; mains $9-14;
☼ lunch & dinner, closed Mon Nov-Jun) Don't look
for ivy plants, this restaurant is talking Ivy
League. Try a salad with flowers intermin-
gled among the lettuce or salmon and shrimp
penne – portions are a bit small so you'll
probably be tempted to finish your meal with
a pecan slice, four-layer chocolate cake or one
of a huge selection of other enticing baked
goods. On sunny days sit in under the arbor
on the outside deck.

Acton's (☎ 542-7525; 268 Main St; lunch mains $10-15,
dinner $18-26; ☼ 11am-2pm & 5-9pm) Acton's fame
spreads as far as Yarmouth as one of the finest
restaurants in the region. The atmosphere is
simple yet elegant, the food colorful. Spectacular salads, and new twists on old favorites
are the house specialties.

Getting There & Away

Acadian Lines stops at Acadia University in
front of Wheelock Hall off Highland Ave.
Kings Transit buses run between Cornwallis
and Wolfville and stop at 209 Main St.

GRAND PRÉ

Grand Pré, at the outskirts of Wolfville, was
the site of one of the most tragic but compelling stories in eastern Canada's history,
the expulsions of the Acadians (see p33).
This historical site has become a symbol of
the preservation of Acadian culture. French
influence shows through more subtly today
in the form of **Domaine de Grand Pré** (opposite)
one of the region's premier wineries.

Sights & Activities

At **Grand Pré National Historic Site** (☎ 902-542-3631;
2205 Grand Pré Rd; admission $5.75; ☼ 9am-6pm May-Oct),
a modern interpretive center explains the
historical context for the deportation from
Acadian, Mi'kmaq and British perspectives
and traces the many routes Acadians took
from and back to Atlantic Canada.

Beside the center, a serene **park** contains
gardens and an Acadian-style stone church.
There's also a bust of American poet Henry
Wadsworth Longfellow who chronicled the
Acadian saga in *Evangeline: A Tale of Acadie*,
and a statue of his fictional Evangeline, now
a romantic symbol of her people.

Beyond the park, you can see the farmland
created when the Acadians built dykes along
the shoreline as they had done in northwest
France for generations. There are 1200 hectares below sea level here, protected by just
over 9000m of dyke. It's a beautiful area and
you'll easily understand why the Acadians
didn't want to leave.

Many people come to town to visit **Domaine de Grand Pré** (☎ 902-542-1753; www.grandprewines.ns.ca; 11611 Hwy 1; tours $6; ⏰ 11am, 3pm & 5pm, free tasting 10am-6pm) vineyards and winery. Tours of the lovely landscaped grounds take about 45 minutes. Otherwise you can do tastings and stroll through the vines by yourself for free.

Sleeping & Eating

Grand Pré House B&B (☎ 902-542-4277; 273 Old Post Rd; s $65-75, d $85-105) The current owners bought this historic home from the original family and added a meditation hut and sauna. This charming, tranquil spot overlooks a horse pasture and the dykelands. With 16 hectares of fields, ponds and winding paths, you might never want to leave.

The Olde Lantern Inn & Vineyard (☎ 902-542-1389, 877-965-3845; www.oldlanterninn.com; 11575 Hwy 1; s $110-130, d $120-140; 🖳) Clean lines and attention to every comfort (such as buttersoft sheets) makes this a great place to stay. The vineyard grounds overlook Minas Basin where you can watch the rise and fall of the Fundy Tides.

Le Caveau (☎ 902-542-1753; 11611 Hwy 1; mains $14-27; ⏰ lunch & dinner) Considered to be the finest Northern European–style restaurant in the province, this Swiss restaurant is on the grounds of Domaine de Grand Pré. The beautiful outdoor patio is paved with fieldstones and shaded with grapevines. Tours with wine tasting ($6) are given at 11am and 3pm.

Shopping

Tangled Garden (☎ 902-542-9811; 11827 Hwy 1; ⏰ 10am-6pm) Impossible to classify, this is probably the best-smelling shopping experience in Nova Scotia. Buy a bottle of herb-infused vinegar or jelly to take away, or stroll the gardens and meditative labyrinth while licking herb-flavored ice-cream.

WINDSOR

Charlie Brown would be happy in Windsor (population 3778); it's the home of Howard Dills' giant pumpkin variety, the world's heftiest jack-o'-lantern fodder. The town is even more proud of being the birthplace of hockey, which is a debatable claim. What's certain is that this small town on the Avon River holds just enough interest for a short stop, but no more. Windsor is also a place of fast banjo picking and bluegrass and is a hangout for aficionados all summer long.

Orientation & Information

Highway 1 becomes Water St in town, and the main intersection is with Gerrish St. The helpful **tourist office** (☎ 902-798-2690; 31 Colonial Rd; ⏰ 8:30am-6:30pm Jul & Aug, 9am-5pm Sat & Sun Jun, Sep & Oct) is just off exit 6 from Hwy 101. The dyke beside the tourist office offers a view of the tidal river flats.

Sights & Activities

Off King St, the **Fort Edward National Historic Site** (☎ 902-798-4706; admission free; ⏰ 10am-6pm Mon-Sat, noon-4pm Sun Jul & Aug) preserves remnants of a British fort dating from 1750. It was used as one of the assembly stations during the expulsion of the Acadians. The grounds are accessible year-round.

The Victorian **Haliburton House** (☎ 902-798-2915; 414 Clifton Ave; adult/student $3/2; ⏰ 9:30am-5:30pm Mon-Sat, 1-5:30pm Sun Jun–mid-Oct) was the home of Judge Thomas Chandler Haliburton (1796–1865), writer of the Sam Slick stories. Although they aren't read much now, many of Haliburton's expressions, such as 'quick as a wink' and 'city slicker,' are still used.

Windsor's claim as the birthplace of ice hockey is very much debated. The evidence is gathered at the **Windsor Hockey Heritage Society** (☎ 902-798-1800; 128 Gerrish St; admission free; ⏰ 10am-5pm Mon-Sat).

An especially ornate Victorian house, the 1890 **Shand House Museum** (☎ 902-798-8213; adult/concession $3/2; ⏰ 9:30am-5:30pm Mon-Sat, 1-5:30pm Sun Jun–mid-Oct) also offers historical displays and a great view from the tower room.

Stop for a visit at **Howard Dill's Farm** (☎ 902-798-2728; 400 College Rd; admission free; ⏰ 8am-4pm). Dill is a four-time world champion pumpkin grower and developer and you can check out his weighty beauties for yourself.

Sleeping & Eating

Avon River Park (☎ 902-684-3299; 955 Hwy 1, Mount Denson; tent/RV sites $10/16) This small campground, just above the Avon River, is a great spot to see the effect of the dramatic Bay of Fundy tides.

Meander In B&B (☎ 902-798-2514, 877-387-6070; www.bbcanada.com/meanderinbandb; 153 Albert St; r $60-80; 🖳) This central 1898 mansion is just the sort of place you'd hope to meander into. The three rooms have a shared bathroom and there's tea with home-baked goods in the evening.

Clockmaker's Inn (☎ 902-792-2573, 866-778-3600, www.theclockmakersinn.com; 1399 King St; d $100-125, ste $150; 🖳) Re-opened in 2005, this is the most stunning B&B in the area. The French chateau–style mansion has curved bay windows, lots of stained glass and sweeping hardwood staircases. Step into the wide entranceway to become even more enamoured of the exceptionally tasteful interior. It's gay friendly and afternoon tea is served every day as is breakfast.

Spitfire Arms Alehouse (☎ 902-792-1460; 29 Water St; mains $7-11; ☺ 11am-midnight) This traditional pub is the best place to eat in town and gets packed with locals and visitors alike. There's live music on weekends and it's OK to bring the kids till around 9pm.

CENTRAL NOVA SCOTIA

Hiking, rafting and rockhounding, without too many tourist traps, characterize Central Nova Scotia, one of the most compelling regions in the province. This region introduces Nova Scotia to those traveling overland from the rest of Canada – do not just bomb past on bleak Hwy 104!

Called the 'Glooscap Trail' in provincial tourism literature, the area is named for the figure in Mi'kmaw legend who created the unique geography of the Bay of Fundy region. Unfortunately, stories and representations of Glooscap are easier to come across than genuine acknowledgments of present-day Mi'kmaq people, some 5000 of whom live in this part of the province.

SHUBENACADIE

Shubenacadie (population 906), or simply 'Shubie,' is best known for the **Shubenacadie Provincial Wildlife Park** (☎ 902-758-2040; www.wildlifepark.gov.ns.ca; 149 Creighton Rd; adult/child 6-17yr/family $4/$1.50/10; ☺ 9am-7pm mid-May–mid-Oct, 9am-3pm Sat & Sun rest of year), a not-to-miss stop if you want to commune with Nova Scotia's wildlife up-close (you can hand-feed the deer and, if you're lucky, pet a moose). The animals were either born in captivity or once kept as 'pets,' and as a result cannot be released into the wild – they live in large enclosures and are very well cared for. Turn off Hwy 102 at exit 11 and follow Hwy 2 to the park entrance.

Wild Nature Camping (☎ 902-758-1631; 20961 Hwy 2; serviced/unserviced sites $20/15) is only about 100m up a hill from the highway and has a lake, trees and a big red barn. It's the countryside without the drive.

MAITLAND

Tidal bore rafting trips leave from this speck of a town at the mouth of the Shubenacadie River. The rafting is done on the white-water that is created by the meeting of the outflow of the river and the blasting force of the incoming Fundy tides.

Wave heights are dependant on the phases of the moon (see below); find out from your rafting company about the tides for the day you want to go since your experience (either mild or exhilarating) will be dictated by this. Outboard powered Zodiacs plunge right through the white-water for the two to three hours that the rapids exist. Prepare to get very, very wet – no experience is needed.

Tours

Shubenacadie River Adventures (☎ 902-261-2222, 800-878-8687; www.shubie.com; 10061 Hwy 15; day rafting with barbecue adult/child $70/65) Also offers mud-sliding.

Shubenacadie River Runners (☎ 902-261-2770, 800-856-5061; www.tidalborerafting.com; 8681 Hwy 215; half-/full-day rafting adult $50/70, child $40/60) The biggest rafting company is hyper-organized and professional in every way.

Sleeping

There are a handful of places to sleep in Maitland but the few eating options have unpredictable opening hours – bring your own food or a full belly.

Wide Open Wilderness Camping (☎ 902-261-2228; www.wowcamping.com; 11129 Hwy 215, Urbania; serviced/

TIDAL BORE

The **tidal bore** is a unique phenomenon to witness. As a result of the extreme Bay of Fundy tides, a tidal bore or wave flows up the feeder rivers when high tide comes in. Sometimes the advancing wave is only a ripple, but with the right phase of the moon it can be a meter or so in height, giving the impression that the Salmon River is flowing backwards. See it from the lookout on Tidal Bore Rd, off Hwy 236 just west of exit 14 from Hwy 102 on the northwest side of Truro. Staff in the adjacent Palliser Motel **gift shop** (☎ 902-893-8951) can advise when the next tidal bore will arrive. There's another one in Moncton, New Brunswick (p171), that's worth checking out.

unserviced sites $27/18) Between Shubenacadie and Maitland, this camping is a bit buggy but the big wooded sites are right at the river.

Terranita B&B (☎ 902-261-2102; www.bbcanada.com /terranitabb; 8098 Hwy 215; r $85-155; ☺ Jun-Oct) This big stone house in the middle of 2 hectares is only minutes from the rafting operators. Special dietary needs are taken into account for the elegant breakfasts.

TRURO

Although Truro (population 11,457) lacks the eye candy aspect of many Nova Scotian towns, it's exceptionally friendly and well serviced. A quick look at the map explains why Truro is known as the hub of Nova Scotia. Several major highways converge here, along with a VIA Rail line; it's also a bus transfer point. You will probably have to pass through this town and it's best if you time it around lunchtime to take advantage of the town's fine eating establishments. Most restaurants are clustered around Prince and Inglis Sts, which are the most picturesque areas. You could also use Truro as a base to ride the tidal bore (see opposite).

Information

Tourist office (☎ 902-893-2922; Victoria Sq, cnr Prince & Commercial Sts; ☺ 8:30am-7:30pm Jul & Aug, 9am-5pm mid-May–Oct) One of the most friendly and helpful tourist offices in Nova Scotia. There's free Internet access.

Sights & Activities

Truro is the tree sculpture capital of Nova Scotia and the tourist office gives out a free guide explaining the more interesting ones around town.

Victoria Park (Park St off Brunswick St) is one pleasant way of escaping Truro. Explore 400 hectares of green space in the center of town, including a deep gorge and two waterfalls. The park attracts dozens of bird species.

Colchester Museum (☎ 902-895-6284; 29 Young St; adult/child $2/1; ☺ 10am-5pm Jul & Aug, 10am-noon & 2-5pm Tue-Fri, 2-5pm Sat Sep-Jun) has exhibits on the founding of Truro, the region's human history and Elizabeth Bishop, a noted poet who grew up in the area.

Jan van der Leest's large collection of melodeons, harmoniums and reed organs is in the **Organery** (☎ 902-893-4824; 53 Farnham Rd; admission by donation; ☺ 11am-4pm May-Oct). There is also a fabulous tearoom on the premises (tea from $1.50).

Festivals

The best time to visit Truro is the second weekend in August when Millbrook First Nation, hosts a **powwow** (☎ 902-897-9199). Campsites and showers are available there; drugs and alcohol are prohibited. Another good time to visit is mid-May for the **Truro International Tulip Festival** (www.townoftruro.ca). This is a great family gathering with bluegrass concerts and a big antique market.

Sleeping

Iron Duck (☎ 902-893-3005; therockwells2@hotmail.com; 242 Kent Rd; r $55-75) The rooms in this simple home of an elderly couple are the best deal in town. The owner makes her own preserves, which she serves at breakfast.

At the Organery (☎ 902-893-4824, 877-822-5655; www.organery.ca; 53 Farhham Rd; r/ste $85/100) After checking out the organs and stopping for tea, why not stay the night at this completely renovated century home. The chatty owners also speak Dutch, German and French.

Royalty B&B (☎ 902-893-3112; www.royaltybandb.ca; 628 Prince St; r $90-125; ⬛) Truro's newest B&B is right in the heart of the historic downtown just steps from restaurants and shops. This nicely remodeled heritage home has a shared kitchen and private entrance for guests.

Eating

Murphy's Fish & Chips (☎ 902-895-1275; 88 Esplanade St; mains $5-9; ☺ 11am-7pm Mon-Thu & Sat, to 8pm Fri, noon-7pm Sun) Considered by some to the best fish-and-chips in Nova Scotia, this place is worth coming to just for the fishing-dock decor.

Wooden Hog (☎ 902-895-0779; 627 Prince St; lunch $7, dinner mains $10-16; ☺ 9am-10pm Mon-Thu, 9am-11pm Fri, 11am-1pm Sat) Blues music is pumped into this western-style café with a big wooden 'hog' – a Harley Davidson – hanging on the back wall. The healthy food makes you feel alright ordering a decadent dessert.

Culina Dea (☎ 902-895-1616; 914 Prince St; mains $6-23; ☺ 9am-3pm Mon-Sat & 5-9pm Thu-Sat) You can dream of whipping up your own creations (the restaurant is also a kitchenwares store) while dining on creative pizzas and nouvelle cuisine.

Getting There & Away

The **bus station** (☎ 902-895-3833; www.acadianbus.com; 280 Willow St; ☺ 8am-10:30pm) is busy with Acadian Lines buses en route to Amherst ($22, two hours, three times daily) and Sydney ($50, five hours, three times daily).

ECONOMY

Known for hiking and clam digging, 'Economy' is considered by most locals to be a conglomeration of Upper, Lower and Central Economy. Hugging the shore of the Minas Basin, the northeast arm of the Bay of Fundy, this area is a place of good views, big tides and happy people.

Sights & Activities

Raspberry Bay Stone (☎ 902-647-2287; www.raspberry baystone.com; Hwy 2, Bass River; ☺ 10am-5pm mid-May–Sep, call ahead rest of year), about 7km east of Economy, is a wonderful combination of an artist's studio, gallery, museum, garden and petting zoo. Heather Lawson was the first female stonemason in Canada.

For more petting zoo plus some mighty fine cheese, stop at **That Dutchman's Farm** (☎ 902-647-2751; www.thatdutchmansfarm.com; Hwy 2, Upper Economy; adult/child $3.30/2.50; ☺ 9am-6pm Apr-Dec). A bag of grain costs only $1 and you can walk the trails of the 50-hectare property while feeding the

birds and animals. Don't miss out learning about cheese-making then sampling the goods at the café (opposite).

Get information about local hikes at the **Cobequid Interpretation Centre** (☎ 902-647-2600; 3248 Hwy 2, near River Phillip Rd; admission free; ☺ 9am-4:30pm Mon-Fri, to 6pm Sat & Sun Jul & Aug). It has good exhibits on the area's ecology and history. Climb a WWII observation tower for a bird's-eye view of the surrounding area.

The most challenging hikes are around Economy Falls. The **Devil's Bend Trail** begins 7km up River Phillip Rd toward the Cobequid Mountains. Turn right and park; the 6.5km (one-way) trail follows the river to the falls. The **Kenomee Canyon Trail** begins further up River Phillip Rd, at the top of the falls. A 20km loop, it takes you up the river to its headwaters in a protected wilderness area. Several streams have to be forded. There are designated campsites, making this a good two-day adventurous trek.

The **Thomas Cove Coastal Trail** is actually two 3.5km loops with great views across the Minas Basin and of the Cobequid Mountains. They begin down Economy Point Rd, 500m east

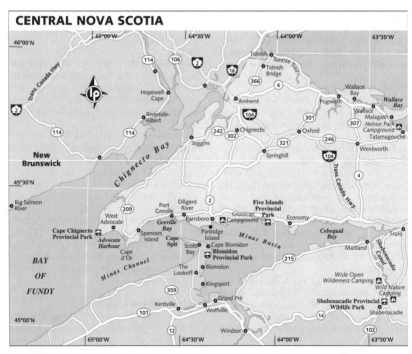

CENTRAL NOVA SCOTIA

of the Cobequid Interpretation Centre. Follow the signs to a parking area. Finally, there are several hikes in **Five Islands Provincial Park** (☎ 902-254-2980; parks.gov.ns.ca; Hwy 2), 7km west of Economy. The 4.5km **Red Head Trail** is well developed with lookouts, benches and great views.

Sleeping & Eating

Five Islands Provincial Park (☎ 902-254-2980; http://parks.gov.ns.ca; Hwy 2; campsites $18) There are 90 sites here – from large grassy sites to smaller forested ones – plus showers, flush toilets and a playground. It's a good place to try clam digging plus enjoy the views of the 90m cliffs along the ocean.

High Tide B&B (☎ 902-647-2788; www3.ns.sympatico .ca/hightide.bb; 2240 Hwy 2, Lower Economy; d $85-95) This friendly, modern bungalow has great views. Janet will have you down on the beach for a clam boil in no time.

Four Seasons Retreat (☎ 902-647-2628, 888-373-0339; www.fourseasonsretreat.ns.ca; 320 Cove Rd, Upper Economy; 1-/2-/3-bedroom cottages $100/145/195; 🖥) Fully equipped cottages are surrounded by trees on and face the Minas Basin. In summer

there's a hot tub near the pool; in winter – or on a chilly night – there are woodstoves.

Several take-away stands selling fried clams pop up along the highway near Five Islands Provincial Park in the summer. The café at **That Dutchman's Farm** (🕙 11am-4pm Jun-Sep) offers sandwiches, soups and plates of the eccentric farmer's own gouda.

PARRSBORO

Parrsboro (population 1529), the largest of the small towns along the Minas Basin shore, is the perfect base for exploring the Minas Basin. Rockhounds come from far and away to look for fossils and semiprecious stones that get turned up daily by the forceful Fundy tides (see boxed text, p113). The Fundy Geological Museum has wonderful exhibits and good programs that take you to the beach areas known as Nova Scotia's 'Jurassic Park.' The annual **Gem & Mineral Show** is in mid-August.

Information

Tourist office (☎ 902-254-3266; 69 Main St; 🕙 10am-7pm Jun-Oct) Has tide information and free Internet access.

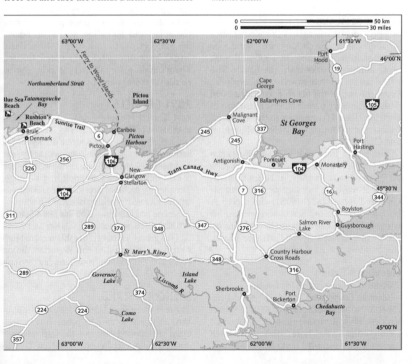

Sights & Activities

FUNDY GEOLOGICAL MUSEUM

This award-winning **museum** (☎ 902-254-3814; www.museum.gov.ns.ca/fgm; 162 Two Islands Rd; adult/child/student/family $5/3/4.25/12; ⊙ 9:30am-5:30pm Jun–mid-Oct, 9am-5pm Tue-Sat mid-Oct–May) uses interactive exhibits to help its visitors 'time travel' to when the fossils littering Parrsboro's beaches were alive. You can look into a lab where dinosaur bones are being cleaned and assembled. Two- to three-hour beach tours (adult/child $11.50/5.75) focus on minerals or fossils; there are up to four tours daily. Check the website for full-day family programs.

PARRSBORO ROCK & MINERAL SHOP & MUSEUM

Browse this impressive **shop** (☎ 902-254-2981; 39 Whitehall Rd; admission free; ⊙ 9am-9pm Mon-Sat, 9am-5pm Sun May-Nov) with its collection of prehistoric reptile fossils, semiprecious stones from Parrsboro and around the world, and even a one-of-a-kind fossilized footprint of the world's smallest dinosaur. Owner and native of Parrsboro Eldon George (see opposite) has an unsurpassed passion for rocks and fossils.

PARTRIDGE ISLAND

Steeped in history, this is the most popular shoreline to search for gems. Samuel de Champlain landed here in 1607 and took away amethyst rocks from the beach. The island is 4km south of town on Whitehall Rd. From the end of the beach a 3km **hiking trail** with explanatory panels climbs to the top of Partridge Island (connected to the mainland by an isthmus) for superb views of Blomidon and Cape Split.

Just before the beach is **Ottawa House Museum** (☎ 902-254-2376; 1155 Whitehall Rd; admission $2; ⊙ 10am-6pm Jun–mid-Sep), a 21-room mansion that was once the summer home of Sir Charles Tupper (1821–1915), who served as both premier of Nova Scotia and prime minister of Canada. The museum has exhibits on the former settlement on Partridge Island, shipbuilding and rum-running.

Sleeping & Eating

Parrsboro is not a haven for foodies.

Glooscap Campground (☎ 902-254-2529; fax 902-254-2313; 1380 Two Island Rd; tent/RV sites $15/20; ⊙ mid-May–Sep) This attractive municipally owned campground on the shore 5km south of town has some nice secluded tent sites.

Riverview Cottages (☎ 902-254-2388; 3575 Eastern Ave; cottage $50-75; ⊙ Apr-Nov) Remodeled and under new British ownership, these country-cute, completely equipped cottages are a steal. You can canoe and fish on the bordering river and there's a big lawn perfect for a barbecue.

Parrsboro Mansion B&B (☎ 902-254-2585, 866-354-2585; www.parrsboromansion.com; 3916 Eastern Ave; r $85-150; 🖳 🛋) The perfect spot for health-minded folks, this striking B&B in a Louisiana–style mansion is equipped with everything from a sauna to an exercise room. The renovated, modern rooms have exceptionally comfy beds.

Harbourview Restaurant (☎ 902-254-3507; 145 Pier Rd; lunch $8-12, dinner mains $12-17; ⊙ 8am-9pm Mon-Sat May-Oct) Locals will tell you that this is the only place worth eating at in town. It serves fresh seafood, good breakfasts and fried fare. The friendly, local atmosphere and views make for a pleasant meal.

Entertainment

Ship's Company Theatre (☎ 902-254-3000, 800-565-7469; www.shipscompany.com; 18 Lower Main St; adult $20-24, student/under 13yr $15/10; ⊙ Jul–mid-Sep) This innovative theater company performs new Canadian and Maritime works 'on board' the MV *Kipawo*, the last of the Minas Basin ferries, now integrated into a new theater. There's high-quality theater for kids, improv comedy, readings and concerts.

PORT GREVILLE

Port Greville is a lovely drive of about 20km to the west of Parrsboro on Hwy 209. Stop for tea, baked goods and a tour at the **Age of Sail Heritage Centre** (☎ 902-348-2030; www.parrsboro.com/aos.htm; Hwy 209; adult/family $2/5; ⊙ 10am-6pm Jun-Sep). It captures the area's shipbuilding heritage. The site also includes a restored 1857 Methodist church and a working blacksmith shop.

Serene and luxurious, **Ebb Tide B&B & Tearoom** (☎ 902-342-2011; www.ebbtide.ca; 8614 Hwy 209; r $75-95; 🖳) is a great base to explore this region. High British tea is served in the Victorian dining room every afternoon from Tuesday through Saturday (May to October).

SPENCERS ISLAND

The legendary ship *Mary Celeste* was built in 1861 at this one-time ship-building center. Originally named *Amazon*, the ship was later renamed before setting out from New York to

LOCAL VOICES

Eldon George

Amateur lapadarian, jeweler and palaeontologist; owner of The Rock & Mineral Shop & Museum (opposite), age 75, Parrsborro

What do you think is the most important environmental issue facing your region today? Here in Parrsborro we have the world's highest tides, which is an amazing thing. Now they are trying to harness this energy with underwater turbines, which will generate electricity. At first the local fishermen were quite worried that this would affect the fishing, but experts have come from England, the US and Canada, and they tell us that the fish can just go straight through without getting harmed. If they can harness this power and bring it to full potential it could bring in all kind of industries. Just think of the millions of kilowatts that have gone to waste already! **Where is your favorite secret spot?** I have lots of secret spots but most I keep to myself – I've found many one-of-a-kind semiprecious stones. The whole coast at Parrsborro changes daily. I think of the tides of the Bay of Fundy as being like 20,000 bulldozers working for me free of charge 365 days a year uncovering layers and bringing them out to the beach. Once the fossils and stones are uncovered they have to be collected or the next storm will take them away.

cross the Atlantic with a full load of alcohol. One month later, the sailing vessel was discovered, sails set and nothing out of place, but with no sign of a single crew-member. The story was later immortalised by mystery writer Sir Arthur Conan Doyle in his short story titled *Mary Celeste*. Today the **Old Shipyard Beach Campground** lets you camp on the very spit of land where the boat was built. The **lighthouse** has a small information desk and museum about the *Mary Celeste*.

Although treeless, RV-dominated and windy, the **Old Shipyard Beach Campground** (☎ 902-392-2487; noreenbob2000@yahoo.com; 774 Beach Rd; serviced/unserviced sites $16/22; ☽ Jun-Oct) has a beachside charm and history to boot. The on-site **restaurant** (mains lunch $3-8, dinner $10-20; ☽ noon-late, closed Mon) here has great seafood, home-made pies and ice-cream. Every chair is different, animal skins and Victorian carpets cover the floor and there's a rickety outdoor terrace.

An antique sailor's cottage right by the beach, **Spencer's Island B&B** (☎ 902-392-2721; spencebb@yahoo.ca; Hwy 209 at Spencers Beach; r $40-60; ☽ Jul-Sep) oozes historic charm. Nautical drawings decorate the walls and a friendly dog welcomes you at the door.

ADVOCATE HARBOUR

This breathtaking place is wedged between Cape d'Or and Cape Chignecto. A 5km-long beach is piled high with driftwood. Behind it, salt marshes reclaimed with dykes by the Acadians are now replete with birds. The main attraction is Cape Chignecto Provincial Park,

opened in 1998 and now the crown jewel of the park system. Spend an extra day in 'town' to recover from the exertions of exploring the park.

Fundy Tides Campground (☎ 902-392-2584; 95 Mills Rd; tent/RV sites $12/18) is flat and un-interesting but has good water views. The **canteen** (☽ 8am-9pm Jul & Aug, 11am-7pm rest of year) serves tasty fishburgers ($6.50) and other delicacies.

Cape Chignecto Provincial Park

The **Cape Chignecto Coastal Trail** is a rugged 60km loop with backcountry – nay, old-growth – campsites. Budget four days and three nights for the hike. The **Mill Brook Canyon Trail** (15km return) and the hike to **Refugee Cove** (20km return) are other challenging overnight hikes. There are some easier hikes and more are being developed. Some hikers have tried to avoid the ups and downs of the trails by taking shortcuts along the beach at low tide and have been cut off by the Bay of Fundy tides. Get a tide table and follow advice from park staff to avoid being trapped on the cliffs.

Park visitors must register and leave an itinerary at the **visitors center** (☎ 902-392-2085; www.capechignecto.net; 1108 West Advocate Rd; hiking permits $3, backcountry sites $18; ☽ 8am-7pm Mon-Thu, 8am-8pm Fri & Sat, 8am-6pm Sun Jul & Aug, 8am-5pm Mon-Thu, 8am-7pm Fri & Sat, 8am-6pm Sun late May-Jun, Sep & Oct). Camping in the backcountry requires reservations. In addition to 51 wilderness campsites at six spots along the coastal trail and 27 walk-in sites near the visitor center, there is also a 12-bed **bunkhouse** (dm $12) and a wilderness **cabin** (up to 4 people $50).

NOVA SCOTIA

CAPE D'OR

This spectacular cape of sheer cliffs was mis-named Cape d'Or (Cape of Gold) by Samuel de Champlain in 1604 – the glittering veins he saw in the cliffs were actually made of copper. Mining took place between 1897 and 1905 and removed the sparkle. Take the side road off Hwy 209 to Cape d'Or then hike down the dirt trail to **Lightkeeper's Kitchen & Guest House** (☎ 902-670-0534; www.capedor.ca; Cape d'Or; s/d with ocean view $70/100; mid-May–mid-Oct). The original lighthouse-keeper's residence is now a laid-back four-room guesthouse. A very cosmopolitan feeling **restaurant** (mains lunch $7-12, dinner $16-18; 11am-4pm & 6-8pm mid-May–Aug, 11am-4pm & 6-8pm Thu-Mon Sep–mid-Oct) pumps out low-volume techno music and serves original seafood, meat and vegetarian creations.

JOGGINS

Cliffs in this area hold extensive deposits of 300-million-year-old fossils. If you look closely you can make out all sorts of sea critters and plants among the layers. If you don't trust your luck finding fossils on your own, go to the **Joggins Fossil Centre** (☎ 902-251-2727; 30 Main St; admission adult/child/senior $5/3/4; 9am-5:30pm mid-Jun–Oct), which has a massive collection of fossils with explanations and help with identifications.

AMHERST

The geographic center of the Maritimes, Amherst's (population 9470) quaint historic brick downtown quickly gives way to modern malls and fast-food joints along the outskirts. This is the travel junction for travelers to Nova Scotia, PEI and New Brunswick but there's little reason to dawdle as you're just a short drive from either the Bay of Fundy shore or the Northumberland Strait (between Nova Scotia and PEI).

Information

Tourist office (☎ 902-667-0696; 51 La Planche St; 10am-6pm Mon-Sat) Specializes in the area.
VIC (☎ 902-667-8429; 8:30am-9pm Jul & Aug, to 8pm Jun & Sep, to 6pm May & Oct, to 5pm Nov-Apr) At exit 1 off Hwy 104, just as you cross the border from New Brunswick. Has heaps of info on all of Nova Scotia.

Sights

The **Cumberland County Museum** (☎ 902-667-2561; 150 Church St; adult/child under 16yr/family $3/free/5; 9am-5pm Mon-Sat May-Sep, closed Mon Oct-Apr) is in the erstwhile home of Father of Confed-

eration, RB Dickey. Exhibits include articles made by prisoners of war at the Amherst Internment Camp during WWI. Leon Trotsky was one of the prisoners of war.

The 490-hectare **Amherst Point Migratory Bird Sanctuary** has more than 200 bird species. From downtown Amherst, turn left off Church St onto Victoria and drive about 6km, crossing the Trans-Canada Hwy (Hwy 104). (From the highway, take exit 3 and turn toward Amherst Point.) A small parking lot, which is the trailhead for paths into the sanctuary, is on your left just after mailbox No 947.

Sleeping & Eating

Treen Mansion (☎ 902-667-2146; 113 Spring St; s/d $65/75) This large Victorian house was built from quarry stones in 1907. The four comfortable rooms have private bathrooms and TVs. Laundry facilities are available.
Hampton Diner Open Kitchen (☎ 902-667-3562; 21386 Fort Lawrence Rd; mains $7-10; 7am-9pm Tue-Sun May-Oct) This classic diner, 700m south of the Amherst VIC and 3km north of downtown Amherst, dates from 1956. Come here for seafood, steaks, burgers or pie.

Getting There & Away

Acadian Lines has bus services to Halifax ($36, three hours, twice daily) that leave from the **Irving Mainway gas station** (☎ 902-667-8435; 213 S Albion St).

The Trans-Canada Hwy (Hwy 104)east of Amherst charges a toll of $3. It's an incentive to use scenic Hwy 2 through Parrsboro instead of dull – but fast – Hwy 104. The Sunrise Trail (Hwy 6) through Pugwash and Tatamagouche to Pictou also avoids the toll.

Amherst's **VIA Rail station** (☎ 800-561-3952), is on Station St, a few minutes' walk from the center of town; see p284 for more details.

SUNRISE TRAIL

Go beach-hopping along this 450km coastline of more than 30 beaches. The Northumberland Strait between Nova Scotia's north shore and PEI is said to have the warmest waters north of the US Carolinas, with summer water temperatures averaging slightly over 20°C. All that coast means that there are plenty of fishing boats and most of them in this region bear lobsters. Small towns and emerald fields along rolling Hwy 6 make this a reasonable highway for cycling.

PUGWASH

Pugwash is renowned for the events that took place at 247 Water St. In July 1957 industrialist Cyrus Eaton (1883–1979) brought together a group of 22 leading scientists from around the world to discuss disarmament issues and science. The meeting was sponsored by Bertrand Russell, Albert Einstein and others, though they did not attend. The Pugwash Conference laid the groundwork for the Partial Test Ban Treaty of 1963. Today the village is a place for contemplating your own peace on the beach or just wandering around this country town.

Built in 1888, the former Pugwash train station, one of the oldest in Nova Scotia, today serves as a **tourist office** (☎ 902-243-2449; 10222 Durham St; ☽ 9am-6pm late Jun-Sep). Wares by local craftspeople are sold along the main street and also at tables set up at the former train station on Saturdays. Pugwash hosts a colorful **Gathering of the Clans** festival each year on July 1. Street names in town are written in Scottish Gaelic as well as in English.

Pleasant **Shillelagh Sheila's Country Inn** (☎ 902-243-2885; www.shillelaghsheilasinn.com; 10340 Durham St; s/d $65/75) is in the heart of town. The food here is phenomenal!

WALLACE

Wallace is prime territory for birding and beachcombing. The tourist information center is at the **Wallace Museum** (☎ 902-257-2191; Hwy 6; ☽ 9am-5pm Mon-Sat, 1-4pm Sun). Granted to the community in 1990, this 1840 home was in one family for generations. With the house came collections of baskets woven by the Mi'kmaq, period dresses and shipbuilding memorabilia, which are now displayed. A section of the **Trans Canada Trail** (TCT; p48) runs behind the museum.

Wallace Bay Wildlife Bird Sanctuary (1km north of Hwy 6 on Aboiteau Rd) protects 585 hectares, including tidal and freshwater wetlands. A 4km walking trail is a nice way to explore some of it and observe the many bird species that flock here, particularly in spring and fall. In the spring, keep your eyes peeled for bald eagles nesting near the parking lot, which is on the left just before the causeway.

WENTWORTH

The Wentworth Valley is a detour off the shore, 25km south of Wallace via Hwy 307. It's particularly pretty in the fall when the deciduous trees change color. The 24-bed **Wentworth Hostel** (☎ 902-548-2379; www.hihostels .ca; 249 Wentworth Station Rd; dm member/nonmember $15/20) is 1.3km west of Hwy 4 on Valley Rd, then straight up steep Wentworth Station Rd. The big rambling farmhouse, built in 1866, has been used as a hostel for half a century. There are two family rooms and a kitchen. It's central enough to be a base for both the Sunrise Trail and much of the Minas Bay shore. Trails for hiking and mountain biking start just outside the door.

TATAMAGOUCHE

Wine, maple syrup, warm beaches and farm fresh produce everywhere; what more could you want? Tatamagouche (population 738) is the largest of several small, charming towns around Tatamagouche Bay, a protected inlet off the Northumberland Strait. With all the good things to eat as well as some fun museums and laid-back vibe, it's no wonder this has become a popular tourist destination.

Information

Fraser Cultural Centre (☎ 902-657-3285; 362 Main St; ☽ 10am-5pm Mon-Fri, 10am-4pm Sat, 11am-3pm Sun mid-Jun–Sep) Tourist information, Internet access (per hour $2) and local history displays. One room is dedicated to local giantess Anna Swan, who achieved fame with Barnum & Bailey's circus in the early 20th century.

Sights & Activities

Sample the free wine that comes with a tour of the scenically located **Jost Winery** (☎ 902-257-2636; www.jostwine.com; off Hwy 6, Malagash; admission free; ☽ tours noon & 3pm mid-Jun–mid-Sep). Enjoy a snack and a glass of wine (try the very sweet icewine – the specialty) at the outdoor patio where there is often free music. Winery signs direct you about 5km off Hwy 6.

In a gorgeous setting on the stream that once provided it with power, the **Balmoral Grist Mill** (☎ 902-657-3016; http://gristmill.museum .gov.ns.ca; 660 Matheson Brook Rd; adult/child 6-16yr $3/2; ☽ 9:30am-5:30pm Mon-Sat, 1-5:30pm Sun Jun–mid-Oct) still grinds wheat in summer. Purchase some to take away or bring your own food for a picnic. To get here from Tatamagouche, turn south on Hwy 311 (at the east edge of town) and then east on Hwy 256. There are plenty of signs along the way.

From the Balmoral Grist Mill, drive further east on Hwy 256, and then north on Hwy 326, to get to the **Sutherland Steam Mill** (☎ 902-

657-3365; http://steammill.museum.gov.ns.ca; off Hwy 326 in Denmark; adult/child 6-17yr $3/2; ☯ 9:30am-5:30pm Mon-Sat, 1-5:30pm Sun Jun–mid-Oct). Built in 1894, it produced lumber, carriages, wagons and windows until 1958. Now it's a fully operational museum.

Blue Sea Beach on the Malagash Peninsula has warm water and fine sand, and a marsh area just inland that's ideal for bird-watching. There are picnic tables and shelters to change in. Small cottages crowd around **Rushton's Beach**, just east of Tatamagouche in Brule, but it's worth a visit to look for seals (turn left at the end of the boardwalk and walk toward the end of the beach) and birdlife in the adjoining saltmarsh.

The old railway from Tatamagouche to Oxford (50km) is now part of the **TCT** (p48), a great route to bike.

The gay-friendly **Tatamagouche Centre** (☎ 800-218-2220; www.tatacentre.ca; Loop 6), which is affiliated with the Uniting Church, offers retreats and short courses on everything from organic gardening to yoga (two-day course including lodging $250), plus guided excursions to First Nations powwows.

Sleeping & Eating

Nelson Park Campground (☎ 902-657-2730; http://centralnovascotia.com/members/nelsonparkcamp/; 153 Loop 6; tent/RV sites $18/25; ⚡) Just 1.5km west of Tatamagouche and right on the bay, tent sites 62 to 71 offer privacy near the water. You can walk or cycle to town on the TCT.

Green Dragon Organic Farm & B&B (☎ 902-657-0081; www.greendragon.ca; 3082 Balmoral Rd; r $75) Even the sheets are organic at this environmentally conscious one-room B&B. Mingle with fallow deer and llamas as you experience life on a 100% organic heritage farm.

Train Station Inn (☎ 902-657-3222, 888-724-5233; www.trainstation.ca; 21 Station Rd; d $90-100, caboose $100-170; ▣) Stay in the old stationmaster's residence above the train station or get a whole caboose! The caboose suites are an eight-year-old boy's dream: period train posters, toy trains, books about locomotives and even train motifs on some of the pillowcases. The dreamer behind the inn, Jim LeFresne, grew up across the tracks and saved the train station from demolition when he was just 18. A dining car serves a limited menu of chicken, steak and lobster dinners ($16 to $25) from Thursday to Saturday mid-June to September. Laundry and kitchen facilities are available.

Sugar Moon Farm (☎ 902-657-3348, 866-816-2753; www.sugarmoon.ca; Alex Macdonald Rd, off Hwy 311, Earltown; mains $9-12, prix fixe $60-70; ☯ 9am-5pm Thu-Mon Jul & Aug, 9am-5pm Sat & Sun Sep-Jun) You must stop here if you love maple syrup. The food – simple, delicious pancakes – is the highlight of this working maple farm, but you can also tour the camp and learn all you ever wanted to know about sugaring. For an exquisite culinary treat, take in a 'Chef's Night': one Saturday night each month a different top chef creates a prix fixe meal. Check online for dates or call to reserve.

Shopping

Lismore Sheep Farm (☎ 902-351-2889; 1389 Louisville Rd, off Hwy 6; ☯ 9am-5pm) A working farm with more than 300 sheep, this is a fun destination even if you don't buy a rug, blanket or socks. From May to October, the barn is open (adult/child $1/50¢) for visitors to pat the lambs and learn all about producing wool.

A lively **farmers' market** (end of Creamery Rd, off Main St) with wares from both farmers and artisans happens each Saturday morning all summer in the historic Tatamagouche Creamery.

PICTOU

Pictou (*pik*-toe; population 3875) is one of the brightest lights on the Sunrise Trail, with plenty of places to stay and several festivals. Most activity borders the waterfront, which is unfortunately blighted by a giant smoking mill in the distance. Many people stop through for a side trip or as a stopover via ferry to/from PEI (p118).

The first Scottish immigrants to Nova Scotia landed here in 1773 which allows Pictou to dub itself the 'Birthplace of New Scotland.' Water St, the main street, is lined with interesting shops and beautiful old stone buildings.

Information

Pictou Public Library (☎ 902-485-5021; 40 Water St; ☯ noon-9pm Tue & Thu, to 5pm Wed, 10am-5pm Fri & Sat) Free Internet access.

Pictou Tourist Information Office (☎ 902-485-6151; 40 Water St; ☯ 8:30am-4:30pm Mon-Fri) In the library.

Town of Pictou (www.townofpictou.com) Links to sights and festivals.

VIC (☎ 902-485-6213; Pictou Rotary northwest of town; ☯ 8am-9:30pm Jul & Aug, 9am-7pm May, Jun & Sep–mid-Dec) A large center situated to meet travelers arriving from the PEI ferry.

Sights & Activities

The beautiful Pictou waterfront, with its ample boardwalks and interesting sights, is the result of a revitalization effort that started in 1989. A replica of the ship *Hector* that carried the first 200 Highland Scots to Nova Scotia is tied up for viewing during the summer.

Hector Heritage Quay (☎ 902-485-4371; 33 Caladh Ave; adult/student/senior/family $5/2/4/12; ☯ 9am-5pm Mon-Sat, noon-5pm Sun mid-May–early Oct) captures the experience of the first Scottish settlers through a re-created blacksmith shop, a collection of shipbuilding artifacts and varied displays about the *Hector* and its passengers. There are guided tours at 10am and 2pm.

You can enjoy picnics and swimming at Caribou/Munroe's Island Provincial Park.

In the old train station, the **Northumberland Fisheries Museum** (☎ 902-485-4972; 71 Front St; adult/student/senior/family $4/2/3/9; ☯ 9am-6pm Mon-Sat, noon-6pm Sun, late May-early Oct) explores the area's fishing heritage. Exhibits include strange sea creatures and the spiffy *Silver Bullet*, an early 1930s lobster boat.

A **monument** on the waterfront recognizes the 2nd Construction Battalion, a battalion of Black soldiers that left for Europe from Pictou and Truro during WWI.

Festivals & Events

Pictou Landing First Nation Powwow (☎ 902-752-4912) Across the Pictou Harbour (a 25-minute drive through New Glasgow), this annual powwow held in the first weekend of June features sunrise ceremonies, drumming and craft demonstrations. Camping and food are available on site, which is strictly alcohol- and drug-free.

Lobster Carnival (☎ 902-485-5150; www.townofpictou.com) Begun in 1934 as 'The Carnival of the Fisherfolk,' this four-day event in early July now offers free entertainment, boat races and lots of chances to feast on lobster.

Hector Festival (☎ 902-485-8848; www.decostecentre.ca) Free daily outdoor concerts, Highland dancing and piping competitions and a *Hector* landing re-enactment all take place in mid-August.

Sleeping

BUDGET

Caribou/Munroe's Island Provincial Park (☎ 902-485-6134; http://parks.gov.ns.ca; 2119 Three Brooks Rd; campsites $18) This park is less than 5km from Pictou, set on a gorgeous beach. Sites 1 to 22 abut the day-use area and are less private; 78 to 95 are gravel and suited for RVs. The rest are wooded and private.

Hostel Pictou (☎ 902-485-8740; www.backpackers.ca; 14 Chapel St; dm $20) Reservations are recommended at this cosy, nine-bed backpacker hostel a block from the Pictou waterfront. It's in a funky 1848 heritage home and the owner works at the post office.

Willow House Inn (☎ 902-485-5740; www.willowhouseinn.com; 11 Willow St; r incl breakfast with/without private bathroom $80/65) It's almost hard to find your way through the multidirectional staircases that crisscross this historic home. Rooms are a mix of lovely wooden antiques and 1960s garage sale fodder, but they're comfy and the breakfasts are fantastic.

MIDRANGE

Auberge Walker Inn (☎ 902-485-1433, 800-370-5553; www.walkerinn.com; 34 Coleraine St; r $80-90, ste $150; ☒) The entrance makes it feel like you are visiting your accountant rather than stay at an Inn; the 1865 brick building has, in past, housed business offices as well as the local library. Twin, double and queen rooms are small and hotel-like; there is one suite with 3.6m ceilings and kitchenette. Breakfast is included.

Dolan's Inn & Guesthouse (☎ 902-485-1337; www.dolans.ca; 168 West River Rd; s/d $80/100, ste $130-180) Choose from one of five modern rooms in the potpourri scented inn or take a two- or three- bedroom guesthouse – great value for families. Located slightly above the town, it catches a cool breeze and makes a pleasant stroll into town.

TOP END

Pictou Lodge (☎ 902-485-4322, 888-662-7484; www.maritimeinns.com; 172 Lodge Rd, off Braeshore Rd; r/f/cottages from $120/240/180; ☒ ☒) This atmospheric 1920s resort is on more than 60 hectares of wooded land between Caribou/Munroe's Island Provincial Park and Pictou. Beautifully renovated ocean-side log cabins have original stone fireplaces; motel units are also available. The light-catching glass art in the windows here add real style.

Customs House Inn (☎ 902-485-4546; www.customshouseinn.ca; 38 Depot St; r $95-140; ☒ ☒) There's something reassuring about sleeping in a stone building this thick and solid. A federal building till 1959, the high-ceilinged rooms here still retain an aura of being offices of someone very important. The decor is as sturdy and elegant as the walls. Identical twin brothers run this inn so don't be alarmed if the innkeeper seems to be everywhere at once!

NOVA SCOTIA

Eating & Drinking

Pictou is no culinary mecca – see other options in New Glasgow (below), a worthy side trip for a good meal.

Carver's Coffeehouse & Studio (☎ 902-382-3332; 41 Coleraine St; light meals $3-6; ☻ 8am-9pm Jun-Sep, 8am-6pm Mon-Sat, noon-5pm Sun rest of year) Nestle among the plants and an eclectic umbrella as you enjoy a strong coffee, beer or light meal. The café doubles as a carving studio for chatty Keith Matheson, who did the detail work on the *Hector*. Try the heated ginger raisin cookies and enjoy the company of local artists.

Pressroom Pub & Grill (☎ 902-485-4041; 50 Water St; mains $7-14; ☻ 11am-midnight) The interior of this place get so busy it does seem like a pressroom. It serves salads, sandwiches, wraps or chowder and extends to a big outdoor patio.

Old Stone Pub (☎ 902-485-4546; 38 Depot St; mains $7-20; ☻ lunch & dinner) In the basement of the Customs House Inn, this pub feels like an 18th-century sailors' hang out. Reasonably priced inventive sandwiches, pastas and seafood are found on the beyond-pub food menu.

Entertainment

deCoste Entertainment Centre (☎ 902-485-8848; www.decostecentre.ca; 91 Water St; tickets about $16; ☻ box office 11:30am-5pm Mon-Fri, 1-5pm Sat & Sun) Opposite the waterfront, this impressive performing arts center stages a range of live shows. Experience some top-notch Scottish music during a summer series of ceilidhs (*kay*-lees) at 2pm from Tuesday to Thursday (adult/child $15/7).

Getting There & Away

Northumberland Ferries (☎ 902-566-3838, 888-249-7245; www.peiferry.com; pedestrian/motorcycle/car $13/36/57; ☻ May-Dec) cruises between Caribou, near Pictou, and Wood Islands, PEI, up to nine times daily (five times in the fall and spring). Note that vehicle fees include all passengers for the 1¼-hour trip. The ferry operates on a first-come, first-served basis.

A **water taxi** (☎ 902-396-8855; one-way/return $10/18) runs twice daily to and from New Glasgow in July and August. In Pictou it leaves from beside the Salt Water Café (opposite the *Hector*) at 1:30pm and 6:30pm; in New Glasgow it departs from the Riverfront Marina at noon and 5pm.

NEW GLASGOW

The largest town on the Northumberland Shore, New Glasgow (population 9432) has always been an industrial center but the lovely historic downtown offers more scenery and good restaurants than your average blue-collar town. The first mine opened in neighboring Stellarton in 1807. An underground explosion in 1992 at the Westray Mine in Plymouth killed 26 men.

The few major local attractions are in Stellarton, a 5km drive away.

Sights & Activities

Museum of Industry (☎ 902-755-5425; http://industry.museum.gov.ns.ca; Hwy 104 at exit 24; adult/child 6-16yr/family $7/3/15; ☻ 9am-5pm Mon-Sat, 10am-5pm Sun Jul-Oct, 9am-5pm Mon-Sat, 1-5pm Sun May & Jun, 9am-5pm Mon-Fri Nov-Apr) This is a wonderful place for kids. There's a hands-on water power exhibit and an assembly line to try to keep up with.

Crombie Art Gallery (☎ 902-755-4440; 1780 Abercrombie Rd; admission free; ☻ 9-11am & 1-4pm Wed Jul & Aug, tours on the hr) This private gallery in the personal residence of the founder of the Sobey supermarket chain has an excellent collection of 19th- and early-20th-century Canadian art including works by Cornelius Krieghoff and the Group of Seven. It's near the paper mill between Pictou and New Glasgow.

Eating

Café Italia (☎ 902-928-2233; 62 Provost St; mains $8-13; ☻ 7:30am-10pm Mon-Thu, till midnight Fri, 11:30am-10pm Sat) Locals fill the booths at this small trattoria. Choose from salads, sandwiches, pasta and pizza. Open in the morning for coffee and snacks, but not breakfast. Pizzas are available for takeout.

Bistro (☎ 902-752-4988; 216 Archimedes St; mains $18-27; ☻ dinner Tue-Sat) The only constant on the menu is creativity in spicing and sauces. This little pink and light-blue gem is considered to have the finest food in the region; try the Tuscany mussels or seared salmon with Pernod and tarragon cream. Reservations are recommended.

ANTIGONISH

This is a lively university town with some good restaurants and old-time charm. All the action is on Main St but beautiful beaches and hiking possibilities north of town could easily keep you busy for a couple of days.

Catholic Scots settled Antigonish (an-tee-guh-*nish*) and established St Francis Xavier University. It's known for the Scottish Highland Games held each July since 1861.

Information

Antigonish Public Library (☎ 902-863-4276; 274 Main St; ☺ 10am-9pm Tue & Thu, 10am-5pm Wed, Fri & Sat) Free Internet access. Enter off College St.

Bookends Used Books (☎ 902-863-6922; 342 Main St) Trashy novels and erudite reading.

VIC (☎ 902-863-4921; 56 West St, cnr Hwy 104 & Hwy 7; ☺ 10am-8pm Jul & Aug, 10am-6pm mid-Jun–early Oct) Brochures, local calls and free Internet access. It's in the Antigonish Mall parking lot.

Sights & Activities

The **Heritage Museum** (☎ 902-863-6160; 20 E Main St; admission free; ☺ 10am-5pm Mon-Sat Jul & Aug, 10am-noon & 1-5pm Mon-Fri Sep-Jun) has exhibits on customs and folklore.

A 4km hiking/cycling trail to the nature reserve at **Antigonish Landing** begins just across the train tracks from the museum, then 400m down Adam St. The landing's estuary is a good bird-watching area where you might see eagles, ducks and ospreys.

The attractive campus of 125-year-old **St Francis Xavier University** is behind the Romanesque **St Ninian's Cathedral** (www.antigonishdiocese.com/ninian1.htm; 120 St Ninian St; ☺ 7:30am-8pm). The **Hall of the Clans** is on the 3rd floor of the old wing of the Angus L MacDonald Library, just beyond the St Ninian's Cathedral parking lot. In the hall, crests of all the Scottish clans that settled this area are displayed. Those clans gather each July for the Antigonish Highland Games.

Festivals & Events

Antigonish Highland Games (www.antigonishhighlandgames.com) An extravaganza of dancing, pipe-playing and heavy-lifting events involving hewn logs and iron balls; held in mid-July.

Evolve (www.evolvefestival.com) Five stages of funk, bluegrass, hip-hop and more, plus workshops on everything from puppetry to media literacy; mid-August.

Sleeping & Eating

Whidden's Campground & Trailer Court (☎ 902-863-3736; www.whiddens.com; 11 Hawthorne St; tent/RV sites $27/31, cottages $102, all incl taxes; ☻) This unusual accommodation complex right in town offers campsites and two-bedroom mobile homes for rent.

Antigonish Highland Heart B&B (☎ 902-863-1858, 800-863-1858; www.bbcanada.com/3241.html; 135 Main St; r $75-85) Be welcomed by the smells of fresh baking bread and by the bright smile of Shebby, the friendly owner. This old (c 1854) house is

well located and is made to feel like home with special touches like rag dolls on the beds.

Sunshine on Main Café (☎ 902-863-5851; 332 Main St; mains $8-13; ☺ 7am-9pm Sun-Thu, 7am-9:30pm Fri & Sat) A great place to stop if you're tiring of fried food, this bright café serves healthy breakfasts, lunches and dinners using plenty of organic ingredients. The huge, multi-ethnic menu has something for everyone.

Gabrieau's Bistro (☎ 902-863-1925; 350 Main St; mains lunch $8-13, dinner $20-26; ☺ 7:30am-9:30pm Mon-Sat) Grab a coffee and pastry in the morning or any of a number of imaginative vegetarian dishes, salads, meats and seafood for lunch or dinner. Locals credit Chef Mark Gabrieau for setting the culinary high-water mark in Antigonish.

Getting There & Away

Acadian Lines bus services stop at **Hollywood Video** (☎ 902-863-6900; 44 James St) near Hwy 104 (Trans-Canada Hwy).

CAPE GEORGE

It's too bad this scenic cape is nicknamed the 'mini-Cabot Trail.' If you've been to the real Cabot trail this area will disappoint in comparison, but the beautiful views of this 72km-route loop make it pretty in its own right. Best not to think about the Cabot trail and enjoy! You can easily spend a full day along this stretch of road. From a well-marked picnic area near **Cape George Point Lighthouse**, a 1km walk leads to the lighthouse itself. It's automated and not that big, but there are views to Cape Breton Island and PEI. Signs at the picnic area also point to longer hikes through forests and coastal areas, including one 32km loop. Signs at all the trail junctions indicate how long it will take to follow alternate routes.

You can also start exploring these trails from the wharf at **Ballantyne's Cove**, one of the prettiest communities in Nova Scotia. To walk from the wharf to the lighthouse and back again is 8km. Also visit **Ballantyne's Cove Tuna Interpretive Centre** (☎ 902-863-8162; 57 Ballantyne's Cove Wharf Rd; admission free; ☺ 10am-7:30pm Jul-Sep) for displays on both the fish and the fishery. A fish-and-chips van parks nearby.

Pomquet

About 16km east of Antigonish, this tiny Acadian community (population 1521) is on a stunning **beach** with 13 dunes that keep growing; waves dump the equivalent of more than 4000 truckloads of sand on the beach each year. Many bird species frequent the salt marshes behind the dunes. Comfortable, modern **Sunflower B&B** (☎ 902-386-2492; www.arichat .com/sunflower; 1572 Monk's Head Rd; r $75-90) is right on the water and has engaging Acadian hosts.

CAPE BRETON ISLAND

Bald eagles soar over wooded, rolling hills and sparkling lakes while whales cavort off the rocky coast of Cape Breton Island, Nova Scotia's princess of nature. While not driving the legendary 300km Cabot Trail around Cape Breton Highlands National Park, hiking the myriad trails or venturing out to sight marine mammals in the salty spray of the Atlantic, get lost in the past; Scottish, Acadian and Mi'kmaq all have firm roots here and welcome exploration.

Fans of music and dance will want to spend several days along the Ceilidh Trail taking in square dances in community halls; there are spectacular hikes near Mabou, in the national park and around Cape North; the French Acadian community of Chéticamp is rich in artistry and community spirit; and the region around the Bras D'Or lakes offers opportunities to explore the history and present of the Mi'kmaq First Nation.

The tourist season on Cape Breton Island is short and congested. Most tourists visit in July and August, and many restaurants, accommodations and VICs only open from mid-June to September. **Celtic Colours** (www.celtic-colours .com), a wonderful roving music festival each October that attracts top musicians from Scotland, Spain and other countries with Celtic connections, helps extend the season into the fall, which is a superb time to visit.

PORT HASTINGS

Cape Breton Island ceased to be a true island when the Canso Causeway was built across the Strait of Canso in 1955. Today, Port Hastings is industrial, modern and neither cute nor quaint. If you must stay the night, try **Harbourview Bed & Breakfast** (☎ 902-625-3224; 209 Granville St, Port Hawkesbury; s/d $65/75) in the area of town with the nicest architecture and views of the causeway; there are rooms in the antique-style Victorian home and in motel-style rooms next door.

Cape Breton's best **VIC** (☎ 902-625-4201; 96 Hwy 4; 8:30am-8:30pm Jun-Aug, 8:30am-7pm Sep, 9am-6pm May, 9am-5pm Oct-Dec) is on your right as you drive onto the island. This is definitely worth a stop: there are few other tourist offices on Cape Breton Island and outside of July and August this might be the only one you'll find open. The staff is very well informed and helpful about everything to do with region.

CEILIDH TRAIL

You'd better have your dancing shoes or be prepared for some serious foot tapping along the Ceilidh Trail, Nova Scotia's road of Scottish fiddlers. Take a hard left immediately after leaving the Port Hastings VIC to get on Hwy 19, which snakes along the western coast of the island.

For a great introduction to local culture, visit the **Celtic Music Interpretive Centre** (☎ 902-787-2708; www.celticmusicsite.com; 5473 Hwy 19; flexible schedule tours $4; 9am-5pm Mon-Fri Jun-Aug). Half-hour tours include some fiddle music and a dance step or two. The staff can tell you on which nights nearby communities have square dances – Cape Bretoners are very friendly and will help anyone to find their feet!

Creignish Craft Works B&B (☎ 902-625-5709; www.bbcanada.com/159.html; 2154 Hwy 19, Creignish; s/d $45/60; May-Oct) in a 'recycled school house,' is also the workshop of Sandra Kuzminski. She'll entertain kids with crafts and point you to the best hidden secrets of Cape Breton Island. Rooms are large and comfortable and there are wonderful sunset views over St George's Bay.

MABOU

The beating heart of the Ceilidh Trail looks pretty small and insignificant at first glance. This one-road town begins to sparkle at night, when the fiddlers and pickers come out to make merry. In the day, get off the highway to explore the hiking trails among lush hills and hidden inlets, take a drink at the single malt whisky distillery or just kick back and absorb the crisp, country ambience.

SIGHTS & ACTIVITIES

Mabou is more a place to experience than to see specific sights. Take any turn off Hwy 19 and see where it takes you.

Glenora Inn & Distillery (☎ 902-258-2662, 800-839-0491; www.glenoradistillery.com; Hwy 19, 9km north of Mabou; guided tours incl tasting $5; 9am-5pm mid-

Jun–mid-Oct, tours on the hr) is the only distillery making single malt whiskey in Canada. After the tour and a tonsil-burning taste of the local beverage, enjoy free ceilidhs in the pub (open 1pm to 3pm and 8pm to 10pm); you can eat there or in the dining room (lunch $9 to $12, dinner prix fixe $40; open 8am to 10pm June to October).

SLEEPING & EATING

Clayton Farm B&B (☎ 902-945-2719; fax 902-945-2078; 11247 Hwy 19; s/d $75/85) Creaky wood floors, light florals, throw rugs and country quilts make this one of the most authentic farmhouse experiences you're likely to have – the decor is rustically perfect. This 1835 farmhouse sits on a working red angus ranch and is run by

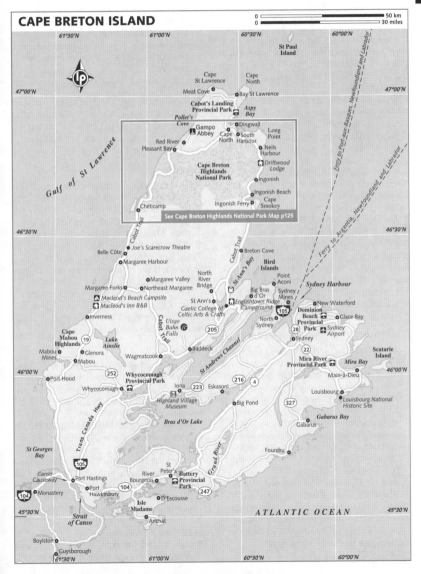

CAPE BRETON ISLAND

NOVA SCOTIA

hard-working Isaac Smith. Paraphernalia of old Cape Breton life and of Isaac's family are casually scattered throughout the common areas and comfortable guest rooms. Isaac likes company and is a treasure trove of history as well as information about the area.

Duncreigan Country Inn (☎ 902-945-2207, 800-840-2207; http://duncreigan.ca; Hwy 19; r $110-195) Nestled in oak trees on the banks of the river, this inn has serene grounds and private, spacious rooms. Some rooms have terraces that open up on the river. Bikes are available to guests and there's a licensed dining room (mains $10 to $23; open 5:30pm to 8:30pm July to October) that serves breakfast to guests (free) or dinner by reservation.

Glenora Inn & Distillery (☎ 902-258-2662, 800-839-0491; www.glenoradistillery.com; Hwy 19, 9km north of Mabou; r $125-150, chalets $175-240) Rooms here are dark, cavelike and perfect for sleeping it off if you've been drinking the rocket fuel sold at the bar. The chalets are a better choice if you want brighter surroundings. Lunch- and dinner-time ceilidhs (mains $9 to $27) are a great accompaniment to gourmet pub food – eat, drink and be merry!

Red Shoe Pub (☎ 902-945-2996; www.redshoepub .com; 11533 Hwy 19; mains $11-17; ☺ 11:30am-midnight Wed 11:30am-2am Thu-Sat, noon-midnight Sun) Gather round a local fiddle player (often from the Rankin family) while enjoying a pint and a superb meal (the Acadian *toutière* pie for $11 is divine). You won't want to leave this window-lit niche, as cosy as a good friend's

---

DETOUR: CAPE MABOU HIGHLANDS

An extensive network of hiking trails between Mabou and Inverness, **Cape Mabou Highlands** extends toward the coast west of Hwy 19. Hikes ranging from 4km to 12km start from three different trailheads. An excellent trail guide ($4) is available at the grocery on Hwy 19 in Mabou and maps are also posted at the trailheads. To reach the Mabou Post Rd trailhead, follow Mabou Harbour Rd 4.5km west from the large white St Mary's Church, then head 7.7km northwest on a gravel road signposted 'Mabou Coal Mines.' This is the start of a spectacular hike (8km to 12km, depending on which return route you choose) along undulating hills and softly grassed dunes – including a dangerous section along high cliffs.

LOCAL VOICES

Mairi (Maddy) Rankin
Musician, age 27, Mabou
What's your favorite secret spot? The Mabou Coal Mines beach and hiking trails. There's a million-dollar view and it's so quiet and away from everything. **If your best friend was coming to visit, where would you go for the weekend?** I'd start in Mabou – there's something going on every night in summer – then we'd stay on Hwy 19 stopping for parties, dances, music and beaches.

---

living room, so go on and indulge in a dessert such as the unforgettable sticky English toffee pudding ($4.50). Don't be afraid to stay on after dinner to get to know some locals and maybe a few travelers too.

INVERNESS

Row upon row of company housing betrays the history of coal mining in Inverness, the first town of any size on the coast. Its history and people are captured evocatively by writer Alistair MacLeod. His books are for sale at the **Bear Paw** (☎ 902-258-2528; Hwy 19), next to the Royal Bank. Proprietor Alice Freeman weaves at a loom at the back of the shop and will happily dispense information to travelers.

Beginning near the fishing harbor there are miles of sandy **beach** with almost comfortable water temperatures in late summer. A **boardwalk** runs 1km along the beach.

SIGHTS

Inverness Miners' Museum (☎ 902-258-3822; 62 Lower Railway St; admission by donation; ☺ 9am-5pm Mon-Fri, noon-5pm Sat & Sun Jul & Aug), in the old train station just back from the beach, presents local history.

Inverness County Centre for the Arts (☎ 902-258-2533; www.invernessarts.ca; 16080 Hwy 19; ☺ 10am-5pm Mon-Wed & Fri, to 7pm Thu, 1-5pm Sat & Sun Jun–mid-Sep, 10am-5pm Mon-Fri rest of year) is a beautiful new establishment with several galleries and an upmarket gift shop featuring work by local and regional artists. It's also a music venue with a floor built for dancing – of course!

SLEEPING & EATING

Macleod's Beach Campsite (☎ 902-258-2433; www .macleods.com; Hwy 19, sites $24-28; ☺ mid-Jun–Oct; 🖳)

This campground has a sweeping pastoral area for RVs and some smaller tent sites nestled in the trees a few hops away from a magnificent white-sand beach. It's about 10km north of Inverness.

Macleods Inn B&B (☎ 902-253-3360; www.macleods.com; Broad Cove Rd, off Hwy 19; r $70-125) Five kilometers north of Inverness, this is a high-end B&B for a not-so-high-end price. Each room is named for a Scottish family and is decorated (in a low-key way) with the accompanying tartan. The house is big and modern but the decoration is in keeping with Cape Breton heritage.

Coal Miner's Café (☎ 902-258-3413; 15818 Central Ave; mains $7-15; ❤ 6am-1am Jun-Oct, 6am-9:30pm rest of year) For eating in town, stop at this bar and café with a great display of old mining photography – the bar wall hangings are devoted to ice hockey.

Casual Gourmet & Bank Head Pub (☎ 902-258-3839; Hwy 19; pub menu $8-13, dinner $15-20; ❤ 7am-9pm Jul & Aug, 11:30am-9pm rest of year) Out of town in the southerly direction, this is a great place to stop for healthy soups, quesadillas, chili and more – at night the dining turns to artfully prepared seafood, meat and vegetarian fare. Like the name says, it's casual and gourmet. Windows wrap around the dining area bringing in sea views and light. Cool little antique trinkets line the window-sills.

MARGAREE VALLEY

Billowing hills and flowing rivers tempt you to veer away from the ocean and into a series of river valleys known for trout and salmon fishing as well as for horseback riding. The region is a confusing collection of towns all called Margaree this or that and centers on Margaree Forks, the intersection of Hwy 19 and the Cabot Trail.

The tiny **VIC** (☎ 902-248-2803; Margaree Forks; ❤ 9am-5pm Mon-Sat Jun-Aug) has extremely helpful staff, who can help with fishing arrangements. Right at the same junction, **Margaree Forks Public Library** (Margaree Forks; ❤ 9:30am-3pm Mon-Fri Jun-Aug) has free Internet.

If you're serious about fishing, consider staying at the wonderfully remote **Big Intervale Fishing Lodge & Cabins** (☎ 902-248-2275; www.margaree.capebretonisland.com/fishinglodge; 3719 Big Intervale Rd; cabin $85). You can go to the rustic lodge just to relax in the mesmerizing outback setting and take a full package including all meals and a fishing guide – check the website for the flexible options. The lodge is open year-round.

CHÉTICAMP

A center of Acadian culture, Chéticamp (population 3000) owes its cultural preservation to its isolation; the road didn't make it this far until 1949. It's a gateway to Cape Breton Highlands National Park, and has some top-notch museums and live music opportunities. The 1893 Church of St Pierre dominates the town with its silver spire and colorful frescoes but the rest of this seaside town is modern and drab.

Chéticamp is known for its arts, particularly hooked rugs, and as a pioneer of the co-operative movement. In 1917 Local fishermen organized themselves into a co-op in order to secure better prices and more independence. It disbanded recently, a victim of the decline of the fishery. But there is still a Credit Union, a Co-op grocery store, and a Co-op Artisanale.

Information

A **tourist information kiosk** (☎ 902-224-3349; ❤ 8am-10pm Jul & Aug, 9am-5pm Mon-Fri Sep & Oct) is adjacent to a sizable parking lot and the waterfront boardwalk, directly across from the liquor store and post office.

Visitor information and Internet access ($2 per hour) are available at Les Trois Pignons museum (below).

Sights & Activities

Les Trois Pignons (☎ 902-224-2642; www.lestroispignons.com; 15584 Cabot Trail Hwy; adult/family $3.50/9; ❤ 8am-7pm Jul & Aug, 9am-5pm May-Jun & Sep–mid-Oct) is an excellent museum – if you aren't familiar with the art of rug-hooking you really should stop by for the fantastic historical displays plus a short rug-hooking demonstration. Artifacts, including hooked rugs, illustrate early life and artisanship in Chéticamp. Almost everything artfully displayed here – from bottles to teacups to rugs – was collected by one eccentric local resident.

La Pirogue Fisheries Museum (☎ 902-224-3349; 15359 Cabot Trail Rd; admission $5; ❤ 9am-7pm May-Oct) tells the story of the local fish industry. The building that houses both this museum and the community development association incorporates green technologies such as solar windows and geothermal heat pumps. In the basement, you can learn how to build a lobster trap or hook a rag rug.

Joe's Scarecrow Theatre (☎ 902-235-2108; 11842 Cabot Trail; admission free; ❤ 8:30am-9pm mid-Jun–early Oct), about 25km south of Chéticamp next to Ethel's Takeout restaurant, is a quasi-macabre outdoor collection of life-sized figures that looks like supernumerary, half-dead Village People. Several other folk-art shops are along the highway between here and Chéticamp.

Whale Cruises (☎ 902-224-3376, 800-813-3376; www .whalecruises.com; Government Wharf; adult/child $29/12) Several operators sell tours from the Government Wharf, across and down from the church. Captain Cal is the most experienced and offers three-hour expeditions up to four times daily. It's wise to reserve your trip a day in advance in midsummer.

Sleeping

Accommodations are tight throughout July and August. It's advisable to call ahead or arrive early in the afternoon. If you're camping, better options are available at the national park campgrounds (right).

Chéticamp Outfitters Inn B&B (☎ 902-224-2776; www.cheticampns.com/cheticampoutfitters; 13938 Cabot Trail Rd; s $55, d $65-95, bungalow $110) Just far enough from town to be relaxing (about 2km) yet close enough to the action, this sunny place offers a range of well-priced choices in true Acadian style. Views stretch from the sea to the mountain, wildflowers burst from every corner of the garden and you might even see a passing moose. Very full breakfasts are served in the panoramic dining area by energetic hosts.

Lawrence Guest House B&B (☎ 902-224-2184; 15408 Cabot Trail; s/d $80/92) This gay-friendly, heritage B&B faces the waterfront and is within walking distance of most attractions. Although simply furnished, there's an authentic antique feel; a full breakfast is served at a large dining table.

Bay Wind Suites (☎ 902-224-2233; www.baywind suites.com; 15299 Main St; ste $190-240) By far the poshest place in town, these romantic, chic suites are worth the splurge. Perched right on a seaside boardwalk, each immaculate unit has a unique theme and is decorated in muted colors and sunlight off the bay. Breakfast is served in your own suite.

Eating

Co-op Artisanale Restaurant (☎ 902-224-2170; 15067 Main St; mains $7-12; ⏰ 9am-9pm) Get your Acadian dishes here. Stewed chicken dinner and *pâté à la viande* (meat pie) are the local specialties. Delicious potato pancakes ($6) with apple sauce, molasses or sour cream are the only vegetarian option. The mark-up on local Jost

wine – sold for $18 per liter – might be the lowest anywhere in Nova Scotia.

All Aboard (☎ 902-224-2288; south entrance, Chéticamp; mains $10; ⏰ 11am-midnight) This excellent local's favorite serves seafood and more at very reasonable prices. It has a fresh, nautical ambience and some creative extras on the menu such as a maple vinaigrette for the salads. There's a kid's and senior's menu as well as sinful desserts.

Harbour Restaurant & Bar (☎ 902-224-2233; 15299 Main St; mains $12-29; ⏰ 8am-10pm) With casual dining over the boardwalk, the menu here is upscale and creative but the prices are very affordable. The wine list is one of the best you'll find in the region and some nights there is live music, wine tastings or other activities. It's located in the same building as Bay Wind Suites (left) and has the same owner.

CAPE BRETON HIGHLANDS NATIONAL PARK

Woodland, tundra, bog and a winding road with a million-dollar view make up Cape Breton Highlands National Park, one of Canada's most dramatic parks. The famous **Cabot Trail** is one of your best bets in the province for spotting moose (or dodging them on the road – look out!) and nesting bald eagles. The drive is at its best along the northwestern shore and then down to Pleasant Bay. Use a low gear to save your brakes – and lessen air pollution – when descending mountains.

Of course it's even better if you can explore on foot, hiking through a tapestry of terrain to reach what feel like forgotten vistas looking out over an endless, icy ocean.

Information

There are two park entrances; one at Chéticamp and one at Ingonish. Purchase an **entry permit** (adult/child under 17yr/up to 7 people in a vehicle $5/2.50/12.50) at either park entrance. A one-day pass is good until noon the next day.

Chéticamp Information Centre (☎ 902-224-2306; www.parkscanada.gc.ca; 16646 Cabot Trail; ⏰ 8am-8pm Jul & Aug, 9am-5pm mid-May–Jun, Sep & Oct) Has displays and a relief map of the park, plus a bookstore. Ask the staff for advice on hiking or camping. It's usually staffed from 8am to 4pm, Monday to Friday, in winter.

Ingonish Information Centre (☎ 902-285-2535; 37677 Cabot Trail; ⏰ 8am-8pm Jul & Aug, 9am-5pm mid-May–Jun, Sep & Oct) On the eastern edge of the park, this center is much smaller than the one at Chéticamp and has no bookstore. Wheelchair-accessible trails are indicated on the free park map available at either entrance.

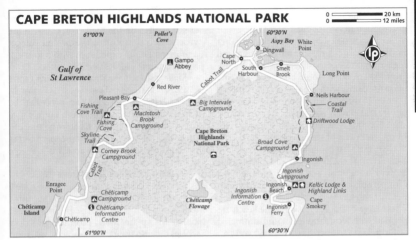

Activities

HIKING

There are more than 25 trails ranging from easy 20-minute strolls to challenging adventures up the mountainside. Two trails on the west coast of the park have spectacular ocean views. **Fishing Cove Trail** gently descends 330m over 8km to the mouth of rugged Fishing Cove River. You can opt for a steeper and shorter hike – 2.8km – from a second trailhead about 5km north of the first. Double the distances if you plan to return the same day. Otherwise, you must preregister for one of eight backcountry sites ($20) at the Chéticamp Information Centre. Reviews of trails in and near the park are available at www.cabottrail.com. Most other trails are shorter and close to the road, many leading to ridge tops for impressive views of the coast. The best of these is **Skyline Trail**, a 7km loop that puts you on the edge of a headland cliff right above the water. The trailhead is about 5.5km north of Corney Brook Campground.

Just south of Neils Harbour (p128), on the eastern coast of the park, the **Coastal Trail** runs 11km round-trip and covers a more gentle but still lovely coastline.

CYCLING

Don't make this your inaugural cycling trip! Although popular for touring, the riding is tough and there are no shoulders in many sections. You must be comfortable sharing the incredible scenery with plenty of RVs. Alternatively you can mountain bike on four inland trails in the park. Only **Branch Pond Lookoff Trail** offers ocean views.

Sea Spray Outdoor Adventures (☎ 902-383-2732; www.cabot-trail-outdoors.com; 1141 White Point Rd, Smelt Brook; half-/full day $25/35; ☺ 9am-5pm Jun–mid-Oct) in Smelt Brook near Dingwall rents bikes and will do emergency repairs on the road. It also offers help planning trips and leads organized cycling, kayaking and hiking tours.

CROSS-COUNTRY SKIING

Best in March and April; there are groomed ski trails (day pass for adult/family $5/10) and possibilities for off-trail skiing. If you stay overnight there's a $10 fee for tenting. Two shelters at Black Brook, south of Neils Harbour, rent for $20 and $30.

Sleeping

Towns around the park offer a variety of accommodations. The park has six drive-in **campgrounds** (backcountry/tent/RV sites $20/21/27) with discounts after three days. Most sites are first-come, first-served, but wheelchair-accessible sites, group campsites and backcountry sites can be reserved for $5. In the smaller campgrounds further from the park entrances, just pick a site and self-register. To camp at any of the three larger ones near the park entrances, register at the closest information center.

The 162-site Chéticamp Campground is behind the information center. Wheelchair-accessible sites are available. When the main campground is full, an overflow area is opened. There are no 'radio free' areas, so peace and quiet is not guaranteed.

Corney Brook (20 sites), 10km further north, is a particularly stunning campground high over the ocean. There's a small playground here, but it would be a nerve-racking place to camp with small kids. MacIntosh Brook (10 sites) is an open field 3km east of Pleasant Bay. It has wheelchair-accessible sites. Big Intervale (10 sites) is near a river 11km southwest of Cape North.

Near the eastern park entrance, you have a choice of the 256-site Broad Cove Campground at Ingonish and the 90-site Ingonish Campground, near Keltic Lodge at Ingonish Beach. Both have wheelchair-accessible sites. These large campgrounds near the beach are popular with local families in midsummer.

From late October to early May, you can camp at the Chéticamp and Ingonish campgrounds for $15, including firewood. In truly inclement weather, tenters can take refuge in cooking shelters with woodstoves. Bring your own food.

Keltic Lodge, a theatrical Tudor-style resort erected in 1940, shares Middle Head Peninsula with **Highlands Links golf course** (☎ 902-285-2600, 800-441-1118; www.highlandslinksgolf.com; round $83), reputed to be one of the best in the world, and the Ingonish Campground. The lodge is worth visiting for its setting and the hiking trail to the tip of the peninsula just beyond the resort. You must have a valid entry permit (see p124) to the national park to go here.

PLEASANT BAY

Pleasant Bay is aptly named: a carved-out bit of civilization hemmed in on all sides by the park and wilderness. It's an active fishing harbor known for its whale-watch tours and Tibetan monastery. If you are in the area on Canada Day (July 1), try to be in the stands for the annual monks versus townpeople baseball game.

Sights & Activities

Gampo Abbey (☎ 902-224-2752; www.gampoabbey.org; 🕑 tours 1:30-3:30pm Mon-Fri Jun 15-Sep 15), 8km north of Pleasant Bay past the village of Red River, is a monastery for followers of Tibetan Buddhism. Students come from all across Canada and the USA for extended meditation programs in this beautiful place in the middle of nowhere. Ane Pema Chödrön is the founding director of the abbey and a noted Buddhist

author, but you aren't likely to see her here as she is often on the road. You can visit the grounds any time during the day but you get a more authentic experience with a tour – a friendly monk escorts you.

Make a stop at the **Whale Interpretive Centre** (☎ 902-224-1411; www.whalecentre.ca; 104 Harbour Rd; adult/family $4.50/14; 🕑 9am-5pm Jun–mid-Oct) at the wharf – it's a tiny little museum but it's nice to get a little biology lesson before getting out to see the real thing. Park entrance permits are for sale here, and Internet access is available at the C@P site downstairs.

Captain Mark's Whale & Seal Cruise (☎ 902-224-1316, 888-754-5112; www.whaleandsealcruise.com; adult/child under 16yr $25/12; 🕑 mid-May–Sep) has three tours daily in the spring, five in the summer and fall. Captain Mark promises not only whales but also time to see seabirds, seals and Gampo Abbey. There's a discount of 25% if you reserve a spot on the earliest (9:30am) or latest (5pm) tour. Tours leave from the wharf next to the Whale Interpretive Centre.

Cabot Trail Whale Watching (☎ 902-224-1976, 877-224-1976; adult/child $44/22; 🕑 May–mid-Oct) uses a Zodiac that gets you lower to the water and thus closer to the whales. It's a much more adventurous approach. It offers a 20% discount if you book the 9am or 6pm tour or if you are staying at Cabot Trail Hostel (see below).

The popular, challenging 20km-return hiking trail to **Pollett's Cove** begins at the end of the road to Gampo Abbey. There are great views along the way and perfect spots to camp when you arrive at the abandoned fishing community. This is not a Parks Canada trail, so it can be rough underfoot.

Sleeping & Eating

Cabot Trail Hostel (☎ 902-224-1976; www.cabottrail.com /hostel; 23349 Cabot Trail; dm $20-24, r $55; 🖳) Bright and basic, this very friendly 18-bed hostel is a good base for exploring Cape Breton Highlands National Park and the beautiful area north of it. There's a common kitchen and barbecue area. The office for Cabot Trail Whale Watching (see left) is here.

Midtrail Motel & Inn (☎ 902-224-2529; www.midtrail .com; 23475 Cabot Trail; motel r $100-120, inn r $175-200) This bubblegum pink complex sits majestically above the Bay of St Lawrence – all rooms have a view of either the bay or the mountains. Motel rooms have lots of light but are standard style while the inn has some finer rooms with hardwood floors and glass detail.

There's a family-style **restaurant** (breakfast, lunch & dinner) on site.

Andrea's Family Restaurant (902-224-2588; cnr Harbour Rd & Cabot Trail; mains $5-7; 11am-6pm May-Oct) Opposite the turnoff to Harbour Rd, this roadside takeout has a covered deck and a surprisingly broad menu. Shop for 'new to you' clothing while you wait for your food.

BAY ST LAWRENCE

Bay St Lawrence is a picturesque little fishing village tucked against the rocky bluffs of Cape North, the very north edge of Cape Breton Island.

Captain Cox (902-383-2981, 888-346-5556; Bay St Lawrence Wharf; adult/child $25/12) has been taking people to see whales aboard the 107.5m *Northern Gannet* since 1986. He leads his professional and fun trips at 10:30am, 1:30pm and 4:30pm in July and August. Call for spring and fall schedules.

Jumping Mouse Campground (902-383-2914; 3360 Bay St Lawrence Rd; campsites $18, cabins for up to 4 people $30; Jun-Sep;) is an eco-friendly campground with just 10 spacious oceanfront sites (no cars allowed). Reservations are accepted for multinight stays and for a beautifully built four-bunk cabin. There's a great common area for meeting other travelers as well as an organized recycling center. The best part: it's nearly bug-free.

South of Bay St Lawrence on protected and warm Aspy Bay, **Four Mile Beach Inn** (902-383-2282, 888-503-5551; www.fourmilebeachinn.com; 1530 Bay St Lawrence Rd; r $120, with kitchen $140) is awash in history and character. The building was a general store for decades and is still full of strange flotsam and jetsam. Three units have kitchen facilities and there are views of Aspy Bay and mountains. Kayaks, canoes and bicycles are available free for guests.

To enjoy Aspy Bay and its spectacular beach just for an afternoon, stop at nearby **Cabot's Landing Provincial Park**.

MEAT COVE

The northernmost road in Nova Scotia finishes at sublimely beautiful Meat Cove, 13km northwest of Bay St Lawrence (the last 7km of the road is gravel). Besides being a place to watch frolicking whales in unbelievably clear water, keep an eye on the earth for orchids – some rare species aren't found anywhere else in Nova Scotia. **Meat Cove Welcome Center** (902-383-2284; 2296 Meat Cove Rd; Internet per hr $2;

9am-7pm Jun-Oct) has iffy opening hours but when it's open you can get information on hiking trails. Leave your car here if there's no room at the trailhead.

From Meat Cove, a 16km **hiking trail** continues northwest to Cape St Lawrence lighthouse and Lowland Cove, an ideal spot for camping. Spend an hour gazing over the ocean, and you're guaranteed to see pods of pilot whales. They frolic here all spring, summer, and into the fall. Carry a compass and refrain from exploring side paths; locals have gotten lost in this area.

Meat Cove Campground (902-383-2379/2658; 2475 Meat Cove Rd; campsites $18; Jun-Oct) is spectacular, perched on a grassy bluff high above the ocean out in the middle of nowhere – single women travelers might feel uncomfortable here alone. There's room for small trailers, but no electricity. Bring some loose change with you: the showers are coin-operated ($1 for 12 minutes) and firewood is $3 for nine pieces. Be prepared for high winds since there are no sheltered sites.

Meat Cove Lodge (902-383-2672; 2305 Meat Cove Rd; d/f $40/50; Jun–mid-Sep) has three rooms in a rustic home at the entrance to Meat Cove, opposite the welcome center. A light breakfast is served.

CAPE NORTH TO SOUTH HARBOUR

Only a few stray houses dot the lonely road between these two wee towns. Skirting the northern perimeter of the national park this forested area juts out into the sea at Aspy Bay. Despite the isolation, there are a few wonderful places to stay as well as a good roadside eating stop.

Sleeping & Eating

Hideaway Campground & Oyster Market (902-383-2116; www.campingcapebreton.com; 401 Shore Rd, South Harbour; sites/cabins $18/40) A gem of a campground with wooded winding trails and an open vista plateau with plenty of tent space. There are a few rustic cabins (with no bedding) and you can get fresh oysters at the little on-site grocery store.

Oakwood Manor B&B (902-383-2317; www.cape bretonisland.com/oakwood; r $60-85; May-Nov) This heritage oak farmhouse lies amid an 80-hectare farm of gentle valley. Picture-perfect barns and farm buildings add to the charm. To get to the B&B, take the Bay St Lawrence road north from Cape North village then turn left at the Oakwood Manor sign down a 1.2km-long gravel road.

Morrison's (☎ 902-383-2051; Cabot Trail, Cape North; mains lunch $6-11, dinner $10-18; ☒ 8am-9pm May-Oct) Part museum, part roadhouse, part restaurant, this is the most fun place to stop for a meal on this stretch. Old logging saws, antlers, fishnets, bottles and other heritage paraphernalia make the ambience, while thick sliced homemade bread and fresh local homemade ingredients make up wonderful seafood dishes and light lunches.

NEILS HARBOUR

On your way south to Ingonish, leave the Cabot Trail to follow the rugged, windswept White Point Rd via Smelt Brook to the fishing villages of White Point and Neils Harbour. These are real gritty, working-people towns and, even though there is some nice architecture and colorful homes, this road feels distinctly off-the-beaten tourist track. You'll pass a number of gorgeous **beaches**.

Chowder House (☎ 902-336-2463; meals $5-10; ☒ 11am-9pm Jul & Aug, 11am-6pm mid-Jun–late Jun & Sep), next to the lighthouse in Neils Harbour, serves the most authentic home-cooked clam or seafood chowder you'll ever sample for under $4.

INGONISH

At the eastern entrance to the national park are Ingonish and Ingonish Beach, small towns lost in the background of motels and cottages. This is a long-standing popular destination, but there are few real attractions other than the park entry, and the beach. There are several hiking trails nearby in the national park (see p124).

The beach at **Ingonish Beach** is lovely, a long, wide strip of sand tucked in a bay surrounded by green hills.

Sleeping & Eating

Driftwood Lodge (☎ 902-285-2558; www3.ns.sympatico .ca/driftwood.lodge; 36125 Cabot Trail, Ingonish; r $30-60, ste with kitchen $60-90) A ramshackle seaside establishment, 8km north of the Ingonish park entrance, this lodge sits on a half-hectare property along a fine-sand beach. It's run by a great mother-and-daughter team.

Muddy Rudder (☎ 902-285-2280; 38438 Cabot Trail, Ingonish Ferry; mains $5-21; ☒ 11am-8pm Jun-Sep) Order a fresh crustacean at the window then watch as it's tossed in a pot of boiling water – five to 10 minutes later it's served to you still steaming. The setting is a step up from a picnic but the food is five-star.

ST ANN'S LOOP

Serene winding roads pass lakes with eagles soaring overhead; artists workshops dot the trail like Easter eggs waiting to be discovered. Although you could skip the drive around St Ann's Bay and take a $5 ferry to Englishtown, you'd be missing a leg of the Cabot Trail that is distinctly satisfying to the senses. If you explore deeper you'll discover walking trails to waterfalls and scenic vistas, Mi'kmaw culture and a decidedly interesting mishmash of characters.

Gaelic College of Celtic Arts & Crafts (☎ 902-295-3411; www.gaeliccollege.edu; 51779 Cabot Trail; 5-day course incl lodging $680-715; ☒ 9am-5pm Jun–mid-Oct), at the end of St Ann's Bay, teaches Scottish Gaelic, bagpipe playing, Highland dancing, weaving and more. The **Great Hall of the Clans Museum** (admission $3) traces Celtic history from ancient

---

DETOUR: DINGWALL

Turn off the Cabot trail to the quaint fishing village of **Dingwall** on the shores of Aspy Bay. Interesting diving for experienced divers can be had off nearby St Paul Island, which has a number of shipwrecks. Check in with **St Paul Island Trading Company** (☎ 902-383-3483; www.saintpaul .ca; 599 Main St) who can organize professional dives and who also operate an appointment-only museum of treasures taken from the wrecks. Contact them for details.

Dingwall also has a popular resort, **Markland Coastal Resort** (☎ 902-383-2264, 800-872-6084; www.marklandresort.com; Cabot Trail at Dingwall; r $140, chalet $230-290; ▯ ⟨⟩). There's a nearly 360-degree view from this minipeninsula lined with fine white sand. Rustic cabins and log rooms are large but pricey – you are paying for the scenery here. The best 'chalets' are, for some reason, the ones with an inferior view. Chamber music (Sunday 4:30pm) and Ceilidhs (Friday 8pm) are performed in the atmospheric Octagon Arts Centre and exquisite dining is available in the resort **dining room** (mains lunch $8-20, dinner $14-36; ☒ breakfast, lunch & dinner).

times to the Highland clearances. Don't leave the area without stopping in at an **artist's workshop** or two; you'll find pottery, leather and pewter workers, painters and more. The artists are easy to find, just keep an eye out for the signs along the main road.

Sleeping & Eating

Englishtown Ridge Campground (☎ 902-929-2598; 866-929-2598; www.englishtown-ridge.com; Hwy 312; serviced/unserviced sites $17/24; ⬛ ⬥) 'Stunning' is one way to describe the site of this campground on a ridge overlooking an ocean inlet. Although open sites have the better view, you might want a wooded site if it's windy. Make sure you have change for the pay showers.

J Kerr's B&B (☎ 902-929-2114; 43627 Cabot Trail, Breton Cove; no prices; ⊙ May-Nov 15) For 26 years Joan Kerr has offered her home to travelers for whatever the traveler decides to pay – and so far she's not discouraged. Rainbow paintings grace the walls, little dog Rocky gets you to toss a ball for him and Joan cooks up a mighty fine breakfast in the morning – any place this friendly and homey is worth quite a bit don't you think?

Chanterelle Country Inn & Cottages (☎ 902-929-2263, 866-277-0577; www.chantrelleinn.com; 48678 Cabot Trail, North River; r $135-225; ⊙ May-Nov; ⬛ ⬥) The Chanterelle is unparalleled as an environmentally friendly place to stay – even the soaps are chemical- and scent-free. The house is in an idyllic setting on 60 hectares atop a hill overlooking rolling pastures and bucolic bliss. The inn and cottages are open, inviting, and well laid out to ensure comfort and privacy. Meals (breakfast and dinner) are served on the screened-in porch, which spans the length of the house and is open to the main dining room and living room. Search for blown-up umbrella-shaped, lemon-yellow chanterelle mushrooms along the forest trails – even if you don't find any, some may turn up on your dinner plate. If you're not staying here, you can reserve for dinner at the highly reputed restaurant (mains $20 to $28, prix-fixe four courses veg/nonveg $32/40; open 6pm to 8pm May to November).

Clucking Hen Deli & Bakery (☎ 902-929-2501; 45073 Cabot Trail; mains $4-14; ⊙ 7am-7pm Jul-Sep, 7am-6pm May, Jun & Oct) A sign reads 'no fowl moods in here.' Listen to the local 'hens' cluck away while you eat a delicious meal of homemade breads, soup and salad. They like to hear a chirp or even a cock-a-doodle-doo from guests too,

so throw in a squawk and get the scoop on local gossip.

NORTH SYDNEY

North Sydney (population 7260) itself is a nondescript service town, though many travelers pass through here by way of the ferry to/from Newfoundland. Although there are good sleeping options, you'll have a hard time finding anything beyond fried seafood and burgers in restaurants.

Reserve accommodations if you're coming in on a late ferry or going out on an early one. Most North Sydney motels and B&Bs are open year-round and it's understood that guests will arrive and leave at all hours.

Four rooms share two bathrooms in **Alexandra Shebib's B&B** (☎ 902-794-4876; www.bbcanada.com/9938.html; 88 Queen St; s/d $45/70), which is a convenient, old-fashioned place good for backpackers who want to walk or take an inexpensive taxi ride to the ferry.

For something a little more elegant in the same area, **Heritage Home B&B** (☎ 902-794-4815, 866-601-9123; www.capebretonisland.com/northside/heritagehome; 110 Queen St; s/d $50/65-80) is in a lovely Victorian home. All rooms overlook the garden or harbor.

Take a sharp right after you descend the ferry ramp and 10 minutes later you'll be at the fabulously frilly **Gowrie House B&B** (☎ 902-544-1050, 800-372-1115; www.gowriehouse.com; 840 Shore Rd, Sydney Mines; s/d/ste $135/145/175; ⊙ Apr-Dec) with its extensive gardens. Off-season discounts of up to 40% are available. Reservations are required for the inn's sumptuous evening feasts (prix fixe $45).

For information about the **Marine Atlantic ferry** (☎ 800-341-7981; www.marine-atlantic.ca) refer to p233 and p255.

Acadian Lines buses to Halifax ($62, seven hours) and points in between can be picked up at the Best Western North Star Hotel opposite the Marine Atlantic ferry terminal. **Transit Cape Breton** (☎ 902-539-8124; adult/child 5-12yr $3.25/$3) runs bus 5 back and forth between North Sydney's Commercial St and Sydney at 8:40am, 12:40pm, 2:40pm and 5:40pm Monday to Saturday.

Around North Sydney

A 15km-drive northwest of North Sydney, **Bird Island Boat Tours** (☎ 902-674-2384, 800-661-6680; www.birdisland.net; 1672 Big Bras d'Or Rd; adult/child under 13yr $33/15) ventures out to the cliff-edged islands

NOVA SCOTIA

of Hertford and Ciboux beyond St Ann's Bay (part of Bird Islands). Depending on which month you take the tour, you'll see colonies of razorbills, kittiwakes, puffins (mid-May to mid-August) or terns.

SYDNEY

The second-biggest city in Nova Scotia and the only real city on Cape Breton Island, Sydney (population 26,083) is the embattled core of the island's collapsed industrial belt. The now-closed steel mill and coal mines were the region's largest employers. Nowadays, the city is a melting pot of Poles, Italians, Africans, Mi'kmaq and more, as well as your standard Scots. The only sizable airport in Cape Breton is here as well as a university and a hopping music scene.

Orientation

Downtown, Charlotte St is lined with stores and restaurants and there's a pleasant boardwalk along Esplanade, while the North End historic district has a gritty charm.

Information

CB Island (www.cbisland.com) Has a virtual tour, trip planner etc.

McConnell Memorial Library (☎ 902-562-3279; cnr Falmouth & Charlotte Sts; ☼ 10am-9pm Tue-Fri, to 5:30pm Sat) Free Internet access.

VIC Sydney River (☎ 902-563-4636; 20 Keltic Dr; ☼ 8:30am-4:30pm Mon-Fri); Waterfront (☎ 902-539-9876; 74 Esplanade; ☼ 9am-7pm Jul & Aug, 9am-5pm Jun & Sep-late Oct)

Sights

There are eight buildings older than 1802 in a two-block radius in North End Sydney. Three are open to the public, including **St Patrick's Church Museum** (☎ 902-562-8237; 87 Esplanade; admis-

sion free; ☼ 9am-5pm Jun-Aug), in the oldest Catholic church on Cape Breton Island. Among artifacts housed here is a not-so-merciful whipping post from the mid-19th century.

The 1787 **Cossit House** (☎ 902-539-7973; http://cossit.museum.gov.ns.ca; 75 Charlotte St; adult/concession $2/1; ☼ 9am-5pm Mon-Sat, 1-5pm Sun Jun–mid-Oct) is the oldest house in Sydney. Just down the road, **Jost Heritage House** (☎ 902-539-0366; 54 Charlotte St; admission free; ☼ 9am-5pm Mon-Sat, 1-5:30pm Sun Jun–mid-Oct) features a collection of model ships as well as an assortment of medicines used by an early-20th-century apothecary.

Cape Breton Centre for Heritage & Science (☎ 902-539-1572; 225 George St; admission free; ☼ 9am-5pm Mon-Sat Jun-Aug, 10am-4pm Tue-Fri Sep-May) explores the social and natural history of Cape Breton Island. Upstairs the **Nova Scotia Centre for Craft & Design** (☎ 902-539-7491; ☼ 9am-4:30pm Mon-Thu, to 4pm Fri) showcases work by local craftspeople.

Sleeping & Eating

Most establishments in Sydney are open year-round.

Gathering House B&B (☎ 902-539-7172, 866-539-7172; www.gatheringhouse.com; 148 Crescent St; s/d $50/65) This welcoming, ramshackle Victorian home is close to the heart of town. The retired hosts like to talk about folklore and pet therapy. Children are welcome.

Paul's Hotel (☎ 902/866-562-5747; www3.ns.sympatico.ca/candb.landry; cnr Pitt St & Esplanade; s/d/tw $60/65/70) This grand old hotel is run by a grand old dame in her '80s. It's one of the oldest hotels in Nova Scotia and has been in the same family for three generations. The price is right for the waterfront location and private bathrooms. Breakfast is served buffet style.

Paradise Found B&B (☎ 902-539-9377, 877-539-9377; www3.ns.sympatico.ca/paradisefound; 62 Milton St;

SYDNEY TAR PONDS

North America's largest toxic waste site lies just three blocks east of the Charlotte St museums, at the end of Ferry St. Since its founding in 1901, the Sydney steel mill has produced some 700,000 tons of toxic sludge, the by-product of burning dirty coal to produce coke for use in the steel plant. The 51-hectare coke-oven site is now a field of rubble contaminated to depths of 25m.

The immense scale and extreme toxicity of the site have thwarted several clean-up attempts. Finally, in 2004, the Canadian and Nova Scotian governments put forward $400 million to finance over 10 years of clean-up. Local residents who put up with an incredible stench of tar in hot weather and suffer from elevated cancer rates (not proven to be linked to the waste site) are happy but still a little skeptical about the progress. Check out the clean-up progress as shown by the 'Tar-O-Meter' at www.tarpondscleanup.ca.

r $95-110) Knowledgeable and hospitable hosts take a lot of pride in this elegant B&B. They'll join you for a several-course breakfast and help plan your travels. The rooms are extra comfortable.

Joe's Warehouse Food Emporium (☎ 902-539-6686; 424 Charlotte St; mains lunch $7-10, dinner $14-25; ⏰ 11:30am-11pm Mon-Sat, 4-11pm Sun Jul & Aug, 11:30am-10pm Mon-Sat, 4-10pm Sun rest of year) This popular restaurant in a converted tire warehouse has a cosy bar, a posh dining room and a casual family restaurant. Beef is the specialty here.

Entertainment

A lot of touring bands make the trek to Sydney. Fiddlers and other traditional musicians from the west coast of the island also perform here or at the Savoy in Glace Bay (below). Gigs are about $5.

Upstairs at French Club (☎ 902-371-0329; 44 Ferry St) This groovy little North End club features rock, Celtic, jazz and movie nights.

Chandler's (☎ 902-539-3438; 76 Dorchester St) This standard, cavernous bar has top-end local and Canadian talent on stage.

Getting There & Away

The Sydney airport is none too busy. A $10 airport improvement fee must be paid at a separate counter by all departing passengers. **Air Canada Jazz** (☎ 902-873-5000; www.flyjazz.ca) flies between Sydney and Halifax ($375 to $800, 45 minutes, four times daily). **Air St-Pierre** (☎ 902-562-3140, 877-277-7765; www.airsaintpierre.com) flies to Sydney ($300, two hours) from early July to early September, on Thursdays and Sundays.

The Acadian Lines bus depot is at 99 Terminal Dr. There are also a number of shuttle services to Halifax.

GLACE BAY

Glace Bay, 6km north of Sydney, would be just another fading coal town were it not for its exceptional **Cape Breton Miners' Museum** (☎ 902-849-4522; www.minersmuseum.com; 42 Birkley St; tour & mine visit adult/child $10/5; ⏰ 10am-6pm Wed-Mon, 10am-7pm Tue Jun-Aug, 9am-4pm Mon-Fri Sep-May); it's off South St less than 2km east from the town center. The highlight of this museum, and this whole region, is the guided adventure under the seafloor to visit closed-down mines. Retired miners, chock-full of old mining tales and character, lead you through the damp shafts – be prepared to be hunched over (the mines aren't very tall) and chilly for about an hour.

There are also exhibits on the lives of early-20th-century miners and their families. The museum's **restaurant** (mains $8-14; ⏰ noon-8pm) is highly recommended and offers a good selection of seafood, sandwiches and burgers; there's a daily lunch buffet from noon to 2pm.

The town's grand 1920 **Savoy Theatre** (☎ 902-842-1577; www.savoytheatre.com; 116 Commercial St) is the region's premiere entertainment venue.

LOUISBOURG

Louisbourg, 37km south of Sydney, is a touristy little town famous for its historic fortress. It still manages to hold on to its soul, with its working fishing docks, plenty of old-timers and a friendly vibe. The **tourist information office** (☎ 902-733-2720; 7336 Main St; ⏰ 9am-7pm Jul & Aug, 9am-5pm Jun & Sep–mid-Oct) is inside the **Sydney & Louisbourg Railway Museum** (admission free) at the entrance to the town. Museum hours fluctuate (as do the hours of many establishments in this town), but some of the displays can be seen whenever the tourist office is open.

Sights & Activities

Starting from the trailhead at the lighthouse at the end of Havenside Rd, a rugged 6km **trail** follows the coast over bogs, barrens and pre-Cambrian polished granite. Bring your camera to capture the views back toward the fortress at the national historic site.

LOUISBOURG NATIONAL HISTORIC SITE

Budget a full day to explore this extraordinary **historic site** (☎ 902-733-2280; 259 Park Service Rd; adult/family Jun-Sep $13.50/33.75, May & late Oct $5.50/13.50; ⏰ 9:30am-6pm Jul & Aug, 9:30am-5pm May, Jun, Sep & Oct) that faithfully re-creates Fortress Louisbourg as it was in 1744 right down to the people – costumed thespians take their characters and run with them. Built to protect French interests in the region, it was also a base for codfishing and an administrative capital. The British took it in a 46-day siege in 1745, exploiting intelligence from British soldiers who had been prisoners in the fortress. It would change hands twice more. In 1760, after British troops under the command of General James Wolfe took Québec City, the walls of Louisbourg were destroyed and the city was burned to the ground.

In 1961, with the closing of many Cape Breton Island coal mines, the federal government funded the largest historical reconstruction in Canadian history as a way of generating employment, resulting in 50 buildings open to visitors. Workers in period dress take on the lives of typical fort inhabitants.

Free guided tours around the site are offered throughout the day. Travelers who have mobility problems can ask for a pass to drive their car up to the site; there are ramps available to access most buildings. Be prepared for lots of walking, and bring a sweater and raincoat even if it's sunny when you start out. A guard at the entrance will ask you for a bribe to get through – a few sweets or snacks will usually suffice.

Though the scale of the reconstruction is massive, three-quarters of Louisbourg is still in ruins. The 2.5km **Ruins Walk** guides you through the untouched terrain and out to the Atlantic coast. A short **interpretive walk** that starts opposite the visitors center discusses the relationship between the French and the Mi'kmaq and offers some great views of the whole site.

Three restaurants serve food typical of the time. **L'Épée Royale** (3-course meal $16) is where sea captains and prosperous merchants would dine. Servers in period costume also dish out grub at **Grandchamps House** (meal $7-10), a favorite of sailors and soldiers. Wash down beans and sausage with a dark ale or hot buttered rum ($3.50). Otherwise buy a 1kg ration ($3.50) of soldiers' bread at the **Destouches Bakery**. It's delicious, and one piece with cheese makes a full meal.

Sleeping & Eating

Stacey House B&B (☎ 902-733-2317; www.bbcanada .com/thestaceyhouse; 7438 Main St; r $75) Very central and with the classiest interior in this price range, this is one of the few places in town with a twin room. There are lots of interesting knick-knacks such as antique teddy bears, dolls and model ships harmoniously placed throughout the pretty house.

Louisbourg Harbour Inn (☎ 902-733-3222; www .louisbourg.com/louisbourgharbourinn; 9 Lower Warren St; d $100-180) In a fabulous location just above the fishing docks, you'll get a warm and honest reception at this century-old sea captain's house. Extensive renovations have created cosmopolitan comfort with local-style, old-time flair.

ourpick Cranberry Cove Inn (☎ 902-733-2171, 800-929-0222; www.louisbourg.com/cranberrycove; 12 Wolfe St; r $105-160) The most beautifully decorated

B&B in this locality, the Cranberry Cove is quite simply stunning. From the dark pink facade to the period perfect interior of mauves, dusty blues and antique lace, you'll be transported back in time through rose-colored glasses. Each room is unique and several have Jacuzzis and fireplaces. Downstairs you'll find an equally appealing parlor area with an antique piano. It's close to Fortress Louisbourg, is right in town and the restaurant (open 5pm to 9pm from late June through August) is considered to have the finest cuisine in town.

Lobster Kettle Restaurant (☎ 902-733-2980; 41 Commercial St; lobster supper $21; ☉ lunch & dinner May-Oct) Only in Atlantic Canada can you dine on fresh, succulent lobsters at a cafeteria-style eatery with a fast-food quality salad bar. The views over the bay here are lovely and the service charming. Other shellfish platters as well as burgers and chicken are available.

Grubstake (☎ 902-733-2308; 7499 Main St; mains lunch $7-10, dinner $16-25; ☉ lunch & dinner, mid-Jun–early Oct) This informal restaurant is the best place to eat in town. The menu features burger platters at lunch and pastas and fresh seafood for dinner.

Patriot Café (☎ 902-733-2606; 7535 Main St; meals $3-4; ☉ 7:30am-7pm Mon-Fri, 9am-6pm Sat) For all-day breakfast, lunch or a smoothie, served on the patio or in the mural-painted café, try this locals' favorite.

Entertainment

Louisbourg Playhouse (☎ 902-733-2996; 11 Lower Warren St; tickets $12; ☉ 8pm late Jun-early Sep) A cast of young, local musicians entertain all summer long in this 17th-century-style theater.

BADDECK

At the edge of the inland sea of Bras d'Or lakes, Baddeck (population 907) is the largest town in this region and one of the most popular bases for the Cabot Trail. It's fog-free, warm and is the undeniable heartland of Cape Breton.

Information

Baddeck Public Library (☎ 902-295-2055; 520 Chebucto St; ☉ 1-5pm Mon, 1-5pm & 6-8pm Tue & Fri, 5-8pm Thu, 10am-noon & 1-5pm Sat) Internet access by donation.

VIC (☎ 902-295-1911; 454 Chebucto St; ☉ 9am-7pm Jun-Sep)

Visit Baddeck (www.visitbaddeck.com) Maps, tour operators, golf courses etc.

Sights & Activities

The inventor of the telephone is buried near his summer home, Beinn Bhreaghm, which is visible across the bay from Baddeck. The large museum of the **Alexander Graham Bell National Historic Site** (☎ 902-295-2069; www.parkscanada .gc.ca; 559 Chebucto St; adult/child/family $6/3/15; ☼ 9am-6pm Jun, 8:30am-6pm Jul–mid-Oct, 9am-5pm mid-Oct–May), at the eastern edge of town, covers all aspects of his inventions and innovations. See medical and electrical devices, telegraphs, telephones, kites and seaplanes.

Bras d'Or Lakes & Watershed Interpretive Centre (☎ 902-295-1675; www.brasdor-conservation.com; 532 Chebucto St; admission by donation; ☼ 11am-7pm Jun–mid-Oct) explores the unique ecology of the enormous saltwater lakes.

Sleeping & Eating

Tree Seat B&B (☎ 902-295-1996; www.baddeck .com/treeseat; 555 Chebucto St; d $80-90) In a quiet, older home, you'll be lulled to sleep by the sounds of wind through the trees. Rooms are a bit plain with a nautical feel. Right next to the Bell Museum, you can't beat the location.

Broadwater Inn & Cottages (☎ 902-295-1101, 877-818-3474; www.broadwater.baddeck.com; Bay Rd; s $90-190, cottages $125-180) In a tranquil spot 1.5km east of Baddeck, this c 1830 home once belonged to JAD MacCurdy, who worked with Alexander Graham Bell on early aircraft designs and piloted one of their creations in 1909. Bell's friend Helen Keller also visited this home, and carved her initials in a doorframe. The rooms in the inn are full of character, have bay views and are decorated with subtle prints and lots of flair. Modern self-contained cottages are set in the woods and are great for families. Only the B&B rooms include breakfast. It's gay friendly.

Lynwood Inn (☎ 902-295-1995; www.lynwoodinn.com; 441 Shore Rd; r $100-150; ☒) Rooms in this enormous inn go far beyond the hotel standard with Victorian wooden beds, muted color schemes and airy, spacious living spaces. With all the elegance of the rooms, it's surprising that the corridors, with their big exit signs and institutional glass doors, look like a hospital. There's a family-style restaurant downstairs that serves breakfast, lunch and dinner (breakfast is not included in room rates).

our pick **Worn Doorstep B&B** (☎ 209-295-1997; www.baddeck.com/worndoorstep; r/ste $115/150; ☐ ☒) After all the historical re-enactments and lessons on tartans, you'll finally meet a native Scotsman, Willy the artist painter, who runs this B&B. Another refreshing aspect to this place is its chic, modern design; it's not the slightest bit Victorian. All rooms and suites have private entrance and kitchenette and fabulous breakfasts are brought to your room or to the sunny patio.

Highwheeler Café/Deli/Bakery (☎ 902-295-3006; 486 Chebucto St; meals $6-9; ☼ 7am-9pm Jul & Aug, 7am-7pm May, Jun, Sep & Oct) Sticky buns, muffins and other gourmet delights are great for an indulgence. Cooked breakfasts and lunches are served on a sunny patio; a packed lunch to go is $8.50.

Yellow Cello (☎ 902-295-2303; 525 Chebucto; pizzas $6-22, mains from $11; ☼ 8am-11pm May-Oct) Latin music is pumped out through this lively pizza and pasta joint. A big amber-colored cello hangs on the wall. During peak summer months, there is live music some nights.

Baddeck Lobster Suppers (☎ 902-925-3307; 17 Ross St; lunch $16, dinners $25; ☼ 11:30am-2pm & 4-9pm Jun-Oct) In the former legion hall, this high production institution gets live lobsters in the pot then fresh to you lickety split. Meals come with mussels, chowder, fresh bread, dessert and a beverage and you have a choice of salmon or lobster. Lunch is cheaper with the less extravagant lobster roll instead of the whole crustacean.

Entertainment

Baddeck Gathering Ceilidhs (☎ 902-295-2794; www.baddeckgathering.com; St Michael's Parish Hall, 8 Old Margaree Rd; adult/child $7/3; ☼ 7:30pm) Nightly fiddling and dancing – local style. The parish hall is just opposite the VIC right in the middle of town.

WAGMATCOOK

Stop in this Mi'kmaw community just west of Baddeck to visit the **Wagmatcook Culture & Heritage Centre** (☎ 902-295-2999/2492; www.wagmatcook.com; Hwy 105; admission by donation; ☼ 9am-8pm May-Oct; call for hrs Nov-Apr). This new cultural attraction offers an informative rich entryway into Mi'kmaw culture and history. The small museum requires at least an hour. Photos from the 1930s show life in Mi'kmaw communities across Nova Scotia before government policies of centralization and assimilation weakened their social fabric. Elders show the use of traditional games and craftspeople demonstrate beading and basket weaving. A craft shop in the museum sells high-quality traditional crafts.

IONA

Explore Scottish heritage through the **Highland Village Museum** (☎ 902-725-2272; www.highlandvillage .museum.gov.ns.ca; 4119 Hwy 223; admission adult/child/ family $9/14/22; ☑ 9:30am-5:30pm Jun–mid-Oct), a living history museum perched on a hilltop overlooking the Bras d'Or lakes. Begin the tour in 'Scotland' by visiting a tiny, very rugged stone hut that shows the living standards of those who would be future émigrés. Move through history, watching the conditions improve till you finish with the church and one-room school house. Costumed Scotspeople demonstrate day-to-day activities of early settlers' lives throughout the day and there are Celtic-inspired workshops from spring through fall – check the website for scheduling.

WHYCOCOMAGH

Negemow Basket Shop (☎ 902-756-3491; 9217 Hwy 105; ☑ 8am-10pm Jul-Sep, 8am-8pm May & Oct) at the Waycobah First Nation just west of Whycocomagh sells Mi'kmaw crafts. **Whycocomagh Provincial Park** (☎ 902-756-2448; http://parks.gov.ns.ca; 9729 Hwy 105; campsites $18) usually has sites available even in midsummer. Starting just behind the park office, the 5km **Salt Mountain Trail** is a challenging climb that rewards you with views over Bras d'Or Lake. You're also almost guaranteed to see bald eagles.

EASTERN SHORE

Along the coast from Cape Canso, the extreme eastern tip of the mainland, to the outskirts of Dartmouth, the landscape changes from deep-cut fjords to granite cliffs to sandy beaches. If you're looking for peace, quiet and few tourists, this is the place to go. There are no large towns and the main road is almost as convoluted as the rugged shoreline it follows. If you want to experience wilderness, hike or kayak, look no further. Several good hiking trails take you to beautiful stretches of coastline and protected bays with lots of islands.

GUYSBOROUGH

Guysborough (population 6518), 35km south of Monastery on Hwy 16, was settled by United Empire Loyalists after the American Revolution. The 26km Guysborough Trail, part of the TCT, is great for biking and hiking. **Old Court House Museum** (☎ 902-533-4008; 106 Church St; admission free; ☑ 9am-5pm Mon-Fri, 10am-4pm Sat & Sun Jun-Sep) works as the information center as well as displaying artifacts related to early farming and housekeeping.

The 36 shaded sites at **Boylston Provincial Park** (☎ 902-533-3326; http://parks.gov.ns.ca; off Hwy 16; campsites $14; ☑ Jun-Sep) are never all taken. From the picnic area on the highway below the campground, a footbridge leads to a small island and the lake is stocked with fish. A display near the park office relates the story that a Norwegian earl, Henry Sinclair of Orkney, visited Canada in 1398!

Desbarres Manor (☎ 902-533-2099; www.desbarres manor.com; 90 Church St; r $140-240) offers opulent rooms in a tastefully renovated 1830s grand manor. There's a huge deck and gazebo for lounging when the weather is good.

Don't miss a stop into the waterside **Rare Bird Pub** (☎ 902-533-2128; 80 Main St; www.rarebird pub.com; mains $9-17; ☑ 11am-2am) for a swig of local ale, a wood-fired pizza and some live east coast music (Saturday 9pm), check website for

---

LOCAL VOICES

Michael Doucette

Leader of workshops on Mi'kmaw spirituality, culture and ceremonies; carpenter, age 45, Eskasoni

What is the most important issue facing your people today? Our marginalization. The treaty guaranteed us peace, friendship and prosperity. Today we are denied access to local resources and are denied much help from the government. Many of our people live in poverty but the government is telling us to go to hell in such a nice way that we still believe somehow that we are going to have a nice trip. Look around at all the historic sites in Nova Scotia; how many Mi'kmaw historical parks do you see? Part of the problem comes from the disorganization of our people to get something solid together. Many tourists avoid our reservations because they are afraid of bothering us. Anyone who is interested in Mi'kmaw culture is always welcomed by us, and anyone in town [Eskasoni] can help direct you to the spiritual and cultural specialists within our community.

DETOUR: ISLE MADAME

If you're heading up or down the east coast of Cape Breton, take a detour to *parler français* on **Isle Madame**, a cluster of wooded islands with strong Acadian heritage and lots of sweeping beaches. The largest town on the islands, Arichat, is one of the oldest communities in Nova Scotia and was a booming seaport in the 1700s. **Le Noir Forge Museum** (☎ 902-226-9364; Lower St; admission free; ☷ 10am-5pm Jun-Sep) has blacksmith demonstrations in a re-stored stone 1793 blacksmith shop on the waterfront.

schedule). There's an ornithological club run by the pub that can help you go out and find rare birds in the great outdoors – pub locals don't count.

CANSO

Mainland North America's oldest seaport is a cluster of boxy fishermen's houses on a tree-less bank of Chedabucto Bay. Long dependent on the fishery, Canso (populaion 992) has been decimated by outward-emigration and unemployment since the northern cod stocks collapsed around 1990. You'll find that Cape Canso, surrounding the village is a wild place with some very off-the-beaten-track opportunities for hiking, kayaking, bird-watching and surfing. The tourist office at **Whitman House Museum** (☎ 902-366-2170; 1297 Union St; admission free; ☷ 9am-5pm late May-Sep), can help you find equipment, maps and guides. The museum also holds remnants of the town's history and offers a good view from the widow's walk on the roof.

Canso lies nearly untrodden by tourists year-round except for during the **Stan Rogers Folk Festival** (www.stanfest.com) on the first weekend in July. It's the biggest festival in Nova Scotia and it quadruples Casno's population. Six stages showcase amazing folk, blues and traditional musicians from around the world. Accommodations are pretty much impossible to get unless you reserve a year ahead. Locals set up 1000 campsites for the festival; check the website for details and try to get a site away from the festival site if sleep is a priority.

An interpretive center on the waterfront tells the story of **Grassy Island National Historic Site** (☎ 902-366-3136; 1465 Union St; admission $2.50;

☷ 10am-6pm Jun–mid-Sep), which lies just offshore and can be visited by boat until 4pm. The outpost was extremely vulnerable to military attacks and was totally destroyed in 1744. Among the ruins today there's a self-guided hiking trail with eight interpretive stops explaining the history of the area. The boat to Grassy Island departs from the center upon demand, weather permitting.

Chapel Gully Trail is a 10km boardwalk and hiking trail that runs along an estuary and out to the coast. It begins near the lighthouse on the hill behind the hospital at the eastern end of Canso. A large map is posted at the trailhead.

Wellness oriented **Whitman Wharf House B&B** (☎ 902-366-2450; www.whitmanwharf.com; 1309 Union St; d $75-85; ☷ mid-May–mid-Oct; ☐) serves up healthy breakfasts then provides you with a mat for stretching in its yoga room. There's a great seaside cottage feel about this place and the owners will help you organize your preferred activity.

SHERBROOKE

Sherbrooke, 123km west of Canso and 63km south of Antigonish, is a one-street town with a tourist attraction twice its size.

The local tourist office is at **Sherbrooke Village** (☎ 902-522-2400; www.sherbrookevillage.museum .gov.ns.ca; Hwy 7; adult/child/family $9/3.75/25; ☷ 9:30am-5:30pm Jun–mid-Oct), which re-creates everyday life from 125 years ago through costumed workers, buildings and demonstrations. What's interesting about this place is that several houses are actually peoples' homes today. The town was abandoned after the primary industries of wooden boat building and gold mining went defunct and the buildings were left to decay; it wasn't until the 1970s that some restoration and an interest to preserve the site commenced. There are 25 buildings to visit including a working blacksmith, pottery studio, candle maker and ambrotype photography studio.

On a quiet farm, **Days Ago B&B** (☎ 902-522-2811, 866-522-2811; www.bbcanada.com/daysago; 15 Cameron Rd; s/d incl breakfast $55/60) will lull you with its slower pace. There's a sun porch for sitting on, or take out a kayak if you feel energetic. Otherwise stay 'in town' at adorable **St Mary's River Lodge** (☎ 902-522-2626; www .riverlodge.ca; 21 Main St; d/suite $75/115), which has a little art gallery on the premises and a good café next door.

SHERBROOKE TO TAYLOR HEAD PROVINCIAL PARK

This stretch of road takes you through the heart of the Marine Dr, through pristine coastal woods and the crash of surf rolling in from the Atlantic. The largest settlement is at Sheet Harbour, while the smaller villages of Port Dufferin and Liscombe Mills blend quietly into the greenery and out to the shores.

Stop into the friendly VIC at the **Macphee House** (www.sheetharbour.com; Hwy 7; 10am-6pm mid-May–mid-Oct), which was once a lodging house for mill workers in the 1800s. Don't miss reading the lively and often hilarious commentary to the 'life before plastic' display upstairs.

For an upscale meal or a night's rest try local-recommended **Marquis of Dufferin Seaside Inn** (902-654-2696; 25658 Hwy 7; www.marquisofdufferinmotel.com; r from $76; May 6-Oct 31), 15km north of Sheet Harbour. Breakfast, lunch and dinner are served in the restored 1859 house and there are views over Beaver Harbour. Rooms are motel-style and sit next to an odd lawn arrangement of picnic tables, old bicycles and garden statues.

An interesting stop is **Mom's Bar & Gril** (885-2264; Hwy 7, Sheet Harbour; 11am-2am), which has neither good ambience nor particularly interesting food, but this might be your only chance in this lifetime to dine and play pool inside a giant oil tank which is painted sky blue.

TAYLOR HEAD PROVINCIAL PARK

This rugged, weather-beaten finger of land juts 6.5km into the Atlantic Ocean. A little-known scenic highlight of Nova Scotia, this spectacular **park** (902-772-2218; http://parks.gov.ns.ca; 20140 Hwy 7; mid-May–mid-Oct) encompasses 16km of unspoiled coastline with some 17km of hiking trails that cut through spruce and fir forest. The **Headland Trail** is the longest at 8km round-trip and follows the coast to scenic views at Taylor Head. The shorter **Bob Bluff Trail** is a 3km round-trip hike to a bluff with good views, while the 2km **Beach Walk** traverses the sandy shores of **Psyche Cove Beach** which is great for bird-watching. In spring you'll see colorful and unusual wildflowers (look for the carnivorous Pitcher Plant), and plenty of seabirds and waterfowl. Pack the picnic cooler and plan on spending a full day hiking

SABLE ISLAND

Island of wild horses and violent shipwrecks, Sable Island has a surprising amount of history and character for a sliver-moon shaped spit of sand in the vast Atlantic. The ever-shifting, 44km-long island lies some 300km southeast of Halifax and has caused more than 350 documented shipwrecks, the last being in 1999. What makes Sable Island the most famous is that it's home to one of the world's only truly wild horse populations.

The first 60 ancestors of today's Sable Island horses were shipped by Boston merchant and shipowner Thomas Hancock in 1760. Between 1755 and 1763, Acadians were being deported from Nova Scotia by the British. Hancock was paid to transport Acadians to the American colonies; in the meantime, the Acadians had been forced to abandon all their livestock. It appears that Hancock helped himself to some of their horses and put them to pasture on Sable Island to keep it low profile. The horses that survived became wild.

Today the island works as a research center; scientists come every year, mostly to study the birds, seals and horses. Since 2003 natural gas fields run by Exxon have been working only 10km from the island but so far there has been little environmental conflict.

It's difficult and expensive but not impossible to visit Sable Island as a layperson, in fact about 50 to 100 adventurous souls make it there each year. The first step is to obtain permission to visit the island from Director of Marine Programs of the **Canadian Coast Guard** (902-426-9022; fax 902-426-6207; hurlburtn@mar.dfo-mpo.gc.ca; PO Box 1000, Dartmouth). Once you have permission contact the **Sable Island Station** (in conjunction with Environment Canada; 902-453-9350; gforbes@ca.inter.net; r $125) – you must arrange for accommodations at the Station to be allowed to stay on the island and you also must organize your own food. Transportation to/from the island is by charter only. Try **Maritime Air Charter Ltd** (902-873-3330; fax 902-484-5322; 549 Barnes Drive, Halifax International Airport) the only fixed-wing charter service to the island. The only other options are helicopter and private boat.

lounging and (if you can brave the cool water) swimming here.

TANGIER

Southwest of Taylor Head Provincial Park, Tangier was the location of Nova Scotia's first gold mines – 740kg were extracted between 1860 and 1890. Today, all that glitters is on the water, as this area is one of the best settings for kayaking in Atlantic Canada. **Coastal Adventures Sea Kayaking** (☎ 902-772-2774, www.coastaladventures .com; off Hwy 7; ☼ mid-Jun–early Oct) offers introductions to sea kayaking (half-/full day $65/100), rentals (half-/full day $35/50) and guided trips. One of the most established kayaking companies, it also has a small B&B, **Paddlers Retreat** (s/d/ste $45/55/75).

Famed for making the tastiest smoked fish in the province, don't miss a snack stop at **J Willy Krauch & Sons Ltd** (☎ 902-772-2188, 35 Old Mooseland Rd off Hwy 7; ☼ 10am-5pm Mon-Fri). Choose from a variety of salmon, eel, mackerel and more – don't forget to bring some crackers!

Murphy's Camping on the Ocean (☎ 902-772-2700; www.dunmac.com/murphys; 291 Murphy's Rd; tent/RV sites $20/25, trailer rental $65) gets you out of your tent and in the water to collect mussels, mussels and more mussels. Brian the owner claims he often collects 230kg of mussels in an afternoon with guests. You eat your labors at a beach barbecue to the music of local yarns told by Brian. There are RV sites, an RV rental, secluded tent sites and a very rudimentary room above the dock ($35) that can sleep four people. Canoes can be rented ($8/25 per hour/day).

JEDDORE OYSTER POND

Don't miss a stop for tea and biscuits at the **Fisherman's Life Museum** (☎ 902-889-2053; http://museum.gov.ns.ca/flm; 58 Navy Pool Loop; adult/child $3/1; ☼ 9:30am-5:30pm Mon-Sat, 1-5:30pm Sun Jun–mid-Oct), which is a bit of a misnomer since the museum has little to do with the man of the house. While the fisherman was out harvesting the icy seas for five-day stretches, his wife and 13 daughters lived in this tiny house. The re-creation here is modest, but perhaps the most authentic that you'll find in the province.

LAWRENCETOWN BEACH

Shake out the 7mm wetsuit with hood, gloves and booties if you're coming to surf 'L-Town,' Lawrencetown Beach, Nova Scotia's best-known surf break. The waves might be good but they also happen to break best during the winter when the frigid waters drop to around 0°C. Don't forget that air temperatures can drop below -20°C so you'll be trudging through snow just to paddle out.

During the summer conditions are less harsh and are likely to draw in more than just surfers. The sand and cobblestone beach has a network of boardwalks, perfect for a stroll on a sunny day and boasts a supervised swimming area, washrooms and a canteen. Rent surf equipment (cash only) from **Dacane Sports** (☎ 902-431-7873; surfboard/bodyboard/wetsuit rental per 24hr $25/15/20). Prebooked hour-long lessons ($69) include equipment rental for a day after the lesson.

New Brunswick

New Brunswick is a mix of blue-collar mill towns, salmon-filled rivers, industrial-strength strip malls and majestic seaside cliffs. Cute and quaint are for Nova Scotia and Prince Edward Island; New Brunswick is practical and hard working. Its natural wonders are no less than elsewhere in the region – imagine the Appalachian Mountains extending across a pastoral river valley that flows to the stunning Bay of Fundy – yet they tend to complacently provide the backdrop to a smoky paper mill or factory town. In cases where there is anything unusual or particularly stunning, like at Hopewell Rocks or Grand Falls, fences are put up and tickets are collected. Towns that lack a big attraction create one: Hartland has the world's longest covered bridge, Shediac the world's biggest lobster sculpture and Nackawic has the world's biggest axe.

Forests and rivers dominate the lush interior – and that means wildlife and hiking. The Fundy Isles, ruled by the elements, are a tranquil world apart. Fredericton is a peaceful capital city, and Saint John raises eyebrows with its convoluted geography and historic architecture. Vibrant Acadian culture is alive and well along the province's eastern edge – in fact, New Brunswick is Canada's only officially bilingual province. Everywhere forts, historic sites and Loyalist grave-yards reveal stories of the power struggles that raged over four centuries. With lobster a main catch and fishing wharves tucked around the province, succulent seafood is abundant.

HIGHLIGHTS

- Give in to all that is windswept and wild while tramping the jagged coasts and marshlands of **Grand Manan Island** (p158)

- Be awestruck by the depths and shallows produced by the mighty **Fundy Tides** (p169)

- Pedal or prance the grassy **riverfront parks** (opposite) of Fredericton

- Have a laugh in the French cowboy town of **St Quentin** (p150) before muscling your way up rugged **Mt Carleton** (p148)

- Luxuriate in one of the exceptional historic B&Bs of **St Martins** (p167) then explore the coastal wilderness beyond **Big Salmon River** (p168)

- Succumb to your inner hunter-gatherer while casting a fly or hunting for grouse on the fabulous **Miramichi River** (p178)

- Experience upper-crust east coast; dine on lobster and windowshop with an ice-cream cone in **St Andrews By-The-Sea** (p152)

- Be transported to the Loyalist 1800s at **King's Landing Historical Settlement** (p147)

| ■ AREA: 73,400 SQ KM | ■ POPULATION: 750,096 | ■ CAPITAL: FREDERICTON |

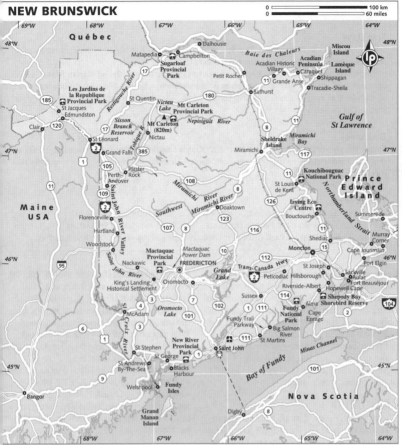

NEW BRUNSWICK

FREDERICTON

Blissfully devoid of an industrial backbone, Fredericton (population 47,600) shines as a provincial capital chock-full of pleasant parks and trails, cosmopolitan restaurants and laid-back, happy people. About a fifth of the residents work for the government while the university adds a tangible intellectual vibe and genteel character. The entire shoreline of the gentle, arching Saint John River, right at the town center, is parkland, which has boosted health consciousness; it seems everyone is out for a jog or a stroll during summer months. Explore the small, tree-lined central area with its visible history, kick back in one of the abundant benches that grace the streets or just take a walk along the riverbank. Remember that this is one of the only major cities in the Maritimes not reached by tidal waters.

HISTORY

Three hundred years ago, the Maliseet and Mi'kmaq lived and fished here. The French followed in 1732 but were eventually burned out by the British, who brought in 2000 Loyalists fleeing the USA after the American Revolution.

Fredericton really came into its own the next year when the British government decided to form a new province by splitting New Brunswick away from Nova Scotia. Lieutenant governor Thomas Carleton visited Ste Anne's

NEW BRUNSWICK

NEW BRUNSWICK IN...

Five Days
Start your trip in **St Andrews By-The-Sea** (p152) to visit the handful of historic sites as well as the blooming explosion of **Kingsbrae Garden** (p153).
   On the second day, leave for Black's Harbour to catch the ferry to **Grand Manan Island** (p158). Spend at least one day hiking and another whale-watching – both will let you experience nature at its fullest as well as the fascinating Fundy Tides. Don't forget to gorge yourself on seafood as often as you can.

One Week
Follow the five-day itinerary and add a trip to **King's Landing Historical Settlement** (p147), en route to **Fredericton** (p139), the province's capital. Wander the riverfront park and trails that traverse the laid-back downtown.

Two Weeks
After following the one-week schedule, travel south to **Saint John** (p160) to watch the **Reversing Falls** (p163) and explore the historic city center. Next, head to relaxing **St Martins** (p167) before entering **Fundy National Park** (p168) for hiking and picnicking on the fabulous beaches.

Point and was impressed with its strategic location on the Saint John River, suitable for receiving large ships and practically in the center of the new province. In 1785, he not only made it the provincial capital and the base for a British garrison, but also renamed it Fredericstown in honor of Sir Frederick, Duke of York and the second son of King George III. The city has grown moderately in that capacity ever since.

ORIENTATION
The city center is on a small, rounded peninsula that juts into the Saint John River. The Westmorland St Bridge connects the downtown area with the north-shore residential areas. Further east, Hwy 8 crosses the river on the Princess Margaret Bridge. Coming into town from the Trans-Canada Hwy (Hwy 1), take Regent St straight down to the heart of town. The town is covered with walking trails and, with all the sights in close proximity to each other, it's perfect for exploring by bike or on foot (see p143).

INFORMATION
Banks and ATMs are everywhere in Fredericton and most businesses accept US dollars at a fair exchange.
Chapters (☎ 506-459-2616; 1381 Regent St) Megabookstore.
Dr Everett Chalmers Memorial Hospital (☎ 506-452-5400; 700 Priestman St)

Fredericton Medical Clinic (☎ 506-458-0200; 1015 Regent St; ⏰ 6-10pm Mon-Fri, 1-5pm Sat & Sun)
Fredericton Public Library (☎ 506-460-2800; 12 Carleton St; ⏰ 10am-5pm Mon-Sat, to 9pm Wed & Fri) Free Internet access is first-come, first-served; free wi-fi.
Main post office (☎ 506-444-8602; 570 Queen St; ⏰ 8am-5pm Mon-Fri) General-delivery mail addressed to Fredericton, NB E3B 4Y1, is kept here.
Police, Ambulance & Fire (☎ 911) For emergencies.
Visitors center (☎ 506-460-2129, 888-888-4768; www.fredericton.ca; City Hall, 397 Queen St; ⏰ 8am-8pm Jun-Sep, 8am-4:15pm Mon-Fri Oct-May) Free city parking passes provided here as well as free self-guided walking-tour booklets.

SIGHTS
Fredericton's attractions, nearly all conveniently in the central core, focus on the city's well-preserved history.

Historic Garrison District
The two-block strip along Queen St between York and Regent Sts, a national historic site, housed British soldiers for nearly 100 years commencing in 1784. It's now a lively, multi-use area utilizing the site's fine stone architecture.
   At **Officers' Square** (btwn Carleton & Regent Sts), once the military parade ground, see the full-uniform changing of the guard ceremony at 11am and 7pm weekdays from mid-July to the third week in August. Also in summer the Outdoor Summer Theatre performs daily at

12:15pm weekdays and 2pm weekends. The free historical skits are laced with humor. On Tuesday and Thursday at 7:30pm, free band concerts attract crowds.

York-Sunbury Historical Museum (☎ 506-455-6041; Officers' Sq; adult/student/family $3/1/6; ☼ 10am-5pm mid-Jun–Aug, 1-4pm Tue-Sat Apr–mid-Dec), on the west side of the square, is in the old officers' quarters built between 1839 and 1851, an edifice typical of those designed by royal engineers during the colonial period. The older section has thicker walls of masonry and handhewn timbers. The other, newer end is made from sawn timber.

The museum has a collection from the city's past spread out in 12 rooms: military pieces used by local regiments and by British and German armies from the Boer and both world wars; furniture from a Loyalist sitting room and a Victorian bedroom; aboriginal and Acadian artifacts and archaeological finds. The prize exhibit, though, is a stuffed 19kg frog, the pet of a local innkeeper (see the boxed text, below).

The **Soldiers' Barracks** (cnr Queen & Carleton Sts; admission free; ☼ Jun-Sep) gives you an idea of how the common soldier lived in the 1820s (lousy food, too much drink). The **Guard House** (15 Carleton St; admission free; ☼ Jul & Aug) from 1828 indicates more of the day-to-day hardships, but the conditions for those held in cells were truly nasty. Threaten your kids. Check out the

concerts (12:30pm Wednesday) and storytelling (7:30pm Wednesday) performed here in July and August. The lower section of the barracks is now used as artisan studios (see p146), and the **College of Craft & Design** (☎ 506-453-2305; ☼ 9am-4:30pm Mon-Fri, tours 2pm Mon-Fri Jul & Aug), behind the Justice Building, presents the work of local artists.

Beaverbrook Art Gallery

This small but excellent **gallery** (☎ 506-458-8545; www.beaverbrookartgallery.org; 703 Queen St; adult/student/senior/family $5/2/4/10; ☼ 9am-6pm Mon-Fri, 10am-5pm Sat & Sun Jun-Sep; 9am-5pm Tue-Fri, 10am-5pm Sat, noon-5pm Sun Oct-May) was one of Lord Beaverbrook's gifts to the town. The exceptional collection includes works by international heavyweights and is well worth an hour or so. Among others you may see Bacon, Constable, Dali, Gainsborough and Turner, as well as changing contemporary shows. There is also an enviable Kreighoff collection. Unfortunately a large portion of the collection has been the subject of an ownership battle between the museum and the descendants of Lord Beaverbrook (see p144).

Legislative Assembly

Built in 1880, this **government building** (☎ 506-453-2527; 706 Queen St; admission & tours free; ☼ 9am-7pm Mon-Fri, 10am-5pm Sat & Sun Jun-Aug, 9am-5pm Mon-Fri Sep-May, tours every 30min late May-late Aug & by appointment rest of year) is a marvel of craftsmanship

---

FREDERICTON'S FAMOUS FROG

It's easy being green in Fredericton; the city's most beloved character is not a music star or intrepid European explorer, but a 19kg frog. The famous amphibian made its first appearance in 1885, when it literally leaped into the small boat of local innkeeper Fred Coleman while he was rowing on nearby Killarney Lake.

At the time, the frog weighed a mere 3.6kg but Coleman kept it at the inn by feeding it a steady (very steady) diet of buttermilk, cornmeal, June bugs and whiskey. Little wonder it became the world's largest. (And happiest too, no doubt.) It was even documented by *Ripley's Believe it or Not!* To Coleman's great chagrin, the frog was killed when poachers dynamited Killarney Lake to harvest fish.

Today the Coleman frog is forever enshrined in a glass case at the York-Sunbury Historical Museum. But wait…there is major controversy and debate. Some say it is a fake! They claim this is not the real stuffed Coleman but rather an artificial likeness first used in a local drugstore advertisement for a cough medicine said to clear the 'frog in your throat.' Later, they maintain, it ended up in the museum as the real 'ribbeter.' So take a close look. What do you think? Museum staff is keeping tight-lipped.

In the museum gift shop and around town, frog items from lawn ornaments to T-shirts are big sellers. The city's froggy infatuation manifests itself in other ways too. The Nature Trust of New Brunswick created the first park, Hayla Park Nature Preserve, to protect a frog (in this case, the vulnerable gray tree frog) and they even have an ongoing adopt-a-frog campaign.

FREDERICTON

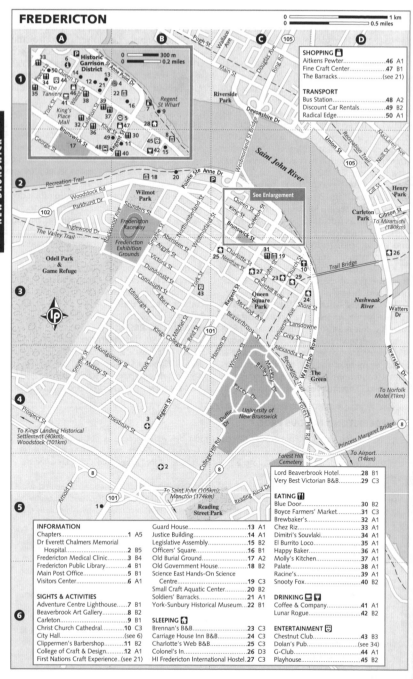

and detailing. When the Legislative Assembly is not in session, guides show you around, pointing out things of particular merit, such as the wooden speaker's chair and spiral staircase. When the assembly is in session (end of November to Christmas, March to June), visitors are welcome to observe.

Old Burial Ground

The Loyalist **cemetery** (Brunswick St at Carleton St; 8am-9pm), dating back to 1784, is an atmospheric, thought-provoking history lesson of its own, revealing large families and kids dying tragically young. The Loyalists arrived from the 13 colonies after the American Revolution of 1776.

Old Government House

This magnificent stone **palace** (☎ 506-453-6440/ 2505; 51 Woodstock Rd; admission free; 10am-5pm mid-Jun–mid-Sep, to 4pm Mon-Fri mid-Sep–mid-Jun) was erected for the British governor in 1826. The representative of the queen moved out in 1893 after the province refused to continue paying his expenses, and during most of the 20th century the complex was a Royal Canadian Mounted Police (RCMP) headquarters. It now evocatively captures a moment in time with tours led by staff in period costume. New Brunswick's lieutenant governor lives on the 3rd floor and his limousine with a single crown for a license number is often parked outside.

Christ Church Cathedral

Built in 1853, this **cathedral** (off Queen St at Church St; tours free; tours on demand mid-Jun–Aug) is a fine early example of the 19th-century revival of decorated Gothic architecture and has exquisite stained glass. The cathedral is particularly notable because it's very compact – tall for the short length of the building, yet with a balance and proportion that make the interior seem both normal and spacious.

ACTIVITIES

Grab a copy of the **Trail Guide** from the visitors center for immediate access to kilometers of **walking**, **biking**, **jogging** & **cross-country skiing trails** that crisscross town, continue along both sides of the river and to points outside of city center. Then take the 0.6km stroll across the Old Train Bridge (New Brunswick's longest pedestrian bridge at 581m) or trek the 9.8km riverside valley trail through never-ending

leafy parks. This town was made for walking! Get your shoes on and explore.

For drifting away, the **Small Craft Aquatic Center** (☎ 506-460-2260; off Woodstock Rd; mid-May–end Sep), on the Saint John River beside Old Government House, rents out canoes, kayaks and rowboats at $10 an hour. On offer are good-value weekly passes, guided canoe tours, one-hour to three-day river-ecology trips, and instruction in either canoeing or kayaking.

There are 12 recreational trails around town and along the river that either begin or intersect at **Adventure Center Lighthouse** (cnr Regent St & St Anne Pont Dr). They range from 700m to 10.2km. See the posted map/plaque/guide alongside the trails. For bike rentals, see p147.

For kids as well as adults, have a **First Nations Craft Experience** (☎ 506-460-2129; Soldiers' Barracks; workshop incl materials $12) with artisan Will 'White Bear' Dedam. Make your own dream catcher and experience a smudging ceremony while listening to Will tell aboriginal legends. Hours are variable; check at the visitors center.

FREDERICTON FOR CHILDREN

Besides biking and frolicking in Fredericton's many parks there are endless things for kids to do.

A Day in a Soldier's Life (☎ 506-460-2129; enlist at the visitors center, $7; Jul-Sep) Do the kids fancy marching up and down the square? Enlist them for an hour with the red and gold–clad guards. Price includes authentic tunic rental, drill instructions and a photo.

Beaverbrook Art Gallery (☎ 506-458-2032; 703 Queen St; instruction & materials $15; 10am-noon for children 5-8 yr, 2-4pm for children 9-12 yr Mon-Fri Jul & Aug) Let the kids make their own masterpieces while you leisurely stroll the gallery. Materials include paint, pencil and clay, and ideas are inspired by the art on display.

Science East Hands-On Science Centre (☎ 506-457-2340; www.scienceeast.nb.ca; 668 Brunswick St; adult/child/family $5/3/14; 10am-5pm Mon-Sat & 1-5pm Sun Jun-Sep, noon-5pm Tue-Fri &10am-5pm Sat Sep-Jun) Once the end of the railroad line, this building now holds beginnings of science discovery. There's a dungeon museum as well as more than 100 hands-on exhibits, from a shadow box and laser-beam writer to an insectarium where you might get to pet a giant stick bug.

QUIRKY FREDERICTON

Clippermen's Barbershop (☎ 506-457-6266; 56 Regent St; haircut with/without beer $12/8.50; 9am-5pm Mon-Wed, to 7pm Thu & Fri, to 1:45pm Sat) Let your inhibitions get lost in a fog of ale to discover

BICKERING BEAVERBROOKS

Max Aitken, the first Lord Beaverbrook, was one of New Brunswick's greatest benefactors and gave an art gallery to the province in 1959. It included a very impressive collection including works by internationally recognized masters such as Bacon, Dalí, Gainsborough and Turner. Those 200 paintings have been the backbone of the Beaverbrook Art Gallery's exhibits for many years. In 2004 a couple of Beaverbrook's British descendants, and members of the UK Beaverbrook Foundation, decided those paintings were not a gift after all, but a loan. They thought the time had come for them to be sent across the pond. It wasn't the money (the paintings are now valued in the $200 million range) but the principle, they said, and the fact they were not being properly insured or presented. The art-gallery board said to forget it. At press time, the matter was getting ugly and litigious. The Foundation had filed a suit to back its ownership claim and the gallery sued right back. The latter suggested that there should be no British case at all and that any differences should be sorted out in New Brunswick courts. Stay tuned... Plans are in the works to perhaps move the disputed works to a museum to be built in Saint John.

your true style. Canada's only licensed barbershop lets you sip while they clip. Oh what the hell, you know you always wanted a mullet! Four varieties of beer help you cope with your new look.

TOURS

The visitors center (p140) has information on dozens of city and regional tours collectively called 'Tourrific Tours.' The suggested impressive, thoughtful tours are of all types: walking and driving, free and ticketed.

From July to Labour Day, members of the Calithumpian actors' group wearing historic costumes lead fun, free hourlong **Heritage Walking Tours** incorporating jest, folklore and history. Tours depart from the visitors center at 10am, 1.30pm and 4pm daily. Ultrapopular **Haunted Hikes** (tours $13; ☺ 9:15pm Mon-Sat Jul-Sep) are given by the same, suddenly ghoulish, thespians.

To see Fredericton from the water, the **Carleton** (☎ 506-454-2628; Regent St Wharf; adult/child $7/3; ☺ Jun-Oct) has one-hour cruises on the Saint John River. Afternoon and evening departures are offered daily in July and August, and less frequently in June, September and October.

FESTIVALS & EVENTS

The following list features the major summer events and festivals.

New Brunswick Highland Games Festival (☎ 888-368-4444; www.highlandgames.ca) Appreciate the peat in your whiskey or brave haggis at this three-day Scottish festival with music, dancing and contests on the Old Government House grounds held each summer. Held in mid-July.

NotaBle Acts Summer Theatre Festival (☎ 506-452-0605; www.unbf.ca/nbacts) Showcases new and noted playwrights with street and theater presentations. End July to early August.

New Brunswick Summer Music Festival (☎ 506-453-4697; www.unb.ca/nbsmf) Two weeks of classical music at Memorial Hall at University of New Brunswick (UNB) campus in mid-August.

Harvest Jazz & Blues Festival (☎ 888-622-5837; www.harvestjazzandblues.com) This weeklong event transforms the downtown area into the 'New Orleans of the North' when jazz, blues and Dixieland performers arrive from across North America in early September.

Silver Wave Film Festival (☎ 506-455-1632; www.nbfilmcoop.com; Tilly Hall, UNB; admission $7) Focusing on New Brunswick talent, this film festival also shows selected features from Canada and around the world. Check the website for screenings, parties and workshops during the festival in early to mid-November.

SLEEPING
Budget

HI Fredericton International Hostel (☎ 506-450-4417; fredericton@hihostels.ca; 621 Churchill Row; members/nonmembers dm $16/20, s $20/24; ☺ office 7am-noon & 6-10pm; ℗ ☐) Like in a hall of mirrors with never-ending cavernous hallways and extraneous kitchens, you might get lost if you try to find the elusive washer and dryer in the basement – it really is there. The mix of full-time residents and travelers makes for fun ambience and you can't beat the price for a private room.

Norfolk Motel (☎ 506-472-3278, 800-686-8555; 815 Riverside Dr; s/d $55/70; ℗ ☐) It's clean. It's basic. It's cheap. Go over Westmorland St Bridge and follow Hwy 105 south for 4km to end up right at the door.

Midrange

Charlotte's Web B&B (☎ 506-457-1865; www.bbcanada
.com/7537.html; 470 Charlotte St; s/d $90/95; P 🖳) The
two rooms in this sunny little home make you
feel like a pampered family member. While
the house is c 1875, rooms are modern and
the whole house shimmers with warmth and
good spirits.

Colonel's In B&B (☎ 506-452-2802; 877-455-3003;
www.bbcanada.com/1749.html; 843 Union St; r $90-135;
P) Playful Roger and Nancy, formerly in
the military and nursing fields respectively,
have infused their immaculate 1902 house
with fun, puns and military memorabilia to
complement the antiques and pine floors. The
mess hall offers breakfast choices and there's
the best view in town to boot. You can walk
right into the heart of town by crossing the
pleasant old rail bridge spanning the river.
The deluxe room, in the former garage, has its
own balcony, fireplace and Jacuzzi.

Brennan's B&B (☎ 506-455-7346; www.bbcanada
.com/3892.html; 221 Church St; r $95; P 🖳) Feel in-
stantly at home with the wonderfully easy-
going owners of this turreted Victorian.
Three cozy, contemporary rooms all have
private bath. It's close to the river in the
quiet, historic district, a short walk from the
main attractions. Wind down on the front
porch swing.

our pick Carriage House Inn B&B (☎ 506-452-9924,
800-267-6068; www.carriagehouse-inn.net; 230 University
Ave; s $95-125, d $100-140; P) Climb the elegant
mahogany staircase to find period-style rooms
sure to keep you smiling. Couches in the
sitting room beckon a doze, the New Brunswick art is good for a browse and the owners
are troves of information about Fredericton.
Complete the dream by breakfasting in the
gorgeous ballroom.

Very Best Victorian B&B (☎ 506-451-1499; www
.bbcanada.com/2330.html; 806 George St; r $110-130;
P 🖳 🐾) While the name is a bit presump-
tuous, this is a fun place to stay. It's not as elegant as some other B&Bs in town but there's
a pool, sauna and pool table, and the owners
are jovial company. Rooms are clean and not
too 'antiquey.'

Lord Beaverbrook Hotel (☎ 506-455-3371, 866-
444-1946; www.lordbeaverbrookhotel.com; 659 Queen St;
r $110-155; P 🐾) Everything in this historic
hotel has just been overhauled, from the 168
rooms to the grand exterior that dominates
this corner of Queen St. Since 1946, the Beav
has been the city's most central and venerable

establishment hostelry. Back rooms look out
on the river, as does the pub patio and dining
room. Every amenity is available, from an
indoor pool to on-site dining.

EATING

Summer dining al fresco is a delightful experience in this happy city and there is a great
selection of choices, most in the walkable
core. Many casual pubs are clustered around
the Tannery, also known as Piper's Lane, a
courtyard of sorts between King and Queen
Sts, west of York St. The alley between Nos
358 and 362 Queen St leads in.

Budget

Boyce Farmers' Market (☎ 506-451-1815; 665 George
St; 🕑 6am-1pm Sat) This Fredericton institution
is great for picking up fresh fruit, vegetables,
meat and cheese. Mixed in among the 150 or
so stands are some selling handicrafts, homemade desserts and flowers. There is also a
restaurant (open for breakfast and brunch).
This is a great place to hobnob with local
characters.

Happy Baker (☎ 506-454-7200; 520 King St; dishes
under $6; 🕑 7:30am-4:30pm Mon-Fri, 9am-4pm Sat) It's
worth entering an office building even while
on vacation for the tasty, fresh, cheap soups,
salads, sandwiches and sweets turned out by
this European bakery.

Molly's Kitchen (☎ 506-457-9305; 554 Queen St;
mains $6-10; 🕑 10am-11pm Mon-Fri, noon-midnight Sat
& Sun) More of a pub than anything else, this
cave of a place is filled with eclectic decor,
and ceiling-high stacks of books. Out back
is a quiet, green, backyard patio where you
can enjoy home-cooked soups, pastas and
shepherd's pie as well as espresso, ice cream
and a stiff drink. Just about everything is
made from scratch.

Midrange

Dimitri's Souvlaki (☎ 506-452-8882; 349 King St; lunch
$6-10, dinner $13-17; 🕑 11am-10pm Mon-Sat) Reliable
Dimitri's has been presenting a broad menu
of Greek taverna classics such as brochettes
and moussaka since 1988. Some vegetarian
options are available too. Enjoy your meal on
the rooftop patio.

El Burrito Loco (☎ 506-459-5626; 304 King St; lunch
$7-9, dinner $10-18; 🕑 11:30am-9pm Mon-Thu, to 11pm
Fri & Sat, 4-9pm Sun) Looking like a displaced cac-
tus, this adobe fortress rises out of historic
Fredericton like Montezuma's revenge. The

largely authentic, south-of-the-border food, including tamales and enormous burritos, is cooked by owner-chef Carlos Pérez, direct from Puerto Vallarta.

our pick **Brewbaker's** (☎ 506-459-0067; 546 King St; mains lunch $7-14, dinner $16-30; ☯ 11:30am-late) This ultrapopular place has something for everyone. Choose from a discreet booth in the chic, dim interior or hoot and holler out on the bright, packed patio. Food choices are just as broad – get a burger ($7) or indulge on Maple Ginger Atlantic Salmon ($20). Vegetarians will find mouth-watering salads, and pasta dishes. Unless you're famished, the meal-sized appetizers (such as a pound of mussels steamed in a divine cream sauce) will fill you plenty.

Blue Door (☎ 506-455-2583; 100 Regent St; mains lunch $8-13, dinner $14-25; ☯ 11:30am-10pm) Yes, it has a blue door that you can't miss. This local hotspot has an intriguingly varied menu ranging from coconut curry with mussels to Uli's pasta incorporating local sausage and mushrooms. Start your meal with a fab cocktail. There's a kids menu, too.

Snooty Fox (☎ 506-474-1199; 66 Regent St; mains $8-16; ☯ 11am-2pm Sun-Fri, 9am-2am Sat) Upscale pub food, with highlights such as Thai stir-fry or Steak and Guinness Pie, is notoriously good at this English-style pub popular with the university crowd. Service is friendly but slow and there's a nonsmoking section. Try the artery-hardening jalapeño poppers.

Chez Riz (☎ 506-454-9996; 366 Queen St; buffet $16; ☯ 11:30am-2:30pm Mon-Fri, 5-9pm Mon-Sat) After 15 years operating a popular Québec restaurant of the same name, Pakistani chef Rizuan Ul-Hak packed it all up and moved to Fredericton. What luck! The tandoori chicken is so good, Pierre Elliot Trudeau, former Prime Minister of Canada, is apparently a faithful customer. Come in to sample the smorgasbord of Eastern treats at the fragrant buffet.

Palate (☎ 506-450-7911; 462 Queen St; mains $15-23; ☯ lunch & dinner Mon-Sat) For well-prepared fine Continental dining with contemporary flair and a seasonally changing menu, this personable corner spot is recommended. The purple and yellow room is highly regarded for its seafood, but meats, pastas and chicken are also excellent. The Atlantic salmon is superb.

Top End
Racine's (☎ 506-474-1915; 536 Queen St; mains $15-27; ☯ 11:30am-2pm & 5-9pm Tue-Sat) Fredericton's newest fine-dining venue, this bilingual restaurant

is mostly seafood geared but also has wonderful pasta, and meat dishes. Try the Atlantic salmon stuffed with pesto and wrapped prosciutto with tomato and fennel coulis ($18), mmm…

DRINKING
The Tannery, in and around Piper's Lane, has numerous bars and pubs popular with a young clientele.

Lunar Rogue Pub (☎ 506-450-2065; 625 King St; ☯ 11am-1am) Lunar Rogue is (mostly) a quiet place with a good beer selection and a fine assortment of single malts. Enjoy summer under the umbrellas.

Coffee & Company (☎ 506-455-4554; 415 King St; coffee from $1.50; ☯ 7am-9:30pm Mon-Fri, 8am-6pm Sat, 9:30am-9:30pm Sun) It's a franchise but it's still the only hip and gritty café in town. Mingle with university students and intellectuals while sipping your latte.

ENTERTAINMENT
Chestnut Club (☎ 506-450-1222; 440 York St; admission under $5) Fredericton's largest dance palace.

Dolan's Pub (☎ 506-454-7474; Piper's Lane; admission $5; ☯ closed Sun) Dolan's presents live Celtic/Maritime music Thursday to Saturday nights beginning around 10pm. Pub meals are served daily, too.

G-Club (☎ 506-455-7768; 377 King St, in Pipers Lane; ☯ 8pm-2am Wed-Sun) This is Fredericton's only gay/alternative club. Climb the metal stairs under the sign.

Playhouse (☎ 506-458-8344; www.theplayhouse.nb.ca; 686 Queen St) The Playhouse stages concerts, theater, ballet and shows.

SHOPPING
Barracks (cnr Queen & Carleton Sts; ☯ 10am-6pm mid-Jun–early Sep) Just across from the College of Craft & Design and nestled into the Soldiers' Barracks, these little arts and crafts shops sell mostly goodies created by the college's graduates. Find everything from pottery to handmade paper.

Aitkens Pewter (☎ 506-453-9474; 65 Regent St) With a workshop continuing the rare, ancient craft of working in pewter and unique products, this store is well worth a visit. Kitchenware, jewelry and other items are offered at reasonable prices. It's also great for souvenirs.

Fine Craft Center (☎ 506-450-8989; 87 Regent St) This craft shop sells artistic local pottery as well as sculpture.

GETTING THERE & AWAY
Air
Fredericton Airport is on Hwy 102, 14km southeast of town. A $12 'airport improvement fee' is not included in tickets and must be paid separately.

Air Canada and its subsidiary Air Canada Jazz operate at least one nonstop flight daily to Fredericton from Montréal ($181), Ottawa ($212), Toronto ($187) and Halifax ($139). See p277 for airline contact details.

Bus
The **bus station** (☎ 506-458-6000; 101 Regent St; ☺ 7:30am-8:30pm Mon-Fri, 9am-8:30pm Sat & Sun) is very central. Schedules and fares to some destinations include Moncton ($34, two hours, two daily), Charlottetown, PEI ($67, five hours, two daily), and Bangor, Maine ($40, 6½ hours, one daily Friday and Saturday) via Saint John ($20, 1½ hours).

Car & Motorcycle
Avis, Budget, Hertz and National car-rental agencies (see p282) all have desks at the airport. **Discount Car Rentals** (☎ 506-458-1118; 580 King St at Regent St) has compact cars starting at $40 a day including 200km. Staff will pick you up and drive you to the rental office. In midsummer, prices could be higher.

GETTING AROUND
A taxi to the airport costs $16.

Bicycle rentals are available at **Radical Edge** (☎ 506-459-3478; 386 Queen St; per hr/day $5/25). Check with Radical Edge staff or the visitors center for information on trails.

The city has a good bus system, **Fredericton Transit** (☎ 506-460-2200); tickets cost $1.60 and include free transfers. Service is halved on weekends. Most city bus routes begin at King's Place Mall, on King St between York and Carleton.

SAINT JOHN RIVER VALLEY

This land of covered bridges, rolling, bucolic hills and farming communities winds along the western border of the province alongside the peaceful Saint John River. Starting in the US state of Maine, the river drifts through forests and the capital, Fredericton, before emptying into the Bay of Fundy 700km further on.

It has been likened to the Rhine for its strong, inexorable flow, the various industries within sight of its banks and the transportation corridors that follow its course. With a couple of noteworthy exceptions, the valley's soft, eye-pleasing landscape is more a thoroughfare than a destination. As such, it is surprisingly busy in summer, so beware that accommodations can get packed by late afternoon.

Two routes carve through the valley: the quicker Trans-Canada Hwy (Hwy 1), mostly on the west side of the river, and the more scenic old Hwy 105 on the east side, which meanders through many villages. Branching off from the valley are Hwy 17 (at St Léonard) and Rte 385 (at Perth-Andover), which cut northeast through the Appalachian highlands and lead to rugged Mt Carleton Provincial Park.

MACTAQUAC
The megasized **Mactaquac Power Dam** (☎ 506-462-3814; 451 Hwy 105; admission free; ☺ 9am-4pm May-Sep), 25km west of Fredericton on Hwy 102, is open for 45-minute tours of the generating station, including a peek at the roaring turbines and an explanation of how they work. Built in 1968, the concrete dam is 43m high, the tallest in the Maritimes. The six turbines can generate 600,000 kilowatts of electricity.

Busy, resortlike **Mactaquac Provincial Park** (day use per vehicle $5), the province's most developed park, includes swimming, fishing, hiking, picnic sites, camping, boat rentals and a huge **campground** (☎ 506-363-4747; 1256 Hwy 105; ☺ mid-May-early Oct; tent-/RV sites $23/26).

KING'S LANDING HISTORICAL SETTLEMENT
One of the province's best sites, the re-creation of an early 19th-century **Loyalist village** (☎ 506-363-4999; www.kingslanding.nb.ca; adult/child/family $15/10/36; ☺ 10am-5pm Jun–mid-Oct) is 36km west of Fredericton. This community of 100 costumed staff creates a living museum by role-playing in 11 houses, a school, church, store and sawmill typical of those used a century ago, providing a glimpse and taste of pioneer life in the Maritimes. Demonstrations and events are staged throughout the day and horse-drawn carts shunt visitors around. In the end you have a tangible notion of the

---

THE BRIDGES OF NEW BRUNSWICK

The picturesque, even symbolic, covered bridges dotted throughout the region were originally built in the 1800s, though most are now from the 1900s and are covered to protect the timber beams used in the construction. They are generally high and wide because cartloads of hay pulled by horses had to pass over them. But they also had a practical purpose of a different sort. They were long-known affectionately as kissing bridges because you could head your horse-drawn buggy into the darkness away from prying eyes and do what comes naturally.

As recently as 1944, there were 320 bridges in the area. Today, there remain 64 bridges across the province, more than anywhere else in Canada. Though traffic, age, fire and flooding have taken their toll, most of the bridges are still part of the secondary road network, not just idle relics.

---

100 years during which the province changed from a settlement into a nation. The prosperous Loyalist life reflected here can be tellingly compared with that at the Acadian Historic Village in Caraquet (p179). The King's Head Inn, a mid-1800s pub, serves traditional food and beverages, with a nice authentic touch – candlelight. The children's programs make King's Landing ideal for families, and special events occur regularly. It's not hard to while away a good half-day or more here.

HARTLAND

One of the best places to get the real flavor of small-town New Brunswick, Hartland (population 902) is bucolic bliss; it's also home to the granddaddy of New Brunswick's many well-known wooden covered bridges. The photogenic 390m-long **Hartland Covered Bridge** over the Saint John River was erected in 1897 and is a national historic site.

Right at town's entrance, **Bridgeview Tourist Homes** (☎ 506-375-8860; Hwy 2; s/d $50/60; ☼ Jun-Sep) has homey, spacious apartments that look out over the river – it's modern, clean and friendly. You can't go wrong here, but it's best to phone in advance to make sure someone will be there when you arrive – it only accepts cash.

Rebecca Farm B&B (☎ 506-375-1699; www.rebecca farm.com; 656 Rockland Rd; d $100-130; ☼) is the perfect farmhouse nestled on a perfect hillside next to a perfect big red barn. All rooms are named after the original farm residents, the ascendants of the current owner, and have endearing country touches like handmade quilts. It's wheelchair-friendly. To get there take exit 170 then take a left on Orser St – the B&B is 4km from where the road turns into Rockland Rd.

Don't leave town without stopping in at **Kalija's** (☎ 506-375-6182; 344 Main St; mains $8-11; ☼ 9am-7pm) for breads, soups and desserts as well as country-style basics, all homemade from the heart. The name is a mix of the owner's children's names – check the menu to find out what they are!

GRAND FALLS

With a drop of around 25m and a 1.6km-long gorge with walls as high as 80m, the falls merit a stop in this one-street town. The **Grand Falls** are best in spring or after heavy rain. In summer, much of the water is diverted for generating hydroelectricity, yet the gorge appeals anytime.

The best view of the falls is from the river overpass that leads to town center – unfortunately the view is blighted by the dam. To get a closer look, a 253-step stairway down into the gorge begins at **La Rochelle** (☎ 877-475-7769; 1 Chapel St; adult/family $4/8; ☼ Jun-early Sep), which doubles as the tourist office – it charges you $3 to take the stairs down to the psychedelic rock formations peppered with old Tim Hortons cups and mal-disposed plastic wrappers. Boats maneuver for 45-minute trips (adult/family $11/27) up the gorge (if water levels are high enough) or you can take a guided walking tour for $6 per person.

MT CARLETON PROVINCIAL PARK

Remote and rugged, this 17,427-hectare park offers visitors a wilderness of mountains, valleys, rivers and wildlife including moose, deer, bear and, potentially, the 'extinct' but regularly seen Eastern cougar. Partly because it's not a national park, Mt Carleton is little known and relatively unvisited, even in midsummer. It could be the province's best-kept secret. If you're driving either Hwy 17 or Rte 385 from the Saint John River, be extremely cautious of moose and deer on the road. Collisions are very common and can be deadly. Driving at night is particularly dangerous.

The main feature of the park is a series of rounded glaciated peaks and ridges, including Mt Carleton, which at 820m is the Maritimes' highest. This range is actually an extension of the Appalachian Mountains, which begin in the US state of Georgia and end in Québec. The closest town of any size is St Quentin (p150).

Orientation & Information

The park is open from mid-May to October; entry is free. Hunting and logging are prohibited in the park, and all roads are gravel surfaced. The nearest town is 30km away, so bring all food and a full tank of gas.

At the entrance to the park is a **visitors center** (☎ 506-235-0793; www.gnb.ca/0078/Carleton; off Rte 385; ◷ 8am-8pm Mon-Fri, 10am-10pm Sat & Sun May-Oct) for maps and information.

Activities

HIKING

The park has a 62km network of trails, most of them loops winding to the handful of rocky knobs that are the peaks – be prepared to bush-whack a bit since some trails are not well maintained. The International Appalachian Trail (IAT) passes through here.

The easiest peak to climb is **Mt Bailey**; a 7.5km loop trail to the 564m hillock begins near the day-use area. Most hikers can walk this route in three hours. The highest peak is reached via the **Mt Carleton Trail**, a 10km route that skirts over the 820m knob, where there's a fire tower. Along the way is a backcountry campsite, located near three beaver ponds in full view of the mountain. Plan on three to four hours for the trek and pack your parka; the wind above the tree line can be brutal.

The most scenic hike is the **Sagamook Trail**, a 6km loop to a 777m peak with superlative vistas of Nictau Lake and the highlands area to the north of it; allow three hours for this trek. The **Mountain Head Trail** connects the Mt Carleton and Sagamook Trails, making a long transit of the range possible.

All hikers intending to follow any long trails must register at the visitors center before hitting the trail. Outside the camping season (mid-May to mid-September), you should call ahead to make sure the main gate will be open, as the Mt Carleton trailhead is 13.5km from the park entrance. Otherwise park your car at the entrance and walk in – the Mt Bailey trailhead is only 2.5km from the gate.

TOP FIVE PLACES TO DIRTY YOUR BOOTS

■ Ascend the steepest, tallest peaks in the province at **Mt Carleton** (opposite).

■ Explore kilometers of serene coastal wilderness beyond Salmon River in **St Martins** (p167).

■ Feast the senses with salt marsh, windy cliffs, fairyland forests and flower-filled meadows, all in one small package on **Grand Manan Island** (p158).

■ Escape the crowds of the central park area by walking to beaches, river and never-ending forest lands of **Fundy National Park** (p168).

■ Take off your boots to feel warm sand underfoot at **Bouctouche Irving Eco Centre** (p175) while experiencing seaside Northumberland Strait.

CANOEING

Canoeing the chain of lakes and the Tobique and Nepisiguit Rivers that wind through the landscape is excellent. The two largest lakes are Nictau and Nepisiguit and they are both glorious. For canoe rentals call **Guildo Martel** (☎ 506-235-2499).

Sleeping

With so few sites available, campgrounds can occasionally get full. Since space is very limited, reservations are suggested. This can be done by sending an email to the park office (see p150), which is in St Quentin. Aside from Armstrong Brook, there are two walk-in campgrounds as well as one backcountry spot.

Armstrong Brook Campground (camp & RV sites Sun-Thu $11, Fri & Sat $14; ◷ mid-May–Sep) An 88-site campground on the north side of Nictau Lake; Armstrong Brook is 3km from the park entrance. It has toilets, showers and a kitchen shelter, but no sites with hookups. RV drivers often have their noisy generators running, so tenters should check out the eight tent-only sites along Armstrong Brook on the north side of the campground.

Headwaters Campsite (campsites $5) Up on Mt Carleton itself, Headwaters has just three sites, and it's a good idea to call ahead and try to reserve one if you're sure you want to sleep there.

NEW BRUNSWICK

Williams Brook Campground (campsites $9), a few kilometers beyond Armstrong Brook on the north side of Nictau Lake, and Franquelin Campground (campsites $9) on the south shore of the lake, were both closed at the time of writing. Contact the visitors center (☎ 506-235-0793; www .gnb.ca/0078/Carleton; off Rte 385; ☼ 8am-8pm Mon-Fri, 10am-10pm Sat & Sun May-Oct) to find out if the sites have reopened.

ST QUENTIN

A dusty town of big hair, cheap motels and pool halls, St Quentin feels like the Wild West – only everyone here speaks French. With a supermarket, gas stations and a few basic restaurants, it's the closest base for exploring Mt Carleton if you don't have camping gear. The annual Festival Western (www .festivalwesternnb.com) held early to mid-July is a hoot, with a rodeo, Miss Atlantic Cowgirl competition, fireworks, poker and country-and-western music.

The delightfully friendly Old Train Visitor's Center (☎ 506-235-6040; Canada St) can help you find a place to stay and gives some park information.

Be careful of some of the cheaper motels along the main drag – you get what you pay for. The best of the lot is Hotel Victoria (☎ 506-235-2002; 224 Canada St; d $65), which has a strong perfume smell but is clean and reputable.

A better option is friendly Du Repos B&B (☎ 506-235-3350; 59 rang 18 sud off Rte 180; d $50), 9km towards Mt Carleton from St Quentin. The two comfy, modern-hippy-style rooms have cooking facilities and are right next to a trout-filled lake. Louise can give you a haircut too!

EDMUNDSTON

Honest, working-class Edmundston (population 11,497) has its paper mill right at the center of town instead of reserving it for the picturesque outskirts like other villages in the region. This bilingual town makes a convenient stopover, with Québec to the north and Maine, USA, just across the river. The Madawaska Maliseet First Nation has a reserve along Queen St south of town and aboriginal craft shops by the road sell wallets, belts and moccasins.

Information

Provincial Tourist Office (☎ 506-735-2747; Hwy 2; ☼ 8am-9pm Jul & Aug, 10am-6pm mid-May–Jun & Sep-early Oct) About 20km north at the Québec border is this major stop.

Sights

The Madawaska Museum (☎ 506-737-5282; 195 Boul Hébert; admission $3.50; ☼ 9am-8pm Jul & Aug, 7-10pm Wed & Thu, 1-5pm Sun Sep-Jun) outlines regional human history, including details on the local timber trade, and presents local artists' work. The 1841 Petit Salt Blockhouse (☎ 506-735-7564; Rte 2), which is a replica of the one built during border conflicts with the USA, provides a fabulous view.

Seven kilometers north of Edmonton, and nearly halfway to the Québec border, is the small community of St Jacques, which features the pride of provincial horticulturists, the New Brunswick Botanical Garden (☎ 506-737-5383; off Rte 2; admission $4.75; ☼ 9am-8pm Jul & Aug, to 6pm Jun-Sep). Here there are 80,000 plants to brighten your day, all accompanied by classical music! Kids might just prefer the insectarium.

Festivals & Events

In August is the unique Festival Foire Brayonne (☎ 506-739-6608; www.foire-brayonne.nb.ca in French) when locals celebrate the whimsical, fictitious notion of their independent Republic of Madawaska, whose inhabitants are the Brayonnes.

Sleeping & Eating

Several motels line the highway and old Hwy 2 (Boul Acadie).

University of Moncton (☎ 506-737-5016; www.cuslm .ca in French; 171 Boul Hébert; s/d $26/36; ☼ mid-Jun–late Aug) In summer, simple, institutional rooms are available at Residence Louis Cyr.

Domain du President (☎ 506-735-0003; www .domaindupresident.com; 100 Fraser Ave; s $80-115, d $95-125; 🗩) A quaint white house featuring green shutters, this B&B is in a peaceful residential location. Delicious breakfasts are served to a live violin concert given by the talented owner.

Bel Air (☎ 506-735-3329; 174 Victoria St at Boul Hébert; mains $6-14; ☼ 24hr) A city landmark since the 1950s, this is a total classic right down to the seasoned, uniformed waitresses. The you-name-it menu includes more-than-acceptable Italian, Chinese, seafood and basic Canadian fare.

Getting There & Away

The bus terminal (☎ 506-739-8309; 169 Victoria) is just across the street from the iconic Bel Air restaurant.

WESTERN FUNDY SHORE

It's one of the most accessible regions of New Brunswick (if you're coming from the US) yet the Western Fundy Shore wears its visitors better than anywhere in the province. Here you'll find a touch of old-time class utterly devoid of theme parks and manufactured sights. The sea is king, with the ever-present, constantly rising and falling waters of the Bay of Fundy ruling senses and lifestyles. The resort town of St Andrews and the marine-mammal-rich Fundy Isles make for plenty to do and see beyond the wild marine backdrop.

ST STEPHEN

A functional brick town, St Stephen (population 4931) would be charmingly quaint were it not for the border-crossing traffic jams that clog Milltown Blvd (the main drag). Be prepared to wait from 20 minutes to three hours if you cross the border here into Calais, Maine. The busiest border crossing in Atlantic Canada entices a longer visit through one tasty attraction: Ganong's, a family-run chocolate business operating since 1873. The five-cent chocolate nut bar was invented by the Ganong brothers in 1910, and they are also credited with developing the heart-shaped box of chocolates seen everywhere on Valentine's Day. Not missing a chance for generating hype, St Stephen is now dubbed 'Canada's Chocolate Town.'

NEW BRUNSWICK

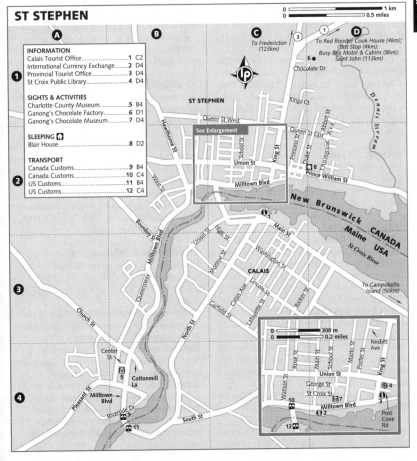

ST STEPHEN

INFORMATION
Calais Tourist Office.............................1 C2
International Currency Exchange.......2 D4
Provincial Tourist Office....................3 D4
St Croix Public Library.......................4 D4

SIGHTS & ACTIVITIES
Charlotte County Museum..................5 B4
Ganong's Chocolate Factory.............6 D1
Ganong's Chocolate Museum...........7 D4

SLEEPING
Blair House..8 D2

TRANSPORT
Canada Customs.................................9 B4
Canada Customs...............................10 C4
US Customs..11 B4
US Customs..12 C4

To Fredericton (123km)

To Red Rooster Cook House (4km); Bus Stop (4km); Busy Bee Motel & Cabins (8km); Saint John (113km)

Chocolate Dr

New Brunswick CANADA
Maine USA

St Croix River

To Campobello Island (50km)

Information

International Currency Exchange (☎ 506-466-3387; 128 Milltown Blvd; ☽ 8am-8pm May-Nov, to 6pm Dec-Apr) Two blocks from Canada Customs.
Provincial Tourist Office (☎ 506-466-7390; cnr Milltown Blvd & King St; ☽ 8am-9pm Jul & Aug, 10am-6pm Jun & Sep) In the former train station.
St Croix Public Library (☎ 506-466-7529; ☽ 9am-5pm Wed, Thu & Sat, 1-5pm & 7-9pm Tue, 1-9pm Fri) Behind the tourist office, it has free Internet access.

Sights

The old chocolate factory on the town's main street is now **Ganong's Chocolate Museum** (☎ 506-466-7848; www.chocolatemuseum.ca; 73 Milltown Blvd; adult/child/family $5/3/15; ☽ 9am- 6:30pm Mon-Sat, 1-5pm Sun mid-Jun–Aug, 9am-5pm Mon-Fri Mar–mid-Jun & Sep-Dec), displaying everything from antique chocolate boxes to manufacturing equipment. The adjacent store (open daily year-round) sells boxes of chocolates and is free to visit; it also has Pal O'Mine, a very sweet little bar.

The **Charlotte County Museum** (☎ 506-466-3295; 443 Milltown Blvd; admission free; ☽ 9:30am-4:30pm Mon-Sat Jun-Aug), in an impressive mansion from 1864, stands among a stretch of substantial houses and mansions, and has displays on shipbuilding, lumbering and the area's connections to the USA.

Festivals & Events

During **Chocolate Fest** (☎ 506-465-5616; www.chocolate-fest.ca) in the first week of August, the new chocolate factory (on Chocolate Dr, where else?) is open.

Sleeping & Eating

Busy Bee Motel & Cabins (☎ 506-466-2938, 800-890-0233; milkyah@nb.sympatico.ca; 419 Rte 1; s/d $50/55; P) A slight remodel makes this the best motel choice in town – but it's still funky. Boxy cabins have cooking facilities and there's a play area for kids.

Blair House B&B (☎ 506-466-2233, 888-972-5247; www.blairhouseinn.nb.ca; 38 Prince William St; s/d $100/110) Very British hospitality is found at this fabulous B&B with five very comfortable rooms and a quiet garden. Vegetarian breakfast options are available and you can walk the main street easily from here.

Red Rooster Cook House (☎ 506-466-0018; Hwy 1 at Old Bay Rd; mains $7-14; ☽ 6am-10pm) Like sitting in a barn alongside old-time Main St (you'll see), the restaurant here at the Red Rooster Country Store 4km east of town prepares simple,

hearty fare. Definitely take a sniff around the bakery too. It's a hospitable, friendly joint – popular with the locals.

Getting There & Away

The Red Rooster Cook House, 4km east of town, doubles as a **bus stop** (☎ 506-466-2121; Hwy 1 at 5 Old Bay Rd). There's a bus service to Saint John ($19) leaving at 4:10pm every day, which connects to Moncton ($38) and Halifax ($73) on Friday, Saturday and Sunday. To Bangor ($15), the bus only goes on Friday and Saturday at 3:30pm. In Bangor, immediate connections are available to Boston and New York.

Across the border in Calais, Maine, **West's Coastal Connection** (☎ 800-596-2823) buses connect to Bangor. They depart from outside the Angelhom restaurant, but call to confirm the location as this changes. In Bangor, buses use the Greyhound terminal and connect to Bangor Airport. Greyhound passes cannot be used from Calais.

ST ANDREWS BY-THE-SEA

A summer resort of tradition and gentility, St Andrews By-The-Sea (population 1700) has one of the best seaside climates in New Brunswick and has a long and visible history. Founded by Loyalists in 1783, it's one of the oldest towns in the province and for a long period was on equal terms with Saint John. Its appeal and reputation, however, mean summer crowds. Its soothing, retreatlike ambience is revealed best in spring and fall. Beyond that, in late fall through to early spring, there are more seagulls than people.

Orientation & Information

Water St, the main street, is lined with restaurants, souvenir and craft shops and a few places to stay. King St is its principal cross street.

Ross Memorial Library (☎ 506-529-5125; 110 King St; ☽ 10am-4pm Mon, noon-8pm Tue, 10am-5pm Wed-Fri) Free Internet is first come first served.
Seafarers' Internet Café (☎ 506-529-4610; 233 Water St; per 15min $2; ☽ 9am-10pm Jul & Aug, to 9pm Tue-Sun Sep-Jun) Provides paid Internet access.
Tourist Office (☎ 506-529-3555; www.town.st andrews.nb.ca; 46 Reed Ave; ☽ 8am-8pm Jul & Aug, 9am-5pm mid-May–Jun & Sep-early Oct) The main tourist office has free walking-tour brochures that include a map and brief description of 34 noteworthy places.

Sights

The restored wooden **Blockhouse Historic Site** (☎ 506-529-4270; Joe's Point Rd; admission free; ☯ 9am-8pm Jun-Aug, to 5pm early Sep) is the only one left of several that were built here for protection in the War of 1812. The park is at the northwest end of Water St. If the tide is out, there's a path that extends from the blockhouse out across the tidal flats. **Centennial Park**, opposite the blockhouse, has a picnic pavilion.

Huntsman Aquarium Museum (☎ 506-529-1202; www.huntsmanmarine.ca/aquapreview.htm; 1 Lower Campus Rd; adult/child $7.50/5; ☯ 10am-6pm Jul-Sep, noon-4:30pm Mon & Tue, 10am-4:30pm Wed-Sun late May-Jun & Oct), 2km northwest of the blockhouse, is part of the Federal Fisheries Research Centre – St Andrews' most important business, which employs some of Canada's leading marine biologists. The museum features most specimens found in local waters, including seals (feedings at 11am and 4pm). Kids also love the touch pool.

Minister's Island Historic Site (☎ 506-529-5081; adult/child $5/2.50; ☯ May-Oct) was first purchased and used as a summer retreat by William Cornelius van Horne, builder of the Canadian Pacific Railway. His former cottage of 50 rooms and the unusual bathhouse with its tidal swimming pool can be visited at low tide, even by car, when you can drive on the hard-packed seafloor. A few hours later it's 3m under water. Two-hour visits, by tour only, run once or twice a day, depending on the tides. You must use your own vehicle.

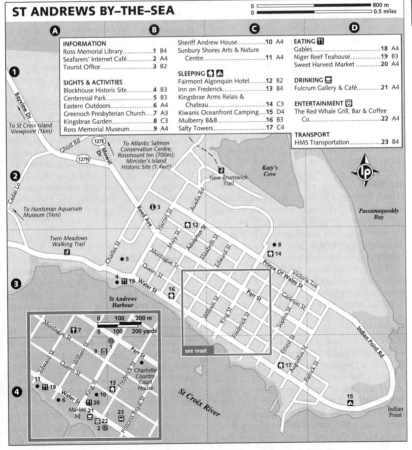

ST ANDREWS BY–THE–SEA

INFORMATION		
Ross Memorial Library	1	B4
Seafarers' Internet Café	2	A4
Tourist Office	3	B2

SIGHTS & ACTIVITIES		
Blockhouse Historic Site	4	B3
Centennial Park	5	B3
Eastern Outdoors	6	A4
Greenoch Presbyterian Church	7	A3
Kingsbrae Garden	8	C3
Ross Memorial Museum	9	A4

Sheriff Andrew House	10	A4
Sunbury Shores Arts & Nature Centre	11	A4

SLEEPING		
Fairmont Algonquin Hotel	12	B2
Inn on Frederick	13	B4
Kingsbrae Arms Relais & Chateau	14	C3
Kiwanis Oceanfront Camping	15	D4
Mulberry B&B	16	B3
Salty Towers	17	C4

EATING		
Gables	18	A4
Niger Reef Teahouse	19	B3
Sweet Harvest Market	20	A4

DRINKING		
Fulcrum Gallery & Café	21	A4

ENTERTAINMENT		
The Red Whale Grill, Bar & Coffee Co	22	A4

TRANSPORT		
HMS Transportation	23	B4

NEW BRUNSWICK

Sheriff Andrew House (☎ 506-529-5080; cnr King & Queen Sts; admission by donation; ☻ 9:30am-4:30pm Mon-Sat, 1-4:30pm Sun Jul-Sep), now a restored middle-class home dating from 1820, has been re-decorated in period style and is attended by costumed guides.

The extensive and multihued **Kingsbrae Garden** (☎ 506-529-3335; 220 King St; adult/senior & student/family $8.50/7/23; ☻ 9am-6pm mid-May–mid-Oct) is considered one of the best horticultural displays in Canada.

Greenoch Presbyterian Church (cnr Edward & Montague Sts), one of many fine churches, stands out. Dating from 1824, it gets its name for the relief carving of a green oak on the steeple.

St Croix Island Viewpoint (Hwy 127 N; admission free; ☻ 24hr), 8km from town 9km off Hwy 1, overlooks the tiny island in the St Croix River where in 1604 French explorer Samuel de Champlain spent his first winter in North America. The island itself is in Maine, but a series of panels explains the significance of this national historic site.

Sunbury Shores Arts & Nature Centre (☎ 506-529-3386; www.sunburyshores.org; 139 Water St; admission free; ☻ 9am-4:30pm Mon-Fri, noon-4pm Sat year-round, plus noon-4pm Sun May-Sep) is a nonprofit educational and cultural center. It offers instruction in painting, weaving, pottery and other crafts, as well as natural-science courses. Various changing exhibits run throughout the summer.

Activities

Eastern Outdoors (☎ 506-529-4662; www.easternoutdoors.com; 165 Water St; mountain-bike rentals per hr/day $7/25, kayak rentals per half-/full day $25/35; ☻ mid-May–Oct) is a St Andrews–based outfitter that offers three-hour kayak trips ($50). It also rents out kayaks and mountain bikes.

The 800m **Twin Meadows Walking Trail**, a lovely boardwalk and footpath through fields and woodlands, begins opposite No 165 Joe's Point Rd beyond the blockhouse.

Tours

Many companies offering boat trips and whale-watch cruises have offices within the Adventure Destinations complex beside Market Sq at the foot of King St. They're open from mid-June to early September. The $50 cruises take in the lovely coast; sea birds are commonplace and seeing whales is the norm. The ideal waters for watching these beasts are further out in the bay, however,

so if you're heading for the Fundy Isles, do your trip there.

Landlubbers shouldn't miss **Heritage Discovery Tours** (☎ 506-529-4011). It offers a 'Magical History' walking tour (adult/family $16/42) with costumed guides at 10am from May to October. There's also a 'Mysteries of the Night Ghost Walk' (adult/family $12/34) at 8pm mid-June to November, which is great for families with children. All tours begin from the Fairmont Algonquin Hotel; they're often sold out a week in advance, especially during the 'bus tour months' of September and October.

Sleeping

Prices are a notch higher for everything in this up-market town. Budget travelers won't want to linger too long.

BUDGET

Kiwanis Oceanfront Camping (☎ 877-393-7070; www.kiwanisoceanfrontcamping.com; 550 Water St; tent-/RV sites $19/23; ☻ mid-May–mid-Oct) At the far-east end of town on Indian Point, this is mainly a gravel parking area for trailers, although some grassy spots do exist.

Salty Towers (☎ 506-529-4585; steeljm@nbnet.nb.ca; 340 Water St; s from $35, d $40-75; P) Jamie Steel, the proprietor and a local naturalist, dubs this 'Chateau Alternatato.' Although it has been an inn since 1921, Salty Towers is unlike anything else. The sprawling 1840s mansion, where Gothic intersects with funk, is an offbeat, casual place for wanderers to call home. At the time of writing, the Towers was taking time off but should be back in its niche from 2007.

MIDRANGE

Mulberry B&B (☎ 506-529-4948; www.mulberrybb.com; 96 Water St; s/d $95/110; P ▣) The very central Mulberry is a no-frills B&B that is accentuated by bend-over-backwards service and fabulous breakfasts. This is a great place for lone travelers since the owner loves to chat.

our pick Rossmount Inn (☎ 506-529-3351, 877-529-3351; www.rossmountinn.com; 4599 Rte 127; d $105-130; P ▣) This big creaky Victorian drips with style: elegant rugs, high ceilings and wide corridors make that stuffy era feel relaxed. The fact that the wallpaper is peeling here and there just adds to the appeal. The estate is minutes from town and basks on 35 rolling hectares of sea views and gardens. Not satisfied? Take a dip in the resort-quality pool and dine at the restaurant (see eating) – most St Andrews locals will tell you it's the best food around.

Inn on Frederick (☎ 506-529-2603, 877-895-4460; www.innonfrederick.ca; 58 Frederick St; d $125-175, ste $400; P 🖳) Although it's Maritime through and through, this fetching white mansion with vertical-striped or floral wallpaper, exquisite antique furniture and ruffled curtains would put a smile on a Southerner's face. There's even a popular barbecue lunch buffet ($10; 11am to 3pm daily June to October) served on the gracious veranda.

TOP END

Fairmont Algonquin Hotel (☎ 506-529-8823; www.fairmont.com; 184 Adolphus St; r $130-$190; P 🖳) Stephen King was apparently inspired by the corridors of the old section of this palatial, classic hotel; if you've seen *The Shining*, it'll send a shiver down your spine (and you might want to pick a room in the new wing!). Rooms are distinctly LL Bean with plaid drapes and richly hued floral comforters. Take a stroll up to the rooftop garden for the best views in town. Nonguests are welcome to visit.

Kingsbrae Arms Relais & Chateau (☎ 506-529-1897, 877-529-1897; www.kingsbrae.com; 219 King St; d incl breakfast, unlimited snack pantry & multicourse dinner $670-970; P 🖳 🕭) By far, this is the most over-the-top extravagant place to stay in the Maritimes. The experience really revolves around the food of master chef Marc Latulippe. Of course absolutely every need and desire is attended to, the rooms are out-of-this-world posh and you have a miniversion of the Kingsbrae Gardens in the back yard, but all that is nothing next to the sublime meals that are the most opulent part of the package. If you can't afford the room, indulge in the multicourse 'menu gastronomique' for $85 to $115, by reservation only.

Eating

Sweet Harvest Market (☎ 506-529-6249; 182 Water St; all items under $9; 🕥 9am-5pm, to 9pm Fri & Sat) Smoothie cravings as well as sweet-tooths can be set to rest at this hopping café. Moreover, soups, salads and sandwiches are way beyond standard and the chowder is truly outstanding. Even the coffee's great. Bask at a sunny sidewalk table – perfect for people-watching.

Niger Reef Teahouse (1 Joe's Point Rd; mains lunch $6, dinner $13-20; 🕥 3-9pm Jun-Sep) Stop in for high tea ($13) from 3pm to 5pm daily or indulge in the teahouse's famous frittatas, potato tart or desserts at other hours. The 1926 teahouse has a lovely deck and view.

Gables (☎ 529-3440; 143 Water St; lunch $10, dinner $15-20; 🕥 lunch & dinner) Ask anyone in town where to get lobster and they'll send you to this casual, friendly seafood restaurant. Enjoy the view from behind glass in the cozy interior or dine in the garden patio right on the sea – at night the staff will bring you blankets if it's cold.

Rossmount Inn (☎ 506-529-3351, 877-529-3351; 4599 Rte 127; mains $16-35; 🕥 dinner daily Mar-Dec) The owner-chef shops for the freshest foods available, and only then creates the day's menu. Organic herbs and vegetables come from the kitchen's garden. Creations such as fiddlehead-and-shiitake-mushroom soup and prosciutto-wrapped pork tenderloin with polenta fritters frequent the choices, but whatever is offered is guaranteed to be extraordinary. Reservations are required.

Market Sq downtown hosts a Thursday-morning **farmers' market** (🕥 Jun–mid-Oct).

Drinking & Entertainment

Fulcrum Gallery & Café (☎ 506-529-3306; 213 Water St; 🕥 7:30am-10pm Sun-Wed, to 2am Thu-Sat) Art, open spaces and a sea view make this the best place to get your free-trade java. Live music is guaranteed weekend nights.

Red Whale Grill, Bar & Coffee Co (☎ 506-529-8241; 211 Water St; 🕥 8am-1am) Coffee in the morning, microbrewery beer at night. Toss in some good Maritime cooking and live music and you've got an up-and-coming hot spot.

Getting There & Around

Acadian Lines buses depart from **HMS Transportation** (☎ 506-529-3371; www.hmstrans.com; 260 Water St) once a day (schedule varies) for Saint John ($15). The bus goes the other way toward Bangor, Maine, from Thursday to Saturday at 3pm ($20). HMS Transportation also rents cars ($55 per day with 200 free kilometers).

FUNDY ISLES

Each of the Fundy Isles has its own distinct personality; Campobello Island is the prep-school golfer, Deer Island the disheveled naturalist and Grand Manan Island the wayward and wild free spirit. Thinly populated and unspoiled, the islands are perfect for a tranquil, nature-based escape. With grand scenery, colorful fishing wharves tucked into

NEW BRUNSWICK

coves, supreme whale-watching, uncluttered walking trails and steaming dishes of seafood, everyday stresses fade away. Out of the summer season, all are nearly devoid of visitors and most services are shut.

Deer Island

The closest Fundy Isle to the mainland, Deer Island (population 1195) has a tinge of a laid-back hippy vibe. It's a modest fishing settlement peppered with artist and craft shops as well as utilitarian fishing-hardware stores. The 16km-by-5km island has been inhabited since 1770, and 1000 people live here year-round. It's well forested and deer are still plentiful. Lobster is the main catch and there are half-a-dozen wharves around the island.

ORIENTATION & INFORMATION

Deer Island can be easily explored on a day trip, but as with all the Fundy Isles, you'll want to linger as long as possible. Narrow, winding roads run south down each side toward Campobello Island and the ferry (drive defensively).

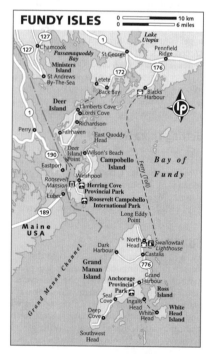

SIGHTS & ACTIVITIES

At **Lamberts Cove** is a huge lobster pound used to hold live lobster (it could well be the world's largest). Another massive pound squirms at Northern Harbor.

At the other end of the island is the 16-hectare **Deer Island Point Park** where Old Sow, the world's second-largest natural tidal whirlpool, is seen offshore a few hours before high tide. Whales pass occasionally.

At the end of Cranberry Head Rd is a **deserted beach**. Most land on the island is privately owned, so there are no hiking trails.

TOURS

Whales usually arrive in mid-June and stay through October. There are several companies offering tours:

Cline Marine Inc (☎ 506-747-0114, 800-567-5880; www.clinemarine.com; 1745 Rte 772, Leonardville; 2½hr tours adult/child $45/30) Offers trips at 9:30am, 12:30pm and 3:30pm in July and August. The 12:30pm tour is most likely to get booked out. Early and late in the season, only the midday trip goes. Boats depart from Richardson Wharf; from the Letete ferry, go 2.8km and turn left.

Eastern Outdoors (☎ 800-565-2925; www.eastern outdoors.com) Operates full-day kayak tours ($89) to see marine mammals, seabirds, islands and beaches. Participants meet at the northern ferry wharf.

Lambert's Outer Island Tours (☎ 506-747-2426; www.outerislandtours.com; adult/child/family $50/30/140) Offers whale-watch tours at 10am, 1pm and 4pm in July and August. It's a smaller operation than Cline Marine and uses a smaller boat. Tours leave from Lord's Cove, 2km from the Letete ferry.

SLEEPING & EATING

Deer Island Point Park (☎ 506-747-2423; www.deeris landpointpark.com; 195 Deer Island Point Rd; campsites $16; ☼ Jun-Sep) Set up your tent on the high bluff and spend an evening watching the Old Sow whirlpool. The campground is directly above the Campobello ferry landing.

Sunset Beach Cottages & Suites (☎ 506-747-2972; www.cottageandsuites.com; 21 Cedar Grove Rd; d $70-100; ☎) In a quiet wooded cove with clear and calm waters, this complex has everything from self-contained cottages to condolike suites. Swim in the heated pool or kayak right from the beach.

45th Parallel Motel & Restaurant (☎ 506-747-2231; parallel45th@hotmail.com; 941 Hwy 772, Fairhaven; mains $9-14; ☼ 11am-9pm early Jun–mid-Sep, noon-2pm Tue & Thu, 5-10pm Fri & Sat, noon-7pm Sun mid-Sep–May) The specialty is seafood at this red-and-white-checkered, country classic. Don't miss seeing Herman, the monster lobster. The motel rooms (single/double $48/58) are a fine bargain, too.

GETTING THERE & AWAY

A free government-run ferry (25 minutes) runs to Deer Island from Letete, which is 14.5km south of St George on Hwy 172 via Back Bay. The ferries run year-round every half-hour from 7am to 7pm, and hourly from 7pm to 10pm. Get in line early on a busy day.

East Coast Ferries (☎ 506-747-2159, 877-747-2159; www.eastcoastferries.nb.ca; ☼ end Jun–mid-Sep), a private company, links Deer Island Point to Eastport, Maine, an attractive seaside town. It leaves for Eastport every hour on the hour from 9am to 6pm; it costs $14 per car and driver, plus $3 for each additional passenger.

For service to Campobello, see below.

Campobello Island

Due to its accessibility and proximity to New England, Campobello Island feels as much a part of the USA as of Canada, and most of the tourists here are Americans. It's a gentler and more prosperous island, with straight roads and better facilities. The wealthy have long enjoyed Campobello as a summer retreat.

Like many moneyed families, the Roosevelts bought property in this peaceful coastal area at the end of the 1800s and it is for this that the island is best known. The southern half of Campobello is almost all park, and a golf course occupies still more.

ORIENTATION & INFORMATION

There isn't even a gas station on the island; to fill their tanks, the 1200 residents of Campobello must cross the bridge to Lubec, Maine. They generally use the same bridge to go elsewhere in New Brunswick, as the Deer Island ferry only runs in summer (see above).

Tourist Office (☎ 506-752-7043; ☼ 9am-7pm Jul & Aug, 10am-6pm late May-Jun & Sep-early Oct) With currency exchange, it's 500m from the bridge.

SIGHTS & ACTIVITIES

The southernmost green area is the 1200-hectare **Roosevelt Campobello International Park** (☎ 506-752-2922; www.fdr.net; Hwy 774; admission free; ☼ 10am-6pm late May-Oct), the site of the Roosevelt mansion and a visitors center. There are free guided tours of the 34-room 'cottage' where Franklin D Roosevelt grew up (between 1905 and 1921) and which he visited periodically throughout his time as US president (1933–45).

Adjacent **Hubbard House** (admission free), built in 1898, is open to visitors. The grounds around all of these buildings are open all the time, and you can peek through the windows when the doors are closed. The park is just 2.5km from the Lubec bridge, and from the front porch of the Roosevelt mansion you can look directly across to Eastport, Maine. You'd hardly know you were in Canada.

Unlike the manicured museum area, most of the international park has been left in its natural state to preserve the flora and fauna that Roosevelt appreciated so much. A couple of gravel roads meander through it, leading to beaches and 7.5km of nature trails. It's a surprisingly wild, little-visited part of Campobello Island. Deer, moose and coyote call it home and seals can sometimes be seen offshore on the ledges near Lower Duck Pond, 6km from the visitors center. Look for eagles, ospreys and loons.

Along the international park's northern boundary is **Herring Cove Provincial Park** (admission free). This park has another 10km of walking trails as well as a campground and a picnic area on an arching 1.5km beach. It makes a fine, picturesque place for lunch.

Ten kilometers north of Roosevelt Park, **Wilson's Beach** has a large pier with fish for sale, and a sardine-processing plant with an adjacent store. There are various services and shops available here in the island's biggest community.

Four kilometers north of Wilson's Beach, **East Quoddy Head** is the second-busiest visitor spot, with a lighthouse at the northern tip of the island. Whales browse offshore and many people sit along the rocky shoreline with a pair of binoculars enjoying the sea breezes.

TOURS

Island Cruises (☎ 506-752-1107, 888-249-4400; 62 Harbour Head Rd, Wilson's Beach; 2½hr tours adult/child $45/28; ☼ mid-Jun–Oct) Offers whale-watch cruises.

Piskahegan River Company (☎ 506-755-6269, 800-640-8944; www.campobello.com/PiskCom/Piskahegan2 .html; 2455 Hwy 774, Wilson's Beach; ☼ Jun–mid-Sep) Operates out of Pollock Cove Cottages. The company offers kayaking tours (three-hour/half-day $30/60) around Campobello, but you must call ahead for reservations.

SLEEPING

Herring Cove Provincial Park (☎ 506-752-7010; fax 506-752-7012; www.tourismnewbrunswick.ca; 136 Herring Cove Rd; tent-/RV sites $22/24; ☯ mid-May–early Oct) This 76-site park on the east side of the island, 3km from the Deer Island ferry, has some nice, secluded sites in a forest setting. It's preferable to Deer Island Point Park and makes a good base for visiting the adjacent international park, plus has a sandy beach and ample hiking.

Owen House B&B (☎ 506-752-2977; www.owenhouse .ca; 11 Welshpool St, Welshpool; d $110-210; ☯ May-Oct) Capturing the essence of Campobello, this nine-room classic overlooks the sea and still holds original furniture and decoration from the mid-1800s. Light bursts in through large windows, a creaky staircase leads to rooms that make you want to curl up with a good book, and Adirondack chairs grace the immaculate waterside garden.

EATING

For such a civilized island, the eating options are surprisingly simple.

Sweet Time Bakery (☎ 506-752-2470; 1001Rte 774, Welshpool; breakfast from $2.75, lunch $4-10, dinner $7-17; ☯ 8am-8pm) This little café-bakery has the best breakfast deal on the island but is also a great spot for wonderfully fresh baked goodies or a simple soup and salad.

Family Fisheries Restaurant (☎ 506-752-2470; Hwy 774, Wilson's Beach; mains $5-20; ☯ lunch & dinner mid-Apr–late Oct) Complete with its own fish market, the specialty is seafood, especially fish-and-chips and chowders. This very casual spot also has sandwiches and burgers but is famed for its massive chicken Caesar salads.

Lupine Lodge (610 Rte 774, Welshpool; mains $14-17; ☯ lunch & dinner). The most chic bet on the island is in a 1915 lodge (built by cousins of the Roosevelts) lined with wood and decorated with moose heads and old snow shoes. The specialty is seafood – fresh fish, scallops and lobster – but steaks are offered too. The deck is a fine place to have a cocktail (and this is the only place on the island serving mixed drinks) and watch the sun sink.

GETTING THERE & AWAY

East Coast Ferries (☎ 506-747-2159, 877-747-2159) connects Deer Island to Campobello Island, costing $14 per car and driver plus $3 per additional passenger. The ferry departs every half-hour between 8:30am and 6:30pm (6pm in June and September). It's a scenic 25-minute trip from Deer Island past numerous islands, arriving at Welshpool, halfway up the 16km-long island.

Grand Manan Island

From windy, jagged cliffs and marshland, to dripping forests and perfect sloping points with storybook lighthouses, Grand Manan has incredible natural diversity within its 30km length. There are dozens of trails to wander and coves to explore, as well as a handful of surprisingly good restaurants where you can sample island-fresh seafood.

In 1831, James Audubon first documented the many birds that frequented the island. About 312 species, including puffins and arctic terns, live here or pass by each year, so birders come in numbers too. Offshore from June onward it's common to see whales feeding on the abundant herring and mackerel.

The island's relative isolation and low-key development mean there are no crowds and little obvious commercialization. Some people make it a day trip, but lingering is highly recommended.

INFORMATION

Grand Manan Library (☎ 506-662-7099; 1144 Rte 776; ☯ 8:30am-4:30pm Mon-Fri) Has free Internet.

Visitor Information Centre (VIC; ☎ 506-662-3442, 888-525-1655; www.grandmanannb.com; 130 Rte 772; ☯ 9am-4pm Mon-Fri, to noon Sat Jun-Oct) At the south edge of North Head.

SIGHTS

In North Head, across the street from the ferry terminal, the **Whale & Sea Bird Research Station** (☎ 506-662-3804; 24 Hwy 776; admission by donation; ☯ 8:30am-5pm Jul & Aug, 10am-4pm mid-May–Jun & Sep) provides good information about the area's marine life. Exhibits include skeletons and photographs.

On the north side of Grand Harbour, the **Grand Manan Museum** (☎ 506-662-3524; 1141 Hwy 776; adult/student $4/2; ☯ 10am-4:30pm Tue-Sat Jun-Sep) has a marine section, displays on the island's geology, antiques and reminders of the Loyalist days, but the highlight is the stuffed-bird collection with examples of species seen on the island. US writer Willa Cather spent summers here for years and some of her belongings, including a typewriter, remain. There's a good selection of books for sale, as well as birding checklists for the island.

LOCAL VOICES

Larry Locke
Retired bank manager, age 61, Grand Manan Island
If your best friend was coming to town where would you go? I just had some friends come over in June and I took them to Southern Head. They said if it was for sale they'd have bought the whole thing. If friends came in August I'd take them out whale-watching or to seine the weir [dip net for herring in the fish parks]. **What is the most important issue in your region today?** Transportation. In the wintertime the ferry to Grand Manan only goes three times a day. Well, the fisheries are still working and that means that they don't have enough transport to get their product to market. Our industry is year-round but the ferry only works in regards to tourism.

Seal Cove flourished during the era of smoked herring (1870–1930), and many wooden structures remain including numerous smokehouses along the harbor. Purse seiners still fish for herring and Connors Brothers has a cannery here, but the biggest catch is lobster.

ACTIVITIES

Grand Manan features more than 18 marked and maintained paths covering 70km of some of the finest **hiking trails** in New Brunswick. The most extensive system is found at the north end of the island, near Long Eddy Point Lighthouse, and several can be linked for an overnight trek. For details, buy *Heritage Trails & Foot Paths on Grand Manan* ($5) at the Grand Manan Museum.

Highly recommended is the slightly pulsequickening (especially in the fog) walk via a footbridge out to the lighthouse at **Swallowtail** on a narrow cliff-edged promontory. The views of the coast and sea are great. To get there , turn right as you leave the ferry – it's only 1km. The walk around and beyond the **Southwest Head** lighthouse along the edge of the 180m cliffs should not be missed. Unlimited hiking possibilities extend in both directions.

Located south of Seal Cove, **Anchorage Provincial Park** (☎ 506-662-7022; btwn Grand Harbour & Seal Cove) is good for bird-watching – wild turkeys and pheasant are common.

TOURS

Several operators run whale-watch trips and guarantee results (see a whale or you get your money back) – this is one of the best places in Atlantic Canada to see the whales. Peak whale-watching begins in mid-July and continues through September.

Adventure High (☎ 506-662-3563; www.adventure high.com; 83 Hwy 776, North Head; ☺ mid-May–Oct) Around 600m to the left of the ferry wharf; offers sea-kayak tours (half-/full day $55/100). The two-hour sunset tour is $40. Adventure High also rents out bicycles (per half-/full day $16/22).

Sea Watch Tours (☎ 506-662-8552, 877-662-8552; www.seawatchtours.com; Seal Cove; adult/child $55/35) Has been around since 1969 and knows these waters. Most of the company's wildlife-viewing tours are long (up to six hours), so take lunch, a motion-sickness pill and a warm sweater. Whale sightings on these trips are almost certain and you often see the endangered northern right whale. In midsummer these tours are often booked out several days in advance. There's a good chance of seeing puffins and seals as well.

SLEEPING

Anchorage Provincial Park (☎ 506-662-7022; btwn Grand Harbour & Seal Cove; tent-/RV sites $22/25; ☺ mid-May–early Oct) The island's best camping is 16km from the ferry. There's a kitchen shelter for rainy days, a playground, Laundromat and long sandy beach. It's possible to book ahead, but the staff never turns anyone away. Get down by the trees to block the wind. Anchorage adjoins some marshes, which comprise a migratory bird sanctuary, and are several short hiking trails.

Shorecrest Lodge (☎ 506-662-3216; www.shorecre stlodge.com; 100 Hwy 776, North Head; r $85-120) This cozy 10-room guesthouse, 700m to the left from the ferry, is owned by a couple from Cape Cod. Rooms are a bit faded but the welcome makes up for that. The dining room has an impeccable reputation and is open for lunch and dinner (mains $19 to $24) by reservation.

Harrington Cove Cottages (☎ 506-662-3868; Rte 776, Harrington Cove; r $90) Up the island, past Seal Cove, are these summery-looking, large cedar cabins, scattered on a hill and affording fine views from their own decks. Cheaper weekly rates are offered.

Manan Island Inn B&B (☎ 506-662-8624; www.man aninn.com; 22 Rte 776, North Head; d $90-140) Right by the ferry terminal, find this salty black-and-white Victorian house with nine rooms. Guests can use the fridge and microwave, as well as the sitting room that evokes another era.

ourpick Compass Rose B&B (☎ 506-662-8570; www .compassroseinn.com; 65 Rte 776; s $85-125, d $95-135; ☽ Jun-Sep) Originally the post and telegraph office for North Head, the Compass Rose is now Grand Manan's finest B&B. It's got everything you'd hope for in a seaside cottage: views from every room, bright yet discreet interiors and a knock-your-socks-off dining room with 180-degree sea views. Fine dinners (mains $16 to $22) and afternoon tea (2pm to 4pm; $3.50) are also available to nonguests by reservation.

EATING

Options are nearly nonexistent in the off-season (from October to early June). That said, there is some fine eating on Grand Manan, often in lodging establishments' dining rooms (see sleeping, previous). Something to sample on the island is dulce, an edible seaweed for which the island is renowned. It's a very popular snack food around the Maritimes and connoisseurs say this is the best there is. It's sold mostly from people's homes; watch for signs.

North Head Bakery (☎ 506-662-8862; 199 Hwy 776, North Head; ☽ 6:30am-5:30pm) Watch as the frosting is drizzled over fresh cinnamon buns and just see if you can turn one down. This wonderful little bakery uses only organic flours and serves steaming free-trade organic tea and coffee. It's a little hard to find, right across the street from the hospital.

Keyser's Café (☎ 506-662-8128; 9 Ferry Wharf Rd; mains $8-14; ☽ 4-10pm Mon-Sat) To your right as you disembark the ferry, this humble-looking place serves up the finest food for miles. The sunny back patio is a blissful spot to enjoy a jug of sangria with a gourmet salad and scallops seared to perfection. Finish off with a massive slice (easily enough for two people) of the house cheesecake. Burgers, steak, fish and other mouth-watering fare are also available.

Mc Laughlin's Wharf Inn (☎ 506-662-8760; 1863 Rte 776, Seal Cove; mains $10-24; ☽ 5-10pm Mon-Sat) It's worth the drive to Seal Cove to dine at this exceedingly (and deservedly) popular waterside inn. This is the kind of place where every table is full of smiles, chatter and good fun. It must be because the food – mostly seafood –

is really exceptional. Don't even try to get a table without a reservation.

GETTING THERE & AWAY

Coastal Transport Ltd (☎ 506-662-3724, 506-456-3842; www.coastaltransport.ca; North Head; round-trip adult/child/car $10/5/30; ☽ daily crossings 6 end Jun–mid-Sep, 3 rest of year) operates the ferry service from Blacks Harbour to Grand Manan. The MS *Grand Manan V*, built in 1990, is larger and quicker, knocking a half-hour off the two-hour trip.

The trip is free on the way over – just board and go. Pay on the way back. Advance-ticket sales are available at North Head and are *strongly* advised. Arrive (very) early. For walk-ons and bicycles, there is never a problem.

If the line of cars at Blacks Harbour is endless, consider doing Grand Manan as a day cruise (board the same boat, but leave the car behind). There's free parking and, depending on the season, you'll have between four and 10 hours on the island between ferries.

BLACKS HARBOUR

Sardine-lovers will note this is home of Connor Brothers, one of the world's largest producers of that delectable little fish-in-a-can. Two thousand people work here. Connor Brothers' trademark brand is Brunswick Sardines and the company runs a **factory outlet store** (☎ 506-456-3897) behind Silver King Restaurant in the center of town. Load up!

Bayview B&B (☎ 506-456-1982; www.bbexpo.com /NewBrunswick/bayview.htm; 391 Deadmans Harbour Rd; s/d with shared bathroom $45/50), a bayside family house about 4km from the Grand Manan ferry, offers three rooms (two with double beds and one with two single beds) in the renovated 18th-century house.

SAINT JOHN

A gritty working port town, Saint John (population 124,981) has an active sense of preservation and heritage without being overly gentrified. The busy downtown is concentrated and walkable, and offers some culture while retaining an intriguing edge. When the sun shines the surrounding hills, jagged bays and bridges glow; when it's foggy the city becomes thick with mysterious atmosphere. Whatever the weather, it's the province's most urban stop.

The protected downtown area reflects Saint John's proud past. It's known as the 'Loyalist City' for the thousands of late-18th-century refugees who settled here, and evidence of this background is plentiful. It has deservedly won honors for maintaining Canada's most intact collection of 19th-century commercial architecture.

Saint John (the name is always spelled out in full, never abbreviated, to avoid confusion with St John's, Newfoundland) is the province's largest city and main industrial center. Sitting on the bay at the mouth of the Saint John River, it is a major year-round port. The dry dock is one of the world's largest and the huge Irving conglomerate is headquartered here. The city has also become a major cruise-ship stopover, hosting dozens of ships annually.

HISTORY

The Maliseet Aboriginal people were here when the British and French began squabbling about furs. Though Samuel de Champlain had landed in 1604, the area remained pretty much a wilderness until 1783, when about 7000 people loyal to Britain arrived from republican America.

The Loyalists were the true founders of Saint John, turning a fort site into Canada's first legal city, incorporated in 1785. Between 1844 and 1848, some 35,000 Irish immigrants arrived, fleeing famine in Ireland, and enough stayed that today they comprise the city's largest ethnic group.

By the mid-19th century Saint John had become a prosperous industrial town, important particularly for its wooden shipbuilding. Though it now uses iron and steel rather than wood, shipbuilding is still a major industry here. In 1877, two-thirds of the city, including most of the mercantile district, was reduced to ashes by fire. It was quickly rebuilt. Today, ethnic diversity is slowly emerging, with small but expanding communities from Latin America, the Caribbean, Lebanon and Asia. Despite this, economic growth is lethargic.

ORIENTATION

Dissected by Saint John River and spread out over an area of 321km, the city feels almost like a handful of separate towns that have been stuck together. Downtown (known as Uptown) Saint John sits on a square peninsula between the mouth of the Saint John River and Courtenay Bay. Kings Sq marks the nucleus of town, and its pathways duplicate the pattern of the Union Jack. Water St borders the redeveloped waterfront area with Market Sq.

The district south of Kings Sq is known as the **South End** with Queens Sq at its heart. On Courtenay Bay, to the east, are the dry dock, shipbuilding yards and much heavy industry. North of town is Rockwood Park, a recreational area.

West over the Harbour Bridge (25¢ toll) is **Saint John West**. Many of the street names in this section of the city are identical to those of Saint John proper, and to avoid confusion, they end in a west designation, such as Charlotte St W. Saint John West has the ferries to Digby, Nova Scotia.

DETOUR: NEW RIVER PROVINCIAL PARK

Just off Hwy 1, about 35km west of Saint John on the way to St Stephen, **New River Provincial Park** (☎ 506-755-4042) has one of the best beaches along the Fundy Shore, a wide stretch of sand bordered on one side by the rugged coastline of Barnaby Head. During camping season the park charges a $5 fee per vehicle for day-use, which includes parking at the beach and Barnaby Head trailhead.

You can spend an enjoyable few hours hiking Barnaby Head along a 6km network of nature trails. The Chittick's Beach Trail leads through coastal forest and past four coves, where you can check the catch in a herring weir or examine tidal pools for marine life. Extending from this loop is the 2.5km Barnaby Head Trail, which hugs the shoreline most of the way and rises to the edge of a cliff 15m above the Bay of Fundy.

The park's **campground** (☎ 506-755-4042; newriver@gnb.ca; 78 New River Beach Rd; tent-/RV sites $22/24; ☒ late May-early Oct) is across the road from the beach and features 100 secluded sites, both rustic and with hookups, in a wooded setting. Drawbacks are the gravel emplacements and traffic noise.

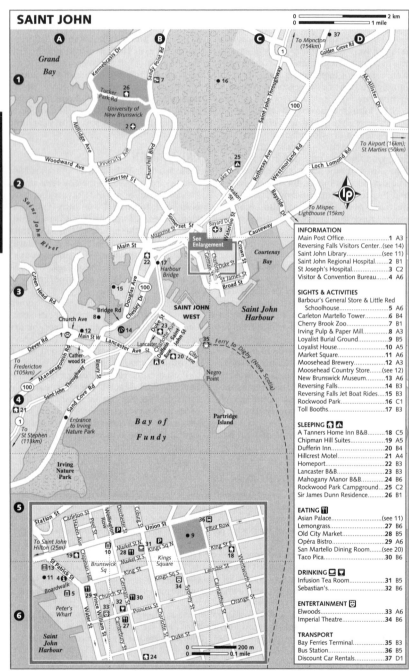

SAINT JOHN

INFORMATION

Main post office (☎ 506-672-6704; 41 Church Ave West, Postal Station B, E2M 4X6; ☺ 8am-5pm Mon-Fri) In Saint John West. Send general delivery mail here.

Police, Fire & Ambulance (☎ 911) For emergencies.

Saint John Library (☎ 506-643-7220; 1 Market Sq; ☺ 9am-5pm Mon & Sat, 10am-5pm Tue & Wed, to 9pm Thu & Fri) Free Internet access.

Saint John Regional Hospital (☎ 506-648-6000; 400 University Ave; ☺ 24hr) Emergency room.

St Joseph's Hospital (☎ 506-632-5555; 130 Bayard Dr; ☺ emergency room 7am-10pm) On the north side of downtown.

Visitor & Convention Bureau (☎ 506-658-2990, 888-364-4444; www.tourismsaintjohn.com; Market Sq; ☺ 9:30am-8pm mid-Jun–Aug, to 6pm Sep–mid-Jun) Knowledgeable, friendly staff. Reversing Falls also has a seasonal visitors center (below).

SIGHTS

New Brunswick Museum

This is a quality **museum** (☎ 506-643-2300; www .gnb.ca/0130; 1 Market Sq; adult/student/family $6/3.25/13; ☺ 9am-5pm Mon-Wed & Fri, to 9pm Thu, 10am-5pm Sat, noon-5pm Sun, closed Mon Nov–mid-May) with a varied collection. There's a captivating section on marine wildlife with an outstanding section on whales including a life-sized specimen. The provincial bird exhibit is comprehensive and the displays on the marine history of Saint John are good, with many excellent models of old sailing ships. There are also hands-on exhibits and worthwhile temporary shows.

Reversing Falls

The Bay of Fundy tides and their effects are a predominant regional characteristic. The falls here are part of that and are one of the best-known sites in the province. However, 'reversing falls' is a bit of a misnomer. When the high Bay of Fundy tides rise, the current in the river reverses, causing the water to flow upstream. When the tides go down, the water flows in the normal way. Generally, it looks like rapids.

The **Reversing Falls Visitors Centre** (☎ 506-658-2937; 200 Bridge Rd; ☺ 8am-7pm mid-May-early Oct), next to the bridge over the falls, can supply a *Reversing Falls Tide Table* brochure that explains where in the cycle you are. You can also watch a film at the **observation deck** (admission $2) upstairs. With all the visitors and tour buses during summer you may find the people-watching more of an event than the flowing water. See above for a more involved experience.

Barbour's General Store & Little Red Schoolhouse

The fun old **general store** (☎ 506-658-2939; Market Sq; admission free; ☺ 9am-6pm mid-Jun–mid-Sep) is packed with the kind of merchandise sold 100 years ago, including old stoves, drugs, hardware and candy. Alongside it, the **Little Red Schoolhouse** is a small museum that's also bound to provoke memories. To get a peek through the Dutch door ask at Barbour's. People aren't allowed in any more as it's full of hornets!

Carleton Martello Tower

In Saint John West, this **national historic site** (☎ 506-636-4011; 545 Whipple St, cnr Fundy Dr; adult/family $3.50/8; ☺ 10am-6pm Jun-Oct) is just off Lancaster Ave, which leads to the Digby ferry terminal. A Martello tower is a circular two-story stone coastal fortification. They were first built in England and Ireland at the beginning of the 19th century. In North America, the British built 16 of them during the early 1800s. Inside, explore the restored powder magazine, barracks and the upper two levels that were added during WWII for the defense of the Saint John Harbour. Go when there's no fog because the view is outstanding.

Loyalist House & Burial Ground

Dating from 1810, **Loyalist House** (☎ 506-652-3590; 120 Union St; adult/child/family $3/1/7; ☺ 10am-5pm Jul-Aug, Mon-Fri only Jun) is the city's oldest unchanged building. The Georgian-style place is now a museum, depicting the Loyalist period and it contains some fine carpentry. The monument to the Loyalists next to the house is striking.

The mood-inducing **cemetery**, with fading tombstones from as early as 1784, is just off Kings Sq, in a park-style setting in the center of town.

Mispec Lighthouse

After the 25-minute drive to the windswept cliff here you'll swear it was 100 miles to a city from this **lighthouse** (Red Head Rd). Take a picnic and stop along the way at Mispec Beach. This exhilarating excursion is not in the tourist information. Cross Courtenay Causeway, turn right onto Bayside Dr, then right onto Red Head Rd. Keep going.

Moosehead Brewery

Moosehead is the country's oldest independent beer maker, dating back to 1867, the year

NEW BRUNSWICK

of Confederation. At the time of research the free tours and tastings had been suspended due to the all-too-familiar contemporary security and insurance fears. Call the **Moosehead Country Store** (☎ 506-635-7020; 49 Main St W; admission free; ⊙ 9am-5pm Mon-Wed, to 9pm Thu & Fri, 10am-5pm Sat) for the latest news. The store has great logo attire for all you mooseheads.

Irving Pulp & Paper Mill

Seeing (and hearing) a modern paper mill is quite an educational experience. To arrange a free tour of **Irving Pulp & Paper Mill**, call ☎ 506-635-7749 during business hours.

ACTIVITIES

Beginning on a boardwalk at Market Sq (behind the Hilton hotel), **Harbour Passage** is a walk and cycle trail that leads around the harbor and naval facility across the toll bridge to Reversing Falls. Informative plaques line the route and it's about 45 minutes one way right after Reversing Falls. In the other direction, it is to be continued along the revamped port lands downtown.

For those with vehicles and an appreciation of nature, **Irving Nature Park** (☎ 506-653-7367; west end of Sand Cove Rd; admission free; ⊙ 8am-dusk early May-early Nov) is a must for its rugged, unspoiled coastal topography. It's also a remarkable spot for bird-watching, with hundreds of species regularly reported. Seals may be seen on rocks offshore. Though the park is said to be on Taylors Island, this is not an island at all but rather a 245-hectare mountainous peninsula protruding into the Bay of Fundy. Seven trails of varying lengths lead around beaches, cliffs, woods, mudflats, marsh and rocks. Good footwear is recommended. The perimeter can be driven on a 6.5km dirt road. It's well worth the 5km drive southwest from downtown to get here. Take Hwy 1 west from town and turn south at Exit 107, Bleury St. Then turn right on Sand Cove Rd and continue for 2km to the entrance.

SAINT JOHN FOR CHILDREN

Saint John is considerably less child-friendly than gardenlike Fredericton or theme park–heavy Moncton. The best place for families is **Rockwood Park** (main entrance 445 Mt Pleasant Ave; admission free; ⊙ 8am-10pm Jun-Sep, to 6pm Oct-May) which houses **lakes** for swimming, **playgrounds**, **horse stables** (☎ 506-633-7659) and **Cherry Brook Zoo** (☎ 506-634-1440; 901 Foster Thurston Dr; admission adult/ child/family $6.50/3.50/16.50; ⊙ 10am-dusk). In 2002 Saint John cut all funding for the zoo so local residents began a monthly sponsorship program. Now the zoo is funded entirely through the program, making it the only 'people's zoo' in Canada. Emphasis is on endangered animals and how to combat extinction. It's a simple place with lots of heart but the animals look overfed and gloomy.

TOURS

Pick up the excellent self-guided historic walking tours pamphlet from either visitors center. The four walks focus on history and architecture. Whale-watching is not an attraction in Saint John, save for the very occasional, very wayward minke.

Reversing Falls Jet Boat Rides (☎ 506-634-8987; www.jetboatrides.com; ⊙ Jun–mid-Oct) Offers two types of trips. The one-hour slow-boat trips (adult/child $32/25) to the Reversing Falls and around the harbor depart from Market Sq. There are also 20-minute jet-boat rides ($30) through the white water at Reversing Falls. Count on getting soaked. For extremists, there is also an open, plastic bubble cage for one that bobs through the turbulence ($100) – it was nice knowing you.

Saint John Transit Commission (☎ 506-658-2855) Runs 2½-hour bus tours (adult/child $16/5) around the city mid-June to early October. Departures and tickets from Reversing Falls Visitors Centre, Barbour's General Store at Market Sq and Rockwood Park Campground. Two tours daily. At 9:30am the bus leaves Reversing Falls and takes 15 minutes to get to each of the other two stops. The trip is reversed from 12:30pm to 1pm.

Words, Walks & Workshops (☎ 506-672-8601; walks free-$5; ⊙ 7pm Tue Jun-Sep) For nearly 30 years David Goss, travel and outdoor columnist, has led themed walks throughout city and nature. The walks have so much flair that locals as well as visitors frequent the fun. Departure locations and hours vary; check with the visitors center.

FESTIVALS & EVENTS

Loyalist Days (☎ 888-364-4444) This eight-day event celebrates the city's Loyalist background with a re-creation of the first arrival, period costumes, parades, crafts, music, food, and fireworks on the last night. Held in the third week of July.

Festival by the Sea (www.festivalbythesea.com) For 10 days this very popular, highly regarded performing-arts event presents hundreds of singers, dancers and other performers from across Canada in concerts and shows put on throughout the city night and day. Many of the performances staged in parks and along the harborfront are free. Early August.

SLEEPING
Budget
Saint John motels sit primarily along Mana-wagonish Rd, 7km west of the downtown, and its continuation Ocean West Way, the old Hwy 100 west of town; this area is industrial and uninteresting but some of the motels have views. Rothesay Ave (Hwy 100 eastbound) has a few more, and though more expensive, they're closer to town.

Rockwood Park Campground (☎ 506-652-4050; www.sn2000.nb.ca/comp/rockwood-park-campground; Lake Drive South; tent-/RV sites $15/20; ❄ mid-May–early Oct) You won't find much privacy at this hillside campground but the views, good amenities and proximity to town make up for it. From here you can also enjoy huge Rockwood Park, with small lakes and part of the university campus. Bus 6 to Mt Pleasant from Kings Sq comes within a few blocks Monday to Saturday.

Sir James Dunn Residence (☎ 506-648-5755; www.unbsj.ca/resconf/; University of New Brunswick, off Sandy Point Rd near Rockwood Park; s/d $34/47, ste d/tr/q $72/78/84; ❄ May-Sep; ℗) This is one of the better deals for campus accommodation in the Maritimes. Out of college-life context dorm rooms are pretty institutional and bland, but they are clean, comfy and private. The two-bedroom suites with kitchenette and TV in the Residence Suites are fantastic if you want to cook your own food. A student card will get you an additional 30% discount. The campus is found 6km north of the city center (take bus 15 from Kings Sq).

Hillcrest Motel (☎ 506-627-5310; 1315 Manawagonish Rd; s/d $50/55; ℗) The small, wood-paneled rooms here are a step up from the area standard, plus there are great views from most units. Check your room first: some non-smoking rooms smell like smoking rooms. The welcome could use a few words from Miss Manners.

Lancaster B&B (☎ 506-672-8861, 888-378-2555; www.lancasterbandb.ca; 523 Lancaster Ave; s/d $65/75; 🖥) On the Westside near the Digby Ferry port, this delightful B&B is a slice of suburban bliss. The heritage home is large, airy and lived in; a fluffy cat wanders the halls and the family members always seem happily at work on some household project. Children are welcome.

Midrange
Consider spending a little more to stay in one of these fantastic midrange options.

Chipman Hill Suites (☎ 506-693-1171; www.chipmanhill.com; office 9 Chipman Hill; ste $50-300) Rest your weary travel heads in an apartment that feels very much like home. Chipman has taken 10 historic properties around downtown, renovated them into mini-apartments with kitchens while leaving all the character intact, and rents them out by the day, week or month. The size and features of each apartment determine their price, but all are a steal and have laundry facilities. This is an excellent choice for families.

our pick **Mahogany Manor B&B** (☎ 506-636-8000, 800-796-7755; www.sjnow.com/mm; 220 Germain St; d $95-110; ℗ 🖥 ♿) This gem of a historic building has wide-open spaces, uncluttered antique-chic rooms and owners who know that service is king. Escape into the jungle of a garden or just hole up and contemplate the comfort and style of your spacious room. Although the B&B has recently changed hands, it's still as professional and gay-friendly as it's always been.

A Tanners Home Inn B&B (☎ 506-634-8917, 877-634-8917; www.tannershomeinn.com; 190 King St E; r $95-110; ℗ 🖥) Be welcomed by Bismark, a giant fluffball of a dog who blends perfectly with the plush windowside couch. Your human hosts are even more charming with a welcome so warm, it stands out even by Maritime standards. Just blocks to downtown, the inn is a lovingly restored former tanner's house from 1878.

Homeport (☎ 506-672-7255; 888-678-7678; www.homeport.nb.ca; 60 Douglas Ave; d $95-125, ste $145-175; ℗) These twin mansions, which are perched above grand, historic Douglas Ave, offer a range of large, well-appointed rooms. You'll also find afternoon tea in the traditional parlor, a great-start morning meal and a flowering garden. Service and smiles make the luxury that much better.

Top End
Dufferin Inn B&B (☎ 506-635-5968; www.dufferininn.com; 357 Dufferin Row; d/ste $155/285; 🖥) Stained-glass windows and mahogany panels create the dark ambience of this 1896 residence of Judge John Babington MacAulay Baxter. The rooms are considerably brighter than the common areas. Today, the inn is German owned and is highlighted by the cooking of chef Axel Begner (p166). The whole inn is smoke-free and relatively environmentally friendly.

NEW BRUNSWICK

EATING
Budget
Old City Market (☎ 506-658-2820; 47 Charlotte St; ⏰ 7:30am-6pm Mon-Thu, to 7pm Fri, to 5pm Sat) Wedged between North and South Market Sts is this sense-stunning, bustling market, which has been home to wheeling and dealing since 1876. Apart from the fresh produce stalls, which are at peak activity on Saturday when local farmers arrive, there are numerous counters selling a range of delectable prepared meals and foods, even lobster.

Midrange
Opéra Bistro (☎ 506-642-2822; 60 Prince St; mains lunch $7-8, dinner $8-14; ⏰ lunch & dinner) The San Martello Dining Room's, hip little sister serves up gourmet sandwiches at lunch and internationally inspired mains such as steamed dim sum ($8) and vegetarian eggplant and red pesto risotto ($12) at dinner. Many consider this the best food in Saint John; and it's undeniably affordable.

Asian Palace (☎ 506-642-4909; Market Sq; lunch specials $8, dinner mains $8-17; ⏰ lunch & dinner) The Palace prepares exquisite Indian fare in a Western-style dining room. Specialties include tandoori (24-hour notice required for the exceptional mogul chicken), spicy curries and vindaloos. There is also a dozen vegetarian selections.

Taco Pica (☎ 506-633-8492; 96 Germain St; mains $10-19; ⏰ 10am-10pm Mon-Sat) Guatemalan, Mexican and Spanish fusion is served at this bright cantina-style café. While the food is just OK, dining among plastic iguanas, sombreros and sunny umbrellas is a fun contrast to the brick-dominated streets of Saint John. Practice Spanish with the waiter and get tropicalized with luscious blended fruit drinks.

Lemongrass (☎ 506-657-8424; 42 Princess St; mains $13-21; ⏰ 11:30am-11pm Mon-Thu, 5pm-11pm Sat & Sun) Amber walls draped with silk scarves bring the Victorian era East, all the way to Thailand. The ambience is spot on and what the food lacks in authenticity it makes up for in flavor. A heated outdoor patio makes alfresco dining possible beyond July and August.

Top End
San Martello Dining Room (☎ 506-635-5968; 357 Dufferin Row; mains $27-34; ⏰ dinner by reservation) At the Dufferin Inn, this restaurant with a German-trained chef serves Euro-inspired dishes using primarily organic ingredients.

Take the time to have a drink in the library before sitting down in the elegant dining room for unique soups and appetizers followed by mains such as red cabbage–stuffed pheasant with sherry sauce ($30). If you want more from the experience, take a cooking class (by reservation; 3½-hour class $40 to $45) with the chef.

DRINKING & ENTERTAINMENT
Saint John is a drinking town. Club action can be found in two main areas: in Market Sq, where the clubs have outdoor patios; and around the corner of Princess and Prince William Sts.

Sebastian's (☎ 506-693-2005; 43 Princess St; martinis from $7; ⏰ 5-10pm Mon-Tue, 5-11pm Wed-Thu, 5pm-2am Fri & Sat) Urban-hardware decor and clean lines call out to be enjoyed with a martini. So order away! The menu lists more than 50 varieties, making this the 'it' spot for cocktails in Saint John. Light meals, from salads to Indian fare to seafood, offer a good landing pad for drinks.

Infusion Tea Room (☎ 506-693-9843; 41 Charlotte St; tea $2-5; ⏰ 7:30am-6pm Mon-Sat) Don't miss this place if you love tea. Choose a steaming pot from the extensive list of black, green, Rooibos, chai and more. The ultimate is the ginseng and lily tea, which is served in a glass pot and opens up into a flower as it steeps. A full British-style high tea can also be reserved (a day in advance) for $20. Soups, sandwiches and light meals ($5 to $7) accompany these liquid delights.

Elwoods (☎ 506-657-3001; 112 Prince William St; ⏰ 11:30am-late) Grab some 'pub food with attitude' ($9 to $15), from burgers to vegan, at this comfy but modern pub with an outdoor patio. Live entertainment happens Friday and Saturday night from 10pm.

Imperial Theatre (☎ 506-674-4100; 24 Kings Sq S; ⏰ box office 10am-7pm Mon-Fri, noon-4pm Sat) Now restored to its original 1913 splendor, the Imperial is the city's premier venue for performances ranging from classical music to live theater. Call for schedule and ticket information.

GETTING THERE & AWAY
Air
The airport is east of town on Loch Lomond Rd toward St Martins. Air Canada has flights to Montréal (one way $180), Toronto ($190) and Halifax ($80) three or four times daily. A 'passenger facility charge' of $10 must be paid at the gate.

Boat

The Bay Ferries' **Princess of Acadia** (☎ 506-649-7777, 888-249-7245; www.bayferries.com; one-way walk-on adult/child/senior $35/15/20, children under 5yr free, car $80) sails between Saint John and Digby, Nova Scotia, year-round. The three-hour crossing can save a lot of driving.

From Saint John between late June and mid-September, departure times are 12:45am, 9am and 4:45pm daily (there's no 12:45am trip on Sunday or Monday). During the rest of the year, ferries only run once or twice daily. There has been some talk of shutting down the ferry but at the time of writing the provincial governments had offered $8 million to keep the ferry running for the next two years only.

Arrive early or call ahead for vehicle reservations (additional fee $5), as the ferry is very busy in July and August. Even with a reservation, arrive an hour before departure. Walk-ons and cyclists should be OK anytime. There's a restaurant and a bar.

Bus

The town's **bus station** (☎ 506-648-3500; 300 Union St; ☉ 7:30am-9pm Mon-Fri, 8am-9pm Sat & Sun) is a five-minute walk from downtown and is served by Acadian Lines. There are services to Fredericton ($20, 1½ hours) and to Moncton ($26, two hours), with one morning and one afternoon trip in each direction. There's also a direct service to Bangor, Maine ($28, 3½ hours), with onward service to Boston and New York on Friday and Saturday.

GETTING AROUND
To/From the Airport

City bus 22 links the airport and Kings Sq. **Diamond Taxi** (☎ 506-648-0666) operates an airport shuttle costing $13. It leaves approximately 1½ hours before all flights, and runs to and from hotels such as the Hilton on Market Sq and the Delta Brunswick on Brunswick Sq. For a taxi, call **Vets** (☎ 506-658-2020), which charges $27 for the first person plus $3 for each additional person.

Bus

Saint John Transit (☎ 506-658-4700) has 30 routes around the city; the fare is $2. The most important is the east–west bus service, which is either bus 1 or 2 eastbound to McAllister Dr and bus 3 or 4 westbound to Saint John West near the ferry terminal. It stops at Kings Sq in

the city center. Another frequent bus service is bus 15 or 16 to the university.

Car & Motorcycle

Discount Car Rentals (☎ 506-633-4440; 622 Rothesay Ave) is opposite the Park Plaza Motel. Avis, Budget, Hertz and National all have car-rental desks at the airport.

Parking meters in Saint John cost $1 an hour from 8am to 6pm weekdays only. You can park free at meters on weekends, holidays and in the evening. The parking meters on Sydney St south of Kings Sq allow up to 10 hours of free parking on weekends and holidays. Park free anytime on back streets such as Leinster and Princess Sts, east of Kings Sq. The **city parking lot** (11 Sydney St) is free on weekends.

EASTERN FUNDY SHORE

While Fundy National Park and Hopewell Rocks swell with tourists during the summer, the area closest to Saint John, around St Martins and through the Fundy Trail, is a rugged, unspoiled paradise that stays relatively peaceful. Hikers, cyclists, kayakers and all nature-lovers will be enchanted with the entire coast which is edged by dramatic cliffs and dramatic tides. It's still not possible to drive directly along the coastline from St Martins to Fundy National Park; a detour inland by Sussex is necessary, unless you're prepared to hike.

ST MARTINS

St Martins (population 374) spreads along the coast with its fine architecture, rolling pastoral hills, endless beaches and exciting sea caves. There's a covered bridge and a prevalent feeling of peace. Once a somnolent wooden shipbuilding center, it's now garnering new attention due to the coastal recreational parkway, opened in 1998. For those with time, littoral Gardner Creek, en route on meandering Rte 825 from Saint John, has 8km of untouched beach.

Sights & Activities

The many fine, oversized homes reflect the wealth of the shipbuilding era (1803–1919). For details, visit the seasonal, unassuming **Quaco Museum** (☎ 506-833-4740; 236 Main St; ☉ noon-5pm Sat & Sun May–mid-Jun, daily mid-Jun–Labour Day, Sat & Sun Labour Day-Oct).

NEW BRUNSWICK

River Valley Adventures (☎ 506-833-2331, 888-871-4244; www.rivervalleyadventures.com; 415 Main St; bikes per hr/day $8/35, kayak tours per 2hr/half-/full day $35/55/80, hiking tours per half-/full day $25/55) are located right across from the tourist office and offer everything you might need for an adventure from bikes to kayaks to guided hikes.

Explore the **caves** at the far end of the vast expanse of beach.

FUNDY TRAIL PARKWAY

The **parkway** (☎ 506-833-2019; www.fundytrailparkway.com; adult/child/family $3/2/10; ☉ 6am-8pm mid-May–Oct) features a rugged section of what has been called the only remaining coastal wilderness between Florida and Newfoundland. The 11km-long parkway to Big Salmon River is a lovely stretch of pavement with numerous viewpoints and picnic areas. Eventually it will extend to Fundy National Park. A separate 16km-long hiking-biking trail also winds its way along.

Pedestrians and cyclists can enter free of charge. In the off-season, the main gate is closed, but you can always park at the entrance and hike or pedal in. On Saturdays, Sundays and holidays an hourly shuttle bus operates from noon to 6pm ferrying hikers up and down the trail between the parkway entrance and Big Salmon River. The shuttle is $3, or free if you paid to enter.

At Big Salmon River is an **interpretive center** (☉ 8am-8pm mid-May–mid-Oct) with exhibits and a 10-minute video presentation. Remains of a sawmill that existed from the 1850s to the 1940s is visible at low tide directly below the interpretive center.

A suspension bridge leads to a vast wilderness hiking area beyond the end of the road. Hikers can make it from Big Salmon River to Goose River in Fundy National Park in three to five days. At last report, no permits or permissions were required to do so. But beyond Big Salmon River, be prepared for wilderness, rocky scree and even a rope ladder or two. Some beach sections are usable only at low tide and the cliffs are unsafe to climb.

Sleeping & Eating

Three family-style beachside restaurants share a complex right on the beach just east of the covered bridge. They all serve standard seafood, fish-and-chips, burgers and ice cream.

Mini Horse Farm B&B (☎ 506-833-6240; www .worldis.com/kathi; 280 West Quaco Rd; d $60; ☉ May-Oct)

An artist couple runs this mini–horse farm that doubles as a B&B. Small kids can take rides on the horses ($5, free for guests) and the farm is a great place to wander (there's a secluded beach nearby) for everyone. Rooms in the cluttered house are nothing luxurious but the charm of the place, the lively owners and the fabulous homemade preserves make up for it.

Quaco Inn B&B (☎ 506-833-4772; www.quacoinn .com; 16 Beach St; r $99-200; ☉ Apr-Nov) This historic mansion has been remodeled to feel quite modern. Built in 1901 after a fire destroyed many of St Martin's luxurious homes, the inn sits just a few meters from the Bay of Fundy. Meals are prepared with fresh ingredients from the garden. Breakfast (from $7) and dinner ($38 to $40) are both served in the 'Tidal Watch' dining room and are also available to nonguests by reservation.

St Martin's Country Inn B&B (☎ 506-833-4534, 800- 566-5257; www.stmartinscountryinn.com; 303 Main St; r $105-165; ☉ Apr-Dec; P &) Decadent architecture, luminous stained-glass windows and sumptuous furnishings make this the most deluxe place in town. Towering atop a small hill, the bay-view mansion is an unmissable landmark. Don't miss a meal in the caught-in-time dining room.

Mrs Brown's Tea Room (☎ 506-833-4499; 133 Main St; full/light afternoon tea $13/9; ☉ 1-5pm) Dedicated to the ritual of a leisurely afternoon tea, this antique-style place complete with floral china, lace tablecloths and bright windows is like stopping by Grandma's for a cuppa. Enjoy with sweet or savory pastries.

FUNDY NATIONAL PARK

This **national park** (☎ 506-887-6000; www.pc.gc .ca/fundy; day permit adult/child/family $7/3.50/17.50) is one of the country's most popular – it gets very, very crowded during July and August. Highlights are the world's highest tides, the irregularly eroded sandstone cliffs and the wide beach at low tide that makes exploring the shore for small marine life and debris such a treat. The park features an extensive network of hiking trails.

Fundy is also home to one of the largest concentrations of wildlife in the Maritimes, including black bear, moose, beaver and peregrine falcons. In late 2004, DNA tests on a hair in the park found it to be that of a cougar, thought by many to be extinct in the region.

Information

Both visitors centers have bookstores and information counters, and sell entry permits and season passes.

Headquarters Visitors Centre (☎ 506-887-6000; ⊙ 10am-6pm mid-Jun–early Sep, 9am-4pm early Sep–mid-Jun) At the south entrance.

Wolfe Lake Information Centre (☎ 506-432-6026; Hwy 114; ⊙ 10am-6pm late Jun-early Sep) North entrance.

Activities

HIKING

Fundy features 120km of walking trails where it's possible to enjoy anything from a short stroll to a three-day trek. Several trails require hikers to ford rivers, so be prepared.

The most popular backpacking route is the **Fundy Circuit**, a three-day trek covering 48km through the heart of the park. Hikers generally spend their first night at Marven Lake and their second at Bruin Lake, returning via the Upper Salmon River. First, stop at the visitors center to reserve your wilderness campsites ($4 per person per night; call ahead for reservations).

Another overnight trek is the **Goose River Trail**. It joins the Fundy Trail, which is accessible by road from St Martins. This undeveloped three-day trek is one of the most difficult in the province. While you can cycle to Goose River, the trail beyond can only be done on foot. For more information, see right.

Enjoyable day hikes in Fundy National Park include **Coppermine Trail**, a 4.4km loop that goes to an old mine site; and **Third Vault Falls Trail**, a challenging one-way hike of 3.7km to the park's tallest falls. On a lighter note, the three-hour, ranger-led **Fundy Night Life Hike** (adult/child/family $12/8/33) at 8pm Saturday in July and August is great, if spooky, fun. Book well in advance.

CYCLING

Mountain biking is permitted on the following six trails: Goose River, Marven Lake, Black Hole, East Branch, Bennett Brook (partially open) and Maple Grove. Surprisingly, at last report there were no bicycle rentals in Fundy National Park or in nearby Alma. Call the visitors centers to find current information on this.

SWIMMING

The ocean is pretty bracing here; luckily, there's a heated saltwater **swimming pool** (☎ 506-887-6014; adult/child $3/1.50; ⊙ 11am-6:30pm late Jun-early Sep) not too far from the park's southern entrance.

Sleeping

Fundy Highlands Inn & Chalets (☎ 506-887-2930, 800-883-8639; www.fundyhighlandchalets.com; 8714 Hwy 114; cabins $65-85; ⊙ May-Oct) Of the park's three roofed options, the well-maintained choices here are recommended. The simple but charming little cabins, all with decks and superlative views, are cheaper than the newly renovated motel-like units (which have bunk beds and a double bed making them perfect for

---

THE TIDES OF FUNDY

The constant ebb and flow of the world's highest tides shape the lives of Fundy residents. Shipping and fishing schedules are set by the tides and, as you'll see, the shoreline metamorphoses the entire landscape every six hours.

A Mi'kmaw legend explains the tide as the effect of a whale's thrashing tail sending the water forever sloshing back and forth. A more prosaic explanation is in the length, depth and gradual funnel shape of the bay itself.

The contrasts between the high and ebb tide are most pronounced at the eastern end of the bay and around the Minas Basin, with tides of 10m to 15m twice daily, 12½ hours apart. The highest tide ever recorded anywhere was 16.6m, the height of a four-story building, at Burncoat Head near Noel, Nova Scotia.

All tides are caused by the rise and fall of the oceans due to the gravitational pull of the sun and the moon. When the moon is full or new, the gravitational forces of the sun and moon are working in concert, and the tides at these two times of the month are higher than average. When one of these periods coincides with the time when the moon is at its closest to earth (perigee, once every 27½ days) the tides are at their most dramatic.

Local schedules are available at regional tourist offices.

families), but both options include kitchenettes. The property is green and quiet and the owners couldn't be more helpful.

The park has five campgrounds and 13 wilderness sites. **Camping reservations** (☎ 800-414-6765, 877-737-3783; reservation fee $7.50) must be made at least three days in advance. The park entry fee is extra and is paid upon arrival.

Just an open field at the northwest entrance to the park, **Wolfe Lake Campground** (campsites $13) has no showers. However, it has the advantages of a covered cooking area and few other campers.

In the interior are the two large **Chignecto Campgrounds** (tent-/RV sites $21/25). The 131-site **Headquarters Campground** (tent-/RV sites $21/27) is near the visitors center. Along the coast, 8km southwest of the visitors center, is **Point Wolfe Campground** (campsites $21) and its 181 sites with sea breezes and cooler temperatures.

To reserve a backcountry site, call either of the visitors centers.

ALMA

The tiny village of Alma (population 290) is a supply center for the park. It has accommodations, restaurants, a small grocery store plus a liquor outlet and Laundromat. Most facilities close in winter, when it becomes a ghost town. Down on the beach is a statue of Molly Kool, the first female sea captain on the continent.

For kayaking tours in and around Fundy, head to **Fresh Air Adventure** (☎ 800-545-0020; www.freshairadventure.com; 16 Fundy View Dr; full-/half-day tours $105/57; ☻ late May–mid-Sep), which offers myriad kayaking tours, from two-hour trips to multi-day excursions.

Stay a night at **Cleveland Place B&B** (☎ 506-887-2213; www.bbcanada.com/137.html; 8602 Main St; r $80-100), right in town center, which is a homey nook with wonderfully friendly hosts. Breakfast is cooked completely from scratch – Jane even grinds her own grain!

It's often booked for dinner weeks in advance, but it's worth trying to get a table at **Tides Restaurant** (☎ 506-887-2313; 8601 Hwy 114; mains $8-23; ☻ lunch & dinner mid-May–Oct) in the dining room at Parkland Village Inn. It prepares top-rate seafood but the ribs aren't far behind. Between the beach, the village wharf and the hummingbirds out the window it's hard to concentrate on cracking a claw. The casual takeout patio has fish-and-chips and cold beer.

Kelly's Bake Shop (☎ 506-887-2460; 8587 Hwy 114; ☻ 7am-8pm Jul & Aug, 10am-5pm Mon-Fri, 9am-6pm Sat & Sun May-Jun & Sep-early Oct) has legendary $1 sticky buns that usually sell out by 1pm.

CAPE ENRAGE & MARY'S POINT

From Alma, old Rte 915 yields two sensational, yet relatively isolated, promontories high over the bay.

See the lighthouse at windblown, suitably named Cape Enrage and wander the beach. **Cape Enrage Adventures** (☎ 506-887-2273; www.capenrage.com) offers kayaking (full/half day $78/52) and rappelling (two hours $50). Have some chowder ($6.50) or a dessert at its tiny yet charming **Keeper's Lunchroom**.

At Mary's Point, 22km east, is the **Shepody Bay Shorebird Reserve** (Mary's Point Rd, off Hwy 915; admission free). From mid-July to mid-August literally hundreds of thousands of shorebirds, primarily sandpipers, gather here. Nature trails and boardwalks lead along the dikes and marsh. The interpretive center is open from late June to early September, but you can use the 6.5km of trails anytime.

HOPEWELL ROCKS

At Hopewell Cape, where the Petitcodiac River meets the Fundy waters in Shepody Bay, is the **Hopewell Rocks Ocean Tidal Exploration Site** (☎ 877-734-3429; off Hwy 114; adult/child/family $7/5/18, shuttle extra $2; ☻ 8am-8pm late Jun–mid-Aug, 9am-5pm mid-May–late Jun & mid-Aug–early Oct). The 'rocks' are unusual erosion formations known as 'flowerpots.' The shore here is lined with these irregular geological forms, as well as caves and tunnels, all of which have been created by erosion from the great tides.

With a parking lot the size of Fredericton it can get extremely crowded, which makes nature feel somewhat like Disneyland. However, an exploratory walk along the beach at low tide is still worthwhile. Check the tide tables at any tourist office, and don't get stranded on the beach when the water rushes in; it's a long wait before you can reach the stairs again! You can't hit the beach at high tide, but the rock towers are visible from the trails above.

In either event, morning is the best time for shutterbugs and has fewer visitors. Note that the ticket is good for the next day too. Admission includes the interpretation center and the expansive wooded property makes for pleasant strolling. The walk to Demoiselle Beach provides a good chance of spotting waterfowl and migratory birds. All told, a quick visit can cheerfully stretch into several hours.

From late June to early September **Baymount Adventures** (☎ 506-734-2660, 877-601-2660; www.baymountadventures.com; adult/child $55/45) offers two-hour kayak tours of the rocks with plenty of birdlife as a bonus, and a cave tour near Hillsborough. The office is 100m beyond the café inside the Exploration Site.

SOUTHEASTERN NEW BRUNSWICK

It might be the geographical heart of the Maritimes, but this corner of New Brunswick isn't exactly the most lovable area in the region. Moncton, known as 'Hub City,' is a major crossroads and, although not pretty, has some unique attractions that make it worth a stop. Southeast, en route to Nova Scotia, are significant historical and birdlife attractions.

MONCTON

Moncton (population 61,045) rises up from a boggy plain and at first glimpse appears to be an industrial monstrosity. Take a closer look. Explore the historic brick downtown area to discover that this university town has more than its share of culture and some of the best food you'll find for miles. As the province's second city and a major transportation and distribution center for Atlantic Canada, Moncton sees a lot of through traffic, especially in summer. Due to a couple of odd attractions – Magnetic Hill and a tidal bore – it's worth a pit stop on your way past.

History

Moncton was originally on a Mi'kmaq portage route from Shediac. In the 1740s the first Acadians settled, to be followed in 1766 by Protestant German immigrants from Pennsylvania. In the mid-1800s it was a major shipbuilding hub, but falling demand for wooden ships led to the closure of Moncton's shipyards in the early 1860s. Later, it became a rail center and during WWII the city served as a transportation hub and training facility for pilots from many Allied countries. Moncton now thrives as a main service center for the Maritimes.

Today, nearly half the bilingual population has French as their mother tongue, thanks to the number of descendants of Acadians.

Orientation & Information

The small downtown area extends north and south of Main St. The river lies just to the south and north of town the Trans-Canada Hwy (Hwy 2) runs east–west. Lengthy Mountain Rd, leading west toward the Trans-Canada Hwy, is lined with service stations and chain restaurants.

Moncton Public Library (☎ 506-869-6000; 644 Main St; ◷ 9am-8:30pm Tue-Thu, to 5pm Fri & Sat) Free Internet access.

St George Street After Hours Medical Clinic (☎ 506-856-6122; 404 St George St; ◷ 5:30-8pm Mon-Fri, noon-3pm Sat, Sun & holidays) No appointment is required to see a doctor. Adjacent to Jean Coutu Pharmacy.

Visitors center (☎ 506-853-3590, 800-363-4558; www.gomoncton.com; Tidal Bore Park; ◷ 9am-8pm Jul & Aug, , to 7pm Jun, to 4:30pm late May & Sep-early Oct) From November to mid-May, find the office at City Hall, 2nd fl, 655 Main St.

Sights

At **Magnetic Hill** (☎ 506-858-8841; cnr Mountain Rd & Hwy 2; entry per car $5; ◷ 8am-8pm mid-May–mid-Sep), incredibly one of Canada's best-known (though not best-loved) attractions, gravity appears to work in reverse. Start at the bottom of the hill in a car and you'll drift upward. You figure it out. After hours and out of season, it's free. It's a goofy novelty, worth the head-scratching laugh, but all the money-generating, spin-off hoopla now surrounding the hill overglamorizes what should be a minor attraction. Family-oriented attractions include a depressing zoo and good water park (adult/child $24/18; half price after 3pm).

Tidal Bore Park (east end of Main St; admission free; ◷ 24hr) features a twice-daily incoming wave caused by the tides of the Petitcodiac River, which are in turn related to the tides in the Bay of Fundy, the world's highest. As the tide advances up the narrowing bay it starts to build up on itself, forming a wave. The height of this oncoming rush can vary from just a few centimeters to about 1m. The size and height of the bore are determined by the tide, itself regulated by the moon. As with the tides, there are two bores a day, roughly 12 hours apart. While this is an interesting occurrence, especially in theory, the bores are often…boring.

The modest **Moncton Museum** (☎ 506-856-4382; 20 Mountain Rd, near Belleview St; admission $1.50; ◷ 10am-8pm Jul-Aug, 9am-4:30pm Mon-Sat & 1-5pm Sun Sep-Jun) outlines local history from the time of the Mi'kmaq and early settlers to the present. Photos and artifacts show the influence of shipbuilding and the railway. Next door is the oldest building in town, the **Free Meeting House** (1821).

At the **Acadian Museum** (☎ 506-858-4088; www .umoncton.ca/maum; Clement Cormier Bldg; adult/student $3/2, all free on Sun; ☷ 10am-5pm Mon-Fri, 1-5pm Sat & Sun Jul & Aug, 1-4:30pm Tue-Fri, 1-4pm Sat & Sun Sep-Jun), on the university campus, you can get brief history of the Acadians through displays depicting the day-to-day life. The first European settlers in the Maritimes had an arduous yet enthralling history that was defined by their expulsion by the British in 1755. An even better museum about Acadian culture is **Monument-Lefebvre National Historic Site**

(☎ 506-758-9783; 480 Central St; adult/child/senior/family $3.50/1.25/3/8.75; ☷ 9am-5pm Jun–mid-Oct), in St Joseph, 25km southeast of Moncton. Exhibits such as paintings, crafts and life-sized models are well done and, unlike those at many similar sites, devote attention to the subjects' lives through to the present.

Tours

Gray Line (☎ 866-276-1111; www.grayline.com) offers bus tours ($40) to Hopewell Rocks, which includes kayaking around the formations.

Sleeping

Basic motels and more expensive chain hotels cluster around the Magnetic Hill area. Prices are high for what you get and the area lacks

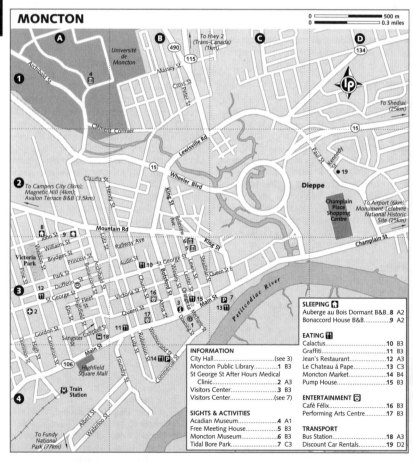

MONCTON

Université de Moncton

To Hwy 2 (Trans-Canada) (1km)

To Shediac (25km)

To Campers City (3km);
Magnetic Hill (4km);
Avalon Terrace B&B (3.5km)

Dieppe

Champlain Place Shopping Centre

To Airport (6km);
Monument-Lefebvre National Historic Site (25km)

Victoria Park

Mountain Rd

Petitcodiac River

Highfield Square Mall

Train Station

To Fundy National Park (77km)

charm (unless you enjoy the whoosh of the freeway) as well eating options beyond fast food. Stay near the historic town center for a more provincial experience.

Campers City (☎ 506-384-7867, 877-512-7868; www .sn2000.nb.ca/comp/camper_city; 138 Queensway Dr; tent-/ RV sites $25/30; Jun-Sep) The nearest campground to the city (around 3km west), at the Mapleton Rd exit from Hwy 2, caters mostly to RVs but has some nice grassy sites for tents at the back.

Bonaccord House B&B (☎ 506-388-1535; www.bb canada.com/4135.html; 250 Bonaccord St; s/d $45/58) Within walking distance of the center is the four-room, ever-popular, bargain-priced Bonaccord House. It's the appealing yellow-and-white house with stately Doric columns on the porch and a yard surrounded by a white picket fence.

Auberge au Bois Dormant B&B (☎ 506-855-6767; www.auberge-auboisdormant.com; 67 John St; r $85-150; P) Acadian owned and gay-friendly, this lovely Victorian peppers in modern flair to delicious perfection. Its downtown location is ideal and the owners are friendly and helpful.

Auberge Canadiana Inn (☎ 506-382-1054; 46 Archibald St; r $95-175; P) This gorgeous old place is steeped in time and character, and the breakfast nook brings the seaside to Moncton – sounds impossible but it's true. The outdoor 2nd-floor veranda is a perfect place to plan or review the day and the center of Main St is a very short walk.

Avalon Terrace B&B (☎ 506-854-6494, 888-833-7177; www.avalonterrace.com; 739 Frampton Lane; d $115-160; P) Near the theme parks of Magnetic Hill, this well-garnished B&B has its own theme: King Arthur. While most rooms in the modern home are decorated with antiques, the ruffled peach Guinevere room veers more towards Vegas. Romance is queen and breakfasts are superb.

Eating & Drinking

Moncton Market (120 Westmorland St, 7am-1pm Sat) It's not really a farmers' market as most items are ready to eat, but the gastronomic array here is mind-boggling. Plan on having your breakfast or lunch here. It's a must if you're in Moncton on a Saturday morning.

Pump House (☎ 506-855-233; 5 Orange Lane; mains $7-13; 11am-1am) Dining next to all those beer vats has got to give you a hankering for a beer or three. The Pump is where the locals

unwind and you can get a good burger, steak-based meal or wood-fired pizza. Of the brews made on the premises, the Muddy River stout is tasty, or be more adventurous and try the blueberry beer.

Calactus (☎ 506-388-4833; 128 St George St; mains $7-13; 11am-10pm) Even carnivorous locals come to pack this vegetarian café. Start your meal with a thick blended smoothie then move on to pizzas, veggie burgers or pastas such as the Portobello cannelloni ($12).

Graffiti (☎ 506-382-4299; 897 Main St; mains $9-16; 11am-11pm Sun-Thu, to midnight Fri & Sat) Graffiti is upscale in everything but price. The kitchen prepares mouth-watering dishes with a Mediterranean or 'new Greek' flair, including seafood, moussaka and a vegetarian couscous, and the room is understatedly refined.

Le Chateau à Pape (☎ 506-855-7273; 2 Steadman St; mains $20-25; dinner from 4pm) For fresh seafood or a steak in a rambling wooden place with a Maritime setting, this is the spot. It's been serving top-rated meals for many years and is right beside Tidal Bore Park. After dinner, stroll along the adjoining Riverfront Promenade.

Entertainment

Free *Marque* or *Mascaret* magazines give rundowns on Moncton's vibrant (read: raucous) nightlife. Central Main St and side streets have several bars with a young crowd, live bands and dancing.

Café Félix (☎ 506-381-9388; 785 Main St; 11am-late Mon-Thu, noon-late Fri & Sat, 10am terrace jazz brunch Sun) French bistro meets Louisiana jazz in this blue-and-red lounge wonderland. The food is Cajun inspired and Friday- and Saturday-night live music (from 7pm) ranges from blues to swing.

Performing Arts Centre (☎ 506-856-4379; 811 Main St; box office 9am-5pm Mon-Fri, to 1pm Sat) The impressive Capitol Theatre, a 1920s vaudeville house, has been restored and is now the city's Performing Arts Centre. It's home to Theatre New Brunswick and the Symphony New Brunswick, which give performances on a regular basis.

Getting There & Away

AIR

Moncton, New Brunswick's busiest airport, is served by discount airline WestJet from cities across Canada. Flights to other parts of Canada tend to be cheaper here than those out of Halifax. Air Canada and its subsidiary Air Canada Jazz fly from Montréal, Toronto, Halifax and Québec City. Greater Moncton Airport is about 6km east of Champlain Place Shopping Centre via Champlain St. Departing passengers must pay an 'airport improvement and reconstruction fee' of $15.

BUS
Acadian Lines stops at the **bus station** (☎ 506-859-5060; 961 Main St; ☒ 7:30am-8:30pm Mon-Fri, 9am-8:30pm Sat & Sun), right in the heart of town. Buses go to Fredericton ($34, two hours, two daily), Charlottetown ($31, 3½ hours, two to three daily), Halifax ($48, four hours, three to four daily) and Bangor, Maine ($43, six hours) with onward service to Boston and New York.

CAR & MOTORCYCLE
If you need wheels, Avis, Budget, Hertz and National all have car-rental desks at the airport or try **Discount Car Rentals** (☎ 506-857-2323; 566 Paul St; ☒ 8am-6pm Mon-Fri, 9am-1pm Sat).

Parking can be a hassle in Moncton: parking meters ($1 per hour) and 'no parking' signs extend far out from downtown. The parking lot at Moncton Market on Westmorland St charges $1/7 per hour/day and is free on Saturday, Sunday and evenings after 6pm. Highfield Sq Mall on Main St provides free parking for its clients, and who's to say you aren't one?

TRAIN
The sparkling **train station** (☎ 506-857-9830, 800-561-3952; 1240 Main St; ☒ 9am-6pm) is right in the heart of town. With VIA Rail, the *Ocean* goes through northern New Brunswick, including Miramichi and Campbellton, and into Québec, on its way to Montréal ($109). It leaves at 5:40pm daily except Tuesday. The train to Halifax ($56) departs daily at 11:40am, except Wednesday.

Getting Around
The airport is served by bus 20 Champlain, which leaves from Champlain Pl nine times on weekdays. A taxi to the center of town costs about $14.

Codiac Transit (☎ 506-857-2008) is the local bus system running daily, except Sunday. Single tickets are $1.75.

SACKVILLE
Sackville (population 5341) is a small university town that's in the right place for a pit stop – for birds and people. The **Sackville Waterfowl Park**, across the road from the university off East Main St, is on a major bird migration route. Boardwalks with interpretive signs rise over portions of it. The **Wildlife Service** (☎ 506-364-5044; 17 Waterfowl Lane, off E Main St; admission free; ☒ 8am-4pm Mon-Fri) has information and a wetlands display at one of the entrances. Enthusiasts should also see the **Tantramar Wetlands Centre** (☎ 506-364-4257; www.weted.com; 223 Main St; admission free; ☒ 8am-4pm Mon-Fri) with its walking trail and educational office. It's behind the high school.

Mel's Tea Room (☎ 506-536-1251; 17 Bridge St; mains $4-10; ☒ 8am-midnight Mon-Sat, 10am-11pm Sun) is the favorite among locals. This tearoom, operating in the center of town since 1919, has the charm of a 1950s diner, including a jukebox and prices to match.

FORT BEAUSÉJOUR NATIONAL HISTORIC SITE
Right by the Nova Scotia border, this **national historic site** (☎ 506-536-0720; www.pc.gc.ca/fortbeausejour; 1.5km west of the visitors center; adult/child/family $3.50/1.75/8.75; ☒ interpretive center 9am-5pm Jun–mid-Oct) preserves the remains of a French fort built in 1751 to hold the British back. It didn't work. Later it functioned as a stronghold during the American Revolution as well as the War of 1812. Only earthworks and stone foundations remain, but the view is excellent, vividly illustrating why this crossroads of the Maritimes was fortified by two empires.

To find out more, visit the **New Brunswick Visitor Centre** (☎ 506-364-4090; 158 Aulac Rd; ☒ 9am-9pm Jul & Aug, 10am-6pm mid-May–early Oct), off Hwy 2 in Aulac, at the junction of roads leading to all three Maritime provinces.

NORTHUMBERLAND SHORE

Folks here, like those further north on the Acadian Peninsula and in northern PEI, claim their waters are the warmest north of Virginia in the USA, because of spin-off currents of the Gulf Stream. Regardless, it ain't Miami by a long shot. New Brunswick's half of the Northumberland Shore stretches from the Confederation Bridge to Kouchibouguac National Park and makes up part of the Acadian Coastal Drive. A good part of the population along this coast is French-speaking.

CAPE JOURIMAIN

Near the bridge to PEI, the **Cape Jourimain Nature Centre** (☎ 866-538-2220; Rte 16; admission free; 8am-8pm May-Oct) sits in a 675-hectare national wildlife area that protects this undeveloped shoreline and its migratory birds. The center has exhibits on climate change, ecology and birdlife. Seventeen kilometers of trails wind through salt marshes, dunes, woods and beach. A four-story lookout provides views of the surroundings and Confederation Bridge.

There's a **New Brunswick Visitor Centre** (☎ 506-538-2133; Hwy 16; 8am-9pm Jul & Aug, 9am-6pm mid-May–Jun & Sep-early Oct) by the bridge.

The **Confederation Bridge** (☎ 902-437-7300; www .confederationbridge.com; car/motorcycle $41/16; 24hr) makes getting to PEI faster, easier and cheaper than travel by ferry. Cash, debit and major credit cards are accepted. If you're cycling or walking, you must pick up the free shuttle across the bridge at the Bridge Facility Building at the junction of Hwys 16 and 955. It leaves every two hours when required. See p200 for more details.

SHEDIAC

A self-proclaimed lobster capital, Shediac (population 4892) is the focal point of the area's beach resorts and home of the annual July **lobster fest**. You can even enjoy it on pizza! The many white lights sprinkled around town all summer lend a festive air.

It seems on any hot weekend that half the province is flaked out on the sand at **Parlee Beach**, turning the color of cooked lobster. South at **Cap Pelé** are vast stretches of more sandy shorelines. Terrific **Aboiteau Beach** is over 5km of unsupervised sand, while others have all amenities and lifeguards.

Shediac Bay Cruises (☎ 506-532-2175, 888-894-2002; www.lobstertales.ca; Pointe-du-Chene wharf) takes passengers out on the water, pulls up lobster traps, then shows you how to cook and eat 'em – all for $54. Conversely, you can fish for mackerel for $35.

For a small town, accommodations are varied and generous, from camping through to lovely old inns. **Le Coin Gretzky** (☎ 506-533-9626; cgretzkybnb@yahoo.ca; 17 Cornwall Point Rd; r $60-90) is a beauty of a place with a wonderful porch

and bright breakfast area. It's central but not right on the main drag.

For sucking a lobster leg, **Fisherman's Paradise** (☎ 506-532-6811; 640 Main St; mains $13-24; 11am-10pm) has them lining up. The convivial atmosphere is perfect for a summer-holiday meal.

BOUCTOUCHE

This small, surprisingly busy town is an Acadian cultural focal point with several unique attractions. The **VIC** (☎ 506-743-8811; Hwy 134; 9am-5pm Jun-Sep) at the town's south entrance features a boardwalk that explains the local oyster industry.

Sights & Activities

Le Pays de la Sagouine (☎ 800-561-9188; www.sagouine .com; 57 Acadie St; adult/child/senior/family $15/11/14/36; 10am-6pm Jul & Aug, 10:30am-4pm mid-Jun–Sep) consists of a cluster of buildings made to appear like a fishing community – it's on a small island in the Bouctouche River. Dedicated to Acadian writer Antonine Maillet, Le Pays de la Sagouine is an immersion course in Acadian history and culture. It hosts live music and theatrical shows. In July and August there's a supper theater at 7pm Monday to Saturday with a variety of musical programs ($46 including dinner). In June and September, the dinner show is usually on Saturdays only (most programs are in French). Friday nights are given over to concerts.

Irving Eco Centre (☎ 506-743-2600; www.irvingeco center.com/main.htm; 1932 Hwy 475; admission free; interpretive center 10am-8pm Jul & Aug, noon-5pm Mon-Thu, noon-6pm Fri, 10am-6pm Sat & Sun mid-May–Jun & Sep-Oct), on the coast 9km northeast of Bouctouche, protects and makes accessible 'La Dune de Bouctouche,' a beautiful, long sand spit jutting into the strait. The interpretive center has displays on the flora and fauna, but the highlight is the 2km boardwalk above the dune. The peninsula itself is 12km long, taking four to six hours to hike over the loose sand and back. Few visitors go beyond the boardwalk, so even a short walk means solitude.

To reduce the impact of the large numbers of visitors in July and August, only the first 2000 persons to arrive each day are admitted to the boardwalk. It reopens to everyone after 5pm. Otherwise the boardwalk is accessible anytime year-round. On Saturdays at 8am during July and August there's a free bird-watch tour. Bicycles are not allowed on the dune, but there's a separate 12km hiking-cycling trail through mixed forest to Bouctouche town, which begins at the Eco Centre parking lot.

Exhibits cover Acadian culture at **Kent Museum** (☎ 506-743-5005; 150 Hwy 475; adult/child $3/1; ⊗ 9am-5pm Mon-Fri & noon-6pm Sat & Sun Jul & Aug, 9:30am-noon & 1-4pm Mon-Fri mid-Jun–end Jun & Sep–mid-Oct), in the former Convent of the Immaculate Conception (1880), 2km east of the center of Bouctouche.

KayaBéCano (☎ 506-743-6265, 888-529-2232; www .kayabecano.nb.ca; 1465 Hwy 475; adult/child $30/15; ⊗ mid-May–early Sep), 2.5km south of Irving Eco Centre, runs two-hour kayak trips that explore the cultured-oyster industry. It also rents out kayaks for self-guided trips along the dune.

KC Irving (1899–1992), founder of the Irving empire, was from Bouctouche, and there's a large bronze statue of him in the town park.

Sleeping & Eating

Aux P'tits Oiseaux B&B (☎ 506-743-8196; oiseau@nbnet .nb.ca; 124 Hwy 475; r with shared bathroom $50-60) This friendly B&B near the Kent Museum features a collection of 500 carved birds mounted through the house. Call ahead as it's usually full all summer.

Auberge Vue de la Dune B&B (☎ 506-743-9893; www.aubergevuedeladune.com; 586 Rte 475; r $90-135; P ⊔ &) Bright modern rooms and Acadian hospitality welcome you to this chef-run inn. The popular 50-seat dining area serves up copious portions of Acadian-inspired seafood ($10 to $25) in a casual café style. Wheelchair access.

Restaurant Le Vieux Presbytère de Bouctouche (☎ 506-743-5568; opposite Kent Museum, Hwy 475; lobster dinner $35; ⊗ 5:30-8:30pm Jun-early Oct) This large restaurant in an old religious residence does casual, social, PEI-style lobster suppers. Reservations are required.

ST LOUIS DE KENT

Blooming with visitors in summer, St Louis (population 991) is ideal as a service base for visiting Kouchibouguac National Park (following).

You can't do better than **Oasis Acadienne B&B** (☎ 506-876-1199; www.kayakouch.com; 10617 Hwy 134; s $40-70, d $55-85; ⊗ May-Oct), a congenial six-room B&B 4km south of Kouchibouguac. It's run by the Kayakouch kayaking people (opposite) and has a dock astride the Kouchibouguac River right in the backyard!

If the national park, 2.5km north, is full, **Daigle's Park** (☎ 506-876-4540; www.campingdaigle .com; 10787 Hwy 134; tentsites $17, RV sites $20-26; ⊗ mid-May–mid-Sep; &) is a good camping alternative. There are some nicely wooded sites for tenters.

KOUCHIBOUGUAC NATIONAL PARK

Coastal highlights – bogs, tidal rivers, beaches and offshore sand dunes extending for 25km – make this park. The sands invite strolling, bird-watching and clam-digging. At the south end of the main beach, seals are often seen offshore.

Kouchibouguac (*koosh*-e-boo-gwack), a Mi'kmaw word meaning 'river of long tides,' also has populations of moose, deer and black bear. Other features are the salt marsh and a bog where there's an observation platform.

Information

The **visitors center** (☎ 506-876-2443; www.pc.gc.ca /kouchibouguac; 186 Hwy 117; park admission per day adult/ child/family $7/3.50/17.50; ⊗ 8am-8pm Jul & Aug, 9am-5pm mid-May–mid-Oct) features interpretive displays and a small theater as well as an information counter and gift shop.

Activities

HIKING

The park has 10 trails, mostly short and flat. The excellent **Bog Trail** (1.9km) is a boardwalk beyond the observation tower, and only the first few hundred meters are crushed gravel. This trail tends to be crowded around the middle of the day and is best done early or late. The **Cedars Trail** (1.3km) is less used. The **Osprey Trail** (5.1km) has a bit of everything. Maybe best is walking the **Kelly's Beach Boardwalk** (600m one way), then turning right and going the 6km to the end of the dune. Take some drinking water. The visitors center has a special all-terrain wheelchair with oversized wheels that park staff loan out free upon request. Otherwise, the boardwalk to Kelly's Beach is wheelchair-accessible.

CYCLING

Kouchibouguac features hiking trails and canoe routes, but what really sets it apart is the 40km of bikeways – gravel paths that wind through the park's backcountry. **Ryan's Rental Center** (☎ 506-876-3733), near the South Kouchibouguac campground, rents out bicycles at $6/28 per hour/day and canoes/kayaks at $30/50 per day. From Ryan's it's possible to cycle a 23km loop and never be on the park road.

SWIMMING & KAYAKING

For swimming, the lagoon area is shallow, warm and safe for children, while adults will find the deep water on the ocean side invigorating. There's also a 'gay beach' in the park, a 45-minute walk to the right from the end of the Kelly's Beach boardwalk.

Kayakouch (☎ 506-876-1199; www.kayakouch.com; 10617 Hwy 134; ☉ mid-Jun–Aug), just 4km south of the national park, rents out kayaks and offers guided kayaking tours.

Sleeping

Kouchibouguac has two drive-in campgrounds and three primitive camping areas totaling 359 sites. The camping season is from mid-May to mid-October and the park is very busy throughout July and August, especially on weekends. **Camping reservations** (☎ 877-737-3783; www.pccamping.ca; reservation fee $8) are taken for 60% of the sites. Otherwise, get on the lengthy 'roll call' waiting list – it can take two or three days to get a site. The park-entry fee is extra.

South Kouchibouguac (tent-/RV sites $18/26; ☉ mid-May–mid-Oct) The largest campground is located 13km inside the park near the beaches, with showers and a kitchen shelter.

Cote-a-Fabien (campsites $14) On the north side of Kouchibouguac River is away from trails and beaches, and doesn't have showers.

The three primitive campgrounds have only vault toilets and a pump for water. These cost $8 per person per night, as does canoe camping.

THE MIRAMICHI

Almost synonymous with fly-fishing, Miramichi connotes both the city and the river as well as an intangible, captivating mystique. The spell the region casts emanates from Acadian and Irish folklore and from the dense forests and wilderness of the area. Residents of the region wrestle a livelihood from the forest, which equals paper, pulp and saw mills. The region produces some wonderful rootsy music and inspires artists including noted writer David Adams Richards, whose work skillfully mines the temper of the region.

MIRAMICHI

The city of Miramichi (population 18,508) is an industrial and somewhat confusing amalgam of Chatham and Newcastle and the villages of Douglastown, Loggieville, Nelson and several others along a 12km stretch of the Miramichi River. Miramichi City, with its Irish background, is an English-speaking enclave in the middle of a predominantly French-speaking region. From here north, it's all mill country. Held in early August, the **Miramichi Folksong Festival** (www.miramichifolksongfestival.com), begun in 1957, is the oldest such festival in North America.

Information

Chatham Tourist office (☎ 800-459-3131; www.miramichi.org; Hwy 11; ☉ 9am-9pm late May-early Oct, 9am-6pm early May & late Oct) On the south side of the river.

Newcastle Public Library (☎ 506-623-2450; 100 Fountain Head Lane; ☉ 1-8pm Tue & Wed, 10am-5pm Thu-Sat) Near Ritchie Wharf; free Internet access.

Newcastle Tourist office (☎ 506-623-2152; ☉ Jun-Aug) Seasonal office downtown at Ritchie Wharf, on the river's north side.

Sights & Activities

Surrounded by two paper mills and sawmills, a **statue** to Lord Beaverbrook (1879–1964), one of the most powerful press barons in British history (see the boxed text, p144), stands in central Newcastle. Among the many gifts he lavished on the province are the 17th-century English benches and the Italian gazebo here. His ashes lie under the statue presented as a memorial to him by the town.

Beaverbrook spent most of his growing years in Newcastle. **Beaverbrook House** (☎ 506-624-5474; 518 King George Hwy; admission free; ☉ 9am-5pm Mon-Fri, 10am-5pm Sat, 1-5pm Sun mid-Jun–Aug), his boyhood home (erected 1879), is now a museum.

Ritchie Wharf, a riverfront boardwalk park nearby, has playgrounds, eateries, a lighthouse, an information center and also boat tours ($9) to **Beaubears Island** in the summer. The island has been a Mi'kmaw campsite, a refugee camp for Acadians during the expulsion, and a ship-building site.

The **Enclosure** (☎ 506-622-8638; 8 Enclosure Rd), 5km southwest of the city of Miramichi, was used as a refugee site in the 1700s by the Acadians. A small **museum** houses artifacts from area archaeological digs. Evidently, one of the ships that brought the Acadians was a sister to the famous *Bounty*.

French Fort Cove Nature Park (☎ 506-624-9121; www.frenchfortcove.com; headless nun tour $8; ☻ May-Sep) sits on the site of an old Acadian settlement that was completely destroyed by the British in 1760. Today it houses around 5km of tranquil walking trails. At night you can accompany costumed guides who tell the eerie tale of 'the headless nun,' who apparently still haunts the area.

Experience Miramichi music with a foot-stomping **Kitchen Party** (☎ 506-773-8010; www .miramichikitchenparty.com; per person $25; ☻ 7pm Tue mid-Jun–Sep). Dates change so check the website.

Sleeping & Eating

Enclosure Campground (☎ 506-622-8638, 800-363-1733; www.sn2000.nb.ca/comp/enclosure-campground; 8 Enclosure Rd; tent-/RV sites $21/27; ☻ May-Oct) Southwest of Newcastle off Hwy 8 is another of Lord Beaverbrook's gifts, a former provincial park called the Enclosure (see above). This riverside park includes a nice wooded area with spacious quasiwilderness sites for tenters.

Sunny Side Inn (☎ 506-773-4232; www.bbcanada.com /sunnysideinn; 65 Henderson St, Chatham; s/d $75/90; ☺) Miramichi's longest operating inn is showing the wear in a Faulty Towers–eque way. The imposing turreted mansion has a chipped-paint exterior and the interior feels like it was being worked on then forgotten. Still, it's comfy and friendly with very big rooms and great breakfasts.

Saddler's Café (☎ 506-773-4214; 1729 Water St, Chatham; mains lunch $7-10, dinner $11-16; ☻ 11:30am-3pm & 5-8pm Tue-Sat) Miramichi residents are fascinated by this place since it's one of the first to steer away from fried specialties to more worldly cuisine such as lobster and mozzarella tart ($10) or warm Thai pineapple salad ($13). The bright interior feels almost Greek and looks out over the river.

Getting There & Away

The **bus station** (☎ 506-622-0445; 60 Pleasant St; ☻ 8:30am-5pm Mon-Fri, 1-3pm Sat & Sun) is in downtown Newcastle. Daily buses leave for Fredericton ($19, 2½ hours), Saint John ($38, five hours) and Campbellton ($23, three hours).

The **VIA Rail station** (☎ 800-561-3952; Station St at George St) is in Newcastle. Trains from Montréal and Halifax stop here.

MIRAMICHI RIVER VALLEY

The Miramichi is actually a complex web of rivers and tributaries draining much of central New Brunswick. The main branch, the 217km-long Southwest Miramichi River, flows from near Hartland through forest to Miramichi City where it meets the other main fork, the Northwest Miramichi. For more than 100 years, the entire system has inspired reverent awe for its tranquil beauty and incredible Atlantic salmon fly-fishing and grouse hunting. Famous business tycoons, international politicians (check for the availability of bullet-proof body gear from the tourist office if Dick Cheney is in town), sports and entertainment stars and Prince Charles have all wet lines here. Even Marilyn Monroe is said to have dipped her legs. The legendary fishery has had some ups and downs with overfishing, poaching and unknown causes (perhaps global warming) affecting stocks, but they now seem back at sustainable levels. The **tourist office** (☎ 506-365-7787; www.doaktown.com) is in the Atlantic Salmon Museum.

Sights

Historic **Doaktown** is the river valley's main center and its unofficial fishing capital. See the **Atlantic Salmon Museum** (☎ 506-365-7787, 866-725-6662; www.atlanticsalmonmuseum.com; 263 Main St, adult/family $5/12; ☻ 9am-5pm Jun–mid-Oct) for its equipment, photos and an aquarium containing river life and, of course, salmon in various growth stages. **Doak Historic Site** (☎ 506-365-2026; 386 Main St; adult/family $5/15; ☻ 9am-6pm Jun-Sep) depicts the area through the mid-1800s with exhibits and demonstrations.

Activities

Sport fishing remains the main activity, but is tightly controlled for conservation. Licenses are required and all anglers must employ a registered guide. A three-day license for non-residents is $40. All fish over 63cm must be released. For more, see www.gnb.ca/0078/fw /angling/summary.asp.

WW Doak & Sons (☎ 506-365-7828; www.doak.com; 331 Main St) is one of Canada's best fly-fishing shops. It sells a staggering number of flies annually, some made on the premises. A wander through here will certainly get an angler pumped.

Despite the presence of the king of freshwaters, there are other pastimes to enjoy.

The **Miramichi Trail**, a walking and cycling path along an abandoned rail line, is now partially complete, with 75km of the projected 200km useable. At McNamee, the pedestrian **Priceville Suspension Bridge** spans the river. It's a popular put-in spot for canoeists and kayakers spending half a day paddling downriver to Doaktown. Several outfitters in Doaktown and Blackville offer equipment rentals, shuttle services and guided trips for leisurely canoe, kayak or even tubing trips along the river.

Sleeping & Eating

Beautiful rustic lodges and camps abound here, many of which replicate the halcyon days of the 1930s and '40s. Click on www .doak.com for links to more accommodations options.

Homestead B&B (☎ 506-365-7912; Hwy 8, Blissfield; r $70-125) In nearby Blissfield, this fifth-generation house dating from 1877 has rooms in the main house as well as a couple of cabins.

Ledges Inn (☎ 506-365-1820, 877-365-1820; www .ledgesinn.com; Rte 8; r $90-150, fishing packages per day from $424) The ultimate for fishing and/or hunting in New Brunswick, this lodge offers it all from lush cabin-style rooms, phenomenal gourmet dining, excellent guides and pampering extras such as massage. Check the website for all sorts of packages, from romantic getaways to wet and wild hunting and fishing adventures.

In addition to sampling superb salmon from local menus, something to try is the fiddlehead, the first shoot of a fern for which the province, and most notably this area, is celebrated.

NORTHEASTERN NEW BRUNSWICK

This strongly Acadian region skirts the Gulf of St Lawrence and whips around the windy tip of the Acadian Peninsula to the Baie de Chaleurs (Chaleur Bay). The northern portion is by far the most scenic while Caraquet is a pleasant enough base town. Campbellton is the thoroughfare to Québec but won't offer much of a first impression if this is your first view of the province. Almost the entire northern interior half of the province is inaccessible,

rocky, river-filled forest. Inland, highways are lined with timberland, making for monotonous driving.

TRACADIE-SHEILA

Unmasking a little-known but gripping story, the **Historical Museum of Tracadie** (☎ 506-393-6366; 399-222 Rue du Couvent; adult/child $3/1; ☺ 9am-6pm Mon-Fri, noon-6pm Sat & Sun) focuses on the leprosy colony, based here from 1868 to as late as 1965. It's the only place in Canada providing details on a leprosarium. The nearby cemetery has the graves of 60 victims of Hansen's Disease (leprosy).

CARAQUET

The Acadian Peninsula, extending from Miramichi and Bathurst out to two islands at the edge of the Baie des Chaleurs, was first settled by the unhappy Acadian victims of colonial battles between Britain and France in the 1700s. The oldest of the Acadian villages, Caraquet (population 1689) was founded in 1757 by refugees from Nova Scotia. It's now the main center of the peninsula's French community and is by far the most attractive town in which to experience Acadian culture. Caraquet's colorful, bustling fishing port, off Boul St Pierre Est, has an assortment of moored vessels splashing at the dock. East and west Boul St Pierre are divided at Rue le Portage.

Information

The **visitors center** (☎ 506-726-2676; 51 Boul St Pierre Est; ☺ 9am-5pm mid-Jun–mid-Sep) and all of the local tour operators are found at the Callefour de la Mer complex, with its Day Adventure Center, restaurant and views down on the waterfront near the fishing harbor.

Sights
ACADIAN MUSEUM

The **Acadian Museum** (☎ 506-726-2682; 15 Boul St Pierre Est; adult/student $3.50/2; ☺ 10am-6pm Mon-Sat, 1-6pm Sun Jun–mid-Sep, to 8pm Jul & Aug) is in the middle of town with views over the bay from the balcony. It has a neatly laid-out collection of artifacts donated by local residents, including common household objects, tools, photographs and a fine wood stove. Most scary is the desk-bed, at which you could work all day and then fold down into a bed when exhaustion strikes! It belonged to a superior at the Caraquet Convent in 1880.

THE LEPERS OF TRACADIE

No one knows how leprosy was introduced into New Brunswick (most cases were in Gloucester and Northumberland Counties). In the 1820s Ursule Landry Benoit of Tracadie was the first to die of the disease. Her hard, scaly flesh and distorting sores were only the beginning of the horror as the disease slowly spread from families to neighbors. Death was not as frightening a prospect as living with the disfigurement and the stigma attached to the condition. Victims became outcasts.

In 1844, New Brunswick chose Sheldrake Island at the mouth of the Miramichi River for the lazaretto that was to help contain the disease. Lepers ranging in age from eight to 46 were forced to leave their homes and families to take up residence. Many escaped from the harsh and isolated conditions of Sheldrake in the years to follow until finally, in 1849, the remaining 31 lepers were transferred to a new lazaretto at Tracadie. By 1868, conditions were bettered again by the arrival of the Religious Hospitallers of Saint Joseph from Montréal. They continued care until the last leper left in 1965. During this period lepers from across Canada (except the Chinese, who were sent to D'Arcy Island in British Columbia) were sent to Tracadie.

STE ANNE DU BOCAGE

Six kilometers west of town is **Ste Anne du Bocage** (☎ 506-727-3604; 579 Boul St Pierre Ouest; admission free; ☥ 8am-9pm May-Oct), one of the oldest religious shrines in the province. On this spot, Alexis Landry and other Acadians settled soon after the infamous expulsion and the graves of some of them are on the sanctuary grounds. Down a stairway by the sea is a sacred spring where the faithful come to fill their water bottles.

ACADIAN HISTORIC VILLAGE

Acadian Historic Village (☎ 506-726-2600, 877-721-2200; www.villagehistoriqueacadien.com; 14311 Hwy 11; adult/senior/family $15/13/36, child under 6yr free; ☥ 10am-6pm early Jun-Sep), 15km west of Caraquet, is a major historic reconstruction set up like a village of old, with 33 buildings and workers in period costumes reflecting life from 1780 to 1880. The museum depicts daily routines in a typical postexpulsion community and makes for an intriguing comparison to the obvious prosperity of the British King's Landing Historic Settlement (p147), west of Fredericton.

A good three to four hours is required to see the site, and you'll want to eat. For that, there are four choices: two snack bars; Dugas House, serving sit-down Acadian dishes; and the dining room at Château Albert, with a menu from 1910.

The village has a program for kids ($30), which provides them with a costume and seven hours of supervised historical activities. If you don't have time to see everything, ask the receptionist to stamp your ticket for re-entry the next day. In September only five or six buildings are open and village admission is reduced to $8/4/18 per adult/student/family. Facing the village parking lot is a **wax museum** (adult incl audio guide $8).

For accommodations for the Château Albert, see opposite.

Activities

Sea of Adventure (☎ 800-704-3966; 2242 Beauport St; ☥ Jul & Aug) offers three-hour whale-watch tours (adult/child $64/41) in rigid-hulled Hurricane Zodiacs seating 12 passengers.

Festivals & Events

The largest annual Acadian cultural festival, **Festival Acadien** (☎ 506-727-2787; www.ville.caraquet.nb.ca in French) is held here the first two weeks of August. It draws 100,000 visitors; more than 200 performers including musicians, actors, dancers from Acadia and other French regions (some from overseas) entertain. The culminating Tintamarre Parade is a real blowout.

Sleeping & Eating

Camping Caraquet (☎ 506-726-2696; www.sn2000.nb.ca/comp/camping-caraquet; 619 Boul St Pierre Ouest; tent-/RV sites $19/25; ☥ mid-Jun–mid-Sep) This former provincial park overlooking the sea is just west of the Ste Anne du Bocage sanctuary. The core of the campground is RVs but there are plenty of tentsites around the perimeter.

Maison Touristique Dugas (☎ 506-727-3195; www.maisontouristiquedugas.ca; 683 Boul St Pierre Ouest; s/d without bathroom $50/60, d with bathroom & cooking facilities $60-70, cabin d $70) There's something for everyone at this large red wooden house with a rear annex, just 1.5km west of Ste Anne du Bocage. There are 11 rooms with shared bathrooms, two apartments with private cooking facilities in the main house, and five cabins with private bathrooms and cooking facilities in the backyard. Children are welcome and you can rent bikes and boats here. Breakfast costs extra.

Château Albert (Acadian Historic Village; www.village historiqueacadien.com/chateauanglais.htm; d $70-125; &) For total immersion in the Acadian Historic Village, spend the night at Château Albert in early-20th-century style – no TV, no phone – but a comfortable, very quiet room. The fee of $160 per couple includes admission to the site and a tool around in a Model T Ford.

Café Phare (☎ 506-727-9469; 186 Boul St Pierre; mains $7-11; ☺ breakfast, lunch & dinner) Good luck even parking for this ultrapopular arty café. The whole place smells like cooking soup and you'll find all the little tables packed with jovial Francophones sipping wine or enjoying an espresso over soups, salads and light mains. There are often art exhibits, poetry readings and the like.

Restaurant Le Caraquette (☎ 506-727-6009; 89 Boul St Pierre Est; mains $6-28; ☺ 6am-11pm Mon-Sat, 7am-11pm Sun) Simple, with a great view and extremely popular with the locals, this is a good choice for breakfast, a basic lunch or more tantalizing seafood selections in the evening.

La Chocolatière (☎ 506-727-3727; 144 Boul St Pierre; mains $9-22; ☺ 5-10pm Mon-Fri, 9am-10pm Sat & Sun) This French-inspired, chic country restaurant serves Acadian as well as European seafood soups and more. Don't leave without popping in for a few delectable handmade chocolates from the shop on the premises.

Getting There & Away
Public transportation around this part of the province is very limited as Acadian Lines buses don't pass this way. Local residents wishing to connect with the bus or train in Miramichi or Bathurst use van shuttles. Ask for details at the tourist office.

GRANDE ANSE
Back along the shoreline west of Caraquet, this small town boasts the unique **Popes Museum** (☎ 506-732-3003; 184 Hwy 11; adult/family $5/10; ☺ 10am-6pm mid-Jun–Aug), which houses images of 263 popes from St Peter to the current one, as well as sundry religious articles. There is also a detailed model of the Basilica and St Peter's Sq in Rome.

At the foot of the cliffs, behind the imposing church, is a beach and picnic spot. To get there edge down Ave Portuaire toward the fishing wharf.

The road west to Bathurst skirts the rugged, scenic shoreline cliffs. Without doubt, stop at easily missed **Pokeshaw Community Park** (admission per car $1), 5.5km west of the Popes Museum (look carefully for signs). Just offshore atop an isolated sea stack created by coastal erosion, thousands of double-crested cormorants nest in summer. In late fall, the birds fly south to their winter home in Maryland. From the parking lot you can look straight across at the birds squawking and swirling. This wonderfully undeveloped park is a terrific place to photograph the coastal cliffs, and you can also picnic and swim.

PETIT ROCHER
Some 20km north of Bathurst in Petit Rocher (population 1966) is the **New Brunswick Mining & Mineral Interpretation Centre** (☎ 506-542-2672; 397 Hwy 134; admission $6; ☺ 10am-6pm late Jun-Aug). This mining museum has various exhibits on the local zinc industry. The tour includes a simulated descent in a mining shaft and takes about 45 minutes.

DETOUR: ACADIAN PENINSULA

The intrepid may head further up the **Acadian Peninsula** to the home of the province's largest fishing fleet at **Shippagan** – crab is the main catch. The **Aquarium & Marine Centre** (☎ 506-336-3013; 100 Aquarium St; adult/family $7/14; ☺ 10am-6pm mid-May–Sep) is a modern and inviting place to learn about sea critters and the people that catch them. Kids will love its touch tanks and seals (fed at 11am and 4pm). High winds and calm seas mean perfect kite-surfing conditions. **Shippagan Kiteboard Centre** (☎ 506-337-0338; www.shippagan.kiteboard.com; 9-15 Allée Maximin, Pionte Canot; courses incl material from $50) offers rentals and classes to all who want to give kiting a whirl.

Continue across the bridge to **Lamèque Island**, a flat land of modern homes, power lines and some good beaches. To really get away from it all, head across yet another bridge to **Miscou Island**, with few habitants, lots of beaches and lovely natural landscapes.

NEW BRUNSWICK

LOCAL VOICES

Serge Comeau

Priest, age 36, Caraquet

What is the most important issue for Acadians today? The cooperation and solidarity between urban and rural communities. Acadians originally settled in small villages; today many Acadians are moving to the city. So how do you keep strong Acadian ties in an urban setting? It's important that our culture doesn't become diluted. **Who is your local hero?** A boy named Louis Mailloux. He was killed in a rebellion here in 1875 when he was only 19 years old. The uprising was because of a ban on teaching French and religion in schools. Mailloux is a symbol of the fight for our language and beliefs – for Acadians our culture exists through these things.

Auberge d'Anjou (☎ 506-783-0587, 866-783-0587; auberge.anjou@nb.aibn.com; 587 Hwy 134; r incl breakfast $65-85) is a fine place with immaculate spaces that are well furnished but quite small. It was the first inn in the area and has been tastefully upgraded. The complex, which included an old convent, is near the large church, which is on the corner of the road to the wharf.

If you do stay a night, **Café Rarti Show** (☎ 506-783-7223; 445 Principal; light mains $5-8; ☺ 10am-11pm Tue-Thu, to midnight Fri & Sat) often has live music and is a hip, social place for beer, wine and a light meal.

CAMPBELLTON

Campbellton (population 7798), on the Québec border, is the second-biggest highway entry point to the Maritimes from the rest of Canada. It's a not-so-scenic town in the midst of a lovely area on the edge of the Restigouche Highlands, a portion of the Appalachian Mountains. The lengthy Restigouche River, which winds through northern New Brunswick and then forms the border with Québec, empties to the sea here. The Baie des Chaleurs is on one side and rolling hills encompass the town on the remaining sides. Across the border is Matapédia and Hwy 132 leading to Mont Joli, 148km into Québec.

Information

Campbellton Public Library (☎ 506-753-5253; 2 Aberdeen St at Andrew St; ☺ 10am-5pm Mon-Fri Jul & Aug, Tue-Sat Sep-Jun) Free Internet access.

Provincial Tourist Office (☎ 506-789-2367; 56 Salmon Blvd; ☺ 8am-9pm Jul & Aug, 10am-6pm mid-May–Jun & Sep-early Oct) Next to City Center Mall, near the bridge from Québec. A park opposite features a huge statue of a salmon surrounded by manmade waterfalls.

Sights

Dominated by Sugarloaf Mountain, which rises nearly 400m above sea level and looks vaguely like its namesake in Rio, **Sugarloaf Provincial Park** (☎ 506-789-2366; 596 Val d'Amours Rd; admission free) is off Hwy 11 at exit 415. From the base, it's just a half-hour walk to the top – well worth the extensive views of town and part of the Restigouche River. Another trail leads around the bottom of the hill. A second attraction of Sugarloaf Provincial Park is the **Alpine Slide** (ride $4; ☺ late Jun-early Sep), which involves taking a chairlift up another hill and sliding down a track on a sled; it's fun but don't expect any adrenaline rush.

Sleeping & Eating

Campbellton Lighthouse Hostel (☎ 506-759-7044; campbellton@hihostels.ca; 1 Ritchie St; dm members/nonmembers $16/20; ☺ mid-Jun–Aug, reception 7-11am & 4-11pm; P) This distinctive, long-running HI hostel is in a converted lighthouse by the Restigouche River, near the Provincial Tourist Office.

Sugarloaf Provincial Park (☎ 506-789-2366; 596 Val d'Amours Rd; tentsites $20, RV sites $22-25; ☺ mid-May–early-Oct) There are 76 sites in a pleasant wooded setting at this park 4km from downtown Campbellton.

Maison McKenzie House B&B (☎ 506-753-3133; www.bbcanada.com/4384.html; 31 Andrew St; d $65-90) The only B&B in town, this large two-story house from 1910 – with an impressive veranda – is four blocks south of the tourist office.

Something Else Restaurant (☎ 506-753-7744; 65 Water St; lunch mains around $10, dinner set menu $25; ☺ 4:30-9pm Sat-Wed, 11am-9pm Thu & Fri) Your best bet for something nonfried, this place serves mussels, salads, pasta and internationally inspired cuisine.

Getting There & Away

The Acadian bus stop is located at the **Pik-Quik convenience store** (☎ 506-753-3100; Water St near Prince William St). The bus departs every day at 11am for Fredericton ($35, 3½ hours) and Moncton ($35, six hours). Then, twice a day (once in the morning and once in the afternoon), an Orléans Express bus leaves for Gaspé ($55) and Québec City ($66, seven hours).

The **VIA Rail station** (☎ 800-561-3952; 113 Roseberry St; ☉ 5:45-10:30am Wed-Mon & 5:45-10pm Thu-Tue) is conveniently central. There's one train every day except Wednesday, going south to Moncton ($60, four hours) and Halifax ($83, nine hours), and one daily, except Tuesday, heading the other way to Montréal ($76, 11 hours).

Prince Edward Island

Move over Mounties, Canada's got a spunky, redheaded feminine side. Wherever you go in Prince Edward Island (PEI), little Anne Shirley, Lucy Maud Montgomery's immortal heroine of *Anne of Green Gables,* is larger than her fictional britches. Ironically, the island itself is a redhead – from tip to tip sienna-colored soil peeks out from under potato plants, and the shores are lined with rose and golden sand. Mi'kmaw legend tells of the Great Spirit of creation who reserved a small amount of red dirt to form 'the fairest of all earthly places,' Prince Edward Island. Today modern technology tells us that the red hue is from a high iron oxide content.

Canada's tiniest province lies in the Gulf of St Lawrence. The crescent-shaped island's deep bays and tidal rivers have created a convoluted shoreline that divides the province into three equal parts. Eastern PEI, known as Kings County, hosts secluded beaches and small fishing villages; its wealth of stunning routes is gaining international renown as a cycling destination. Queens County, covering most of central PEI, has cemented its reputation for verdant countryside and as the center of Anne fever; having some of Canada's finest beaches only increases the area's appeal. Prince County, which makes up western PEI, is a fascinating and gorgeous place to explore the cultures and history of the French Acadians and Mi'kmaq aboriginal peoples. Despite the splendor, most visitors fall in love with PEI's charm and relaxed atmosphere.

PRINCE EDWARD ISLAND

HIGHLIGHTS

- Wear a bib and get lobster juice up to your elbows at a traditional PEI **lobster supper** (p205) in New Glasgow

- Admire PEI's lack of hills while cycling the red-dirt, nearly bump-free, 279km **Confederation Trail** (p200)

- Paddle peacefully past the sandstone cliffs, endless beaches and patchwork fields of **Prince Edward Island National Park** (p201)

- Wiggle your feet and make a squeak on the 'singing' sands of **Basin Head Beach** (p198)

- Shop, stroll and be transported back to the birth of Canada in **Old Charlottetown** (p186)

- Explore Mi'kmaw culture, eat a traditional meal and shop for crafts in the village of **Lennox Island First Nation** (p213)

- Be taken away into the pages of *Anne of Green Gables* while visiting the Green Gables House in **Cavendish** (p206)

- Step-dance to bagpipes and fiddles at a Scottish **ceilidh** (p195) in Summerside

| ■ AREA: 5700 SQ KM | ■ POPULATION: 137,800 | ■ CAPITAL: CHARLOTTETOWN |

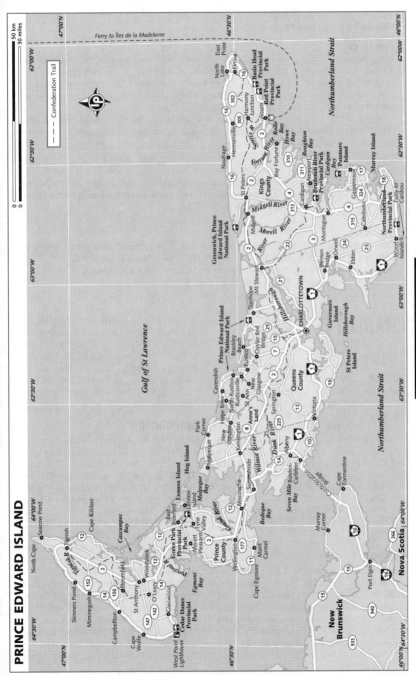

PRINCE EDWARD ISLAND IN...

Two Days

Spend the better part of a day wandering through the historic, leafy streets of **Old Charlottetown** (below). Ascend the grand stairs of **Province House** (opposite) to see Canada's birthplace, then gawk at the harbor view from the veranda of **Beaconsfield House** (p189), before chilling out under some shade in Victoria Park's **waterfront gardens** (p189). Drive out of town for a **lobster supper** (see the boxed text, p205) at New Glasgow or St Anns.

Next morning, pack your beach gear and plop yourself on one of the exquisite beaches of **Prince Edward Island National Park** (p201) then explore the magnificent dunes at **Greenwich** (p199).

Four Days

Follow the two-day itinerary then spend a day visiting the Anne-related sights near **Cavendish** (p206). Enjoy your last day exploring the coast by kayak from **North Rustico** (p204) or cycling the Confederation Trail around **Mt Stewart** (p200).

One Week

After enjoying your four-day itinerary, allow a few days to tour **Kings County** (p195), with stops at **Orwell** (p195), **Montague** (p196) and the illustrious **Basin Head Beach** (p198).

Alternatively, delve into the Acadian and Mi'kmaw cultures of **Prince County** (p209) while en route from **Summerside** (p209) to the **North Cape** (p214).

CHARLOTTETOWN

It's been said that Charlottetown (population 32,200) is too small to be grand and too big to be quaint. In fact, PEI's capital is just about the perfect size; it's compact enough for a newcomer to navigate, while hip eateries, eclectic shopping and the city's elegant historical sites are only a leisurely stroll apart. Quiet colonial and Victorian streets lined with gracious trees, elegant 19th-century mansions and the island's signature redbrick facades occasionally give way to contemporary buildings that give the city an intriguing mix of old and new. Charlottetown's history, natural beauty and short visiting season ensure that its streets are packed with visitors every July and August.

HISTORY

Charlottetown is named after the exotic consort of King George III. Her African roots, dating back to Margarita de Castro Y Sousa and the Portuguese royal house, are as legendary as they are controversial. The idea that this English queen had an African ancestry is still too much for many historians to handle.

While many believe the city's splendid harbor was the reason Charlottetown became the capital, the reality was less glamorous. In 1765 the surveyor-general selected Charlottetown because he thought it prudent to bestow the poor side of the island with some privileges. Thanks to the celebrated 1864 conference, however, Charlottetown is etched in Canadian history as the country's birthplace.

ORIENTATION

University Ave is the city's largest street; its southern terminus is punctuated by historic Province House, which marks the entrance to Old Charlottetown. Befitting the transition is the stark juxtaposition of the house and the modern Confederation Centre of the Arts.

Parallel to University Ave is Queen St, which runs west of the Confederation Centre. Queen St and the adjacent blocks on Grafton, Richmond and Sydney Sts are home to Charlottetown's finest restaurants and shops.

Majestic Great George St runs south from Province House, past impressive St Dunstan's Basilica to Peake's Wharf and Confederation Landing Park. The waterfront is the hub of summer activity, hosting various festivals.

To the west of town, on the waterfront, is the verdant Victoria Park and its sweeping promenade.

INFORMATION

Bookstores
Bookman (☎ 902-892-8872; 177 Queen St) Huge selection of rare secondhand books.
Reading Well Bookstore (☎ 902-566-2703; 87 Water St) Features local authors.

Emergency
Police, Ambulance & Fire (☎ 911)
Royal Canadian Mounted Police (☎ 902-368-9300; 450 University Ave) For nonemergencies.

Internet Access
Numerous cafés throughout the city have wi-fi as do many hotels and B&Bs.
Confederation Centre Public Library (☎ 902-368-4642; cnr Queen & Grafton Sts; ⏲ 10am-8pm Tue-Thu, to 5pm Fri & Sat, 1-5pm Sun) Free Internet access.
Timothy's World Coffee (☎ 902-628-8503; 137B Kent St; per hr $5; ⏲ 7am-7pm Mon-Fri, 9am-6pm Sat, 11:30am-5pm Sun)

Internet Resources
Visit Charlottetown (www.visitcharlottetown.com) A helpful website with upcoming festival information, city history and visitor information.

Medical Services
Polyclinic Professional Centre (☎ 902-629-8810; 199 Grafton St; ⏲ 5:30-8pm Mon-Fri, 9:30am-noon Sat) Charlottetown's after-hours, walk-in medical clinic. Non-Canadians must pay a $40 fee.
Queen Elizabeth Hospital (☎ 902-894-2111; 60 Riverside Dr; ⏲ 24hr) Emergency services.

Money
PEI wants your tourist dollar; banks and ATMs are everywhere.
TD Canada Trust (☎ 902-629-2265; 192 Queen St; ⏲ 8am-6pm Mon-Wed, to 8pm Thu & Fri, 9am-3pm Sat)

Post
Main post office (☎ 902-628-4400; 135 Kent St)

Tourist Information
Visitors center (☎ 902-368-4444, 888-734-7529; www.peiplay.com; Founders' Hall; ⏲ 9am-8pm Jun, to 10pm Jul & Aug, 8:30am-6pm Sep–mid-Oct, 9am-4:30pm Mon-Fri mid-Oct–May) Located in Founders' Hall, this is the island's main visitors center. It has all the answers and a plethora of brochures and maps, too.

SIGHTS
All of the major sights are within the confines of Old Charlottetown, which makes wandering between them as rewarding as wandering through them.

Province House National Historic Site
Charlottetown's centerpiece is the imposing, yet welcoming, neoclassical **Province House** (☎ 902-566-7626; 165 Richmond St; admission free; ⏲ 9am-6pm Jul & Aug, to 5pm Jun-Sep, 9am-5pm Mon-Fri Oct-May). The symmetry of design is carried throughout, including two brilliant skylights reaching up through the massive sandstone structure. It was here in 1864, within the Confederation Chamber, that 23 representatives of Britain's North American colonies first discussed the creation of Canada (see opposite). Along with being the 'birthplace of Canada,' the site is home to Canada's second-oldest active legislature.

Several rooms have been restored, and in July and August you may find yourself face to face with Canada's first prime minister: actors in period garb wander the halls and regularly perform reenactments of the famous conference. Enjoy the *Great Dream*, a 17-minute film about the monumental 1864 conference.

Confederation Centre Art Gallery & Museum
In a modern building that dominates Queen St between Grafton St and Victoria Row at Richmond St, the **Confederation Centre** (☎ 902-628-1864; www.confederationcentre.com; 145 Richmond St) serves not only as Charlottetown's theater complex, but as its art and exhibition hall as well. The **art gallery** (admission free; ⏲ 9am-5pm mid-Jun–Oct, 11am-5pm Wed-Sat & 1-5pm Sun rest of year) focuses on Canadian Art and has a special exhibit on LM Montgomery. Check the website for gallery exhibits and live performances throughout the year.

PRINCE EDWARD ISLAND

TOP FIVE
GENTLE LANDSCAPES OF PRINCE EDWARD ISLAND

- Purple, pink and white lupins taking over the countryside in late June and July
- Pink sands, singing sands, migrating sands
- The green tangle of potato fields
- Red cliffs and green fields dotted with wildflowers meeting a steel-blue sea
- The symphony of fall foliage

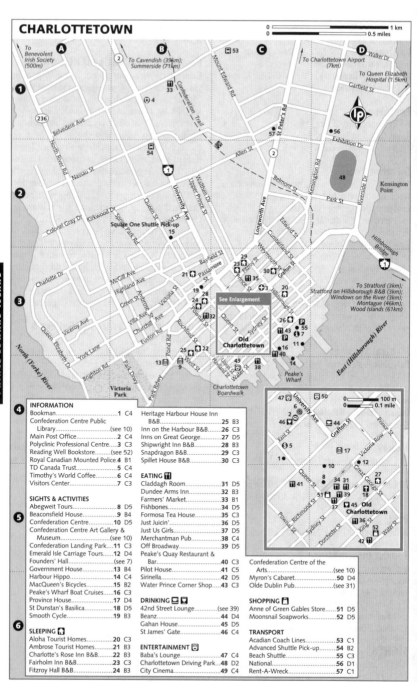

CHARLOTTETOWN

Founders' Hall

Opened in 2001, this high-tech multimedia **exhibit** (☎ 902-368-1864, 800-955-1864; 6 Prince St; adult/child 6-17 yr/family $7/3.75/17; ☼ 9am-8pm Mon-Sat Jul & Aug, 9am-5pm Mon-Sat & to 4pm Sun mid-May–mid-Oct), housed in an old train station, deluges your senses with facts and fun about Canada's history since 1864. It's sure to entertain children, and the child in you.

Beaconsfield House

With its crowning belvedere, intricate gingerbread trim and elegant 19th-century furnishings, **Beaconsfield House** (☎ 902-368-6603; 2 Kent St; adult/student/family $4.25/3.25/14; ☼ 10am-5pm Jul & Aug) is the finest Victorian mansion in Charlottetown. Have a wander or sit on the veranda and be stunned by the view. Hours vary September to June.

St Dunstan's Basilica

Rising from the ashes of a 1913 fire, the three towering stone spires of this neo-Gothic **basilica** (☎ 902-894-3486; 45 Great George St; admission free; ☼ 8am-5pm) are now a Charlottetown landmark. The marble floors, Italian carvings and decoratively embossed ribbed ceiling are surprisingly ornate.

Government House

Within the sprawling gardens of Victoria Park is **Government House** (☎ 902-368-5480; admission free; ☼ 10am-4pm Mon-Fri Jul & Aug). This striking colonial mansion, with its grand hall, Palladian window and Doric columns, has been home to PEI's lieutenant governors since 1835. In 2003 the Hon JL Bernard broke with an almost-170-year-old tradition and opened its doors to the public.

ACTIVITIES

Just strolling the peaceful streets of Charlottetown is enough to keep most visitors occupied.

Cycling is the 'it' thing to do on PEI and Charlottetown is no exception. Rent bikes, and get touring maps, cycle routes and some friendly advice at **Smooth Cycle** (☎ 902-566-5530, 800-310-6550; www.smoothcycle.com; 308 Queen St; rentals per half-/full day $17/25, week $110). **MacQueen's Bicycles** (☎ 902-368-2453; www.macqueens.com; 430 Queen St; per day/week $25/125) also rents a variety of quality bikes with children's models at half price. Leisurely pedal the town or, depending on the condition of those thighs, head north to Prince Edward Island National Park (50km round-trip) for the day. Both of these operators also offer excellent customized islandwide tours of the Confederation Trail.

WALKING TOUR

A $1 pamphlet containing three detailed walking tours of the Historic Districts of Charlottetown is available at the visitors center – the walks focus on architecture.

Our walk takes you down to the sea and past some of the more important historic sites. It will take you all day if you stop at all the sights.

Begin at the **visitors center** (**1**; p187) where you can park your car (get the ticket validated at the visitors center) if you need to. Enter the adjacent **Founders' Hall** (left) to go through the Time Tunnel to 1864 when the Fathers of the Confederation were planning the union of Canada.

Once you've reached our era again, stroll the boardwalk past **Confederation Landing Park** (**2**) to **Peake's Wharf Waterfront Merchants** (**3**), where you can browse an interesting collection of boutiques, craft shops and cafés.

Turn right at Queen St, right again onto Water then left on Great George Street. Two blocks later you arrive at **St Dunistan's Basilica** (**4**; left), one of Canada's largest churches. Peek inside to admire the ornate Italian carvings before crossing over to the **Inns on Great George** (**5**; p192), a cluster of 12 heritage buildings that now form a large inn – the main building that has the inn's lobby is called the Pavilion and housed some of the Charlottetown Conference Delegates in 1864 (see p186).

Continue up Great George St to the **Province House** (**6**; p187) to go back in time once more to the Confederation Conference, this time via costumed actors in the actual location of the conference. Come out onto Victoria Row, where you could stop for lunch before going into the **Confederation Centre Art Gallery & Museum** (**7**; p187) to experience fine examples of Canadian art. Walk down two blocks on Queen St, along the series of little shops and cafés, then turn right on Dorchester St. On your left

PRINCE EDWARD ISLAND

WALK FACTS

Start Visitors center
Finish Victoria Park
Distance 2.7km
Duration 5½ to six hours

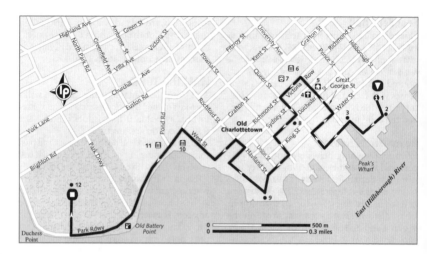

PRINCE EDWARD ISLAND

at No 55–7 is **McPhee Hostelry (8)**, which was a well-known tavern in the early 19th century – the entrance for carriages is still there.

Turn left on Pownal St then, two blocks down, turn right onto Water St. At Haviland St turn left and amble along seaside **Charlottetown Boardwalk (9)**. This area was an active shipping center in the late 19th century and was famous for the construction of wooden ships. At the Boardwalk's end you arrive at Sydney St. Turn left on Rochford St at the first intersection then take your first left onto Richmond St then the next right onto West St. After two blocks you come to historic **Beaconsfield House (10**; p189). Browse the museum, books, genealogical records and stop for tea and scones on the scenic porch before going down Kent St toward **Government House (11**; p189) and **Victoria Park (12)** to relax in Charlottetown's prettiest setting.

To return you could either take the Jump-on Jump-off Trolley (see p194) back to the visitors center or discover your own route back on foot.

CHARLOTTETOWN FOR CHILDREN

Full of parks, peaceful corners and ice-cream shops, Charlottetown is a great place to bring the kids. See opposite for PEI's International Children's Theatre Festival.

Harbour Hippo (☎ 902-628-8484; www.harbourhippo .com; Lower Prince St Wharf; adult/child/under 4yr $23/16/free; ☺ Jun-Sep, 55min tours every 1¼hr, 10:15am-8pm) is an amphibious vessel that drives you around the historic district then plunges into the sea for a harbor tour. There's a lively commentary.

TOURS

Abegweit Tours (☎ 902-894-9966; adult/child under 11yr $9.50/1; ☺ tours Jun-Oct) One-hour double-decker bus tours through Charlottetown leave from the Confederation Centre. The six-hour north shore tour ($65) will pick you up if you're staying in town.

Confederation Players (☎ 902-368-1864; 6 Prince St; adult $5; ☺ tours Jul & Aug, Tue-Sat mid-Jun–Sep). There is no better way to tour Charlottetown. Playing the fathers and ladies of Confederation, actors garbed in 19th-century dress educate and entertain through the town's historic streets. Tours leave from the visitors center, and there are Great George St, Merchants & Mansions and Waterfront storytelling tours.

Emerald Isle Carriage Tours (☎ 902-394-3780; cnr Great George & Richmond Sts; 30/45/60min tours $60/70/100; ☺ tours 10am-11pm Jun-Oct) Experience Charlottetown by horse and carriage. A costumed guide narrates the voyage.

Peake's Wharf Boat Cruises (☎ 902-566-4458; 1 Great George St; 70min cruise $16; ☺ tours 1pm, 6:30pm & 8pm Jun-Aug) Observe sea life, hear interesting stories and witness a wonderfully different perspective of Charlottetown from the waters of its harbor. An excellent seal-watch trip ($22) departs at 2:30pm, returning at 5pm.

FESTIVALS & EVENTS

Charlottetown Festival (☎ 902-566-1267; www .confederationcentre.com/festival.asp) This theatrical festival from mid-May to mid-October features free outdoor performances, a children's and dance programs.

Festival of Lights (☎ 902-368-1864, 800-955-1864) Buskers roam the historic waterfront by day, while Canada's best musicians perform by night – all in celebration of their country's birthday. There's free entertainment and fireworks on July 1. Held from June 30 to July 3.

PEI's International Children's Theatre Festival (☎ 800-803-1421; Beaconsfield House, Victoria Park; admission $6.50; ☺ shows 11am Mon-Fri) shows a different play for every day of the week, from mid-July to early September. Get swept away in the fun at this interactive theater festival. Although geared toward younger children, big kids will enjoy it too.

Old Home Week (☎ 902-629-6623; www.peipro vincialexhibition.com) Held at the Provincial Exhibition grounds, this mid-August event features carnival rides, musical entertainment, games of chance, harness racing and traditional livestock shows.

Festival of the Fathers (☎ 902-368-1864, 800-955-1864) On the waterfront, this three-day festival celebrates Charlottetown's history by recreating the enchanting events of the Victorian era. Expect musicians, dances, traditional food, carriage rides and humorous street games. Held on the weekend before Labour Day.

PEI International Shellfish Festival (☎ 866-955-2003; www.peishellfish.com) Now one of the island's largest festivals, this massive kitchen party, set on the Charlottetown waterfront, merges great traditional music with incredible seafood. Don't miss the oyster-shucking championships or the chowder challenge. It's held on the third weekend in September.

SLEEPING

This town is B&B heaven. The quantity of gorgeous Victorians makes for a mind-boggling array of period charm. During peak season (July and August) things book up quickly so it's wise to book ahead; in the off-season rates can drop dramatically and it's possible to sleep in some of the most elegant accommodations for not much more than the price of a motel room.

Budget

Ambrose Tourist Homes (☎ 1-800-665-6072; www .ambrosetouristhome.com; 17 Passamore St; s/d $35/45; ☺ May-Nov; ▢) The neighbors yell day and night right below your window and the lobby reeks of cigarette smoke. On the upside, this clean, cheap place has comfy beds, wi-fi and a friendly owner who will pick up wheels-less folks at bus stations and airports.

Aloha Tourist Homes (☎ 902-892-9944; www.aloha amigo.com; 234 Sydney St; s/d/tw without bathroom $35/ 55/70) The newly remodeled rooms in these two heritage homes are great value. A fully equipped kitchen, along with friendly management and central location make for budget perfection.

Spillett House B&B (☎ 902-892-5494; www.spillet thouse.pe.ca; 157 Weymouth St; s/d without bathroom $50/60; ▢) Yes, you can stay in a lovely heritage B&B on a budget. This well-loved home with hardwood floors, spacious rooms and comfortable antique furnishings is perfectly located in Old Charlottetown. Kids are welcome and there are storage facilities for bicycles.

Midrange

Snapdragon B&B (☎ 902-368-8070, 866-235-7164; www.thesnapdragon.com; 177 Fitzroy St; d $95-150; ▢) This uncluttered B&B is furnished simply but tastefully and is surrounded by a wonderful garden full of flowers. Owners Laura and Steve are light-hearted folk who make guests feel right at home.

Inn on the Harbour B&B (☎ 902-367-4499, 877-333-9933; www.innontheharbourpei.com; 3 Hillsborough St; d $100-200; ▢) It lacks the sumptuous charms of heritage B&Bs but this modern, comfortable inn sits on an enviable site near the waterfront and Founders' Hall. There's a meeting room on-site for business travelers.

Heritage Harbour House Inn B&B (☎ 902-892-6633, 800-405-0066; hhhouse@attglobal.net; 9 Grafton St; d/ste $125/175; ▢) A two-minute walk from Victoria Park is this family-friendly B&B-turned-inn. Country furnishings, modern amenities and balconies complete each of the large new rooms built onto this elegant old home. Spanish and Japanese are spoken and there are laundry facilities on the premises.

ourpick Fitzroy Hall B&B (☎ 902-368-2077; www .fitzroyhall.com; 45 Fitzroy St; d $125-170, ste $209-250) A perfect blend of elegance and comfort, this house is as grand as they come while the welcome is warm and down to earth. The innkeepers have put some serious thought into how to make their guests comfortable: the answer is found with refined antiques, muted color schemes, and details such as hidden alcoves with fridges and hotpots for guests to keep cold drinks or make tea.

Charlotte's Rose Inn B&B (☎ 902-892-3699; www .charlottesrose.ca; 11 Grafton St; d/ste $145/$195; ▢) You won't find more charming hosts than in this 1884 home in one of the most lovely and peaceful areas of old Charlottetown. The decadent Victorian has true English flair with bodacious rose-printed wallpaper, big fluffy beds and grand bathrooms. The upstairs suite sleeps four and has a full kitchen; guests in this room can opt out of the large B&B breakfasts.

PRINCE EDWARD ISLAND

Top End

Shipwright Inn B&B (☎ 902-368-1905, 888-306-9966; www.shipwrightinn.com; 51 Fitzroy St; r & ste $150-290; 🖳) Massive suites and rooms have a modern decor but retain an antique nautical-country charm. Included in the luxury is afternoon tea and cakes and there are aromatherapy oils in all the bathrooms that you can add to your massaging jet tub. Prices go down considerably from November to April.

Fairholm Inn B&B (☎ 902-892-5022, 888-573-5022; www.fairholm.pe.ca; 230 Prince St; ste $165-285; 🖳) This national historic inn was built in 1838 and is a superb example of the Picturesque movement in British architecture. Take tea while enjoying the morning sun in the lovely conservatory, wander the gardens or hole up with a book in the library. Luxurious English fabrics, beautiful Prince Edward Island artwork and extravagant antiques, including grandiose beds, fill each of the five-star suites. Light a fire, soak in your tub and sink back into the elegant days of the 19th century.

Inns on Great George B&B (☎ 902-892-0606, 800-361-1118; www.innsongreatgeorge.com; 58 Great George St; d $180-290) A colorful collage of celebrated buildings, built along Charlottetown's most famous street, has rooms ranging from plush and historic to bold and contemporary. It's both gay- and family-friendly. A babysitting service is available.

EATING

Radiating from Queen St, venerable restaurants pepper Old Charlottetown. The quality is high, as can be the price. Pubs dole out some great food and provide good value. During summer Victoria Row's pedestrian mall and the waterfront are hot spots.

Budget

Farmers' Market (☎ 902-626-3373; 100 Belvedere Ave; 🕑 9am-2pm Sat, plus Wed Jul & Aug) Come hungry and empty-handed. Enjoy prepared island foods or peruse the cornucopia of fresh organic fruit and vegetables.

Formosa Tea House (☎ 902-566-4991; 186 Prince St; snacks $3, mains $6; 🕑 lunch & dinner) Taiwanese vegetarian treats are served in this Victorian gone East. Sip an Almond Milk Tea (hot or cold) among Buddhas and copper dragons. Snacks such as veggie sushi ($3) and Asian noodle soups fill you up without emptying your pocket.

Just Juicin' (☎ 902-894-3104; 62 Queen St; wraps $5; 🕑 breakfast & lunch) Although the smoothies star, the pita wraps here are the best quick eats in town. The smoothie concoctions are as refreshing as they are tasty and will put a serious bounce in your step.

Just Us Girls (☎ 902-566-1285; 106 Queen St; light mains from $6; 🕑 8am-9pm) Girls just want…well-composed salads, light mains, decadent desserts and a fancy cocktail to wash it all down. Of course browsing hip clothing, fancy soaps and sparkly jewelry while we wait for our meal makes us even happier. The food is so good here that the clientele has gone co-ed, as you'll see from all the well-adjusted men dining on the sidewalk-side patio at lunchtime.

Midrange

Peake's Quay Restaurant & Bar (☎ 902-368-1330; 2 Great George St; mains lunch $8-12, dinner $15-20; 🕑 11am-2am late May-Sep) The atmosphere here is fantastic in summer. Patrons pack the huge balcony overlooking the town's historic waterfront to enjoy local seafood and nightly live Celtic music.

Water Prince Corner Shop (☎ 902-368-3212; 141 Water St; meals $8-13; 🕑 9:30am-8pm May, Jun & Oct, 9am-10pm Jul-Sep) When locals want seafood they head to this inconspicuous, sea-blue eatery near the wharf. It is deservedly famous for its scallop burgers but it's also the best place in town for fresh lobster.

Sirinella (☎ 902-628-2271; 83 Water St; mains lunch $8-14, dinner $12-26; 🕑 lunch & dinner Mon-Fri, dinner Sat) Cross the threshold of this diner-looking restaurant and you are transported to seaside Italy. It's nothing fancy, just little round, white-clothed tables, some Mediterranean oil paintings and incredibly authentic Italian fare.

Merchantman Pub (☎ 902-892-9150; 23 Queen St; mains $9-22; 🕑 11.30am-10pm Mon-Sat) The crammed-together tables fill quickly at this locals' favorite. In addition to great traditional pub grub, you can also dine on Asian-influenced creations such as Thai peanut curry or Madras chicken sauté.

Pilot House (☎ 902-894-4800; 70 Grafton St; mains $11-30; 🕑 11:30am-10pm Mon-Sat) The oversized wood beams and brick columns of the historic Roger's Hardware building provide a bold setting for fine dining or light pub fare. Lunch specials are creative, delicious and a bargain at $10. Throw in some vegetarian selections and Pilot House has something for everyone.

Fishbones (☎ 902-628-6569; 49 Water St; mains lunch $10-15, dinner $17-20; ⏱ 11am-11:30pm May-Oct) Catch live jazz nightly through the summer at this indoor-outdoor sidewalk restaurant. Open windows and fake (yet tasteful) trees make it feel like summer here. Oysters are the house specialty but you do pay for the music and decor – everything seems to be a few dollars more here.

our pick **Off Broadway** (☎ 902-566-4620; 125 Sydney St; mains $12-35; ⏱ 11am-11pm Mon-Sat, to 10pm Sun) Slip into an art-deco booth, draw the burgundy curtains and pretend you are escaping the paparazzi – if you were famous, this is where you'd go. The dark yet chic ambience is matched by fine mains such as lobster crepes ($15) or seafood coconut curry ($21). Don't leave without taking a cocktail or dessert in the even more elaborate upstairs lounge (see below).

Top End
Claddagh Room (☎ 902-892-9661; 131 Sydney St; mains $20-27; ⏱ dinner) Get your Irish fix at this relaxed-atmosphere restaurant with some of the finest seafood you're likely to find. The Irish-inspired Galway Bay Delight features a coating of fresh cream and seasonings over scallops and shrimp that have been sautéed with mushrooms and onions, then flambéed with Irish Mist liqueur.

Dundee Arms Inn (☎ 902-892-2496; 200 Pownal St; mains dinner $22-29; ⏱ lunch & dinner, plus breakfast Jun-Sep) The historic inn is home to chef Patrick Young who, using local fresh ingredients, comes up with fabulous creations such as pork tenderloin marinated in island maple syrup.

DRINKING
Charlottetown has an established and burgeoning drinking scene. Historic pubs dot the old part of town, while the budding café scene and newer bars are found around University Ave and Kent St. Most bars and pubs have a small cover charge (about $5) on weekends, or when there is live music.

our pick **42nd Street Lounge** (☎ 902-566-4620; 125 Sydney St) Upstairs at Off Broadway restaurant, brick, velvet, warm shadows and the elegance of old make this hip place perfect for a drink and conversation. Sink into a comfy sofa and let the night begin. The gregarious bartender is known for his Jaeger Rita martinis.

Gahan House (☎ 902-626-2337; 126 Sydney St) Within these historic walls the pub owners brew PEI's only homegrown ales. Sir John A's Honey Wheat Ale is worth introducing to your insides, as is the medium- to full-bodied Sydney Street Stout.

Beanz (☎ 902-892-8797; 38 University Ave; ⏱ 10am-5pm Sat-Thu, to 6pm Fri) It's a trendy spot with local artwork, which blends, brews and steams the best hot beverages in Charlottetown.

ENTERTAINMENT
From early evening to the morning hours, Charlottetown serves up a great mix of theater, music, island culture and fun. To tap into the entertainment scene, pick up a free monthly copy of the *Buzz*.

Live Music
Throughout Charlottetown and PEI various venues host traditional ceilidhs (*kay*-lees). They are sometimes referred to as 'kitchen parties' and usually embrace gleeful Celtic music and dance. If you have the chance to attend one, don't miss it. The Friday edition of the *Guardian* newspaper lists times and locations of upcoming ceilidhs.

Benevolent Irish Society (☎ 902-963-3156; 582 North River Rd; admission $8; ⏱ 8pm Fri mid-May–Oct) On the north side of town, this is a quirky place to catch a ceilidh. Come early, as seating is limited.

Olde Dublin Pub (☎ 902-892-6992; 131 Sydney St; admission $5) A traditional Irish pub with a jovial spirit and live entertainment nightly during the summer. Celtic bands and local notables take to the stage and make for an engaging night out.

Baba's Lounge (☎ 902-892-7377; 81 University Ave; admission $5) This welcoming, intimate venue hosts great local bands playing their own tunes. Occasionally there are poetry readings as well.

Myron's Cabaret (☎ 902-892-4375; 151 Kent St; admission from $5) At the opposite end of the spectrum, Myron's believes that bigger is better. The line of stylish 20-somethings strung out the door must agree. Three cavernous floors reverberate with heavy metal and alternative music pumped out by local bands and DJs.

Theater
Confederation Centre of the Arts (☎ 902-566-1267, 800-565-0278; www.confederationcentre.com; 145 Richmond St) This modern complex's large theater and outdoor amphitheater host concerts, comedic performances and elaborate musicals. *Anne of*

Green Gables – The Musical has been entertaining audiences here as part of the Charlottetown Festival since 1964, making it Canada's longest-running musical. You'll enjoy it, and your friends will never have to know.

Cinemas

City Cinema (☎ 902-368-3669; 64 King St) A small independent theater featuring Canadian and foreign-language films.

Sports

Charlottetown Driving Park (☎ 902-892-6823; 46 Kensington Rd; admission free; ⊙ Thu May-Dec, Thu & Sat Jun-Sep) Just north of the town center, this park allows you to witness human, horse and buggy in the spectacle of harness racing, a popular Maritime-province pastime.

SHOPPING

Local arts and crafts are an island institution. Shops abound along Victoria Row and the waterfront.

Moonsnail Soapworks (☎ 902-892-7627; 85 Water St) This little shop and artist's studio produces an amazing array of soaps, jewelry and artwork. Lather up with its red-clay and kelp bar!

Anne of Green Gables Store (☎ 902-368-2663; 110 Queen St; ⊙ 9am-9pm Mon-Sat, 11am-7pm Sun May-Sep, 10am-5pm Mon-Fri Oct-Apr) For those who haven't had their fill of LM Montgomery.

GETTING THERE & AWAY

Air

Charlottetown Airport is 8km north of the city center at Brackley Point and Sherwood Rds. A taxi to/from town costs $12, plus $4 for each additional person. Air Canada flies daily to Toronto (from $250 round-trip), Halifax (from $175) and Montréal (from $130). See p277 for airport information.

Bus

The only intra-island bus transportation to and from Charlottetown is the **Beach Shuttle** (☎ 902-566-3243; one way/return $12/20), which makes stops between Charlottetown and Cavendish, leaving from the visitors center. For buses and shuttles traveling to Halifax, see p76. Acadian Lines (p281) buses also travel to elsewhere on the mainland.

Car & Motorcycle

With next to no public transportation available, rental cars are the preferred method for

most travelers going to/from Charlottetown. During the summer cars are in short supply, so book ahead.

Nationwide companies such as Avis, Budget, National and Hertz have offices in town and at the airport. Note that the airport desks are strictly for people with reservations.

Your best option in Charlottetown is **National** (☎ 902-368-2228; cnr Kensington Rd & Exhibition Dr). New compact cars with unlimited kilometers and insurance rent for $60 per day. **Rent-A-Wreck** (☎ 902-566-9955; 57A St Peter's Rd) is another good option. It has compact used cars, including insurance and 200km free per day, for the same price.

GETTING AROUND

Bicycle

Riding is a great way to get around this quaint town. Both **Smooth Cycle** (☎ 902-566-5530, 800-310-6550; www.smoothcycle.com; 308 Queen St; rentals per half-/full day $17/25, week $110) and **MacQueen's Bicycles** (☎ 902-368-2453; www.macqueens.com; 430 Queen St; per day/week $25/125) rent bikes. See p189 for more details.

Car & Motorcycle

During the summer, traffic snarls to a halt on University St and finding parking becomes an art form. That said, the municipal lots near the visitors center and Peake's Wharf charge $6 per day. One loonie ($1) gets you two hours at any of the town's parking meters, which operate between 8am and 6pm on weekdays.

Public Transportation

Trius Tours (☎ 902-566-5664; one-way fare $1.50) runs the anemic city transit within Charlottetown. One bus makes various loops through the city, stopping sporadically at the Confederation Centre between 9:20am and 2:40pm.

The Jump-on, Jump-off Trolley (adult/family $10/20), designed for tourists, stops at all the main attractions plus a handful of shops and restaurants. It runs daily from 9am to 5pm and you can get on and off as many times as you like; passes are for two days.

Taxi

Fares are standardized and priced by zones. Between the waterfront and Hwy 1 there are three zones. Travel within this area is about $5, plus $1 per extra person. **City Taxi** (☎ 902-892-6567) and **Yellow Cab PEI** (☎ 902-566-6666) provide good service.

EASTERN PEI

You can make your own tracks across Kings County, the eastern third of the province and PEI's most underrated and undertouristed region. From stretches of neatly tended homesteads to the sinuous eastern shore with picturesque harbors and beaches (which lack the winds found along the north shore), natural spaces, country inns and fine dining await. Majestic tree canopies seem to stretch endlessly over scenic heritage roads.

ORWELL

Surrounded by rolling green fields, Orwell is found 28km east of Charlottetown, via Hwy 1.

The main reason to stop here is **Orwell Corner Historic Village** (☎ 902-651-8510; off Hwy 1; adult/child under 12yr $7.50/free; ☷ 10am-5:30pm daily late Jul-Sep, 9am-4:30pm Mon-Fri late May-late Jun), a living re-creation of a 19th-century farming community. Painstaking restoration and workers in 19th-century dress bring everything – from the schoolhouse to the shingle mill – alive. Watch a smithy in action, or visit the massive draft horses that grace the barn. If possible, come on a Wednesday and take part in a traditional **ceilidh** (admission $10; ☷ 8pm).

Be sure to leave time to visit the gabled house and 57-hectare property of the **Sir Andrew MacPhail Homestead** (☎ 902-651-2789; 269 MacPhail Park Rd; admission free; ☷ 11am-5pm Tue-Sun mid-Jun–mid-Sep), which is 1km down the road.

Rachel's Motel & Cottages (☎ 902-659-2874, 800-559-2874; www.holidayjunction.com/canada/pei/cpe0014.html; 4827 Hwy 1; d/2-bedroom cottages $55/60; ☷ mid-May–mid-Oct), south of Orwell, just west of the Lord Selkirk Provincial Park turnoff, is a fine accommodations choice. There are well-kept rooms with small kitchenettes as well as two-bedroom cottages. It's set back from the highway and has a large playground.

Rainbow Lodge B&B (☎ 902-651-2202, 800-268-7005; 7521 Hwy 1; s/d $65/80) leaps at you from the roadside with a giant rainbow mural, fluttery garden pinwheels and blooms of flowers. It's certainly the 'most out' accommodation on PEI but don't pass up the cheery rooms just because you're straight.

WOOD ISLANDS

'Woods' is the first place where you set foot on PEI if you arrive by ferry, and one of the first things you'll see is the **visitors center** (☎ 902-962-7411; Plough Waves Centre, cnr Hwy 1 & Rte 4; ☷ 8:30am-6pm late May–mid-Oct, to 9pm mid-Jun–Aug, 10:30am-6pm mid-May–late May & mid-Oct–late Oct, closed Nov–mid-May) about 1km up from the terminal.

If you want a bite to eat and the idea of limp ferry hot dogs doesn't whet your appetite, stop at **Crabby's Seafood** (☎ 902-962-3228; Fisherman's Wharf; mains from $4; ☷ noon-6pm Jun-Sep) on the wharf just outside the ferry terminal. This little fishmonger not only sells delectably

---

DETOUR: PANMURE ISLAND

A favorite detour from Rte 17 is to **Panmure Island**, a flat, bird-filled haven of beaches, highlighted by **Panmure Island Provincial Park** (☎ 902-838-0668; serviced/unserviced campsites $19/22; ☷ Jun–mid-Sep), the now well-filled-in causeway that links the island with the mainland. On one side of the spit sheltered St Mary's Bay offers safe swimming, while the opposite ocean side has vast stretches of secluded dunes and views out to sea. You can camp here and the park has every amenity for its 44 sites (most unserviced). **Panmure Island Lighthouse** (☎ 902-838-3568; tours $5; ☷ 9:30am-5pm Jul-Aug, variable Jun & Sep), Prince Edward Island's oldest wooden lighthouse, is as picture-perfect as they come with fields of lupin and grazing horses in front. Take a tour before forgetting your worries on the endless beach.

There's an annual **Powwow** (☎ 902-892-5314; www.ncpei.com/powwow-trail.html; ☷ mid-Aug) held each year with drumming, crafts and a sweat tent – it attracts around 5000 visitors so don't expect any secluded beaches!

Those without camping gear should seriously consider staying at the grandiose **Maplehurst Properties** (☎ 902-838-3959; www.maplehurstproperties.com; Rte 347; d $135-190; ☷ May-Oct) on the ocean side of Panmure. Marsha Leftwich has mustered every glimmer of her native Southern hospitality to create an exceptional B&B that drips with gorgeous chandeliers as well as fresh baked muffins and treats. Everything is bright, modern and really, really big in this newly built Georgian colonial mansion. Spend the day as a beach bum then sleep it off like royalty!

PRINCE EDWARD ISLAND

POINTS EAST COASTAL DRIVE

The 374km Points East Coastal Drive is a circuitous country road that's nearly empty on weekdays. Tour past lupin-studded fields, vertical red cliffs, antique lighthouses and Prince Edward Island's sandiest delights: the mountainous dunes at Greenwich that border the Gulf of St Lawrence and the musical sands of Basin Head along the northeastern seaboard. The east coast from Bay Fortune to Montague rewards visitors with crisp bays, rolling hills and gourmet treats. The best thing to do on this road trip? Leave the car and hop on a bike (p199); the eastern parts of the Confederation Trail are the island's most beautiful.

fresh crustaceans by the pound, he'll also steam them for you, right there, and you can shamelessly dig in at his shopside picnic table. If you make a mess of yourself, there's warm soapy water to wash up with. You won't find a better deal on cooked shellfish on all of PEI.

Don't rush to or from the ferry. The **Wood Islands Provincial Park** and its 1876 lighthouse are well worth the short walk. The museum, actually inside the lighthouse, is one of the best of its type on the island. Cruise the re-created lighthouse-keeper quarters, learn about rum running and the mystery of the 'Burning Ship' (see the boxed text, opposite).

Northumberland Ferries (☎ 902-566-3838, 888-249-7245; www.peiferry.com; pedestrian/motorcycle/car $13/36/57; ☼ May-Dec) crosses to Caribou near Pictou, Nova Scotia, up to nine times daily (five times in the fall and spring). You only pay going from PEI – see p116 and p200 for more details.

MONTAGUE & AROUND

The fact that Montague isn't flat gives it a unique, inland feel. Perched on either side of the Montague River, the busy little town is the service center for Kings County; its streets lead from the breezy, heritage marina area to modern shopping malls, supermarkets and fast-food outlets.

At Pooles Corner there is a large **tourist office** (☎ 902-838-0670; cnr Rtes 3 & 4; ☼ 8am-7pm late Jun-late Aug, 9am-4:30pm late May–mid-Jun & Sep–mid-Oct). Along with the usual tourist office services, there are several museum-quality exhibits.

Back in town, the statuesque former post office and customs house (1888) overlooks the marina, and houses the **Garden of the Gulf Museum** (☎ 902-838-2467; 564 Main St S; adult/child under 12yr $3/free; ☼ 9am-5pm Mon-Fri early Jun-late Sep). PEI's oldest museum lets you glimpse pioneer days and early-20th-century life.

Across the marina is a restored train station, which marks a terminus on the Confederation Trail (see p200). The only things pulling up now are exhausted people – the trains stopped in 1984. The station contains a small information booth, an ice-cream stand and **Cruise Manada** (☎ 902-838-3444, 800-986-3444; adult/child under 14yr $20/10; ☼ mid-May–Sep), which offers popular boat tours to PEI's largest seal colony, and takes a peek at mussel farms too.

Next to the tourist office, **Ricky's Bike Rentals** (☎ 902-962-3085; Montague Waterfront, per hr/half-/full day $7/15/30) sets up a mobile shop in his colorful van. The Confederation Trail is a 30-second pedal away.

Just north of town, development meets nature at **Brudenell River Provincial Park** (☎ 902-652-8966; off Rte 3; tentsites $19, RV sites $22-25; ☼ late May–mid-Oct), which is a park and resort complex. Options range from kayaking and nature walks to horseback riding and golf. The campground is nicely sheltered and close to the Confederation Trail.

Boudrealaut's White House Tourist Home (☎ 902-838-2560, 800-436-3220; Rte 17 off Rte 4; s/d $50/65) is run by the most energetic 83-year-old we've ever met. The rooms are simple but comfortable and after you are given maps, menus and activity ideas for the area, you are pretty much left on your own. There's bicycle storage and kids are welcome. For a more upscale experience, check into **Knox's Dam B&B** (☎ 838-4234; knoxsdambandb@hotmail.com; cnr Rtes 353 & 320, Montague; d/ste $80/125) which has the luck of being constantly serenaded by the babble and flow of Knox' Dam on the Montague river. The big red Victorian has three artfully decorated rooms and a sunny downstairs breakfast room. There's good trout fishing at the dam.

As famous for its chowder and mussels as it is for its scenic deck, **Windows on the Water Café** (☎ 902-838-2080; 106 Sackville St, Montague; mains dinner $15-22; ☼ lunch & dinner May-Oct) cooks up a tempting array of seafood, chicken and vegetarian dishes. Lobsters here are precooked so it's best to go elsewhere for a lobster dinner (see the boxed text, p205).

BAY FORTUNE

Although the scenery of pine forests and patchwork fields meeting gentle, dark surf is spectacular, most people come to Bay Fortune to eat. **Inn at Bay Fortune** (☎ 902-687-3745; www .innatbayfortune.com; Rte 310; r from $150, ste $200-335; ☺ Jun–Oct), on 19 hectares where the bay opens up onto the Northumberland Strait, has some of the most upscale rooms and cottages on PEI as well as what many believe to be the island's best restaurant (meals from $60). Chef Warren Barr is known for lively combinations of local ingredients that capture the essence of the best PEI flavors. The menu changes daily according to season, with highlights such as tartare of PEI scallops with strawberry and balsamic salsa or pavé of crispy beef short ribs with roasted organic shitake mushrooms. You can dine in the elegant restaurant or take a special reservation at the chef's table in the kitchen where you can watch as seven sublime courses are created for you. Rooms are modern with country flair; the most fun rooms, tiny units in a tower with nearly 360-degree views, are the least expensive. The price goes up with size, culminating in private cottages.

SOURIS

Embracing the waters of Colville Bay is the quaint town of Souris (*sur*-rey; population 1248). It owes its name to the French Acadians and the gluttonous mice who repeatedly ravaged their crops. Thankfully it's now known more for its local musicians and fantastic music festivals than for hungry field rodents.

This bustling fishing port makes a great base for your east coast adventures. The coast, Confederation Trail and nearby Scenic Heritage Rd (The Glen) provide tremendous cycling options, and the waters are perfect for kayaking. This is also the launching point for ferries to the Îles de la Madeleine in Québec.

Information

Provincial Tourist Office (☎ 902-687-7030; Main St; ☺ 9am-9pm Jul & Aug, to 4:30pm mid-Jun–early Oct) In the Matthew & McLean building next to the CIBC Banking Centre.

Sights & Activities

Built of red island sandstone in 1901, the distinctive rounded tower of **St Mary's Catholic Church** (cnr Chapel & Longworth Sts) still looms over Souris. Another historic building that's worth a peak is the **Town Hall** on Main St.

A Place to Stay Inn (p198) rents bicycles ($4 per hour, $12/20 per half-/full day).

Festivals & Events

The reputation of the **PEI Bluegrass & Oldtime Music Festival** (☎ 902-569-3153; www.bluegrasspei .com/rollobay.htm; Rte 2) continues to grow. Held in early July, it's one of Atlantic Canada's top music festivals, with acts drawn from as far away as Nashville. Come for just a day, or camp out for all three.

PRINCE EDWARD ISLAND

THE BURNING SHIP OF NORTHUMBERLAND STRAITS

If you happen to be driving along the Northumberland Straits on a fog-bound autumn night, look over the dark waters for a 'phantom ship' in flames out at sea. Whether or not you believe in ghosts, this eerie vision has been documented for more than 200 years. In western Prince County, Canoe Cove, and Charlottetown; and particularly from Wood Islands to Murray Harbour, fishermen and landlubbers have been spotting what looks like a three-masted sailing vessel in full blaze. Any attempt to rescue the ship causes the mirage to vanish into the horizon. Similar cases have been reported from districts near Prince Edward Island: Pictou Island and Malagash in Nova Scotia and around Bouctouche in New Brunswick. An intriguing aspect of eyewitnesses' accounts is that they occur mostly from September through November and are generally a harbinger of a storm. On certain occasions very large numbers of people have witnessed the same appearance.

While the 'phantom ship' has taken guises of being the ghost of one of a slew of ships lost at sea, some people suggest that it is perhaps a manifestation of St Elmo's Fire, a fog bank that reflects the moonlight or mirage completely unique to the area. Whatever the reason, Mi'kmaq legend also references sea-bound fireballs on the Strait so chances are the phenomenon has been in existence long before written records.

Check out the fascinating room at the Wood Island Lighthouse (p195), dedicated to the burning ship, for first-hand, detailed accounts.

Sleeping & Eating

A Place to Stay Inn (☎ 902-687-4626; apts1@pei.aibn.com; 9 Longworth St; dm $22, s/d $65/70; ☼ closed Feb) A B&B and a hostel, this superb facility is located beside St Mary's Catholic Church. It has a full kitchen, laundry facilities, bicycle rental, a lounge and TV room. The owner is a treasure trove of information.

McLean House Inn (☎ 902-687-1875; www.mclean houseinn.com; 16 Washington St; tw/d incl light breakfast $95/110; ☼ May-Nov) The view from, and atmosphere of, this beautiful mansard home make it perfect for a lazy afternoon. Head to the sunroom, grab some wicker and sink into a book. Ask for the Colville Bay room (No 303). The house is a little hidden, down a side street opposite the tourist office.

Mathew's House Inn (☎ 902-687-3461; www.mathew houseinn.com; 15 Breakwater St; d $100-180; ☼ late Jun-Sep) Owned by the same family from its construction in 1885 until the late 1980s, this home has retained its old-time feel perhaps more than any other B&B on the island. Lovingly restored, meticulously clean and decorated with the finest antiques, this is a truly unique place to stay. The affable, multilingual hosts give you a full- or light-breakfast option and will cook authentic Italian dinners for guests on request. Children are welcome.

Bluefin Restaurant (☎ 902-687-3271; 10 Federal Ave; meals $7-13; ☼ breakfast, lunch & dinner) Near McLean House Inn, this local favorite is known for its heaped servings of traditional island food. Its lunch special runs from 11am to 1pm.

Getting There & Away

CTMA Ferries (☎ 418-986-3278, 888-986-3278; www.ctma .ca; one-way fare adult/child/vehicle $42/21/79) runs ferries (five hours) to Québec's Îles de la Madeleine.

BASIN HEAD PROVINCIAL PARK

While this **park** (off Rte 16; admission free) is home to the **Basin Head Fisheries Museum** (☎ 902-357-7233; adult/student $4.50/2; ☼ 9am-6pm Jul & Aug, to 5pm Jun-Sep), its star attraction is the sweeping sand of golden **Basin Head Beach**. Most islanders rank this as their favorite beach. The sand is also famous for its singing – well, squeaking. Five minutes of joyous 'musical' footsteps south from the museum and you have secluded bliss – enjoy! Unfortunately the sand only performs when dry so if it's been raining, it's no show. Atop the beach, the museum traces the island's fishing history and features an interpretive center and a coastal ecology exhibit.

EAST POINT & AROUND

Built the same year Canada was unified, the **East Point Lighthouse** (☎ 902-357-2106; adult/child $2.50/1; ☼ 10am-6pm mid-Jun–Aug) continues to stand guard over the northeastern shore of PEI. After being blamed for the 1882 wreck of the British *Phoenix*, the lighthouse was moved closer to shore. The eroding shoreline is now chasing it back. Teetering on the cliff is the old assistant's house. It has a restored radio room and a gift shop.

The wooded coast and lilting accents of the north shore make for an interesting change of pace. **North Lake** and **Naufrage** harbors are intriguing places to stop and, if you feel so inclined, join a charter boat in search of a 450kg tuna.

For a truly fabulous, out-of-the-way place to stay, try **Johnson Shore Inn B&B** (☎ 902-687-1340; www.johnsonshoreinn.com; off Rte 16; d $125-300; ☼ May-Nov), perched on a knobby point of the never-ending red cliffs of Hermanville. With

PRINCE EDWARD ISLAND

sunrise on one side and sunset on the other, you can sit back and concentrate on little more than bird chirps and the passing of the sun; this is the essence of peace and quiet. Rooms are elegant, the food (dinner is by request) divine. It's gay-friendly and a great place for retreats.

ELMIRA

Ever expanding, the **Elmira Railway Museum** (☎ 902-357-7234; Rte 16A; adult/student/family $3/2/10; ☼ 10am-6pm Jul & Aug, to 5pm Fri-Wed mid-Jun–mid-Sep) includes a quirky **miniature-train ride** (adult/student/ family $7/4/15) that winds through the surrounding forest. This magnificently restored station marks the eastern end of the Confederation Trail (see p200).

GREENWICH

Massive, dramatic and ever-shifting sand dunes epitomize the amazing area west of Greenwich. These rare parabolic giants are fronted by an awesome beach – a visit here is a must. Saved by Parks Canada in 1998, this 6km section of shore is now part of Prince Edward Island National Park (p201).

Avant-garde meets barn at the **Greenwich Interpretation Centre** (☎ 902-961-2514; Hwy 13; ☼ 9:30am-7pm late Jun-Aug, 4:30pm mid-May–mid-Jun & Sep–mid-Oct), where pictorial and audiovisual exhibits detail the dune system and the vast archaeological history of the site. While it's interesting inside, there's nothing better than wandering in the midst of the tree-eating sand dunes. The environment and flora are extremely sensitive, so be careful to stay on the trails.

ST PETERS TO MT STEWART

The region between these two small towns is a hotbed for cycling. The section of the Confederation Trail (see the boxed text, p200) closest to St Peters flirts with the shoreline and rewards riders with an eyeful; it's the only part of the trail that skirts the ocean like this. In Mt Stewart, a funky speck of a town, three riverside sections of the Confederation Trail converge, giving riders and hikers plenty of attractive options within a relatively compact area. Both the Confederation Trail and a **provincial tourist office** (☎ 902-961-3540; Rte 2; ☼ 8am-7pm late Jun-late Aug, 9am-4:30pm mid-Jun & Sep–Oct) are found next to the bridge in St Peters, the larger of the two villages.

Although designed for guests of the Christian center, the austere rooms of **Midgell Centre** (☎ 902-961-2963; 6553 Rte 2; dm & s without bathroom $20; ☼ mid-Jun–mid-Sep) are available to visitors. Depending on the setup, you may be in a dorm or private room. Communal kitchens in each building add value to this great budget option – it's near St Peters and Greenwich.

Trailside Inn, Café & Adventures B&B (☎ 902-676-3130, 888-704-6595; www.trailside.ca; 109 Main St; d $80; ☼ mid-May–mid-Oct) is smack-dab in the middle of things and makes a great place to stay. Rooms feel like home in a college rental sort of way. You can also rent bicycles (per two/ four/12 hours $10/17/25) and the licensed **café** (mains $8-18; ☼ breakfast, lunch & dinner) serves up delectable desserts, chowder and other light fare. On weekends, the intimate café hosts local musicians. The **Hillsborough River Eco-Centre** (☎ 902-676-2811; 104 Main St; admission $2; ☼ 9am-4pm Mon-Sat) across the street, has displays on the wildlife, environment and cultural history of the Hillsborough River area.

In St Peters, **Bayside Restaurant & Suites** (☎ 902-961-2954, 866-961-2954; www.baysidecountryinn .com; Rte 16; mains lunch $6-11, dinner $13-18; ☼ 8am-9pm May–mid-Nov) offer clean suites and condo units (suites $135 to $175) to rest weary thighs; these spacious apartments sleep four to six people. Conveniently, you can eat here too although there's not much more than standard fried fish and burgers.

To take a well-earned trail break or eat out in style drop in to **Inn at St Peters** (☎ 902-961-2135, 800-818-0925; www.innatstpeters.pei.ca; 1168 Greenwich Rd; cottages $365-390) with its luxurious cottages, water views and chic dining area. Cottage prices include breakfast and dinner at the very respected **restaurant** (mains lunch/dinner from $17/22; ☼ breakfast, lunch & dinner May-Oct); if this is beyond your budget (and the prices are steep for what you get) you should consider at least lunch at this fine-dining establishment.

CENTRAL PEI

With Prince Edward Island National Park and Anne, the island's most famous (albeit fictional) citizen, Central PEI draws in the lion's share of the province's tourism. And it's no wonder; nowhere on the island is the mix of nature and history more astounding. A beautiful mélange of colorful fields, quaint villages and forests undulates northward before meeting the dramatic coastal landscapes.

Everything is less than an hour from Charlottetown so you can have it all: live it up at city theaters, bars and restaurants then relax during the day in pastoral peace.

BORDEN-CARLETON

The only place remotely like Borden-Carleton on PEI is Cavendish; the two towns have completely artificial mall-like centers that revolve around tourism. The main reason to stop here (besides shopping for trinkets and ice-cream) is to stop at the **Gateway Village Visitor Information Centre** (☎ 902-437-8570; Hwy 1; ☼ 8:30am-8:30pm Jun–mid-Sep, to 6pm late May & early Oct–mid-Oct, to 9am-4:30pm Wed-Sun mid-Oct–mid-May), near the PEI side of the bridge. Here you can pick up oodles of free maps and brochures, take advantage of tidy restrooms and visit the excellent introductory exhibit called **Our Island Home** (☼ May-Nov). Staff can point you to the Confederation Trail (below), which lurks nearby.

Just 5km out of 'town' in the small hamlet of Albany is **Robinson's Farm Market Potato Farm Tours & Corn Maze** (☎ 902-437-2676; Rte 1A; admission free, activities $3-5; ☼ 11am-7pm Jun-Nov, corn maze late Jul-Oct), the most fun potato farm you're ever likely to find. Pick a potato and have it cooked into a French fry, take a hay-wagon ride or feed the funny goats. The highlight is the corn maze in which whole families get lost. Stock up on fresh fruits and veggies at the market when you're done playing.

After frolicking at Robinson's potato farm, stay the night with another farming family. **Carleton Cove B&B** (☎ 902-855-2795; carleton-cove@pei .sympatico.ca; Rte 10, Albany; s/d $50/60; ☼ Jun-Nov) feels like grandma's house with shimmery polyester bedspreads, flowered wallpaper and stuffed animals everywhere.

If you are leaving PEI to go to New Brunswick, you will most likely journey across the 12.9km **Confederation Bridge** (☎ 902-437-7300; www.confederationbridge.com; car/motorcycle $41/16; ☼ 24hr). Sadly, the 1.1m-high guardrails rob you of any hoped-for view. The toll is only charged on departure from PEI, and includes all passengers; cash, debit and major credit cards are accepted.

Cyclists and pedestrians are banned from the bridge and must use a demand-driven **shuttle service** (☎ 902-437-7349; pedestrians/cyclists $4/8; ☼ 24hr); call ahead to reserve in advance if you're with a large group. Go to the bridge operations building near the tollgates; the operators guarantee you won't have to wait more than two hours for the shuttle at any time. For details on getting to PEI from New Brunswick, see p175.

If you're planning to travel one way on the bridge and the other by ferry, it's cheaper to take the ferry to PEI and return via the bridge.

VICTORIA

A place to wander and experience more than 'see,' the shaded, tree-laden lanes of this delightful little fishing village scream out character and charm. The entire village still fits neatly in the four blocks laid out when the town was formed in 1819. Colorful clapboard and shingled houses are home to more than one visitor who was so enthralled by the place

---

CYCLING THE CONFEDERATION TRAIL

Like one of the province's many lighthouses, the 357km-long Confederation Trail acts as a beacon, calling North American and European cyclists. Thanks to its origins as the bed of Prince Edward Island's (PEI) railway the route is almost entirely flat, as it meanders around hills and valleys. There are some sections of the trail that are completely canopied in lush foliage, and in late June and the early weeks of July the trail is lined with bright, flowering lupins. There's perhaps no better way to enjoy the fall change of colors on the island than by riding the trail.

The 279km tip-to-tip route from Tignish (p213), near North Cape, to Elmira (p199), near East Point, is extremely rewarding and passes through countless idyllic villages, where riders can stop for meals or rest for the night. Some of the most popular sections are near Mt Stewart, St Peters (p199) and Harmony Junction. Note that the prevailing winds on PEI blow from the west and southwest, so cycling in this direction is easier. Branches connect the trail to the Confederation Bridge (above), Charlottetown (p189), Souris (p197) and Montague (p196).

Provincial tourist offices have excellent route maps and the island's website (www.gov.pe.ca /visitorsguide/index.php3?number=1014339) offers a plethora of planning and trail information. The bicycle-rental shops in Charlottetown (p189) also run superb islandwide tours.

they decided to stay. There's a profusion of art, cafés and eateries, as well as an excellent **summer theater festival**.

We dare you to just eat one of the sublime handmade Belgian chocolates at **Island Chocolates** (☎ 902-658-2320; 13 Main St; ⌖ 10am-8pm Mon-Sat, noon-8pm Sun Jun-Sep)! Call ahead to arrange for a tour of the factory or just stop in for coffee and hand-dipped decadence.

Next to the theater, **Victoria Village Inn & Restaurant** (☎ 902-658-2483; 22 Howard St; d/tw/tr incl breakfast $90/90/140) has an unforgettable staircase that has one word of Lewis Carroll's poem 'Jabberwocky' on each stair ledge…'t'was brillig and the slithy toves…' This place is so comfy, you may even shed a tear saying goodbye to the plush sofas in the striking sitting room. Throw in the amazing cuisine of chef Stephen Hunter and you have a winner. His casual fine-dining **restaurant** (mains $14-19; ⌖ dinner) has a deceptively decadent menu. Vegetarian selections and theater packages are also available. Reservations are highly recommended.

Landmark Café (☎ 902-658-2286; cnr Main & Howard Sts; mains $10-20; ⌖ 11am-whenever) kind of feels like you just walked into someone's kitchen. You know a place must be good when the sign on the door says 'Welcome Back,' and this nook-like café certainly is full of locals. Order a soup or healthy main (from meat to veggie dishes) and admire the trinket-filled shelves that contain everything from French vintage KFC tubs to monkeys carved from coconuts.

Music, comedy and storytelling take center stage at the wonderfully antique-feeling **Victoria Playhouse** (☎ 902-658-2025, 800-925-2025; 20 Howard St; adult/youth & senior $20/18; ⌖ shows 8pm Jul-Sep) on Monday; engaging theater productions are on other days.

PRINCE EDWARD ISLAND NATIONAL PARK

Heaving dunes and red sandstone bluffs provide startling backdrops for some of the island's finest stretches of sand; welcome to **Prince Edward Island National Park** (☎ 902-672-6350; www.pc.gc.ca/pei; day pass adult/child under 17yr/family $5/2.50/12.50). This dramatic coast, and the narrow sections of wetland and forests behind it, are home to diverse plants and animals, including the red fox and endangered piping plover.

The park is open year-round, but most services only operate between late June and

the end of August. Entrance fees, charged between mid-June and mid-September, admit you to all the park sites except the House of Green Gables (p206). If you are staying for longer than five days, it's worth considering a seasonal pass. The park maintains an information desk at the Cavendish Visitor Centre (p206). Failing that, the provincial tourist office at Brackley Beach (p203) also provides information.

The following sights are organized from east to west, first covering the park-run facilities, then the private operations inside and out of the park.

Sights & Activities

Beaches lined with marram grasses and wild roses span almost the entire length of the park's 42km coastline. In most Canadians' minds, the park is almost synonymous with the beaches. **Dalvay Beach** sits to the east, and has some short hiking trails through the woods. The landscape flattens and the sand sprawls outward at **Stanhope Beach**. Here a boardwalk leads from the campground to the shore. Backed by dunes, and slightly west, is the expansive and popular **Brackley Beach**. On the western side of the park, the sheer size of **Cavendish Beach** makes it the granddaddy of them all. During summer this beach sees copious numbers of visitors beneath its hefty dunes. If crowds aren't your thing, there are always the pristine sections of sand to the east.

A unique wrinkle in the Gulf Stream ensures the waters here are some of the warmest

PRINCE EDWARD ISLAND

AROUND PEI NATIONAL PARK

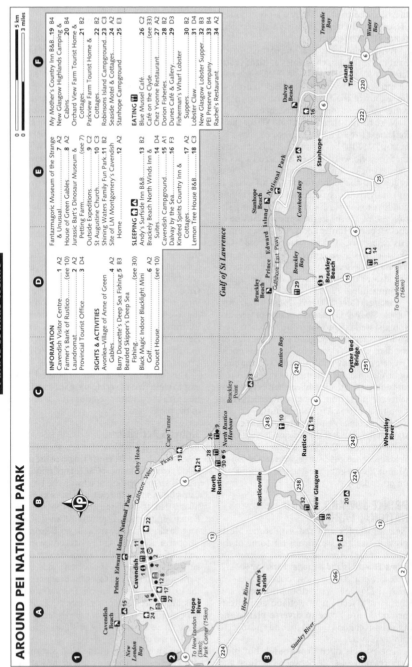

INFORMATION
Cavendish Visitor Centre..............1 A2
Farmer's Bank of Rustico.........(see 10)
Laundromat......................................2 A2
Provincial Tourist Office.................3 D4

SIGHTS & ACTIVITIES
Avonlea–Village of Anne of Green
  Gables..4 A2
Barry Doucette's Deep Sea Fishing.5 B3
Bearded Skipper's Deep Sea
  Fishing....................................(see 30)
Black Magic Indoor Blacklight Mini
  Golf...6 A2
Doucet House...........................(see 10)

Fantazmagoric Museum of the Strange
  & Unusual....................................7 A2
House of Green Gables....................8 A2
Jurassic Bart's Dinosaur Museum &
  Petting Farm...........................(see 7)
Outside Expeditions........................9 C2
St Augustine Church......................10 C3
Shining Waters Family Fun Park...11 B2
Site of LM Montgomery's Cavendish
  Home...12 A2

SLEEPING 🛏
Andy's Surfside Inn B&B...............13 B2
Brackley Beach North Winds Inn &
  Suites.......................................14 D4
Cavendish Campground.................15 A1
Dalvay by the Sea.........................16 F3
Kindred Spirits Country Inn &
  Cottages...................................17 A2
Lemon Tree House B&B.................18 C3

My Mother's Country Inn B&B....19 B4
New Glasgow Highlands Camping &
  Cabins......................................20 B4
Orchard View Farm Tourist Home &
  Cottages...................................21 B2
Parkview Farm Tourist Home &
  Cottages...................................22 B2
Robinsons Island Campground.....23 C3
Seaside Motel & Cottages.............24 A2
Stanhope Campground.................25 E3

EATING 🍴
Blue Mussel Café..........................26 C2
Café on the Clyde...................(see 33)
Chez Yvonne Restaurant...............27 A2
Dorion Fisheries...........................28 B2
Dunes Café & Gallery....................29 D3
Fisherman's Wharf Lobster
  Suppers.....................................30 B2
Lobster Claw.................................31 D4
New Glasgow Lobster Supper......32 B3
PEI Preserve Company..................33 B4
Rachel's Restaurant.......................34 A2

0 ———— 5 km
0 ———— 3 miles

on the east coast north of Virginia. Lifeguards are on duty at Cavendish, Brackley and Stanhope Beaches in midsummer, but take care, as undertows and rip currents are quite common. You may see small red jellyfish, known locally as bloodsuckers. Don't worry, they're not – at worst, they may irritate the skin. Last words of warning: don't forget the sunscreen!

Sleeping

Parks Canada operates three highly sought-after **campgrounds** (☎ 800-414-6765; tent sites $22, RV sites $25-27; ☺ early Jun-late Aug), which are spread along its length. They all have kitchen shelters and showers. For an additional fee of $10, you can reserve a campsite, but you must do so at least three days in advance by phone or via the website www.canadiancamping.ca. You can request a campground, but not a specific site; you must accept whatever is available when you arrive. While 80% of sites can be booked in advance, the remaining sites are first-come, first-served, so it's wise to arrive early.

Stanhope Campground, on Gulfshore East Parkway, is nestled nicely in the woods behind the beach of the same name. There is a well-stocked store on-site.

Robinsons Island Campground, also located on Gulfshore East Parkway, is open from late June. The most isolated of the three sites, it's set at the end of Brackley Point. It's not too much fun if the wind gets up.

The proximity of Cavendish Campground, off Rte 6, to the sights makes it the most popular. It has exposed oceanfront sites and ones within the shelter and shade of the trees. Don't be lured by the view – it's nice, but sleep is better.

The communities listed following also provide excellent accommodation options in or around the park.

DALVAY BY THE SEA

Standing proudly near the east end of the park, and overlooking the beach named after it, is **Dalvay by the Sea** (☎ 902-672-2048; Gulfshore East Parkway; d incl breakfast & dinner $260-360; ☺ Jun-Oct), a historic mansion. Built in 1895 this majestic building is now owned by Parks Canada, and operated as an inn. Although it's in desperate need of a remodel, it's easily the most luxurious and stunning accommodation on the north shore. Each room's antique furnishings are unique, but spare; it's the majestic main hall, full of fine carpets and antiques, that is

the real stunner. Unfortunately, a turn from the grand entrance brings you to a shabby lobby full of furniture that looks as though it's been through several yard sales. The **dining room** (dinner mains $18-30; ☺ breakfast, lunch & dinner Jul & Aug) prepares remarkable dishes ranging from hazelnut-and-sage-crusted rack of lamb to fresh island lobster. It is open to nonguests, and both lunch and afternoon tea are reasonably priced. The inn also rents bicycles (per hour/half-day/day $5/12/20).

BRACKLEY BEACH

Brackley Beach is the largest town with an entrance to the western portion of PEI National Park. There's a **provincial tourist office** (☎ 902-672-7474; cnr Rtes 6 & 15; ☺ 8am-9pm Jul & Aug, 9am-4:30pm Jun & Sep-early Oct) 4km before the park entrance.

While out this way do not miss a stop at **Dunes Café & Gallery** (☎ 902-672-2586; Rte 15; mains dinner $16-25; ☺ 11:30am-10pm Jun-Sep, 10am-6pm May & Oct), a complete change of pace from Anne art and fish-and-chips. Honestly, where else on the island can you enjoy Vietnamese rice-noodle salad in the shade of a giant Buddha? Come in for a coffee, a meal or just to roam the eclectic mix of Asian and island art in the sprawling glass gallery and garden. The staff encourages people to kick back and relax in the garden or rooftop sitting areas.

Multitask by doing your laundry as you eat at **Lobster Claw** (☎ 902-672-2950; Rte 6; breakfasts from $4, mains lunch & dinner $8-16; ☺ breakfast, lunch & dinner), a restaurant connected to washer and dryer happiness. Good-value breakfasts are copious, while lunches and dinner are just standard seafood and Maritime fare.

If you plan on using Brackley Beach as a base to explore the park, **Brackley Beach North Winds Inn & Suites** (☎ 902-672-2245, 800-901-2245; www.peisland.com/northwinds; r/ste incl breakfast $100/200; ☺ Jun–mid-Sep; 🖭) is as good a place as any and has everything from honeymoon suites to family units. It's got a corporate vibe but the management is warm as well as being very professional.

RUSTICO

The Acadian settlement at Rustico dates back to 1700, and several fine historic buildings speak of this tiny village's former importance. Most prominent is **St Augustine's Church** (1830), the oldest Catholic church on PEI. The old cemetery is on one side of the church, the solid red-stone **Farmer's Bank of Rustico** (☎ 902-963-3168; Rte 243; admission free; ⊙ 9:30am-5:30pm Mon-Sat, 1-5pm Sun Jun-Sep) is on the other. The bank operated here from 1864 to 1894; it was a forerunner of the credit-union movement in Canada. Beside the bank is **Doucet House**, an old Acadian dwelling that was relocated here.

Resting above the riverbank, **Lemon Tree House B&B** (☎ 902-963-3053, 877-848-7042; www.vir tuo.com/lemontree; Stead Rd; d/ste $85/130, 1-/2-bedroom cottages $105/120; ⊙ Apr-Oct; 💻) is an adorable buttercup-yellow cottage on 1.2 hectares of gentle wood. Rooms are basic with some frilly lace around the windows and wall-to-wall carpet. Feeling brave? Have a dip in the water.

NEW GLASGOW

New Glasgow is a quiet town that spreads elegantly across the shores of the River Clyde. This is the favorite lobster-supper getaway for folks from Charlottetown although it's becoming equally respected for its luscious preserves. The bucolic pace and breezes off the grand, meandering river make this a wonderful place to escape.

At **New Glasgow Lobster Supper** (☎ 902-964-2870; Rte 258; lobster dinners $26-32; ⊙ 4-8:30pm Jun–mid-Oct) you can make a right mess with the lobster, while also gorging on an endless supply of great chowder, mussels, salads, breads and homemade desserts (see boxed text, opposite).

Café on the Clyde (☎ 902-964-4300; mains dinner $13-17; ⊙ 9am-8pm mid-Jun–late Sep, to 4pm late May–early Jun & late Sep–mid-Oct) is perhaps the best casual dining option near the national park. Sun reflects in off the River Clyde and makes this place glow. The vegetarian wraps with a hint of feta truly hit the spot and local fare, such as a cheesy potato pot pie with maple bacon cream, is quite creative. The café is an addition to the famous **PEI Preserve Company** (⊙ 9am-5pm, to 9pm mid-Jun–late Sep). While the preserves are a tad pricey, we think they're worth every penny; if you're not going to buy, at least come in to browse the free samples. Don't pass the orange ginger curd or the raspberry champagne preserves. Both café and preserve company are off Hwy 13, at the junction of Rtes 224 and 258.

If there was ever a doctorate awarded in campsite planning, it would go to **New Glasgow Highlands Camping & Cabins** (☎ 902-964-3232; les .andrews@pei.sympatico.ca; Rte 224; tent-/RV sites $26/29, cabins $50; ⊙ Apr-Oct; 💻). The campground is likely the nicest on PEI, with 20-odd sites properly spaced in the forest, each with its

own fire pit. For rainy days there are light-cooking facilities in the lodge. Add a Laundromat, a small store, a heated swimming pool and a mystifying absence of bugs and you're laughing. There are also bright cabins, each with two bunks, a double bed, a sofa and a picnic table; bathrooms are shared. The word is out, so book ahead. Quiet campers are appreciated here; rowdy folk should look elsewhere. The campgrounds are 1.7km east of PEI Preserve Company.

My Mother's Country Inn B&B (☎ 902-964-2508, 800-278-2071; www.mymotherscountryinn.com; 397 Simpson Mill Rd; d $90-200, t/q $125/250; ⊙ Jun–mid-Oct; 💻) is another reason to linger in New Glasgow. An oasis within 20 hectares of rolling hills, brisk streams and enchanting woodlands, this is pure, rural delight. The house is the essence of country style with sea green– and ochre-painted walls, bright pastel quilts, wood floors and plenty of light. A big red bard waits to be photographed by a storybook brook. PEI quaintness moves into an era beyond Green Gables? You be the judge.

ST ANN

St Ann is so small you hardly even know you've arrived. Yet on a summer evening, follow the traffic and wafts of lobster steam to **St Ann's Parish** (☎ 902-621-0635; Rte 224; supper $24-30; ⊙ 4:30-8:30pm mid-Jun–Oct), which rivals New Glasgow as PEI islanders' favorite lobster supper (see the boxed text, opposite).

In 1963, St Ann's had a $35,000 mortgage to pay so the inventive Father Denis Gallant decided to serve lobster dinners in the basement of the church to raise money to help pay it off. Early the next year, the basement was set up to serve approximately 100 people lobster suppers one day a week; the price was $1.50. Voila! The tradition of PEI lobster suppers was born. Today, the food is pricier but is prepared fresh daily. The church employs approximately 30 locals during peak season.

NORTH RUSTICO

Popeye and Olive Oyl would feel very much at home in North Rustico. Rickety, boxy fishermen's houses painted in navies, brick reds and beiges line a deep harbor that is simply packed with fishing vessels. A walk east from the pier along the boardwalk, and out to North Rustico Harbour, is a great way to take in the sights, sounds and smells of this little village.

In the center of town, near the post office and bank, is one of the best-known, busiest restaurants in the province.

Activities

Whether you're a beginner or more advanced, this is a great area for **kayaking**. Leave Anne, and all those who love her, behind and hit the ocean with PEI's leading adventure-tourism provider, **Outside Expeditions** (☎ 902-963-3366, 800-207-3899; www.getoutside.com; 374 Harbourview Dr; mid-Jun–mid-Oct), situated at the far end of the harbor in a bright yellow fishing shed. The 1½-hour introductory Beginner Bay tour ($39) begins with a lesson in kayaking techniques. The most popular trip is the three-hour Harbour Passage tour ($55), which operates three times daily (9am, 2pm and 6pm). Trips are run in the off-season, whenever at least four people want to go.

If your idea of ocean activity is reeling in a big one, look for the plethora of **deep-sea fishing operators** (adult/child $30/20; trips 8am, 1:15pm & 6pm Mon-Sat, 1:15pm & 6pm Sun Jul-Sep) along Harbourview Dr. The best known is **Bearded Skipper's Deep Sea Fishing** (☎ 902-963-2334; beardedskipper@pei sympatico.ca; behind Fisherman's Wharf Restaurant) with Cap'n Norm Peters whose salty grey beard and 30 years of experience have made him a local legend. Younger companies such as **Barry Doucette's Deep Sea Fishing** (☎ 902-963-2465; North Rustico Wharf) are also recommended. All fishing trips are three to 3½ hours and include all gear.

Sleeping & Eating

Andy's Surfside Inn B&B (☎ 902-963-2405; Gulfshore W Pkwy; d with/without bathroom $75/45; Jun-Nov) Inside the national park, 2.7km toward Orby Head from North Rustico, is this large, rambling house overlooking Doyle's Cove. It has been an inn since the 1930s, and the kitchen is open to those who want to bring home a few live lobsters. Sit back on the porch, put your feet up, and thank your lucky stars; they even speak Japanese here.

Orchard View Farm Tourist Home & Cottages (☎ 902-963-2302, 800-419-4468; www.peionline.com/al/orchard; 7602 Rte 6; d without bathroom $55, 2-bedroom cottages $160; May-Oct) As with most tourist home rooms and B&Bs in this region, frills and flowery wallpaper abound. Thankfully, the cottages are more austere; they include kitchens and have views over the fields to the not-so-distant ocean. Outside you'll be able to enjoy bona fide farm life in the company of grain, soybeans and hogs.

Fisherman's Wharf Lobster Suppers (☎ 902-963-2669; 7230 Main St; lobster dinners $27; lunch Jul–mid-Oct, dinner mid-May–mid-Oct) During the dinner rush in July and August this huge place has lines of people out the door. It's a fun, casual, holiday-style restaurant offering good value – that is if you don't wreck your shirt (see the boxed text, below)! Come hungry, as there are copious servings of chowder, tasty local mussels, rolls and a variety of desserts to go with your pound of messy crustacean. If things go your way, you may get a table with an ocean view.

Blue Mussel Café (☎ 902-963-2152; Harbourview Dr; mains dinner $14-22; lunch & dinner late Jun-late Sep) This place is relatively small, but its location, pan-fried scallops and steamed mussels will leave a big impression. It's en route to Outside Expeditions.

LOBSTER SUPPERS

You don't need to change out of your jeans or get the kids a babysitter to gorge yourself on Prince Edward Island's (PEI) most ambrosial shellfish. The classic PEI dining experience is a no-frills lobster supper, held in dining halls, churches and community centers throughout the island. The lobster, just like its eager devourers, is unadorned with sauces and fanfare; the suppers are a place to enjoy these critters in the buff (or perhaps a little melted butter) for their own divine flavors and texture. Kids are not only welcome, they are well catered for with half-sized suppers and other menu options such as beef or scallops. Just to make sure no one goes hungry, there is a slew of accompaniments, from chowder to mussels to PEI potato salad to oven-fresh rolls. Held daily for dinner from roughly mid-June to mid-October, approximately 10 locations hold lobster suppers. The most renowned are in **New Glasgow** (☎ 902-964-2870; Route 258), see opposite; **St Ann** (☎ 902-621-0635; St Ann's Parish, Rte 224, St Ann), see opposite and **North Rustico** (☎ 902-963-2669; 7230 Main St), see above. The cost of dinner depends on the market price of lobster but generally hovers around $28 for an all-inclusive meal with a 455g crustacean.

If you'd rather do the cooking and make a mess of your lobster in private, head straight to **Dorion Fisheries** (☎ 902-963-2442; Harbourview Dr; 🕙 mid-May–mid-Oct). It has great seafood straight off the boat and at market prices.

CAVENDISH

Anyone familiar with *Anne of Green Gables* might have lofty ideas of finding Cavendish as a quaint village bedecked in flowers and country charm; guess again. While the Anne and Lucy Maud Montgomery sites are right out of the imagination-inspiring book pages, Cavendish itself is a mishmash of manufactured attractions with no particular town center. The junction of Rte 6 and Hwy 13 is the tourist center and the area's commercial hub. When you see the service station, wax museum, church, cemetery and assorted restaurants, you know you're there. This is the most visited community on PEI outside of Charlottetown and, although an eyesore in this scenic region, it is kiddie wonderland. To get out of the world of fabricated and fictional free-for-all, head to beautiful **Cavendish Beach**; it gets crowded during summer months but with perfect sand and a warm (ish) ocean in front, you won't really care.

Information

Cavendish Visitor Centre (☎ 902-963-7830; 🕙 8am-8pm Jul–mid-Sep, 9am-4.30pm mid-May–Jun & mid-Sep–mid-Oct) Situated at the junction, near the police station, municipal offices and post office, this outlet has a wealth of information on the area, along with a craft shop, exhibits on the national park and a courtesy phone to make reservations. It's open until 9pm in July and August.
Laundromat (☎ 902-963-2370; 8934 Rte 6; 🕙 8am-9pm mid-May–Sep) At Cavendish Tourist Mart.

Sights

Cavendish is the hometown of Lucy Maud Montgomery (1874–1942), author of *Anne of Green Gables*. Here she is simply known as Lucy Maud or LM. Owned by her grandfather's cousins, the now-famous **House of Green Gables** (☎ 902-672-7874; Rte 6; adult/child under 17yr/family $5.75/3/14.50; 🕙 9am-8pm late Jun-late Aug, to 5pm early May–mid-Jun & Sep-Oct) and its Victorian surrounds inspired the setting for her fictional tale. In 1937 the house became part of the national park and it's now administered as a national heritage site. Hours vary November to May.

If you haven't read the 1908 novel, you really should try while you are on the island –

not just to enjoy it, but to try to understand all the hype. The story revolves around Anne Shirley, a spirited 11-year-old orphan with red pigtails and a creative wit, who was mistakenly sent from Nova Scotia to PEI. The aging Cuthberts (who were brother and sister) were expecting a strapping boy to help them with farm chores. In the end, Anne's strength of character wins over everyone in her path.

The site celebrates Lucy Maud and Anne with exhibits and audiovisual displays. The trails leading from the house through the green, gentle creek-crossed woods are worthwhile. The Haunted Wood and Lover's Lane have maintained their idealistic childhood ambience. If you did read the book as a child, you will be taken into that land of dreams that only Anne could have created.

To delve deeper into Anne fantasy, visit **Avonlea – Village of Anne of Green Gables** (☎ 902-963-3050; www.avonlea.ca; Rte 6; admission adult/senior/child/family $19/17/13/55; 🕙 9am-5pm mid-Jun–mid-Sep; 🚻) where costumed actors perform dramatic moments and scenes from *Green Gables* chapters. Beyond the theatrical exploits, the park offers you cow-milking demonstrations, a ride in a horse-drawn wagon and other period farm activities. Check the website for the day's schedule.

The **Site of LM Montgomery's Cavendish Home** (☎ 902-963-2231; Rte 6; admission adult/child $3/1; 🕙 9am-5pm May-Oct, to 6pm Jul & Aug) is considered hallowed ground to Anne fans worldwide. Raised by her grandparents, Lucy Maud lived in this house from 1876 to 1911 and it is here that she wrote *Anne of Green Gables*. The land is now owned and tended to by Lucy Maud's grandson, who also runs a small museum and bookshop.

If you're traveling with kids or just have a fascination with kitsch, you could try some of the many other establishments that cluster around Green Gables on Rte 6. All are open daily from July to Labour Day. **Black Magic Indoor Blacklight Mini Golf** (Rte 6; adult/child $6/5; 10am-10pm) fulfils lifelong dreams of golfing in the dark while the **Fantazmagoric Museum of the Strange & Unusual** (adult/child $6/5; 10am-10pm) takes you far from Anne's Land to the sands of fake Egypt and a detailed replica of King Tut's tomb. Kids will love **Jurassic Bart's Dinosaur Museum & Petting Farm** (adult/child $6/5; 10am-6pm) to look at dinosaur remains and the highlight: Jurassic poop. **Shining Waters Family Fun Park** (over/under 158cm $16/14, 3yr & under free; 10am-7pm) is probably the most fun indulgence of all with 12 hectares of pirate ships, children's discos, waterslides and greasy food. There are more opportunities than these to explore your inner kid so bust out the credit card and enjoy.

Tours

As one would suspect, most operators have an Anne-themed tour. **Cavendish Tours** (902-566-5466; half-/full-day tours $50/60) offers a half-day tour that visits Green Gables and takes in North Rustico and New Glasgow. The full-day tour adds the Lucy Maud Montgomery Birthplace and Silver Bush (p208).

Sleeping & Eating

While accommodations are numerous, remember that this is the busiest and most expensive area you can stay. There are more bargains east, toward North Rustico.

Parkview Farm Tourist Home & Cottages (902-963-2027, 800-237-9890; www.peionline.com/al/parkview; 8214 Rte 6; B&B s/d $50/60, cottages $155;) With no frills and set on a working dairy farm, 2km east of Cavendish, this place has ocean views and you can stroll straight down to the sea. Each of the seven cottages (available May to mid-October) has a kitchen and a barbecue, as well as a balcony to catch the dramatic comings and goings of the sun. The B&B rooms are open all year-round and are funky but homey. Kids will love the chance to get to know the farm animals.

Seaside Motel & Cottages (902-963-2724, 888-351-2724; www.peionline.com/al/seaside; Grahams Lane; motel units $90, s/d without bathroom $45/50, 1-/2-/3-bedroom cottages $90/100/110;) This family-style place, at the west entrance to Cavendish Beach, overlooks New London Bay. With all the buildings encircling a large grass field, it has a bit of an OK Corral feel to it. Most of the motel rooms have small kitchens. A heated pool, a playground and nature trails add to its appeal.

A YEN FOR ANNE

Cuter than Pokémon and able to leap cultures in a single bound, *Akage no An* (Red-haired Anne) has secured a magical throne in Japanese pop culture. The novel was introduced to Japan in the 1950s and quickly found its way into the school curriculum with the idea that its wholesomeness and positive themes would build hope after the devastation of WWII. Beyond cheerleading the nation, Anne remained steadfast in Japanese culture by capturing their hearts with her courage and free spirit. Today *Akage no An* has become a Japanese girl's rite of passage and visiting Prince Edward Island (PEI) a pilgrimage.

Japanese homage to Anne has appeared in many forms. She became an animated character in 1979 and a musical version of *Akage no An* toured Japan in the 80s and 90s. In 1981 23 Anne enthusiasts visited PEI and later established the 'Buttercups,' an Anne fan club; today the club has more than 200 members. *Philosophy of Anne* books are available to young Japanese readers wanting to get more understanding of Anne, and the School of Green Gables – a social work and nursing college in Okayama – tries to instill Anne ideology in its students.

But the biggest Anne shrine of them all is Canadian World, a PEI theme park that re-creates Green Gables down to the patchwork quilts and a little red-haired Canadian girl who will answer questions. Unfortunately the park, located in an out-of-the-way collapsed mining town, has become too much like Canada: lots of open spaces and few people. It is now on the verge of bankruptcy and covered in weeds. Perhaps Japan's fascination with Green Gables isn't enough to fill a theme park. Critics say the park lacks the 'real' Anne's spunk and imagination; which can only be found by visiting PEI.

PRINCE EDWARD ISLAND

our pick **Kindred Spirits Country Inn & Cottages**
(☎ 902-963-2434, 800-461-1755; www.kindredspirits.ca;
Memory Lane; B&B d incl breakfast $75-200, cottages $200-
265; 🖳 🐾) A huge, immaculate complex, this
place has something for everyone, from a
storybook-quality B&B to deluxe cottages.
Rooms are every Anne fan's dream with dotty
floral prints, glossy wood floors and fluffy,
dreamlike beds. Downstairs the lounge has a
fireplace that'll make you wish it would snow
and couches, perfect for snuggling up with a
mug of cocoa. Elegant cottages are private and
range from honeymoon perfection to family
bliss. The place has been run by the same family for more than 20 years and, in the spirit of
Anne, they never turn away a kindred spirit –
if you love Anne, they'll make it possible for
you to stay in the room of your dreams.

Chez Yvonne Restaurant (☎ 902-963-2070; 8947 Rte
6; mains $9-13; 🕙 breakfast, lunch & dinner Jun-Sep) Chez
Yvonne has been serving steak and seafood
dinners to tourists since the 1970s. This place
is well known for its home cooking, especially
its bread and rolls, which are baked on the
premises. It's your best bet in town if you're
looking for something un-fried.

Rachel's Restaurant (☎ 902-963-3227; Rte 6; mains
$12-18; 🕙 breakfast, lunch & dinner Jun-Oct; 👍) This
new establishment seats 200 and serves up
family meals of pastas, pizzas and steaks. Its
corporate, chain-restaurant feel fits right in
with the attractions of town; the best seating
is out on the ocean-view deck.

Getting Around
The **Cavendish Red Trolley** (all-day ticket $3; 🕙 10am-
6pm late Jun-Aug) runs hourly along Hwy 13 and
through Cavendish, making various stops including the Cavendish Visitor Centre, Cavendish Beach and the House of Green Gables.

NEW LONDON & PARK CORNER
New London and Park Corner both have
strong ties to Lucy Maud Montgomery, and
are thus caught up in the everything-Anne
pandemonium. The area of these towns and
between is a winding bucolic wonderland with
the occasional peek at the sea.

In New London, 10km southwest of Cavendish, is the **Lucy Maud Montgomery Birthplace**
(☎ 902-886-2099; cnr Rtes 6 & 20; admission $2; 🕙 9am-
6pm Jul & Aug, to 5pm mid-May–Jun & Sep–mid-Oct). The
house is now a museum that contains some
of her personal belongings, including her
wedding dress.

Almost 10km northwest of New London is
the village of Park Corner and the **Lucy Maud
Montgomery Heritage Museum** (☎ 902-886-2807;
4605 Rte 20; adult/child $2.50/1; 🕙 9:30am-6pm Jul & Aug,
to 4:30pm mid-Jun–Labour Day). It's believed to be
the home of Lucy Maud's grandfather and
there's a lot of Anne paraphernalia. Take a
guided tour; there's a guarantee that if you're
not absolutely fascinated, you don't pay the
admission.

Almost 500m down the hill from here, surrounded by a luscious 45-hectare property, is
the charming home Lucy Maud liked to call
Silver Bush. It was always dear to her and she
chose the parlor for her 1911 wedding. Silver
Bush hosts the **Anne of Green Gables Museum**
(☎ 902-886-2884; 4542 Rte 20; adult/child under 17yr $3/1;
🕙 9am-6pm Jul & Aug, to 5pm mid-May–Jun & Sep-early
Oct). It contains such items as her writing desk
and autographed 1st-edition books. Horse-
drawn carriages roll past the alluring Lake of
Shining Waters ($3).

Red Road Country Inn B&B (☎ 902-886-3154, 800-
249-1344; www.redroadcountryinn.com; Rte 6 btwn Kensington & New London; d $95-140, ste $160-190; 🕙 mid-Jun–Jan;
🐾) is great option for Anne fans not wanting
to stay in Cavendish. Slip into some wicker
and sip tea above undulating pea-green fields
that meet quiet blue inlets.

Blue Winds Tea Room (☎ 902-886-2860; 10746 Rte
6, New London; meals from $7; 🕙 11am-8pm Fri-Sun Jul &
Aug, to 6pm mid-May–Jun & Sep–mid-Oct), just 500m
southwest of Lucy Maud's birthplace, is a
pretty tearoom surrounded by English gardens. Of course like everything else in this
region, they've got to be 'Anne,' so order a
raspberry cordial ($3.50) or some New Moon
Pudding ($5); both recipes have been taken
from Lucy Maud's journals. You can get a
healthy meal too; the soup, salads, quiche and
chicken curry are delicious and a pleasure to
eat in such a well-appointed setting. Afternoon high tea ($12) is every Thursday from
2pm to 5pm and Sunday brunch ($10.50) is
11:30am to 2pm.

MALPEQUE
It's famed for large, sweet, fleshy oysters but
Malpeque is also visited for it's typical Maritime scenery of weathered fishing boats, neatly
stacked lobster traps and fishermen's houses.
About 10 million oysters are harvested each
year from the controlled 'farms' of the bay.
Arrive in late afternoon or early morning for
the best light on the water.

Cabot Beach Provincial Park (☎ 902-836-8945; www.gov.pe.ca/visitorsguide/explore/parks; off Hwy 20; sites $19-25; ☿ mid-Jun–mid-Sep), 4km north of Malpeque village, is one of the larger parks on the island. There's picnicking, a beach on Malpeque Bay, and plentiful campsites on a long grassy hill. Aerial pesticide spraying on nearby potato fields can be a downside when the wind is blowing the wrong way.

Speaking of oysters, if you want to slurp (or chew) a few, there's no better place than **Malpeque Oyster Barn** (☎ 902-836-3999; 12 oysters around $18; ☿ 11am-9pm Jul-Sep). You can buy them by the dozen as fresh as they come. With a chaser of cold beer, it doesn't get better than this. You can also get chowder and mussels.

KENSINGTON

A friendly hub town, Kensington is about halfway between Summerside and Cavendish. There's a great **Welcome Center** (☎ 902-836-3031; Kensington Railyard; ☿ 9am-5pm Jun-Oct) at the old rail station that is surrounded by a handful of local craft shops, and a **farmers' market** (☿ 10am-2pm Jun-Sep) is held in the old freight shed behind the train station on Saturday mornings.

Shipwright's Café (☎ 902-836-3403; cnr Rtes 6 & 233; mains lunch $11-20, dinner $25-33; ☿ lunch & dinner Jun-Oct; ⚇) on the road toward Cavendish, is what many consider to be the best restaurant in this corner of PEI. You'll be instantly charmed by the magnificent Victorian then become more impressed once you get your meal: island lamb, oysters, mussels and 'vegetarian flair' are prepared using mostly organics grown on the grounds. After dinner, stroll through the gardens in full-bellied bliss.

WESTERN PEI

From edible seaweed to space-age windmills; from the heart of Acadian PEI to the province's liveliest Mi'kmaq community, Western PEI holds an enormous amount of contrast in a small space. Malpeque and Bedeque Bays converge to almost separate the western third of PEI from the rest of the province. This region sits entirely within the larger Prince County, and it combines the sparse pastoral scenery of Kings County's interior with some of Queens County's rugged coastal beauty.

The cultural history here stands out more than elsewhere on the island. On Lennox Island a proud Mi'kmaq community is working to

foster knowledge of its past, while French Acadians are doing the same in the south, along Egmont and Bedeque Bays.

SUMMERSIDE

While it lacks the elegance and cosmopolitan vibe of Charlottetown, Summerside (population 14,654) is a simpler, seaside-oriented place with everything you need in one small, tidy package. Recessed deep within Bedeque Bay and PEI's second-largest 'city', this tiny seaside village possesses a modern waterfront and quiet streets lined with leafy trees and grand old homes. The two largest economic booms in the province's history, shipbuilding and fox breeding, shaped the city's development in the 19th and early 20th centuries. Unfortunately, like Charlottetown, its outskirts are plagued by unsightly development. You'll find most sights of interest along, or near to, Water St, which runs parallel to the waterfront.

Information

Provincial Tourist Office (☎ 902-888-8364; Spinnaker's Landing; ☿ 9am-7pm late Jun-late Aug, to 4:30pm early–mid-Jun & Sep–mid-Oct) The walking-tour pamphlet details the town's finer 19th-century buildings.
Rotary Regional Library (☎ 902-436-7323; 192 Water St; ☿ 10am-5pm Wed-Sat, to 9pm Tue, 1-5pm Sun) For free Internet access, visit the library in the city's old train station.

Sights & Activities

The **Confederation Trail** (p200) makes its way right through town and passes behind the library on Water St.

SPINNAKER'S LANDING

This redeveloped **waterfront** is the highlight of Summerside. A continually expanding

PRINCE EDWARD ISLAND

PRINCE EDWARD ISLAND

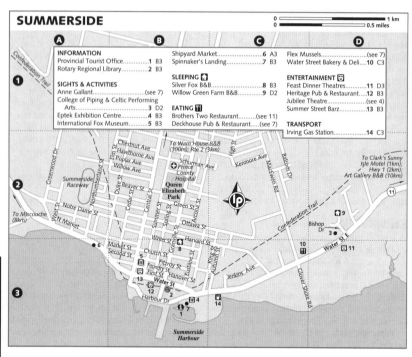

SUMMERSIDE

INFORMATION
Provincial Tourist Office.............1 B3
Rotary Regional Library.............2 B3

SIGHTS & ACTIVITIES
Anne Gallant.............................(see 7)
College of Piping & Celtic Performing
Arts..3 D2
Eptek Exhibition Centre.............4 B3
International Fox Museum..........5 B3

Shipyard Market.......................6 A3
Spinnaker's Landing..................7 B3

SLEEPING
Silver Fox B&B...........................8 B3
Willow Green Farm B&B............9 D2

EATING
Brothers Two Restaurant..........(see 11)
Deckhouse Pub & Restaurant.....(see 7)

Flex Mussels.............................(see 7)
Water Street Bakery & Deli....10 C3

ENTERTAINMENT
Feast Dinner Theatres...........11 D3
Heritage Pub & Restaurant....12 B3
Jubilee Theatre.......................(see 4)
Summer Street Barz................13 B3

TRANSPORT
Irving Gas Station..................14 C3

boardwalk allows you to wander and enjoy the pretty harbor and its scenic surroundings. There are some lovely eateries, a stage for live music in the summer, and numerous shops. A mock lighthouse provides adults with a nice lookout and some local information, while a large model ship is a dream playground for children. Backing all of this is the modern **Eptek Exhibition Centre** (☎ 902-888-8373; 130 Harbour Dr; admission by donation; ⌚ 10am-4pm), which features local and traveling art exhibitions.

SHIPYARD MARKET
Continue along the boardwalk from Spinnaker's Landing to aptly named **Shipyard Market** (⌚ mid-Jun–mid-Sep), which was built on the site of an old shipbuilding facility. This market provides the backdrop to daily **live music** (admission by donation; ⌚ 5pm to 8pm Jul–mid-Sep) which has a daily theme: Irish music Wednesday, Acadian Friday, fiddlers Saturday etc. The highlight of this complex is woodcarving demonstrations by Bill Gallant; watch while he forms one of those tree sculptures that seem to be everywhere in the Maritimes.

There's also a **farmers' market** Saturday from 10am to 1pm from early July to the end of August.

COLLEGE OF PIPING & CELTIC PERFORMING ARTS
In celebration of Celtic dance and music, this **school** (☎ 902-436-5377; www.collegeofpiping.com; 619 Water St E; ⌚ 9am-9pm late Jun-Aug) provides visitors with free 20-minute miniconcerts Monday to Friday at 11:30am, 1:30pm and 3:30pm – expect bagpipes, singing and dancing. Inspired? Put on some warm clothes and enjoy the two-hour ceilidhs (adult/student $12/7) that take place every night at 7pm in the covered amphitheater.

INTERNATIONAL FOX MUSEUM
This tiny **museum** (☎ 902-436-2400; 286 Fitzroy St; admission by donation; ⌚ 10am-5pm Jun-Sep) recounts the role of Summerside in the world's first successful captive breeding of the silver fox in 1890 – and the obscene flows of money and controversy that followed it. The museum is upstairs in the historic Holman Homestead (1855).

Courses

If scarlet sunsets and fairytale lighthouses inspire you to pull out a brush and palette, call on local painter **Anne Gallant** (☎ 902-436-1588 Spinnaker's Landing; adult/child $20/15; ⓨ children 1-2pm, adults 2:30-4pm Jun-Oct). All materials are supplied and you'll leave the class with a finished painting.

Festivals

Summer on the Waterfront Festival (☎ 902-888-2500, 800-708-6505; www.jubileetheatre.com; 124 Harbour Dr) Held at the Jubilee Theatre from July to mid-September, this festival hosts local and well-known Canadian musical acts. It showcases everything from theatrical comedy to live jazz, blues and pop music performances.

Sleeping

The wonderful selection of places to stay in Summerside makes this a good base for exploring the region.

Clark's Sunny Isle Motel (☎ 902-436-5665, 877-682-6824; www.sunnyislemotel.com; 720 Water St E; d/tw $50/60; ⓨ May-Oct) Great service, immaculate gardens and a lovely trail to the beach sets Clark's apart from other motels in the area. Ask for a room out back.

Willow Green Farm B&B (☎ 902-436-4420; www.willowgreenfarm.com; 117 Bishop Dr; d $50-100) With the Confederation Trail at its back door and the College of Piping & Celtic Performing Arts out its front, this rambling farmhouse is a great place to stay. Rooms are bright and the bold country interior is a refreshing change from busy period decors. Read by the wood stove, or check out some of the more interesting farm animals. Book ahead; this place fills quickly.

Warn House B&B (☎ 902-436-5242, 888-436-7512; www.warnhouse.com; 330 Central St; tw $85, d $95-115) Set in from the road, among trees next to the old cemetery, Warn House is extremely comfortable and welcoming. Lounge under a tree or on the lovely veranda. Original Canadian art adorns the walls and there's even a place to store bicycles.

Art Gallery B&B (☎ 902-887-2683, 877-388-2683; www.bbcanada.com/artgallery; 407 Mac Murdo Rd, North Bedeque; d $90; ⓨ May-Oct; 🖳) East of town, stay in pastoral paradise only minutes from waterfront Summerside. Owner Arno Freitag is a muralist and painter and you'll find his works displayed throughout the sunny hallways of this elegant farmhouse. The upstairs reading nook inspires long journal entries or hours with a book.

ourpick Silver Fox B&B (☎ 902-436-1664, 800-565-4033; www.silverfoxinn.net; 61 Granville St; d $125-140; 🖳) With opulent details such as antique lace curtains and navy-and-gold-striped wallpaper, this Queen Anne Revival B&B feels like a stylish 1920s or '30s re-creation of the Victorian era. Even if you're not staying here you shouldn't miss taking tea in the very British, very posh tearoom (tea $1.50; open noon to 4pm Monday to Saturday) complete with koi ponds and patio flower gardens; high tea ($29 for two people), served on a three-tiered serving plate, is available by reservation.

Eating

Eating options are not as fine as sleeping, but you won't go hungry.

Water Street Bakery & Deli (☎ 902-536-5055; 605 Water St E; lunch $4-6; ⓨ 7am-6:30pm Mon-Sat) This is the best place in town for a quick and tasty sandwich or a slice of pizza.

Deckhouse Pub & Restaurant (☎ 902-436-0660; 150 Harbour Dr; mains $7-13; ⓨ 11am-11pm Jun–mid-Sep) Step off the Spinnaker's Landing boardwalk and onto one of the Deckhouse's two outdoor decks, for a great meal in harborfront surroundings. Live music adds to the atmosphere on weekends. It's well known for the hand-battered fish-and-chips.

Flex Mussels (☎ 902-436-6049; Spinnaker's Landing; per lb around $8; ⓨ 10am-10pm Jul & Aug, to 5:30pm Jun & Sep) Mussel-lovers apply here. More than 20 flavors of fresh steamed mussels served with hand-cut PEI fries are served at this little takeout café. Try the Thai steam with lemongrass and coconut milk or the Dubliner with Guinness and caramelized onions.

Brothers Two Restaurant (☎ 902-436-9654; 618 Water St E; mains $10-15; ⓨ lunch Mon-Fri, dinner daily) Brothers Two's service, pasta, steak and fresh seafood have made it a local favorite for more than 30 years. The vegetarian stir-fry and island blue mussels steamed in garlic and white wine are both excellent. If you want in on the laughter coming from below, check out Feast Dinner Theatres (below).

Entertainment

Jubilee Theatre (☎ 902-888-2500, 800-708-6505; www.jubileetheatre.com; 124 Harbour Dr) This modern theater is in the same complex as the Eptek Exhibition Centre and holds the Summer on the Waterfront Festival (left).

Feast Dinner Theatres (☎ 902-436-7674; 618 Water St; dinner & show $32; ⓨ 6:30pm Mon-Sat Jun-Dec) Most locals start to giggle when they speak of their last time at Feast Dinner Theatres. It's located below Brothers Two Restaurant, and is the longest-running dinner theater in Atlantic Canada. Music, script and improvisation combine with audience participation to make a memorable evening. The food's not too shabby either.

Heritage Pub & Restaurant (☎ 902-436-8484; 250 Water St) This traditional pub hosts local bands (no cover) on Friday, and occasionally on Saturday.

Summer Street Barz (☎ 902-436-7400; 12 Summer St; admission $4) This is the only true nightclub in town, and it casts a pretty wide net. Thumping beats resonate from the basement, the cracks of pool cues echo from the core, and twangs of country ring from the rafters. Oh, and there's a sports bar too. Things don't pick up until after midnight on Friday and Saturday.

Getting There & Away

To reach Cavendish (36km) and Charlottetown (71km) from Summerside by car, it's quickest to head north on Hwy 1A and then follow Rte 2 to your turnoff.

Acadian Lines (p281) stops at the **Irving gas station** (☎ 902-436-2420; 96 Water St) in the center of town and has services to Charlottetown ($11, one hour), Moncton ($30, two hours) and Halifax ($56, 3½ hours). On request, bus shuttles pick up at the Esso station on Hwy 1A at the end of Water St E.

RÉGION ÉVANGÉLINE

The strongest French Acadian ancestry on the island is found here, from Miscouche to Mont Carmel. Some 6000 residents still speak French as their first language, although you'll have trouble discerning this region from others in the province. There is one notable exception: the red, white, blue and yellow star of the Acadian flag hangs proudly from many homes. It was in Miscouche, on August 15, 1884, that the Acadian flag was unfurled for the very first time. The yellow star represents the patron saint of the Acadians, the Virgin Mary. Renewed efforts are underway to preserve the unique Acadian culture on the island. See the Culture chapter (p37) for more information on Acadians.

A favorite stop on this stretch is the **Bottle Houses** (☎ 902-854-2987; Rte 11, Cape Egmont; admission adult/child $5/2; ☼ 9am-8pm Jul & Aug, 10am-6pm Jun & Sep), the artful and monumental recycling

project of Edouard Arsenault. More than 25,000 bottles of all shapes and sizes (that Edouard collected from the community) are stacked in white cement to create a handful of buildings with light-filled mosaic walls.

In Miscouche, the worthwhile **Acadian Museum** (☎ 902-432-2880; 23 Maine Dr E; adult/student/family $4.50/3.50/15; ☼ 9:30am-7pm Jul & Aug, to 5pm Mon-Fri & 1-4pm Sun Sep-Jun) uses 18th-century Acadian artifacts, texts, visuals and music to enlighten visitors about the tragic and compelling history of the Acadians on PEI since 1720. The introspective video introduces a fascinating theory that the brutal treatment of the Acadians by the British may have backhandedly helped preserve a vestige of Acadian culture on PEI.

Not far from the Acadian Museum, **Lecky's B&B** (☎ 902-436-3216, 888-220-4059; www.lecky.ca; d $70-100) is a never-ending maze of ramshackle hallways and comfy rooms decorated in every style from country antique to '60s orange and blue. Five-course lobster and steak dinners come highly recommended and are available by reservation. The friendly owners are helpful with finding local ceilidhs in the area.

TYNE VALLEY

Arbored in trees and undulating up and down gentle slopes, this area is one of the most scenic in the province. The village, with its cluster of ornate houses, gentle river and art studios, is definitely worth a visit. If you're a lover of oysters and your timing is right, enjoy the **Tyne Valley Oyster Festival** (www.exhibitions -festivalspeiae.com/tynevalleyoysterfestival .html), held in early August. This is a locals-oriented affair but that makes it all the more fun. Horse pulls, a strong-man contest, fiddling competitions, step dancing and an oyster-shucking race are all part of the hoopla. Even if you miss the festival, don't miss trying the Malpeque oysters while in town.

Green Park Provincial Park, 6km north of the village along Rte 12, hosts the **Green Park Shipbuilding Museum & Historic Yeo House** (☎ 902-831-7947; Rte 12; adult/child under 13yr $5/free; ☼ 9am-5pm mid-Jun–mid-Sep). The museum and restored Victorian home, along with a re-created shipyard and partially constructed 200-ton brigantine, combine to tell the story of the booming shipbuilding industry in the glory days of the 19th century.

The **park** (☎ 902-831-7912; off Rte 12; tent-/RV sites $19/25, cabins with shared bathroom $35; ☼ mid-Jun–

mid-Sep) has 58 campsites spread within a mixed forest. The 12 cabins just beyond the campsite are a steal.

Doctor's Inn B&B (☎ 902-831-3057; www.peisland.com/doctorsinn; 32 Allen Rd; d without bathroom incl breakfast $60-75) is an old country home on a hectare of organic market gardens; as you might guess, the meals made with all that fresh produce are fabulous. One of the rooms has a small pullout bed to help accommodate children. Its dining room (four-course meal guests/nonguests $45/55; hours by reservation) is known to prepare the finest meals in the region. Cooked over a wood stove, the *tournedos rossini* (beef tenderloin and liver pâté with a red-wine sauce), *sole almandine* (fillet of sole coated with white wine and toasted almonds) and organic vegetables from the garden are all superb; wine is included.

Not surprisingly the specialty at **Landing Oyster House & Pub** (☎ 902-831-3138; 1327 Port Hill Station Rd; mains $8-13; ☺ lunch & dinner Tue-Sun Mar-Dec, also Mon in Jul) is 15 deep-fried oysters – definitely indulge. Live bands (cover $3 to $5) play here on Friday night, and also Saturday during July and August.

LENNOX ISLAND

Set in the mouth of Malpeque Bay, sheltered behind Hog Island, is Lennox Island and its 245 Mi'kmaq (mig-*maw*) aboriginal people. While working hard to promote awareness and understanding of their past, both in and out of their own community, they are also making renewed efforts to preserve their culture. Projects such as the Lennox Island Aboriginal Ecotourism Complex are manifestations of this hard work. A trip to the island is rewarding and highly recommended. The island is connected by a causeway making it accessible from the town of East Bideford off Rte 12. There is a large celebration here at the end of June and another, for St Ann's day, on the last Sunday in July.

The **Lennox Island Aboriginal Ecotourism Complex** (☎ 866-831-2702; 2 Eagle Feather Trail; adult/student $4/3; ☺ 10am-6pm Mon-Sat, noon-6pm Sun late Jun-early Sep) is an all-purpose modern building that opens its doors to anyone interested in Mi'kmaq culture. Inside there is a worthwhile 15-minute audiovisual exhibit, and information about the two excellent **interpretive walking trails** around the island. These trails consist of two loops, forming a total of 10km, with the shorter one (3km) wheelchair-

accessible. If you want to delve deeper into the First Nations experience, you can take part in **workshops** – from basket weaving to Mi'kmaw language studies. Workshops are arranged on an individual basis so contact the ecotourism complex for scheduling and prices. **Minegoo Café** (Ecotourism Centre; mains from $8; ☺ 10am-6pm Mon-Sat, noon-6pm Sun mid-May–mid-Oct) serves traditional Mi'kmaw food as well as standard fare with all the freshest local ingredients; the setting, looking over Malpeque Bay, is spectacular. The new **Lennox Island Hostel** (Ecotourism Centre; dm $20), which inhabits the upper level of the Ecotourism complex, sleeps 14, is spotless and has the same views as the café.

Up the hill from the ecotourism complex, and across from St Ann's Church (1898), is the **Lennox Island Mi'kmaq Cultural Centre** (8 Eagle Feather Trail). It operates in unison with the ecotourism complex and houses artifacts along with displays about the history and culture of the Mi'kmaq.

Mi'kmaq Kayak Adventures (☎ 902-831-3131, 800-500-3131; 3hr tours $60; ☺ tours 9am, 1pm, 5pm & sunset Jul & Aug, by appointment May, Jun & Sep) operates from the ecotourism complex but at the time of writing it was unsure if these tours would continue. Call the center to find out about availability.

TIGNISH

Tignish is a quiet town tucked up near the North Cape; it sees only a fraction of PEI's visitors. The towering **Church of St Simon & St Jude** (1859) was the first brick church built on the island. Have a peek inside – its ceiling has been restored to its gorgeous but humble beginnings, and the organ (1882) is of gargantuan proportions. Of its 1118 pipes, the shortest is 15cm, while the longest is nearly 5m!

The Confederation Trail (see p200) begins (or ends!) two blocks south of the church on School St – the other end is in Elmira, 279km east. The **Tignish Cultural Centre** (☎ 902-882-1999; 305 School St; admission free; ☺ 8am-4pm Mon-Fri), near the church, has a good exhibition of old maps and photos, tourist information and a library with Internet access.

Tignish Heritage Inn (☎ 902-882-2491, 877-882-2491; www.tignish.com/inn; d $80-115; ☺ mid-May–mid-Oct) is behind the church, off Maple St. Hiding among the trees is this charming four-story brick convent-turned-inn (1868). The high ceilings, spacious rooms and modern amenities make staying here a simple choice. The

---

DETOUR: PIONEER FARM

Ever dreamed of ditching it all and living off the land? Jim and Judy Bertling actually did it, and in the process created **Pioneer Farm** (☎ 902-859-2229; www.pioneerfarm.ca; 2km off Rte 14, Glenwood; admission $5; ☺ 1-5pm Sun & Mon Jul & Aug, other times by appointment). On 60 hectares of secluded oceanfront woodland, the farm uses only wind and solar power, grows its own veggies and raises its own free-range turkeys and chickens in order to live, and make an example of an environmentally responsible lifestyle. While all this is interesting and good, you'll be most tickled by the barnyard personalities that cavort around the grounds: meet eternally surprised-looking Spirit the llama, Jasmine the gentle Jersey cow and Thumbelina the gregarious pygmy goat; Moses the donkey acts as a guard dog. There's a plethora of things to do here, from just stopping in for a quick tour to llama treks where you can 'take a llama to lunch,' on a picnic to a nearby lake.

To get the full experience stay a night or three (you won't want to leave) in the 100% natural cottage ($110, sleeps six). Help with farm chores, go kayaking or just melt into the simple life – it'll be an experience you'll never forget.

---

lower two floors are comfortable, if a little old-fashioned. The 3rd floor has more contemporary decor.

NORTH CAPE

The drive toward North Cape seems stereotypically bucolic, until the moment your eyes rise above the quaint farmhouses to see the heavens being churned by dozens of science fiction–worthy white blades. Strangely, expecting the surreal sight takes nothing away from it.

The narrow, windblown North Cape is not only home to the **Atlantic Wind Test**, but also to the longest **natural rock reef** on the continent. At low tide, it's possible to walk out almost 800m – exploring tide pools and searching for seals along the way. It's all classic PEI red that glows at sunset. With all that shallow rock, the functioning 1866 **lighthouse** is one of the most important on PEI; the chain-link fence and radio tower cut down its photogenic qualities but many a seafarer is glad the lighthouse has everything it needs.

The **Wind Energy interpretive center** (☎ 902-882-2991; adult/student/family $5/3/13; ☺ 9:30am-8pm Jul & Aug, to 6pm mid-May–Jun & Sep–early Oct), at the northern end of Rte 12, provides high-tech displays dedicated to wind energy, and informative displays on the history of the area. The aquarium is always a hit with kids. The **Black Marsh Nature Trail** (2.7km) leaves the interpretive center and takes you to the west side of the cape – at sunset these crimson cliffs simply glow against the deep blue waters.

For a bit of fun, check out **Captain Mitch's Deep Sea Fishing & Boat Tours** (☎ 902-882-2883; Hwy 12; adult/child $20/10; ☺ Jul & Aug). The captain's a ˊ

lively lobster fisherman who will take you out to his ocean playground of spray, seals and seabirds. Tours leave from Seacow Pond Harbour, 6.5km south of North Cape.

Sleeping & Eating

Island's End Motel (☎ 902-882-3554; Doyle Rd; d $65-75) Your closest option near North Cape, off Rte 12, and your only option if you're here in the off-season, is the friendly Island's End. The owner, Neil, takes a lot of pride in his place and it shows. It's simple and comfortable.

Wind & Reef Restaurant & Lounge (☎ 902-882-3535; mains lunch $8-15, dinner $12-37; ☺ lunch & dinner) 'Vast' scarcely describes the 180-degree views from this place. It's located above the interpretive center with views to forever and attracts visitors as well as locals out for a treat. The food is Maritime family fare with a smattering of upscale platters.

WEST COAST

Along the west coast, you may be puzzled at the sight of horse and rider dragging rakes in the shallows off shore. They are collecting Irish moss, a valuable purplish seaweed that gets uprooted and blown to shore in storms. Less visible collectors are harvesting the moss at sea.

Along Rte 14, in the village of Miminegash, is the **Irish Moss Interpretative Centre** (☎ 902-882-4313; Rte 14; admission $2; ☺ 10am-7pm early Jun-late Sep), begun by local women long involved in the harvesting of Irish moss. Almost half the world's Irish moss supply (which becomes carageenan) comes from PEI, and goes into everything from ice cream and toothpaste to cough syrup and automobile tires! Still

PRINCE EDWARD ISLAND

tempted? The **Seaweed Pie Cafe** (meals $5-12), at the center, serves a special seaweed pie ($4.50) although nothing about the fluffy, creamy creation reeks of the beach.

Between Miminegash and West Point, Rte 14 hugs the shore and provides stunning vistas. It's perhaps the finest drive on the island – if you're not on a motorcycle, you'll wish you were.

Off Hwy 14, the striking, black-and-white-striped **West Point Lighthouse** (☎ 902-859-3605, 800-764-6854; www.westpointlighthouse.com; ☑ mid-May–Sep), dating from 1875, has been restored. Between 1875 and 1955 there were only two lighthouse keepers. Today the staff is made up of their direct descendants. There's a small **museum** (adult/child/family $2.50/1.50/7; ☑ 9am-9pm mid-May–end Sep), where you can climb the tower for a breathtaking view. Part of the former lighthouse keepers' quarters have been converted into a nine-room **inn** (d $90-145); the Tower Room ($140) is actually in the old lighthouse tower. Rooms are pretty basic, but with the beach and mystique of the place you won't be fussed. The **restaurant** (meals $8-18; ☑ 8am-8pm mid-May–mid-Oct) is famous for its clam chowder.

Cedar Dunes Provincial Park (☎ 902-859-8785; tent-/RV sites $19/22; ☑ late Jun–mid-Sep) is worth a leisurely stop even if you're not staying here. There's tent space in an open grassy field adjacent to West Point Lighthouse. The red-sand beach, with its dunes and beach grass, is an island gem.

Newfoundland & Labrador

Here's what they say: God created the world in six days. On the seventh day, he didn't rest, no sir. He spent it throwing rocks in the water to make Newfoundland.

Locals relay the story with relish, practically daring you to come over to their island. It won't be easy. You'll have to ferry through the bad-ass waters of the Cabot Strait or fly into a fog-swallowed airport. But you're finished piddling around in the Maritimes, right? Ready to go one step beyond, where the cliffs are craggier, historic sites more ancient, people quirkier and food more wild?

The Rock is it: as remote and haunting as it gets in Atlantic Canada. This place even has its own time zone, for crissake, an offbeat half-hour ahead of its Maritime brethren. And so you know what's what: the chilly chunk of northern land known as Labrador joined Newfoundland in province-dom in 2001, thus the name became Newfoundland and Labrador. Whatever the tag, this place's landscape is unreal: massive razor-sided fjords cut inland, where glaciers have sculpted the terrain and scattered boulders like marbles on a playground. Tiny fishing villages (called outports) cling to the tortuous shore, some so isolated they're reachable only by boat.

Newfoundland and Labrador's visiting season is short, with many services shut between October and May. Icebergs drift down from April through early July, while whales swim by in July and August. Hiking, sea kayaking and popping fresh berries into your mouth happen all summer long.

HIGHLIGHTS

- Share the waves with whales and puffins at **Witless Bay Ecological Reserve** (p229)
- Hoist a drink and soak up the history of North America's oldest city, **St John's** (opposite)
- Explore Leif Eriksson's 1000-year-old Viking pad at the sublime **L'Anse aux Meadows National Historic Site** (p248)
- Hike the mountains and kayak the fjordlike lakes at **Gros Morne National Park** (p244)
- Try out the outport life in **Burgeo** (p255)
- Learn Basque whaling history then walk alongside ancient whale bones at **Red Bay** (p259)
- Get your French fix – wine, chocolate éclairs and baguettes – in **St-Pierre** (p237)
- Try **cod tongues**, **caribou tenderloin** and **bakeapple jam** throughout the province

| AREA: 405,720 SQ KM | POPULATION: 510,000 | CAPITAL: ST JOHN'S |

NEWFOUNDLAND

ST JOHN'S

Encamped on the steep slopes of a harbor, with bright scarlet, pine and periwinkle houses crowding its hilly crooked streets, St John's (population 99,200) often is described as looking like a mini San Francisco. Yet the vibe of Newfoundland's largest city and capital remains small-town. Its citizens are happy to share conversation over a drink or meal, and seem genuinely excited you've come all this way to see their land.

Highlights include view-gaping from Signal Hill, walking the seaside North Head Trail, absorbing provincial culture at The Rooms and listening to live music and hoisting a pint (or shot of rum) in George St's pubs. Many visitors take advantage of the city's beyond-the-norm eating and lodging options by making St John's their base camp for explorations elsewhere on the Avalon Peninsula. Cape Spear (p229), Witless Bay Ecological Reserve (p229) and Ferryland (p230) are easy day trips.

St John's is North America's oldest city and Britain's first overseas colony. Its possessive name is simply short for its lifeblood, St John's Harbour.

HISTORY

St John's excellent natural harbor, leading out to what were once seething seas of cod, prompted the first European settlement here in 1528. Sir Humphrey Gilbert landed in town

55 years later, and proudly claimed the land for Queen Elizabeth I. The many Spanish, French and Portuguese settlers living around the harbor then were not amused.

During the late 1600s and much of the 1700s, St John's was razed and taken over several times as the French, English and Dutch fought for it tooth and nail. After Britain's ultimate victory on Signal Hill in 1762, things finally settled down and St John's started to take shape throughout the 1800s.

Since then four fires have ripped through the city, the last in 1892. Each time locals rebuilt with their pride and, more importantly, their sense of humor, intact.

Despite the centuries of turmoil, the harbor steadfastly maintained its position as the world trade center for salted cod well into the 20th century. By mid-century, warehouses lined Water St, and the merchants who owned them made a fortune. Come the early 1960s, St John's had more millionaires per capita than any city in North America. Many called it the Codfish Republic, a riff on Central America's Banana Republics, and said these merchants got rich off the backs of the outport fishing communities, which only seemed to get poorer.

Today St John's wharves still act as service stations to fishing vessels and cruise ships from around the world, though it's the offshore oil industry that now drives the economy.

ORIENTATION

While the streets of St John's can be confusing, it is nearly impossible to get lost thanks to the massive landmark of Signal Hill to the northeast. This sight is visible throughout much of the hilly city, and simply walking downhill will inevitably take you to the harbor. One of the city's oldest sections sits on the harbor at the base of Signal Hill. This small group of houses is known as the Battery.

Water and Duckworth Sts, which run parallel to each other and the waterfront, are the main thoroughfares, lined with restaurants, shops and bars. Boozer-packed George St is between the two.

Memorial University of Newfoundland (MUN) is located about 2km northwest of downtown.

INFORMATION
Bookstores

Afterwards (☎ 709-753-4690; 245 Duckworth St) Used books, comics and magazines.

Second Page Bookstore (☎ 709-722-1742; 363 Water St) Perfect for a secondhand book or pristine A-Ha poster.

Emergency
Police, Ambulance & Fire (☎ 911)
Royal Newfoundland Constabulary (☎ 709-729-8000; 1 Fort Townshend St) For nonemergencies.

Internet Access
There's not a lot. Your best option is the public terminal at the visitors center (p220;

free access for 15 minutes). Both Coffee & Company (p227) and Hava Java (p226) have free wi-fi.

Internet Resources
City of St John's (www.stjohns.ca) The 'Tourism' category has descriptions of and links to attractions, accommodations, eateries, events and scenic drives.

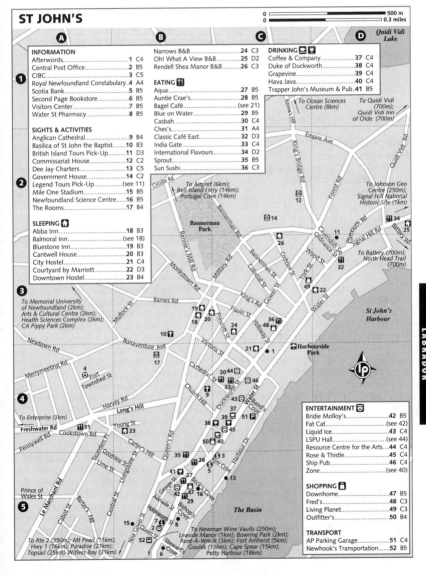

ST JOHN'S

0 — 500 m
0 — 0.3 miles

INFORMATION	
Afterwords	1 C4
Central Post Office	2 B5
CIBC	3 C5
Royal Newfoundland Constabulary	4 A4
Scotia Bank	5 B5
Second Page Bookstore	6 B5
Visitors Center	7 B5
Water St Pharmacy	8 B5

SIGHTS & ACTIVITIES	
Anglican Cathedral	9 B4
Basilica of St John the Baptist	10 B3
British Island Tours Pick-Up	11 D3
Commissariat House	12 C2
Dee Jay Charters	13 C5
Government House	14 C2
Legend Tours Pick-Up	(see 11)
Mile One Stadium	15 B5
Newfoundland Science Centre	16 B5
The Rooms	17 B4

SLEEPING	
Abba Inn	18 B3
Balmoral Inn	(see 18)
Bluestone Inn	19 B3
Cantwell House	20 B3
City Hostel	21 C4
Courtyard by Marriott	22 D3
Downtown Hostel	23 B4

Narrows B&B	24 C3
Oh! What A View B&B	25 D2
Rendell Shea Manor B&B	26 C3

EATING	
Aqua	27 B5
Auntie Crae's	28 B5
Bagel Café	(see 21)
Blue on Water	29 B5
Casbah	30 C4
Ches's	31 A4
Classic Café East	32 D3
India Gate	33 C4
International Flavours	34 D2
Sprout	35 B5
Sun Sushi	36 C3

DRINKING	
Coffee & Company	37 C4
Duke of Duckworth	38 C4
Grapevine	39 C4
Hava Java	40 C4
Trapper John's Museum & Pub	41 B5

ENTERTAINMENT	
Bridie Molloy's	42 B5
Fat Cat	(see 42)
Liquid Ice	43 C4
LSPU Hall	(see 44)
Resource Centre for the Arts	44 C4
Rose & Thistle	45 C4
Ship Pub	46 C4
Zone	(see 40)

SHOPPING	
Downhome	47 B5
Fred's	48 C3
Living Planet	49 C4
Outfitter's	50 B4

TRANSPORT	
AP Parking Garage	51 C4
Newhook's Transportation	52 B5

Quidi Vidi
Lake

To Ocean Sciences
Centre (8km)

To Quidi Vidi
(700m);
Quidi Vidi Inn
of Olde (700m)

To Johnson Geo
Centre (250m);
Signal Hill National
Historic Site (1km)

To Battery (700m);
North Head Trail
(700m)

St John's
Harbour

Harbourside
Park

Bannerman
Park

To Airport (6km);
Bell Island Ferry (14km);
Portugal Cove (14km)

To Memorial University
of Newfoundland (2km);
Arts & Cultural Centre (2km);
Health Sciences Complex (2km);
CA Pippy Park (2km)

The Basin

To Rte 2 (350m); Mt Pearl (11km);
Hwy 1 (16km); Paradise (21km);
Topsail (25km) Witless Bay (31km)

To Newman Wine Vaults (250m);
Leaside Manor (1km); Bowring Park (2km);
Rent-A-Wreck (3km); Fort Amherst (5km);
Goulds (13km); Cape Spear (15km);
Petty Harbour (18km)

To Enterprise (3km)

Prince of
Wales St

NEWFOUNDLAND & LABRADOR

HOW TO SPEAK NEWFANESE

One recent visitor described the local accent as Irish meets Canadian while chewing a mouthful of cod. Well said.

Two hundred years ago, coastal fishing families from Ireland and England made up almost the entire population. Since then, as a result of living in isolated outposts, their accents have evolved into almost 60 different dialects. Strong, lilting inflections, unique slang and colorful idioms pepper the language, sometimes confounding even residents.

The authoritative source is the *Dictionary of Newfoundland English* (www.heritage.nf.ca /dictionary), or visit www.offdarock.com/newfieslang.asp, a website devoted to local sayings. In the meantime, here are a few translations:

- 'Oweshegettinonbys': pronounced 'how's she getting on, boys?' ie how are you?
- 'Where you longs to': where are you from?
- 'Long may yer big jib draw': good luck

Current (www.currentmag.ca) Website of the free alternative magazine covering local arts and politics.

Medical Services

Health Sciences Complex (☎ 709-777-6300; 300 Prince Phillip Dr) A 24-hour emergency room.
Water St Pharmacy (☎ 709-579-5554; 335 Water St) Also sells walking trail maps.

Money

Banks stack up near the Water St and Ayre's Cove intersection.
CIBC (☎ 709-576-8800; 215 Water St)
Scotia Bank (☎ 709-576-6000; 245 Water St)

Post

Central post office (☎ 709-758-1003; 354 Water St)

Tourist Information

Newfoundland & Labrador Tourism (☎ 800-563-6353; www.newfoundlandandlabradortourism.com; PO Box 8730, St John's, NF A1B 4K2) This helpful website and 24-hour telephone line are great sources of province-wide tourism information.

Visitors center (☎ 709-576-8106; www.stjohns.ca; 348 Water St; ◷ 9am-4:30pm Mon-Fri, to 5pm Sat & Sun mid-Jun–Sep, Mon-Fri only rest of year) Has free provincial and city roadmaps, plus local walking tour and hiking trail maps.

SIGHTS

Most sights listed here are downtown or within a few kilometers, but don't forget about Cape Spear, Bell Island and other attractions in surrounding towns; see Around St John's, p228.

Signal Hill National Historic Site

A trip up **Signal Hill** (www.pc.gc.ca/signalhill; Signal Hill Rd; admission free; ◷ 24hr), the city's most famous landmark, is worth it for the glorious view alone, though there's much more to see.

An **interpretive center** (☎ 709-772-5367; adult/child under 17yr $3.95/1.95; ◷ 8:30am-8pm mid-Jun–early Sep, to 4:30pm rest of year) features interactive displays on the site's storied history. The last North American battle of the Seven Years' War took place here in 1762, and Britain's victory ended France's renewed aspirations for control of eastern North America.

You can see cannons and remains of the late 18th-century British battery at **Queen's Battery & Barracks** further up the hill. The tiny castle topping the hill is **Cabot Tower** (admission free; ◷ 9am-9pm mid-May–early Sep, to 5pm rest of year), built in 1900 to honor both John Cabot's arrival in 1497 and Queen Victoria's Diamond Jubilee. Here Italian inventor Guglielmo Marconi gleefully received the first wireless transatlantic message from Cornwall, England, in 1901. There are guides and displays in the tower; an amateur radio society operates a station here in summer.

In midsummer, several dozen soldiers dressed as the 19th-century Royal Newfoundland Company perform a **tattoo** (admission $2; ◷ 11am & 3pm Wed-Sun Jul–mid-Aug) on O'Flaherty Field next to the interpretive center. It wraps up with the firing of historic cannons.

An awesome way to return to downtown is along the **North Head Trail** (1.7km) that connects Cabot Tower with the harborfront Battery neighborhood. The walk departs from the tower's parking lot and traces the cliffs, imparting tremendous sea views and sometimes whale spouts. Because much of the trail runs along the bluff's sheer edge, it isn't something to attempt in icy, foggy or dark conditions.

Quidi Vidi

Over Signal Hill, away from town, is the tiny, picturesque village of **Quidi Vidi**. Here you'll find the oldest cottage in North America, the 1750s-era **Mallard Cottage** (☎ 709-576-2266; 2 Barrows Rd; admission free; 🕙 9:30am-4:30pm May-Sep, call for hours Oct-Apr). It's now a national heritage site and a very cluttered antique/junk shop. Something is sure to charm you; profits go to maintenance.

Built in 1762 and still symbolically guarding the bay from up the hill is **Quidi Vidi Battery** (☎ 709-729-2977; Cuckhold's Dr; admission $3; 🕙 10am-5:30pm Jun–mid-Sep). Built by the French after they took St John's, the battery was quickly claimed by the British and remained in military service into the 1800s. Period-garbed interpreters dole out historical information.

Inland from the village, **Quidi Vidi Lake** is the site of the city-stopping St John's Regatta (p224). The **Royal St John's Regatta Museum** (☎ 709-576-8921; cnr Lakeview Ave & Clancy Dr, off Forest Rd; admission free; 🕙 Jul & Aug) is on the 2nd floor of the boathouse. Opening hours vary. A popular walking trail leads around the lake.

Quidi Vidi Brewing (☎ 709-738-4040; www.iceberg beer.com; 15 Barrows Rd; admission incl 1 bottle & tastings $6; 🕙 noon-5pm Mon-Sat) is a microbrewery located in an old fish-processing plant on the tiny wharf. It's a swell place to slake one's thirst.

By car, take Forest Rd from the city and follow it past the lake until it turns into Quidi Vidi Village Rd. Locals prefer you to park on the outskirts of town and walk in.

The Rooms

Not many museums offer the chance to see a giant squid, hear a 40-part choral installation and peruse historical photos all under one roof. But that's **The Rooms** (☎ 709-729-0917; www.therooms.ca; 9 Bonaventure Ave; adult/child 6-16yr $5/3; 10am-5pm Mon, Tue, Fri & Sat, to 9pm Wed & Thu, noon-5pm Sun), the newly opened provincial museum, art gallery and archives. Frankly, the building is much more impressive to look at than look in, since its frequently changing exhibits are sparse. But whoa! The views from this massive stone-and-glass complex, which lords over the city from a breath-sapping hilltop, are eye poppers; try the 4th-floor café for the best vistas. There's free admission Wednesday evenings and the first Saturday each month.

Johnson Geo Centre

Nowhere in the world can geo-history, going back to the birth of the earth, be accessed so easily as in Newfoundland, and the **Geo Centre** (☎ 709-737-7880; www.geocentre.ca; 175 Signal Hill Rd; adult/child 5-17yr $10.25/4.60; 🕙 9:30am-5pm Mon-Sat, 1-5pm Sun, closed Mon mid-Oct–mid-May) does a grand job making snore-worthy geologic information perk up with appeal via its underground, interactive displays.

The center also has an exhibit on the *Titanic*, and how human error and omission caused the tragedy, not just an iceberg. For instance, the ship's owners didn't supply her with enough lifeboats so as not to 'clutter the deck,' and the crew ignored myriad ice warnings. What any of this has to do with geology remains unclear, but who cares? It's fascinating.

Basilica of St John the Baptist

Built in 1855, the soaring twin spires of the **basilica** (☎ 709-754-2170; www.thebasilica.ca; 200 Military Rd; admission free; 🕙 8am-3pm Mon-Fri, to 6pm Sat, to 12:30pm Sun) pierce the sky and are visible all the way from Signal Hill. Inside, 65 unique stained-glass windows illuminate the remarkable polychromatic Italianate ceiling and its gold-leaf highlights. Free half-hour tours are offered 10am to 5pm Monday to Saturday in July and August, according to demand. Ask about the **Basilica-Cathedral Museum**, which holds a small collection of sacred vessels, paintings and books.

Anglican Cathedral of St John the Baptist

Serving Canada's oldest parish (1699), the **Anglican cathedral** (☎ 709-726-5677; www.sji.ca/ca thedral; 22 Church Hill; admission free; 🕙 10:30am-noon & 2-4:30pm Mon-Fri Jun-Sep) is one of the finest examples of ecclesiastical Gothic architecture in North America. Although originally built in the 1830s, all but its exterior walls were reduced to ashes by the Great Fire of 1892. It was rebuilt in 1905. The Gothic ribbed ceiling, graceful stone arches and long, thin stained-glass windows are timeless marvels. Students offer tours, organists play **concerts** (🕙 1:15pm Wed), and church ladies serve **high tea** ($8; 🕙 2:30-4:30pm Mon-Fri, Jul & Aug) in the crypt.

Fort Amherst

Across from Signal Hill, and dwarfed by massive cliffs, are the remains of a centuries-old **fort** (Fort Amherst Rd; admission free; 🕙 24hr). You can almost touch the icebergs and whales, and the views along the rugged coast are incredible. You'll discover remnants of WWII gun batteries and a lighthouse (1810), the first in Newfoundland.

NEWFOUNDLAND & LABRADOR

LOCAL VOICES

Brian Chaulk

Radio operator at Cabot Tower and naval architecture student at Memorial University, age 24, St John's

What is the most important issue facing Newfoundland today? The economy. We've seen a gutting of our primary industries like wood mills and fishing. The codfish industry shut down in 1992 (see p236) and we've tried to replace it with shellfish. But the shellfish industry concentrates money to those who can buy larger ships. With codfishing, if you had a boat and two or three hooks you could go out. The offshore oil industry is picking up some of the slack, but it's bringing prosperity mostly to St John's versus the smaller communities. We have a lot of outmigration to Alberta. Many of my friends are there. **Do you have any local heroes?** Danny Williams, our current premier. He has really taken a stand for Newfoundland. He recently took down all the Canadian flags until the province was able to reach an accord with the federal government and we were able to receive our fair share of natural resource money.

Newman Wine Vaults

Dating from the 1780s, the dark, cool **wine vaults** (☎ 709-739-7870; www.historictrust.com; 436 Water St; admission by donation; 10am-4:30pm Tue-Sat mid-Jun–Aug) are where the Newman company aged its port until 1996 (when EU regulations forced the process back to Portugal). Tour guides relay fun stories like how English noblemen, who wanted to be buried in their homeland, got shipped back after death in barrels of port, since the alcohol preserved their bodies. There are no tastings, but you can purchase bottles.

Commissariat House

Near Gower St, this 1820s late-Georgian **mansion** (☎ 709-729-6730; King's Bridge Rd; adult/child under 13yr $3/free; 10am-5:30pm Jun-Sep) was used by the supplies officer of the British military. The house has been restored to 1830s style and contains many period pieces.

Government House

Set among a stand of chestnut, maple and oak trees is the Palladian-style **Government House** (☎ 709-729-4494; www.mun.ca/govhouse; Military Rd; dawn to dusk). Built at the same time as the White House, but at four times the cost, the austere mansion (1831) with its prominent corner quoins and window surrounds is home to the province's lieutenant governor. The interior maintains original furnishings and is open for free tours (10am Wednesday and Thursday); you must book in advance.

CA Pippy Park

The feature-filled, 1343-hectare **CA Pippy Park** (☎ 709-737-3655; www.pippypark.com) coats downtown's northwestern edge. Recreational facilities include walking trails, picnic areas, playgrounds and a campground. **Memorial University**, the province's only university, is here too.

The university's **botanical garden** (☎ 709-737-8590; www.mun.ca/botgarden; adult/child 6-18yr $5/1.15; 10am-5pm May-Nov) is at Oxen Pond, at the park's western edge off Mt Scio Rd. There's a cultivated garden and a nature reserve. Together, these and the park's **Long Pond** marsh give visitors an excellent introduction to the province's flora, habitats (including boreal forest and bogs) and animals (look for birds at Long Pond and the occasional moose).

The **Fluvarium** (☎ 709-754-3474; www.fluvarium.ca; Nagle's Pl; adult/child 5-14yr/family $5.50/3.50/17.50; 9am-5pm Mon-Fri, noon-5pm Sat & Sun May-Oct, to 4:30pm Nov-Apr), a glass-sided cross-section of a 'living' river, is located across the street from the campground. Viewers can peer through large windows to observe the undisturbed goings-on beneath the surface of Nagle's Hill Brook. Numerous brown trout and the occasional eel can be seen. If there has been substantial rain or high winds, all visible life is lost in the murkiness.

There's also a demonstration **fish hatchery**. Opening times vary, but feeding time is scheduled at 4pm, and tours are offered hourly except at 4pm. Outside there are interpretive trails; it's possible to walk all the way to Quidi Vidi Lake from here.

ACTIVITIES

Excellent walking and hiking trails zigzag across the area. The **Grand Concourse** (☎ 709-737-1077; www.grandconcourse.ca) is an ambitious

95km-long network of trails all over town and linking St John's with nearby Mt Pearl and Paradise via downtown sidewalks, trails, river corridors and old railway beds. Most hiking is done in the CA Pippy Park and Quidi Vidi Lake areas. Maps ($2.60) are available from newsstands and **Water St Pharmacy** (☎ 709-579-5554; 335 Water St). The visitors center also gives away a photocopied map. Don't miss the sea-hugging North Head Trail (p220).

The epic **East Coast Trail** (☎ 709-738-4453; www.eastcoasttrail.com) stretches 220km from Fort Amherst south to Cappahayden; a further 300km is to be developed. It's part easy coastal walking, part tough wilderness trail. Maps ($23.95) are available from **Outfitter's** (☎ 709-579-4453; 220 Water St), **Downhome** (☎ 709-722-2070; 303 Water St) and the website, which also has details on free weekly guided hikes. An excellent stretch runs along the coast from Cape Spear (p229).

Golf and cross-country skiing enthusiasts can partake in CA Pippy Park (opposite). For sea kayaking in the vicinity, see p229.

ST JOHN'S FOR CHILDREN

St John's will keep the wee ones entertained, rain or shine. CA Pippy Park (opposite) is a kids' haven, with a huge playground, lots of trails and of course, the Fluvarium. The ever-hungry ducks at the pond in **Bowring Park** (Waterford Bridge Rd) love company, as do the sea creatures at the Ocean Sciences Centre (p228). Just knowing a cannon will blast at the end of the tattoo should keep them riveted at Signal Hill (p220). The various boat tours (right) are also a great bet, but inquire if there are icebergs and whales in the area first.

TOP FIVE ANIMALS YOU'LL SPOT IN NEWFOUNDLAND

- Moose: behold the antlers but beware of Bullwinkle on the roads.

- Humpback whale: seeing one launch in a mighty breach is mind-blowing.

- Puffin: who can resist the funny-looking love child of the penguin and parrot?

- Caribou: enjoy glimpses of these impressive beasts usually only seen in the High Arctic.

- Atlantic salmon: true, it'll most likely be sighted on your dinner plate, but you'll see them wild, too.

While geology may not initially spark their interest, the fact that the Johnson Geo Centre (p221) is underground may do the trick. Another rainy-day option is the **Newfoundland Science Centre** (☎ 709-754-0823; www.nlsciencecentre.com; Murray Premises, Beck Cove; adult/child 3-18yr/family $6/4.25/20; 10am-5pm Mon-Fri, 10am-6pm Sat, noon-6pm Sun) with dinosaurs, a planetarium and space exhibits (check out the astronaut toilet or calculate your age on Mars).

QUIRKY ST JOHN'S

Explore the city's dark corners, its folklore and paranormal activity on the super-popular **St John's Haunted Hike** (☎ 709-685-3444; www.hauntedhike.com; tours $5; 9.30pm Sun-Thu Jun–mid-Sep), led by the black-caped Reverend Thomas Wyckham Jarvis Esq. He'll spook you with tales of headless captains, murderesses and other ghosts.

TOURS
Boat

For most tours, you need to head out of town to Petty Harbour (p229) or Witless Bay (p229). The **Dee Jay Charters** (☎ 709-753-8687; www.deejaycharters.ca; Pier 7, Harbour Dr; 2hr tours adult/child under 16yr $40/20; 10am, 2pm & 6pm Jun-Sep) boat sneaks into Quidi Vidi and makes a run down to Cape Spear in search of icebergs in June, whales in July and August and seabirds all season.

Bus

British Island Tours (☎ 709-738-8687; www.britishislandtours.com; 2½hr tours adult/child 5-15yr $23/13; 9:15 & 1:15 May-early Oct) These tours aboard a double-decker bus include Signal Hill and Quidi Vidi. Pick-up is from the Fairmont Hotel on Cavendish Sq and Mile One Stadium.

City Hostel (☎ 709-754-4789; www.hostels.com; 246 Duckworth St) The hostel (see also p224) arranges city tours ($39, three hours) and Colony of Avalon/Cape Spear tours ($69, five hours).

Legend Tours (☎ 709-753-1497; www.legendtours.ca; adult/child 13-18yr $59/35; 66 Glenview Tce; Apr-Oct) This award-winning operator covers St John's, Cape Spear and the Northeast Avalon Peninsula. The commentary is richly woven with humor and historical tidbits. Pick-up is from the Fairmont Hotel on Cavendish Sq.

Walking

There are self-guided walking tours available from the visitors center (p220) that traverse the city's east and west sides and downtown, as well as the St John's Haunted Hike (above). The East Coast Trail (left) offers free guided hikes.

NEWFOUNDLAND & LABRADOR

FESTIVALS & EVENTS

For the full slate of events, check with the **visitors center** (☎ 709-576-8106; www.stjohns.ca/city services/events/calendar.jsp).

St John's Day Celebration (☎ 709-576-8106; www.st johns.ca) Four days of jazz and blues concerts, parades, street dances and sporting events begin around June 18 to commemorate the city's birthday.

Sound Symposium (www.soundsymposium.com) Seven days of concerts, workshops, dance, theater and film experiments in the second week of July every other year; next symposium is in 2008.

George Street Festival (☎ 709-576-8106; www.st johns.ca) The mighty George St becomes one big nightclub for a fabulous week of daytime and night-time musical performances in late July.

Newfoundland & Labrador Folk Festival (☎ 709-576-8508; www.nlfolk.com) This intimate, three-day event in Bannerman Park celebrates traditional Newfoundland music, dancing and storytelling over the first weekend of August.

Royal St John's Regatta (☎ 709-576-8921; www.st johnsregatta.org) The streets are empty, the stores are closed and thousands migrate to the shores of Quidi Vidi Lake on the first Wednesday in August. This rowing regatta officially began in 1825 and is now the oldest continuously held sporting event in North America.

SLEEPING

Scores of tiny inns and B&Bs offer great value in the heart of St John's; they're usually better options than the hotels and motels. Parking is available at or near all accommodations. The city's hefty 17% tax is not included in prices listed here unless stated otherwise.

For more lodging options, see the city's website (www.stjohns.ca/visitors/accommodation/index.jsp).

Budget

CA Pippy Park (☎ 709-737-3669; www.pippypark.com; Nagles Place; campsites $18-28; ◎ May-Sep) Despite being conveniently close to town and the university, just off Allandale Rd at Higgins Line, this campground is quiet and surprisingly verdant.

City Hostel (☎ 709-754-4789; www.hostels.com; 246 Duckworth St; incl tax dm $27.60, r $55.20; 🖳) Located above the Bagel Café, this place is pretty spiffy for a hostel, with its dark hardwood floors, comfy blankets, free wi-fi and dorms containing four beds at most. It also arranges tours (p223).

Downtown Hostel (☎ 709-754-7658; www.geocities .com/downtownhostel; 25 Young St; dm $23, r $56) It's a

toss-up who has more character, the energized owner Carola or the building itself. Crooked homemade furniture resists the steeply plunging floors, and electrical cords and world maps adorn the walls.

Midrange

All rooms listed in this category have private bathrooms.

Oh! What A View B&B (☎ 709-576-7063; www.oh whataview.com; 184 Signal Hill Rd; d incl breakfast from $85; 🖳) It's a 20-minute hike (uphill) from the town center, but oh, it really is a stunning view. Several common balconies take in the harbor below. The rooms are bright and modern, if a bit small. Ask for room No 8 with its Juliet balcony or No 3 with its straight shot of the water.

Cantwell House (☎ 709-754-8439, 888-725-8439; www.cantwellhouse.nf.net; 25 Queen's Rd; d incl breakfast from $85; 🖳) Take tea from a seat on Cantwell's deck and stare out over a colorful collage of row houses to the blue harbor. A friendly atmosphere combines with a sense of privacy in the Victorian ambience.

Narrows B&B (☎ 709-739-4850, 866-739-4850; www .thenarrowsbb.com; 146 Gower St; r incl breakfast $85-125) Warm colors mix with elegant trims and large wooden beds in the rooms of this welcoming B&B. There are modern amenities throughout and a gorgeous sitting room and balcony where guests can mingle and swap whale stories.

Abba Inn (☎ 709-754-0058, 800-563-3959; www.ab bainn.com; 36 Queen's Rd; d incl breakfast from $85-185; 🖳) The Abba shares the same building as the Balmoral (below), and they even share reservations (ie if one is full, they'll hook you up with the other). They have similar amenities and ambience.

Balmoral Inn (☎ 709-754-5721, 877-428-1055; www .balmoralhouse.com; 38 Queen's Rd; r incl breakfast $89-179; 🖳) While the Balmoral is a typical B&B in many ways (cherub statues, long wooden antique tables), its owners live off-site and breakfast is self-serve, so it's more relaxed and private than many B&Bs. Each room has super-comfy mattresses and wired high-speed Internet access.

Bluestone Inn (☎ 709-754-7544, 877-754-9876; www .thebluestoneinn.com; 34 Queen's Rd; d incl breakfast $89-189; 🖳) Built from the same historic stone as Cabot Tower and Government House, the Bluestone provides towering plasterwork ceilings, fireplaces and original artwork in its rooms. The harbor view from the gabled room on the 3rd floor is stunning – Dame Judi Dench is one of many who have enjoyed it.

Courtyard by Marriott (☎ 709-722-6636, 866-727-6636; www.marriott.com/yytcg; 131 Duckworth St, r city view/harbor view from $139/159;) Situated right smack downtown, the Courtyard outfits each room with a minirefrigerator, large TV and wired high-speed Internet access, and there are free laundry facilities.

Top End

Leaside Manor (☎ 709-722-0387, 877-807-7245; www .leaside.nf.ca; 39 Topsail Rd; r $99-129, ste $150-325, apt $179-249;) Owner Elaine Hann has done a knock-out job redecorating this old merchant's home to be plush but tasteful. The higher-end rooms have a canopied bed, fireplace and Jacuzzi, which explains why the *Globe & Mail* designated Leaside one of Canada's 'most romantic destinations.' It's about a half-hour walk from downtown; to be closer, inquire about the downtown apartments.

Rendell Shea Manor B&B (☎ 709-738-7432, 877-738-7432; www.rendellshea.com; 82 Cochrane St; d $140-230) Thank the Great Fire of 1892 for sparing this historic home. It's opposite Government House and full of 19th-century opulence. Superb architecture, grand canopy beds, fireplaces and mighty bathtubs embellish the rooms.

EATING

St John's has moved beyond fried fish. Thai, Japanese, Indian, Latin and even vegetarian restaurants have popped up, providing a good variety. Don't worry, though, you can still get your fish-and-chips fix near Freshwater and Harvey Rds, where the chip shops cluster.

Budget

Auntie Crae's (☎ 709-754-0661; 272 Water St; sandwiches $4-7; 8am-7pm) Come to this specialty food store for a cuppa joe, groceries, chowder or a sandwich. Relax with your goodies in the adjoining Fishhook Neyle's Common Room.

Ches's (☎ 709-726-2373; 5-9 Freshwater Rd; meals $5-9; 9am-2am Sun-Thu, 9am-3am Fri & Sat) Ches's and its fish-and-chips are an institution in Newfoundland. No frills, just cod that will melt in your mouth.

International Flavours (☎ 709-738-4636; 4 Quidi Vidi Rd; meals $8-9; 11am-7pm Tue-Sat) Pakistani owner Talat ladles out a whopping spicy plateful of dahl, curry and/or basmati rice for her daily set meal (one with meat, the other without).

Midrange

Bagel Café (☎ 709-739-4470; 246 Duckworth St; breakfasts $7-11; 7am-10pm) It's the Bagel Café by day, Figg's Restaurant by night, but frankly it's the breakfast we're after, available any time. Eggs 'n' fishcakes, omelets and piles of home-fry potatoes get dished up in the dim lighting to tattooed guys and prim older ladies alike.

Casbah (☎ 709-738-5293; 2 Cathedral St; mains lunch $7-14, dinner $11-22; lunch Mon-Fri, dinner daily, brunch Sat & Sun) Fun, sassy waitstaff serve fun, sassy food in colorful Casbah. They keep everyone happy by offering small, medium and large plates, which might contain maple-roasted pumpkin soup or halibut burger with wasabi mayo.

Sun Sushi (☎ 709-726-8688; 186 Duckworth St; sushi rolls $4-7; noon-9:30pm Mon-Thu, to 10pm Fri & Sat) Ahh, sushi has finally come to the province, pleasing the townsfolk tremendously, which is why this place is always hopping.

SCRUNCHEONS, TOUTONS & FLIPPER PIE: A GASTRONOMIC GUIDE

Get ready for a whole new culinary vocabulary when you enter Newfoundland. Lesson number one: having a 'scoff' is local parlance for eating a big meal.

Two of Newfoundland's favorite dishes are fish 'n' brewis and jig's dinner. Fish 'n' brewis is a blend of salted fish, onions, scruncheons (aka fried pork fat) and a unique near-boiled bread. Jig's dinner is a right feast comprising a roast (turkey or possibly moose) along with boiled potatoes, carrots, cabbage, salted beef and pea-and-bread pudding. A touton is fried dough that you dip in gooey molasses.

Cod tongues are the tender, fleshy bits between the lower jaws served battered and fried, while cod cheeks are just that: cheeks from the fish. Fishcakes are a blend of cod, potato and onion mushed together and fried – delicious. Seal flipper pie, on the other hand, is for the brave; the strong flavor of seal meat is definitely an acquired taste.

To finish off your meal, try figgy duff, a thick fig pudding boiled in a cloth bag.

And the final lesson in gastro terminology: when you're done eating, pat your stomach and say, 'I'm full as an egg.'

NEWFOUNDLAND & LABRADOR

LOCAL VOICES

Terry O'Rourke

Co-owner of the Duke of Duckworth pub (below), age 49, St John's

What is the most important issue facing Newfoundland today? Young people are leaving. Many go to the mainland once they get an education. Right now we don't have the resources to satisfy their needs. Hopefully we will if the oil industry takes off (see boxed text, p236). **What is the most defining characteristic of your province?** The resourcefulness of the people. They've survived here for hundreds of years and against all odds. Just get in your car and travel to the outports. People had to diversify, especially once the fishing industry collapsed. Now they have interpretive centers to keep their sense of community alive, and to show off their history and culture. **As a pub owner surrounded by food and drink, can you recommend any local favorites?** We have wonderful beers: India, Jockey, Dominion Ale and Blue Star are local brands. For food, it's jig's dinner (p225). Ya gotta do it.

Sprout (☎ 709-579-5485; 364 Duckworth St; mains $6-10; ⏱ 11:30am-9pm Tue-Fri, 9am-9pm Sat, 9am-3pm Sun) It's almost unheard of in Newfoundland: full-on vegetarian food. So savor your marinated tofu burger, spinach pesto melt sandwich and brown rice *poutine* (fries served under gravy and bean curd) before leaving town.

Classic Café East (☎ 709-726-4444; 73 Duckworth St; dinner mains $13-19; ⏱ 8am-10pm) Soak up harbor views while wolfing down Newfie standards: toutons, fish 'n' brewis, seafood chowder and fishcakes, plus omelets and sandwiches.

India Gate (☎ 709-753-6006; 286 Duckworth St; mains $11-15; ⏱ lunch & dinner) This is the local Indian favorite. For $11 the weekday all-you-can-eat lunch special is a steal; it runs from 11:30am to 2:30pm – with loads of vegetarian options.

Top End

Aqua (☎ 709-576-2782; 310 Water St; mains dinner $21-32; ⏱ lunch & dinner) The mains at this hip bistro incorporate local seafood and wild game, resulting in inventive dishes such as caribou with warm bakeapple coulis, molasses-glazed salmon and prosciutto-wrapped cod.

Blue on Water (☎ 709-754-2583; 319 Water St; mains dinner $22-33; ⏱ 7:30am-11pm Mon-Fri, 9am-11pm Sat, 9am-10pm Sun) Blue is another high-end, casual-toned restaurant using locally sourced ingredients for dishes such as lobster with spinach mashed potatoes or cod tongues and scruncheons.

DRINKING

George St is the city's famous party lane. Water and Duckworth Sts also have plenty of drinkeries, but the scene is slightly more sedate. Expect most places to charge a small cover (about $5) on weekends or when there's live music. Don't forget to try the local Screech (opposite).

Coffee shops seep in between the restaurants and bars along Water St.

our pick **Duke of Duckworth** (☎ 709-739-6344; 325 Duckworth St, McMurdo's Lane) 'The Duke,' as it's known, is an unpretentious English-style pub that represents all that's great about Newfoundland and Newfoundlanders. Stop in on a Friday night, and you'll see a mix of blue-collar, white-collar, young, old, even band members from Great Big Sea plunked down on the well-worn, red-velour bar stools. The kitchen cooks the ultimate in chicken pot pie, fish cakes and other comfort foods, and 14 beers (including the local Quidi Vidi) flow through the taps. It's no wonder there are locals out there racking up $1000 tabs every few months.

Trapper John's Museum & Pub (☎ 709-579-9630; 3 George St) It's not the most polished pub in town, but it sure is the most fun place to become an Honorary Newfoundlander, which happens after you kiss Stubby the Puffin (a variation on the usual codfish). The animal traps enshrined throughout grant the 'museum' status.

Grapevine (☎ 709-754-8463; 206 Water St) Dark, swanky Grapevine is a wine and cocktail bar with great music and martinis; there's live music on Tuesday.

Quidi Vidi Inn of Olde (☎ 709-576-2223; 67 Quidi Vidi Village Rd, Quidi Vidi) This quirky yet beloved little pub sits just out of town in Quidi Vidi. If only the 2000 spoons on the wall could talk…

Hava Java (☎ 709-753-5282; 216 Water St; ⏱ 7:30am-11pm Mon-Fri, 9am-11pm Sat & Sun) The atmosphere at this place is refreshingly antifranchise and pro tattoo; it just focuses on making the best coffee in town.

If you need that leather lounger to truly enjoy your espresso, head to **Coffee & Company** (☎ 709-576-3606; 204 Water St; ☽ 7:30am-11pm).

ENTERTAINMENT

Perhaps because this is such an intimate city, word-of-mouth and flyers slapped on light poles seem to be the major vehicle for entertainment information. Venues are close together – have a wander and enjoy.

Live Music

Cover charges range from $5 to $8.

Ship Pub (☎ 709-753-3870; 265 Duckworth St) Attitudes and ages are checked at the door of this little pub, tucked down Solomon's Lane. You'll hear everything from jazz to indie, and even the odd poetry reading.

Rose & Thistle (☎ 709-579-6662; 208 Water Street) Well-known local folk musicians like Ron Hynes strum here.

Bridie Molloy's (☎ 709-576-5990; 5 George St) This polished Irish pub hosts an older crowd and offers Irish and Newfoundland music six nights a week.

Fat Cat (☎ 709-739-5554; George St) Blues radiates from this cozy bar nightly during the summer.

Nightclubs

St John's true nightclubs, which only open late on Friday and Saturday night, cater to energetic straight and gay crowds. Cover charges vary, but are typically between $5 and $10.

Zone (☎ 709-754-2492; 216 Water St) This is the premier gay dance bar in Newfoundland. Straights are equally welcome to soak up the fun energy; located above Hava Java.

Liquid Ice (☎ 709-754-2190; 186b Water St) If you like your house, drum and bass or hip-hop, wade into this gay-friendly nightspot.

Theater

Arts & Culture Centre (☎ 709-729-3900, 800-663-9449; www.artsandculturecentre.ca; cnr Allandale Rd & Prince Phillip Dr) Live theater and dance performances are staged regularly; near CA Pippy Park.

Resource Centre for the Arts (☎ 709-753-4531; www.rca.nf.ca; 3 Victoria St) Sponsors theater, dance and visual art by Newfoundland artists, all of which is staged downtown in the former longshoremen's union hall (aka LSPU Hall).

Shakespeare by the Sea Festival (☎ 709-691-7287; www.nfld.com/~sbts/menu.html; adult/child under 12yr/student $15/5/10; ☽ 6pm early Jul–mid-Aug) Live outdoor productions are presented at Bowring Park amphitheater. Note there are no advance sales.

SHOPPING

You'll find traditional music, berry jams and local art in the nooks and crannies of Water and Duckworth Sts.

Fred's (☎ 709-753-9191; 198 Duckworth St; ☽ 9:30am-9pm Mon-Fri, 9:30am-6pm Sat, noon-5pm Sun) This is the premier music shop in St John's. It features brilliant local music such as Buddy Wasisname and The Other Fellers.

Living Planet (☎ 709-739-6810; 116 Duckworth St) For quirky tourist T-shirts and buttons even locals are proud to wear.

Downhome (☎ 709-722-2070; 303 Water St) It specializes in local goods such as jams, woolen wear and the coveted *How to Play the Musical Spoons* CD.

Outfitter's (☎ 709-579-4453; 220 Water St) A camping and gear shop where you can purchase maps for the East Coast Trail.

GETTING THERE & AWAY
Air

Air Canada, WestJet, Continental and Provincial are the main carriers; see p277 and p280 for contact details.

GETTING SCREECHED IN

Within a few days of your arrival in St John's, you'll undoubtedly be asked by everyone if you've been 'screeched in,' or in traditional Newfoundland slang, 'Is you a screecher?' It's not as painful as it sounds, and is, in fact, locals' playful way to welcome visitors to the province.

Screeching derives from the 1940s when new arrivals were given their rites of passage, and from pranks played on sealers heading to the ice for the first time. Today the ceremony takes place in local pubs, where you'll gulp a shot of rum (there's actually a local brand called Screech), recite an unpronounceable verse in the local lingo, kiss a stuffed codfish and then receive a certificate declaring you an 'Honorary Newfoundlander.' Sure it's touristy, but it's also good fun. The more the merrier, so try to get screeched in with a crowd.

Bus

DRL Coachlines (☎ 709-263-2171; www.drlgroup.com) operates the only cross-island bus route on Newfoundland. It sends one bus per day from St John's to Port aux Basques ($130, cash only; 13½ hours) via the 905km-long Hwy 1, making 25 stops en route. It leaves at 7:45am from Memorial University's Student Centre.

Newhook's Transportation (☎ 709-682-4877, in Placentia 709-227-2552; 13 Queen St) provides service down the southwestern Avalon Peninsula to Placentia, making a stop at the Argentia ferry terminal ($20, two hours, twice daily).

Car & Motorcycle

Avis, Budget, Dollar, National and Hertz (see p282) have offices at the airport. **Enterprise** (☎ 709-722-9480; 229 Kenmount Rd) and **Rent-A-Wreck** (☎ 709-753-2277; 909 Topsail Rd) are a 10- to 20-minute drive from the airport but often have lower rates.

Share Taxis

Leaving once or twice a day, these large vans typically seat 15 and allow you to jump on or off at any point along their routes. **Fleetline Bus Service** (☎ 709-722-2608) provides daily service, except Sunday, to Carbonear ($16, three hours) and the lower Conception Bay area. **Shirran's** (☎ 709-468-7741) daily service plies the Bonavista Peninsula, including Trinity ($35, three hours) and Bonavista ($40, 3½ hours). **Foote's Taxi** (☎ 709-832-0491) travels daily down the Burin Peninsula as far as Fortune ($40, five hours).

GETTING AROUND
To/From the Airport

The airport is 6km north of St John's on Portugal Cove Rd (Rte 40). A government flat rate applies for trips from the airport to town. The official service is **Citywide Taxi** (☎ 709-722-7777), and depending on your destination it will cost either $17.50 or $20, plus $2.50 for each extra passenger. Taxis from town to the airport run on meters and should cost around $14.

Car & Motorcycle

The city's one-way streets and unique intersections can be confounding. Thankfully, citizens are incredibly patient. A loonie ($1) will get you an hour at the parking meters that line Water and Duckworth Sts. **AP Parking Garage** (cnr Baird's Cove & Harbour Dr; ☎ 6:30am-11pm) charges $1 for 30 minutes or $9 per day.

Public Transportation

The **Metrobus** (☎ 709-722-9400; www.metrobus.com; 1-way fare $2, book of 10 tickets $18) system covers most of the city. Maps and schedules are online and in the visitors center. A useful bus is the No 3, which circles town via Military Rd and Water St before heading to the university.

Taxi

Except for the trip from the airport (left), all taxis operate on government-standardized meters. A trip within town should cost around $5. **Jiffy Cabs** (☎ 709-722-2222) and **Citywide Co-op** (☎ 709-726-6666) provide dependable service.

AROUND ST JOHN'S
North of St John's

Right out of *20,000 Leagues Under the Sea*, the **Ocean Sciences Centre** (☎ 709-737-3708; www.osc.mun .ca; admission free; ☼ 10am-5pm Jun-early Sep) is operated by Memorial University and examines the salmon life cycle, seal navigation, ocean currents and life in cold oceanic regions. The outdoor visitors' area consists of local sealife in touch tanks. It's about 8km north of St John's just before Logy Bay. From the city, take Logy Bay Rd (Rte 30), then follow Marine Dr to Marine Lab Rd and take it to the end.

Secluded and rocky, **Middle Cove** and **Outer Cove** are just a bit further north on Rte 30 – they're perfect for a beach picnic.

North at the head of **Torbay Bight** is the enjoyably short **Father Troy Path**, which hugs the shoreline. The view from **Cape St Francis** is worth the bumpy gravel road from Pouch Cove. There's an old battery and you may just luck out and see a whale or two.

West of St John's

West of town on Topsail Rd (Rte 60), just past Paradise, is **Topsail** and its panoramic views of Conception Bay and its islands.

Bell Island (www.bellisland.net) is the largest of Conception Bay's little landmasses, and it makes an interesting day trip. It's a 14km drive from St John's to Portugal Cove to the **ferry** (☎ 709-895-6931; per passenger/car $3.75/6.25; ☼ hourly 6am-11pm), and then a 20-minute crossing. Bell Island has the distinction of being the only place on the continent to get nailed by German forces in WWII. Its pier and 80,000 tons of iron ore were torpedoed by U-boats in 1942. At low tide, you can still see the aftermath. The island sports a pleasant mélange of beaches, coastal vistas, lighthouses and trails. Miners here used to work in shafts under the sea at the world's largest submarine iron mine. The **Iron Ore Mine & Museum** (☎ 709-488-2880; adult/child under 12yr $7/3; ☻ 11am-7pm Jun-Sep) details the operation and gives visitors the chance to go underground; dress warmly.

South of St John's

CAPE SPEAR

A 15km drive southeast of town leads you to the most easterly point in North America. The coastal scenery is spectacular, and you can spot whales through much of the summer. The area is preserved as the **Cape Spear National Historic Site** (☎ 709-772-5367; www.pc.gc.ca/capespear; Blackhead Rd; adult/child under 17yr $3.95/1.95; ☻ mid-May–mid-Oct) and includes an **interpretive center** (☻ 9:30am-8pm mid-May–early Sep, 10am-6pm early Sep–mid-Oct), the refurbished 1835 **lighthouse** (☻ 10am-6pm mid-Jun–mid-Oct) and the heavy gun batteries and magazines built in 1941 to protect the harbor during WWII. A trail leads along the edge of the headland cliffs, past 'the most easterly point' observation deck and up to the lighthouse. You can continue all the way to Maddox Cove and Petty Harbour along the East Coast Trail; even walking it a short way is tremendously worthwhile.

Heed all signs warning visitors off the rocks by the water, as rogue waves have been known to sweep in.

You reach the cape from Water St by crossing the Waterford River south of town and then following Blackhead Rd for 11km.

GOULDS & PETTY HARBOUR

In **Goulds**, at the junction of Rte 10 and the road to Petty Harbour in Bidgood's Plaza, is **Bidgood's** (☎ 709-368-3125; ☻ 9am-9pm Mon-Sat, 11am-5pm Sun). This supermarket purveys traditional Newfoundland specialties that will either intrigue or repulse you. It has a religious following among locals who come to buy such delicacies as fresh seal flipper, caribou steak and moose in a jar. For the faint of heart, there are partridgeberry and bakeapple jams.

Its back lapping up against steep rocky slopes, movie set–beautiful **Petty Harbour** is filled with weathered boats, wharves and sheds on precarious stilts. The tall ship *Scademia* departs from here and goes out searching for whales and icebergs; contact **Adventure Tours** (☎ 709-726-5000; www.netfx.ca/scademia; 2hr tours adult/child 3-13yr $40/20; ☻ 1pm May-Sep).

AVALON PENINSULA

The Avalon Peninsula looks like a geographical afterthought – floating at sea and tethered to the rest of Newfoundland by nothing more than a narrow isthmus, at points just 5km wide – but this place certainly pulls its weight. Not only does it hold half of the province's population, but it also houses four of the province's six seabird ecological reserves, one of its two wilderness reserves and 28 of its 41 national historic sites.

The landscape along the coastline's twisty roads is vintage fishing-village Newfoundland. Many visitors day trip to the peninsula's sights from St John's, which is easily doable, but there's something to be said for escaping the 'big city' and burrowing under the quilt at night in Brigus, Ferryland or Dildo (you read right).

Much of the East Coast Trail (p223) runs through the area; keep an eye out for free guided hikes. The ferry to Nova Scotia leaves from Argentia.

SOUTHEASTERN AVALON PENINSULA

This area, sometimes called the South Shore, is known for its wildlife, archaeology, boat and kayak tours and unrelenting fog. Scenic Rtes 10 and 90, aka the Irish Loop, lasso the region.

Witless Bay Ecological Reserve

This is a prime area for whale-, iceberg- and bird-watching, and several boat tours will take you to see them from the towns of **Bay Bulls** (31km south of St John's) and **Bauline East** (15km south of Bay Bulls). There is a **visitors center** (☎ 709-334-2609; Rte 10; ☻ 9am-7pm Jul & Aug, to 4pm mid-late Jun & Sep) in Foodland Plaza in Bay Bulls.

Four islands off Witless Bay and southward are preserved as the **Witless Bay Ecological Reserve** and represent one of the top seabird breeding areas in eastern North America. Every summer, more than a million pairs of birds gather here, including puffins, kittiwakes, storm petrels and the penguinlike murres. Tour boats sail to the islands, hugging the shore beneath sheer cliffs and giving you a shrieking earful as well as an eyeful.

The best months for trips are June and July, when the humpback and minke whales arrive to join the birds' capelin- (a type of fish) feeding frenzy. If you really hit the jackpot, in early summer an iceberg might be thrown in too.

Tours from Bay Bulls visit Gull Island, which has the highest concentration of birds. Tours from Bauline East head to nearby Great Island, home to the largest puffin colony. Bauline East is closer to the reserve, so less time is spent en route.

To no one's surprise, kayaking has also taken off in the area. You don't just see a whale in a kayak, you feel its presence.

You can't miss the boat tour and kayak operators – just look for signs off Rte 10. Reservations are suggested. The following are recommended tour companies, all operating from May through September:

Colbert's Seabird Tours (☎ 709-334-2098; Rte 10, Bauline East; 1hr tours adult/child 5-12yr $20/10) Several departures daily for the 10-minute ride to see puffins and whales.

Gatherall's (☎ 800-419-4253; www.gatheralls.com; Northside Rd, Bay Bulls; 1½hr tours adult/child 5-9yr/child 10-17yr $49/16/20.50) A fast, large catamaran gives you as much time at the reserve as O'Brien's. It's also more stable and a wise choice for people prone to seasickness.

O'Brien's (☎ 709-753-4850, 877-639-4253; www .obriensboattours.com; south side of Bay Bulls; 2hr tours adult/child 4-9yr/child 10-17yr $50/20/25) Several daily departures throughout the summer. A more expensive but exhilarating option is the two-hour tour in a high-speed Zodiac ($80). Three-hour guided kayak tours are $59, and there's a shuttle service from St John's ($20).

Ocean Adventure Tours (☎ 709-334-3998; www .oceanadventure.ca; Rte 10, Bauline East; 1hr tours adult/child 7-12yr $20/10) It's a 10-minute ride to the Great Island.

Stan Cooke Sea Kayaking (☎ 709-579-6353, 888-747-6353; www.wildnfld.ca; Harbour Rd, Cape Broyle; 4hr tours $69) Located further south near Ferryland, Stan offers great guided tours for beginners and advanced paddlers.

La Manche Provincial Park

Diverse bird life, along with beaver, moose and snowshoe hare, can be seen in this lush park only 53km south of St John's. A highlight is the 1.25km trail to the remains of La Manche, a fishing village that was destroyed in 1966 by a fierce winter storm. Upon arrival, you'll see the beautiful newly built suspension bridge dangling over the narrows – it's part of the East Coast Trail. The trail head is at the park's fire-exit road, past the main entrance.

There is excellent **camping** (☎ 709-685-1823; Rte 10; campsites $13, per vehicle $5; mid-May–mid-Sep), with many sites overlooking large La Manche Pond; the latter is good for swimming.

Ferryland

Ferryland, one of North America's earliest settlements, dates to 1621, when Sir George Calvert established the Colony of Avalon. A few Newfoundland winters later he was scurrying for warmer parts. He settled in Maryland and eventually became the first Lord Baltimore. Other English families arrived later and maintained the colony despite it being razed by the Dutch in 1673 and by the French in 1696.

The seaside surrounds of the **Colony of Avalon Archaeological Site** (☎ 709-432-3200; www.heritage .nf.ca/avalon; Rte 10; adult/child 5-14yr/family $8/5/20; 9am-7pm mid-Jun–early Sep, 10am-5pm mid-May–early Jun & mid-Sep–mid-Oct) only add to the rich atmosphere, where you'll see archaeologists unearthing everything from axes to bowls. The **visitors center** houses interpretive displays and many of the artifacts that have been recovered.

The village's former courthouse is now the small **Historic Ferryland Museum** (☎ 709-432-2711; Rte 10; adult/child under 12yr $2/1; 9am-5pm mid-Jun–early Sep). The towering hill behind the museum was where settlers would climb to watch for approaching warships or to escape the Dutch and French incursions. After seeing the view, you'll understand why the settlers named the hill 'the Gaze.'

Once a convent, **Downs Inn** (☎ 709-432-2808, 877-432-2808; acostello@nf.sympatico.ca; Rte 10; d with/without bathroom $75/65; mid-May–mid-Nov) has four rooms. A full breakfast is included, and everything is close by.

Fantastic **Lighthouse Picnics** (☎ 709-363-7456; www.lighthousepicnics.ca; Rte 10; picnic for 2 $40; 11:30am-6pm Tue-Sun Jun-Sep) has hit upon a novel concept: it provides a blanket and picnic meal (say, a curried chicken sandwich, mixed-green salad, and lemonade from a Mason jar) that visitors then wolf down while sitting in a field overlooking the ocean. It's located at Ferryland's old lighthouse, which you'll see as you enter town.

Avalon Wilderness Reserve

Dominating the interior of the region is the 1070-sq-km **Avalon Wilderness Reserve** (☎ 709-635-4520; www.env.gov.nl.ca/parks/wer/r_aw/; free permit required). Illegal hunting dropped the region's caribou population to around 100 in the 1980s. Twenty years later, there are countless thousands roaming the area. Permits for hiking and canoeing are available at La Manche Provincial Park (left).

Even if you don't trek into the wilds, you are still bound to see caribou along Rte 10 between Chance Cove Provincial Park and St Stevens. Seeing one of these impressive beasts is a treat rarely experienced by those not living in the far north of Canada, Russia or Finland.

Mistaken Point Ecological Reserve

This **ecological reserve** (☎ 709-438-1100; www.env .gov.nl.ca/parks/wer/r_mpe/), which Unesco has short-listed for world heritage site designation, protects 575-million-year-old multicelled marine fossils – the oldest in the world. The name comes from the blinding fog that blankets the area and has caused many ships to lose their way over the years. The reserve is reached by a 45-minute hike from the bumpy gravel road between Portugal Cove South (turn off Rte 10 from here) and **Cape Race**. It was the lighthouse keeper at Cape Race who received the fateful last message from the *Titanic*.

Along Route 90

The area from St Vincent's to St Mary's provides an excellent chance of seeing whales, particularly humpbacks, which feed close to shore. The best viewing is from **St Vincent's beach**. Halfway between the two villages is **Point La Haye Natural Scenic Attraction**, a dramatic arm of fine pebbles stretching across the mouth of St Mary's Bay – it's perfect for a walk.

   Salmonier Nature Park (☎ 709-229-7888; www .env.gov.nl.ca/snp; Rte 90; adult/child under 18yr $3.45/free; ☷ 10am-6pm Jun-early Sep, 10am-4pm Mon-Fri early Sep–Jun) rehabilitates injured and orphaned animals for release back into the wild. A 2.5km trail through the woods takes you past indigenous fauna and natural enclosures with moose, caribou and beaver. There's an **interpretive center** and touch displays for children. The park is on Rte 90, 12km south of the junction with Hwy 1.

CONCEPTION BAY

Fishing villages stretch endlessly along Conception Bay's scenic western shore, a mere 80km from St John's. Found among the bay's bright boats and fishing nets is Brigus, the regional highlight in all its English-y, rock-walled glory. For information on share taxis from the capital, see p228. The **regional tourism association** (☎ 709-596-3474; www.baccalieutourism .com) provides accommodation and hiking-trail information.

Brigus

Resting on the water and surrounded by rock bluffs is the heavenly village of Brigus (population 780). Its idyllic stone-walled streams meander slowly past old buildings and colorful gardens before emptying into the serene Harbour Pond. Famous American painter Rockwell Kent lived here during WWI, before his eccentric behavior got him deported on suspicion of spying for the Germans in 1915. The path toward his old cottage makes a great walk.

Captain Robert Bartlett, the town's most famous son, is renowned as one of the foremost arctic explorers of the 20th century. He made more than 20 arctic expeditions, including one in 1909, when he cleared a trail in the ice that enabled US commander Robert Peary to make his celebrated dash to the North Pole. Bartlett's house, **Hawthorne Cottage** (☎ 709-528-4004; www.pc.gc.ca/hawthornecottage; cnr Irishtown Rd & South St; adult/child 6-16yr/family $3.70/2.45/8.40; ☷ 9am-7pm Jul & Aug, to 5pm Wed-Sun mid-May–Jun & Sep–mid-Oct), is a national historic site and museum.

On the waterfront, below the church, is the **Brigus Tunnel**, which was cut through rock in 1860 so Robert Bartlett could easily access his ship in the deep cove on the other side.

In July and August, a **walking theater** (☎ 709-528-4817, 709-528-4004; ☷ 2:30pm Sun) presents Brigus' history with costumes, dancing and skits – a steal for $5. There are no advance sales.

A clean, comfortable and child-friendly farmhouse, **Brookdale Manor** (☎ 709-528-4544; www .bbcanada.com/5274.html; Farm Rd; s/d $55/65; ☷) sits

---

FAIRY LAND

Perhaps because of the province's Irish influence, fairies play a big role in local lore, especially around the Avalon Peninsula. The populace's superstition certainly helped local rum-runners back in the day. After getting their booze ashore, rum-runners would put burlap over their horses' hooves to quiet them and then cart the alcohol inland using lanterns to lead the way. Villagers would see lights floating in the distance but didn't hear anything – fairies, they thought, and stayed far away.

Some superstitions dictate that you take crackers with you – supposedly fairies won't spirit you away if you appease them with a crisp Saltine.

NEWFOUNDLAND & LABRADOR

just outside the village. The **Brittoner** (☎ 709-528-3412; www.bbcanada.com/4385.html; 12 Water St; r incl breakfast $60-70; ☺ May-Oct), an old-fashioned Victorian home, backs onto Harbour Pond. The loft is ideal for families.

Every perfect village needs a perfect eatery. At **North St Café** (☎ 709-528-1350; 29 North St; light meals $6-9; ☺ 11am-6pm May–mid-Oct), quiche, fish cakes, scones and afternoon tea are all on order.

Cupids

Cupids is the oldest English colony in Canada, settled in 1610. Visitors can take a 20-minute tour of the **archaeological dig site** (☎ 709-528-1344; www.baccalieudigs.ca; Seaforest Dr; adult/child 5-12yr $2/1; ☺ 9am-4:45pm, late Jul–mid-Oct). The **Cupids Museum** (☎ 709-528-3500; adult/child 5-12yr $2/1; ☺ 10am-5pm mid-Jun–mid-Oct) displays the artifacts uncovered.

Harbour Grace

A mixed crowd of historic figures has graced this harbor town (population 3400) over the past 500 years. Notables include the pirate Peter Easton and aviatrix Amelia Earhart. Learn about them at the redbrick customs house that is now the small **Conception Bay Museum** (☎ 709-596-5465; Water St; admission $3; ☺ 10am-5pm mid-Jun–early Sep). You can also visit the airstrip Amelia launched from in 1932 – **Harbour Grace Airfield** (☎ 709-596-5901; Earhart Rd) – when she became the first woman to cross the Atlantic solo.

It's hard to miss the large ship beached at the mouth of the harbor. This is the SS *Kyle* (1913), wrecked during a 1967 storm. Locals liked the look of it so much they actually paid to have it restored instead of removed.

North of Harbour Grace

The largest town north of Harbour Grace is Carbonear. Unfortunately, the most interesting thing about Carbonear itself is the remote island offshore. The windswept **Carbonear Island** has had a tumultuous history, with international battles, pirate intrigues and shipwrecks.

Clinging to cliffs at the northern end of the peninsula are the remote and striking villages of **Bay de Verde** and **Grates Cove**. Hundreds of 500-year-old rock walls line the hills around Grates Cove and have been declared a national historic site. Further offshore, in the distance, is the inaccessible **Baccalieu Island Ecological Reserve**, which is host to three million pairs of Leach's storm petrel – making this the largest such colony in the world.

TRINITY BAY

Thicker forests, fewer villages and subdued topography typify the shores of Trinity Bay and give the west coast of the peninsula a much more serene feeling than its eastern shore.

Heart's Content

The **Cable Station Provincial Historic Site** (☎ 709-583-2160; Rte 80; adult/child under 13yr $3/free; ☺ 10am-5:30pm late May-Sep) tells the story of the first permanent transatlantic cable that was laid here in 1866. The word 'permanent' is significant, because the first successful cable (connected in 1858 to Bull Arm, on Trinity Bay) failed shortly after Queen Victoria and US President James Buchanan christened the line with their congratulatory messages.

Dildo

Oh, go on – take the obligatory sign photo, and then we'll move on. For the record, no one knows definitively how the name came about; some say it's from the phallic shape of the bay.

Joking aside, Dildo is a lovely village and its shore is a good spot for whale-watching. Pothead (no joke) whales come in by the pod, and humpback whales can also be seen in summer. The **Dildo Interpretation Centre** (☎ 709-582-2687, 709-596-1906; Front Rd; adult/child $2/1; ☺ 10am-6pm Jul-Sep) has exhibits on the area's 19th-century codfish hatchery, as well as the ongoing Dorset Eskimo archaeological dig on Dildo Island.

Two flawlessly restored oceanside houses comprise **Inn by the Bay** (☎ 709-582-3170; www.innbythebaydildo.com; 78 Front Rd; d incl breakfast $80-150; ☺ May-Dec), the most luxurious spot to stay on the northern Avalon Peninsula. Within the Inn, the elegant **Veranda Sunroom** (mains $14-18), complete with commanding view, is open to guests for dinner.

CAPE SHORE

The ferry, French history and lots of birds fly forth from the Avalon Peninsula's southwesterly leg. Newhook's Transportation (p228) connects the towns of Argentia and Placentia to St John's.

Argentia

Argentia's main purpose is to play host to the **Marine Atlantic ferry** (☎ 800-341-7981; www .marine-atlantic.ca; adult/child 5-12yr $76/38, per car/ motorcycle $157/79) which connects Argentia with North Sydney in Nova Scotia – a 14-hour trip. It operates from mid-June to late September with three crossings per week. The boat leaves North Sydney at 6am Monday, 7am Wednesday and 3:30pm Friday. It returns from Argentia at 11:59pm Monday, 9am Thursday and 8:30am Saturday. Cabins (four-berth $138) are available. Vehicle fares do not include drivers.

A provincial **visitors center** (☎ 709-227-5272; Rte 100; ⏱ hrs vary to coincide with ferry sailings) is 3km from the ferry on Rte 100.

Placentia

In the early 1800s, Placentia (www.placentia .ca; population 4400) – then Plaisance – was the French capital of Newfoundland, and the French attacks on the British at St John's were based here. Near town, lording over the shores, is **Castle Hill National Historic Site** (☎ 709-227-2401; www.pc.gc.ca/castlehill; adult/child 6-16yr $3.95/1.95; ⏱ 10am-6pm mid-May–mid-Oct), where remains of French and British fortifications from the 17th and 18th centuries provide panoramic views over the town and the surrounding waters.

The fascinating **graveyard** next to the Anglican church holds the remains of people of every nationality who have settled here since the 1670s. The **O'Reilly House Museum** (☎ 709-227-5568; 48 Orcan Dr; admission $2; ⏱ 9am-8pm Mon-Fri, noon-8pm Sat & Sun mid-Jun–Aug), within a century-old Victorian home, gives you more of an inside look at the town and its past luxuries. Wander past the other notable buildings, including the **Roman Catholic church** and the **stone convent**. A boardwalk runs along the stone-skipper's delight of a beach.

The plain but central **Harold Hotel** (☎ 709-227-2107; Main St; r $69-89) is a decent lodging option. Its **restaurant** (meals $7-15) serves great pizza.

Cape St Mary's

At the southeastern tip of the peninsula is **St Mary's Ecological Reserve**, one of the most accessible bird colonies on the continent. Visit the **interpretive center** (☎ 709-277-1666; www.env.gov .nl.ca/parks/wer/r_csme/; adult/child 6-18yr/family $5/2/10; ⏱ 9am-5pm mid-May–mid-Oct, longer hours in summer) and snag a map for the 1.4km trail to Bird Rock, the third-largest gannet-nesting site in North America. Its near-vertical cliffs provide ideal nesting conditions for nearly 70,000 seabirds, including kittiwakes, murres and razorbills. Guides are here during summer.

EASTERN NEWFOUNDLAND

Two peninsulas grasp awkwardly out to sea and comprise the sliver that is Eastern Newfoundland. The beloved, well-touristed Bonavista Peninsula projects northward. Historic fishing villages freckle its shores, and windblown walking trails swipe its coast. The **Discovery Trail Tourism Association** (☎ 709-466-3845; www.thediscoverytrail.org/hikediscovery) has put together a hiking guidebook and maps for the area; several trails are less than 5km, and they go to a maximum of 17km.

While Clarenville is the Bonavista Peninsula's access point and service center, there's not much on offer besides a **visitors center** (☎ 709-466-3100; 379 Hwy 1; ⏱ 8am-8pm Jun-Aug, 9am-6pm mid-May–late May & Sep).

To the south juts the massive but less-traveled Burin Peninsula, another region of fishing villages; these towns struggle harder to find their way in the post-cod world. The ferry for France – yes, France, complete with wine, éclairs and brie – departs from Fortune and heads to the nearby French islands of St-Pierre and Miquelon (p237) – a regional highlight.

TRINITY

Let's set the record straight: Trinity is the Bonavista Peninsula's most popular stop, a historic town of crooked seaside lanes, storybook heritage houses and gardens with white picket fences. **Trinity Bight** (www.trinitybight .com) is the name given to the 12 communities in the vicinity, including Trinity, Port Rexton and New Bonaventure.

While Trinity is movie-set lovely, some visitors have complained its perfection is a bit boring. But if you like historic buildings and theater along with your scenery, this is definitely your place. It's a tiny town (population 250) and easily walkable.

First visited by Portuguese explorer Corte-Real in 1500 and established as a town in 1580, Trinity is one of the oldest settlements on the continent.

Information

Post office (☎ 709-464-2240; 1 Garland Rd)
RBC Royal Bank (☎ 709-464-2260; Rte 230)
Trinity Medical Clinic (☎ 709-464-3721) On the road out of town.

Sights & Activities

Historical site lovers can gorge on buildings scattered throughout the village. The six main venues have a combined **admission ticket** (adult/child under 12yr $7.50/free).

The **Trinity Historical Society** (☎ 709-464-3599; ☒ 10am-5:30pm mid-Jun–mid-Sep) runs three of the sites. The **Lester Garland House** (West St) was rebuilt to celebrate cultural links between Trinity and Dorset, England – major trading partners in the 17th, 18th and 19th centuries. The **Trinity Museum** (Church Rd) displays more than 2000 pieces, including North America's second-oldest fire wagon. The **Green Family Forge** (Church Rd) is an iron-tool-filled blacksmith museum.

The provincial government operates the other trio of **sites** (☎ 709-464-2042; ☒ 10am-5:30pm mid-Jun–mid-Oct), which include costumed interpreters: the **Lester Garland Premises** (West St) depicts an 1820s general store; the **Interpretation Centre** (West St) provides a comprehensive history of Trinity; and **Hiscock House** (Church Rd) is a restored merchant's home from 1910.

Further afield is **Fort Point**, where you'll find four cannons, the remains of the British fortification from 1745. There are 10 more British cannons in the water, all compliments of the French in 1762.

The **Skerwink Trail** (5km) is a fabulous loop that affords spectacular coastal vistas. It's accessible from the church in Trinity East, off Rte 230.

Tours

Atlantic Adventures (☎ 709-464-2133; www.atlantic adventures.com; 2½hr tours $42; ☒ Jun-Aug) Several conventional whale-watch tours leave daily from the wharf near the Dock Restaurant.

Ocean Contact (☎ 709-464-3269; www.oceancontact .com; Village Inn, Taverner's Path; 3hr tours adult/child under 13yr/child 13-15yr $70/45/55; ☒ mid-Jun–mid-Sep) Renowned scientist Dr Peter Beamish offers more than just whale-watching. His high-tech boat uses 'rhythm-based communication' to interact with whales. Seeing one jump on cue is as mind-boggling as it is exhilarating.

Trinity Walking Tours (☎ 709-464-3723; Clinch's Lane; adult/child $8/free; ☒ 10am Mon-Sat Jun-Aug) These entertaining and educational tours start behind Hiscock House.

Sleeping & Eating

There are numerous fine inns and B&Bs. Space gets tight in summer, so book ahead.

Village Inn (☎ 709-464-3269; www.oceancontact.com; Taverner's Path; r incl breakfast $70-90) This inn has classic country rooms with bright windows, antique furnishings and weathered floorboards. The dining room (mains $9 to $16; open breakfast, lunch and dinner) is open to non guests (after 9am) and makes great traditional meals along with partridgeberry pie and vegetarian options.

Eriksen Premises (☎ 709-464-3698, 877-464-3698; www.trinityexperience.com; West St; r incl breakfast $80-115; ☒ May-Oct) This Victorian home offers elegance in accommodations and dining (mains $13 to $22; open lunch and dinner). It also books two nearby B&Bs: Kelly's Landing (four rooms) and Bishop White Manor (nine rooms).

Artisan Inn & Campbell House B&B (☎ 709-464-3377, 877-464-7700; www.artisaninntrinity.com; High St; d $110-115, apt $135-230; ☒ May-Oct) Adjacent to each other and managed by the same group, these places are gorgeous. The three-room inn hovers over the sea on stilts; the flower-surrounded, three-room B&B also provides ocean vistas.

Dock Restaurant (☎ 709-464-2133; www.atlantic adventures.com; Dock Lane; mains $8-16; ☒ breakfast, lunch & dinner May-Oct) This scenic spot sits next to the wharf and prepares great chowder and seafood.

Entertainment

Rocky's Place Lounge (☎ 709-464-3400; High St) Fiddle and caller let loose at Rocky's Place on Wednesday at 10pm. Learn traditional dance, or relax and watch the show.

Alongside the Lester Garland Premises is the celebrated **Rising Tide Theatre** (☎ 888-464-3377; www.risingtidetheatre.com; Water St; matinee/evening tickets $13/17; ☒ Tue-Sun mid-Jun–mid-Oct), which hosts the 'Seasons in the Bight' theater festival and the **Trinity Pageant** (adult/child under 15yr $11/free; ☒ 2pm Wed, Sat & Sun), an entertaining outdoor drama on Trinity's history.

Getting There & Around

Trinity is 259km from St John's and is reached via Rte 230 off Hwy 1. **Shirran's Taxi** (☎ 709-468-7741; $35) makes the trip daily from St John's.

BONAVISTA

'O buona vista!' ('Oh, happy sight!'), shouted John Cabot upon spying the New World from his boat on June 24, 1497. Or so the story goes.

NEWFOUNDLAND & LABRADOR

From all descriptions, this pretty spot (population 4000) is where he first set foot in the Americas. Today Bonavista's shoreline, with its lighthouse, puffins and chasms, continues to rouse visitors.

Information

Bonavista Community Health Centre (☎ 709-468-7881; Hospital Rd)

Post office (☎ 866-607-6301; 28 Church St)

Scotiabank (☎ 709-468-1070; 1 Church St)

Sights & Activities

Cape Bonavista Lighthouse (☎ 709-468-7444; Rte 230; adult/child under 13yr $3/free; ☼ 10am-5:30pm mid-Jun–Oct) is a brilliant red-and-white-striped lighthouse dating from 1843. The interior has been restored to the 1870s and is now a provincial historic site. A **puffin colony** lives just offshore; the birds put on quite a show around sunset.

At **Dungeon Park** (Cape Shore Rd, off Rte 230; admission free), you can stare out to distant sea stacks and watch thunderous waves roll through and slam the coast. Nowhere is the power of water more evident than at the Dungeon, a deep chasm 250m in circumference that was created by the collapse of two sea caves.

Ryan Premises National Historic Site (☎ 709-468-1600; www.pc.gc.ca/ryanpremises; Ryans Hill Rd; adult/child 6-16yr $3.95/1.95; ☼ 10am-6pm mid-May–late Oct) is a restored 19th-century saltfish mercantile complex. The slew of white clapboard buildings honors five centuries of fishing in Newfoundland via multimedia displays and interpretive programs.

An impressive full-scale replica of the ship on which Cabot sailed into Bonavista is at **Ye Matthew Legacy** (☎ 709-468-1493; www.matthewlegacy.com; Roper St; adult/child 6-16yr/family $6.50/2.25/15.75; ☼ 10am-6pm, to 9pm Fri mid-May–Sep). The interpretation center provides details on the amazing vessel and voyage.

Outside town near **Maberly** on Rte 238, there's an offshore island where thousands of puffins, kittiwakes and murres roost. A gorgeous 17km coastal hiking trail runs between Maberly and Little Catalina (part of the Discovery Trail; see p233).

Sleeping & Eating

The town website (www.bonavista.net) provides further lodging options. Minimal best describes the dining scene.

White's B&B (☎ 709-468-7018; www.bbcanada.com/3821.htm; 21 Windlass Dr; r $50-60; 🖳) Low-key White's

has three rooms to choose from, all with either private or en-suite bathroom. Enjoy the bike rentals, barbecue use and ocean view.

Harbourview B&B (☎ 709-468-2572; 21 Ryans Hill Rd; r $60; ☼ May-Oct) The name doesn't lie: you get a sweet view at this simple, four-room B&B. Two rooms share a bathroom.

Cabot's Loft B&B (☎ 709-468-1855; www.cabotsloft.net; 19 Ryans Hill Rd; r $105-135) Owned by the local cop, Cabot's offers two cushy rooms with lots of elbow room, hardwood floors and yep, good sea views. There's also a self-contained unit with full kitchen and laundry facilities.

Marsh's Snack Bar (☎ 709-468-2639; Rte 230; snacks $5-9; ☼ 10am-1am) Marsh's serves fish-and-chips and other snacks out by the lighthouse.

Getting There & Around

Bonavista is a scenic 50km drive north of Trinity along Rte 230. **Shirran's** (☎ 709-468-7741; $40) drives up daily from St John's.

BURIN PENINSULA

It's not exactly lively on the Burin Peninsula, as the crapped-out fishing economy has made its presence felt. Still, the coastal walks inspire, and the region is a low-key place to spend a day or two before embarking toward the baguettes of France (p237).

Information & Orientation

Although Marystown (population 5900) is the largest town on the peninsula, there's not much to see besides the **visitors center** (☎ 709-279-1887; www.theheritagerun.com; Rte 210; ☼ 9am-9pm mid-Jun–early Sep, 9am-4:30pm Mon-Fri early Sep–mid-Jun).

Burin (population 2470) is the most attractive town on the peninsula, and has a gorgeous elevated boardwalk over the waters of its rocky shoreline. **St Lawrence** (population 1550) is known for fluorite mining and scenic coastal hikes. In **Grand Bank** (population 2840), there's an interesting self-guided walk through the historic buildings and waterfront; each summer it's home to an entertaining theater festival. Just south is **Fortune** (population 1600), the jump-off point for St-Pierre.

Sights

The huge sail-like structure thrusting into the air marks the **Provincial Seamen's Museum** (☎ 709-832-1484; www.therooms.ca; Marine Dr, Grand Bank; adult/child $2.50/free; ☼ 9am-5pm May–mid-Oct). It deserves a visit. It depicts both the era of

NEWFOUNDLAND & LABRADOR

GONE FISHIN': NEWFOUNDLAND'S COD MORATORIUM

For hundreds of years, Newfoundland's waters – especially the Grand Banks (p45) to the south and east – were known as a place where you could dip your bucket and then hoist it back up filled with fat, slippery codfish. The English, French, Spanish and others all sailed over to cast their lines. Right up through the late 20th century, codfishing was the province's primary industry.

That all changed in 1992, the year the government imposed the codfishing moratorium. Fish stocks had been declining over the years, and the government decided to take action. With the swipe of a pen, codfishing was made illegal within a 320km radius of provincial shores. Twenty thousand fishermen and plant workers were out of work overnight in what has been called the largest layoff in Canadian history.

It was to be a temporary measure at first, but the hoped-for cod rebound never happened. Well over a decade later, scientists warn that stocks remain critically low and could take decades to come back. Fisherfolk say that while it may be true, they are being unfairly penalized. Just outside the 320km no-fishing zone, they reason, big trawlers from other countries continue to scoop up cod, and that's why stock numbers remain depleted.

Whether the moratorium is right or wrong, the impact on the local way of life has been staggering. Families who fished for generations have had to scramble to find new livelihoods. Many end up leaving the province to get work, fostering a trend known as 'outmigration.'

Alberta exerts the biggest pull, particularly the oilsands industry in Fort McMurray. Just about every Newfoundlander has a family member or friend who's headed west for at least part of the year to earn big bucks driving trucks for the booming mine companies. Although the money is good, the lifestyle prompts a new set of problems: families are split, drugs are prevalent, and money that's easily come by is also easily spent.

While many locals have left the province – regions round St Anthony, Stephenville and the Burin Peninsula have seen their populations drop by more than 20% since 1992 – others have found resourceful ways to stay put. A group of former fishermen in Burgeo started a successful tomato greenhouse and now sell their wares to provincial grocery stores. Some communities have converted their boats and fish plants to process crab and shrimp instead of cod. Newfoundland also is developing its own oil industry offshore from St John's. Finally, many communities are generating jobs by turning to tourism, an industry that was practically nonexistent prior to the moratorium.

the banking schooner and the changes in the fishery over the years. Kids will adore the model sailing ships.

Burin Heritage Museum (☎ 709-891-2217; Seaview Dr, Burin; admission free; ☽ 8:30am-5pm May-Oct, closed weekends Sep & Oct) has displays in two historical homes telling of life's highs and lows in remote outports.

Just 4km from Fortune, **Fortune Head Ecological Reserve** (off Rte 220; admission free; ☽ 24hr) protects fossils dating from the planet's most important period of evolution, when life on earth progressed from simple organisms to complex animals. It happened some 550 million years ago, at the juncture of the Precambrian and Cambrian eras. A guide is on site from 8am to 4pm and can explain it all in greater detail. Or visit the **interpretive center** (☎ 709-832-2810; adult/child 2-12yr $5/3; ☽ 7am-8pm, to 9pm Wed) in town by the St-Pierre ferry dock.

Activities

The Burin Peninsula offers good **hikes** due to its varied coastline. Ask at the Burin Heritage Museum about locating the **Cook's Lookout** trailhead. It's a 20-minute walk from town to the panoramic view. Off Pollux Cr in St Lawrence, the rugged, breath-draining **Cape Trail** (4km) and **Chamber Cove Trail** (4km) shadow the cliff edges and offer amazing vistas down to rocky shores and some famous WWII shipwrecks. Another good (and easier) trail is the **Marine Hike** (7km) that traces Admiral's Beach near Grand Bank. It leaves from Christian's Rd off Rte 220.

Sleeping & Eating

Eating and sleeping options are spread thinly. For those heading to St-Pierre, Grand Bank and Fortune are the best bases (Grand Bank is nicer but further, at 8km from the ferry dock).

Sound of the Sea B&B (☎ 709-891-2115, 866-891-2115; www.soundofthesea.com; 16A Seaview Dr, Burin; d $60-70) This old merchant's home overlooks the harbor and is only steps away from the town's beautiful boardwalk. The loft with a pullout sofa is perfect for families.

Fortune Inn B&B (☎ 709-832-1774, 888-275-1098; 89 Bayview St, Fortune; s/d with shared bathroom $71/77; ☯ May-Oct) Antiques, shmantiques – who needs 'em? The nine rooms in this ex–apartment building are cheaply furnished (linoleum floors, drab colors), but they're clean and functional and, most importantly, they're only a 750m walk to the St-Pierre ferry.

Inn by the Sea B&B (☎ 709-832-0202, 888-932-0202; www.theinnbythesea.com; 22 Blackburn Rd, Grand Bank; s/d $79/89; ☯ Jun–mid-Oct; 🖳) Each of the four rooms has a plump queen-sized bed, private bathroom and desk with laptop hookup.

Sharon's Nook & the Tea Room (☎ 709-832-0618; Water St, Grand Bank; meals $5-9; ☯ 7:30am-9pm Mon-Sat, 11am-7:30pm Sun) This countrified eatery serves up lasagna, chili, sandwiches and heavenly cheesecake.

Getting There & Around

The Burin Peninsula is accessed via Rte 210 off Hwy 1. The drive from St John's to Grand Bank is 359km and takes just over four hours. **Foote's Taxi** (☎ 709-832-0491, 800-866-1181) travels from St John's down the peninsula as far as Fortune ($40, five hours).

ST-PIERRE & MIQUELON

Twenty-five kilometers offshore from the Burin Peninsula floats a little piece of France. The islands of St-Pierre and Miquelon aren't just Frenchlike with their berets, baguettes and Bordeaux, they *are* France, governed by and financed by the *tricolore*.

Citizens here take their national pride very seriously – some even feel it's their duty to maintain France's foothold in the New World. Locals kiss their hellos and pay in euros, while pastry shops waft sweet smells from every corner. French cars – Peugeots, Renaults and Citroens – crowd the tiny one-way streets. It's an eye-rubbing world away from Newfoundland's nearby fishing communities.

St-Pierre is the more populated and developed island, with most of its 5600 residents living in the town of St-Pierre. Miquelon is larger geographically but has only 700 residents.

The fog-mantled archipelago has a 20th-century history as colorful as its canary, lime and lavender houses (see boxed text, p238). Going further back: Jacques Cartier claimed the islands for France in 1536, after they were discovered by the Portuguese in 1520. At the end of the Seven Years' War in 1763, the islands were turned over to Britain, only to be given back to France in 1816. And French they've remained ever since.

ORIENTATION & INFORMATION

While French is widely spoken, many people are bilingual. Canadian visitors need only official photo identification and a birth certificate, while EU citizens and Americans need passports. Other nationalities should confirm with their French embassy if a visa is needed prior to arrival.

Note that time on the islands is half an hour ahead of Newfoundland Time. Calling the islands is an international call, meaning you must dial ☎ 011 in front of the local number. The only calling cards that work on the islands are ones bought there. You'll also need a round plug 220V electrical adapter.

Merchants gladly accept the loonie, though they return change in euros. If you're staying for a while, it's probably easiest to get euros from the local ATMs. Prices are quoted in euros (€) and things are generally more expensive than in Newfoundland. Alcohol is the exception, but daytrippers take heed: you are not allowed to return to Canada with booze unless you pay duties on it. To merit the duty-free waiver, you must stay on the islands at least 48 hours.

Almost all shops and business close between noon and 1:30pm. Some stores are also closed on Saturday afternoons, and most are closed on Sunday.

The **visitors center** (☎ off the islands 508-410-200; www.st-pierre-et-miquelon.info; place du Général de Gaulle; ☯ 7:30am-6pm Jun-Sep, 8:30am-noon & 1:30-5:30pm Mon-Fri Oct-May) provides a great St-Pierre town map showing all banks, restaurants etc. Staff can also provide information and bookings for tours, which are the best way to see the islands. Much can also be seen on foot.

SIGHTS & ACTIVITIES

In St-Pierre, the best thing to do is just walk around and soak it up – when you're not eating, that is. Pop into stores and sample goods

---

ST-PIERRE'S BOOZY BACKSTORY

When Prohibition dried out the USA's kegs in the 1920s, Al Capone decided to slake his thirst – and that of the nation – by setting up shop in St-Pierre.

He and his mates transformed the sleepy fishing harbor into a booming port crowded with imported-booze-filled warehouses. Bottles were removed from their crates, placed in smaller carrying sacks and taken secretly to the US coast by rumrunners. The piles of Cutty Sark whiskey crates were so high on the docks, clever locals used the wood both to build and heat houses. At least one house remains today and is known as the 'Cutty Sark cottage'; most tours drive by.

St-Pierre still imports enough alcohol to pickle each and every citizen a few times over. It remains legendary to Newfoundland mainlanders as the home of cheap alcohol, including a type of grain alcohol that reputedly cleans engines or can be mixed with water to create a local moonshine. Not surprisingly, it is illegal in Canada.

---

you'd usually have to cross an ocean for. Despite meticulous research involving scores of chocolate éclairs, croissants and gateaux, there is no clear winner on the best pastry shop. You'll have to conduct your own tests.

While pastries are important, allow enough time for the magical **Île aux Marins** (3hr tours adult/child €16/12; 9am & 2pm May-Sep), a beautiful abandoned village out in the harbor. A bilingual guide will walk you through colorful homes, a small schoolhouse museum and the grand church (1874) that make up this island museum. For details on this and the many other island-spanning tours, check with the visitors center.

Hotel/Motel Robert (508-412-419; admission free; 10/12 rue du 11 Novembre) has a small lobby museum with a collection of rum-running artifacts, including Al Capone's straw hat. The **cemetery** (ave Commandant Roger Birot) with its above-ground mausoleums is interesting to wander through.

Miquelon, 45km away, is less visited and less developed. The village of **Miquelon**, centered on the church, is at the northern tip of the island. From nearby **l'Étang de Mirande** a walking trail leads to a lookout and waterfall. From the bridge in town, a scenic 25km road leads across the isthmus to the wild and uninhabited island of **Langlade**. There are some wild horses and smaller animals such as rabbits, and around the rocky coast and lagoons you'll see seals and birds.

FESTIVALS & EVENTS

From mid-July to the end of August, folk dances are often held in St-Pierre's square.
Bastille Day (July 14) The largest holiday of the year.
Basque Festival (mid-August) A weeklong festival with music, marching and invigorating street fun.

SLEEPING & EATING

There are just over a dozen accommodations on St-Pierre and Miquelon. Hotels are more expensive than the inns (auberges). Book ahead in summer. Not surprisingly, there is a profusion of great eateries – indulge.

Chez Hélène B&B (508-413-108; 15 rue Beaussant, St-Pierre; r with shared bathroom €45) This is the brightest of choices, near all the action, with rooms overlooking the harbor. Room No 6 has a wee balcony for taking everything in.

Auberge Quatre Temps B&B (508-414-301; www.quatretemps.com; 14 rue Dutemple, St-Pierre; s/d with private bathroom €48/56;) Let's start by saying there's a bar inside and it's open all day. There's also bike rental, wireless Internet, a restaurant and fine terrace. The hitch is it's a 15-minute walk from the ferry dock, but it's worth it.

Maxotel (508-416-457; girmaxro@cheznoo.net; 42 rue Sourdeval, Miquelon; s/d €54/61) The simple two-bedroom apartments that can sleep up to four people (€86) have kitchens and sit near the sea. It's a 10-minute walk from the wharf.

Hotel Île de France (508-410-350; www.hotelile defrance.net; 6 rue Maître Georges Lefèvre, St-Pierre; s €80, d €88-96) Spacious and simple rooms fill this centrally located hotel; breakfast is included. It's home to a smart, colorful restaurant (mains €8 to €17; open noon to 2pm and 7pm to 10:30pm) serving traditional French fare, wine and pizzas. The lunch specials (€10) are a delicious bargain.

Le Maringouin'fre (508-413-679; 22 rue du Général Leclerc, St-Pierre; meals €5-8; 11am-10:15pm, closed Mon) This is the perfect place for a cheaper meal or fantastic crepes.

Le Cabestan (508-412-100; 1bis rue Marcel Bonin; mains €17-27; noon-2pm & 7-9pm) The traditional Basque meals using hot peppers are superb. Cool down afterward with the crème brûlée.

NEWFOUNDLAND & LABRADOR

GETTING THERE & AWAY

Air

Air Saint-Pierre (☎ 508-410-000, 877-277-7765; www .airsaintpierre.com) flies to St John's ($144), Montréal ($544) and Halifax ($271). There are two to three flights weekly to each city.

Boat

From Fortune on Newfoundland, **St-Pierre Tours** (☎ 709-832-0429, 800-563-2006; www.spmexpress .net; 5 Bayview St, Fortune) operates two ferries to St-Pierre. From July to early September, the MV *Atlantic Jet* (adult/child two to 11 years $93.50/46.75 round-trip, one hour) departs at 2:45pm. It returns from St-Pierre at 1:30pm. The smaller MV *Arethusa* (same price; 1½ hours) makes the journey Monday to Saturday, leaving Fortune at 7:30am and returning from St-Pierre at 2:45pm, thus making a day trip possible. The ferries also run on a reduced schedule from late April through June and September to mid-October; call for times. The boats carry foot passengers only. Leave your car in the parking lot by the ferry (per day $6).

GETTING AROUND

The MV *Atlantic Jet* also serves Miquelon (adult/child €19.50/9.50 round-trip, one hour) from St-Pierre on Tuesday, Friday and Sunday. Other ferries ply the route to Langlade (adult/child €15/7.50 round-trip) and Île aux Marins (adult/child €3/2.30 round-trip) every day.

Locamat Testeur (☎ 508-413-030; 10 rue Richerie) rents bicycles (per half-/full day €10/13.50) and scooters (per half-/full day €24/34).

CENTRAL NEWFOUNDLAND

Central Newfoundland elicits fewer wows per square kilometer than the rest of the province, but that's because huge chunks of the region are pure bog-land and trees. The islands of Notre Dame Bay – particularly Twillingate, when icebergs glide by – are exceptional exceptions.

TERRA NOVA NATIONAL PARK

Backed by lakes, bogs and hilly woods, and fronted by the salty waters of Clode and Newman Sounds, **Terra Nova National Park** (☎ 709-533-2801; www.pc.gc.ca/terranova; Hwy 1; adult/child 6-16yr/family per day $5.45/2.70/13.60) is spliced by the Trans-Canada Hwy (Hwy 1) running through its interior. It's not nearly as dramatic as the province's other national park (see Gros Morne, p244), though it does offer moose, bear, beaver and bald eagles, as well as relaxed hiking, paddling, camping and boat tours.

Information

Visitor Information Marine Centre (☎ 709-533-2942; Hwy 1; ⊙ 9am-8pm late Jun-Aug, 10am-5pm mid-May–mid-June & Sep–mid-Oct) Oodles of park information and interesting displays; 1km off Hwy 1 at Salton's Day-Use Area, 80km east of Gander.

Sights & Activities

The **Marine Centre's** aquariums, underwater cameras and touch tanks let you explore the ocean's secrets.

Terra Nova's 14 hiking trails total almost 100km; pick up maps at the visitors center. Highly recommended is the **Malady Head Trail** (5km), which climaxes at the edge of a headland cliff offering stunning views of Southwest Arm and Broad Cove. **Sandy Pond Trail** (3km) is an easy loop around the pond – your best place to spot a beaver.

The epic **Outport Loop** (55km) provides access to backcountry campgrounds. The loop in its entirety is rewarding, but be warned: parts are unmarked, not to mention mucky. A compass, a topographical map and ranger advice are prerequisites for this serious route.

There are **canoe rentals** (☎ 709-677-2221; fees vary; ⊙ 10am-6pm mid-Jun–early Sep) at Sandy Pond, where you can also swim. Inquire about the **Sandy Pond-Dunphy's Canoe Route** (10km), a great paddle with only one small portage.

Sea kayaking has taken off in the park, thanks to its 200km shoreline. Terra Nova Adventures (see below) offers **kayak rentals** (per day single/double kayak $45/55). At Burnside, 15km from the park's western gate, boats (see below) leave for the **Beothuk archaeological sites**, Bloody Reach and Beaches. Also in the region is **Salvage**, a photographer's-dream fishing village with well-marked walking trails. It's near the park's north end on Rte 310, about 26km from Hwy 1.

Tours

Burnside Heritage Foundation (☎ 709-677-2474; www.burnsideheritage.ca; 4½hr tours $35; ⊙ mid-Jun–Sep) Fascinating boat tours to the famous archaeological remains of the extinct Beothuk tribe. While waiting for the boat, you can visit the field laboratory and museum ($2), open from 9am to 8pm.

Ocean Watch Tours (☎ 709-533-6024; www3.nf
.sympatico.ca/oceanwatch; ☻ mid-May–Oct) Three-hour
research trips (adult/child under 13yr $45/22.50) Allows
you special interaction with the wildlife, including whales
and – hold on – plankton! Tours leave at 9am from behind
the Marine Centre. The two-hour fjord tour ($35/17.50) is
less science, more fun; it leaves at 1pm and 4pm.

Terra Nova Adventures (☎ 709-533-9797, 888-533-
8687; www.theoutfitters.nf.ca; ☻ May–early Sep) Next to
Ocean Watch, popular 2½-hour kayak tours (adult/youth
$50/35) leave at 10am and 1:30pm. There are also seven-
hour coastal tours ($119/95) and do-it-yourself rentals.
All tours are subject to demand.

Sleeping

Camping is the only option within the park
itself. For those with aspirations of a bed, the
town of Eastport has B&Bs; it's near the park's
north end on Rte 310, about 16km from Hwy
1. For camping reservations (recommended
on summer weekends), call or go online to
Parks Canada (☎ 905-426-4648, 877-737-3783; www.pc
camping.ca; reservation fee $10.90).

Malady Head Campground (campsites $14-17)
Located at the park's northern end, Malady
Head is fairly basic (though it has showers)
and quiet.

Newman Sound Campground (campsites $17-26)
This is the park's main (noisier) campground,
with a grocery store, Laundromat and bicycle
rentals.

Backcountry camping (free permit required; campsites
per day/season $9/62) There are eight backcountry
sites: half of them sit along Newman Sound's
southern shore and are reached by paddling,
hiking, water taxi or Ocean Watch Tours;
the other half are inland and accessed by
canoe.

Doctor's Inn B&B (☎ 709-677-3539; www.doctors-inn
.nf.ca; 5 Burden's Rd, Eastport; r $70-95; ☻ May-Oct; ☒)
Yes, there really is a doctor in this big old
rambling house, as well as a flowery patio,
gazebo and five fine rooms featuring private
bathrooms.

GANDER

Gander (population 9600) sprawls across
the juncture of Hwy 1 and Rte 330, which
leads to Notre Dame Bay. It is a convenient
stopping point, but doesn't have much else
to offer.

Gander essentially germinated from its
airport. The site was chosen by the British in
the 1930s because of its proximity to Europe
and its fogless weather. Most recently, Gander gained attention for its hospitality to the
thousands whose planes were rerouted here
after the September 2001 terrorist attacks in
the USA.

There is a **visitors center** (☎ 709-256-7110; www
.gandercanada.com; ☻ 8:30am-8pm mid-Jun–Sep, 8:30am-
5pm Mon-Fri Oct–mid-Jun) on Hwy 1 at the central
exit into town.

For aviation fanatics, the **North Atlantic Aviation Museum** (☎ 709-256-2923; www.naam.ca; Hwy 1;
adult/child 6-15yr $4/3; ☻ 9am-9pm late Jun-early Sep,
9am-5pm Mon-Fri early Sep-late Jun) has exhibits detailing Newfoundland's air contributions to
WWII and the history of navigation. Just east
on Hwy 1 is the sobering **Silent Witness Monument**, a tribute to 248 US soldiers whose plane
crashed here in December 1985.

Sinbad's Hotel & Suites (☎ 709-651-2678; www
.steelehotels.com; Bennett Dr; s/d $83/94) has clean,
comfortable hotel rooms within the center
of Gander. For meals, make it **Giovanni's Café**
(☎ 709-651-3535; 71 Elizabeth Dr; light meals $5-9; ☻ 7am-
10pm Mon-Fri, 8:30am-10pm Sat, 11am-4pm Sun), with
coffee, wraps, sandwiches and salads.

DRL Coachlines (☎ 709-263-2171; www.drlgroup
.com) has its stop at the **airport** (☎ 709-651-3434)
Buses leave for St John's ($50, 5¼ hours) at
5:02pm and Port aux Basques ($75, 8¼ hours)
at 12:48pm.

TWILLINGATE ISLAND &
NEW WORLD ISLAND

This area of Notre Dame Bay gets the most
attention, and deservedly so. Twillingate
(which actually consists of two barely separated islands, North and South Twillingate;
combined population 3500) sits just north of
New World Island. The islands are reached
from the mainland via an amalgamation of
short causeways. It's stunningly beautiful,
with every turn of the road revealing new
ocean vistas, colorful fishing wharves or
tidy groups of pastel houses hovering on
cliffs and outcrops. An influx of whales and
icebergs every summer only adds to the appealing mix.

Information

Twillingate website (www.twillingate.net) Good
resource with accommodation, attraction and tour
information.

Visitors center (☎ 709-628-7454; Rte 340;
☻ 8:30am-8:30pm Jun-Sep, to 4:30pm Mon-Fri Oct)
Located in Newville, on New World Island, it has maps and
information on trails and walks.

Sights & Activities

Without a doubt, your first stop on Twillingate Island should be **Prime Berth** (☎ 709-884-2485; www.twillingatetourism.com; Walter Elliott Causeway; admission $5; ⏰ 10am-5pm Jun–mid-Sep). Run by an engaging fisherman, this private fishing museum, with its imaginative and deceivingly simple concepts, is brilliant, and fun for scholars and school kids alike.

The **Long Point Lighthouse** (☎ 709-884-2247; admission free; ⏰ hours vary) provides dramatic views of the coastal cliffs. Travel up the winding steps, worn from lighthouse-keepers' footsteps since 1876, and gawk at the 360-degree view. This is an ideal vantage point for spotting icebergs in May and June.

The town of Twillingate's **museum** (☎ 709-884-2825; www.tmacs.ca; off Main St; admission $1; ⏰ 9am-8pm Jul & Aug, to 8pm early May-Jun & Sep–mid-Oct) is housed in a former Anglican rectory and tells the history of the island since the first British settlers arrived in the mid-1700s. It also displays articles brought back from around the world by local sea captains. Another room delves into the seal hunt and its controversy. There's a historic **church** next door.

In **Little Harbour**, en route to the town of Twillingate, a short trail leads to the secluded and picturesque **Jone's Cove**. Toward Durrell, the **Iceberg Shop** (☎ 709-884-2242; Main St; admission free; ⏰ 9am-9pm May-Sep), with its iceberg interpretation center, ice-cream and gregarious owner, is worth a peek.

Don't neglect a tour of the exceptionally scenic **Durrell** and its **museum** (☎ 709-884-2780; adult/child $2/1; ⏰ 9am-8pm Jul & Aug, to 5pm Jun & Sep), dwelling atop Old Maid Hill. Bring your lunch; there are a couple of picnic tables and a spectacular view.

On New World Island, **Dildo Run Provincial Park** (☎ 709-635-4520; Rte 340, Virgin Arm; campsites $13, per vehicle $5; ⏰ Jun–mid-Sep) has fine picnicking and camping set in a wooded area by a bay. Due to currents, swimming is not recommended.

Tours

Fun two-hour tours (per adult/child $35/20) to view icebergs and whales depart daily from mid-May to early September.

Twillingate Adventure Tours (☎ 709-884-5999; www.daybreaktours.com; off Main St) Departure from Twillingate's wharf.

Twillingate Island Boat Tours (☎ 709-884-2242; www.icebergtours.ca; Main St) Departure from the Iceberg Shop.

Festivals & Events

Fish, Fun & Folk Festival (www.fishfunfolkfestival .com) Traditional music and dance, some of which goes back to the 16th century, merrily take over Twillingate in late July.

Sleeping

Despite having about a dozen accommodation options, Twillingate gets very busy in the summer. Book early.

Captain's Legacy B&B (☎ 709-884-5648; www.captainslegacy.com; Hart's Cove; r $75-95; ⏰ mid-May–Oct) A real captain name Peter Troake once owned this historic 'outport mansion,' now a gracious four-room B&B overlooking the harbor.

Paradise B&B (☎ 709-884-5683, 877-882-1999; www .bbcanada.com/8246.html; 192 Main St; r $80-89; ⏰ mid-May–Sep) Set on a bluff overlooking Twillingate's harbor, Paradise offers the best view in town. You can wander down to the beach below, or relax on a lawn chair and soak it all up. Oh, the three rooms are comfy too. Angle for room No 1.

Harbour Lights Inn B&B (☎ 709-884-2763; www .harbourlightsinn.com; 189 Main St; d $109-139; ⏰ May–mid-Oct; ☐) South African hospitality greets you in this historical and popular nine-bedroom home. It's located right on the harbor and has amenities such as TVs, Jacuzzis and wi-fi access.

Eating & Entertainment

R&J Restaurant (☎ 709-884-2212; 110 Main St; meals $8-13; ⏰ 8am-11pm) Sink your teeth into fish 'n' brewis, shrimp, scallops or battered fish. Pizzas and burgers are also available.

All Around the Circle Dinner Theatre (☎ 709-884-5423; Crow Head; adult/child under 13yr $27/13.50; ⏰ 7pm Mon-Sat Jun–mid-Sep) Six of Newfoundland's best not only cook you a traditional meal, they also leave you in stitches with their talented performances. It's just south of the Long Point Lighthouse.

Getting There & Away

From the mainland, Rte 340's causeways almost imperceptibly connect Chapel Island, tiny Strong's Island, New World Island and Twillingate Island.

FOGO ISLAND & CHANGE ISLANDS

Fogo Island (☎ 709-266-2237; www.town-fogo.ca) is larger (population 560), but the neighboring **Change Islands** (☎ 709-621-4181; www.changeislands .ca) have just as much character.

ROUND OR FLAT?

Despite Columbus' stellar work in 1492 (when he sailed the ocean blue without falling off the earth's edge), and despite modern satellite photos that confirm his findings of a rounded orb, the folks at the Flat Earth Society aren't buying it. A spinning, spherical world hurtling through space would only lead to our planet's inhabitants living a confused and disorientated life, they say.

In 'reality,' the stable and calming flat earth is said to have five striking corners: Lake Mikhayl in Tunguska (Siberia); Easter Island; Lhasa (Tibet); the South Pacific island of Ponape; and Brimstone Head on Fogo Island, right here in Newfoundland. So climb up the craggy spine of Brimstone Head, stare off the abyss to earth's distant edge and judge for yourself if the earth is round or flat. If nothing else, you're guaranteed a stunning view of Iceberg Alley.

Sights & Activities

Settled in the 1680s, Fogo Island is an intriguing and rugged place to poke around. Backed by rocky hills, the village of **Joe Batt's Arm** is a flashback to centuries past.

Nearby is **Tilting**, perhaps the most engaging village on the island. The Irish roots run deep here and so do the accents. The inland harbor is surrounded by picturesque fishing stages and flakes, held above the incoming tides by weary stilts. There's also the great coastal **Turpin's Trail** (9km) that leaves from Tilting, near the beach at **Sandy Cove**.

On the opposite end of the island is the village of **Fogo** and the indomitable **Brimstone Head** (see boxed text, above). After you take in the mystical rock's view, do another great hike in town: the **Lion's Den Trail** (5km), which visits a Marconi radio site. Keep an eye out for the small group of caribou that roam the island.

The popular **Brimstone Head Folk Festival** (☎ 709-266-2218) takes place in mid-August.

The Change Islands are home to the **Newfoundland Pony Refuge** (☎ 709-621-4400; 12 Bowns Rd; admission free; ⏰ 8am-8pm Jun-Sep, by appointment rest of year), established to increase numbers of the native, endangered Newfoundland Pony. Only 88 registered beasts of breeding age remain in the province, and this is the largest herd. The small creatures are renowned as hardy workers (especially in winter) with gentle temperaments.

Sleeping

Peg's B&B (☎ 709-266-2392; www.bbcanada.com/7887 .html; 60 Main St, Fogo; s $65, d $70-75; ⏰ May-Nov) Right in the heart of Fogo village, this bright four-room place offers up a friendly atmosphere and harbor views.

Foley's Place B&B (☎ 709-658-7288, 866-658-7244; www.foleysplace.ca; 10A Kelley's Island Rd, Tilting; r $75; 🖥) The four rooms in this traditional, 100-year-old home are brightly colored, modernly furnished and have en-suite bathrooms.

Getting There & Away

Route 335 takes you to the town of Farewell, where the ferry sails to the Change Islands (20 minutes) and then onward to Fogo (45 minutes). Four boats leave between 9am and 8:30pm. Schedules vary, so check with **Provincial Ferry Services** (☎ 709-621-3150, 709-627-3448; www.gov.nl.ca/ferryservices). The round-trip fare to Fogo is $20.25 for car and driver, and $7.50 for additional passengers. It's about $3 less to the Change Islands.

LEWISPORTE

Stretched out Lewisporte (population 3300), known primarily for its ferry terminal, is the largest town on Notre Dame Bay. Other than the boat to Labrador, there really isn't much reason to visit – though as a distribution center it does have all the goods and services.

The simple **Brittany Inns** (☎ 709-535-2533, 800-563-8386; www.brittanyinns.com; Main St; r $72-79; 🖥) has 34 rather stark but clean rooms. Several have kitchenettes.

Oriental Restaurant (☎ 709-535-6993; 131 Main St; meals $6-11; ⏰ 11:30am-11pm) is a pretty straightforward place, and you get a chance at a few vegetables.

DRL Coachlines (☎ 709-263-2171; www.drlgroup.com) stops at Brittany Inns on Main St. Departures for St John's ($56, six hours) leave at 3:54pm and Port aux Basques ($71, 7½ hours) at 1:25pm.

Between mid-June and mid-September, the **MV Sir Robert Bond** (☎ 709-724-9173, 866-535-2567; www.labradormarine.com) runs a weekly vehicle-and-passenger service to the Labrador towns of Cartwright (adult/child five to 12 years $73/36.50, per car/motorcycle $118/60, 24 hours) and Goose Bay (adult/child five to 12 years $118/59, per car/motorcycle $194/97, 46 hours, including a seven-hour stop in Cartwright). The boat leaves Lewisporte on Friday at noon. This ferry route likely will vanish should the Labrador highway between Cartwright and Goose Bay ever get completed.

GRAND FALLS-WINDSOR

The sprawl of two small pulp-and-paper towns has met and now comprises the community of Grand Falls-Windsor (population 13,340). The Grand Falls portion, south of Hwy 1 and near the Exploits River, is more interesting for visitors.

Information

Visitors center (☎ 709-489-6332; www.grandfalls windsor.com; Hwy 1; ☾ 10am-5pm late May–mid-Oct) Just west of town at exit 17.

Sights

The **Mary March Provincial Museum** (☎ 709-292-4522; www.therooms.ca; cnr St Catherine & Cromer Aves; adult/child under 19yr $2.50/free; ☾ 9am-4:45pm May–mid-Oct) is accessed from exit 18A south and is worth visiting. Exhibits concentrate on the recent and past histories of Aboriginal peoples in the area, including the extinct Beothuk tribe.

Set next to Rush Pond, not far from the visitors center, is Beothuk Park and the **Loggers' Life Provincial Museum** (☎ 709-486-0492; www .therooms.ca; exit 17, Hwy 1; adult/child under 19yr $2.50/free; ☾ 9:15am-4:30pm late May–mid-Sep). Here you can experience the life of a 1920s logging camp – smells and all!

Overlooking Grand Falls is the **Salmonid Interpretation Centre** (☎ 709-489-7350; adult/child 5-11yr/child 12-18yr $5/2/3; ☾ 8am-dusk mid-Jun–mid-Sep), where you can watch Atlantic salmon start their mighty struggle upstream to spawn. Unfortunately, they do so under the pulp mill's shadow. To get there, cross the river south of High St and follow the signs.

Sleeping & Eating

Hill Road Manor B&B (☎ 709-489-5451, 866-489-5451; www.hillroadmanor.com; 1 Hill Rd; $99-109; ⚐) Elegant furnishings, cushiony beds that will have you gladly oversleeping and a vibrant sunroom combine for a stylish stay. Kids are welcome.

Kelly's Pub & Eatery (☎ 709-489-9893; 18 Hill Rd; meals $7-11) Hidden neatly behind the smoky pub is this great countrified spot. It makes the best burgers in town and the stir-fries are not too shabby either.

Getting There & Away

DRL Coachlines (☎ 709-263-2171; www.drlgroup.com) has its bus stop at the **Highliner Inn** (☎ 709-489-5639; exit 17, Hwy 1 Service Rd). Departures for St John's ($63, 6½ hours) leave at 3:15pm and Port aux Basques ($67, seven hours) at 2:14pm.

CENTRAL SOUTH COAST

Route 360 runs 130km through the center of the province to the south coast. It's a long way down to the first settlements at the end of **Bay d'Espoir**, a gentle fjord. Note there is no gas station on the route, so fill up on Hwy 1. **St Alban's** is set on the west side of the fjord. You'll find a few motels with dining rooms and lounges around the end of the bay.

Further south is a concentration of small fishing villages. The scenery along Rte 364 to **Hermitage** is particularly impressive, as is the scenery around **Harbour Breton**. It's the largest town (population 2080) in the region and huddles around the ridge of a gentle inland bay.

Southern Port Hotel (☎ 709-885-2283; www.south ernporthotel.ca; Rte 360, Harbour Breton; r $80-85; ⚐) provides spacious, standard-furnished rooms; even-numbered ones have harbor views. Two doors down is **Scott's Snackbar** (☎ 709-885-2406; mains $7-15; ☾ 10:30am-11pm Sun-Thu, to 1am Fri & Sat), serving burgers and home-cooked dishes; it's licensed.

Thornhill Bus Service (☎ 709-885-2144, 866-538-3429) connects Harbour Breton with Grand Falls ($35, 2½ hours), leaving at 7:15am. Government passenger ferries serve Hermitage, making the western south-coast outports (see p256) accessible from here.

NORTHERN PENINSULA

The Northern Peninsula points upward from the body of Newfoundland like an extended index finger, and you almost get the feeling it's wagging at you saying, 'Don't you dare leave this province without coming up here.'

Heed the advice. This area could well be crowned Newfoundland's star attraction. The province's two world heritage sites are these: Gros Morne National Park, with its fjord-like lakes and geological oddities, rests at the peninsula's base, while the sublime, 1000-year-old Viking settlement at L'Anse aux Meadows stares out from the peninsula's tip.

Connecting these two famous sites is the **Viking Trail** (☎ 877-778-4546; www.vikingtrail.org), aka Rte 430, an attraction in its own right that holds close to the sea as it heads resolutely north past Port au Choix' ancient burial grounds and the ferry jump-off to big brooding Labrador. It's no wonder many people base their entire Newfoundland trip around this extraordinary region and usually end up coming back for more, year after year.

The region is gaining hugely in tourism, yet the crowds are nowhere near what you'd get at a Yellowstone or Banff. Still, it's wise to book ahead in July and August.

It's a five- to six-hour drive from Deer Lake to St Anthony. Bus transportation is possible, if a bit irregular, along the entire route.

DEER LAKE

There's little in Deer Lake (population 4770) for the visitor, but it's a convenient place to fly into or jump off the bus for trips up the Northern Peninsula. Rocky Harbour (71km) is north on Rte 430, while Hwy 1 connects Deer Lake to Port aux Basques (268km) in the south and Gander (299km) to the east.

The **visitors center** (☎ 709-635-2202; ⊗ 9am-7pm) sits right on Hwy 1.

B&Bers can hunker down at **Watkins House** (☎ 709-635-3723; 17 Phillip Dr; r $40-55); follow the signs off exit 15 from Hwy 1. **Driftwood Inn** (☎ 709-635-5115; www.driftwoodinn.net; 3 Nicholsville Rd; r $84-107) is also a hospitable option. It has **Jungle Jim's** (meals $8-12; ⊗ lunch & dinner) downstairs. It's about 2.5km from the **Irving Big Stop gas station** (☎ 709-635-2130), off exit 15; a taxi from the airport costs $7.

DRL Coachlines (☎ 709-263-2171; www.drlgroup.com) stops at the Irving Big Stop on Hwy 1. Note that DRL's bus isn't synchronized with shuttle services (p252) heading up the Northern Peninsula from Corner Brook. But if you call ahead they may work things out for you.

For air services to Deer Lake, see p277. The airport is just off Hwy 1. Avis, Budget and Hertz rent cars at the airport; for costs and contact information, see p282.

GROS MORNE NATIONAL PARK

This **national park** (☎ 709-458-2417; www.pc.gc.ca/ grosmorne; per day adult/child 6-16yr/family $8.90/4.45/17.80; ⊗ day-use facilities mid-May–mid-Oct) stepped into the world spotlight in 1987, when Unesco granted it world heritage designation. To visitors, the park's stunning flat-top mountains

and deeply incised waterways are simply supernatural playgrounds. To geologists, this park is a blueprint for our planet and supplies evidence for theories such as plate tectonics. Specifically, the bronze-colored Tablelands are made of rock that comes from deep within the earth's crust. Nowhere in the world is such material as easily accessed as in Gros Morne (it's usually only found at unfathomable ocean depths). Such attributes have earned the park its 'Galapagos of Geology' nickname.

There is enough to do in and around the park to easily fill several days. The hiking, kayaking, camping, wildlife-spotting and boat tours are fantastic.

Orientation

Several small fishing villages dot the shoreline and provide amenities. Bonne Bay swings in and divides the area: to the south is Rte 431 and the towns of Glenburnie, Trout River and Woody Point; to the north is Rte 430 and Norris Point, Rocky Harbour and Sally's Cove. Rocky Harbour is the largest village and is quite central, as are Norris Point and Woody Point.

Information

Park admission includes the trails, Discovery Centre and all day-use areas. It also goes toward the cost of a campsite.

Discovery Centre (☎ 709-453-2490; Rte 431, Woody Point; ⊗ 9am-6pm Jun-Aug, to 9pm Sun & Wed Jun-Aug, 9am-5pm late May & Sep–mid-Oct) Has interactive exhibits and a multimedia theater explaining the area's ecology and geology. There's also an information desk with maps, daily interpretive activities and a small café.

Main Visitor Centre (☎ 709-458-2066; Rte 430, near Rocky Harbour; ⊗ 9am-9pm late Jun-early Sep, to 5pm mid-May–mid Jun & mid-Sep–mid-Oct) As well as issuing day and backcountry permits, it has maps, books, Viking Trail materials and an impressive interpretive area.

Park Entrance Kiosk (Rte 430; ⊗ 10am-6pm mid-May–mid-Oct) By the park entrance near Wiltondale.

Sights

Dominating the southwest corner of the park are the unconquerable and eerie **Tablelands**. This massive flat-topped massif was part of the earth's mantle before tectonics raised it from the depths and planted it squarely on the continent. Its rock is so unusual that plants can't even grow on it. You can view the barren, golden phenomenon up close on Rte 431, or catch it from a distance at the stunning **photography lookout** above Norris Point.

West of the Tablelands, dramatic volcanic sea stacks and caves mark the coast at **Green Gardens**.

At the wharf in Norris Point is the **Bonne Bay Marine Station** (☎ 709-458-2550; www.bonnebay .mun.ca; adult/child 5-18 yr $5/4; ☒ 9am-5pm Jun–mid-Oct, closed Mon & Tue early Sep–mid-Oct), a research facility that's part of Memorial University. Every half-hour there are interactive tours, and the aquariums display the marine ecological habitats in Bonne Bay. For kids, there are touch tanks and a rare blue lobster.

Further up the coast past Sally's Cove, waves batter the rusty and tangled remains of the **SS Ethie**. The story of this 1919 wreck, and the subsequent rescue, was inspiration for a famous folk song.

The Long Range Mountains continue to loom large over the Viking Trail as you head north along the coast. When you're hit with a sudden feeling of disbelief, you have reached **Western Brook Pond**, the park's premier fjord. Its sheer 700m cliffs plunge to the blue abyss and dramatically snake into the mountains. See p246 for information about the excellent boat tours.

Nearby at Broom Point is a **restored fishing camp** (Rte 430; admission free; ☒ 10am-6pm mid-May– mid-Oct). The three Mudge brothers and their families fished here from 1941 until 1975, when they sold the entire camp, including boats, lobster traps and nets, to the national park. Everything has been restored and is now staffed by guides.

Only 20km north, the gentle, safe, sand-duned beach at **Shallow Bay** seems almost out of place, as if transported from the Caribbean by some bizarre current. The water, though, provides a chilling dose of reality, rarely getting above 15°C.

Inquire at the visitor centers about the free interpretive programs, guided walks and evening presentations put on by park staff throughout summer.

Activities

Hiking and kayaking can also be done via guided tours (p246).

HIKING

Twenty maintained trails of varying difficulty snake through 100km of the park's most scenic landscapes. The gem is the **James Callahan Gros Morne Trail** (16km) to the peak of Gros Morne, the highest point in the area at 806m.

While there are sections with steps and boardwalks, this is a strenuous seven- to eight-hour hike, and includes a steep rock gully that must be climbed to the ridgeline of the mountain. Standing on the 600m precipice and staring out over 10 Mile Pond, a sheer-sided fjord, can only be described as sublime.

Green Gardens Trail (16km) is almost as scenic and challenging. The loop has two trailheads off Rte 431, with each one descending to Green Gardens along its magnificent coastline formed from lava and shaped by the sea. Plan on six to eight hours of hiking or book one of the three backcountry camping areas, all of them on the ocean, and turn the hike into an overnight adventure. A less strenuous day hike (9km) to the beach and back is possible from this trail's Long Pond Trailhead.

Shorter scenic hikes are the **Tablelands Trail** (4km), which extends to Winterhouse Brook Canyon; **Lookout Trail** (5km), which starts behind the Discovery Centre and loops to the site of an old fire tower above the tree line; **Lobster Cove Head Trail** (2km), which loops through tidal pools; and **Western Brook Pond Trail** (6km), the park's most popular trail, which is an easy hike to the western end of the fjord and back.

The granddaddies of the trails are the **Long Range Traverse** (35km) and **North Rim Traverse** (27km), serious multiday treks over the mountains. Permits and advice from park rangers are required. For backcountry campsite information, see p246.

If you plan to do several trails, invest $12 in a copy of the *Gros Morne National Park Trail Guide,* a waterproof map with trail descriptions on the back.

KAYAKING

Kayaking in the shadow of the Tablelands and through the spray of whales is truly something to be experienced. Tour operators Long Range Adventures (p246; per day single/double $45/55) and Gros Morne Adventures (p246; per day single/double $50/60) provide rentals for experienced paddlers.

SKIING

Many trails in the park's impressive 55km cross-country ski-trail system were designed by Canadian Olympic champion, Pierre Harvey. Contact the Visitor Centre (opposite) for trail information and reservations for backcountry huts.

NEWFOUNDLAND & LABRADOR

Tours

Most tours operate between June and September; book in advance. Kayaking is best in June and July.

Bon Tours (☎ 709-458-2016; www.bontours.ca; Main St, Rocky Harbour) The Western Brook Pond boat tour (two hour trip adult/child $38/16) at 10am, 1pm and 4pm is phenomenal. The dock is a 3km walk from Rte 430 via the easy Western Brook Pond Trail.

Gros Morne Adventures (☎ 709-458-2722, 800-685-4624; www.grosmorneadventures.com; Norris Point) It offers daily guided sea-kayak tours (two-hour/three-hour $45/55) in Bonne Bay, plus full-day and multiday kayak trips and hiking, skiing and snowshoeing tours. Check the website for many additional options.

Long Range Adventures (☎ 709-458-3104, 709-458-7732; www.longrangeadventures.com; Sally's Cove) Another multi-adventure outfitter offering daily guided sea kayaking (2½-hour tour $45), hiking and mountain-bike tours, plus winter activities. Locally owned Long Range also includes options for budget travelers, such as the three-day Fidgety Fox Tour (hike Gros Morne day one, kayak through day two, and take the Western Brook Pond Boat Tour on day three; shared hostel accommodations included for $289).

Trout River Pond Boat Tours (☎ 709-451-7500; www.troutriverpondboattour.com; Trout River; 2hr tours adult/child 7-17yr $35/18) Runs daily up Trout River Pond past the Tablelands.

Festivals & Events

Gros Morne Theatre Festival (☎ 709-243-2899; www.theatrenewfoundland.com; various locations; tickets $8-23) Nine productions of Newfoundland plays, staged both indoors and outdoors throughout the summer (from late May to mid-September).

Writers at Woody Point Festival (☎ 709-453-2900; www.writersatwoodypoint.com; tickets $20) Authors from across Newfoundland, Canada and the world converge at the Woody Point Heritage Theatre to do readings in mid-August.

Sleeping

While Rocky Harbour is central and has the most options, don't overlook the surrounding communities.

BUDGET

Gros Morne Hostel (☎ 709-458-3104, 709-458-7732; Sally's Cove; dm $20, s/d $28/38) The Long Range Adventures folks (see above) rent out two extra rooms in their house: one has four dorm beds, the other a queen-size bed. It's tight quarters, but the hosts' goodwill smooths out the roughness. Free bike use for guests.

Aunt Jane's Place B&B (☎ 709-453-2485; www.grosmorne.com/victorianmanor; Water St, Woody Point; r with shared bathroom $50-60, r with private bathroom $70; ☷ mid-May–mid-Oct) This historic house oozes character. It sits beachside, so you may be woken early in the morning by the heavy breathing of whales.

Anchor Down B&B (☎ 800-920-2208; www.theanchordown.com; Pond Rd, Rocky Harbour; r with/without bathroom $65/50; ⬛) The home and its five rooms are pretty simple, but guests have raved about excellent hospitality and cooking from the friendly hosts.

Four developed **campgrounds** (☎ 905-426-4648, 877-737-3783; www.pccamping.ca; campsites $17-23, reservation fee $10.90) lie within the park: **Berry Hill** (☷ mid-Jun–mid-Sep), the largest, is most central; **Lomond** (☷ late May–mid-Oct) is good and closest to the southern park entrance; **Trout River** (☷ early Jun–mid-Sep) is average and closest to the Tablelands; and **Shallow Bay** (☷ early Jun–mid-Sep) has ocean swimming (and mosquitoes).

There's a primitive **campground** (campsites $14; ☷ all year) at superb Green Point. Numerous **backcountry campsites** ($9) are spread along trails; reserve them at the Visitor Centre.

MIDRANGE

Middle Brook Cottages (☎ 709-453-2332; www.middlebrookcottages.com; off Rte 431, Glenburnie; cottages $99-129; ☷ Mar-Nov; ♿) These all-pinewood, spic-'n'-span cottages are both perfectly romantic and perfectly kid-friendly. They have kitchens and TVs, and you can splash around the swimming hole and waterfalls behind the property.

Gros Morne Cabins (☎ 709-458-2020; www.grosmornecabins.com; Main St, Rocky Harbour; 1-/2-bedroom cabins $109/139) While backed by tarmac, these cabins are fronted by nothing but ocean. Each of the 22 beautiful log cabins has a kitchen and pullout sofa for children. Bookings can be made next door at Endicott's variety store.

TOP END

Sugar Hill Inn (☎ 709-458-2147; www.sugarhillinn.nf.ca; 115-119 Sexton Rd, Norris Point; d $89-135, ste $175-225; ☷ Mar-Oct) Slide into the sauna or hot tub after a day in the Tablelands, then savor a gourmet meal in the scenic guests-only dining room. All that's left to do is retire to your corner of luxury for a well-deserved snooze.

Eating

Good eats exist within all of the park's many communities.

Earle's Video & Convenience (☎ 709-458-2577; Main St, Rocky Harbour; mains $6-12; ☺ 9am-11pm) Earle is an institution in Rocky Harbour. Besides selling groceries and renting videos, he has great pizza, moose burgers and traditional Newfoundland fare that you can chomp on the patio.

Lighthouse Restaurant (☎ 709-453-2213; Water St, Woody Point; mains $8-14; ☺ 10am-7pm May-Sep, later Fri & Sat) The ladies at this diner cook up a storm in back and deliver Gros Morne's best fish-and-chips, cod tongues and other Newfie dishes, along with cold beer.

Java Jack's (☎ 709-458-3004; Main St, Rocky Harbour; mains $8-19; ☺ 7:30am-8:30pm May-Oct, later Jul & Aug) Jack's provides Gros Morne's best coffees, wraps and soups by day. By night, the upstairs dining room fills hungry, post-hike bellies with fine seafood, caribou and vegetarian fare.

Old Loft Restaurant (☎ 709-453-2294; Water St, Woody Point; mains dinner $15-21; ☺ noon-9pm Jul & Aug, to 7pm May, Jun & Sep) Set on the water in Woody Point, this tiny place is popular for its traditional Newfoundland meals and seafood.

Getting There & Around

For shuttle and bus services to Rocky Harbour, Woody Point and Trout River from Corner Brook, see p252.

PORT AU CHOIX

Port au Choix (population 1000), dangling on a stark peninsula 13km off the Viking Trail, houses a large fishing fleet, quirky museum and worthy archaeological site that delves into ancient burial grounds.

Sights & Activities

The **Port au Choix National Historic Site** (☎ 709-861-3522; www.pc.gc.ca/portauchoix; Point Riche Rd; adult/child 6-16 yr $7.15/3.45; ☺ 9am-6pm mid-Jun–Aug, to 5pm early Jun & Sep– mid-Oct) sits on ancient burial grounds of three different Aboriginal groups, dating back 5500 years. The modern visitors center tells of these groups' creative survival in the area and of one group's unexplained disappearance 3200 years ago.

Phillip's Garden, a site with vestiges of Paleo-Eskimo houses, is a highlight. Two trails will take you there. One is the **Phillip's Garden Coastal Trail** (4km), which leaves from Phillip Dr at

the end of town. From here you hopscotch your way over the jigsaw of skeletal rock to the site 1km away.

If you continue, it's another 3km to the **Point Riche Lighthouse** (1871). A plaque next to the tower recounts the many French and English conflicts in the area between the 1600s and 1900s. In 1904, France relinquished its rights here in exchange for privileges in Morocco (ah, the days when the world was a Monopoly board). The lighthouse is also accessible via the visitors center road.

The other way to reach the sites is via the **Dorset Trail** (8km). It leaves the visitors center and winds across the barrens through stunted trees, passing a Dorset Paleo-Eskimo **burial cave** before finally reaching Phillip's Garden and linking to the Coastal Trail.

At the edge of town is Ben Ploughman's capricious **Studio Gargamelle/Museum of Whales & Things** (☎ 709-861-3280; www.bensstudio.ca; Rte 430; adult/student $3/2; ☺ 9am-5pm Mon-Sat Jun-Sep). His engaging, knowledgeable and humorous manner complements the ever-evolving whale museum he's creating, which includes an impressive, wired-together whale skeleton. Have a look at his artwork – *Crucifixion of the Cod* is a classic.

Sleeping & Eating

Jeannie's Sunrise B&B (☎ 709-861-2254, 877-639-2789; www.jeanniessunrisebb.com; Fisher St; s/d with shared bathroom $55/65, s/d with private bathroom $65/75; 🖳) Jeannie radiates hospitality through her six spacious rooms, free Internet access, bright reading nook and demeanor as sweet as her breakfast muffins.

Dot's Pantry (☎ 709-861-3735; Fisher St; dishes $7-10; ☺ 7am-5:30pm Mon-Sat) Mmm, baked goods and fish-and-chips to fuel your Port au Choix hikes.

Anchor Café (☎ 709-861-3665; Fisher St; mains $12-18; ☺ 11:30am-8pm Sun-Thu, to 9pm Fri & Sat) You can't miss this place – the front half is the bow of a boat – and don't, because it has the best meals in town. The luncheon specials offer good value and the dinner menu has a wide array of seafood.

ST BARBE TO L'ANSE AUX MEADOWS

As the Viking Trail nears St Barbe, the waters of the gulf quickly narrow and give visitors their first opportunity to see the desolate shores of Labrador. Ferries (p259) take advantage of this convergence and ply the route between St Barbe and the Labrador Straits. At Eddies Cove, the road sadly leaves the coast and heads inland.

As you approach the northern tip of the peninsula, Rte 430 veers off toward St Anthony, and two new roads take over leading to several diminutive fishing villages that provide perfect bases for your visit to L'Anse aux Meadows National Historic Site. Route 436 hugs the eastern shore and passes through (from south to north) St Lunaire-Griquet, Gunners Cove, Straitsview and L'anse aux Meadows village. Rte 437 heads in a more westerly direction through Pistolet Bay, Raleigh and Cape Onion.

Sights & Activities

It's all about the Vikings up here.

L'ANSE AUX MEADOWS
NATIONAL HISTORIC SITE

The premise may seem dull – visiting a bog in the middle of nowhere, staring at the spot where a couple of old sod houses once stood – but somehow this **Viking site** (☎ 709-623-2608; www.pc.gc.ca/lanseauxmeadows; Rte 436; adult/child 6-12yr/family $10.40/5.20/26; ⏰ 9am-6pm Jun–mid-Oct) lying in a forlorn sweep of land turns out to be one of Newfoundland's most stirring attractions.

Its historic significance is absolute: it's the home of the first Europeans to land in North America. They were Vikings from Scandinavia and Greenland, who sailed over some 500 years before Columbus. That they settled, constructed houses, fed themselves and even smelted iron out of the bog to forge nails, attests to their ingenuity and fortitude. That it was all accomplished by a group of young-pup 20-somethings, led by Leif Eriksson, son of Eric the Red, is even more impressive.

The remains of the Vikings' waterside settlement – eight original wood-and-sod buildings, looking pretty much as they did in AD 1000 – are what visitors can see, plus three replica buildings inhabited by costumed docents. The latter have names like 'Thora' and 'Bjorn' and simulate Viking chores such as spinning fleece and forging nails.

Allow two or three hours to walk around and absorb the ambience, as well as browse the interpretive center. While there, be sure and see the introductory film, which tells the captivating story of Norwegian explorer Helge

Ingstad, who rediscovered the site in 1960, ending years of searching.

Also worthwhile is the 3km trail that winds through the barren terrain and along the coast surrounding the interpretive center.

NORSTEAD

Can't get enough of the long-bearded Viking lifestyle? Stop by **Norstead** (☎ 709-623-2828; www.norstead.com; adult/child 6-12yr/family $8/5/25; Rte 436; ⏰ 10am-6pm Jun-late Sep), just beyond the turnoff to the national historic site. It's a re-creation of a Viking village with costumed interpreters (more than at L'Anse aux Meadows) smelting, weaving, baking and telling stories around real fires throughout four buildings. Sounds cheesy, but they pull it off with class. There's also a large-scale replica of a Viking ship on hand.

Sleeping

Straitsview, Gunners Cove and St Lunaire-Griquet are all within 12km of the national historic site.

Tickle Inn (☎ 709-452-4321; www.tickleinn.net; Rte 437, Cape Onion; r incl light breakfast $55-75; ⏰ Jun-late Sep) This delightful seaside inn, built in 1890, is surrounded by a white picket fence, oodles of grass and your own private beach. Sit in the parlor, feel the warmth of the Franklin wood-stove and enjoy great home-cooked meals.

St Brendan's Motel (☎ 709-623-2520; www.stbrendansmotel.com; Rte 436, St Lunaire-Griquet; s/d $70/75; ⏰ Jun–mid-Oct) The pine-green exterior of this 11-room motel doesn't look like much, but the rooms (with TV, coffeemaker and refrigerator) are snug and the setting peaceful.

Snorri Cabins (☎ 709-623-2241; www.snorricabins.com; Rte 436, Straitsview; 2-bedroom cabins $75; ⏰ May-Nov) These cabins offer simple comfort and great value. They're perfect for families, with a full kitchen, sitting room and a pull-out sofa.

Dockside Motel (☎ 709-877-2444; www.docksidemotel.nf.ca; Rte 430, St Barbe; s/d $70/75, 2-bedroom cabins $85) This place is literally next door to the ferry landing in St Barbe and has 15 rooms, 10 cabins and a restaurant.

Valhalla Lodge B&B (☎ 709-623-2018, 877-623-2018; www.valhalla-lodge.com; Rte 436, Gunners Cove; r $85-90; ⏰ mid-May–late Sep) Set on a hill overlooking the ocean, this lodge is only 8km from the Viking site. Put your feet up on the deck and watch icebergs in comfort. This very view inspired Pulitzer Prize–winning author E Annie Proulx as she wrote *The Shipping News* here.

Eating

Fishermen's Galley (☎ 709-623-2431; Rte 436, St Lunaire-Griquet; sandwiches $4-8, mains $10-19; ☺ 11am-9pm) Operated by a fisherman and set on the water, this pinewood-paneled dining room serves comforting seafood casseroles and cod burgers, along with fajitas and vegetarian stir-fry.

Northern Delight (☎ 709-623-2220; Rte 436, Gunner's Cove; meals $9-15; ☺ breakfast, lunch & dinner late Apr–mid-Oct) Dine on local favorites such as turbot cheeks and pan-fried cod, fresh lobster and mussels, or just have a 'Newfie Mug-up' (bread, molasses and a strong cup of tea). There's live music on various evenings.

ourpick Norseman Restaurant & Art Gallery (☎ 709-623-2018; Rte 436, L'Anse aux Meadows village; dinner mains $12-22; ☺ 9am-10pm mid-May–late Sep) This casual, red-hued room may well be the best restaurant in all of Newfoundland. Relish the butternut squash soup, peruse a few vegetarian options or sink your teeth into tender Labrador caribou tenderloin. Waterfront views complement the food and drinks.

ST ANTHONY

Hallelujah! You've made it to the end of the road; your windshield has helped control the insect population and you have seen two world heritage sites. After such grandeur, St Anthony (population 2700) may be a little anticlimactic. It's not what you'd call pretty, but it has a rough-hewn charm.

Grenfell is a big name around here. Sir Wilfred Grenfell was a local legend and, by all accounts, quite a man. This English-born and -educated doctor first came to Newfoundland in 1892 and, for the next 40 years, traveling by dog-sled and boat, built hospitals and nursing stations and organized much-needed fishing cooperatives along the coast of Labrador and around St Anthony.

Information

Grenfell Interpretation Centre (☎ 709-454-4010; West St, opposite the hospital; ☺ 9am-8pm Jun-late Sep, 9am-5pm Mon-Fri Oct-May) Visitor information.

Sights & Activities

A number of local sites pertaining to Wilfred Grenfell are subsumed under the **Grenfell Historic Properties** (www.grenfell-properties.com; adult/family $6/12). The **Grenfell Interpretation Centre** is a modern exhibit recounting the historic and sometimes dramatic life of Grenfell. Its handicraft shop has some high-quality carvings and artwork, as well as embroidered parkas made by locals – proceeds go to maintenance of the historic properties. Out back, near the **Dockhouse Museum** and playground, try to spot the odd footprint from Grenfell's beloved dog-sled team in the exterior walls of the carpentry building.

Grenfell's beautiful mansion is now the **Grenfell Museum** (☺ 9am-8pm Jun-Aug, to 5pm Sep), located behind the hospital. Past the wraparound porch, dyed burlap walls and antique furnishings envelop memorabilia including a polar bear rug and, if rumors are correct, the ghost of Mrs Grenfell.

The main road through town ends at **Fishing Point Park**, where a lighthouse and towering headland cliffs overlook the sea. The **Iceberg Alley Trail** and **Whale Watchers Trail** both lead to cliff-top observation platforms – the names say it all.

Tours

Northland Discovery Tours (☎ 709-454-3092, 877-632-3747; www.discovernorthland.com; 2½hr tours adult/child 5-12yr/child 13-17yr $45/20/25; ☺ 9am, 1pm & 4pm late May-late Sep) offers highly recommended cruises for whale- or iceberg-viewing that leave from the dock behind the Grenfell Interpretation Centre on West St. The best 'berg-viewing is in May and June; whales swim by in July and August.

Sleeping & Eating

Fishing Point B&B (☎ 709-454-2009; l.budgell@nf.sympatico.ca; Fishing Point Rd; s/d with shared bathroom $50/60) This tiny, old-fashioned place clings to the rocks en route to the lighthouse and offers the best harbor view in St Anthony. Get up early, grab some coffee and watch the boats head out to sea.

Haven Inn (☎ 709-454-9100, 877-428-3646; www.haveninn.ca; 14 Goose Cove Rd; r $82-123) What it lacks in charm, it makes up in size and amenities. Some of the 35 rooms have fireplaces and Jacuzzi tubs. In the dining room (meals $7 to $18; open 7am to 9pm), you'll get a good view of the harbor and fare like poached salmon with rice pilaf.

Lightkeeper's Café (☎ 877-454-4900; Fishing Point Park; meals $8-20; ☺ lunch & dinner mid-Jun–Sep) This little gem of an eatery sits in the shadow of the lighthouse and is often graced by the sight of icebergs and whales. The chowder and scallops are legendary.

Getting There & Away

Flying to St Anthony is technically possible, but the airport is nearly an hour away. If you're leaving St Anthony by car, you have two options: backtrack entirely along Rte 430, or try the sections of Rte 432 that run down the east coast and Hare Bay. This will meet up with Rte 430 near Plum Point, between St Barbe and Port aux Choix.

The Viking Express (p252) bus picks up at the **Irving Station** (☎ 709-454-2601; Main St) across from the Vinland Motel on West St, leaving for Corner Brook ($55, seven hours) at 10am Sunday, Tuesday and Thursday.

WESTERN NEWFOUNDLAND

Western Newfoundland presents many visitors with their first view of the Rock – a rather forbidding one, where wood houses cling for dear life to jagged shoreline outcrops – thanks to the ferry landing at Port aux Basques. From here, pokey fishing villages cast lines to the east, while Newfoundland's second-largest city raises its wintry head (via its ski mountain) to the northeast.

CORNER BROOK

Corner Brook is happenin' baby – Jean-Claude Van Damme parks his yacht in the harbor, and Oprah just bought a place out by the ski resort! Or so the rumors go as development comes to the handsome Humber Valley. Actually, Newfoundland's second-largest town (population 23,000) is pretty sleepy, though skiers, kayakers and anglers will find plenty of action.

Orientation

The town splashes up the hills at the eastern end of Humbert Arm's 40km-long waters. The smoke-belching pulp and paper mill, the town's lifeblood, marks the center point of downtown. The primary commercial streets run nearby, including Main, Park, West and Broadway Sts.

Information

CIBC Bank (☎ 709-637-1700; 9 Main St)
Post office (☎ 709-637-8807; 14 Main St)
Public library (☎ 709-634-0013; Sir Richard Squires Bldg, Mt Bernard Ave; ☉ 1-8pm Mon & Tue, 10am-8pm Wed, 10am-5pm Thu-Sat) Free Internet access.
Visitors center (☎ 709-639-9792; www.cornerbrook .com; cnr Confederation Dr & West Valley Rd; ☉ 9am-9pm mid-May–mid-Oct, 9am-5pm mid-Oct–mid-May) Just off Hwy 1 at exit 5. Has a craft shop.

Sights & Activities

Marble Mountain (☎ 709-637-7616; www.skimarble .com; Hwy 1) is the lofty reason that most visitors come to Corner Brook. Located in the Humber Valley 8km east of town, it offers Atlantic Canada's best skiing, along with snowboarding and tubing. See p52 for further details.

DRIFTING DOWN ICEBERG ALLEY

Each year 10,000 to 40,000 glistening icebergs break off Greenland's glaciers and enter the Baffin and Labrador currents for the three-year trip south to Newfoundland's famed 'Iceberg Alley.' This 480km-long, 98km-wide stretch of sea runs along the province's north and east coast and is strewn with 'bergs in late spring and early summer. Fogo and Twillingate Islands in Notre Dame Bay and St Anthony on the Northern Peninsula are some of the best places for sightings. Even St John's is graced with a few hundred of the blue-and-white marvels most years (though sometimes the waters remain barren due to climate and current shifts).

To see where the behemoths lurk, check:

- www.icebergfinder.com: the provincial tourism association's website showing where the 'bergs are floating; you can get weekly email updates on their locations and plan your trip accordingly.

- www.ice-glaces.ec.gc.ca: Canadian government's website providing daily iceberg bulletins.

Locals harvest some smaller 'bergs, and if you ask in restaurants you may get a piece along with your drink. Considering the glacial ice may be more than 15,000 years old, it is indeed an ice cube to savor.

When the white stuff has departed, the **Steady Brook Falls Trail** (500m) leads from the ski area's rear parking lot, behind the Petro-Canada station, to a cascade of water that tumbles more than 30m. **Fishing** and **kayaking** in the nearby Humber River are also popular. Inquire at the Marble Inn (p252) to get outfitted.

A tribute to James Cook for his work in surveying the region in the mid-1760s, the **Captain James Cook Monument** (Crow Hill Rd, off Atlantic Ave), a national historic site, is northwest of downtown. Cook's names for many of the islands, ports and waterways, such as the Humber Arm and Hawke's Bay, remain today. While the cliff-top monument is admirable, it's the panoramic view over the Bay of Islands that is the real payoff. The route here is convoluted, but well-marked.

Another scenic walk is the **Corner Brook Stream Trail** (2km), which gently follows the stream's banks and part of Glynmill Pond. It starts in the parking lot of the Glynmill Inn (right).

Within historic Humbermouth Station, the **Railway Society of Newfoundland** (☎ 709-634-2720; Station Rd, off Humber Rd; admission $2; ⊙ 9am-8pm Jun-Aug) has a good-looking steam locomotive and some narrow-gauge rolling stock that chugged across the province from 1921 to 1939.

The **Corner Brook Arts & Culture Centre** (☎ 709-637-2580; www.artsandculturecentre.ca; University Dr) features a 400-seat performing-arts facility and an **art gallery** (admission free; ⊙ 9am-5pm) of local works.

Sleeping

Bell's Inn (☎ 709-634-1150, 888-634-1150; www.bellsinn.ca; 2 Ford's Rd; r incl breakfast $60-110) Gordon Bell's rambling green house tops a hill that's a 15-minute walk from downtown. The eight smallish, comfy rooms will all have private bathrooms; Nos 1 and 4 have harbor views. Sip your morning coffee on the breezy veranda.

Glynmill Inn (☎ 709-634-5181, 800-563-4400; www.glynmillinn.ca; 1 Cobb Lane; d $95-115, ste $115-160) Lawns, gardens and graciousness surround the Tudor-style Glynmill. It originally was built for the engineers supervising the pulp mill's construction in the 1920s, at that time the largest project in the history of papermaking. The inn retains an elegant but down-to-earth ambience.

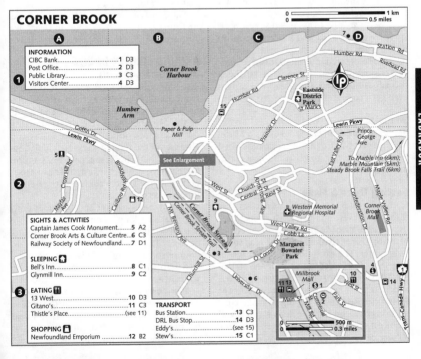

CORNER BROOK

Marble Inn (☎ 709-634-3007, 877-497-5673; www
.marbleinn.com; 21 Dogwood Dr, Steady Brook; ste $89-129,
cottages $129-199; 🖳) Located on the Humber
River across from Marble Mountain, this locally owned inn provides outdoor enthusiasts
with peaceful snoozing in the main lodge's
suites or in the surrounding cedar cottages.
Seasonal activities on-site include salmon
fishing, kayaking and river rafting; a free shuttle bus carts guests to the ski hill.

Eating & Drinking

Thistle's Place (☎ 709-634-4389; in Millbrook Mall;
sandwiches $5-9; 🕑 9am-9pm Mon-Fri, to 6pm Sat) Walk
through the front flower shop to reach the
smoked meat, curried chicken and whole-
wheat veggie wraps at the wee café out the
back. Coffees, cakes, breakfasts and Internet
access ($2 per 15 minutes) are also avail-
able here.

Gitano's (☎ 709-634-5000; in Millbrook Mall; tapas
$6-10, mains $17-25; 🕑 lunch Wed-Fri, dinner Mon-Sat)
Behind Thistle's and owned by the same
family, Gitano's dishes up Spanish-themed
mains such as *estofado* (stewed sweet potatoes,
chickpeas and figs over couscous), tapas (try
the Newfie shrimp rolls) and pastas. Live jazz
wafts through on weekends.

13 West (☎ 709-634-1300; 13 West St; mains dinner
$20-30; 🕑 lunch Mon-Fri, dinner Mon-Sun) Inventive
dishes grace the plates at this bistro, such as
linguini smothered in scallops, cashews, curried cream sauce and chutney. The $10 lunch
specials with dessert are a deal. Vegetarians
even get a couple of choices.

Shopping

Newfoundland Emporium (☎ 709-634-9376; 7 Broadway) Step over Moose, the owner's moose-sized
Newfoundland dog, to get at the local crafts,
music and literature.

Getting There & Away

Corner Brook is a major hub for bus services
throughout Newfoundland. Most operators
use the **bus station** (☎ 709-634-4710) in the center
of town, adjacent to the Millbrook Mall shopping center. The exceptions are DRL, which
stops at the **Confederation Dr Irving station**
(☎ 709-634-7422) across from the visitors center;
and Stew's and Eddy's, who share an office at
9 Humber Rd. Those hoping to make connections between these various stations will
require a taxi. Reservations are essential for
all services.

DRL Coachlines (☎ 709-263-2171; www.drlgroup
.com) buses heading eastward to St John's ($93
cash only, 10½ hours) depart at 11:25am. At
5:55pm services leave for Port aux Basques
($38, three hours). **Stew's** (☎ 709-886-2955, 709-
634-7777) runs a shuttle van to Burgeo ($33 cash
only, two hours) departing at 3pm Monday
through Thursday and at 4pm Friday. **Eddy's**
(☎ 709-634-7777) shuttles travel to Stephenville
($17, 1¼ hours) four times. **Gateway** (☎ 709-
695-3333) shuttles operate weekdays, departing for Port aux Basques ($30, three hours)
at 3:30pm. Returns depart from Port aux
Basques at 8am.

Martin's (☎ 709-453-2207) shuttles operate
weekdays, departing for Woody Point ($14,
1½ hours) and Trout River ($16, two hours)
at 4:30pm. Returns depart Woody Point and
Trout River at 9am. A different **Martin's** (☎ 709-
458-8201) shuttle departs for Rocky Harbour
($18, 1½ hours), also at 4:30pm weekdays.
Returns depart Rocky Harbour at 9am.

The **Viking Express** (☎ 709-634-4710) bus to St
Anthony ($55, seven hours) departs at 4pm
Monday, Wednesday and Friday. Stops in-
clude Deer Lake ($10, 45 minutes) and Rocky
Harbour ($18, two hours).

The **Star Taxi** (☎ 709-634-4343) shuttle picks
up from various hotels en route to Deer Lake
Airport ($18, 45 minutes) three times daily.

AROUND CORNER BROOK
Blomidon Mountains

The Blomidon Mountains, heaved skyward
from a collision with Europe around 500
million years ago, run along the south side
of the Humber Arm. They're tantalizing
for hikers, providing many sea vistas and
glimpses of the resident caribou population.
Some of the trails, especially ones up on
the barrens, are not well marked, so topographical maps and a compass are essential
for all hikers.

One of the easiest and most popular trails
begins at a parking lot on the left side of Rte
450 (500m from the Blow Me Down Brook
bridge). The trail can be followed for an
hour or so; for more avid hikers it continues
well into the mountains, where you're on
your own.

Blow Me Down Provincial Park (☎ 709-681-2430;
Rte 450; campsites $13, per vehicle $5; 🕑 mid-May–mid-Sep)
has beaches and scenery. The park lies near
the twisty end of Rte 450, which heads west
from Corner Brook for some 60km.

Stephenville

As the drive into town past deserted hangars, piles of tires and tract housing portends, Stephenville (population 7100) is in the running for Newfoundland's least appealing town. Not much reason to stop, except for the **Stephenville Theatre Festival** (☎ 709-643-4982; www.stf.nf.ca). It roars into town from mid-July to mid-August toting along the Bard, Broadway and to stir the pot, some cutting-edge Newfoundland plays.

Port au Port Peninsula

The large peninsula west of Stephenville is the only French area of the province. It became known as the French Shore in the early 1700s. Today, the culture is strongest along the western shore between **Cape St George** and **Lourdes**. Here children go to French school, preserving their dialect, which is now distinct from the language spoken in either France or Québec.

In **Port au Port West**, near Stephenville, the gorgeous **Gravels Trail** (3km) leads along the shore, passing secluded beach after secluded beach. Nearby in Felix Cove, stop at **Alpacas of Newfoundland** (☎ 709-648-9414; admission free; Rte 460) and meet the fluffy namesake critters.

Barachois Pond Provincial Park

This popular **park** (☎ 709-649-0048; Hwy 1; campsites $13, per vehicle $5; ☻ mid-May–mid-Sep), sitting just south of Rte 480 on Hwy 1, is one of the few in the province to offer a backcountry experience. From the campground, the **Erin Mountain Trail** (4.5km) winds through the forest and up to the 340m peak, where there are backcountry campsites and excellent views. Allow two hours for the climb.

Not far away are a couple of leisurely nature trails and a nice swimming area.

PORT AUX BASQUES

It's all about the ferry in Port aux Basques (population 4600). Most visitors come here to jump onto the Rock from Nova Scotia, or jump off for the return trip. That doesn't mean the town isn't a perfectly decent place to spend a day or night. Traditional wood houses painted bright in aqua, scarlet and sea green clasp the stony hills. Laundry blows on the clotheslines, boats moor in backyard inlets and locals never fail to wave hello to newcomers.

Port aux Basques (occasionally called Channel-Port aux Basques) was named in the early 16th century by Basque fishers and whalers who came to work the waters of the Strait of Belle Isle.

The town is a convenient place to stock up on food, fuel and/or money before journeying onward.

Orientation

When leaving the ferry, turn left after crossing the bridge and head southeast along Caribou Rd to reach the town center. You'll find postal and banking services along the crooked roads in this older section of town. Other services – grocery stores, gas stations, the hospital and visitors center – are on the opposite side of town, to the northwest.

Information

Bank of Montréal (☎ 709-695-5600; 83 Main St)
Hospital (☎ 709-695-2175; Grand Bay Rd)
Post office (☎ 800-267-1177; 3 Main St)
Public Library (☎ 709-695-3471; Grand Bay Rd; ☻ hours vary, closed Sun & Mon) Free Internet access.
Shopper's Drug Mart (☎ 709-695-7051; Main St; ☻ 10am-9pm Mon-Fri, 10am-6pm Sat, 1-5pm Sun)
Visitors center (☎ 709-695-2262; www.gateway tonewfoundland.com; Hwy 1; ☻ 6am-8pm mid-May–mid-Oct) Information on all parts of the province.

Sights & Activities

Downtown is the small **Gulf Museum** (☎ 709-695-7604; 118 Main St; adult/family $4/7; ☻ 10am-7pm early Jul-late Aug), stuffed with shipwreck artifacts. The showpiece is the astrolabe. This striking brass navigational instrument, made in Portugal in 1628, is designed on a principle discovered by the ancient Greeks to allow for charting of the heavenly bodies. The device is in remarkable condition and is one of only about three dozen that exist in the world.

To the west of town is **Grand Bay West Beach** (Kyle Lane). The long sweeping shore is backed by grassy dunes, which are breeding grounds for the endangered piping plover. The **Cormack Trail** (11km) leaves from here and flirts with the coast all the way to JT Cheeseman Provincial Park (p255).

Scott's Cove Park (Caribou Rd), with its restored boardwalk, candy-colored snack shacks and boat-shaped amphitheater, is the place to mingle with townsfolk and listen to live music. The **Railway Heritage Centre** (☎ 709-695-7560; off Hwy 1; tours $3.50; ☻ 10am-8pm Jul & Aug) also makes an appealing stop.

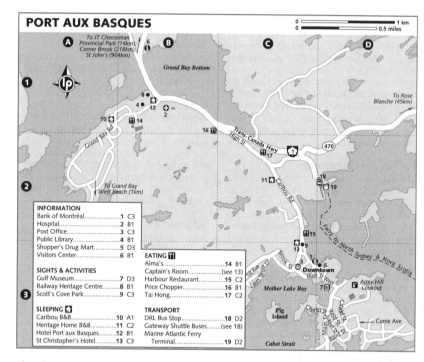

PORT AUX BASQUES

INFORMATION	
Bank of Montréal	1 C3
Hospital	2 B1
Post Office	3 C3
Public Library	4 B1
Shopper's Drug Mart	5 D3
Visitors Center	6 B1

SIGHTS & ACTIVITIES	
Gulf Museum	7 D3
Railway Heritage Centre	8 B1
Scott's Cove Park	9 C3

SLEEPING	
Caribou B&B	10 A1
Heritage Home B&B	11 C2
Hotel Port aux Basques	12 B1
St Christopher's Hotel	13 C3

EATING	
Alma's	14 B1
Captain's Room	(see 13)
Harbour Restaurant	15 C2
Price Chopper	16 B1
Tai Hong	17 C2

TRANSPORT	
DRL Bus Stop	18 D2
Gateway Shuttle Buses	(see 18)
Marine Atlantic Ferry Terminal	19 D2

NEWFOUNDLAND & LABRADOR

Sleeping

With all the ferry traffic, reservations are a good idea.

Heritage Home B&B (☎ 709-695-3240; www.bb canada.com/2665.html; 11 Caribou Rd; r $45-65; ☻ May-Oct) Up on the bluff overlooking the harbor, the five-room Heritage Home is the closest lodging to the ferry (a 10-minute walk). Cottony quilts and glossy wood furnishings fill the small, sunny rooms; only one has a private bathroom.

Caribou B&B (☎ 709-695-3408; www.bbcanada.com /2225.html; 42 Grand Bay Rd; r $55-65; ☻ May-Sep) It's similar to Heritage Home in ambience, but three of the five rooms have private bathrooms. The weep-worthy partridgeberry breakfast muffins compensate for the extra distance from the ferry.

Hotel Port aux Basques (☎ 709-695-2171, 877-695-2171; www.hotelpab.com; 1 Grand Bay Rd; r $75-70, ste d $99-130) The closest competition to St Christopher's, this hotel is older but has more character. For those in need of pampering, the suites will do the trick. Kids stay free.

St Christopher's Hotel (☎ 709-695-3500, 800-563-4779; www.stchrishotel.com; Caribou Rd; s/d $88/93; 🖳)

It's the most professional digs in town, with a small fitness room, high-speed wired Internet access, public Internet terminals and a fine seafood restaurant called the Captain's Room (meals $9 to $15; open for breakfast, lunch and dinner). Odd-numbered rooms have harbor views.

Eating

Alma's (☎ 709-695-3813; Grand Bay Rd, in the mall; meals $4-12; ☻ 8am-8pm Mon-Wed, 8am-9pm Thu-Fri, 8am-7pm Sat, 11am-7pm Sun) Follow the locals into this no-frills family diner for heaping portions of cod, scallops, fishcakes and berry pies. It serves breakfasts, burgers and sandwiches, too.

Harbour Restaurant (☎ 709-695-3238; 121 Caribou Rd; meals $6-12; ☻ 8am-11pm, to 1am Fri & Sat) While you'll get better food and service elsewhere, you can't beat the harborside view here. Pizzas and *donairs* (spiced beef in pita bread) share the menu with the fried chicken and fish-and-chips.

Tai Hong (☎ 709-695-3116; 77 High St; meals $7-12; ☻ 11am-11pm) Vegetarians, this standard Chinese fare is as good as it gets (though vegetables are scarce).

Price Chopper (☎ 709-695-5000; High St; ⏰ 8:30am-6pm Mon-Tue & Sat, 8:30am-9pm Wed-Fri, 11am-5pm Sun) Stockpile groceries at the Chopper.

Getting There & Away

The **Marine Atlantic ferry** (☎ 800-341-7981; www.marine-atlantic.ca; adult/child 5-12yr $27/13.50, per car/motorcycle $77/39) connects Port aux Basques with North Sydney in Nova Scotia. It operates year-round, typically with two sailings daily during winter and three or four sailings between mid-June and mid-September. Departure times vary day-by-day. Daylight summer crossings take approximately six hours, while winter and night sailings are about seven hours. A four-berth cabin will set you back $99.

DRL Coachlines (☎ 709-263-2171; www.drlgroup.com) has a stop at the **ferry terminal** (☎ 709-695-4216). Buses leave at 8am for Corner Brook ($38, 3½ hours) and St John's ($130, 13½ hours); cash only.

If you're hoping to make connections in Corner Brook for the Northern Peninsula, you're best catching the Gateway bus (p252).

AROUND PORT AUX BASQUES

Cape Ray

Adjacent to JT Cheeseman Provincial Park 14km north of town is Cape Ray. The coastal scenery is engaging, and the road leads up to the windblown **Cape Ray Lighthouse** (admission free; ⏰ 10am-9pm Jul & Aug). This area is the southernmost known Dorset Paleo-Eskimo site, dating from 400 BC to AD 400. Thousands of artifacts have been found here and some dwelling sites can be seen.

There is also some fine hikes in the area. The Cormack Trail (p253) will eventually stretch north from here to Flat Bay near Stephenville. The **Table Mountain Trail** (12km) is more like a rugged road (don't even think about driving up it) and begins on Hwy 1 opposite the exit to Cape Ray. The hike leads to a 518m plateau, where there are ruins from a secret US radar site and airstrip from WWII. It's not a hard hike, but allow three or four hours.

John T Cheeseman Provincial Park (☎ 709-695-7222; Rte 408; campsites $13, per vehicle $5; ⏰ late May–mid-Sep) rests next to the beach and has top-notch facilities.

South Coast

Visitors often ignore Rte 470, and that's a shame because it's a beauty. Heading east out of Port aux Basques for 45km and edg-ing along the shore, the road rises and falls over the eroded, windswept terrain, looking as though it's following a glacier that plowed through yesterday.

Isle aux Morts (Island of the Dead) got its label compliments of the many shipwrecks that occurred just offshore over some 400 years. Named after a family famous for daring shipwreck rescues, the **Harvey Trail** (7km) twists along the rugged shore and makes a stirring walk. Look for the signs in town.

Another highlight is the last settlement along the road, **Rose Blanche**, an absolutely splendid, traditional-looking village nestled in a cove with a fine natural harbor – a perfect example of the classic Newfoundland fishing community. From here follow the signs to the restored **Rose Blanche Lighthouse** (☎ 709-956-2052; www.roseblanchelighthouse.ca; adult/student/family $3/2/7; ⏰ 9am-9pm May-Oct). Built in 1873, it's the last remaining granite lighthouse on the Atlantic seaboard. The **Hook, Line & Sinker** (☎ 709-956-2005; meals $6-10; ⏰ 11am-9pm) café is right next door and is a delightful spot for lunch or dinner.

For those without a vehicle, **Gateway** (☎ 709-695-3333) offers flexible van tours from Port aux Basques that visit Rose Blanche. Prices start at $75 and go up depending on how many villages you want to visit en route. For those planning to launch their trip to the South Coast Outports (p256) from Rose Blanche, the one-way fare is $45.

SOUTH COAST OUTPORTS

If you have the time and patience, a trip across the South Coast and its wee fishing villages – called outports – is the best way to witness Newfoundland's unique culture. These little communities are some of the most remote settlements in North America, reachable only by boat as they cling to the convoluted shore. An anomaly is Burgeo, connected by an easy road trip; it has an unspoiled, isolated feel, yet good amenities for travelers. But hurry: the outports are dwindling as government pressure and lack of employment force residents to relocate to more accessible areas.

ORIENTATION & INFORMATION

Burgeo (population 1700) is the largest town and acts as a service center. It's also the only one accessible by road, other than the journey-starting and -ending towns of Rose Blanche (p255) and Hermitage (p243). The tiny outports in between include **Lapoile, Grand Bruit, Ramea, Grey River, François** and **McCallum**.

The visitors center (p253) in Port aux Basques has tourist information on the region. Several outports have a combined website (www.bbsict.com) with lodging and activity information.

SIGHTS & ACTIVITIES

When the sun is out and the sea shimmers between endless inlets and islands, Burgeo is a dream. Climb the stairs to **Maiden Tea Hill** and look out in admiration. The 7km of white-sand beaches at **Sandbanks Provincial Park** may be the best in the entire province. At least the piping plover who dawdle there think so.

Boat tours (2hr per person $25) and **sea-kayak rentals & tours** (per day single/double kayak $70/90, guide per hr $20) are available from Burgeo Haven B&B.

The other outports are great areas for remote camping, hiking and fishing; ask locals about arranging a guide.

SLEEPING & EATING

Other than in Burgeo, you'll likely have to bunk with a local family, which is easy enough to line up. The locals are very helpful.

Sandbanks Provincial Park (☎ 709-886-2331; off Rte 480, Burgeo; campsites $13, per vehicle $5; ☺ late May–mid-Sep) Two-thirds of the 25 campsites are nestled in the forest, while the remainder are in a grassy area. The flies can be brutal.

Blue Mountain Cabins (☎ 709-492-2753; www.bluemountaincabins.ca; Grand Bruit; s/d $70/75; ☺ Jun-Oct) There are just two cottages here. Meals are offered to guests at modest prices, and the hostess can arrange hiking trips.

Gillett's Motel (☎ 709-886-1284; www.gillettsmotel.ca; 1 Inspiration Rd, Burgeo; d $75; ☺) The sole motel in town is, well, motel-like, with all the usual room amenities (TVs, Internet capabilities). It's just fine, as is the on-site Galley Restaurant (meals $7 to $15), where you'll eat cod likely caught that morning.

Burgeo Haven B&B (☎ 709-886-2544; www.burgeohaven.com; 111 Reach Rd, Burgeo; d with/without shared bathroom $70/80; ☐) Right across from Maiden Tea Hill, this large house backs onto an inlet and offers a serene setting. There's free wi-fi, and some of the five rooms have views.

Joy's Place (☎ 709-886-2569; Reach Rd, Burgeo; meals $6-11; ☺ 11am-11:30pm) Near Burgeo Haven B&B,

Joy whips up fried chicken, Chinese dishes, burgers and pie in addition to her ever present fish dishes.

GETTING THERE & AWAY

Lonely, 148km-long Rte 480 shoots off of Hwy 1 south of Corner Brook and then runs straight into Burgeo. Note there is no gas station and barely any civilization, just glacier-cut boulders and ponds and a whole lotta moose. Stew's (p252) shuttle van runs between Corner Brook and Burgeo.

Access to the other towns is by boat only. While the following ferries run all year, the route described below is for mid-May through September. If hours are not given here, it is because departures are not regular. Schedules change, so check with **Provincial Ferry Services** (☎ 709-292-4302; www.tw.gov.nl.ca/ferryservices). Note that the ferries do not take vehicles (except Burgeo to Ramea).

And yes, the schedule below is confusing, but with careful planning a trip through is doable.

Starting at Rose Blanche, ferries leave for Lapoile ($3.75, 1½ hours) and Grand Bruit ($4.75, 2½ hours) at 3:30pm daily (except Tuesday and Thursday). On the same days there are two boats from Lapoile to Grand Bruit ($3.50, one hour). From Grand Bruit to Burgeo ($5.50, three hours), boats only leave Tuesday at 8:45am.

From Burgeo you have a couple of options. One to three ferries daily go to Ramea ($3.75, 1½ hours) and one daily (except Tuesday and Thursday) ferry to Grey River ($5.25, 2½ hours). If you take the Ramea boat, your only options from there to Grey River ($4, 1½ hours) are on the 8am and 3:30pm sail-

---

DETOUR: FRANÇOIS

Tiny **François** (www.francoisnf.com) dumbfounds as you enter its narrow waterway and are suddenly met by towering walls of rock all around. These cliffs are cut with trails that make for great, if challenging, hikes. Sea kayaking and boat tours through abandoned outports and a lost whaling station are offered by **Pinnacle Tours** (☎ 709-842-3336; www.pinnacletours.org). For lodging, you'll stay with a local family. See the town website for further information; see above for ferry schedules.

ings each Tuesday or Thursday. From Grey River there are daily (except Tuesday and Thursday) sailings to François ($4.75, two hours) at 4:45pm. Ferries leave François for McCallum ($4.75, 2½ hours) and Hermitage ($6.75, four hours) at 7am Thursday. If you disembark in McCallum your next chance to reach Hermitage (1½ hours) is the following Thursday at 9:45am.

At Hermitage, you'll have to suss out transportation back to Rte 360. You can then hook up with **Thornhill Bus Service** (☎ 866-538-3429), which runs between Harbour Breton and Grand Falls, and connects with DRL in the latter.

LABRADOR

It's called the Big Land, and with 293,000 sq km stretching northward, it's easy to see why. The place is primeval-looking, consisting of undulating, rocky, puddled expanses with little vegetation. If you ever wanted to see what the world looked like before man stepped on it, this is it. Adding to the Great Northern effect: four huge caribou herds, including the world's largest (some 750,000 head), migrate across Labrador to their calving grounds each year.

Inuit and Innu have occupied Labrador for thousands of years, and until the 1960s the population was still limited to them and a few longtime European descendants known as 'liveyers.' They eked out an existence for centuries by fishing and hunting from their tiny villages that freckled the coast. The interior was virgin wilderness.

Over the past few decades, the economic potential of Labrador's vast natural resources has not gone unnoticed. Several have been tapped, such as the massive iron-ore mines in Wabush and Labrador City and the hydro-electric dam at Churchill Falls.

The northern coast of the province remains essentially unchanged, however, and is a great place to explore the Inuit- and Aboriginal-influenced villages. There are no roads, so you'll have to get there by supply ferry. Actually, a lack of roads and facilities is common throughout this behemoth region, so planning ahead is essential.

Labrador (population 27,000) is a cold, wet and windy place, and its bugs are murderous. Note that the Labrador Straits (not including

the Québec portion) are on Newfoundland Time, while the rest of Labrador (starting at Cartwright) is on Atlantic Time, ie 30 minutes behind Newfoundland. Québec is on Eastern Time, which is an hour behind Atlantic Time. These variations can make ferry and airplane schedules a headache.

LABRADOR STRAITS

And you thought the Northern Peninsula was commanding? Sail the 18km across the Strait of Belle Isle and behold a landscape even more windswept and black-rocked. Clouds rip across aqua-and-gray skies, and the water that slaps the shore is so cold it's purplish. This ain't no place for sissies, but it is a definite place for visitors, easy to reach and exalted with sights like Red Bay, Battle Harbour and a slew of great walking trails that meander past shipwreck fragments and old whale bones.

'Labrador Straits' is the colloquial name given to the communities that comprise the southern coastal region of Labrador. Note that your first stop in the region (population 4700) will not actually be in Labrador at all, as the ferry terminal and airport are both in Blanc Sablon, Québec. Once in Labrador, Rte 510 is the road that connects the Straits communities. South of Red Bay, it is sealed and open all year. From Red Bay north to Cartwright, it's gravel and not open in winter, though this may change. Check with the **Department of Transportation & Works** (☎ 709-729-2300; www.roads.gov.nl.ca).

Blanc Sablon to L'Anse au Clair

After arriving by ferry or plane in Blanc Sablon and driving a few minutes north on Rte 510 you come to Labrador and the gateway town of L'Anse au Clair. Here you will find the Straits' excellent **visitors center** (☎ 709-931-2013, 877-931-2013; www.labradorcoastaldrive.com; Rte 510, L'Anse au Claire; ☒ 9am-5pm mid-Jun–mid-Oct) in an old church that doubles as a small museum. Be sure and pick up hiking trail maps for the region.

The town makes a good a pre- or post-ferry base. Norm at **Beachside Hospitality Home** (☎ 709-931-2338; normanletto@yahoo.ca; 9 Lodge Rd; r $38-45) will play the accordion for you before you tuck under the quilt at this three-bedroom, two-bathroom B&B.

The modern, well-kept **Northern Light Inn** (☎ 709-931-2332, 800-563-3188; www.northernlightinn .com; 56 Main St; s/d $85/105) is a tour-bus favorite.

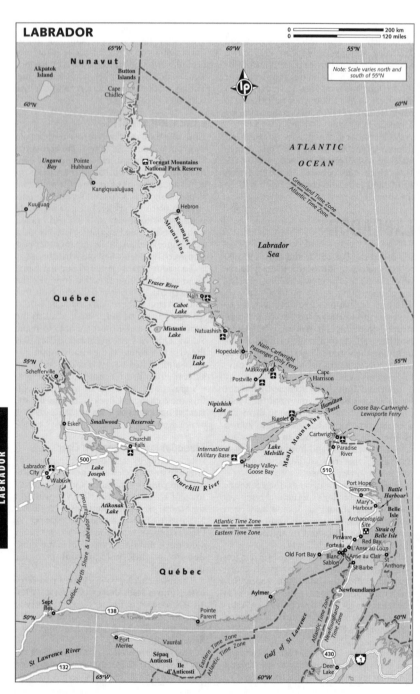

LABRADOR

0 —————— 200 km
0 —————— 120 miles

Note: Scale varies north and south of 55°N

Nunavut

Akpatok Island

Button Islands

Cape Chidley

ATLANTIC OCEAN

Ungava Bay

Pointe Hubbard

Torngat Mountains National Park Reserve

Kuujjuaq

Kangiqsualujjuaq

Hebron

Greenland Time Zone
Atlantic Time Zone

Kaumajet Mountains

Labrador Sea

Québec

Fraser River

Cabot Lake

Nain

Mistastin Lake

Natuashish

Harp Lake

Hopedale

Nain-Cartwright Passenger Only Ferry

Makkovik

Cape Harrison

Postville

Scefferville

Nipishish Lake

Rigolet

Hamilton Inset

Goose Bay-Cartwright-Lewisporte Ferry

Esker

Smallwood Reservoir

Churchill Falls

International Military Base

Lake Melville

Cartwright

Paradise River

Labrador City

500

Lake Joseph

Wabush

Happy Valley-Goose Bay

Churchill River

510

Mealy Mountains

Port Hope Simpson

Battle Harbour

Mary's Harbour

Belle Isle

Atikonak Lake

Atlantic Time Zone

Eastern Time Zone

Archaeological Site

Strait of Belle Isle

Pinware
Red Bay

Forteau
L'Anse au Loup

Old Fort Bay

Blanc Sablon
L'Anse au Clair

St Barbe

St Anthony

Québec

Aylmer

Newfoundland

Sept Iles

138

Pointe Parent

Atlantic Time Zone
Newfoundland Time Zone

Eastern Time Zone
Atlantic Time Zone

Gulf of St Lawrence

430

1

Port Menier

Vauréal

St Lawrence River

132

Sépaq Anticosti Ile d'Anticosti

Deer Lake

Québec North Shore & Labrador Railroad

DETOUR: QUÉBEC'S LOWER NORTH SHORE

The Lower North Shore is the name given to the wild, remote chunk of La Belle Province that extends south of Blanc Sablon. Route 138 (the Québec incarnation of Labrador's Rte 510) runs down the coast here for 74km. It's a beautiful drive with several roadside waterfalls and lookouts from which to see the crashing surf and offshore puffin colonies. The road ends abruptly at Old Fort Bay, and is not connected to further destinations in Québec.

For those wanting to do more than just drive through the region, the **Coaster's Association** (☎ 877-447-2006; www.coasters association.com) provides information on attractions and accommodations.

The even-numbered rooms have harbor views. The **dining room** (mains $12-18; ☺ breakfast, lunch & dinner) is your best bet for food in town.

The **MV Apollo** (☎ 866-535-2567; www.labrador marine.com; adult/child 5-12yr $11.25/6, per car/motorcycle $22.50/11.50) sails the two hours between St Barbe in Newfoundland and Blanc Sablon between May and early January. From early July to mid-September, when things are at their busiest, the boat runs two or three times a day between 8am and 6pm; at other times service drops to once or twice daily. Schedules vary wildly day to day for this journey. Note that the ferry terminal in Blanc Sablon operates on Newfoundland Time and not Eastern Time, which the rest of Blanc Sablon follows.

Provincial Airlines (☎ 800-563-2800; www.provincial airlines.ca) has flights to Blanc Sablon from St John's ($244) and St Anthony ($153). Just to confuse you, departure times from the airport are on Eastern Time versus Labrador Straits (ie Newfoundland) Time.

Rental cars are available at the airport from **Eagle River Rent-a-Car** (☎ 709-931-2352) and **National** (☎ 709-461-2777).

Forteau to Pinware

Continuing northeast on Rte 510 you'll pass Forteau, L'Anse Amour, L'Anse au Loup and Pinware.

Forteau-based **Labrador Adventures** (☎ 709-931-2055; chancock@labradorstraits.net; tours $15-85) provides truly knowledgeable guides for Straits-oriented hikes or day tours by SUV.

This is a terrific way to see the area, especially if you're short on time or car-less. Forteau's **Overfall Brook Trail** (4km) shadows the coast and ends at a 30m waterfall.

Six houses total comprise the village of L'Anse Amour, but it holds more than its share of sights. **L'Anse Amour Burial Mound** (L'Anse Amour Rd), a pile of stones placed here by the Maritime Archaic Aboriginals, is the oldest burial monument in North America. Only a small roadside plaque marks the 7500-year-old site. Down the same road is **Point Amour Lighthouse Provincial Historic Site** (☎ 709-927-5825; L'Anse Amour Rd; admission $3; ☺ 10am-5:30pm May-late Sep). Taking four years to build and with 127 steps to climb, this is the tallest lighthouse in Atlantic Canada. When you dizzily reach the top, you will be bestowed with a spectacular 360-degree view of the coastline. The lighthouse keeper's house has exhibits on maritime history. The HMS *Raleigh* went aground here in 1922 and was destroyed in 1926. The easy, 15-minute **Raleigh Trail** takes you by the site and warship fragments on the beach.

Past L'Anse au Loup is the **Battery Trail** (2km), which meanders through a stunted tuckamore forest to the summit of the Battery, unfurling panoramic sea views.

The road veers inland at Pinware, and skirts along the western side of the Pinware River, until it crosses a one-lane iron bridge, and then runs along the eastern side, high above the rushing whitewater. This stretch of the Pinware is renowned for its **salmon fishing**, and there are lodges with guiding services. About 10km before reaching Red Bay, the land becomes rocky and barren, except for the superfluity of blueberries and bakeapples (and pickers) in August.

Forteau's family-friendly **Seaview Cabins** (☎ 709-931-2840; bradleyhancock@hotmail.com; 33 Main St; cabins $89-95) have been renovated recently. Four of the eight cabins are 'luxury,' ie larger and with water views; two have Jacuzzis. Inquire at the **restaurant** (meals $6-16; ☺ breakfast, lunch & dinner) across the street. While there, chow down on the famous fried chicken and fantastically tender caribou. A grocery store and jam factory are also on-site.

Red Bay

Spread between two venues, brilliant **Red Bay National Historic Site** (☎ 709-920-2051; www.pc .gc.ca/redbay; Rte 510, Red Bay; adult/child 6-16yr/family $7.15/3.45/18.05; ☺ 9am-6pm early Jun–mid-Oct) uses

---

BAKEAPPLE BONANZA

You keep hearing about it: bakeapple jam, bakeapple pie, bakeapple syrup. But what's a bake-apple?

We'll tell you this much: it's not a red fruit that's been placed in the oven. Rather, a bakeapple (sometimes called a cloudberry) is an orangey-yellow fruit similar in shape and size to a large raspberry. It grows wild on small plants in moist northern tundra and boglands – ie Labrador. The taste is often compared to apricot and honey.

Bakeapples ripen in mid-August, and that's when aficionados from Newfoundland pile over to the Labrador Straits and start picking. Get your fill – breakfast, lunch and dinner – at Forteau's **Bakeapple Folk Festival** (adult/child $5/3), a three-day event in mid-August featuring music, dance, crafts and buckets of the eponymous fruit. Or buy bakeapple products at the Seaview Restaurant (p259), where they're made on-site.

---

different media to chronicle the discovery of three 16th-century Basque whaling galleons on the sea bed here. Well preserved in the ice-cold waters, the vestiges of the ships tell a remarkable story of what life was like here some four centuries ago. Red Bay was the largest whaling port in the world, with more than 2000 men residing here. Have a look at the reconstructed *chalupa* (a small Basque dingy used for whale hunting) and some of the other relics in the museum. Then hop in a small boat ($2) to nearby **Saddle Island**, where there is a self-guided interpretive trail around the excavated land sites. Allow at least two or three hours for the museum and island.

Across the bay, the amazing 15-minute **Boney Shore Trail** skirts the coast and passes ancient whale bones (they pretty much look like rocks) scattered along it. The **Tracey Hill Trail** (4.6km) climbs a boardwalk and 670 steps to the top of American Rockyman Hill for a bird's-eye view of the harbor.

Basinview B&B (☎ 709-920-2002; blancheearle@ hotmail.com; 145 Main St; r $46-75) is a simple four-room, shared-bathroom lodging in town.

Remember, Red Bay is the end of paved road. It's pink gravel from here on up to Cartwright.

Battle Harbour

Sitting on an island in the Labrador Sea is the elaborately restored village and saltfish premises of **Battle Harbour** (☎ 709-921-6216; www .battleharbour.com; adult/child 6-12yr $7/3.50; ☼ Jun–mid-Sep). Now a national historic district, it used to be the unofficial 'capital' of Labrador during the early 19th century, when fishing schooners lined its docks. Another claim to fame: this is the place where Robert E Peary gave his first

news conference after reaching the North Pole in 1909.

It's accessed by boat ($40 round-trip) from Mary's Harbour (departures 11am and 7pm, one hour) and you can come for the day or spend a few nights. Accommodations are spread among various heritage homes and cottages, operated by the **Battle Harbour Inn** (☎ 709-921-6325; www.battleharbour.com; Battle Harbour; dm/s/d/cottage $25/90/100/150; ☼ Jun–mid-Sep). A store and **restaurant** (meals $8-18, ☼ breakfast, lunch & dinner) are on-site.

Mary's Harbour to Cartwright

After departing Mary's Harbour you'll pass through Port Hope Simpson 51km up the gravel road, and then there's nothing for 186km until Cartwright. And that, friends, is the literal end of the road. Stay tuned, though: a gravel road supposedly will be built connecting Cartwright to Goose Bay by 2008.

Cartwright-based **Experience Labrador** (☎ 877-938-7444; www.experiencelabrador.com; ☼ Jul-Sep) offers multiday kayaking trips (two-day tour $300) along the northern coast, where you paddle the endless sands of the Wonderstrands that mesmerized the Vikings so long ago.

Other than that, Cartwright is about the ferry. Passenger boats (opposite) depart for the remote villages that sprinkle the northern coast. Vehicle ferries (p242) stop here on their route between Goose Bay and Lewisporte.

The simple **Cartwright Hotel** (☎ 709-938-7414; www.cartwrighthotel.ca; 3 Airport Rd, Cartwright; r $88-106) has 10 rooms, a **dining room** (meals $6-17; ☼ 6am-10pm) and lounge.

NORTHERN COAST

North of Cartwright up to Ungava Bay there are a half-dozen small, semitraditional Inuit communities accessible only by sea or air along the rugged, largely unspoiled mountainous coast.

In 1993 on the shores of Voisey's Bay, near Nain, geologists discovered stunningly rich concentrations of copper, cobalt and especially nickel. A giant mine has been built to extract the goods, and it is expected to pump $11 billion into the provincial economy over 30 years. This likely will open up the north – for better or worse.

Sights & Activities

The first port of call on the north coast is **Makkovik**, an early fur-trading post and a traditional fishing and hunting community. Both new and old-style crafts can be bought.

Further north in **Hopedale** visitors can look at the old wooden Moravian mission church (1782). This **national historic site** (admission $5; ☽ 8:30am-8pm Jun-Sep) also includes a store, residence, some huts and a museum collection; it's all operated by the **Agvituk Historical Society** (☎ 709-933-3777).

Natuashish is a new town that was formed when the troubled village of Utshimassit (Davis Inlet) was relocated to the mainland in 2002. The move was made after a 2000 study showed that 154 of 169 youths surveyed had abused solvents (ie sniffed gasoline) and that 60 of them did it on a daily basis.

The last stop on the ferry is **Nain**, and it's the last town of any size as you go northward. Fishing has historically been the town's main industry, but this is changing due to the Voisey's Bay nickel deposit.

From Nain, you can try to arrange boat transportation to **Torngat Mountains National Park Reserve**. The mountains are popular with climbers because of their altitude (some of the highest peaks east of the Rockies) and isolation. **Nature Trek Canada** (☎ 250-653-4265; www.naturetrek.ca/labrador; ☽ Jul-Sep) runs multiday tours in the area. The **Kaumajet Mountains** also make for an out-of-this-world hiking experience – inquire at the Amaguk Inn.

Sleeping & Eating

Most travelers use the ferry as a floating hotel. For those wishing to get off and wait until the next boat, it usually means winging it for a room, as only Hopedale and Nain have official lodging.

Amaguk Inn (☎ 709-933-3750; Hopedale; r/ste $115 /165) This recently renovated 18-room inn also

has a dining room (meals $11 to $16), and a lounge where you can get a cold beer.

Atsanik Lodge (☎ 709-922-2910; atsaniklabrador@ msn.com; Sand Banks Rd, Nain; s/d $115/125) This large lodge and its restaurant (meals $13 to $18) are your best bet in Nain.

Getting There & Away

Air Labrador (☎ 800-563-3042; www.airlabrador.com) and **Provincial Airlines** (☎ 800-563-2800; www.provincial airlines.ca) serve most of the northern coast's villages from Goose Bay.

The MV *Northern Ranger* plies this section of coast from mid-June to mid-November. It leaves once per week, making the three-day (one way) journey between Goose Bay and Nain, stopping in Makkovik, Hopedale and Natuashish along the way. In warmer months, it also runs south from Goose Bay to Cartwright. Check with **Labrador Marine** (☎ 866-535-2567; www.labradormarine.com) for the ever-evolving schedule and fares.

CENTRAL LABRADOR

Making up the territorial bulk of Labrador, the central portion is an immense, sparsely populated and ancient wilderness. Paradoxically, it also has the largest town in Labrador, Happy Valley-Goose Bay (www.happyvalley-goose bay.com), home to a military base. The town (population 8000) has all the usual services, but unless you're an angler or hunter, there isn't much to see or do and it is very isolated.

Goose Bay was established during WWII as a staging point for planes on their way to Europe, and has remained an aviation center. The airport is also an official NASA alternate landing site for the space shuttle.

All sights and accommodations listed here are located in Happy Valley-Goose Bay.

Sights & Activities

Officially opened by Queen Elizabeth II in 1997, the **Labrador Interpretation Centre** (☎ 709-497-8566; Portage Rd, North West River; admission $3; ☽ 1-4pm Wed-Sun) is the provincial museum, which holds some of Labrador's finest works of art.

The **Northern Lights Building** (☎ 709-896-5939; 170 Hamilton River Rd; admission free; ☽ 10am-5:30pm Mon-Sat, to 9pm Fri) hosts a military museum, interesting lifelike nature scenes and simulated northern lights.

The **Labrador Heritage Society Museum** (☎ 709-497-8858; www.labheritage.ca; off Rte 500; admission $2; ☽ 8:30am-4:30pm Wed-Sun mid-Jun–Sep) includes a traditional trapper's shelter, samples of animal furs and local minerals and details on the ill-fated Wallace-Hubbard expedition into Labrador's interior.

Sleeping & Eating

TMT's B&B (☎ 709-896-4404; gordon.coles@persona .ca; 451 Hamilton River Rd; r per person $35) Family atmosphere and home cooking await you at TMT's.

Aurora Hotel (☎ 709-896-3398; www.aurorahotel .com; 382 Hamilton River Rd; s/d from $79/89; ✇) The Aurora's comfy rooms sit at the crossroads of the airport and sea port. Enjoy a caribou burger in the restaurant (meals $8 to $18; open breakfast, lunch and dinner) or head to the lounge for drinks.

Royal Inn & Suites (☎ 709-896-2456; www.royal innandsuites.ca; 5 Royal Ave; d $83-110, ste $105-135; ▣) The Royal is a good-looking place with a variety of rooms to choose from. Many of them have kitchens as well as high-speed Internet capabilities. A light breakfast is also included.

Getting There & Away

AIR
Air Labrador (☎ 800-563-3042; www.airlabrador.com) and **Provincial Airlines** (☎ 800-563-2800; www.pro vincialairlines.ca) both have flights serving Goose Bay from St John's ($360) as well as Deer Lake ($309).

BOAT
You can reach Goose Bay by two different ferries: the vehicle carrier MV *Robert Bond* (p242) and the passenger-only MV *Northern Ranger* (p261).

CAR & MOTORCYCLE
Your options by car from Happy Valley-Goose Bay are westward along the gravel of Rte 500 to Churchill Falls and then on to the twin cities of Labrador City and Wabush. The drive from Goose Bay to Labrador City takes about 10 hours. There are no services until Churchill Falls, so stock up. The road can also be very, very rough. Before leaving, contact the **Department of Transportation & Works** (☎ 709-729-2300; www.roads.gov.nl.ca) for the latest conditions.

Trucks can be rented at the airport from **National** (☎ 709-896-5575), but due to conditions on Rte 500, you cannot buy insurance.

LABRADOR WEST
Just 5km apart and 15km from Québec, the twin mining towns of **Labrador City** (population 7700) and **Wabush** (population 2000) are referred to collectively as Labrador West, and this is where the western region's population is concentrated. The largest open-pit iron ore mine in the world is in Labrador City, and another operates in Wabush. The landscape is massive and the celestial polychromatic artwork can take up the entire night sky.

Information
Visitors center (☎ 709-944-7631; www.labradorwest .com; 1365 Rte 500; ✇ 9am-9pm mid-Jun–early Sep, 9am-5pm Mon-Fri mid-Sep–early Jun) Just west of Labrador City.

Sights & Activities
In the same building as the visitors center is **Gateway Labrador** (☎ 709-944-5399; www.gateway labrador.ca; adult/student $3/2.50; ✇ 9am-9pm Jun-early Sep, 9am-5pm Mon-Fri, noon-5pm Sat & Sun Sep-May) and

---

LOCAL VOICES

Brigitte Schloss
Former coordinator of the Native Teacher Training Program in Labrador and professor of education at Memorial University, age 79, St John's

What sort of changes have you seen in Labrador since you first began working there in 1950? The north coast [around Makkovik and Nain] has totally changed. My first year there we didn't have mail for three months at a time. We only had fresh meat to eat. Now they have bananas in the stores! It has opened up a lot, but not always for the best. The fish have disappeared. Resettlement has done away with the traditional [Inuit] way of life. **What is the most important issue facing Labrador today?** Development, especially in places like Voisey's Bay (p260). The mining companies say, 'We are going to leave the place the way we found it.' But there is very little topsoil there; it takes 100 years for a tree to grow. The land is sometimes robbed. **What is the most defining characteristic of Labrador?** There is so much space and fresh air. And the people have a thoughtful quietness and wisdom for coping with life.

its **Montague Exhibit Hall**, where 3500 years of human history and culture, including the fur trade, are represented with intriguing artifacts and displays.

Just out of town the landscape is a vast expanse of low, rolling, forested mountains interspersed with flat northern tundra. The **Wapusakatto Mountains** are 5km from town, and parts have been developed for skiing. For trail information and fees for world-class cross-country skiing (the Canadian nation team trains in the region), check with the **Menihek Nordic Ski Club** (☎ 709-944-5842; http://home.crrstv .net/menihek); for alpine skiing, check with the **Smokey Mountain Ski Club** (☎ 709-944-2129; www .smokeymountain.ca).

From Wabush, 39km east on Rte 500 is **Lac Grand Hermine Park** (☎ 709-282-5369; admission $3; ☼ Jun–mid-Sep), with a beach and fine scenery. The **Menihek hiking trail** (15km) goes through wooded areas with waterfalls and open tundra. Outfitters can take anglers to excellent **fishing** waters.

If big holes and trucks the size of apartment buildings make your heart flutter, you can tour the **mines** (admission free; ☼ 1:30pm Wed & Sun Jul-Sep) by contacting the visitors center (opposite).

Sleeping & Eating

PJ's Inn by the Lake (☎ 709-944-3438; www.pjsinnby thelake.com; 606 Tamarack Dr, Labrador City; s/d incl breakfast $50/60; ☐) Pete and Jo's home is your home: they'll let you use their treadmill, rowing machine and/or guitar. The three rooms each have their own bathroom; the Green Room has a Jacuzzi.

Carol Inn (☎ 709-944-7736, 888-799-7736; carolinn@ crrstv.net; 215 Drake Ave, Labrador City; r $85) All 20 of the rooms at this place have kitchenettes and

air-conditioning. There's also a fine dining room (meals $20 to $30; open dinner Tuesday to Saturday), pub (meals $8 to $12; open 8am to midnight) and small pizza franchise.

Wabush Hotel (☎ 709-282-3221; www.wabushhotel .com; 9 Grenville Dr, Wabush; s/d $95/114) Centrally located in Wabush, this chalet-style 68-room hotel has spacious and comfortable rooms. The dining room (meals $9 to $21; open 6:30am to midnight) has a popular dinner buffet.

Getting There & Away

AIR

Air Labrador (☎ 800-563-3042; www.airlabrador.com), **Provincial Airlines** (☎ 800-563-2800; www.provincial airlines.ca) and **Air Canada** (☎ 888-247-2262; www .aircanada.com) fly into the twin cities' airport.

CAR & MOTORCYCLE

Fifteen kilometers west from Labrador City along Rte 500 is Fermont, Québec. From there Rte 389 is mainly paved (with some fine gravel sections) and continues south 581km to Baie Comeau. See opposite for information on Rte 500 heading east.

Budget (☎ 709-282-1234) has an office at the airport; rental cars may not be driven on Rte 500.

TRAIN

The **Iron Ore Company of Canada** (☎ 709-944-8400, ask for operator & then 'train service') operates the Québec North Shore & Labrador Railroad, a once-weekly train (adult/child under 12 years $64/32, round-trip $116) linking Sept Îles, Québec, with Labrador City's depot on Airport Rd. The train leaves Sept Îles on Thursday at 9am and travels nine hours through stunning forest and gorges.

Directory

CONTENTS

ACCOMMODATIONS

In Atlantic Canada, you'll be choosing from a wide range of B&Bs, motels, hotels, hostels and campgrounds. Provincial tourist offices (p273) publish comprehensive accommodation directories as well as posting directory listings on their websites. The tourist offices of Prince Edward Island and Nova Scotia also take bookings online (the latter via a dedicated website at www.checkinnovascotia.com).

In this book we list options in all price categories. The budget category comprises campgrounds, hostels and simple hotels and B&Bs where you'll likely share a bathroom. Rates rarely exceed $90 for a double.

Midrange accommodations, such as most B&Bs, inns, motels and some hotels, gener-ally offer the best value for money. Expect to pay between $90 and $160 for a comfortable, decent-sized double with a private bathroom and TV.

Top-end accommodations (more than $160 per double) offer an international standard of amenities including fitness and business centers and other upmarket facilities.

Most properties have rooms set aside for nonsmokers, and some smaller properties, especially B&Bs, ban smoking altogether. Air-conditioning is not a standard amenity, and you probably won't miss it given the region's cool temperatures. If you want air-conditioning, be sure to ask about it when you book.

Prices listed in this book are for peak-season travel (July and August) and, unless stated otherwise, do not include taxes (14% to 17%). It's best to book ahead in during peak season, holidays (p269) and major events (p269), as rooms can be scarce. In winter, many proper-ties close; those that remain open drop prices by as much as 50%.

Online agencies such as www.orbitz.com, www.expedia.com, www.travelocity.com and www.hotels.com may fetch better rates than booking directly with a hotel. **Tripadvisor** (www.tripadvisor.com) is a handy resource that features reader and published reviews and simultaneously searches the above-mentioned agencies for rates. **Travelaxe** (www.travelaxe .com) adds in filters to help you narrow down your search (eg distance, price, comfort level); it requires a free software download. Also check hotel websites listed throughout this book for special online rates.

For details about how to get your lodging taxes refunded, see p271.

BOOK ACCOMMODATION ONLINE

For more accommodation reviews and rec-ommendations by Lonely Planet authors, check out the online booking service at www.lonelyplanet.com. You'll find the true, insider lowdown on the best places to stay. Reviews are thorough and independent. Best of all, you can book online.

PRACTICALITIES

- Electrical supply is 110V AC, 50/60 Hz.

- The Toronto-based *Globe and Mail* (www.theglobeandmail.com) is still the big news around these parts. Regional dailies include the *Halifax Chronicle-Herald* (www.thechronicleherald.ca), *Charlottetown Guardian* (www.theguardian.pe.ca), *New Brunswick Telegraph-Journal* (www .telegraphjournal.com) and *St John's Telegram* (www.thetelegram.com).

- *Maclean's* (www.macleans.ca) is Canada's weekly news magazine. St John's–based *Downhome* (www.downhomelife.com) is a folksy, *Reader's Digest*–style monthly for Atlantic Canada.

- The Canadian Broadcasting Corporation (CBC) is the dominant nationwide network for both radio and TV. The Canadian TV Network (CTN) is the major competition.

- The NTSC system (not compatible with PAL or Secam) is used for videos.

- Canada officially uses the metric system, but imperial measurements are used for many day-to-day purposes. To convert between the two systems, see the chart on the inside front cover.

B&Bs

B&Bs play a central role in Atlantic Canada's lodging scene, and in small towns they're often the only option. B&Bs are essentially converted private homes whose owners live on-site. People who like privacy may find B&Bs too intimate, as walls are rarely soundproof and it's usual to mingle with your hosts and other guests.

Standards vary widely, sometimes even within a single B&B. The cheapest rooms tend to be small with few amenities and a shared bathroom. Nicer ones have added features such as a balcony, fireplace and an en suite bathroom. Not all B&Bs accept children. Minimum stays (usually two nights) are common and many B&Bs are only open seasonally (May to October). Online booking agencies:

Bed & Breakfast Online (www.bbcanada.com) B&Bs throughout Canada, with many in Atlantic Canada.
Select Inns of Atlantic Canada (www.selectinns.ca) Midrange to top-end B&Bs.

Camping

Atlantic Canada is filled with campgrounds – some federal or provincial, others privately owned. The official camping season runs from May to September, but exact dates vary by location.

Government campsites are nearly always better and cheaper. Private campgrounds are generally geared to trailers (caravans) and recreational vehicles (RVs). Nightly fees in national and provincial parks range from $11 to $25 for tents and up to $35 for full hookup sites.

Several national parks participate in Parks Canada's **camping reservation program** (☎ 905-426-4648, 877-737-3783; www.pccamping.ca). For provincial parks check the following:

New Brunswick (www.tourismnewbrunswick.ca)
Newfoundland (www.env.gov.nl.ca/parks)
Nova Scotia (www.parks.gov.ns.ca)
Prince Edward Island (www.gov.pe.ca/visitorsguide)

Home Stays

How do you feel about staying on couch of a perfect stranger? If it's not a problem, consider joining an organization that arranges home stays. Usually you pay a fee (less than $100) to become a member, and then the stay itself is free.

Couch Surfing (www.couchsurfing.com)
Hospitality Club (www.hospitalityclub.org)

Hostels

Atlantic Canada has independent hostels as well as those affiliated with Hostelling International (HI). All have dorms (per person $10 to $25), which can sleep from two to 10 people, and many have private rooms (from $30/40 per single/double) for couples and families.

Bathrooms are usually shared, and facilities include a kitchen, lockers, Internet access, laundry room and common TV room. Most hostels, especially those in big cities, are open 24 hours. If not, ask if you can make special arrangements if you're arriving late.

For additional information and online reservations:

Hostelling International Canada (www.hihostels.ca)
Hostels.com (www.hostels.com) Includes independent hostels.

Hotels & Motels

Although most motel rooms won't win any style awards, they're usually clean and comfortable and offer good value for travelers. Many regional motels remain your typical 'mom and pop' operations, but plenty of North American chains have also opened up around the region.

Most hotels are part of international chains, and the newer ones are designed for either the luxury market or businesspeople. Rooms have cable TV and Internet access; many also have swimming pools and fitness and business centers.

Chains in Atlantic Canada:

Best Western (☎ 800-780-7234; www.bestwestern atlantic.com) Midrange.

Choice Hotels (☎ 800-424-6423; www.choicehotels.ca) Midrange.

City Hotels (☎ 800-563-2489; www.cityhotels.ca) Midrange.

Delta (☎ 877-814-7706; www.deltahotels.com) Top end.

Fairmont (☎ 800-257-7544; www.fairmont.com) Top end.

ACTIVITIES

Everywhere you go you'll find outfitters and tour operators eager to set you up for everything from cycling and sea kayaking to whale-watching and fishing. For details, see the Outdoors chapter.

BUSINESS HOURS

Standard business hours are 9am to 5pm Monday to Friday. Bank hours are generally 10am to 5pm Monday to Friday and sometimes 9am to noon on Saturday. Post offices are generally open 8:30am to 5pm on weekdays.

Most places serve lunch between 11:30am and 2:30pm Monday to Friday and dinner from 5:30pm to 9:30pm daily, later on weekends. Some are closed on Monday. A few serve breakfast from 7:30am to 10am on weekdays and brunch from 10am to 2pm on Saturday and/or Sunday.

Pubs are generally open from 11am to 2am daily, although exact times vary by province. Bars welcome patrons from around 5pm until 2am nightly, while music and dance clubs open their doors at 8pm or 9pm, though often on Friday and Saturday only. Most close at 2am.

Shops are generally open from 10am to 6pm Monday to Saturday. Many shops also open on Sunday from noon to 5pm, although

this is less prevalent on Prince Edward Island and in New Brunswick, and not at all the case in Nova Scotia.

Reviews in this book do not list hours unless they differ from these standard periods.

CHILDREN

Traveling around Atlantic Canada with the tots can be child's play, especially if you don't overpack the schedule. Lonely Planet's *Travel with Children* offers a wealth of tips and tricks. The website **Travel With Your Kids** (www.travel withyourkids.com) is another good, general resource.

Practicalities

Children who are traveling to Canada without both parents need authorization from the nonaccompanying parent (see p276).

Once in Canada, kids receive a wide range of discounts on attraction admissions and transportation fares. Usually kids aged six to 17 are half price; younger children are free. Ask about 'family' admissions if your posse consists of two adults and two or more kids.

Kids often stay for free in hotels and motels. B&Bs are not so gracious, and may even refuse to accept pint-sized patrons. Ask when booking.

Baby food, infant formula, milk, disposable diapers (nappies) and the like are widely available in drugstores and supermarkets. Breastfeeding in public is legal. In all vehicles, children under 18kg must be restrained in safety seats (p283).

Sights & Activities

The great outdoors yields endless possibilities for wee ones' entertainment such as wildlife-watching (whales! dolphins!), hiking and canoeing. Many national parks offer nature walks or other programs specially for children.

In the cities take 'em to parks, playgrounds or kid-friendly museums. For specific suggestions, see the For Children sections throughout the regional chapters of this book. In addition, most tourist offices can lead you to resources for children's programs, childcare facilities and pediatricians.

CLIMATE CHARTS

For general advice on climate and when to travel in Atlantic Canada, see p22. The climate charts (opposite) provide a snapshot of the region's weather patterns.

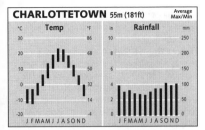

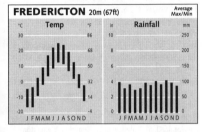

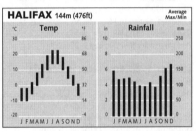

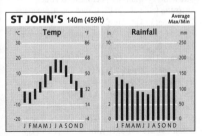

CUSTOMS

Canadian customs allows each person over 18 (entering Alberta, Manitoba and Québec) or 19 (everywhere else) to import duty-free either 1.5L of wine, 1.14L of liquor or 24 350mL beers, as well as 200 cigarettes, 50 cigars, 200g of tobacco and 200 tobacco sticks. You can also bring in gifts valued at up to $60 in total. If you spend at least 48 hours outside Canada you again become eligible for these allowances.

Personal effects – including camping gear, sports equipment, cameras and laptop computers – can be brought into Canada without much trouble.

Importing or exporting money up to a value of $10,000 is fine, but larger amounts must be reported to customs.

Under most circumstances, it is illegal to bring firearms, pepper spray or mace into Canada, or to import fruit, vegetables and plants. Check with a Canadian consulate in your home country if you intend to travel with any of these. Don't attempt to bring in illegal drugs, including marijuana, as sentences can be harsh.

If you're traveling with a dog or cat, carry a signed and dated certificate from a veterinarian to prove that it has had a rabies shot in the past 36 months.

For more information, contact the **Canada Border Services Agency** (CBSA; ☎ 506-636-5064, in Canada 800-461-9999; www.cbsa.gc.ca).

DANGERS & ANNOYANCES

Check the Health chapter for possible health risks and p283 for road conditions and driving hazards.

Crime

Atlantic Canada is a safe place to live and travel. Violent crime does occur, of course, but the four Atlantic provinces post some of Canada's lowest crime rates, and the rates are much lower than in the USA. While smash-and-grab thefts are uncommon, it's always wise to keep valuables out of view in your parked car, especially in the cities.

Insects

Blackflies pester from late May through June, though in northern areas like Labrador that timeframe pushes to mid-July through August. Mosquitoes bother from early spring until early fall. Ticks are around from March to June.

Generally, bug populations are greatest deep in the woods, near water and the further north you go. In clearings, along shorelines or anywhere there's a breeze you'll be fairly safe. Mosquitoes are at their peskiest around sundown. For campers, a tent with a zippered screen is essential. If you're venturing into the backcountry, a 'bug jacket' (essentially a mesh jacket/head-net), available at most camping stores, is recommended. For additional information, see p287.

Ocean Currents & Tides

Currents in the Bay of Fundy create an amazingly strong rip, and the undertow can be just as perilous on Atlantic beaches. The beaches at Prince Edward Island National Park can also be dangerous.

If you go beach hiking along the Bay of Fundy beware of becoming cut off by a rising tide. The water level can rise as much as 30m in just over an hour.

Weather

On winter days, you'll need to bundle up well. For information on avoiding and treating hypothermia, see p287.

DISCOUNT CARDS

If you're a student, never leave home without an **International Student Identity Card** (ISIC; www.isiccard.com), which entitles you to discounts on travel insurance and admission to museums and other sights. The International Youth Travel Card (IYTC), for those under 26 but not students, and the International Teacher Identity Card (ITIC), for full-time educators, offer similar savings. They are all issued by student unions, hostelling organizations and youth-oriented travel agencies.

Discounts are also commonly offered for seniors, children, families and the disabled. In these cases, however, no special cards are issued (you get the savings on-site when you pay). Automobile Association members (p281) also receive various travel-related discounts.

If you plan on visiting nine or more national parks or historic sites, look into getting a **National Parks of Canada Pass** (www.pc.gc.ca/voyage-travel/carte-pass/index_e.asp; adult/child 6-16yr/senior $62.40/31.70/53.50).

EMBASSIES & CONSULATES
Canadian Embassies & Consulates Abroad

Canada has diplomatic representation in almost every country throughout the world. The embassy or high commission is always located in the capital city while consulates, which handle visas and many other travel-related services, are located in other major cities.

Check the website of **Foreign Affairs Canada** (www.international.gc.ca), which has links to all Canadian embassies and consulates overseas.

Australia (☎ 02-6270-4000; www.dfait-maeci.gc.ca /australia/contact-en.asp; Commonwealth Ave, Canberra, ACT 2600)

France (☎ 01-44-43-29-00; www.dfait-maeci.gc.ca /canada-europa/france/; 35 av Montaigne, 75008 Paris)

Germany (☎ 030-203120; www.dfait-maeci.gc.ca/can ada-europa/germany/; Friedrichstrasse 95, 10117 Berlin)

Ireland (☎ 01-417-4100; www.dfait-maeci.gc.ca /canada-europa/ireland/; 65 St Stephen's Green, Dublin 2)

Italy (☎ 06-44-59-81; www.dfait-maeci.gc.ca/canada -europa/italy/; Via G B de Rossi 27, Rome 00161)

Japan (☎ 03-5412-6200; www.dfait-maeci.gc.ca/asia /main/japan/tokyo-en.asp; 3-38 Akasaka 7-chome, Minato-ku, Tokyo 107-8503)

Mexico (☎ 55-247 900; www.dfait-maeci.gc.ca/mexico -city/; Schiller 529, Col Polanco, Rincón del Bosque, 11580 México, DF)

Netherlands (☎ 070-311-1600; www.dfait-maeci.gc.ca /canada-europa/Netherlands/; Sophialaan 7, 2514 JP The Hague)

New Zealand (☎ 04-473-9577; www.dfait-maeci.gc.ca /newzealand; 61 Molesworth St, Thorndon, Wellington)

UK (☎ 020-7258-6600; www.dfait-maeci.gc.ca/canada-eur opa/united_kingdom/; 1 Grosvenor Sq, London W1K 4AB)

USA (☎ 202-682-1740; www.canadianembassy.org; 501 Pennsylvania Ave NW; Washington DC 20001)

Embassies & Consulates in Canada

All embassies are in Ottawa, Canada's capital, though some countries (USA, UK, France) also maintain consulates in Halifax, Moncton and St John's. Contact the relevant embassy to find out which consulate is closest to you.

Australia (☎ 613-236-0841; www.ahc-ottawa.org; 50 O'Connor St, Suite 710, Ottawa, ON K1P 6L2)

France (☎ 613-789-1795; www.ambafrance-ca.org; 42 Sussex Dr, Ottawa, ON K1M 2C9)

Germany (☎ 613-232-1101; www.ottawa.diplo.de; 1 Waverley St, Ottawa, ON K2P 0T8)

Ireland (☎ 613-233-6281; www.irishembassyottawa .com; 130 Albert St, Ottawa, ON K1P 5G4)

Italy (☎ 613-232-2401; www.ambottawa.esteri.it; 275 Slater St, 21st fl, Ottawa, ON K1P 5H9)

Japan (☎ 613-241-8541; www.ca.emb-japan.go.jp; 255 Sussex Dr, Ottawa, ON K1N 9E6)

Mexico (☎ 613-233-8988; www.embamexcan.com; 45 O'Connor St, Suite 1500, Ottawa, ON K1P 1A4)

Netherlands (☎ 613-237-5030; www.netherlandsem bassy.ca; 350 Albert St, Suite 2020, Ottawa, ON K1R 1A4)

New Zealand (☎ 613-238-5991; www.nzembassy.com; 99 Bank St, Suite 727, Ottawa, ON K1P 6G3)

UK (☎ 613-237-2008; www.britishhighcommission.gov.uk; 80 Elgin St, Ottawa, ON K1P 5K7)

USA (☎ 613-238-5335; http://ottawa.usembassy.gov; 490 Sussex Dr, Ottawa, ON K1N 1G8)

FESTIVALS & EVENTS

Atlantic Canada parties loudly in summertime and is quiet the other seasons. The following list is a sampling of shindigs. For festival highlights see Top Ten Bashes (p24). Also see Holidays (right) and the Festivals sections in destination chapters.

July

Antigonish Highland Games (p119) Pipe playing and log lifting; Antigonish.

Atlantic Jazz Festival (p71) Free outdoor concerts; Halifax.

Loyalist Days (p164) Historic costumes and parades; Saint John.

Royal Nova Scotia International Tattoo (p71) Scottish bagpipers blow their horns; Halifax.

August

Festival by the Sea (p164) Singing, dancing and other performing arts; Saint John.

Halifax International Busker Festival (p71) Comics, mimics, daredevils and more; Halifax.

Miramichi Folksong Festival (p177) North America's oldest folk fest; Miramichi.

Newfoundland & Labrador Folk Festival (p224) Traditional Newfie music and storytelling; St John's.

September

Atlantic Film Festival (p72) Atlantic Canada's best films get screened; Halifax.

Canadian Deep Roots Festival (p105) Rawk to Mi'kmaw, Acadian and other unique music; Wolfville.

Festival of the Fathers (p191) Re-live Victorian times; Charlottetown.

FOOD

Seafood (think fish-and-chips, lobster and scallops) and unique regional dishes (fiddleheads and cod tongues) fill Atlantic Canada's tables. See the Food & Drink chapter for the skinny on the cuisine (though you may not be after indulging).

GAY & LESBIAN TRAVELERS

Same-sex marriage is legal in Canada, although attitudes remain more conservative in the Atlantic region than in Canada's largest cities.

Halifax is Atlantic Canada's gay and lesbian epicenter; see p75. Moncton, Fredericton and St John's also have gay communities, albeit smaller. Many accommodations throughout the region (particularly B&Bs) are gay and lesbian friendly; check **Purple Roofs** (www .purpleroofs.com) for listings.

The website www.gaycanada.com enables you to search by province or city for queer-friendly businesses and resources. Another site worth checking is www.queercanada.ca.

HOLIDAYS
Public Holidays

Canada observes 11 national public holidays and more at the provincial level. Banks, schools and government offices remain closed on these days. For important festivals and major events, see left.

NATIONAL HOLIDAYS

New Year's Day January 1

Good Friday March or April

Easter March or April

Victoria Day Monday before May 25

Civic Holiday First Monday of August; also known as Natal Day

Canada Day July 1; called Memorial Day in Newfoundland

Labour Day First Monday of September

Thanksgiving Second Monday of October

Remembrance Day November 11

Christmas Day December 25

Boxing Day December 26

PROVINCIAL HOLIDAYS

Newfoundland also has a slew of provincial holidays:

St Patrick's Day Monday nearest March 17

St George's Day Monday nearest April 23

Discovery Day Monday nearest June 24

Orangemen's Day Monday nearest July 12

School Holidays

Kids break for summer holidays in late June and don't return to school until early September. University students get even more time off, usually from May to early or mid-September. Most people take their big annual vacation during these months.

INSURANCE

No matter how long or short your trip, make sure you have adequate travel insurance. At a minimum, you need coverage for medical emergencies and treatment, including hospital stays and an emergency flight home. Medical treatment for non-Canadians is exhorbitant; simply visiting an emergency room will set you back a whopping $500, and that's before any treatment or medication. For more information, see p285.

Also consider insurance for luggage theft or loss. If you already have a home owners or renters policy, check what it will cover and only get supplemental insurance to protect against the rest. If you have prepaid a large portion of your vacation, trip cancellation insurance is worthwhile.

Worldwide coverage to travelers from more than 44 countries is available online at www .lonelyplanet.com/travel_services. Also check the following providers:

Insure.com (☎ 800-556-9393; www.insure.com)

Travel Guard (☎ 800-826-4919; www.travelguard.com)

Travelex (☎ 800-228-9792; www.travelex.com)

For information about vehicle insurance, refer to p282.

INTERNET ACCESS

It's easy to find Internet access in the region's main cities, and you'll be surprised at the access available in remote areas, thanks to the government's **Community Access Program** (C@P; http://cap.ic.gc.ca/index.htm). Libraries, schools and community agencies in practically every town throughout the region provide free high-speed Internet terminals for public use, travelers included. The only downside is that usage time is limited (usually 30 minutes), facilities have erratic hours, and you may not be able to upload photos (it depends on the facility).

Internet cafés are limited to the main tourist areas, and access generally costs $3 to $8 per hour. If you're traveling with your own laptop computer, you'll find that many of the newer and recently renovated hotels and B&Bs let you plug in from your room, usually via a high-speed broadband connection. Properties that don't offer in-room access often have an Internet terminal for guest use in the lobby.

We have listed public C@P sites and Internet cafés in the regional Information sections throughout this book. Lodgings offering guest terminals with free Internet access are identified with an Internet icon (🖳).

For more information on traveling with a laptop and the gadgets you might need, see www.teleadapt.com. For information on finding wireless hotspots in Atlantic Canada, see www.wififreespot.com/can.html or www.hotspot-locations.com. To find Internet cafés beyond those listed in this book, check www.netcafes.com.

Remember: while on the road, it's advisable to set up a trip-specific email address with a free, web-based provider such as Hotmail (www .hotmail.com) or Yahoo (www.yahoo.com). And be wary of doing banking and other personal transactions from public Internet terminals, as keystroke-capturing software could be in place as could other nonsecure features.

See p25 for a list of websites about traveling in Atlantic Canada.

LEGAL MATTERS

Should you be arrested or charged with an offense, you have the right to keep your mouth shut and to hire a lawyer (contact your embassy for a referral). If you cannot afford one, ask to be represented by public counsel. There is a presumption of innocence.

If driving, you need to carry your driver's license (p281) and carefully obey road rules (p283). Drunk driving is a criminal offense. If caught, you may face stiff fines, have your license suspended and experience other nasty consequences. Consuming alcohol anywhere other than at a residence or licensed premises is also a no-no, which puts parks, beaches and the rest of the great outdoors off limits, at least officially.

When it comes to illegal drugs, the sensible thing to do is to avoid them entirely, as penalties may entail heavy fines, possible jail time and a criminal record. The decriminalization of marijuana possession for personal use remains a subject of intense and ongoing debate.

Abortion is legal.

MAPS

Canadian company **Mapart** (www.mapart .com) and **Rand McNally** (www.randmcnally .com) publish maps for the Atlantic region as a whole as well as for its larger cities; they're

---

LEGAL AGE

▪ Driving a car: 16

▪ Smoking tobacco: 18

▪ Homosexual consent (for males): 18

▪ Consent for other sexual activity: 14

▪ Voting in an election: 18

▪ Drinking alcoholic beverages: 19

sold at bookstores and gas stations. Most tourist offices distribute good, free provincial road maps. If you are a member of the Canadian Automobile Association (CAA; p281) or one of its international affiliates, you can get CAA's high-quality maps for free from any local office. For downloadable maps and driving directions, try **Mapquest** (www .mapquest.com), **Yahoo** (http://maps.yahoo .com) or **Google** (http://maps.google.ca).

For extended hikes or multiday backcountry treks, it's a good idea to carry a topographic map. The **Centre for Topographic Information** (http://maps.nrcan.gc.ca) publishes them; check the website for vendors. You can also download maps from www .geobase.ca.

MONEY

All prices quoted in this book are in Canadian dollars ($), unless stated otherwise.

Canadian coins come in 1¢ (penny), 5¢ (nickel), 10¢ (dime), 25¢ (quarter), $1 (loonie) and $2 (toonie or twoonie) denominations. The gold-colored loonie features the loon, a common Canadian water bird, while the two-toned toonie is decorated with a polar bear.

Paper currency comes in $5 (blue), $10 (purple), $20 (green) and $50 (red) denominations. The $100 (brown) and larger bills are less common, and are tough to change.

Thanks to an unstable world economy, wars and other destabilizing factors, the Canadian dollar has seen fluctuations in recent years, bottoming out in January 2002 when one loonie was worth a mere US$0.62. By late 2006, it had rebounded and almost achieved parity with the US dollar; see Quick Reference on the inside front cover of this book for specifics. Good websites to check for the latest rates are www.xe.com/ucc and www .oanda.com.

Some businesses near the US–Canadian border and in big cities accept payment in US dollars, with change given in Canadian dollars. Don't expect the exchange rate to be in your favor.

For an overview of how much things cost in Atlantic Canada, see p22.

ATMs

Many grocery and convenience stores; airports; and bus, train and ferry stations have ATMs. Most are linked to international networks, the most common being Cirrus, Plus, Star and Maestro.

Most ATMs also spit out cash if you use a major credit card. This method tends to be more expensive because, in addition to a service fee, you'll be charged interest immediately. For exact fees, check with your own bank or credit-card company.

Visitors heading to Atlantic Canada's more remote regions won't find an abundance of ATMs, so it is wise to cash up beforehand.

Cash & Personal Checks

Most Canadians don't carry large amounts of cash for everyday use, relying instead on credit and debit cards. Still, carrying some cash, say $100 or less, comes in handy when making small purchases. In some cases, cash is necessary to pay for rural B&Bs and shuttle vans; inquire in advance to avoid surprises. Shops and businesses rarely accept personal checks.

Credit Cards

Major credit cards such as MasterCard, Visa and Amex are widely accepted in Atlantic Canada, except in remote, rural communities where cash is king. You'll find it hard or impossible to rent a car, book a room or order tickets over the phone without having a piece of plastic. Carry copies of your credit-card numbers separately from the cards and immediately report lost or stolen cards:

Amex (☎ 866-296-5198; http://home.american express.com)

MasterCard (☎ 800-307-7309; www.mastercard.com)

Visa (☎ 800-847-2911; www.visa.com)

Taxes & Refunds

Canada's federal goods and services tax (GST), variously known as the 'gouge and screw' or 'grab and steal' tax, adds 7% to just about every transaction. To make matters worse, most provinces also charge a provincial sales tax (PST). New Brunswick, Nova Scotia and Newfoundland and Labrador have combined the GST and PST into a harmonized sales tax (HST) of 14%. Prince Edward Island's PST is 10%. Unless otherwise stated, taxes are not included in prices given.

If you've spent at least $200 on short-term accommodations and nonconsumable goods, you can have the GST and HST refunded if you leave Canada within 60 days from the date of purchase. The only other hitch is that each eligible receipt must be for at least $50 before taxes.

At the airport or land border crossing have your original receipts (credit-card slips alone are not sufficient) stamped by a customs agent, then mail them with a tax-rebate application (widely available at tourist offices, shops, hotels and on the Internet) to the address on the form. Allow a couple of months for processing. Don't be misled by private companies that distribute 'official tax refund' booklets at visitors centers and duty-free shops. These companies offer to obtain your refund for you and then take up to 20% for their 'services'. It's usually just as fast and easy to do it yourself.

For full details, check with the **Visitors' Rebate Program** (☎ 902-432-5608, in Canada 800-668-4748; www.cra-arc.gc.ca/visitors). It's possible that the refund program will be abolished in the near future; at the time of writing, the Canadian legislature was to vote on it.

Tipping

In restaurants and bars, leaving a 15% tip on the pretax bill is standard; see the boxed text (p58) for further details.

At hotels, tip bellhops about $1 to $2 per bag. Leaving a few dollars for the room cleaners is always a welcome gesture. Cab drivers, hairdressers and barbers also expect a tip, usually 10% to 15%.

Traveler's Checks

Traveler's checks are becoming more and more obsolete in the age of ATMs. Still, they may come in handy as a backup. Traveler's checks issued in Canadian dollars are generally treated like cash by businesses. Traveler's checks in most other currencies must be exchanged for Canadian dollars at a bank or foreign-currency office. For lost or stolen checks call the issuer:

Amex (☎ 866-296-5198)
MasterCard (☎ 800-223-9920)
Visa (☎ 800-227-6811)

POST

Canada's national postal service, **Canada Post/ Postes Canada** (☎ 416-979-8822, 866-607-6301; www .canadapost.ca), is neither quick nor cheap, but it is reliable. Stamps are available at post offices, drugstores, convenience stores and hotels.

Postcards or standard 1st-class airmail letters up to 30g cost 51¢ within Canada, 89¢ to the USA and $1.49 to all other countries.

Travelers often find they have to pay high duties on items sent to them while in Canada, so beware. Poste restante mail can be held for collection; call post offices for details.

SHOPPING

Each province has its own crafts council that publishes a guide to local wares and studios, available at visitors centers. Or check online for information:
New Brunswick (www.nbcraftscouncil.com)
Newfoundland (www.craftcouncil.nf.ca)
Nova Scotia (www.craft-design.ns.ca)
Prince Edward Island (www.peicraftscouncil.com)

Everything you buy is subject to tax, but some purchases may qualify for a refund (see p271).

Art & Jewelry

Wood carving has a long tradition along the French Shore of Nova Scotia. Newfoundland, Labrador and Chéticamp, in Cape Breton, are famous for handmade hooked rugs. Soapstone carvings, Labradorite (a multihued stone) jewelry and porcupine quill work are also well-known artwork in the region.

Edibles

Nova Scotia's smoked salmon is a real treat. Digby chicks, a pungent smoked herring, are a more off-beat alternative. Purveyors also can pack fresh lobster to ship to your home. Wines from Nova Scotia help wash it all down. Sweet treats include maple syrup from New Brunswick and partridgeberry and bakeapple jams from Newfoundland and Labrador.

Fashion

Colorful woolen items – sweaters, mittens, booties, hats, blankets – are handcrafted in Newfoundland and Prince Edward Island and make great gifts.

Music

Fiddle-playing, Celtic-tinged folk music from Cape Breton and Newfoundland fills many returning travelers' suitcases.

SOLO TRAVELERS

There are no particular problems or difficulties traveling alone in Atlantic Canada. Going alone to cafés and restaurants is quite acceptable. People in the region are friendly and easy to talk to. Women don't need to be afraid of initiating a conversation, even with men. Unless you're overtly coquettish, it most likely won't be interpreted as a sexual advance. For more specific advice for women travelers, see p275.

TELEPHONE

Coin-operated public pay phones are fairly plentiful. Local calls cost 25¢ (sometimes 35¢). Dialing the operator (☎ 0), directory assistance (☎ 411 for local calls, 1 + area code + 555-1212 for long-distance calls) or the emergency number (☎ 911) is free of charge from public phones; directory assistance may incur a charge from private phones.

Cell Phones

As in the USA and Europe, cell phones are ubiquitous. The only foreign phones that will work in North America are tri-band models, operating on GSM 1900 and other frequencies. If you don't have such a phone, your best bet may be to buy a prepaid one at a consumer electronics store or via online retailers such as **Telestial** (www.telestial.com) or **Planetfone** (www.planetfone.com). Most cost less than $125, including voicemail, some prepaid minutes and a rechargeable SIM card. **Aliant** (www.aliant.net) is the local provider in Atlantic Canada and also offers options.

US residents frequently can upgrade their domestic cell-phone plan to extend to Canada, including coverage in the Atlantic region. **Verizon** (www.verizonwireless.com) provides good results.

Reception can be poor in rural areas no matter who your service provider is.

Phone Codes

Canadian phone numbers are made up of a three-digit area code followed by a seven-digit local number. When dialing a number within the same area code, just dial the seven-

digit number. Long-distance calls must be preceded by ☎ 1.

For direct international calls, dial ☎ 011 + country code + area code + local phone number. The country code for Canada is ☎ 1 (the same as for the USA, although international rates still apply for all calls made between the two countries).

Toll-free numbers commence with ☎ 800, ☎ 877 or ☎ 866 and must be preceded by 1. Some of these numbers are good throughout Canada and the USA, others only work within Canada, and some work in just one province.

Phonecards

Prepaid phonecards usually offer the best per-minute rates for long-distance and international calling. They come in denominations of $5, $10 or $20 and are widely sold in drugstores, supermarkets and convenience stores. Beware of cards with hidden charges such as 'activation fees' or a per-call connection fee. A surcharge ranging from 30¢ to 85¢ for calls made from public pay phones is common.

TIME

Nova Scotia, New Brunswick, Prince Edward Island and Labrador all follow Atlantic standard time, which is one hour ahead of eastern standard time (used from Québec to Florida) and half an hour behind Newfoundland. For time comparisons, if it's noon in Halifax, it is 11am in New York City and Montréal, 12:30pm in Newfoundland and 4pm in London. Refer to the World Time Zones map (pp302–3) for additional data. Variations are noted in the relevant destination chapters.

Atlantic Canada observes daylight saving time (DST). At the time of research, the schedule was being adjusted. DST now will begin the second Sunday in March (when clocks are put forward one hour) and end the first Sunday in November, but check with the **Institute for National Measurement Standards** (www.nrc.ca/inms) for updates.

TOURIST INFORMATION

Atlantic Canada's provincial tourist offices all maintain comprehensive websites packed with visitor information. Staff also field telephone inquiries and, on request, will mail out free maps and directories about accommodations, attractions and events.

AREA CODES

Telephone area codes in Atlantic Canada are province-wide:

■ New Brunswick (☎ 506)

■ Newfoundland and Labrador (☎ 709)

■ Nova Scotia (☎ 902)

■ Prince Edward Island (☎ 902)

DIRECTORY

For detailed information about a specific area, you'll need to contact a local tourist office, aka visitors center. Just about every city has at least a seasonal (June to August) branch with helpful staff and racks of free pamphlets and maps. Visitor center addresses are listed in the Information sections for individual destinations throughout this book.

Provincial tourist offices:

Newfoundland & Labrador Tourism (☎ 800-563-6353; www.newfoundlandandlabradortourism.com)
Prince Edward Island Tourism (☎ 902-368-4444, 800-463-4734; www.peiplay.com)
Tourism New Brunswick (☎ 506-753-3876, 800-561-0123; www.tourismnewbrunswick.ca)
Tourism Nova Scotia (☎ 800-565-0000; www.novascotia.com)

TOURS

Group travel can be an enjoyable way to go, especially if you're traveling solo. Try to pick a tour that will suit you in terms of age, interest and activity level. For additional packages, check the Tours section for individual destinations throughout this book.

Arctic Odysseys (☎ 206-325-1977, 800-574-3021; www.arcticodysseys.com) Arctic-oriented company with yacht trips up the Newfoundland and Labrador coast.
Backroads (☎ 510-527-1555, 800-462-2848; www.backroads.com) Guided and self-guided bicycle tours worldwide, including Nova Scotia and Prince Edward Island.
Elderhostel (☎ 800-454-5768; www.elderhostel.org) Nonprofit organization offering study tours for active people over 55, including bus and walking tours in Atlantic Canada.
Freewheeling Adventures (☎ 902-857-3600, 800-672-0775; www.freewheeling.ca) Nova Scotia–based company with bicycle tours throughout Atlantic Canada, including bike-and-yoga getaways.
Routes to Learning (☎ 613-530-2222, 866-745-1690; www.routestolearning.ca) Explore Newfoundland's Vikings, New Brunswick's Acadians or Nova Scotia's lighthouses with this Canadian nonprofit's educational tours.
Salty Bear Adventure Tours (☎ 902-202-3636, 888-425-2327; www.saltybear.ca) Backpacker-oriented van tours through the Maritimes with jump-on/jump-off flexibility. There's a two-day circuit around Nova Scotia, or a more stimulating four-day route into Cape Breton and beyond.

TRAVELERS WITH DISABILITIES

You'll find access ramps and/or lifts in many public buildings. Most public restrooms feature extra-wide stalls that are equipped with hand rails. Many pedestrian crossings have sloping curbs. Newer and recently remodeled hotels, especially chain hotels, have rooms with extra-wide doors and bathrooms. We have designated wheelchair-accessible properties with a wheelchair icon (♿) throughout this book.

Interpretive centers at national and provincial parks are usually accessible, and many parks have trails that can be navigated in wheelchairs. Some car-rental agencies offer hand-controlled vehicles and vans with wheelchair lifts at no additional charge, but you must reserve in advance.

Getting around on public transport is possible but requires some planning. The best place to start is **Access to Travel** (www.accesstotravel.gc.ca), with information on accessible air, bus, rail and ferry transportation. The site's 'travel resources' link leads to other useful websites sorted by province. In general, most transportation agencies can accommodate people with disabilities if you make your needs known when booking.

Other organizations specializing in disabled travelers' needs:

Access-Able Travel Source (☎ 303-232-2979; www.access-able.com) A useful website with many links.
Canadian Paraplegic Association (☎ 613-723-1033; www.canparaplegic.org) Information about facilities for mobility-impaired travelers in Canada.
Mobility International (☎ in the USA 541-343-1284, in the UK 020-7403-5688; www.miusa.org) Advises disabled travelers on mobility issues and runs an educational exchange program.
Society for Accessible Travel & Hospitality (☎ 212-447-7284; www.sath.org) More useful links.

VISAS

For information about passport requirements, see p276.

Citizens of dozens of countries – including the USA, most Western European and Commonwealth countries, as well as Mexico, Japan, South Korea and Israel – don't need visas to enter Canada for stays of up to 180 days. US permanent residents are also exempt.

Nationals of around 150 other countries, including South Africa and China, need to apply to the Canadian visa office in their home country for a temporary resident visa (TRV). The website maintained by **Citizenship & Immigration Canada** (CIC; www.cic.gc.ca) has full details, including office addresses and the latest requirements. A separate visa is required if you plan to study or work in Canada.

Single-entry TRVs ($75) are usually valid for a maximum stay of six months from the date of your arrival in Canada. Multiple-entry TRVs ($150) allow you to enter Canada from all other countries multiple times while the visa is valid (usually two or three years), provided no single stay exceeds six months.

Visa extensions ($75) need to be filed with the **CIC Visitor Case Processing Centre** (☎ in Canada 888-242-2100; ☽ 8am-4pm Mon-Fri) in Alberta at least one month before your current visa expires.

Visiting St-Pierre & Miquelon

For details on visiting these French territories off Newfoundland's coast, see p237.

Visiting the USA

Visitors to Canada who also plan to spend time in the USA should know that admission requirements are subject to rapid change. Check with a US consulate in your home country or the visa website maintained by the **US State Department** (www.unitedstatesvisas.gov) for the latest eligibility requirements.

Under the US visa-waiver program, visas are not currently required for citizens of 27 countries – including most EU members, Australia and New Zealand – for visits of up to 90 days (no extensions allowed), as long as you can present a machine-readable passport. Passports issued after October 26, 2005 must also contain digitized information. If you don't have such a passport, you will need to apply for a US visa in your home country. Canadians do not need visas, though they may need passports; check the website above to assess the ever-changing situation. Citizens of all other countries need to apply for a US visa in their home country before arriving in Canada.

All visitors, regardless of their country of origin, are subject to a US$6 entry fee at land border crossings. Note that you don't need a Canadian multiple-entry TRV for repeated entries into Canada from the USA, unless you have visited a third country.

In 2004, the US Department of Homeland Security introduced a new set of security measures called US-VISIT. When you arrive by air or sea, you will be photographed and have your two index fingers scanned. Eventually this biometric data will be matched when you leave the USA. The goal is to ensure that the person who entered the USA is the same as the one leaving it and to catch people who've overstayed the terms of their admission.

At the time of writing, this procedure also was being implemented at 154 land border crossings, including those with Atlantic Canada. For full details about US-VISIT, check with a US consulate in your country or see www.dhs.gov/us-visit.

VOLUNTEERING

Visitors can volunteer their services on an organic farm, usually in exchange for free room and board. Check with **World-Wide Opportunities on Organic Farms** (www.wwoof .ca; application fee $40) for locations in Atlantic Canada. Visitors can also volunteer with scientists from **Earthwatch** (☎ 800-776-0188; www .earthwatch.org) to monitor mammal populations and the impact of climate change in Nova Scotia. Two-week trips cost $2449, including meals and accommodation.

WOMEN TRAVELERS

Atlantic Canada is generally a safe place for women to travel, even alone and even in the cities. In bars and nightclubs, solo women are likely to attract a lot of attention, but if you don't want company, most men will respect a firm 'no thank you.' Note that carrying mace or pepper spray is illegal in Canada.

Physical attack is unlikely, but if you are assaulted, call the police immediately (☎ 911) or contact a rape crisis center. A complete list is available from the **Canadian Association of Sexual Assault Centres** (☎ 604-876-2622; www.casac.ca). Hotlines in major Atlantic cities:

Fredericton (☎ 506-454-0437)
Halifax (☎ 902-425-0122)
St John's (☎ 709-726-1411)

Transportation

CONTENTS

Flights, tours and rail tickets can be booked online at www.lonelyplanet.com/travel _services.

GETTING THERE & AWAY

For information on tours, see p274.

ENTERING THE COUNTRY

Passengers arriving in Canada by plane receive the standard immigration and customs forms to fill out. After landing you first go through immigration, then through customs. In the post–9/11 world, officials can be very strict and you may be asked a series of ques-

---

THINGS CHANGE...

The information in this chapter is particularly vulnerable to change. Check directly with the airline or a travel agent to make sure you understand how a fare (and ticket you may buy) works, and be aware of the security requirements for international travel. Shop carefully. The details given in this chapter should be regarded as pointers and are not a substitute for your own careful, up-to-date research.

---

tions. Questioning may be more intense at land border crossings and your car may be searched.

Having a criminal record of any kind, including a DUI (driving under the influence) charge, may keep you out of Canada. If this affects you, you should apply for a 'waiver of exclusion' at a Canadian consulate (p268) in your country. The process costs $200 and takes several weeks.

Like many countries, Canada is concerned about child abduction. For this reason, single parents, grandparents or guardians traveling with anyone under the age of 18 should carry proof of legal custody, or a notarized letter from the non accompanying parent authorizing the trip. Unaccompanied children will also need a notarized letter of consent from both parents or legal guardians. This is in addition to their passport and/or proof of citizenship.

Passport

Most international visitors require a passport to enter Canada. US citizens are the exception, though they, too, will soon need one.

As it stands now, US citizens must have a valid passport to re-enter the USA by air or sea from Canada. Through December 31, 2007, they can still re-enter at land borders by showing proof of US citizenship (such as a certified copy of their birth certificate or certificate of naturalization) plus photo identification (preferably a current valid driver's license). However, starting in 2008, US citizens will likewise need a passport to cross land borders. Permanent US residents must carry their green card. If entering Canada from a third country, US citizens and permanent residents must have a passport.

At the time of research, the aforementioned deadlines were being debated and there was talk of postponing them. For updates, it is recommended that travelers check the websites for the **US State Department** (www .travel.state.gov) and **Citizenship & Immigration Canada** (www.cic.gc.ca).

Visitors from selected countries also require a visa to enter Canada (see p274).

AIR
Airports & Airlines

Halifax has the region's largest airport and it's the only one so far to have US preclearance privileges (ie nonstop passengers to the US are processed through customs prior to departure, thus ensuring a no-fuss arrival on the US side). Moncton is also busy, and may offer lower fares than Halifax. For visitors heading to Newfoundland, Deer Lake is a great option if you are centering your travels on the west coast.

Atlantic Canada's main airports:

Charlottetown, Prince Edward Island (YYG; ☎ 902-566-7997; www.flypei.com)

Deer Lake, Newfoundland (YDF; ☎ 709-635-3601; www.deerlakeairport.com)

Fredericton, New Brunswick (YFC; ☎ 506-460-0920; www.frederictonairport.ca)

Halifax, Nova Scotia (YHZ; ☎ 902-873-4422; www.hiaa.ca)

Moncton, New Brunswick (YQM; ☎ 506-856-5444; www.gma.ca)

St John's, Newfoundland (YYT; ☎ 709-758-8581; www.stjohnsairport.com)

Sydney, Nova Scotia (YQY; ☎ 902-564-7720)

AIRLINES FLYING TO & FROM NOVA SCOTIA, NEW BRUNSWICK & PRINCE EDWARD ISLAND

The region is not particularly well serviced, and flight and airline choices are limited.

Most visitors will need to fly into Montréal or Toronto, and then connect with another flight to reach their destination in Atlantic Canada. Most flights are via the national flagship carrier Air Canada; it's one of the world's safest airlines, though locals often gripe about its stiff prices. Subsidiary Air Canada Jazz operates most flights to and within the Atlantic region.

Other companies that are based in Canada and are serving international destinations are the charter airline Air Transat and discount airline WestJet. There are numerous US airlines that also serve Atlantic Canada, which are worth researching.

Airlines operating to/from the region:

Air Canada & Air Canada Jazz (AC; ☎ 888-247-2262; www.aircanada.com)

Air St-Pierre (PJ; ☎ 902-873-3566, 877-277-7765; www.airsaintpierre.com)

Air Transat (TS; ☎ 866-847-1919; www.airtransat.com)

American Airlines (AA; ☎ 800-433-7300; www.aa.com)

Continental Airlines (CO; ☎ 800-231-0856; www.continental.com)

Delta Airlines (DL; ☎ 800-241-4141; www.delta.com)

Lufthansa (LH; ☎ 800-563-5954; www.lufthansa.com)

Northwest Airlines (NW; ☎ 800-225-2525; www.nwa.com)

United Airlines (UA; ☎ 800-241-6522; www.united.ca)

WestJet (WS; ☎ 888-937-8538; www.westjet.com)

Zoom (Z4; ☎ 866-359-9666; www.flyzoom.com)

TRANSPORTATION

CLIMATE CHANGE & TRAVEL

Climate change is a serious threat to the ecosystems that humans rely upon, and air travel is the fastest-growing contributor to the problem. Lonely Planet regards travel, overall, as a global benefit, but believes we all have a responsibility to limit our personal impact on global warming.

Flying & Climate Change

Almost every form of motorized travel generates CO_2 (the main cause of human-induced climate change), but planes are by far the worst offenders, not just because of the sheer distances they allow us to travel, but because they release greenhouse gases high into the atmosphere. The statistics are frightening: two people taking a return flight between Europe and the USA will contribute as much to climate change as an average household's gas and electricity consumption over a whole year.

Carbon Offset Schemes

Climatecare.org and other websites use 'carbon calculators' that allow travelers to offset the level of greenhouse gases they are responsible for with financial contributions to sustainable travel schemes that reduce global warming – including projects in India, Honduras, Kazakhstan and Uganda.

Lonely Planet, together with Rough Guides and other concerned partners in the travel industry, support the carbon offset scheme run by climatecare.org. Lonely Planet offsets all of its staff and author travel.

For more information check out our website: www.lonelyplanet.com

Tickets

Online agencies, such as the ones listed below, are good places to start searching for low-cost fares, but they are best when used in conjunction with other search engines. One of these is **ITA Software** (www.itasoftware.com), a search matrix that sorts results by price, while also alerting to downsides such as long layovers, tight connections or overnight travel. No software download is required. Note this site does not actually sell tickets, which must be bought from a travel agent or the airline.

Another handy tool is **Sidestep** (www.sidestep.com), whose search includes low-cost carriers that are not covered by companies such as Expedia and Orbitz. This site requires a free software download that may contain spyware.

And don't forget about travel agents, whose knowledge can be especially helpful when planning extensive trips or complicated routes.

Cheap Tickets (www.cheaptickets.com)
Expedia (www.expedia.com)
Hotwire (www.hotwire.com)
Info-Hub Specialty Travel Guide (www.infohub.com/travelnow.html)
LowestFare (www.lowestfare.com)
Orbitz (www.orbitz.com)
Priceline (www.priceline.com)
STA Travel (www.sta.com)
Travelocity (www.travelocity.com)
Yahoo! Travel (www.travel.yahoo.com)

Australia & New Zealand

There are no nonstop flights from Australia or New Zealand to Atlantic Canada. The most straightforward route is from Sydney to Los Angeles, then to your Canadian destination. Air Canada, Air New Zealand and Qantas are the dominant airlines on this route, but

---

United Airlines and American Airlines also offer flights.

Australia

Flight Centre (☎ 133-133; www.flightcentre.com.au)
STA Travel (☎ 1300-733-035; www.statravel.com.au)

New Zealand

Flight Centre (☎ 0800-243-544; www.flightcentre.co.nz)
Go Holidays (www.goholidays.co.nz)
STA Travel (☎ 0508-782-872; www.statravel.co.nz)

Continental Europe & the UK

Most visitors will have to fly into Toronto, Ontario, or Montréal, Québec, then switch to a regional carrier (most likely Air Canada or WestJet) to reach their final Atlantic destination. In summer, Air Transat flies direct to Halifax from Germany and the UK. Air Canada and Zoom also both fly nonstop to Halifax from the UK. Lufthansa flies into St John's via Toronto.

France

Lastminute (☎ 0892-705-000; www.fr.lastminute.com)
Nouvelles Frontières (☎ 0825-000-747; www.nouvelles-frontieres.fr)

Germany

Just Travel (☎ 089-747-3330; www.justtravel.de)
Lastminute (☎ 01805-284-366; www.lastminute.de)

Italy

CTS Viaggi (☎ 06-462-0431; www.cts.it)

Netherlands

Airfair (☎ 020-620-5121; www.airfair.nl)

THE UK

Bridge the World (☎ 0870-444-7474; www.b-t-w.co.uk)
North South Travel (☎ 01245-608-291; www.northsouthtravel.co.uk) Donates a percentage of profits to projects in the developing world.
Quest Travel (☎ 0870-442-3542; www.questtravel.com)
Travel Bag (☎ 0870-890-1456; www.travelbag.co.uk)

The USA

Most flights to Atlantic Canada from the USA depart from east coast cities such as New York or Boston. If you are flying from elsewhere in the USA, you'll likely have to stop over and change planes on the east coast or in Toronto or Montréal. US carriers United, American, Continental, Delta and Northwest fly to Halifax. In addition,

---

DEPARTURE TAX

Tickets for flights departing from Atlantic Canada, whether purchased in Canada or abroad, should include departure taxes. Passengers sometimes have to pay an 'airport-improvement fee' (usually $10 or $15) on-site, especially in New Brunswick. Details are given in the Getting There & Away sections for destinations throughout this book.

Continental flies to St John's; Northwest flies to Charlottetown; and Delta flies to Fredericton.

Bargain hounds should also consider WestJet, which flies to Toronto from cities in Florida, California and Arizona, and then onward to Moncton, Halifax, St John's and Charlottetown (but connections may not be easy).

STA Travel (☎ 800-781-4000; www.statravel.com)
Travel Cuts USA (☎ 800-592-2887; www.travelcuts.com)

LAND
Border Crossings
The three major border crossings into Atlantic Canada are between Maine, USA, and New Brunswick at Calais/St Stephen, Madawaska/Edmundston and Houlton/Woodstock. The website for the **Canadian Border Services Agency** (www.cbsa-asfc.gc.ca/general/times/menu-e.html) has details on estimated wait times. In general, waits rarely exceed 30 minutes, except during the peak summer season and holidays.

When returning to the USA, check the website for the **US Department for Homeland Security** (http://apps.cbp.gov/bwt) for border wait times.

For information on documents needed to enter Canada, see p276.

Bus
Greyhound (☎ 800-231-2222; www.greyhound.com) and its Canadian equivalent, **Greyhound Canada** (☎ 800-661-8747; www.greyhound.ca), operate the largest bus network in North America, with services to 3600 destinations. Alas, the Atlantic provinces are not among them, so you'll have to take Greyhound to a gateway city such as Montréal or Bangor (Maine) and then switch to an **Acadian Lines** (☎ 902-454-9321, 800-567-5151; www.acadianbus.com) bus. The changeover is pretty seamless, and Acadian even honors Greyhound's discounted Discovery Pass (p281). From Halifax, Acadian runs once daily to Montréal ($138, 18 hours) and Bangor ($80, 10 hours), where there are sporadic connections for New York and Boston.

Car & Motorcycle
The USA's extensive highway network connects directly with the Canadian system at numerous key points along the border. These Canadian highways then go on to meet up with the east–west Trans-Canada Hwy, an excellent way to traverse the country.

If you're driving into Canada, you'll need the vehicle's registration papers, proof of liability insurance and your home driver's license. Cars rented in the USA usually can be driven into Canada and back, but make sure your rental agreement says so. If you're driving a car registered in someone else's name, bring a letter from the owner authorizing use of the vehicle in Canada. For general information about border crossings, see left. For details about driving within Canada, see p281.

Train
Via Rail (☎ 888-842-7733; www.viarail.ca), Canada's national rail line, offers one service to the Atlantic region: a Montréal to Halifax train (advance purchase adult/child two to 11 years $133/66, 21 hours) that runs daily except Tuesday, and includes several stops in New Brunswick and Nova Scotia. It leaves Montréal at 6:30pm, and arrives in Halifax at 4:20pm the next day.

Visitors coming from the USA can hop aboard America's national rail line, **Amtrak** (☎ 800-872-7245; www.amtrak.com), and its daily service connecting New York City with Montréal. The North America Rail Pass (p284) is valid on both Amtrak and VIA Rail.

SEA
Ferry
Various ferry routes connect Atlantic Canada to the USA and even France.

To reach Nova Scotia, the high-speed **Cat** (☎ 902-742-6800, 888-249-7245; www.catferry.com; ☼ late May–mid-Oct) zips across the water to Yarmouth from two towns in Maine. On Monday to Thursday, it departs at 8am from Bar Harbor, Maine (adult/child six to 13 years US$63/43, car/bicycle US$105/16, three hours), and returns at 1pm (4:30pm Wednesday) from Yarmouth. On Friday to Sunday it departs at 2:30pm from Portland, Maine (adult/child six to 13 years US$89/59, car/bicycle US$149/27, 5½ hours), and returns at 9am from Yarmouth. Security fees (each way $10) also apply.

In New Brunswick, East Coast Ferries links Deer Island to Eastport, Maine (p157).

From Newfoundland's Burin Peninsula, you can reach the French territory of St-Pierre & Miquelon (p239).

TRANSPORTATION

GETTING AROUND

AIR

Airlines in Nova Scotia, New Brunswick & Prince Edward Island

Most regional flights within the Maritimes are operated by Air Canada's subsidiary, Air Canada Jazz. Small provincial airlines fly out to the more remote portions of the region. Fares in such noncompetitive markets can be high.

See the Getting There & Away sections of the destination chapters for specific route and fare information. The following are the main carriers flying within Atlantic Canada:

Air Canada & Air Canada Jazz (AC; ☎ 888-247-2262; www.aircanada.com) Flights throughout the region.

Air Labrador (WJ; ☎ 709-738-5441, 800-563-3042; www.airlabrador.com) Flights within Newfoundland and Labrador.

Air St-Pierre (PJ; ☎ 902-873-3566, 877-277-7765; www.airsaintpierre.com) Flights from the French island of St-Pierre to St John's, Halifax, Sydney and Moncton.

Provincial Airlines (PB; ☎ 800-563-2800; www.provincialairlines.ca) Service throughout Newfoundland and Labrador, as well as to Halifax.

WestJet (WS; ☎ 888-937-8538; www.westjet.com) Nationwide discount carrier with a route between St John's and Halifax.

Air Passes

Overseas travelers planning to do a lot of flying within Canada, or around the USA and Canada, might save some money by buying an air pass. **Star Alliance** (www.staralliance.com) members Air Canada, United Airlines and US Airways have teamed up to offer the North American Airpass (three coupons US$399), which is available to anyone not residing in the USA, Canada, Mexico, Bermuda or the Caribbean. It's sold only in conjunction with an international flight operated by any Star Alliance–member airline. Check the website for details.

BICYCLE

The Maritime provinces, particularly Prince Edward Island, are ideal for bicycle touring. See p50 for more on routes and resources.

Cyclists must follow the same rules of the road as vehicles, but don't expect drivers to always respect your right of way. Helmets are mandatory in New Brunswick, Prince Edward Island and Nova Scotia.

Emergency roadside assistance is available from the **Better World Club** (☎ 866-238-1137; www.betterworldclub.com). Membership costs $40 per year, plus a $10 enrollment fee, and entitles you to two free pick-ups and transport to the nearest repair shop (or home) within a 50km radius.

Most airlines will carry bikes as checked luggage without charge on international flights, just as long as they're in a box. On domestic flights they usually charge between $30 and $65. Always check details before you buy the ticket.

If you're traveling on an Acadian bus, you must put your bike in a box ($6) and pay a transportation fee ($5). VIA Rail will transport your bicycle for $20, but only on trains offering checked-baggage service, such as the Halifax to Montréal train.

Purchase

Buying a bike is easy, as is reselling it before you leave. Specialist bike shops have the best selection and advice, but general sporting-goods stores may have lower prices. Some bicycle stores and rental outfitters also sell used bicycles. Check the notice boards in hostels and universities; these are also the best places to sell your bike.

Rental

Outfitters renting bicycles exist in most tourist towns; many are listed throughout this book. Rentals cost around $25 per day; this usually includes a helmet and lock. Most companies require a security deposit of $20 to $200.

BOAT

The watery region hosts an extensive ferry system. For details, see the Getting There & Away and Getting Around sections of the destination chapters. Walk-ons and cyclists should be OK anytime, but call ahead for vehicle reservations or if you require a cabin berth. This is especially important during peak season (July and August). Main operators:

Bay Ferries (☎ 506-649-7777, 888-249-7245; www.bayferries.com) Year-round service between Saint John, New Brunswick, and Digby, Nova Scotia; p167.

CTMA Ferries (☎ 418-986-3278, 888-986-3278; www.ctma.ca) Daily ferries to Québec's Îles de la Madeleine from Souris, Prince Edward Island; p198.

Coastal Transport (☎ 506-662-3724, 506-642-0520; www.coastaltransport.ca) Ferry from Blacks Harbour to Grand Manan in the Fundy Isles, New Brunswick; p160.

East Coast Ferries (☎ 506-747-2159, 877-747-2159; www.eastcoastferries.nb.ca) Connects Deer Island to Campobello Island, both in the Fundy Isles, New Brunswick; p158.

Labrador Marine (☎ 866-535-2567; www.labrador marine.com) Connects Newfoundland to Labrador; p257.

Marine Atlantic (☎ 800-341-7981; www.marine -atlantic.ca) Connects Port aux Basques (p255) and Argentia (p233) in Newfoundland with North Sydney, Nova Scotia.

Northumberland Ferries (☎ 902-566-3838, 888-249-7245; www.peiferry.com) Connects Wood Islands, PEI, and Caribou, Nova Scotia; p118.

Provincial Ferry Services (☎ numbers vary; www .tw.gov.nl.ca/ferryservices) Operates coastal ferries throughout Newfoundland.

BUS

Greyhound Canada does not operate within the Atlantic provinces. The main bus lines in the region:

Acadian Lines (☎ 902-454-9321, 800-567-5151; www .acadianbus.com) Operates a network throughout Nova Scotia, New Brunswick and Prince Edward Island.

DRL Coachlines (☎ 709-263-2171; www.drlgroup.com) Runs a cross-island route on Newfoundland from St John's to Port aux Basques.

Bus frequency ranges from one to two buses per day along most routes. Buses generally are clean, comfortable and reliable. They usually have onboard toilets, air-conditioning (bring a sweater), reclining seats and onboard movies.

A series of small, regional shuttle vans comprises the rest of bus service in the area. These services are detailed in the Getting There & Away sections of the destination chapters. For major shuttle routes see Halifax (p76), Charlottetown (p194), St John's (p228) and Corner Brook (p252).

Bus Passes

Neither Acadian nor DRL offer any special discount passes, though Acadian does honor Greyhound's Discovery Pass (www.discov erypass.com), valid for travel in both the USA and Canada. Note that for short-haul trips, the pass is not necessarily more economical than buying individual tickets. However, it can be worthwhile for onward, long-haul travel.

Costs

Bus travel normally is cheaper than train travel. Operators lop 15% off regular fares for seniors and students, while children under 12 pay half price. Advance purchase discounts do not apply on Atlantic bus lines.

Sample fares on Acadian include Halifax to North Sydney ($62, seven hours); Halifax to Charlottetown ($54, 5½ hours); and Charlotte-town to Moncton ($31, 3½ hours). Sample fares on DRL include St John's to Corner Brook ($93, 10½ hours); and St John's to Port aux Basques ($130, 13½ hours).

Reservations

Tickets must be bought at bus terminals for Acadian and on the bus (cash only) for DRL; there are no phone or online sales. Show up at least 30 to 45 minutes prior to departure.

CAR & MOTORCYCLE
Automobile Associations

The main motoring organization is the **Canadian Automobile Association** (CAA; ☎ 800-268-3750; www.caa.ca), and membership can be quite useful. CAA's services, including 24-hour emergency roadside assistance, are also available to members of its international affiliates such as AAA in the USA, AA in the UK and ADAC in Germany. The club offers trip-planning advice, free maps, travel-agency services and a range of discounts on hotels and car rentals.

In recent years, the **Better World Club** (☎ 866-238-1137; www.betterworldclub.com), which donates 1% of its annual revenue to environmental clean-up efforts, has emerged as an alternative. It also offers roadside assistance for bicycles.

Bring Your Own Vehicle

Requirements for bringing your car into Canada are discussed on p279. It's also easy to rent a car (see p282).

Driver's License

In most Canadian provinces, visitors can legally drive for up to three months with their home driver's license. However, if you'll be spending considerable time in Canada, get an International Driving Permit (IDP), valid for one year. Just grab a passport photo and your home license, and stop by your local automobile association, which will issue you one for a small fee. IDPs may give you greater credibility with traffic police and ease the car-rental process, especially if your home license doesn't have a photograph or is not written in English or French.

TRANSPORTATION

TRANSPORTATION

Fuel & Spare Parts

Most gas stations are self-service and finding one is generally not a problem, except in sparsely populated areas such as Labrador and Newfoundland's south coast.

Finding spare parts can be a tall order away from the big cities. When traveling in remote regions, always bring some tools and at least a spare tire. Roadside emergency assistance (p281) is useful, too.

Gas is sold in liters (see the inside front cover for a metric conversion chart). At the time of writing, the average for midgrade fuel was $1.15 per liter (about C$4.40 per US gallon). Prices are higher than in the USA, so fill up before you cross the border. Prices also are a bit higher in Newfoundland than in the Maritimes, so tank up again before heading that way.

Insurance

Canadian law requires liability insurance for all vehicles. The minimum requirement is $200,000. If you already have auto insurance at home, or if you have purchased travel insurance, make sure that the policy has adequate liability coverage for where you'll be driving. Americans traveling to Canada in their own car should ask their insurance company for a Nonresident Interprovince Motor Vehicle Liability Insurance Card, which is accepted as evidence of financial responsibility anywhere in Canada. Although not mandatory, it may come in handy in case of an accident.

Car-rental agencies will provide liability insurance. Sometimes adequate coverage is already included in the base rental rate, but always ask to be sure. Insurance against damage to the car itself, called Collision Damage Waiver (CDW), reduces or eliminates the amount you'll have to reimburse the rental company. It's optional but, although it's expensive ($12 to $15 per day), it's unwise to drive without it. Certain credit cards, especially the gold and platinum versions, cover CDW for a certain rental period, if you use the card to pay for the rental, and decline the policy offered by the rental company. Check with your card issuer to see what coverage it offers in Canada.

Personal accident insurance (PAI) covers you and any passengers for medical costs incurred as a result of an accident. If your travel-insurance or your health-insurance policy at home does this as well (and most do, but check), then you can do without PAI.

Rental

As anywhere, rates for car rentals vary considerably by model and pick-up location, but you should be able to get an economy-size vehicle for about $35 to $55 per day. Expect surcharges for rentals that originate at airports, additional drivers and one-way rentals. Child safety seats are compulsory (reserve them when you book) and cost about $8 per day.

Car-rental prices can double in July and August, and it's essential to book ahead in prime tourist spots such as Charlottetown or St John's, as there often just aren't enough cars to go around.

To rent your own wheels in Canada you need to be at least 25 years old and hold a valid driver's license and a major credit card.

International car-rental companies usually have branches at airports and in city centers; note that ferry terminals often do not have branches.

Avis (☎ 800-437-0358; www.avis.com)
Budget (☎ 800-268-8900; www.budget.com)
Dollar (☎ 800-800-4000; www.dollar.com)
Enterprise (☎ 800-736-8222; www.enterprise.com)
Hertz (☎ 800-263-0600; www.hertz.com)
National (☎ 800-227-7368; www.nationalcar.com)
Rent A Wreck (☎ 800-327-0116; www.rentawreck.com)
Thrifty (☎ 800-847-4389; www.thrifty.com)

Local agencies may offer lower rates; they also are more likely to rent to drivers under 25. About 100 independent agencies are represented by **Car Rental Express** (☎ 604-714-5911, 888-557-8188; www.carrentalexpress.com), which may yield savings of up to 25% off rates charged by the large chains.

Fly-drive packages often work out to be cheaper than on-the-spot rentals. Check with the airlines and travel agencies when booking.

MOTORCYCLE

Nova Scotia's tourism office produces a free **motorcycle guide** (☎ 800-565-0000; www.novascotia.com/ride). Rentals can be steep: a Harley 1200 Sportster costs about $175 per day:
Big Moose Harley-Davidson (☎ 207-797-6061, 800-427-5393; www.bigmooseharley.com) Rents hogs out of Portland, Maine, that you can ride into Canada; convenient if you're taking the Nova Scotia–bound ferry from Portland.
Vineland Motorcycle Tours (☎ 866-425-6305; www.vintour.ca) Rents hogs out of Halifax.

RECREATIONAL VEHICLES

Rentals cost roughly $160 to $250 per day in high season for midsize vehicles:

Canadream Campers (☎ 403-291-1000, 800-461-7368; www.canadream.com) Rentals from Halifax.

Islander RV (☎ 709-364-7368, 888-848-2267; www.islanderrv.com) Rentals from St John's.

Road Conditions & Hazards

Winter travel can be hazardous due to giant potholes, heavy snow and ice. The website maintained by the **CAA** (www.caa.ca) has useful tips on winter driving, and the website for **Transport Canada** (☎ 800-387-4999; www.tc.gc.ca/road) provides links to road conditions and construction zones for each province.

Distances between services can be long, so keep your gas topped up whenever possible. Remember that much of Atlantic Canada is wilderness. This means that moose, deer and other critters may insist on sharing the road with you. Moose, in particular, present a real danger. Smacking into a beast the height of a horse and weighing 400kg can be deadly. Heed the warning signs, keep your speed down and travel during the day rather than at night.

Road Rules

Canadians drive on the right-hand side of the road. Seat-belt use is compulsory at all times. Children under 18kg must be strapped in child-booster seats, except infants, who must be in rear-facing safety seats. Motorcyclists must wear helmets and drive with their headlights on.

Distances and speed limits are posted in kilometers. The speed limit is generally 40km/h to 50km/h in cities, and 90km/h to 110km/h outside town. You must slow down to 60km/h when passing emergency vehicles.

Turning right at red lights after coming to a full stop is permitted in all provinces, except where road signs say otherwise. Motorists in Atlantic Canada usually stop to let pedestrians cross the street, unlike in other provinces.

Driving while talking on a cell phone is (still) legal everywhere except in Newfoundland and Labrador.

The highest permissible blood-alcohol level for drivers is 0.08%.

HITCHHIKING

Hitching is never entirely safe in any country and we don't recommend it. That said, in remote and rural areas of Atlantic Canada it is not uncommon to see people thumbing for a ride. If you do hitch, understand that you are taking a small but potentially serious risk. Remember that it's safer to travel in pairs and be sure to let someone know where you are planning to go.

Ride-share services offer an alternative to hitching. **Autotaxi** (www.autotaxi.com) is a free web-based bulletin board for ride-sharing within Canada and to the USA. You can advertise a ride yourself or make arrangements with drivers going to your destinations.

LOCAL TRANSPORTATION

Bicycle

Cycling is more of a recreational activity than a means of local transportation in Atlantic Canada. City bike paths are not common. Still, most public transportation allows bicycles to be brought on at certain times of day. See p50 and p280 for more on cycling in the region.

Bus

The only cities in the region with municipal bus services are Fredericton, Saint John, Moncton, Halifax, Sydney and St John's. The Annapolis Valley has an excellent regional bus service between Wolfville and Bridgetown. Elsewhere the private car is king.

Taxi

All the main cities have taxis, which are detailed in the Getting Around sections throughout this book. Taxis usually are metered, with a flag-fall fee of $2.50 and a per-kilometer charge around $1.75. Drivers expect a tip of between 10% and 15%. Taxis can be flagged down or ordered by phone.

TRAIN

Train travel is limited within the region. Prince Edward Island and Newfoundland have no train services. Nova Scotia and New Brunswick are served along **VIA Rail**'s (☎ 888-842-7245; www.viarail.ca) Montréal-to-Halifax route. For a train schedule, check the website. Most stations have left-luggage offices.

Western Labrador is also accessible by train: a privately owned service operated by the **Iron Ore Company of Canada** (☎ 709-944-8400, ask for operator & then 'train service') goes once weekly from Sept Îles, Québec, to Labrador City ($64). See p263 for details.

Train buffs should also check out **Canada by Rail** (www.canadabyrail.ca), an excellent portal packed with information on regional excursion trains, railroad museums and historical train stations.

Classes

On VIA Rail, fares are lowest in comfort class, which is offered on all trains, and buys you a fairly basic, if indeed quite comfortable, reclining seat with a headrest. Blankets and pillows are provided for overnight travel.

VIA Rail also offers various sleeping-car classes, including compartments with upper or lower pull-out berths, and private single, double or triple roomettes.

On the Montréal-to-Halifax train, there is also the 'Easterly' class which includes meals and educational presentations onboard. It's offered May through October only.

Costs

Taking the train is more expensive than the bus, but most people find it a more comfortable way to travel. Buying tickets five days in advance can yield 30% to 40% savings. Students can also save with an ISIC card (p268), though the savings has mostly to do with flexibility (ie the ability to make last-minute bookings and no-fee ticket changes). Seniors over 60 can shave 10% off the price of regu-

lar tickets. Kids age two to 11 years pay half of the adult fare. See VIA Rail's website for further promotions.

Sample advance-purchase fares from Montréal to New Brunswick include Campbellton ($76, 11 hours), Miramichi ($90, 14½ hours) and Moncton ($109, 16 hours); fares to Nova Scotia include Amherst ($116, 17½ hours), Truro ($124, 19 hours) and Halifax ($133, 21 hours).

Reservations

Tickets and train passes are available for purchase online, by phone, at VIA Rail stations and from many travel agents. Seat reservations are highly recommended, especially in summer and for sleeper cars.

Train Passes

The Canrailpass buys 12 days of comfort-class travel within a 30-day period beginning with the first day of travel. It costs $926 during peak season (June to mid-October), and $579 at other times.

The North America Rail Pass allows unlimited travel in the USA and Canada for 30 consecutive days and costs $1149 from June to mid-October and $815 at all other times. All passes can be purchased through VIA Rail.

Health

CONTENTS

There's a high level of hygiene in Atlantic Canada, so most common infectious diseases will not be a significant concern for travelers. Also, excellent medical care is widely available.

BEFORE YOU GO

INSURANCE

The Canadian health-care system is one of the finest in the world. Benefits are generous for Canadian citizens, but foreigners aren't covered. Make sure you have travel-health insurance if your regular policy doesn't apply when you're abroad. For more information, check the **Lonely Planet website** (www.lonelyplanet.com/travel_services/insurance/travel_insurance.cfm). Find out in advance if your insurance plan will make payments directly to providers or reimburse you later for overseas health expenditures.

ONLINE RESOURCES

There is a wealth of travel-health advice on the Internet. The World Health Organization publishes a useful book, called *International Travel and Health,* which is revised annually and is available online at no cost at www.who.int/ith. Another website of general interest is **MD Travel Health** (www.mdtravelhealth.com), which provides complete travel-health recommendations for every country, is updated daily and is available at no cost.

It's usually a good idea to consult your government's travel-health website, if one is available, before departure:
Australia (www.smarttraveller.gov.au)
UK (www.dh.gov.uk/policyandguidance/healthadvicefortravellers/fs/en)
USA (www.cdc.gov/travel/)

IN CANADA

AVAILABILITY & COST OF HEALTH CARE

For immediate medical assistance in most areas, dial ☎ 911 or ☎ 0 for an operator who will direct you to the appropriate service. In general, if you have a medical emergency, the best bet is to find the nearest hospital and go to its emergency room. If the problem isn't urgent, you can call a nearby hospital and

---

RECOMMENDED VACCINATIONS

No special vaccines are required or recommended for travel to Canada. All travelers should be up-to-date on routine immunizations, listed below.

Vaccine	Recommended for	Dosage	Side effects
chickenpox	travelers who've never had chickenpox	two doses one month apart	fever; mild case of chickenpox
influenza	all travelers during flu season (November to March)	one dose	soreness at the injection site; fever
measles	travelers born after 1956 who've had only one measles vaccination	one dose	fever; rash; joint pains; allergic reactions
tetanus-diphtheria	all travelers who haven't had booster within 10 years	one dose lasts 10 years	soreness at injection site

ask for a referral to a local physician, which is usually less expensive than a trip to the emergency room.

Pharmacies are abundantly supplied, but you may find some medications that are available over-the-counter in your home country require a prescription in Canada. Many Americans find that prescription drugs cost less in Canada than at home.

INFECTIOUS DISEASES

There are some infectious diseases that are uncommon outside North America. Most are acquired by mosquito bites, tick bites or environmental exposure.

Giardiasis

This parasitic infection of the small intestine occurs throughout North America and the world. Giardiasis has symptoms that may include nausea, bloating, cramps, and diarrhea, and may last for weeks. Avoid drinking directly from lakes, ponds, streams and rivers, which may be contaminated by animal or human feces.

HIV/AIDS

This infectious disease occurs throughout Canada.

Lyme Disease

In general, the risk of contracting lyme disease is low, but it is important to take precautions. The infection is transmitted by deer ticks, which are only 1mm to 2mm long, and are found in Nova Scotia as well as southern parts of Canada. Most cases occur in late spring and summer. The first symptom is usually an expanding red rash that is often pale in the center, known as a bull's-eye rash. However, in many cases, no rash is observed. Flu-like symptoms are common, including fever, headache, joint pains, body aches and malaise. When the infection is treated promptly with an appropriate antibiotic, usually doxycycline or amoxicillin, the cure rate is high. For prevention tips, see Tick Bites (opposite).

Rabies

Rabies is a viral infection of the brain and spinal cord that is almost always fatal. In Canada most cases of human rabies relate to exposure to bats. Rabies may also be contracted from raccoons, skunks, foxes, and unvaccinated cats and dogs. All animal bites and scratches must be promptly and thoroughly cleansed with large amounts of soap and water, and local health authorities contacted to determine if there is a risk of rabies. If there is

---

MEDICAL CHECKLIST

- Acetaminophen/paracetamol (Tylenol) or aspirin
- Anti-inflammatory drugs (eg ibuprofen)
- Antihistamines (for hay fever and allergic reactions)
- Motion-sickness medication
- Antibacterial ointment (eg Neosporin or Bactroban) for cuts and abrasions
- Steroid cream or cortisone (for poison ivy and other allergic rashes)
- Bandages, gauze, gauze rolls
- Adhesive or paper tape
- Scissors, safety pins, tweezers
- Thermometer
- Pocket knife
- DEET-containing insect repellent for the skin
- Permethrin-containing insect spray for clothing, tents, and bed nets

Bring medications in their original containers, clearly labeled. A signed, dated letter from your physician describing all medical conditions and medications, including generic names is also a good idea. If carrying syringes or needles be sure to have a physician's letter documenting their medical necessity.

any possibility, however small, that you have been exposed to rabies, you should seek preventative treatment, which consists of rabies-immune globulin and rabies vaccine, and is quite safe. In particular, any contact with a bat should be discussed with health authorities, as bats have small teeth and may not leave obvious bite marks.

West Nile Virus
Infections were unknown in Canada until recently, but West Nile virus has now been observed in many provinces, including Québec, Ontario, Saskatchewan, Alberta and Manitoba. At the time of writing there was no evidence of the virus in any of the Atlantic provinces.

The virus is transmitted by Culex mosquitoes, which are active in late summer and early fall, and generally bite after dusk. Most infections are mild or asymptomatic, but the virus may infect the central nervous system, leading to fever, headache, confusion, lethargy, coma, and sometimes death. There is no treatment for West Nile virus.

For the latest update on areas affected by West Nile, go to the website of **Health Canada** (www.westnilevirus.gc.ca). For prevention tips, see Mosquito Bites (right).

ENVIRONMENTAL HAZARDS
Cold Exposure
Cold exposure may be a significant problem, especially in the northern parts of the region. To prevent hypothermia, keep all body surfaces covered, including the head and neck. Synthetic materials such as Gore-Tex and Thinsulate provide excellent insulation. Since the body loses heat faster when wet, stay dry at all times. Change inner garments promptly when they become moist. Keep active, but get enough rest. Consume plenty of food and water. Be especially sure not to have any alcohol. Caffeine and tobacco should also be avoided.

Watch out for the 'Umbles': stumbles, mumbles, fumbles and grumbles, important signs of impending hypothermia. If someone appears to be developing hypothermia, you should insulate them from the ground, protect them from the wind, remove wet clothing or cover with a vapor barrier such as a plastic bag, and transport them immediately to a warm environment and a medical facility. Warm fluids (not coffee or tea) may be given if the person is alert enough to swallow.

Mammal Bites
Most animal injuries are directly related to a person's attempt to touch or feed the animal. Any bite or scratch by a mammal, including bats, should be promptly and thoroughly cleansed with large amounts of soap and water, followed by application of an antiseptic such as iodine or alcohol. The local health authorities should be contacted immediately for possible postexposure rabies treatment.

Mosquito Bites
When traveling in areas where West Nile or other mosquito-borne illnesses have been reported, keep yourself covered (wear long sleeves, long pants, hats and shoes rather than sandals). Apply a good insect repellent, preferably one with DEET, to exposed skin and clothing. Products containing lower concentrations of DEET are as effective, but for shorter periods of time. In general, adults and children over 12 years should use preparations containing 25% to 35% DEET, which last about six hours. Children aged between two and 12 years should use preparations containing no more than 10% DEET, applied sparingly, which will last about three hours. Neurologic toxicity has been reported from DEET, especially in children, but appears to be extremely uncommon and generally related to overuse. DEET-containing compounds should not be used on children under age two. Insect repellents containing certain botanical products, including oil of eucalyptus and soybean oil, are effective but last only 1½ to two hours. Products based on citronella are not effective.

For additional protection, you can apply permethrin to clothing, shoes, tents, and bed nets. Permethrin treatments are safe and remain effective for at least two weeks, even when items are laundered. Permethrin should not be applied directly to skin.

Tick Bites
To protect yourself from tick bites, follow the same precautions as for mosquitoes, except that boots are preferable to shoes, and pants should be tucked in. Be sure to perform a thorough tick check at the end of each day, with the aid of a friend or mirror. Ticks should be removed with tweezers, grasping them firmly by the head. Insect repellents based on botanical products cannot be recommended to prevent tick bites.

HEALTH

Behind the Scenes

THIS BOOK

This guidebook was commissioned in Lonely Planet's Oakland office, and produced by the following:

Commissioning Editor Emily K Wolman
Coordinating Editor Holly Alexander
Coordinating Cartographer Barbara Benson
Coordinating Layout Designer Indra Kilfoyle
Managing Editor Melanie Dankel
Managing Cartographers Alison Lyall, Adrian Persoglia
Assisting Editors Yvonne Byron, Jackey Coyle, Kate Evans and Kate Whitfield
Assisting Cartographer Owen Eszeki
Cover Designer Rebecca Dandens
Project Manager Fabrice Rocher
Language Content Coordinator Quentin Frayne

Thanks to Helen Christinis, Sally Darmody, Rachel Imeson, Wayne Murphy and Celia Wood

THANKS
KARLA ZIMMERMAN

The legendary Newfoundland hospitality is no exaggeration. Many, many thanks to the following kind souls for home-cooked dinners, vehicle tours and patience in answering my endless questions: Bryan Curtis, Rob Makowichuk, Alison Croome, Debrah Wirtzfeld, Robbie Hicks, Vyda, Dana, Jim and Murray Scott, Ken Brown, Dave MacDonald, Daine Hewitt, Bonnie Goudie, Carmen Hancock, Anita Power, Elaine Hann, Brigitte Schloss, Brian Chaulk, Terry O'Rourke and Gillian Marx. Über gratitude to Celeste Brash for beyond the call of duty authoring help. Thanks to editor Emily Wolman for patience and idea-slinging. Thanks most of all to Eric Markowitz, who is, quite simply, the world's best partner-for-life.

CELESTE BRASH

My husband Josh, my kids Jasmine and Tevai and my soul sister Chandra brought out the best of the Maritimes. Suzanne Grenager and Lou Schel-

SEND US YOUR FEEDBACK

We love to hear from travelers – your comments keep us on our toes and help make our books better. Our well-traveled team reads every word on what you loved or loathed about this book. Although we cannot reply individually to postal submissions, we always guarantee that your feedback goes straight to the appropriate authors, in time for the next edition. Each person who sends us information is thanked in the next edition – and the most useful submissions are rewarded with a free book.

To send us your updates – and find out about Lonely Planet events, newsletters and travel news – visit our award-winning website: **www.lonelyplanet.com/contact**.

Note: we may edit, reproduce and incorporate your comments in Lonely Planet products such as guidebooks, websites and digital products, so let us know if you don't want your comments reproduced or your name acknowledged. For a copy of our privacy policy visit www.lonelyplanet.com/privacy.

lenberg helped me with local's only info from Halifax to Lunenburg. Thanks to Cathie from Yarmouth Backpackers, and all the folks at Nova Scotia, New Brunswick and Prince Edward Island Tourism. In PEI thanks to Kim and Elrie Jay for adopting me. Local voice victims: you are great sports! Emily Wolman, editor-extraordinaire, came along for part of the trip with her wonderful partner Abbot. Most thanks to Karla Zimmerman for fortitude and camaraderie.

ACKNOWLEDGMENTS

Many thanks to the following for the use of their content:

Seafood chowder recipe from *Taste of Nova Scotia* © 2006, www.tasteofnovascotia.ns.ca

THE LONELY PLANET STORY

The story begins with a classic travel adventure: Tony and Maureen Wheeler's 1972 journey across Europe and Asia to Australia. There was no useful information about the overland trail then, so Tony and Maureen published the first Lonely Planet guidebook to meet a growing need.

From a kitchen table, Lonely Planet has grown to become the largest independent travel publisher in the world, with offices in Melbourne (Australia), Oakland (USA) and London (UK). Today Lonely Planet guidebooks cover the globe. There is an ever-growing list of books and information in a variety of media. Some things haven't changed. The main aim is still to make it possible for adventurous travelers to get out there – to explore and better understand the world.

At Lonely Planet we believe travelers can make a positive contribution to the countries they visit – if they respect their host communities and spend their money wisely. Every year 5% of company profit is donated to charities around the world.

Index

INDEX

INDEX

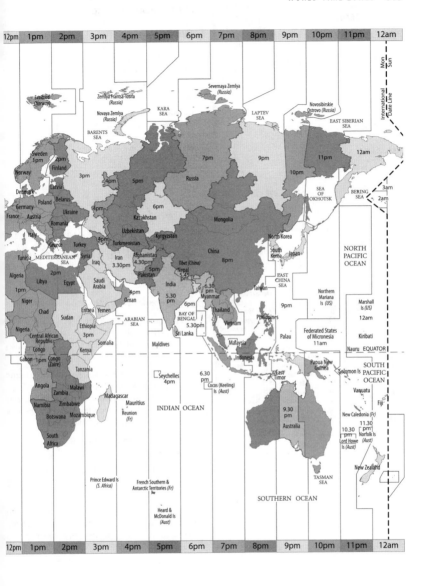

Mon
Sun

International Date Line

Svalbard
(Norway)

Zemlya Frantsa-Iosifa
(Russia)

Severnaya Zemlya
(Russia)

Novaya Zemlya
(Russia)

KARA
SEA

LAPTEV
SEA

Novosibirskie
Ostrovo (Russia)

EAST SIBERIAN
SEA

BARENTS
SEA

Sweden
1pm

2pm

Norway Finland

3am

12am

11pm

Denmark Latvia

3pm

4pm

5pm

7pm

9pm

10pm

2am

Germany Poland Belarus
France Austria Ukraine

4pm

Russia

SEA
OF
OKHOTSK

BERING
SEA

Italy Romania

6pm

Kazakhstan

Mongolia

Greece Turkey

4pm

Turkmenistan

Kyrgyzstan

North Korea

Tunisia MEDITERRANEAN
SEA
Syria

4pm

Uzbekistan

China

South
Korea Japan

NORTH
PACIFIC
OCEAN

Algeria
Libya

2pm

Iraq
Iran
3.30pm

Afghanistan
(4.30pm)

Tibet (China)

8pm

EAST
CHINA
SEA

Egypt

Saudi
Arabia

Pakistan

5pm

Nepal
5.45
pm

Taiwan

Niger

1pm

4pm

Oman

India

5.30
pm

6.30
pm
Myanmar

Northern
Mariana
Is (US)

Marshall
Is (US)

Chad

Sudan

Eritrea Yemen

ARABIAN
SEA

6pm

Thailand

Philippines

9pm

12am

Nigeria

Ethiopia

BAY OF
BENGAL
5.30pm

Vietnam

Palau

Federated States
of Micronesia
11am

Kiribati

Central African
Republic

3pm

Somalia

Sri Lanka

Malaysia

Congo
Gabon

1pm

Kenya

Maldives

Indonesia

Nauru EQUATOR

Congo
(Zaire)

Tanzania

Papua New
Guinea

Solomon Is

SOUTH
PACIFIC
OCEAN

Angola

Seychelles
4pm

6.30
pm
Cocos (Keeling)
Is (Aust)

East
Timor

Vanuatu

Zambia

Malawi

Namibia

Zimbabwe

New Caledonia (Fr)

Fiji

Botswana Mozambique

Madagascar

Mauritius
Reunion
(Fr)

INDIAN OCEAN

9.30
pm

Australia

11.30
pm
Norfolk Is
(Aust)

South
Africa

10.30
pm
Lord Howe
Is (Aust)

New Zealand

Prince Edward Is
(S. Africa)

French Southern &
Antarctic Territories (Fr)

TASMAN
SEA

SOUTHERN OCEAN

Heard &
McDonald Is
(Aust)

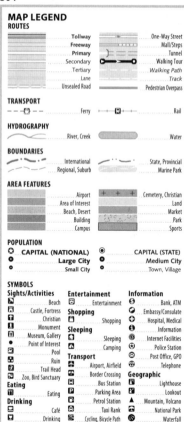

MAP LEGEND

ROUTES

Tollway		One-Way Street
Freeway		Mall/Steps
Primary		Tunnel
Secondary		Walking Tour
Tertiary		Walking Path
Lane		Track
Unsealed Road		Pedestrian Overpass

TRANSPORT

Ferry ·········· Rail

HYDROGRAPHY

River, Creek ·········· Water

BOUNDARIES

International ·········· State, Provincial
Regional, Suburb ·········· Marine Park

AREA FEATURES

Airport		Cemetery, Christian
Area of Interest		Land
Beach, Desert		Market
Building		Park
Campus		Sports

POPULATION

○ CAPITAL (NATIONAL)	◉ CAPITAL (STATE)
● Large City	● Medium City
● Small City	○ Town, Village

SYMBOLS

Sights/Activities
Beach
Castle, Fortress
Christian
Monument
Museum, Gallery
Point of Interest
Pool
Ruin
Trail Head
Zoo, Bird Sanctuary

Eating
Eating

Drinking
Café
Drinking

Entertainment
Entertainment

Shopping
Shopping

Sleeping
Sleeping
Camping

Transport
Airport, Airfield
Border Crossing
Bus Station
Parking Area
Petrol Station
Taxi Rank
Cycling, Bicycle Path

Information
Bank, ATM
Embassy/Consulate
Hospital, Medical
Information
Internet Facilities
Police Station
Post Office, GPO
Telephone

Geographic
Lighthouse
Lookout
Mountain, Volcano
National Park
Waterfall

LONELY PLANET OFFICES

Australia

Head Office
Locked Bag 1, Footscray, Victoria 3011
☎ 03 8379 8000, fax 03 8379 8111
talk2us@lonelyplanet.com.au

USA

150 Linden St, Oakland, CA 94607
☎ 510 893 8555, toll free 800 275 8555
fax 510 893 8572
info@lonelyplanet.com

UK

72–82 Rosebery Ave,
Clerkenwell, London EC1R 4RW
☎ 020 7841 9000, fax 020 7841 9001
go@lonelyplanet.co.uk

Published by Lonely Planet Publications Pty Ltd
ABN 36 005 607 983

Printed by Hang Tai Printing Company Limited
Printed in China